DONALD S. MIDDLETON has taught electronic communications for 39 years and is Emeritus Professor of Electronics at the University of Southern Colorado. He has written two other books in the field of F.C.C. license testing and has held various offices in the Electronic Section of the Colorado Vocational Association and the American Relay League.

PREPARING FOR THE FCC LICENSE EXAM

A Self-Instructional Handbook

Donald S. Middleton

A SPECTRUM BOOK

Prentice-Hall, Inc., Englewood Cliffs, New Jersey 07632

Library of Congress Cataloging in Publication Data

Middleton, Donald S.
    Preparing for the FCC license exam.

    (A Spectrum Book)
    1. Radio—Programmed instruction. 2. Radio—
Examinations, questions, etc. 3. Radio operators—
United States. I. Title.
TK6553.M489   621.3845'076   81-10665
ISBN 0-13-697219-5   AACR2
ISBN 0-13-697201-2 (pbk.)

This publication is dedicated to my former students who are missionaries proclaiming the gospel of Jesus Christ in South America.

This Spectrum Book is available to businesses and organizations
at a special discount when ordered in large quantities. For
information, contact Prentice-Hall, Inc., General Publishing Division,
Special Sales, Englewood Cliffs, N.J. 07632

© 1982 by Prentice-Hall, Inc., Englewood Cliffs, New Jersey 07632

A SPECTRUM BOOK

10   9   8   7   6   5   4   3   2   1

Printed in the United States of America

ISBN 0-13-697201-2 {PBK}

ISBN 0-13-697219-5

Prentice-Hall International, Inc., *London*
Prentice-Hall of Australia Pty. Limited, *Sydney*
Prentice-Hall of Canada, Inc., *Toronto*
Prentice-Hall of India Private Limited, *New Delhi*
Prentice-Hall of Japan, Inc., *Tokyo*
Prentice-Hall of Southeast Asia Pte. Ltd., *Singapore*
Whitehall Books Limited, Wellington, *New Zealand*

Contents

Preface
Auto-tutorial Instructions

Part I - The Second Class Radiotelephone License

Part II - The First Class Radiotelephone License

Preface

At this writing, the FCC has proposed to eliminate the First Class license.
The decision may be made before the end of 1981.
Regardless of their decision, the information contained in this book
should be helpful to anyone employed as an AM, FM, or
TV broadcast engineer.

This auto-tutorial course in FCC license theory is designed to prepare a student for the GENERAL RADIOTELEPHONE OPERATOR LICENSE examination.

There are three elements to this examination:
1. Element 1 consists of 20 questions concerning Basic Law.
2. Element 2 consists of 20 questions concerning Basic Operating Practice.
3. Element 3 consists of 100 questions on Basic Radiotelephone.

THE GENERAL RADIOTELEPHONE OPERATOR LICENSE qualifies an individual to be the chief engineer at AM, FM, and TV broadcast stations. This license is also required by any individual working with studio to transmitter links (STL) at a broadcast station. In addition, any one responsible for servicing and maintaining two-way radio transmitting equipment must have this license.

IMPORTANT-Because of the simplicity of Element 1 and Element 2, the student is asked to make his or her own preparation for these two elements using the two marked tests in the Appendix. Additional information is also given in Chapter 32 and Chapter 33 of *Electronic Communication* by Robert L. Shrader. Note that Element 1 and 2 are integral parts of the General class Radiotelephone license examination.

Advanced post secondary students with a background in the fundamentals of electricity and electronics should be able to make an adequate preparation for the General Radiotelephone examination using Part 1 in one semester. Secondary students will take two semesters for their license study. (Part 1)

This text is divided into 34 units that somewhat correspond to the chapter topics treated in the text *Electronic Communication* by Robert L. Shrader, a McGraw Hill publication of 1980 (4th Ed.). This same text has been programmed by the author of this book and is used for the programmed recheck. Each unit recheck is followed by a unit examination. Part 1 and Part 2 are concluded with a final examination. These Unit and Final examinations are found in the TEST SECTION following the book index.

It should be stated here that Part 2 provides useful information for the broadcast engineer that is no longer tested on by the F.C.C.

The flow chart below shows the plan for each unit:

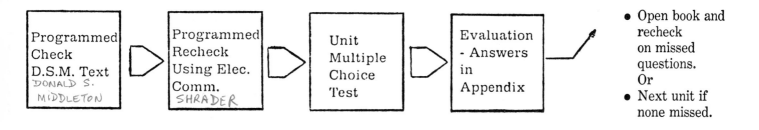

Upon the successful completion of all units of part 1, the student may elect to present him/herself to the office of the Federal Communications Commission for the General Radiotelephone examination. If a student plans to go on to the Part 2 study, that student may find this information useful in passing the examination.

The author wishes to acknowledge a debt of gratitude to the many students who have shared their problems with the F.C.C. examinations during the last 32 years as Pueblo Junior College grew to a University. This has enabled the author to learn of the full scope of Federal Communications Commission examinations on a year to year basis.

Also the encouragement and suggestions of Robert L. Shrader, the author of 'Electronic Communication', are acknowledged with thanks. Although this is a direct study of Federal exams, students pick up much 'nice to know' information from Electronic Communication.

I would like to acknowledge the help and enthusiasm of the University of Southern Colorado Publications Department personnel. My thanks goes to Bill Diachin for help in the layout, Julie Bible who did the typesetting, and Jerry Bible of the Print Shop who gave his special attention to the schematic diagrams.

My special thanks goes to Bill Ryan, a brilliant student, who contributed his talent in putting together the unit on Basic Digital Circuits and spent many hours in proof reading.

There are several 'pluses' to well-written auto-tutorial study over locked step education:

1.) It's self paced and no one need be snowed or bored.
2.) A student can enter training any semester and does not have to wait to fit into a time sequence program.
3.) The learning retention is higher. No more than a few new ideas are presented before a student is asked to make a written response.
4.) A student receives a mental pat on the back every few minutes as in most cases the next frame gives the same answer as the written response.
5.) When laboratory experiments are integrated into the study, only a small quantity of a variety of lab equipment is required since all students don't get to the same experiments at the same time.

Those who have trouble in reading or in disciplining their time find programmed training difficult.

Donald S. Middleton
WØNIT/WØENA

AUTO-TUTORIAL INSTRUCTIONS

1. Auto-tutorial materials are given to you in the same form as in the frames that follow. These materials are presented not as a test but as an educational experience. Not more than a few new ideas are presented in each _____ . (Complete the statement. The correct answer is given at the beginning of the next frame on the next page)

3. (answer or response) As you proceed through the programmed text material, make written responses as required before going to the next frame. This is a learning experience and not a _____ .

5. (answer or response) Communications majors at Colleges and Universities may wish to reinforce their learning experience by incorporating laboratory experiments and audio/visual review tapes. Laboratory experiments and audio/visual review tapes could be used to a good advantage by _____ majors at Colleges and Universities.

7. (multiple choice) If this handbook is used in a classroom situation, the instructor is a resource individual available for further discussion should the student be unable to make the proper test question choice after an open book recheck of missed questions. The instructor would discuss missed test questions only after the student has made an _____ recheck.

9. (advanced) In order to make problem and circuit analysis responses; a pencil, scratch paper, and a calculator should be used. Problem and circuit analysis responses require the use of a _____ .

2. (**frame**) Some frames are informational and require no response. Most frames will require a written _____ from you. (The correct answer is given at the beginning of frame 3 on page vii.)

4. (**test**) After the initial programmed instruction of a particular unit, the student is asked to complete a recheck programmed study utilizing Shrader's *Electronic Communication*. In this second study of the same unit, certain sections of the book are referred to that give specific information related to the unit being studied. Like the original programmed instruction, the recheck study calls for a (n) _____ for most frames.

6. (**Communications**) At the completion of each unit of instruction an F.C.C. style multiple choice test is given. This test can be evaluated by checking with the examination answers in the appendix at the back of the handbook. The examination for each part of the book is found at the end of the part. All tests are of the _____ style.

8. (**open book**) Some students may prefer to write their responses on a separate sheet of paper rather than in the blanks provided. This would enable them to use the unit for a review when studying for the Advanced Radiotelephone Exam. By using a separate sheet of paper for the written responses, the units can be used later for a review of the _____ Radiotelephone exam.

10. (**pencil, scratch paper, calculator**) Note that the programmed instruction is paged so that the immediate succeeding frames are not exposed. Pages 1 through 210 are printed on the right hand pages. Then the book is turned upside down and pages 211 through 411 are printed on the right hand pages coming the other way. Part 2 starting with page 328 continues in the same direction. Now start Unit 1 study. Good Luck!

PART I
THE SECOND-CLASS RADIOTELEPHONE LICENSE

UNIT 1 CURRENT, VOLTAGE, AND RESISTANCE

1. All matter is thought to be composed of small indivisible atoms containing elementary electrical particles. Positively charged **protons** and neutral **neutrons** are tightly bound in the nucleus of the atom. Negatively charged **electrons** are found in energy level orbits or shells around the atomic nucleus. Protons, neutrons, and electrons are elementary _____ particles.

4. (protons) The outer valance negative electron of the copper atom is loosely bound to the parent atom. If under the influence of an electrical field, heat, or light; the electron becomes a free electron, there is one more positive proton than negative electrons left in the system. This unbalanced system is called an ion and has a net_____charge.

7. (ampere) A material like carbon restricts the flow of electrons. This characteristic is known as **resistance**. The unit of resistance is the ohm and the symbol is R or the greek letter Ω (omega). The greater comparative resistance of carbon is due to the lack of _____ electrons.

10. (gold) The color number representation is as follows:

Note the example

Black	zero	Green	five
Brown	one	Blue	six
Red	two	Violet	seven
Orange	three	Grey	eight
Yellow	four	White	nine

Gold 5% tolerance
Silver 10% tolerance

Orange (3 zeros) — Silver 10%
Yellow (4) Violet (7)
Value 47000 ohms
Tolerance 10%

If the third strip was red the value of the resistance above would be_____ ohms.

13. (carbon) In the example shown the type, value and tolerance is _____, _____, and_____.

Double width black Red Black Gold

15. (6 ohms) The resistance of a wire is inversely proportional to cross sectional areas assuming the same type and lengths of wire are compared. This means that a wire of twice the circular mil area has one half the resistance and a wire of one half the circular mil area has twice the resistance. Wire of four times the cicular mil area would have_____ the resistance.

16. (one-fourth) The resistance of a wire is inversely proportional to the diameter squared assuming the same type and same lengths are compared. For example, a wire of twice the diameter has one-fourth $(1/2^2)$ the resistance. Wire of one-third the diameter has 9 ($\frac{1}{1/3^2}$) times as much resistance. Wire of one-half the diameter has _____ times as much resistance.

19. (400 x 2^2 or 1600) Wire size goes by numbers. No. 2 wire is very large wire for example (diameter 266 mils). No. 30 wire has a very small diameter (10 mils). The diameter of No. 16 wire is_____ than that of No. 4.

22. (low or minimum) Electrical pressure that causes electrons to flow through a wire is called **electromotive force, voltage,** or **potential.** If a voltage is applied across two points that are not connected together by a wire there exists lines of force between the two points called **electrostatic lines.** Before electrostatic lines can exist between two points a_____must be applied.

1

2. (electrical) There are over one hundred different kinds of atoms called elements. Different elements like silver and copper are made of atoms having a different number of elementary particles in the nucleus and shells. The atoms of the various elements all have one thing in common. The number of negative electrons in the shells exactly equal the number of positive protons in the nucleus. Therefore, it can be said that the net electrical charge of an atom is _____.

5. (positive) Some metals like copper have many such free electrons and are good electrical conductors while other metals like carbon have fewer free electrons having their valence electrons tightly bound to the atom and are not good electrical conductors. Conduction in metals consist of a flow of free electrons. Free electrons come from the _____ shell of an atom.

8. (free) The common carbon resistors are made by mixing and baking ceramic clay with carbon. The amount of ohmic resistance is determined by the ratio of the carbon to the binding clay. The unit of resistance is the_____.

11. (4700) A useful memory crutch for the color code is as follows:

BETTER	BE	RIGHT	OR	YOUR	GREAT	BIG	VENTURE	GOES	WEST
L	R	E	R	E	R	L	I	R	H
A(O)	O(1)	D(2)	A(3)	L(4)	E(5)	U(6)	O(7)	E(8)	I(9)
C	W		N	L	E	E	L	Y	T
K	N		G	O	N		E		E
			E	W			T		

The value and tolerance for the resistor shown is _____

Brown   Brown
    Black

14. (wire wound, 2 ohms, 5%) The resistance of a wire of constant cross sectional area is directly proportional to its length. That means a wire twice as long has twice as much resistance. If a wire is half as long as another wire of the same type and cross sectional area it has half as much resistance. If 1000 feet of wire has a resistance of 2 ohms, 3000 feet of wire of the same type and size has a resistance of_____ ohms.

17. (four) Now let us combine two resistance factors in a problem. A piece of wire 10 mil (10/1000 of an inch) in diameter and 1 inch long has a resistance of 1 ohm. Another wire of the same type but having a diameter of 5 mils (5/1000 of an inch) in diameter and 1/2 inch long would have a resistance of 2 ohms. (1 ohm (original resistance) x 1/2 (because length is 1/2 as great) x $2^2/1$)   Note that 5 mils is one half of 10 mils. When you invert 1/2 and square it you get 4. If the length in the problem above was changed to 2 inches and the diameter was changed to 2 1/2 mils (2.5/1000 inches) the new resistance would be_____ ohms.

20. (smaller) Since the resistance of wire is inversely proportional to the diameter squared and wire with a small diameter has large size numbers, it can be said that No. 30 wire has a higher resistance than No. 4 wire for example. The resistance of No. 2 wire has_____ resistance for the same length and type than No. 16.

23. (voltage, electromotive force or potential) The unit of electrical pressure (voltage, electromotive force, or potential) is the volt. The symbol is E or V. This concludes Unit 1.

3.   (zero or neutral) Note the arrangement of a copper atom.

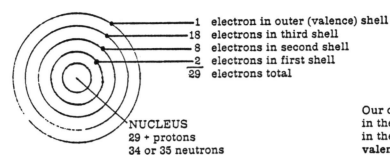

1 electron in outer (valence) shell
18 electrons in third shell
8 electrons in second shell
2 electrons in first shell
$\overline{29}$ electrons total

NUCLEUS
29 + protons
34 or 35 neutrons

Our chief interest in Electronics is in the negative electron or electrons in the outer shell. They are called **valence** electrons.

In the copper atom shown above there are equal numbers of electrons and _____.

6.   (outer or valence) The rate of the flow of free electrons is called **current**. If the quantity of 6.28 billion billion electrons pass a given point in a wire in one second it is said that one **ampere** of current flows. The symbol for current is I standing for intensity of flow. The basic unit of current then is the _____.

9.   (ohm) Most carbon resistors are color coded so their resistances in ohms can quickly be determined by the colors of their stripes. The color of the stripe closest to an end of the cylindrical resistor indicates the first significant number.
The next stripe color indicates the second significant number. In most cases the third stripe color indicates the number of zeros to be added to the first two significant numbers.
A fourth stripe of gold indicates 5% tolerance in the manufacturer and of silver 10% tolerance. No fourth stripe indicates 20% tolerance.
A precision made resistor would have a fourth stripe of_____.

12.   (100 ohms 20% tolerance) Some resistors are wire wound on a ceramic form. Although the same color code is used the stripe closest to an end of the cylindrical form is double width to indicate a wire wound resistor. Note the example below:

Orange (3)   Black (O or no zeros)

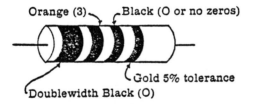

Gold 5% tolerance
Doublewidth Black (O)

Value 03 or 3 ohms
Tolerance 5%

If the first stripe is single width the resistor is a ___CARBON___ resistor.

18.   ($1 \times 2 \times 4^2/1$ or 32) If a certain wire 40 feet in length has a resistance of 10 ohms per foot it follows that its total resistance would be 40 X 10 or 400 ohms. If a second wire of the same length and type had a diameter of twice as great then its resistance would be $1/2^2$ x 400 ohms or 100 ohms. (2.5 ohms per foot). If the diameter in the above problem was changed to 1/2 as great, the new resistance would be _____ ohms.

21.   (less) As current flows through a wire heat energy is dissipated. This results in a power loss. More power is lost in wires having small diameters (large size numbers) because of the higher resistance of small wire. This means that the power lost in No. 18 wire is greater than that lost in No. 6 wire. There would be a _____ loss of power in No. 2 wire compared to No. 18 wire.

3

UNIT 1 CURRENT, VOLTAGE AND RESISTANCE

RECHECK PROGRAMMED INSTRUCTION USING SHRADER'S ELECTRONIC COMMUNICATION

1. The field created between two points caused by the excess and deficiency of charged electrical particles is called an_____field. Sec. 1-2

3. (current) The electron moving force is called _____. Sec. 1-5

5. (resistance) If an atom loses an electron it becomes an _____. Sec. 1-10

7. (conductors) The four factors that determine resistance are type of material, temperature _____, and _____ Sec. 1-12

9. (2.5 Ω)A piece of silver wire 5 mils in diameter and 1 inch long has a resistance of 1 ohm. Another of the same type 2.5 mils in diameter and 1/2 inch long would have a resistance of_____ Sec. 1-12

11. (16 x 30 x 10 or 4800 ohms) A certain type of wire of uniform size has a resistance of 27 ohms per foot. Another wire of the same type and length but having a diameter of 1/3 the first wire would have _____ times the resistance. Sec. 1-12

13. (Four) A third stripe of gold is used for a_____ of_____ Sec. 1-13.

15. (tolerance, 10%) A double width first stripe indicates the resistor is_____. Sec. 1-13

17. (1 Ω ,5%) The wire shown in table 1-3 that can safely carry high current with minimum loss is gauge no. _____. Sec. 1-15

2. (electrostatic) The progressive movement of free electrons along a wire is called _____.
Sec. 1-5

4. (electromotive force, voltage, or potential) The opposing effect that hinders free electron movement is called _____ Sec 1-5

6. (ion) Metals having many free electrons are good_____Sec. 1-12

8. (length and cross section area) If a certain wire of uniform size has a resistance of .25 ohm per foot, 10 foot of the same wire will have a resistance of _____ . Sec. 1-12

10. (2 Ω)A piece of wire 30 feet long has a resistance per foot of 10 ohms. If a second wire has the same length but a diameter of 1/4 the first wire the resistance of the second wire is_____. Sec. 1-12.

12. (nine) If you double the diameter, the area is_____times as great. Sec. 1-12

14. (multiplier, 0.1) A fourth stripe of silver indicates a_____of_____ Sec. 1-13

16. (wire wound) The resistance shown is a wire wound resistor having a value and tolerance of _____ , _____. Sec. 1-13

18. (Zero) This completes the recheck material for Unit 1.

5

1. The copper wire which would carry current with a minimum loss would be
   a. No. 14
   b. No.12.
   c. No. 20.
   d. No. 16.
   e. No. 4.

2. A certain type of wire of certain dimensions has a resistance of 36 ohms per foot. Another wire of the same type and length but having a diameter of one third the first wire would have
   a. one third the resistance.
   b. one ninth the resistance.
   c. 3 times the resistance.
   d. 9 times the resistance.
   e. the same resistance.

3. A piece of silver wire 10 mils in diameter and 1 inch long has a resistance of 1 ohm. A piece of the same type of silver wire 5 mils in diameter and ½ inch long would have a resistance of
   a. .25 ohms.
   b. 4 ohms.
   c. 2 ohms.
   d. 10 ohms.
   e. none of these.

4. The stripes on a certain resistor are double width black, red, black and gold. The resistance value is
   a. 20 ohms.
   b. 120 ohms.
   c. 12 ohms.
   d. 2 ohms at 10% tolerance.
   e. none of these.

5. When there is a difference of potential between two points there exists
   a. an electrostatic field.
   b. current flow.
   c. low resistance between points.
   d. 100 volts of EMF.
   e. none of these.

6. When an electron leaves an atom
   a. H² is formed.
   b. an ion forms.
   c. a proton is left.
   d. a neutron is left.
   e. none of these.

7. A certain wire 36 feet long, has a resistance of 12 ohms per foot. If a second wire has the same length but a diameter of 1/3 the first wire, the resistance of the second wire is
   a. 3,888 ohms.
   b. 120 ohms.
   c. 1296 ohms.
   d. 72 ohms.
   e. none of these.

8. The illustration below indicates

black   red   black   gold

   a. 6 ohms of resistance.
   b. a resistor with a 10% tolerance.
   c. 2 ohms of resistance.
   d. 10 ohms of resistance.
   e. none of these.

9. A certain wire 36 feet long, has a resistance of 12 ohms per foot. If a second wire has the same length but a cross sectional area of 1/3 the first wire, the resistance of the second wire is
   a. 3,888 ohms.
   b. 120 ohms.
   c. 2,190 ohms.
   d. 72 ohms.
   e. 1296 ohms.

UNIT 2
DIRECT CURRENT CIRCUITS

1. The relationship between current, voltage, and resistance is stated by **Ohm's Law.** It should be remembered that voltage is also electrical pressure, electromotive force or potential. The law states that current varies directly with voltage and inversely with resistance. This means that if you double the electrical pressure across a fixed resistance, you also double the current flow and vice versa if you cut the voltage to one-half the current is cut in half. This also means that if you double the resistance leaving the voltage constant, the current is cut in half or if the resistance is cut in half the current doubles. If the voltage across a resistor is increased from 100 volts to 300 volts the current would be__________times as great.

7. **(2 A)** To solve for E in the formula $I = \frac{E}{R}$ we multiply both sides of the equation by R. Note:

$$I \times R = \frac{E \times R}{R} \text{ and } E = IR$$

It's unfortunate but there are many terms for E. For practical purposes these terms may be used interchangeably and are as follows: Electromotive force, potential, potential difference, voltage, voltage drop, IR drop (because E = IR) and electrical pressure. The unit for electromotive force is the __________.

13. **(IR)** R would be equal to__________.

19. **(12 - 4.25 or 7.75 ohms)** It is sometimes necessary to figure the individual branch resistance of a parallel circuit when you know the other branch resistances and the total resistance. An example is given below:

$$R_t = \frac{1}{\frac{1}{R1} + \frac{1}{R2} + \frac{1}{R3}}$$ For convenience, invert both sides of the equation: $$\frac{1}{R_t} = \frac{1}{R1} + \frac{1}{R2} + \frac{1}{R3}$$

Substituting $\frac{1}{8} = \frac{1}{20} + \frac{1}{80} + \frac{1}{R3}$ and $\frac{1}{R3} = \frac{1}{8} - \frac{1}{20} - \frac{1}{80}$ and

$\frac{1}{R3} = \frac{10}{80} - \frac{4}{80} - \frac{1}{80}$ therefore $\frac{1}{R3} = \frac{5}{80}$

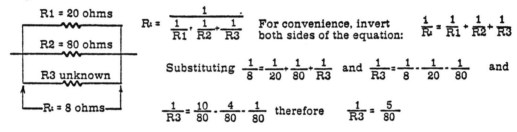

If we cross multiply 5 X R3 = 1 X 80 or 5R3 = 80 and R3 = 80/5 or 16 ohms.

If in the example above R1 was 20 ohms, R2 was 4 ohms, Rt was 2 ohms, then R3 would be__________ohms.

25. **(700 v)** Note that voltage drop is measured across a resistor. If you wished to measure current it would be necessary to insert a current ammeter in series with the circuit resistors as shown.

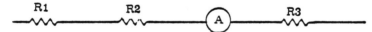

The ammeter can be placed anywhere in the series circuit. For example the ammeter could have been placed between __________ and __________ in the illustration above.

31. **(zero volts)** Before we complete this unit we need to deal with power in DC circuits. Power is the rate of doing work and the unit is watt. Power is equal to the product of the voltage and current or I X E. Using Ohm-s Law, we can change,

$$P = I \times E \text{ to } P = E/R \times E \text{ since } I = E/R \text{ or } P = E^2/R$$

Also using P = I X E we can derive P = I X IR (since E = IR) or $P = I^2R$
There are__________formulas for DC power.

37. **(maximum)** Further use of the formula $P = I^2R$ is made in the following example.

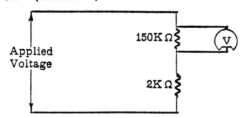

Suppose the measured voltage across R1 was 150 volts. The series circuit current would be 150v/150k ohms or 1 ma. (E/R). The total circuit power would then be $.001^2$ X 152K ohm or .152 watts (P = circuit current squared X total circuit resistance). If the voltage across R1 was measured as 300 v, then the total circuit power would be__________ watts.

2. **(three)** If the resistance is increased three times and the potential is left unchanged, the current would be _____ as great.

8. **(volt)** In a series circuit the sum of the voltage drops is equal to the source voltage. Note the example.

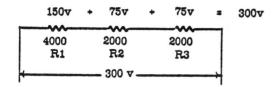

150v + 75v + 75v = 300v

4000 R1   2000 R2   2000 R3

300 v

The total current in this circuit is equal to the voltage source divided by the total resistance or

$$I = \frac{300v}{4000 + 2000 + 2000} \quad \frac{300}{8000}$$

= .0375 A or 37.5 ma.

Since the current is the same in every part of a series circuit, the same current flows through R1, R2, and R3.

The voltage drop across R1 can be figured by the formula E = IR or .0375 X 4000 = 150 v. The 75 volt drop across R2 and R3 is found by multiplying .0375 A times _____ ohms.

14. **(E/I)** It has already been pointed out that the total resistance in a series circuit is equal to the sum of the individual series resistances. In a parallel circuit, the total resistance is less than the resistance of the lowest parallel resistance. By formula the total resistance can be found as shown:

$$R_t = \frac{1}{\frac{1}{R1} + \frac{1}{R2} + \frac{1}{R3}}$$

The total resistance in a parallel circuit is equal to the reciprocal of the sum of the reciprocals of the individual parallel resistances.

The total resistance of resistors connected in _____ is greater than the resistance of any of the individual resistors.

20. **(5 ohms)** In the parallel series combination below the voltage drop across each of the parallel resistors is the same. The voltage drop across the series resistor added to the parallel circuit voltage drop equals the source voltage.

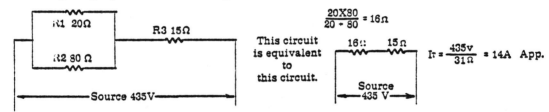

R1 20Ω

R2 80 Ω

R3 15Ω

Source 435V

$$\frac{20 \times 80}{20 + 80} = 16\Omega$$

This circuit is equivalent to this circuit.

16Ω   15Ω

Source 435 V

$$I_T = \frac{435v}{31\Omega} = 14A \text{ App.}$$

The voltage drops across the equivalent parallel resistance would be 14 (I) X 16 (R) or 224 volts. The voltage drop across the 15 ohms resistor would be I X R or 14 X 15 or 210 v. The parallel resistance voltage drop plus the series resistance voltage drop equals 224 + 210 or 434 volts (the approximate source voltage). The 1 volt difference is due to using an approximate current value. The sum of the voltage drops in the equivalent circuit above is equal to _____.

26. **(R1 and R2)** Direct current meters have positive and negative terminals and are called D'Arsonval meters. Assuming current flows from negative to positive the negative terminal must be connected closest to the negative side of the source of EMF. If a meter is pinned backwards it is connected wrong in the circuit. Thus a _____ meter can be used to tell the direction of current through a DC circuit.

32. **(three)** If P = E²/R we can solve for R by multiplying both sides of the equation by R and then dividing both sides of P.

$$R \times P = \frac{E_2}{R} \times R \qquad \frac{R \times P}{P} = \frac{E^2}{P} \qquad \text{and } R = \frac{E^2}{P}$$

By this formula we find that a 2 watt 12 volt lamp has a resistance of _____.

38. **(.608 watts)** Whereas power is the rate of doing work, energy may be thought of as the ability to do work or as work itself. The unit of energy is the watt hour or kilowatt hour. Energy in a DC circuit is equal to the voltage times the current times the time in hours. (or power X hours). If the supply voltage to an electrical device is 120 V.D.C. with a current of 2 amperes, the energy used in 10 hours would be _____ watthours or _____ kilowatt hours.

3. (one third) Ohm's law can be stated mathematically as:

I (intensity of current) $= \frac{E \text{ (electromotive force)}}{R \text{ (resistance)}}$ OR $E \cdot IR$ OR $R = I$

There are_____mathematical forms of Ohm's law.

9. (2000 ohms) If 2 amperes of current is caused to flow through a 10 ohm resistor the voltage drop would be I X R or 2 X 10 = 20 volts.

500 ma or .5 amperes flowing through a 100 ohm resistor would result in a potential difference of _____volts.

15. (series) If a 12 ohms, 24 ohm, and 36 ohm resistor are connected in parallel the total resistance will be less than 12 ohms. Solution is as follows:

$$R_t = \cfrac{1}{\frac{1}{R1}+\frac{1}{R2}+\frac{1}{R3}} = \cfrac{1}{\frac{1}{12}+\frac{1}{24}+\frac{1}{36}} = \cfrac{1}{\frac{6}{72}+\frac{3}{72}+\frac{2}{72}} = \cfrac{1}{\frac{11}{72}} = 1 \times \frac{72}{11} = \frac{72}{11} \quad \text{or} \quad 6.54 \text{ ohms}$$

72 was used as the lowest common denominator.

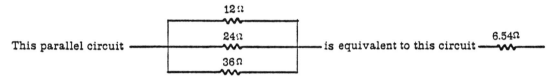

This parallel circuit ———— is equivalent to this circuit ——— 6.54Ω ———

The total resistance of 10 ohm, 20 ohm, and 40 ohms resistors in parallel is_____ohms.

21. (435 v or the source voltage) The voltage drop across R3 in the circuit shown would be_____.

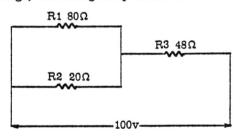

27. (DC or D'Arsonval) If a voltage is applied across one resistor in a series string there will be current flow in that resistor only. The other resistors will not draw any current. Therefore, there will be the same voltage across the whole string as across the one resistor. The example below illustrates this:

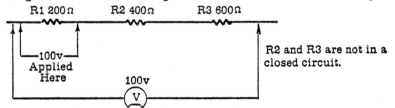

R2 and R3 are not in a closed circuit.

If in the example above 200 V was applied across R1, the voltmeter would read_____V.

33. (144/2 or 72 ohms) Using the same formula a 3 watt, 6 volt lamp would have a resistance of _____ ohms.

39. (2400, 2.4) This completes the programmed text material for Unit 2.

4. **(three)** Using I = E/R. the current flow I through a 1000 ohms resistor R having 10 volts E across it would be 10/1000 or .010 amperes - stated in decimal terms ten-thousandths amperes. This may also be stated as ten milli (a prefix meaning thousandths) amperes or simply 10 ma. .120 amperes may be stated as_____milliamperes.

10. **(50V)** Note that 500 ma was converted to .5 amperes for solution. All units must be in basic form when used in Ohm's Law.

    To solve for R in the formula I = E/R it's convenient to invert both sides of the equation thus:

    Now multiply both sides by E

    $$\frac{1}{I} = \frac{R}{E}$$ $$\frac{1 \times E}{I} = \frac{R \times E}{E}$$ or $$R = \frac{E}{I}$$

    The basic units for E, R, and I are _____

16. **(40/7 or 5.71 ohms)** Two parallel resistors have a total equivalent resistance of their product divided by their sum or

    $$R_t = \frac{R1\ R2}{R1 + R2}$$

    Equal parallel resistors have a total equivalent resistance equal to the value of one resistor divided by the number of parallel resistors or

    $$R_t = \frac{R1}{n}$$ For example, four 8 ohm resistors have an equivalent resistance of 8/4 or 2 ohms.

    The total resistance of a 20 ohm and a 80 ohms resistor connected in parallel is_____ohms.

22. **(75 v)** Current flow through a series circuit made up of three resistors has the same current flow in all parts of the circuit. Therefore, the voltage drop across each resistor is directly proportional to the resistance. Note the examples:

    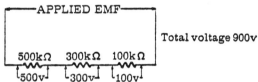

    Total voltage 900v

    If in the example below there is a 100 volt drop across the 100 kilohm resistor, there would be a_____ volt drop across the 400 kilohm resistor.

    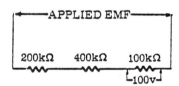

28. **(200 V)** A Wheatsone bridge consists of two parallel paths or branches. Each path consists of two resistors. Note the circuit below:

    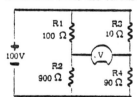

    Considering the negative side of the voltage source as a reference 9/10 of the voltage is dropped across R2 in the R1R2 path because R2 having a resistance value of 900 ohms is 9/10 of the total series resistance in the path. 900 ohms = 9/10 of 900 + 100. In like manner. 9/10 of the voltage across R3 and R4 is dropped across R4. (90 = 9/10 of 90 + 10) Therefore, 90 volts appears both to the left and right of the voltmeter. Consequently, the meter reads zero. The bridge is

    balanced if the ratio of R1 to R2 is equal to the ratio of_____.

34. **(12ohms)** If a 12 volt battery has an internal resistance of .6 ohm and was connected to a 12 volt, 2 watt lamp the current flow would be 12v/72.6 ohms or .165 amperes (165 ma). Internal resistance is considered to be in series with the voltage source as shown.

    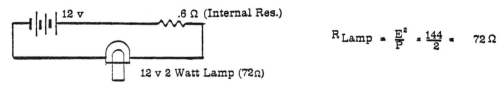

    12 v 2 Watt Lamp (72Ω)

    $$R_{Lamp} = \frac{E^2}{P} = \frac{144}{2} = 72\ \Omega$$

    If a 6 volt battery with an internal R of 1.2 ohms was connected to a 6 volt 3 watt lamp the current would be_____.

KEY TO MULTIPLE CHOICE EXAMS
PART I

FINAL EXAMINATION

1E, 2D, 3A, 4B, 5A, 6C, 7E, 8B, 9D, 10D, 11E, 12B, 13B, 14A, 15E, 16B, 17D, 18C, 19C, 20A, 21D, 22B, 23A, 24C, 25A, 26B, 27D, 28A, 29E, 30C, 31B, 32C, 33B, 34A, 35D, 36C, 37A, 38D, 39A, 40C, 41C, 42B, 43A, 44A, 45E, 46C, 47C, 48B, 49C, 50C, 51A, 52E, 53C, 54D, 55C, 56A, 57A, 58C, 59E, 60A, 61C, 62B, 63D, 64B, 65C, 66C, 67A, 68B, 69A, 70B, 71D, 72B, 73B, 74D, 75C, 76C, 77B, 78D, 79A, 80A, 81B, 82D, 83E, 84C, 85C, 86D, 87E, 88B, 89D, 90A, 91A, 92B, 93A, 94C, 95E, 96B, 97A, 98C, 99D, 100B, 101A, 102C, 103E, 104D, 105E, 106E, 107C, 108D, 109A, 110D, 111E, 112A, 113B, 114C, 115B, 116D, 117D, 118B, 119B, 120E, 121E, 122E, 123A, 124C, 125C, 126C, 127A, 128E, 129A, 130B, 131A, 132B, 133B, 134C, 135A, 136D, 137A, 138B, 139A, 140C, 141E, 142D, 143B, 144D, 145E, 146B, 147A, 148C, 149E, 150D, 151B, 152A, 153B, 154C, 155A, 156C, 157D, 158E, 159B, 160A, 161C, 162B, 163C, 164C, 165D, 166D, 167B, 168C, 169C, 170C, 171B, 172B, 173A, 174E, 175A, 176D, 177D, 178D, 179B, 180E, 181A, 182C, 183C, 184B, 185A, 186E, 187B, 188E, 189C, 190A, 191D, 192B, 193B, 194E, 195C, 196D, 197A, 198D, 199B, 200D, 201E, 202B, 203C, 204B, 205E, 206B, 207A, 208C, 209C, 210E, 211E, 212E, 213C, 214C, 215E, 216C, 217B, 218D, 219B, 220B, 221D, 222A, 223A, 224C, 225B, 226A, 227C, 228C, 229C, 230A, 231D, 232B, 233A, 234E, 235C, 236A, 237D, 238C, 239E, 240A, 241B, 242D, 243A, 244C, 245A, 246A, 247B, 248A, 249A, 250E, 251B, 252D, 253B, 254A, 255C, 256C, 257D, 258B, 259D, 260D, 261B, 262C, 263A, 264B, 265B, 266A, 267D, 268B, 269B, 270D, 271D, 272C, 273B, 274E, 275D, 276E, 277B, 278B, 279B, 280C, 281A, 282C, 283C, 284A, 285D, 286C, 287B, 288B, 289B, 290D, 291A, 292D, 293D, 294A, 295E, 296D, 297B, 298A, 299D, 300E.

PART II

UNIT 1 - 1D, 2D, 3A, 4B, 5B, 6E, 7E, 8E, 9D, 10A, 11C, 12B, 13A
UNIT 2 - 1A, 2B, 3E, 4D, 5B, 6B, 7B, 8B, 9D, 10C, 11B, 12A, 13A, 14B, 15B, 16C, 17A, 18E, 19B, 20C, 21D, 22B, 23C, 24C
UNIT 3 - 1D, 2A, 3C, 4D, 5D, 6E, 7E
UNIT 4 - 1C, 2D, 3B, 4C, 5B, 6D, 7C, 8B, 9C, 10C, 11B, 12D, 13E
UNIT 5 - 1B, 2E, 3B, 4D, 5B, 6E, 7C, 8E, 9C
UNIT 6 - 1E, 2E, 3B, 4A, 5C, 6E, 7B, 8C, 9E, 10B, 11B, 12A, 13B, 14D, 15B, 16B, 17A, 18A, 19D, 20D, 21D, 22D, 23D, 24A, 25C, 26C, 27A, 28C
UNIT 7 - 1C, 2E, 3A, 4B, 5D, 6B, 7E, 8C
UNIT 8 - 1B, 2E, 3D, 4B, 5E, 6A, 7C, 8B, 9C, 10D, 11C, 12C, 13C, 14E, 15C, 16A, 17C, 18B, 19E, 20D, 21B, 22D, 23B

PART II FINAL EXAMINATION

1D, 2A, 3B, 4D, 5D, 6C, 7E, 8B, 9D, 10B, 11C, 12E, 13B, 14A, 15E, 16D, 17C, 18A, 19D, 20C, 21B, 22C, 23C, 24E, 25C, 26D, 27B, 28B, 29E, 30B, 31A, 32B, 33B, 34D, 35C, 36A, 37E, 38B, 39C, 40E, 41D, 42D, 43E, 44B, 45A, 46A, 47C, 48E, 49A, 50B, 51C, 52D, 53D, 54D, 55E, 56C, 57C, 58A, 59C, 60C, 61D, 62B, 63B, 64B, 65E, 66B, 67C, 68B, 69C, 70C, 71B, 72E, 73C, 74A, 75B, 76E, 77A, 78D, 79B, 80C, 81B, 82A, 83B, 84B, 85A, 86A, 87B, 88B, 89A, 90C, 91A, 92C, 93B, 94D, 95E, 96B, 97C, 98C, 99D, 100C, 101B, 102B, 103C, 104C, 105B, 106E, 107A, 108C, 109B, 110E, 111C, 112A, 113C, 114E, 115B, 116D, 117B, 118D, 119D, 120A, 121B, 122C, 123A, 124C, 125D, 126E, 127D, 128C, 129A, 130C, 131E, 132B, 133C, 134B, 135D.

5. **(120 ma)** If 100 volts was placed across a 1000 ohm resistor, the current flow would be_____ amperes or_____ ma.

11. **(volt, ohm, ampere)** If 100 volts forces a current of .1 amperes (100 ma) through a resistor, its resistance can be figured as 1000 ohms since R = E/I or 100/ .100 = 1000 ohms. If 100 volts forces a current flow of .01 amperes through a resistor, the value of resistance must be_____ohms.

17. **(16 ohms)** The total resistance of a 7.5 ohm resistor connected in parallel with another 7.5 ohm resistor is_____ ohms.

23. **(400)** There would be a_____volt drop across the 200K ohm resistor.

29. **(R3 to R4)** Suppose we didn't know the resistance ratio but knew the value of two resistors in different branches and two branch currents. From this we should be able to calculate the voltage to the left of the voltmeter (with respect to the negative terminal of the source) and to the right of the voltmeter. The voltmeter should then register the difference of the two voltages. See the example below:

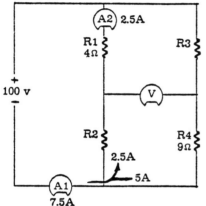

If the total current shown is 7.5 amperes, then the current through R3 and R4 is 5 amperes. The voltage drop across R1 is 2.5A X 4 ohms (I X R) or 10 volts. The voltage drop across R2 is 90 V (100v - 10v). So the voltage to the left of the voltmeter is 90+v. (With reference to the negative side of the source).

The voltage drop across R4 is 5A X 9 ohms (I X R) or 45v. So the voltage at the right side of the voltmeter is +45v (with reference to the negative side of the source voltage). Therefore, the voltmeter will read the differnce of the two voltages of _____volts.

35. **(6V/13.2 ohms or 454 ma)** If two lamps were connected in parallel as shown, the current flow would be_____.

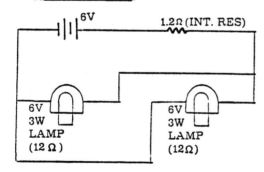

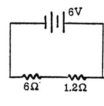

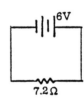

R Lamp = $\frac{E^2}{P}$

KEY TO MULTIPLE CHOICE EXAMS
PART I

UNIT 1 - 1E, 2D, 3C, 4E, 5A, 6B, 7A, 8C, 9E

UNIT 2 - 1B, 2C, 3E, 4B, 5D, 6B, 7E, 8D, 9E, 10D, 11E, 12B, 13B, 14A, 15E, 16B, 17C, 18D,

UNIT 3 - 1C, 2A, 3C, 4C, 5C

UNIT 4 - 1A, 2B, 3D, 4D, 5B, 6B, 7E, 8A, 9E, 10C, 11C, 12C

UNIT 5 - 1A, 2B, 3B, 4B, 5D, 6A, 7B, 8A, 9A, 10E, 11C, 12B, 13C, 14B, 15C, 16E, 17A, 18D, 19E, 20B, 21C, 22A

UNIT 6 - 1A, 2A, 3D, 4C, 5B, 6C, 7D, 8B, 9A, 10E, 11A

UNIT 7 - 1A, 2E, 3C, 4C, 5C, 6C, 7D, 8B, 9C, 10E, 11D, 12B, 13C, 14C, 15B, 16D, 17A, 18C, 19A, 20E, 21C, 22D, 23D, 24C, 25A, 26B, 27A

UNIT 8 - 1E, 2C, 3B, 4E, 5B, 6A, 7C, 8C, 9B, 10C, 11D, 12B, 13C, 14D, 15A, 16E, 17B, 18D, 19C, 20A, 21E, 22C, 23E, 24A, 25B, 26B, ·27A

UNIT 9 - 1B, 2E, 3C, 4C, 5D, 6C, 7B, 8B, 9B, 10A, 11D, 12C, 13A, 14C, 15A, 16B, 17D, 18A, 19B, 20A, 21A 22A, 23B, 24D, 25E, 26A, 27C, 28C, 29D, 30D, 31B, 32C, 33A, 34E

UNIT 10 - 1E, 2B, 3A, 4D, 5A, 6A, 7B, 8C, 9A, 10C, 11B, 12E, 13A, 14B, 15D, 16C, 17A, 18E, 19B, 20A, 21A, 22C, 23E

UNIT 11 - 1B, 2D, 3B, 4A, 5A, 6C, 7E, 8E, 9A, 10C, 11D, 12E, 13C, 14A, 15D, 16E, 17E, 18D, 19C, 20D, 21A, 22A, 23E, 24E, 25B, 26D, 27A, 28C, 29A, 30A, 31B, 32B, 33D, 34C, 35B, 36B, 37A, 38A, 39D, 40D, 41B, 42B, 43B, 44A, 45C, 46E, 47E, 48D, 49B, 50E, 51C

UNIT 12 - 1A, 2C, 3D, 4C, 5B, 6C, 7C, 8C, 9C, 10C, 11A, 12C, 13A, 14E, 15A, 16E, 17B, 18D, 19B, 20A, 21D 22B, 23B, 24C, 25D, 26E

UNIT 13 - 1D, 2D, 3A, 4B, 5C, 6A, 7A, 8A, 9A, 10A, 11D, 12A, 13A, 14E, 15B, 16A, 17E, 18A, 19C, 20D, 21C, 22E, 23E, 24E, 25C, 26D, 27B

UNIT 14 - 1C, 2B, 3D, 4B, 5E, 6D, 7C, 8A, 9C, 10B, 11D, 12D, 13A, 14B, 15C, 16A, 17E, 18E, 19D, 20A, 21A, 22D, 23B, 24C, 25A, 26B, 27B, 28C, 29E, 30C, 31C, 32A, 33A, 34A, 35B, 36C, 37C, 38C, 39D, 40B, 41B, 42D, 43E, 44E, 45B

UNIT 15 - 1E, 2C, 3B, 4A, 5B, 6C, 7A, 8E, 9B, 10C, 11C, 12B, 13B, 14D, 15B, 16C, 17A, 18D, 19A, 20B, 21D, 22C, 23B, 24C, 25D, 26B, 27C, 28D, 29D, 30D, 31C, 32C, 33B, 34A, 35C, 36C, 37B, 38B, 39A, 40B, 41B, 42C, 43B, 44A, 45D, 46A, 47A, 48D, 49E, 50A, 51B, 52A, 53E, 54A, 55D, 56A, 57D, 58D, 59C, 60C, 61E, 62C, 63A, 64B, 65E, 66D

UNIT 16 - 1C, 2D, 3B, 4D, 5A, 6B, 7C, 8B, 9E, 10A, 11D, 12B, 13B, 14E, 15B, 16C, 17C, 18B, 19A, 20E, 21B, 22E, 23C, 24A, 25D, 26B, 27B, 28E, 29C, 30B, 31E, 32C, 33D, 34A, 35C, 36D, 37B, 38D, 39D, 40B, 41D

UNIT 17 - 1E, 2B, 3C, 4C, 5D, 6B, 7E, 8A, 9C, 10D, 11B, 12C, 13A, 14C, 15B, 16B, 17C, 18E, 19A, 20E, 21A, 22E, 23E, 24C, 25C, 26A, 27D, 28D, 29C, 30E, 31B

UNIT 18 - 1C, 2D, 3A, 4B, 5D, 6A, 7E, 8B, 9C, 10B, 11D, 12A, 13C, 14A, 15A, 16C, 17B, 18A, 19B

UNIT 19 - 1C, 2A, 3C, 4C, 5C, 6A, 7E, 8E, 9D, 10B, 11B, 12E. 13E, 14B, 15A, 16E, 17C, 18A, 19D, 20E, 21C, 22B, 23E, 24C, 25E, 26A, 27E, 28A, 29B, 30B, 31D, 32A, 33A, 34A, 35A, 36C, 37C, 38A, 39A 40C, 41D, 42A, 43B, 44A, 45D, 46B, 47A, 48A, 49E, 50E, 51B, 52B, 53D, 54D, 55E, 56B, 57B, 58A, 59A, 60D

UNIT 20 - 1C, 2C, 3C, 4E, 5D, 6D, 7D, 8B, 9A, 10D, 11E, 12D, 13A, 14A, 15A, 16B, 17B, 18B, 19E, 20C, 21B, 22A, 23C, 24B, 25A, 26B, 27E, 28E, 29B, 30A, 31A, 32A, 33B, 34A, 35D, 36C, 37B, 38B, 39B, 40A, 41B, 42B

UNIT 21 - 1C, 2D, 3C, 4D, 5D, 6C, 7A, 8B, 9B, 10E, 11A, 12E, 13D, 14D, 15D, 16D, 17E, 18B, 19E, 20E, 21C, 22A, 23B, 24D

UNIT 22 - 1B, 2B, 3C, 4C, 5A, 6C, 7D, 8C, 9B, 10D, 11A, 12D

UNIT 23 - 1E, 2C, 3B, 4C, 5B, 6B, 7D, 8B, 9A, 10A, 11D

UNIT 24 - 1C, 2D, 3A, 4B, 5E, 6E

UNIT 25 - 1D, 2E, 3B, 4A, 5A, 6B, 7D, 8A, 9D, 10A, 11E

UNIT 26 - 1C, 2C, 3D, 4B, 5A, 6B, 7A, 8B, 9B, 10E, 11A, 12B, 13B, 14A, 15C, 16B, 17A, 18E, 19B, 20E, 21D, 22C, 23A, 24E

6. (.1 A, 100 ma) If 12 volts was placed across 6 ohms of resistance, the current would be_____ amperes.

12. (10,000 ohms or 10 kilohms) A memory crutch for the three forms of Ohm's law is shown below:

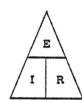

Cover the factor you are wanting to find.
It will be equal to the uncovered product
or quotient. For example: I = E/R as shown

E would be equal to_____.

18. (3.75) The total circuit resistance of two parallel resistors connected in series with another resistor can be figured by use of both parallel and series formulas. Note the example:

This circuit   is equivalent to   this circuit

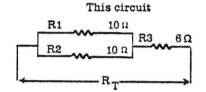

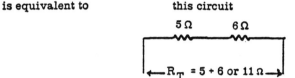

In the circuit shown, R3 must equal to:

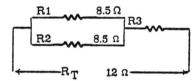

 ohms

24. (200) The total voltage drop across the three resistors would be_____.

30. (45 volts) If A1 is 12.5 amperes and A2 is 2.5 amperes the voltmeter would read_____.

36. (.825 amperes or 825 ma) Since P=I²R, a resistor in a series string dissipates the most power in the form of heat if it has a minimum value. Minimum resistance provides maximum current and power is proportional to current squared. It follows that a resistor in a series string dissipates less power in the form of heat if its resistance is a_____value.

REVIEW SHEET ON FCC EXAM

"Numbers to Remember"

Item	Freq. Tolerance	Power Tolerance	100% Modulation	Channel Width
AM BC Stn	20 cycles or .002% at 1000 Khz	Plus 5% Minus 10%	Ant. Ipk X 2	10 Khz
FM BC Stn.	2000 cycles	Plus 5% Minus 10%	75 Khz	200 Khz
TV BC Stn	1000 cycles	-------	Aural 25 Khz	6 Mhz
Int'n'tl BC	.003%			
Non. Com. Ed. FM. BC Stn	2000 cycles			
STL	.005%			
FM other than FM BC	.01%			

Miscellaneous

Required full scale accuracy of plate meters in final 2%

Portion of antenna ammeter scale considered to be accurate . . . . Upper 2/3

Maximum carrier shift permissible for AM BC Stn 5%

Ratio of peak unmodulated antenna I to 100% modulated (AM) peak ant. I . . . . .1 to 2

Ratio of eff. unmodulated antenna I to 100% modulated (AM) eff. I . . . . 1 to 1.225

Ratio of peak unmodulated ant. P to 100% modulated (AM) peak P . . . . 1 to 4

Ratio of average unmodulated ant. P to 100% modulated (AM) average P. . . . . 1 to 1.5

Ratio of antenna I or P unmodulated to modulated I or P for FM . . . . 1 to 1.

Current tolerance for directive antenna array 5%

Aspect ratio 4 to 3, Field frequency ' 60/sec. , Frames..30/sec.

Standard number of lines . . . . 525.   FM BC dev. ratio 75 to 15 or 5

NBFM deviation plus or minus 5 kc.   NBFM dev. ratio 5 to 3 or 1 2/3

RECHECK PROGRAMMED INSTRUCTION USING SHRADER'S ELECTRONIC COMMUNICATIONS.

1.   Current varies diectly as the_____and inversely as the_____ Sec. 2-1

4.   (IR, E/I) Work problem 2, page 22. Sec. 2-2.

7.   (2/3 as much) If the student has trouble with basic mathematics, he should read SEC. 2-3 and 2-4 and work the problems on page 26. The answers are on page 28.

10. (.378W or 378mw) Work problem 3, page 29. Sec. 2-6 & 2-7.

13. (high or maximum) If on the other hand we reduce the resistance value across an emf to one-half value, we double the current. The power heat loss would consequently double. $(P = I^2 \cdot 2^2 \times R - 1/2)$ $2^2 \times 1/2 = 2$ or twice the original power loss. Maximum power loss results when the circuit resistance is_____.

16. $(P = I^2R, P = IE, P = E^2/R)$ Work problem 15, page 30. Sec. 2-6 & 2-7.

19. (series) There is only one current path in a_____circuit. Sec. 2-10.

22. (zero) In problem 2, page 37, the voltage drops across the 30 ohm, 60 ohm and 150 ohm resistors are _____,_____ , and_____. Sec. 2-11.

25. (13.3v, 39.9Ω) Work problem 4, page 37. Sec. 2-12.

28. (.009 ohm) The complete formula to solve for the total resistance of any number of parallel resistances is_____. Sec. 2-15.

31. (545.45 ohms) Work problem 6, page 41. Sec. 2-15.

34. (.02A, .008A, .4v) Note in the example below that there is no voltage drop across resistors that are not part of a circuit.

The voltage drop across R2 and R3 is_____.

There is no current flow in R2 and R3.

COMBINATIONAL LOGIC GATES AND THEIR TRUTH TABLES

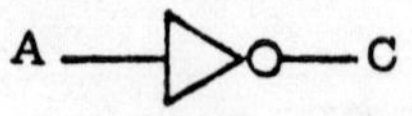

NOT GATE

Input	Output
A	C
1	0
0	1

NOT TRUTH TABLE

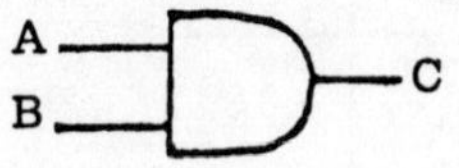

AND GATE

Inputs		Output
A	B	C
0	0	0
0	1	0
1	0	0
1	1	1

AND TRUTH TABLE

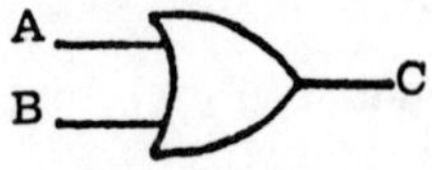

OR GATE

Inputs		Output
A	B	C
0	0	0
0	1	1
1	0	1
1	1	1

OR TRUTH TABLE

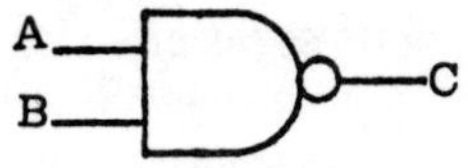

NAND GATE

Inputs		Output
A	B	C
0	0	1
0	1	1
1	0	1
1	1	0

NAND TRUTH TABLE

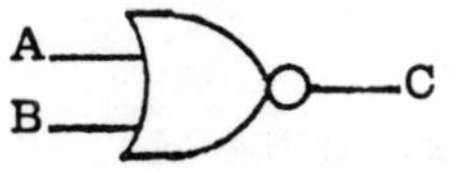

NOR GATE

Inputs		Output
A	B	C
0	0	1
0	1	0
1	0	0
1	1	0

NOR TRUTH TABLE

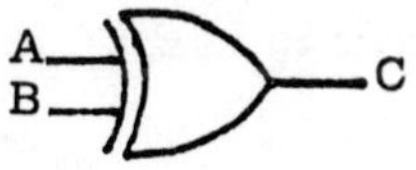

XOR GATE

Inputs		Output
A	B	C
0	0	0
0	1	1
1	0	1
1	1	0

XOR TRUTH TABLE

2. (Voltage, resistance) This is a statement of_____Law. Sec. 2-1.

5. (100v/1000 ohms or .1 ampere) Work problem 3, page 22. Sec. 2-2.

8. Work problem 1, page 29. Sec. 2-6 & 2-7.

11. (400 watts) When current flows through a wire some power is lost as_____. Sec. 2-6 & 2-7

14. (low or a minimum) Work problem 5, page 30. Sec. 2-6 & 2-7.

17. (192 ohms 120v rating) A voltmeter measures the difference of potential between two points and therefore is connected_____a circuit. Sec. 2-9.

20. (series) In a parallel circuit, the current flowing in each load is_____of the other load or loads. Sec. 2-10.

23. (3v, 6v, and 15v) In complex circuits; solution by Ohm's law for voltage, current, and resistance in a particular part of a circuit can be made if there are_____(number) known factors for that part of the circuit. Sec. 2-12.

26. (7.68A) A 12.6v automobile battery is connected across a 12.6v 100 watt lamp. If the internal resistance of the battery is .14 ohms, the current in the circuit would be_____.

29. $(R = \dfrac{1}{1/R1 + 1/R2 + 1/R3})$ Work problem 3, page 41. Sec. 2-15.

32. (40.5v) Work problem 1, page 44. Sec. 2-17.

35. (zero) in a parallel circuit consisting of two series resistors in each path, a voltage difference between the connecting points A and B below can be measured with a voltmeter.

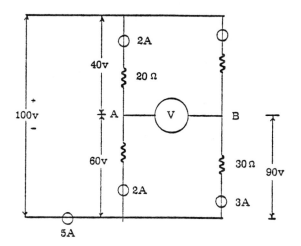

The voltage drop across points A and B is _____.

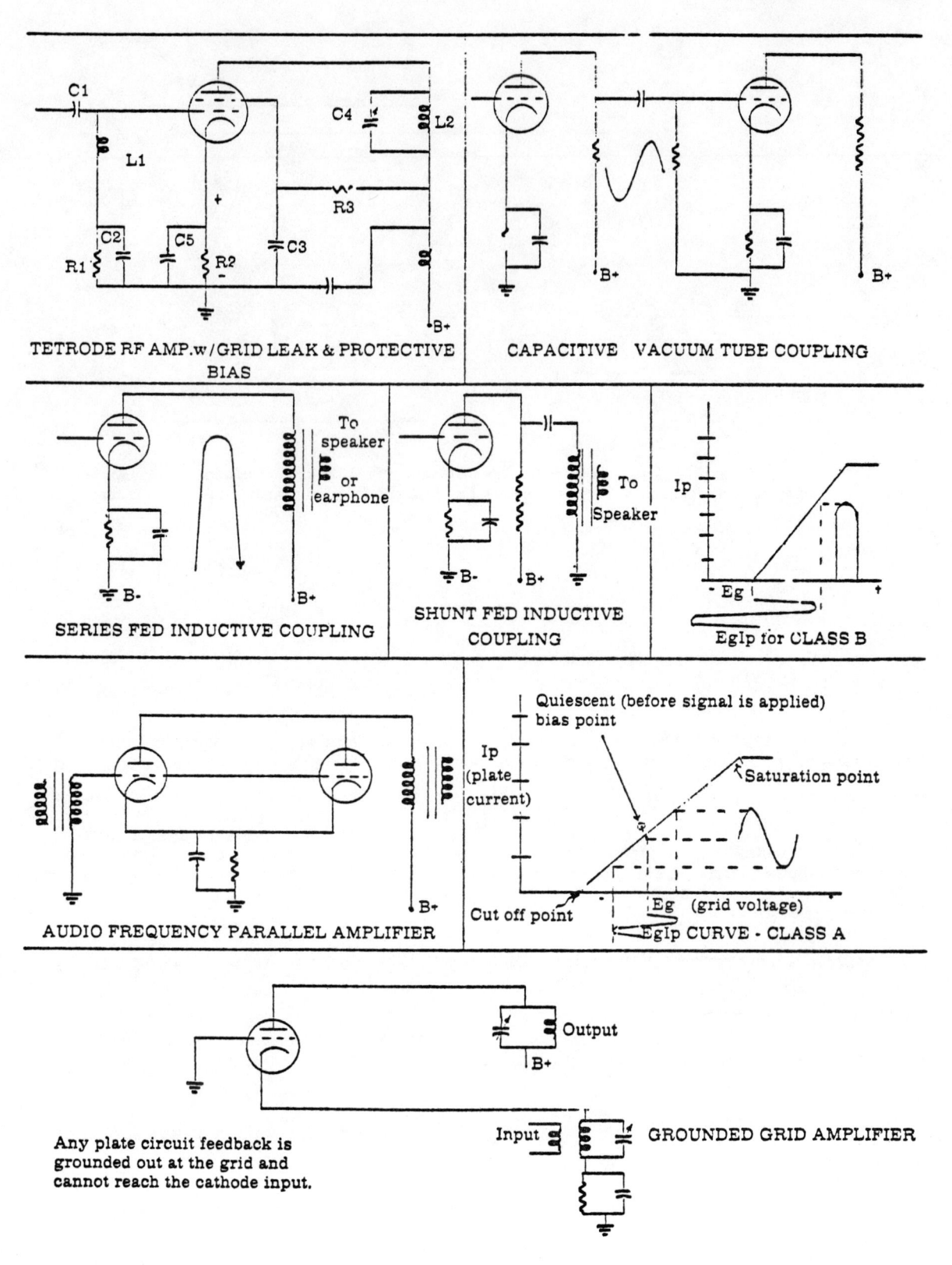

TETRODE RF AMP.w/GRID LEAK & PROTECTIVE BIAS

CAPACITIVE VACUUM TUBE COUPLING

SERIES FED INDUCTIVE COUPLING

SHUNT FED INDUCTIVE COUPLING

EgIp for CLASS B

To speaker or earphone

To Speaker

Ip

- Eg +

AUDIO FREQUENCY PARALLEL AMPLIFIER

Quiescent (before signal is applied) bias point

Saturation point

Ip (plate current)

Cut off point

Eg (grid voltage)

EgIp CURVE - CLASS A

Output

B+

Any plate circuit feedback is grounded out at the grid and cannot reach the cathode input.

Input

GROUNDED GRID AMPLIFIER

407

3.   (Ohm's) By formula E =_____and R =_____. Sec. 2-1.

6.   (120V) Work problem 10, page 23. Sec. 2-2.

9.   (90 watts) Work problem 2, page 29. Sec. 2-6 & 2-7.

12.   (heat) Since power lost in heat is directly proportional to current squared and directly proportional to resistance ($P = I^2R$),doubling the resistance across a constant emf would actually reduce the power loss as it would cut the current in half. In this case,the power loss due to heat would be one half as great. (I^2 - 1/2 squared X R - double).$(1/2)^2$X2= 1/2 original value. Therfore, we conclude that for minimum power heat loss, the resistance should be_____.

15.   (2.074 kwh) Power is equal to_____,_____, and _____.(three formulas) Sec. 2-6 and 2-7.

18.   (across) A D.C. ammeter (D'Arsonval type) can be used to tell the direction of current through a circuit and is always connected in_____in the circuit. Sec. 2-9.

21.   (independent) The algebraic sum of all voltages in a series circuit is always_____. Sec. 2-11.

24.   (two) Work problem 3, page 37. Sec. 2-11.

27.   (7.32 amperes) Work problem 1, page 41. Sec. 2-14.

30.   (180, 150) Work problem 4, page 41. Sec. 2-15.

33.   (.167A, .167A, .1A, 20v) Work problem 2, page 44. Sec. 2-17.

36.   (30v) This completes the recheck material for Unit 2.

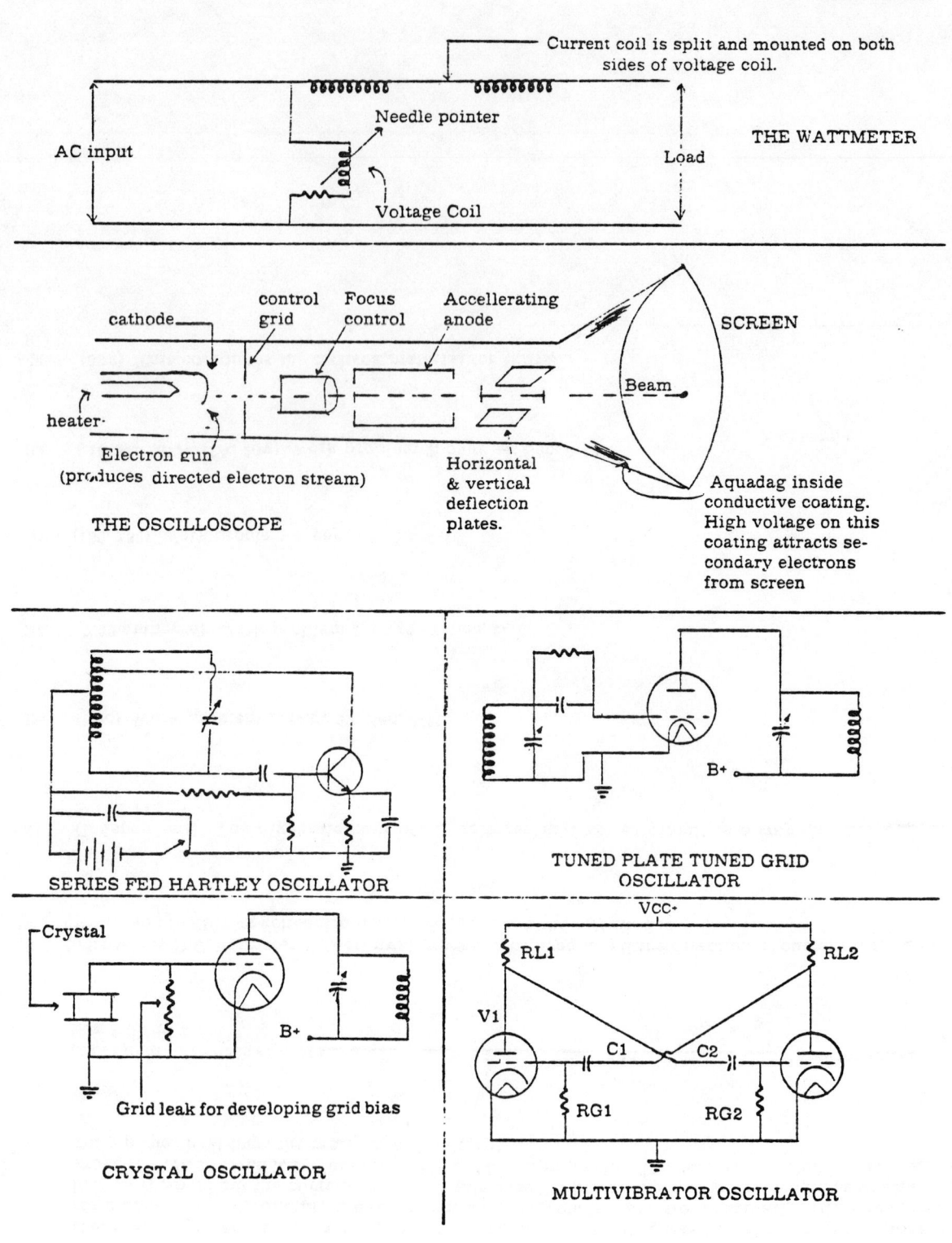

Current coil is split and mounted on both sides of voltage coil.

AC input

Needle pointer

Voltage Coil

Load

THE WATTMETER

cathode

control grid

Focus control

Accellerating anode

SCREEN

Beam

heater

Electron gun
(produces directed electron stream)

Horizontal & vertical deflection plates.

Aquadag inside conductive coating. High voltage on this coating attracts secondary electrons from screen

THE OSCILLOSCOPE

SERIES FED HARTLEY OSCILLATOR

TUNED PLATE TUNED GRID OSCILLATOR

B+

Crystal

B+

Grid leak for developing grid bias

CRYSTAL OSCILLATOR

Vcc·

RL1

RL2

V1

C1

C2

RG1

RG2

MULTIVIBRATOR OSCILLATOR

Unit 2 TEST - D-C ckts.

1. In the diagram below, R3 is equal to

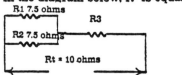

    a. 7.5 ohms.
    b. 6.25 ohms.
    c. 5 ohms.
    d. 10 ohms.
    e. 25 ohms.

2. To tell the direction of direct current flow, it would be best to use
    a. a compass   c. a D'Arsonval meter   e. a dynamometer.
    b. litmus paper.   d. a pedometer.

3. In the diagram below R2 would have a value of

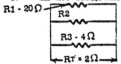

    a. 1 ohm.
    b. 2 ohms.
    c. 3 ohms.
    d. 4 ohms.
    e. 5 ohms.

4. The voltage across the 15 ohm resistor is approximately

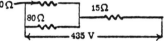

    a. 125 volts.   c. 435 volts.
    b. 210 volts.   d. 140 volts.
                     e. 160 volts

5. In the diagram shown, the voltage is

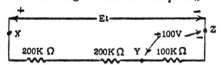

    a. 150 volts x to z.
    b. 300 volts x to z.
    c. 200 volts x to z.
    d. 500 volts x to z.
    e. 75 volts x to z.

6. In the diagram below the voltmeter should read

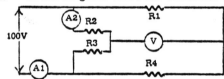

A1-7.5A
A2-2.5A
R2- 4Ω
R4- 9Ω

    a. 10 volts.
    b. 45 volts.
    c. 90 volts.
    d. 100 volts.
    e. none of these.

7. If in the diagram above A1 was changed to 5 amperes, the voltmeter should read

    a. 54 volts   c. 36 volts   e. none of these
    b. 90 volts   d. 76 volts.

8. The measured input to a transmitter was 242 watts. In 31 hours the energy consumed would be

    a. 242 watts.   c. 31 kilowatts.   e. 18 watts
    b. 7.5 kilowatts.   d. 7.5 kilowatt hours.

9. In order for R3 to dissipate the least amount of heat it should be

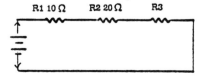

    a. 10 ohms.
    b. 20 ohms.
    c. 30 ohms.
    d. low as possible
    e. high as possible

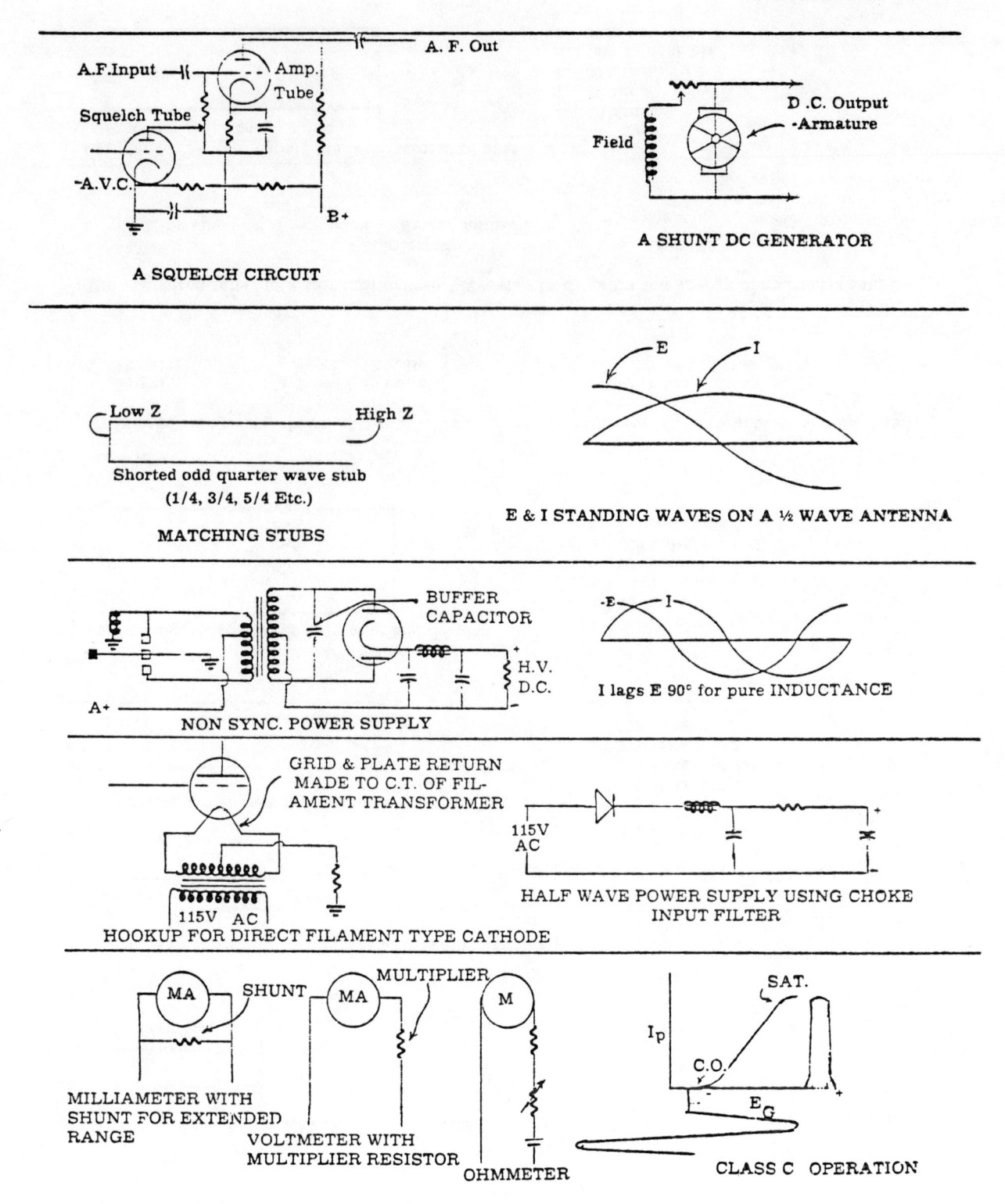

A.F.Input — Amp. Tube — A. F. Out

Squelch Tube

-A.V.C.

B+

A SQUELCH CIRCUIT

Field — D.C. Output — Armature

A SHUNT DC GENERATOR

Low Z — High Z

Shorted odd quarter wave stub
(1/4, 3/4, 5/4 Etc.)

MATCHING STUBS

E   I

E & I STANDING WAVES ON A ½ WAVE ANTENNA

BUFFER CAPACITOR

H.V. D.C.

A+

NON SYNC. POWER SUPPLY

E   I

I lags E 90° for pure INDUCTANCE

GRID & PLATE RETURN MADE TO C.T. OF FILAMENT TRANSFORMER

115V AC

HOOKUP FOR DIRECT FILAMENT TYPE CATHODE

115V AC

HALF WAVE POWER SUPPLY USING CHOKE INPUT FILTER

MA SHUNT

MILLIAMETER WITH SHUNT FOR EXTENDED RANGE

MA MULTIPLIER

VOLTMETER WITH MULTIPLIER RESISTOR

M

OHMMETER

SAT.

I_p

C.O.

E_G

CLASS C OPERATION

10. A bleeder resistor is used across a filter capacitor. If the current through the bleeder resistor is 20 ma and the voltage across the filter capacitor is 300 volts, the power dissipated by the resistor is

   a. 300 watts.   c. 60 watts.   e. none of these
   b. 20 watts   d. 6 watts

11. In the diagram below the voltmeter should read

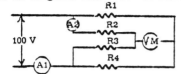

A1 = 12.5 A
A² = 2.5 A

R² = 4 Ω
R⁴ = 9 Ω

   a. 10 volts
   b. 45 volts.
   c. 80 volts.
   d. 100 volts.
   e. 0 volts.

12. If 100 v. D.C. is applied at point W with respect to ground, a voltmeter connected from point X to Z would read

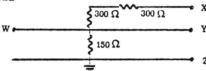

   a. 150 volts.
   b. 100 volts.
   c. 75 volts.
   d. 50 volts.
   e. 25 volts.

13. If you wanted to use a voltmeter to find the power dissipated by the appliation of a voltage from W to ground, you should

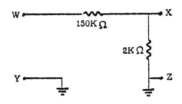

   a. measure the voltage across Y to Z. Square this voltage and divide by 2 K.
   b. measure the voltage across W to X. Divide by 150K. Square this result and multiply by 152K.
   c. measure the voltage across W to X and multiply this by 152K.
   d. measure the voltage across X to Y and multiply this by 150K.
   e. None of these.

14. Energy is measured in units of

   a. kilowatt hours   c. ampere hours.   e. volts
   b. kilowatts.   d. watts.

15. In order to dissipate the greatest amount of power, the load resistance should be

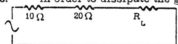

   a. 10 ohms.   c. 30 ohms.   e. low as possible.
   b. 20 ohms.   d. high as possible

16. A 12 volt battery has an internal resistance of .6 ohms. If a 2 watt 12 volt lamp is connected across the battery, the current is

   a. 220 ma.   c. 32 ma.   e. none of these
   b. 165 ma.   d. 78 ma.

17. A 6 volt battery has a 1.2 ohms of internal resistance. If it is connected across two 3 watt - 6 volt light bulbs in parallel, the current through the circuit is

   a. .24 amps.   c. .83 amps.   e. none of these
   b. .35 amps.   d. 6.0 amps.

18. In the diagram below

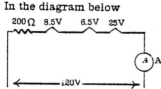

   a. there is no need for the dropping resistor.
   b. the resistance should have a value of 100 ohms
   c. the resistance should have a value of 50 ohms.
   d. the circuit is ok.
   e. the circuit will not work.

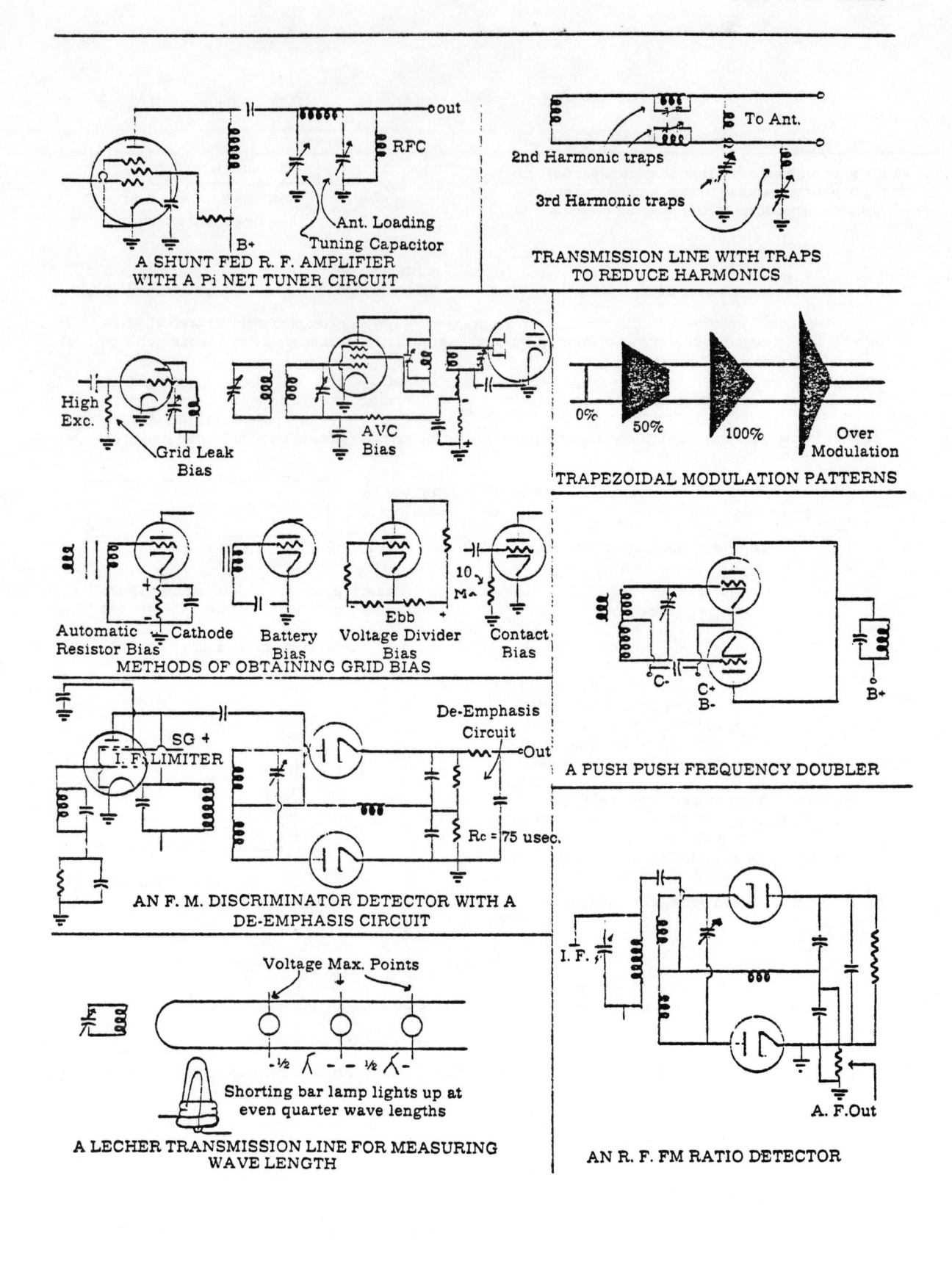

A SHUNT FED R. F. AMPLIFIER
WITH A Pi NET TUNER CIRCUIT

TRANSMISSION LINE WITH TRAPS
TO REDUCE HARMONICS

2nd Harmonic traps

3rd Harmonic traps

To Ant.

High Exc.

Grid Leak Bias

AVC Bias

TRAPEZOIDAL MODULATION PATTERNS

0%   50%   100%   Over Modulation

Automatic Resistor Bias — Cathode

Battery Bias

Voltage Divider Bias

Ebb

Contact Bias

METHODS OF OBTAINING GRID BIAS

A PUSH PUSH FREQUENCY DOUBLER

SG +

I. F. LIMITER

De-Emphasis Circuit

Out

Rc = 75 usec.

AN F. M. DISCRIMINATOR DETECTOR WITH A
DE-EMPHASIS CIRCUIT

Voltage Max. Points

Shorting bar lamp lights up at
even quarter wave lengths

A LECHER TRANSMISSION LINE FOR MEASURING
WAVE LENGTH

I. F.

A. F. Out

AN R. F. FM RATIO DETECTOR

1. When current goes through a wire heat is generated and two fields surround the wire. One field is an electrostatic field and is the kind of field that exist when a potential is connected across the two plates of a capacitor. The other field is electromagnetic. It is like the major field surrounding a coil carrying current.

Cross section of wire carrying current. The dot indicates the tip of the arrow showing current is flowing out of the wire. Radial lines show the electrostatic field. Concentric circles show electromagnetic lines.

In summary, when current flows through a wire heat and fields are generated. The two fields are the _____ and the _____ .

3. (60 ampere turns) The number of lines produced per square inch at some point by an electromagnet is called **flux density**. The symbol is B. In general a greater MMF produces a greater flux density. Therefore, the electromagnetic lines of force are directly proportional to the _____ .

5. (relay) If a core retains its magnetism after the exciting emf is cut off, it is said to have the property of retentivity. The magnetism that remains is called residual magnetism. A core material with high retentivity will have a great amount of _____ magnetism.

7. (300 ohms) In the example (FR.6), the dropping resistor of 500 ohms of resistance with a current flow of .1A would dissipate 5 watts of power in the form of heat. ($P = I^2 R$ or $.1^2 X 500$). It could also be figured as 5 watts using current and voltage. ($P = IE$ or $.1 X 50$). The dissipation of the 300 ohm resistance in the second problem would be _____ .

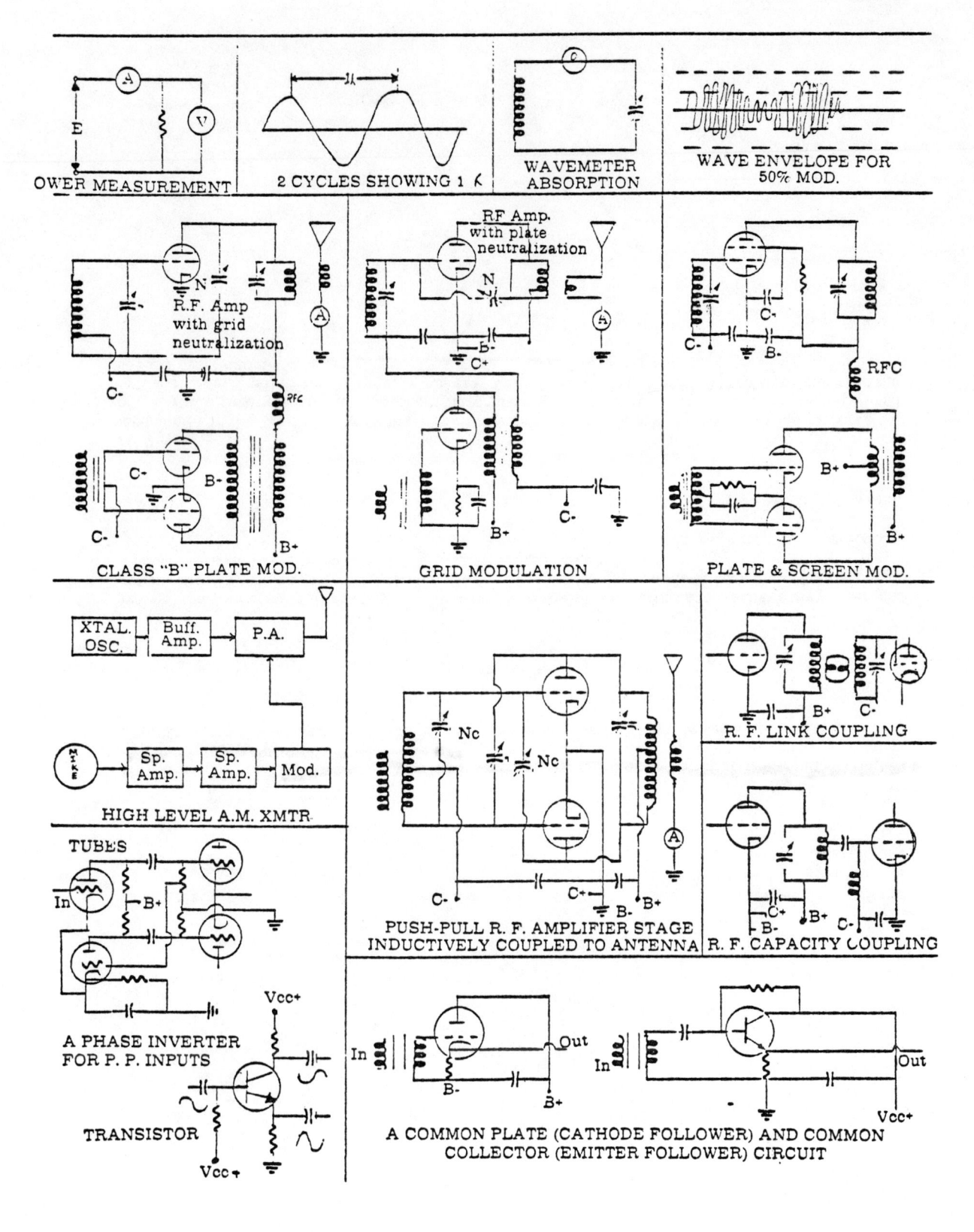

OWER MEASUREMENT

2 CYCLES SHOWING 1 λ

WAVEMETER ABSORPTION

WAVE ENVELOPE FOR 50% MOD.

R.F. Amp with grid neutralization

RF Amp. with plate neutralization

CLASS "B" PLATE MOD.

GRID MODULATION

PLATE & SCREEN MOD.

HIGH LEVEL A.M. XMTR

PUSH-PULL R. F. AMPLIFIER STAGE INDUCTIVELY COUPLED TO ANTENNA

R. F. LINK COUPLING

R. F. CAPACITY COUPLING

A PHASE INVERTER FOR P. P. INPUTS

TRANSISTOR

A COMMON PLATE (CATHODE FOLLOWER) AND COMMON COLLECTOR (EMITTER FOLLOWER) CIRCUIT

2. (electrostatic and electromagnetic) If a wire carrying current is wrapped into a coil, it becomes a strong electromagnet with a north and south pole. The magnetizing force of an electromagnet is called <u>magnetomotive force</u>. The unit is <u>ampere turns</u> (the product of the current in amperes and the number of turns). The symbol is H. A 600 turn coil carrying .1 ampere would have magnetomotive force (MMF) of _____ ampere turns.

4. (electromotive force) The ability of a material to conduct lines of force is called **permeability** Iron has approximately 10,000 times the permeability of air. This makes it useful as a core in an electromagnet. The illustration below shows how an electromagnet can be used with an iron core to form a relay (electromagnetic switch.)

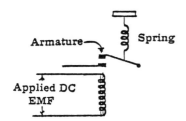

The points are held apart by a spring. When the coil is demagnetized (no emf applied) the switch is open. When an emf is applied the top movable contact is pulled into the bottom stationary contact by the electromagnetic force which is greater than the force of the spring. The top contact is connected to its circuit by a movable magnetic metal called an armature.

An electromagnetic switch is called a _____ .

6. (residual) If the resistance of an electromagnetic coil is known, and the required current for its operation as a DC relay is known it is possible to calculate the value of the dropping resistance needed to operate the relay from a certain voltage source. Note the example below.

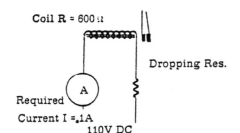

To find the value of the dropping resistance we proceed as follows:
The sum of the voltage drops in a series circuit equals the source voltage.
In this case, E (across the coil) + E (across the resistor) = 110v.

E (across the coil) = .1 X 600 or <u>60v.</u>

E (across the resistor) = 110v - 60v or <u>50v.</u>

If the voltage across the dropping resistance is 50 volts and the current is .1 amperes, the resistance must be E/I or 50/.1 or **500 ohms.**
If the coil resistance of the circuit above was 800 ohms, then the dropping resistance would have to have a value of _____ .

8. (3 watts) This concludes Unit 3.

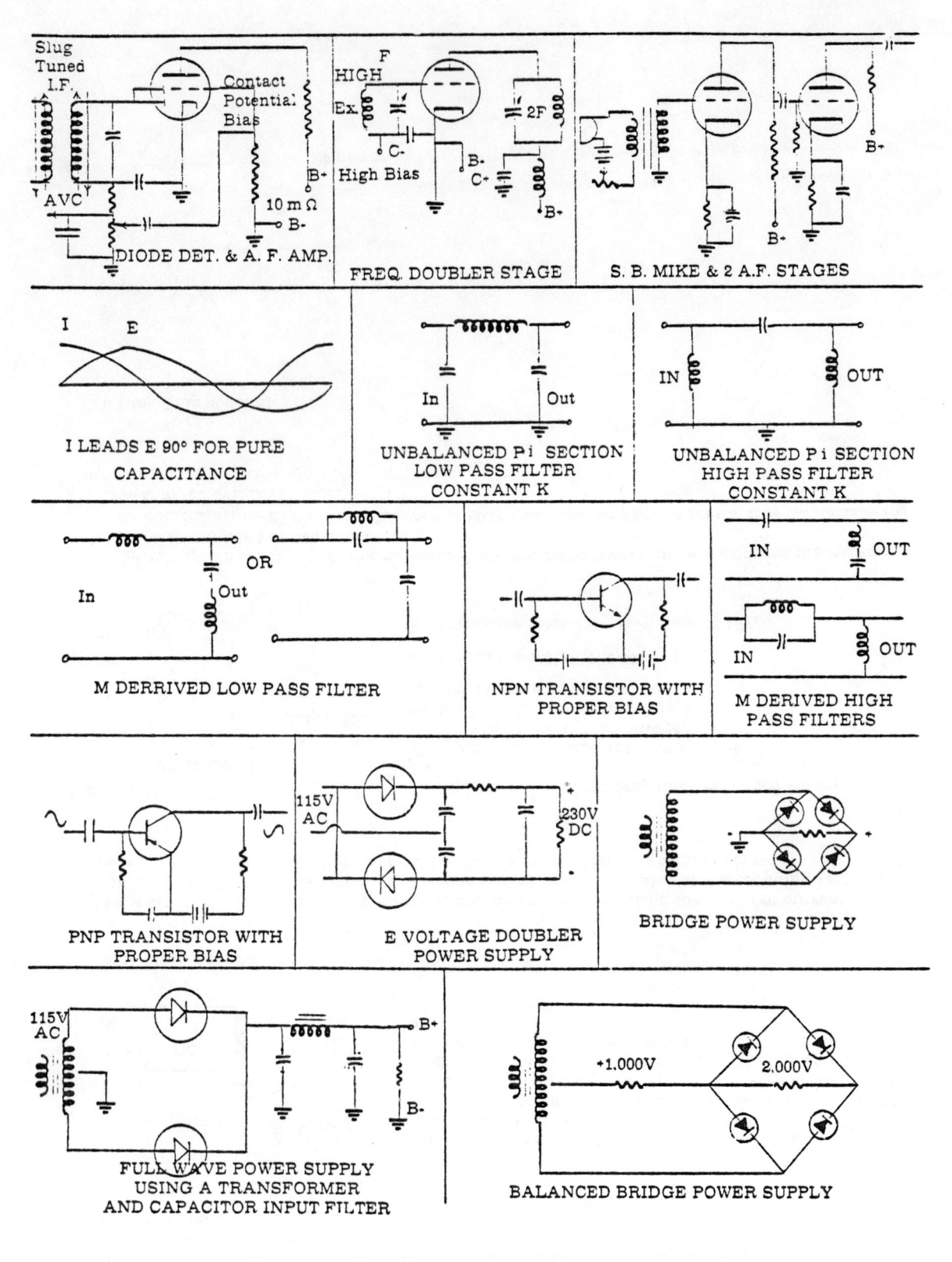

DIODE DET. & A. F. AMP.

FREQ. DOUBLER STAGE

S. B. MIKE & 2 A.F. STAGES

I LEADS E 90° FOR PURE
CAPACITANCE

UNBALANCED Pi SECTION
LOW PASS FILTER
CONSTANT K

UNBALANCED Pi SECTION
HIGH PASS FILTER
CONSTANT K

M DERRIVED LOW PASS FILTER

NPN TRANSISTOR WITH
PROPER BIAS

M DERIVED HIGH
PASS FILTERS

PNP TRANSISTOR WITH
PROPER BIAS

E VOLTAGE DOUBLER
POWER SUPPLY

BRIDGE POWER SUPPLY

FULL WAVE POWER SUPPLY
USING A TRANSFORMER
AND CAPACITOR INPUT FILTER

BALANCED BRIDGE POWER SUPPLY

RECHECK PROGRAMMED INSTRUCTION USING SHRADE'S ELECTRONIC COMMUNICATION

1. Electrons at rest have an_____ field. Electrons in motion produce an_____.
   Sec. 3-2.

3. (lines) The force that produces flux in a coil is called_____ and its common unit is_____
   Sec. 3-4

5. (H) The ability of a material to carry lines of force is called_____ Sec. 3-5.

7. (residual magnetism) If in figure 2-23. a 400 ohm coil was used,the dropping resistance would have to
   have a value of_____.

9. (7.5 watts) This concludes Unit 3 recheck.

$I = \dfrac{E}{R}$, $\quad E = IR$, $\quad R = \dfrac{E}{I}$

$P = IE$, $\quad P = I^2R$, $\quad P = \dfrac{E^2}{R}$

$R = \dfrac{E^2}{P}$, $\quad I = \sqrt{\dfrac{P}{R}}$, $\quad E = \sqrt{PR}$

J (Energy in coil) $= \dfrac{LI^2}{2}$

J (Energy in cap.) $= \dfrac{CE^2}{2}$

$F = \dfrac{.159}{\sqrt{LC}}$. $\quad X_1 = 2\pi FL$. $\quad X_C = \dfrac{1}{2\pi FC}$

$C = \dfrac{1}{4\pi^2 F^2 L}$, $\quad L = \dfrac{1}{4\pi^2 F^2 C}$

$\dfrac{Tp}{Ts} = \dfrac{Ep}{Es}$, $\quad \dfrac{Tp}{Ts} = \dfrac{Is}{Ip}$, $\quad \dfrac{Tp}{Ts} = \sqrt{\dfrac{Zp}{Zs}}$

$T = RC$, $\quad T = \dfrac{L}{R}$

$Q = CE$ (Coulombs). $\quad Q = \dfrac{X_L}{R}$ (Quality)

W.L. $= \dfrac{V}{F}$, $\quad F = \dfrac{V}{W.L.}$

$P = \dfrac{1}{F}$, $\quad F = \dfrac{1}{P}$

V.A. $= \dfrac{Mu\, R_L}{R_L + R_P}$, $\quad Mu = \dfrac{Ep}{Eg}$

$P_{AF} = \dfrac{M^2}{2} P_{DC}$, $\quad P_{SB} = \dfrac{M^2}{2} P_{Car.}$

$I_{Mod.ant.} = \sqrt{1 + \dfrac{M^2}{2}} \times I_{Unmod\text{-}ant.}$

Operating Power out $= I^2R$ (Direct method)

Operating power out $= Ep\, Ip\, F$ (Indirect)

S.W.R. $= \dfrac{E\, Max}{E\, Min.}$, $\quad \dfrac{I\, Max}{I\, Min.}$

$Z = 276 \log \dfrac{D}{r}$, $\quad Z = \sqrt{Z1\, Z2}$.

$Gm = \dfrac{\Delta Ip}{\Delta Eg}$, $\quad Rp = \dfrac{\Delta Ep}{\Delta Ip}$

$E_{RMS} = \dfrac{Epk}{\sqrt{2}}$

$(\triangle Y)$ $\quad Es = Ep\, TR\ \sqrt{3}$

P.I.V. $= (E_{total\ sec.} \times 1.414) - E_{cond.\ tube}$

$Db = 10 \log \dfrac{P1}{P2}$

$Db = 20 \log \dfrac{E1}{E2}$

$Db = 20 \log \dfrac{I1}{I2}$

Motor speed (RPM) $=$

$\quad S = \dfrac{F \times 60}{Pairs\ of\ poles.}$

% Mod (AM) $= \dfrac{E\,max\text{-}pk - Emin\text{-}pk}{E\,max\text{-}pk + E\,min\text{-}pk} \times 100$

% mod (WB FM) $= \dfrac{Deviation}{75\ Khz} \times 100$

% Regulation $= \dfrac{E_{NL} - E_L}{E_L} \times 100$

% Freq. Tol $= \dfrac{Permitted\ Freq.\ Variation}{Correct\ Frequency} \times 100$

% Efficiency $= \dfrac{Pout}{Pin} \times 100$

2. (electrostatic, electromagnetic) The B or flux density of a magnetic field is a measure of the number of _____ per square inch. Sec. 3-3.

4. (electromotive force, ampere turns) This magnetizing force is represented by the letter_____. Sec. 3-4.

6. (permeability) The remaining magnetism in a material after the exciting force is cut off is called _____. Sec. 3-7.

8. (480 ohms) In this case the minimum power dissipation of the resistance would be_____.

SERIES	PARALLEL

SERIES

$$Ct = \frac{C1 \cdot C2}{C1 \cdot C2}$$

$$Ct = \frac{1}{\frac{1}{C1} + \frac{1}{C2} + \frac{1}{C3}}$$

$$Ct = \frac{C1}{n} \quad \text{(When all are equal)}$$

$$Rt = R1 + R2 + R3 \ldots + Rn$$

$$Z = \sqrt{R^2 + (XL - XC)^2}$$

$$I = \frac{E\,Line}{Z}$$

$$E_{Line} = \sqrt{E_R^2 + (E_{XL} - E_{XC})^2}$$

$$E_R = I R$$

$$E_{XC} = I x_C$$

$$E_{XL} = I x_L$$

$$Z = \sqrt{R^2 + X_L^2}$$

$$Z = \sqrt{R^2 + X_C^2}$$

$$E = IZ$$

$$Z = \frac{E}{I}$$

$$Lt = L1 + L2 + L3 \ldots + Ln \quad \text{(No coupling)}$$

$$Lt = L1 + L2 \pm 2M$$

$$M = K\sqrt{L1\,L2}$$

$$K = \frac{M}{\sqrt{L1\,L2}} \qquad P.F. = \frac{R}{Z} = Cos\phi = \frac{T.P.}{A.P.}$$

PARALLEL

$$Rt = \frac{1}{\frac{1}{R1} + \frac{1}{R2} + \frac{1}{R3} + \ldots}$$

$$Rt = \frac{R1 R2}{R1 + R2}$$

$$Rt = \frac{R1}{n} \quad \text{(When all are equal)}$$

$$Ct = C1 + C2 + C3 \ldots + Cn$$

$$Z = \frac{E}{I_{Line}}$$

$$Z = \frac{1}{Y}$$

$$I_{Line} = \sqrt{I_R^2 + (I_{XC} - I_{XL})^2}$$

$$I_R = \frac{E}{R}$$

$$I_{XC} = \frac{E}{x_C}$$

$$I_{XL} = \frac{E}{X_L}$$

$$Y = \sqrt{G^2 + (B_C - B_L)^2}$$

$$G = \frac{I}{R}$$

$$B_C = \frac{1}{X_C}$$

$$B_L = \frac{1}{X_L}$$

$$Y = \frac{1}{Z} \qquad P.F. = \frac{G}{Y}$$

$$Lt = \frac{1}{\frac{1}{L1} + \frac{1}{L2} + \frac{1}{L3} + \frac{1}{L4} \ldots} \quad \text{(with no coupling)}$$

TRANSISTORS

$$A = \frac{Ic}{Ie} \qquad \text{(Current gain for common base circuit - .98 typical)}$$

$$B = \frac{Ic}{Ib} \qquad \text{(Current gain for common emitter circuit} \pm 49)$$

$$A = \frac{B}{1 + B}$$

$$B = \frac{A}{1 - A}$$

UNIT 3   TEST: MAGNETISM

1. A DC relay having a resistance of 700 ohms is made to operate with a current of .1 ampere. When operated from a 120 volt DC line the dropping resistor dissipates
    a. 8 watts
    b. 4 watts
    c. 5 watts
    d. 3 watts
    e. 25 watts

2. Residual magnetism is
    a. the magnetic force which remains when the magnetizing force is removed
    b. the magnetic force apparent when a magnetizing force is applied
    c. permanent
    d. DC current
    e. none of these

3. A coil to a relay has an impedance of 600 Ω , and operates on .1 amp. To operate correctly, a series resistor must be placed in the circuit. With 110V applied, the power dissipation of the resistor would be
    a. 1 watt
    b. 2 watts
    c. 5 watts
    d. 6 watts
    e. 8 watts

4. A coil to a relay has an impedance of 500 Ω , and operates on .1 amp. To operate correctly, a series resistor must be placed in the circuit. With 120V applied, the value of the dropping resistance should be
    a. 500
    b. 600
    c. 700
    d. 800
    e. none of these

5. The dropping resistor in question #4 should be able to dissipate
    a. 5 watts
    b. 6 watts
    c. 7 watts
    d. 8 watts
    e. none of these

9. Station identification should be made clearly and distinctly so that
   a. other stations may clearly identify all calls.
   b. there is no unnecessary repetition.
   c. the FCC can monitor.
   d. all the above.
   e. none of the above.

10. General specifications for obstruction marking and lighting for towers can be obtained from
    a. the F.C.C.
    b. the F.A.A.
    c. the instrument of authorization.
    d. the C.A.P.
    e. the local police.

11. The specifications for obstruction marking and lighting for a particular station can be obtained from
    a. the F.C.C.
    b. the F.A.A.
    c. the instrument of authorization
    d. the C.A.P.
    e. the local police.

12. If an operator is calling a station and it does not answer within a reasonable time, the operator should
    a. call the F.C.C.
    b. keep calling.
    c. leave the transmitter on with no signal.
    d. use more power.
    e. wait a while and call later.

13. An operator can use his station without regard to certain provisions
    a. in times of disaster.
    b. after midnight local time.
    c. on Sunday.
    d. during the quiet hours.
    e. under no circumstances.

14. If a licensed operator permits an unlicensed person to speak over his station.
    a. the station licensee is responsible.
    b. the chief enginer is responsible.
    c. the whole staff is responsible.
    d. the operator is responsible.
    e. none of these.

15. A useful word list for identifying letter is called a
    a. syllabus.
    b. phonetic alphabet.
    c. mnenomic expression.
    d. lexicon.
    e. none of these.

16. A licensed operator normally exhibits his authority to operate a station by
    a. posting a letter from the F.C.C.
    b. posting his license at the station.
    c. posting a statement from the station manager.
    d. posting a statement from the chief engineer.
    e. his ID tag.

17. When testing a station on the air, an operator should.
    a. indicate he is testing.
    b. identify.
    c. be brief.
    d. all of the above.
    e. none of the above.

Unit 4 ALTERNATING CURRENT

1. So far we have only dealt with current going in one direction or direct current. **Alternating current** alternates direction - first going one direction and then another. It is abbreviated **AC**. As it goes in one direction, its amplitude varies from zero to some maximum value and then back to zero before it changes direction. Two directional current through a wire is called _____.

3. **(effective or RMS value)** The word effective simply means the value of AC sine wave voltage that will produce the same heat effect when placed across a resistor as an equal value of DC voltage. R.M.S. means root mean square and refers to the mathematical process of deriving the effective value. The average value is actually the mathematical average of the instantaneous value of voltage during either half cycle or alternation. If it took 50 DC volts across a certain resistance to dissipate 10 watts of power, it would take _____ AC volts to dissipate the same power.

5. ($\sqrt{2}$) Frequency is defined as the number of cycles per second. The unit of frequency is the **Hertz**. Therefore, Hertz means the number of _____ per second.

7. (3,000) 30 gigaHertz means 30,000,000,000 Hertz. It also means 30,000 megaHertz. 3 gigaHertz means _____ megaHertz. (Ask yourself - How many million are there in a billion?)

9. (VLF, LF, MF, HF, VHF, UHF, SHF, EHF) The MF range includes the frequencies of the standard AM broadcast band (600 to 1600 Khz). The MF range is from _____ Khz to _____ Khz.

11. **(30 to 300 MHz).** In radio circuitry it is often necessary to use different insulators (non-conductors) for the different frequencies being used. One common insulator used for VHF circuitry is mica. Many of the plastic insulators are used for the higher radio frequencies. A common VHF insulator is _____.

1   An unattended transmitter
    a. needs no license.
    b. should be inaccessible to unauthorized persons.
    c.   is illegal.
    d. should be identified every ten minutes.
    e. none of these.

2. Wilco means
    a. your last message received, understood, and will be complied with.
    b. this conversation is ended and no response is expected.
    c. my transmission is ended, and I expect a response from you.
    d. I have received all of your last transmission.
    e. repeat.

3. Out or clear means
    a. your last message received, understood, and will be complied with.
    b. this conversation is ended and no response is expected.
    c. my transmission is ended, and I expect a response from you.
    d. I have received all of your last transmission.
    e. repeat.

4. Roger means
    a. your last message received, understood, and will be complied with.
    b. this conversation is ended, and no response is expected.
    c. my transmission is ended, and I expect a response from you.
    d. I have received all of your last transmission.
    e. repeat.

5. When using a microphone in a noisy location one should
    a. yell into a microphone.
    b. cup his hands around the microphone.
    c. use lots of bass response.
    d. use a non directional microphone.
    e. none of these.

6. When an operator shouts into a microphone the received signal is often
    a. more intelligible.
    b. lacking one sideband.
    c. undermodulated.
    d. distorted.
    e none of these.

7. Radio transmitters should be left off when signals are not transmitted
    a. to reduce interference.
    b. to test modulation.
    c. to measure the power output.
    d. to measure frequency deviation.
    e. none of these.

8. Well known words and phrases should be used by an operator for
    a. FCC monitoring.
    b. accuracy.
    c. saving time.
    d. a and b.
    e. b and c.

2. **(alternating current)** A complete train of events in AC is called a cycle. A typical 115 volt 60 cycle per second cycle is shown below in graphical form. The three typical amplitude values are given for the positive half cycle.

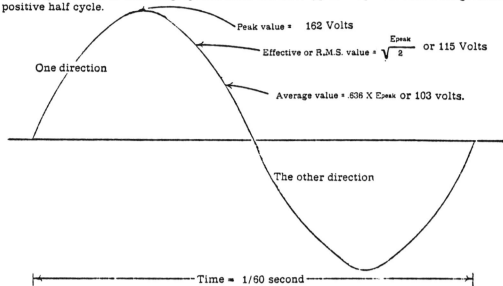

Peak value = 162 Volts

Effective or R.M.S. value = $\sqrt{\dfrac{E_{peak}}{2}}$ or 115 Volts

One direction

Average value = .636 X E_{peak} or 103 volts.

The other direction

|◄————————————— Time = 1/60 second ————————————►|

The effective AC root mean square (R.M.S.) value is the usual value referred to when AC voltage is given. When we speak of 115 volts of AC, it is understood to mean the effective or RMS value. When you divide the peak value by the square root of 2, its like multiplying the peak value by .707 and this gives you the _____ value.

4. **(50 effective or RMS volts)** In order to find RMS AC voltage, the peak voltage must be divided by _____ .

6. **(cycles)** Bidirectional voltage above 10,000 Hertz is called radio frequencies. The radio frequency ranges are as given:

Very Low Frequency	VLF	10,000 to 30,000 Hertz (cycles per second) or 10 - 30 Khz
Low Frequency	LF	30,000 to 300,000 Hertz (cycles per second) or 30 - 300 Khz
Medium Frequency	MF	300,000 to 3,000,000 Hertz (cycles per second) or 300 - 3,000 Khz
High Frequency	HF	3,000,000 to 30,000,000 Hertz (cycles per second) or 3 - 30 MHz
Very High Frequency	VHF	30,000,000 to 300,000,000 Hertz (cycles per second) or 30 - 300 MHz
Ultra High Frequency	UHF	300,000,000 to 3,000,000,000 Hertz (cycles per second) or 300 - 3,000 MHz.
Super High Frequency	SHF	3,000,000,000 to 30,000,000,000 Hertz (cycles per second) or 3 - 30 GHz
Extremely High Frequency	EHF	30,000,000,000, to 300,000,000,000 Hertz (cycles per second) or 30 - 300 GHz

    Note. kilo (k) means times 1,000; mega (M) means times 1,000,000 and giga (G) means times 1,000,000,000. It is important to memorize the ascending order of these ranges, as many F.C.C. examinations ask about two or three of these ranges. 3 megahertz means _____ kiloHertz. (Ask yourself - how many thousands are there in a million?)

8. **(3,000 MHz)** It is important to use a large M for mega since the small m is used for the prefix milli. Now write the ascending order of ranges using abbreviations starting with VLF. VLF, _____ , _____ , _____ , _____ , _____ , _____ , and _____ .

10. **(300 to 3,000 kHz)** The VHF range includes the frequencies of the low band of TV channels (channels 2 through 13). The frequency range of VHF is from _____ MHz to _____ MHz.

12. **(mica)** In the list of radio frequency ranges, two things should be noted about each range. First the highest frequency in the range is ten times the lowest frequency and second each succeeding range starts on the highest frequency of the preceeding range.

    This concludes Unit 4.

17. If a licensee is notified that he has violated an FCC rule or provision of the Communications Act of 1934, he must reply within
    a. 10 days to the F.C.C. in Washington DC.
    b. 10 days to the office originating the notice.
    c. 15 days to the F.C.C. in Washington DC.
    d. 15 days to the office originating the notice.
    e. 30 days to the Washington DC office.

18. If an operator wishes to obtain a hearing on an order for suspension of his license, he must make application within
    a. 10 days of receipt of the notice.
    b. 15 days of receipt of the notice.
    c. 20 days of receipt of the notice.
    d. 30 days of the receipt of the notice.
    e. 60 days of the receipt of the notice.

19. The maximum penalty for violation of the Act or Rule is
    a. $10,000 and/or 1 year, $500 a day.
    b. $1,000 and/or 2 years in jail, $500 a day.
    c. $25,000 and/or 1 year in jail, $100 a day.
    d. $100,000 and/or 2 years in jail, $1000 a day.
    e. none of these.

20. Any emission radiation or induction which endangers a radio communications service is termed
    a. static
    b. superfluous signal.
    c. harmful interference.
    d. induced emission.
    e. none of these.

Unit 4   ALTERNATING CURRENT

Recheck Programmed Instruction Using Shrader's Electronic Communication

1.   The type of alternating current wave form generated by power companies is the _____ wave. Sec. 4-2.

3.   (alternation) You can find the effective voltage of a sine wave by dividing the peak voltage by $\sqrt{2}$ or by multiplying it by _____ . Sec. 4-4.

5.   (cycles) KiloHertz means _____ Hertz. Sec. 4-6.

7.   (1,000,000) One common insulator used at higher radio frequencies is _____ Sec. 4-6.

9.   (LF, 300 kHz - 3 MHz, HF, 30 - 300 MHz, UHF, 3 - 30 GHz, EHF) This completes the recheck on Unit 4.

9. It is usual for log corrections to be made by
   a. the F.C.C.
   b. the F.A.A.
   c. the person making the entry
   d. the station secretary.
   e. none of these.

10. Errors in the station log must be corrected by
    a. striking out the erroneous portion.
    b. making a corrective explanation and initialling
    c. the chief engineer
    d. a and b above
    e. b and c above.

11. A program may be rebroadcasted by another broadcast station
    a. by F.C.C. permission
    b. by permission of the originating station
    c. if its non commercial.
    d. by FM only
    e. without express permission.

12. A message or signal that cannot be transmitted is
    a. an unidentified message or signal.
    b. an obscene message or signal.
    c. a false message or signal.
    d. one of profanity.
    e. any of the above

13. Willfull or malicious interference
    a. can be used in an emergency.
    b. can be used to jam foreign broadcast.
    c. is discouraged but not prohibited
    d. is prohibited.
    e. none of these.

14. Top priority in mobile communications is given to
    a. urgent communications.
    b. direction finding.
    c. government priority.
    d. security.
    e. distress.

15. An operator's license may be suspended if he has
    a. violated a provision of the act.
    b. willfully damaged radio apparatus.
    c. transmitted superfluous signals.
    d. obtained a license by fraud.
    e. all the above.

16. The contents of a message may be divulged to anyone provided that the message pertains to
    a. public broadcasts.
    b. amateur communications
    c. ships in distress.
    d. all of the above.
    e. none of the above.

2.   (sine) One-half cycle is referred to as an _____ . Sec. 4-3.

4.   (.707) The $\sqrt{2}$ is 1.414. 1 divided by 1.414 is .707. Hertz means_____ per second. Sec. 4-6.

6.   (1,000) Gigahertz means a billion Hertz and megaHertz means a _____ Hertz. Sec. 4-6.

8.   (mica) Study table 4-1. memorize the table. Now starting with VLF. complete the table below.

VLF	10 - 30 Khz
_____	30 - 300 Khz
MF	_____
_____	3 - 30 MHz
VHF	_____
_____	300 MHz to 3 GHz
SHF	_____
_____	30 - 300 GHz

ELEMENT 1 EXAMINATION

1. F.C.C. permits and licenses may be obtained by
   a. a written request by mail.
   b. applying to the F.C.C. in Washington D.C.
   c. submitting an application to the appropriate F.C.C. field office.
   d. applying to the F.A.A.
   e. none of these.

2. When a licensee qualifies for a higher grade of F.C.C. license.
   a. he may retain his present license.
   b. his present license will expire in 5 years.
   c. his present license will expire in 1 year.
   d. his present license will be cancelled.
   e. he must find employment requiring the higher license.

3. Commercial licenses are only issued to citizens and other nationals of the USA, except in the case of
   a. aliens having USA visas.
   b. aliens having USA relatives.
   c. aliens holding aircraft pilot certificates issued by F.A.A.
   d. aliens of English descent.
   e. none of these.

4. If a license or permit is lost, the operator should
   a. notify the F.C.C.
   b. Apply for a duplicate.
   c. make a reasonable search.
   d. explain how the permit was lost.
   e. all the above.

5. Radio stations in the USA are inspected by the
   a. F.C.C.
   b. F.A.A.
   c. National Bureau of Standards
   d. B.L.M.
   e. H.E.W.

6. The usual term of a radio operators license is
   a. 1 year.
   b. 2 years.
   c. 3 years.
   d. 4 years
   e. 5 years.

7. A license may be renewed
   a. during the last of its period.
   b. during a 1 year grace period.
   c. any time after it is issued.
   d. a and b above.
   e. b and c above.

8. Logs may be kept by
   a. anyone in possession of the facts.
   b. employees.
   c. engineers.
   d. all of the above.
   e. none of the above.

1. The RMS voltage of a sine wave is equal to
   a. Peak/ $\sqrt{2}$
   b. Peak X $\sqrt{2}$
   c. Peak to Peak/ $\sqrt{2}$
   d. Peak to Peak X $\sqrt{2}$
   e. averaged value

2. The SHF range is
   a. 30,000 Mhz to 300,000 Mhz
   b. 3,000 Mhz to 30,000 Mhz
   c. 300 Mhz to 3,000 Mhz
   d. 300 Khz to 3,000 Khz
   e. none of these

3. The EHF range of frequencies is
   a. 3 Mhz to 30 Mhz
   b. 30 Mhz to 300 Mhz
   c. 300 Mhz to 3,000 Mhz
   d. 30,000 Mhz to 300,000 Mhz
   e. none of these

4. The common VHF insulator is
   a. black rubber
   b. bakelite   d. mica
   c. paper   e. cotton

5. The MF range is
   a. 10 to 30 Khz
   b. 300 to 3,000 Khz   d. 300 to 3,000 Mhz
   c. 3 to 30 Mhz   e. none of these

6. The VHF range is
   a. 3 Mhz to 30 Mhz
   b. 30 Mhz to 300 Mhz
   c. 300 Mhz to 3,000 Mhz
   d. 30,000 to 300,000 Mhz
   e. none of these

7. The UHF range is
   a. 300 to 3,000 Khz
   b. 3 to 30 Mhz   d. 30 to 300 Ghz
   c. 30,000 Khz to 300 Mhz   e. none of these

8. 20 volts equals:
   a. 28.28 Peak volts
   b. 56.56 peak volts   d. 100 peak volts
   c. 32 peak volts   e. 70.7 peak volts

9. The SHF range is
   a. 10 to 30 Khz
   b. 30 to 300 Khz   d. 3 to 30 Mhz
   c. 300 to 3,000 Mhz e. 3 to 30 Ghz

10. The VHF range extends
    a. from 300 to 3,000 Khz
    b. from 3,000 to 30,000 Khz
    c. from 30,000 Khz to 300 Mhz
    d. from 300 to 3,000 Mhz
    e. from 3,000 to 300,000 Khz

11. SHF (super high frequency) refers to the frequency range between
    a. 300,000 Mhz and 300,000 Mhz
    b. 30,000 Khz and 3,000 Mhz
    c. 3,000 Mhz and 30,000 Mhz
    d. 3,000 Mhz and 30,000 Khz
    e. 300 to 3,000 GHZ

12. A good high frequency insulator is
    a. rubber
    b. bakelite   d. glass
    c. mica   e. none of these

Appendices

1.   Inductance is the property of a circuit which opposes any change of current through it. If the current tends to rise a back voltage is induced that opposes the increase. If, on the other hand, the current tends to decrease a voltage is induced that opposes the decrease. This action is the basis of **Lenz's Law.** This law states essentially that the induced field around a conductor is opposed by the existing field produced by an applied EMF. The inductance of a conductor can be increased by wrapping the conductor in coil form. The opposition to the change of current in a circuit is called _____.

5.   **(.625 henrys)** If a certain coil has 400 turns and an inductance of .4 henry, an increase of turns to 500 turns would also produce an inductance of .625 henrys. Since $(500/400)^2$ X .4 is the same as $(2000/1600)^2$ X .4). In either case we square 5/4. If a certain coil has 200 turns with an inductance of .1 henry, an increase to 300 turns would result in an inductance of _____ henry's.

9.   **(.9 henries)** The total inductance of four 6H inductors (coils) connected in parallel would be 6/4 or 1.5H. The total inductance of five 1H inductors connected in parallel without coupling would be _____

13.   **(.5 $\sqrt{L1 \ X \ L2}$)** If two coils are connected in series and there is coupling between them the total inductance is determined by the coefficient of coupling and whether the fields rise and fall together (in phase) or rise and fall out of phase. By formula:

$$Lt = L1 + L2 \pm 2M. \qquad \text{\small PLUS OR MINUS}$$

You add 2 X mutual inductance if the fields are in phase and subtract 2 X mutual inductance if they are out of phase. Note the example below:

Fields in phase   K = .5

```
    ─────ʘʘʘ──────────ʘʘʘ──
          1H            4H
```

L = 1H + 4H + 2M $M = .5 \sqrt{1 \ X \ 4} = .5 \ X \ 2 = 1H.$
L = 1H + 4H + (2 X 1H) = 7H.

If the fields were out of phase it would be necessary to subtract 2M and the total inductance would be _____

17.   **(N to P or M to O)** The restriction to the flow of alternating current through an inductance or coil is called **inductive reactance.** The unit is the ohm and the symbol is **XL.** By formula $XL = 2\pi FL$

                     Where XL = inductive reactance in ohms.
                            F = frequency in hertz (cycles per second)
                            L = inductance in henrys.

It can be seen that the inductive reactance is directly proportional to frequency and inductance. 2π is a constant and therefore not a variable factor. If the frequency doubled in a purely inductive circuit the impedance to the flow of AC current (inductive reactance) would also _____.

21.   **(100 turns)** On the other hand the current ratio secondary to primary is inversely proportional to the secondary to primary turns ratio assuming no transformer power loss. Note below:

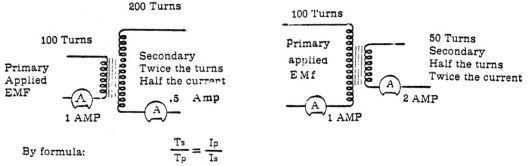

By formula: $\dfrac{Ts}{Tp} = \dfrac{Ip}{Is}$

If the secondary current is 1/4 the primary current the secondary turns would be _____ times the primary turns.

126. Grounded grid amplifiers are often used in high frequency circuits because
   a. they eliminate harmonic generation.
   b. they are good parasitic oscillators.
   c. they eliminate parasitics.
   d. grid neutralization can be used.
   e. they do not have to be neutralized.

127. The input to a push pull amplifier is 1000 volts at 3 amperes. If the efficiency factor is 80%, the power output would be
   a. 3000 watts.
   b. 3750 watts.
   c. 4000 watts.
   d. 2400 watts.
   e. none of these.

128. Long sections of wave guides are not placed parallel to the earth in order to
   a. eliminate capacitance between wave guide and ground.
   b. eliminate inductance between wave guide and ground.
   c. eliminate dust and moisture accumulation.
   d. reduce harmonic energy.
   e. accelerate R.F. current flow.

129. The power output of a directional broadcast antenna is calculated by multiplying the antenna current squared by the radiation resistance. These measurments are made at
   a. the common feed point.
   b. either tower.
   c. the tower having the highest radiation resistance.
   d. the tower having the highest antenna current.
   e. the tower having the lowest radiation resistance.

130. A certain 1/2 wave 800 ft. antenna radiates with an E. R. P. of 500 watts. The field strength of the signal 1 mile away is 336 mv per meter for the fundamental frequency and 47 microvolts per meter for the second harmonic. The second harmonic is attenuated
   a. 67 dbs.
   b. 70 dbs.
   c. 77 dbs.
   d. 80 dbs.
   e. 120 dbs

131. Two coaxial feedlines are used to feed two in phase antennas operating on 98.3 MHz. The total coaxial cable length required would be approximately
   a. 6 meters.
   b. .3 meters.
   c. 4.21 meters.
   d. 3 meters.
   e. none of these.

132. On 5 different occasions the ratios of the base current to the reference current of one element of a directive broadcast antenna array are as shown. The out of tolerance ratio is
   a. 3.8A and 1A.
   b. 4.2A and 1.27A.
   c. 3A and .79A.
   d. 3.35A and .91A.
   e. 3.79A to 1A.

133. A 3/4 wave transmission line is shorted at one end. The impedance at the other end is
   a. infinity.
   b. very low.
   c. very high.
   d. zero.
   e. 52 ohms.

134. If a TV broadcast transmittr is modulated 23% by a 1 KHz aural tone, the deviation is
   a. 17.25 KHz.
   b. 5.75 KHz.
   c. 23 KHz.
   d. 30 KHz.
   e. 1 KHz.

135. If the operating power of the video transmitter at a TV station is 37 KW, the aural operating power should be approximately
   a. 37 kw.
   b. 74 kw.
   c. 18.5 kw
   d. 7.4 kw.
   e. none of these.

2. **(inductance)** There are two kinds of inductance. Self inductance is apparent when a changing EMF is applied to a simple coil. In this case the opposition to current change is manifest in the same circuit that an EMF is applied to. The unit of self inductance is the **Henry** and the symbol is **L.** Mutual inductance results when a primary coil is coupled by its field to a second coil. The unit of mutual inductance is also the **Henry.** The symbol is **M.** The unit of self and mutual inductance is the _____.

6. **(.225 henries)** The formula for the approximate inductance of a coil is:

$$L = \frac{r^2 N^2}{9r + 10\,l}$$

    Where L is inductance in henries
    N is the number of turns
    r is the coil radius
    l is the coil length

    This formula shows that the inductance is not only directly proportional to the turns squared, but also to a ratio of the radius (or diameter) to coil length. If you pulled the turns of an air coil apart you would decrease its inductance. Conversely pushing the turns closer together and decreasing the coil length would _INCREASE_ its inductance.

10. **(1/5 henry)** In the example below four inductors are connected in a complex circuit. Let us solve for the total inductance L. The equivalent circuits are shown on the right.

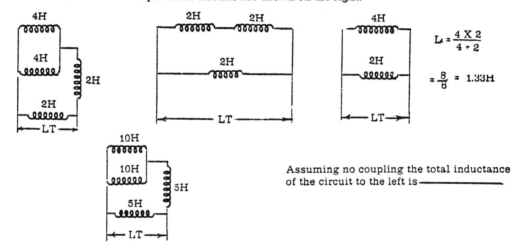

$$L = \frac{4 \times 2}{4 + 2}$$

$$= \frac{8}{6} = 1.33H$$

Assuming no coupling the total inductance of the circuit to the left is _____

14. **(3H)** Note another example:

    6H   6H

    K = .5 (50% linkage)
    Fields are in phase

    L = L1 + L2 + 2M $M = .5\sqrt{L1 \times L2} = .5\sqrt{36} = 3H$

    L = 6 + 6 + (2X3) = 18 henries or 3L1 or 3L2

    It always works out that the total inductance of two coils of equal inductance connected in series with their fields in phase and a coefficient of coupling of .5 is 3L1 or 3L2. If the K was 1 in the problem above the total inductance would be_____henrys or_____times L1.

18. **(double)** When AC voltage is applied to a pure inductance, the current is caused by the inductance to lag the voltage by 90 degrees. (regardless of the amount of inductance). This means that the sine wave current amplitude would reach its maximum value 1/2 of a cycle later than the voltage reached its maximum value. (one cycles is 360 degrees). Note the illustration:

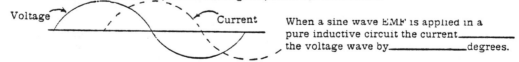

When a sine wave EMF is applied in a pure inductive circuit the current_____ the voltage wave by_____degrees.

22. **(four)** If there is 100 turns in the primary, a primary current of 1 ampere, and a secondary current of .5 ampere; we can use the formula to solve for the secondary current as shown:

$$\frac{Ts}{Tp\,(100)} = \frac{Ip(1)}{Is\,(.5)} \quad \text{or} \quad \frac{Ts}{100} = \frac{1}{5} \quad \text{and} \quad \frac{Ts}{100} = 2 \qquad Ts = 200 \text{ turns.}$$

    Note half as much current in the secondary - twice as many secondary turns. If in the example above Tp = 100, Ip = 1 ampere, and Is = .25 amperes; then there would be_____secondary turns.

117. If the gain of A is infinite, the amplification factor is
    a. 17.
    b. 16.
    c. 15.
    d. 6.5.
    e. infinite.

118. A T network between the antenna ammeter and the phasing control is used to
    a. divide the power.
    b. eliminate the need for separate antenna tuning.
    c. change the power for nighttime operation.
    d. match impedances.
    e. all of the above.

119. The station to transmitter antenna link must be
    a. a folded dipole.
    b. a simple dipole.
    c. a vertical antenna.
    d. directional.
    e. a horizontal antenna.

120. An Austin Ring transformer is used for
    a. isolation of the R.F. from the tower lights.
    b. a balanced modulator.
    c. a bridge rectifier in three phase circuits.
    d. reducing harmonics.
    e. preventing parasitic oscillations.

121. The frequency of the pilot subcarrier used in FM stereo multiplex transmitting is
    a. 3.85 Khz.
    b. 19 Khz.
    c. 6 Mhz.
    d. 4.5 Mhz.
    e. none of these

122. The chrominance sub carrier frequency used color TV broadcasts is
    a. 19 Khz.
    b. 4.2 Mhz.
    c. 3.58 Mhz.
    d. 4.5 Mhz.
    e. 10.7 Mhz.

123. The color burst on the back porch of the horizontal sync pulse is used
    a. to sync the TV receiver color oscillator.
    b. to sync the TV receiver vertical oscillator.
    c. to provide signal for the TV receiver color killer.
    d. to operate the red gun in the CRT.
    e. to operate the blue gun in the CRT.

124. The suppressor grid in a vacuum tube
    a. reduces interelectrode capacitance.
    b. is the second element from the cathode.
    c. is usually tied to the cathode.
    d. controls the electron flow from cathode to anode.
    e. all of the above.

125. The E.R.P. from a certain transmitter is 3.93 watts. The antenna field gain is 1.2 and is fed with 130 ft of RG 58 having a loss of 4.68 db/100 ft. The transmitter output power is approximately
    a. 2 watts.
    b. 5 watts.
    c. 10 watts
    d. 11 watts.
    e. none of these

3. **(henry)** There is a greater opposition to change in current if more turns are used in a coil. The inductance is directly proportional to the number of turns squared. If the turns of a single layer coil are doubled the inductance is quadruppled. If the turns are trippled the inductance is _____ times as great.

7. **(increase)** The inductance of a coil is directly proportional to the turns squared and to the ratio of the RADIUS or DIAMETER to the LENGTH of the coil.

11. **($\frac{10 \times 5}{10 + 5}$ or 50/15 = 3.33H)** The inductance of a coil can be increased by using a laminated iron core made of thin slices of iron. Iron has a greater permeability than air. The iron core provides a sort of secondary, but the induced currents in the core called eddy currents will produce minimal power heat loss if they are constructed by using laminations instead of solid iron. When an iron core coil is used, eddy current power losses are reduced by using _____ iron cores.

15. **(24 henrys, 4L1)** It is also true that the total inductance of two equal inductances connected in series with a K of 1 and the fields in phase is equal to 4L1 or 4L2. Now let us look at an example with fields out of phase (field rises in L1 as it falls in L2). Suppose L1 was .4H and connected in series with L2 having an inductance of .8H. If the fields were out of phase and the mutual inductance is .2H then

    L would equal L1 + L2 - 2M. or = .8 + .4 - (2 X.2) = .8H.

    We subtract 2M because the fields are out of phase. If a .5H and .9H inductor was connected in series with a mutual inductance of .3H and the fields were out of phase, the total inductance would be _____ henrys.

19. **(lags, 90 degrees)** When two coils are coupled together they form a transformer. The voltage induced from a primary to a secondary winding is directly proportional to the turns ratio.

    By formula: $\frac{Ts}{Tp} = \frac{Es}{Ep}$

    Where Tp = primary turns
    Ts = secondary turns
    Ep = primary voltage
    Es = secondary voltage

    The secondary to primary voltage ratio is therefore equal to the secondary to primary _____ ratio.

23. **(400 turns)** This concludes unit five.

110. The voltage drop across a vacuum tube is determined by

    a. the B+ voltage.
    b. the plate current flow.
    c. the dynamic resistance of the tube.
    d. the load resistance.
    e. all of these.

111. The rules and regulations require constant monitoring of

    a. the frequency.
    b. the modulation percentage.
    c. a and b.
    d. the crystal oven temperature.
    e. none of these.

112. Deviation is defined as

    a. deviation above or below the carrier frequency.
    b. deviation above and below the carrier frequency.
    c. 1.5 Khz.
    d. 5 Khz.
    e. 25 Khz.

113. Changing the phase in antenna currents will change

    a. the radiated power.
    b. the transmission line losses.
    c. the directional pattern.
    d. the wavelength.
    e. all the above.

114. If there is no dip in the grid current of an RF amplifier as the plate circuit is tuned through resonance, this indicates

    a. parasitic oscillations.
    b. self oscillation.
    c. insufficient RF excitation.
    d. the antenna coupling is loose.
    e. normal operation.

115. An FM broadcast transmitter is modulated 80% by a 1000 Hz sine wave. If the modulation audio was changed to 10 Khz and the same modulation percentage was used the deviation would be

    a. 75 Khz.
    b. 60 Khz.
    c. 100 Khz.
    d. 15 Khz.
    e. 10 Khz.

116. Split tuning can be remedied by

    a. using close coupling.
    b. neutralization.
    c. degeneraive feedback.
    d. using loose coupling.
    e. parasitic chokes.

4. **(nine)** If a certain coil has 1200 turns and an inductance of .5 henry, an increase of turns to 1600 turns would produce an inductance of $(1600/1200)^2$ X .5 or $(4/3)^2$ X .5 = .89 henrys. If a certain coil has 1600 turns with an inductance of .4 henry; an increase of turns to 2000 turns would produce an inductance of $(2000/1600)^2$ X .4 or _____ henrys.

8. **(radius or diameter, length)** When coils are connected together in series or parallel without any coupling of electromagnetic lines the total inductance is figured in much the same manner as resistance is figured in series or parallel.

   L (Series) = L1 + L2 + L3 . . . .

   _____1_____

12. **(laminated)** The amount of coupling between two coils is indicated by the coefficient of coupling. If there is complete linkage of lines primary to secondary the coefficient is 1 or 100%. If the linkage is 50% the coefficient is .5. The mutual inductance present when a secondary coil is coupled to a primary coil is determined by the amount of coupling and the self inductance of the primary and secondary. By formula

   $$M = K \sqrt{L1 \times L2}$$

   Note the illustration below:

   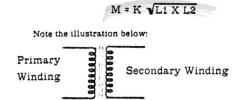

   Primary Winding   Secondary Winding

   Where M = mutual inductance
   L1 = self inductance of primary
   L2 = self inductance of secondary
   K = coefficient of coupling

   If all primary lines cut secondary winding K is equal to 1.

   If the coefficient was 75% then the mutual inductance would equal $.75 \times \sqrt{L1 \times L2}$. If the coefficient (K) was 50% the mutual inductance would be _____.

16. **(.8 henry)** For maximum total inductance the current flowing through two series coils must flow the same direction in each coil so that their fields are in phase.

   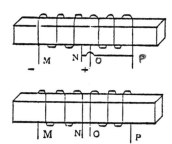

   In this case even though the coils are wound in opposite directions current would flow in the counter clockwise direction in both coils when viewed from the left end (or clockwise in both viewed form the right end.)

   In the example to the left, you should connect ___N to P___ to ___M to O___ for maximum inductance.

20. **(turns)** Let us solve for the secondary turns with the following known values: Ep = 6v. Es = 24v. Tp = 50
   Using our formula: $\dfrac{Ts}{Tp (50)} = \dfrac{Es (24)}{Ep (6)} = \dfrac{Ts}{50} = \dfrac{24}{6}$

   If we cross multiply, 6 Ts = 24 X 50 and 6Ts = 1200

   $Ts = \dfrac{1200}{6} = 200$ turns.

   If the secondary voltage was 12 volts there would be _____ turns in the secondary.

Element 4 Examination

102. To complete one frame it takes

    a. 1/525 seconds.
    b. 1/30 seconds.
    c. 1/60 seconds.
    d. 15,750 seconds.
    e. 167 seconds.

103. The 100% modulation is indicated by

    a.    b.    c.    d.    e.

104. The blanking pulse

    a. regulates the time constant of the horizontal oscillator
    b. drives the CRT grid positive.
    c. drives the CRT grid negative.
    d. blanks the beam as it moves left to right.
    e. none of these.

105. If a full wave power supply using mercury vapor tubes delivered 3000 volts to the filter circuit, the output voltage would be approximately

    a. 1.414 X 3000 volts.
    b. .900 X 3000 volts.
    c. 1500 volts.
    d. 500 volts.
    e. none of these.

106. The output ripple frequency of a 200 volt 3 phase full wave power supply would be

    a. 60 hertz.
    b. 120 hertz.
    c. 30 hertz.
    d. 180 hertz.
    e. 360 hertz.

107. A series RLC circuit consists of 15 ohms of resistance, 25 ohms of capacitive reactance, and 10 ohms of inductive reactance. In such a circuit

    a. the total current leads the total voltage.
    b. the total voltage leads the total current.
    c. there is a 90 degree phase displacement.
    d. the circuit is resonant.
    e. none of these.

108. The standard broadcast station primary service area is

    a. within any 2 mile radius.
    b. within an area which does not go below a power of .5 mw.
    c. within a ground wave area which shows no fading or noise.
    d. half the distance of line of sight distance.
    e. within 100 miles.

109. One advantage of a grounded grid RF amplifier is that it

    a. doesn't require any plate voltage.
    b. doesn't require any neutralization.
    c. is a natural two to one frequency divider.
    d. is rich in harmonic energy.
    e. is self biasing.

Unit 5   Inductance and Transformers

Recheck Programmed Instruction Using Shrader's Electronic Communications

1. The property of a coil opposing any change of current through it is called

    _____, Sec. 5-1.

3. (electromagnetic) The unit of inductance is the _____ and the symbol for self inductance is _____ Sec. 5-2.

5. (inductance) This means that with twice the turns you have four times the inductance. By formula:

    $$\frac{L2}{L1} = \left(\frac{T2}{T1}\right)^2$$

    Let us solve in a problem for L2 when turns are added. Assuming L1 = .4H, T1 = 1600 turns, we can solve for the new inductance L2 when turns are added to give 2000 turns.

    $$\frac{L2}{.4} = \left(\frac{2000}{1600}\right)^2 \text{ and } \frac{L2}{.4} = \left(\frac{5}{4}\right)^2$$

    $$\frac{L2}{.4} = \frac{25}{16} \quad 16L2 = 10 \quad L2 = .625H.$$

    A certain coil having 400 turns and an inductance of .5 henry has added turns for a total of 600 turns. The new inductance would be _____. Sec. 5-3.

7. (current) A low frequency choke coil has greater inductance if it has an _____ core. Sec. 5-6.

9. ($.5\sqrt{L1\ L2}$) The mutual inductance of a 2H coil with 50% of its lines cutting an 8 H coil, is _____ henrys. Sec. 5-7.

11. (66 2/3%) If a .4H and a .6H coil were connected in series with a mutual inductance of .2H, the total inductance with the fields in phase would be _____ henrys and the total inductance with the fields out of phase would be _____ Sec. 5-9.

13. (N to P or M to O) The total inductance of five 1 henry coils connected in series without coupling would be _____ and connected in parallel without coupling would be _____. Sec. 5-10.

15. (increase) The formula for inductive reactance shows that it is directly proportional to the frequency and to the inductance. The impedance to the flow of current (inductive reactance in this case) would be _____ if the frequency doubled. Sec. 5-12.

17. (7,536 ohms, 31,400 ohms) When a pure inductance is connected to a sine wave generator, the current lags the voltage by _____ degrees. Sec. 5-13.

19. (inductance) In its simplest form a transformer consists of a _____ wire and a _____ wire. Sec. 5-15.

21. (laminated) The primary of a transformer has 100 turns with an applied EMF of 115 volts. If the secondary voltage is 460 volts, the number of secondary turns would be _____ Sec. 5-21.

23. (less) The primary of a transformer has 100 turns with a current flow of 1 ampere. If the secondary current is .4 amperes, the number of secondary turns (assuming 100% power transfer) would be _____ Sec. 5-24.

95. Y or admittance is the reciprocal of

   a. susceptance.
   b. resistance.
   c. conductance.
   d. reactance.
   e. impedance.

96. A 500 watt AM BC station modulated 80% would have a side band power of

   a. 520 watts.
   b. 160 watts.
   c. 400 watts.
   d. 50 watts.
   e. none of these.

97. The field gain of a multielement transmitting antenna is the ratio of the signal strength it would produce in a certain receiving antenna to the signal produced in that same antenna by

   a. a yaggi antenna.
   b. A Marconi antenna.
   c. a simple dipole.
   d. a trap antenna.
   e. a cubical quad antenna.

98. An International Broadcasting station has an operating power of 1000 watts. The modulated RF amplifier has an efficiency of 80% and the modulator an efficiency of 20%. The plate power dissipation of the modulator when modulated 90% would be

   a. Approximately 506 watts.
   b. Approximately 2531 watts.
   c. 2025 watts.
   d. 1000 watts.
   e. none of these.

99. A transmitter produces a 500mv per meter signal at one mile. If the power is increased to 3 times, the field strength would be 500 mv per meter at

   a. 1 mile.
   b. 2 miles.
   c. 9 miles.
   d. 1.73 miles.
   e. none of these.

100. An open transmission line has an impedance of 500 ohms. If the conductor spacing remains the same but the conductor wire size is increased the resulting impedance of the line would be

   a. 500 ohms.
   b. More than 500 ohms.
   c. Less than 500 ohms.
   d. Zero.
   e. Infinity.

101. A de-emphasis network is used to

   a. cancel even harmonics.
   b. compensate for high frequencies.
   c. compensate for low frequencies.
   d. provide FM demodulation.
   e. provide AM modulation.

2.   (inductance) Energy is stored in an inductance in the form of an _____field. Sec. 5-2.

4.   (henry, L) In a single layer air coil _____ is directly proportional to the turns squared and to ratio of the radius or diameter to the coil length. Sec. 5-3.

6.   (1.125H) The energy stored in a coil is directly proportional to the product of the inductance and the _____squared. Sec. 5-5.

8.   (iron) The mutual inductance of a primary, secondary system having a K of .5 would be equal to _____ (give formula). Sec. 5-7.

10.   (two) Two coupled coils of 3H and 12H of inductance with a mutual inductance of 4 H would have a coefficient of coupling of _____ Sec. 5-9.

12.   (1.4H, .6H) Two coils connected in series will have a maximum inductance if they are coupled with their fields in phase. This means that the current must flow through the coils in the same direction.

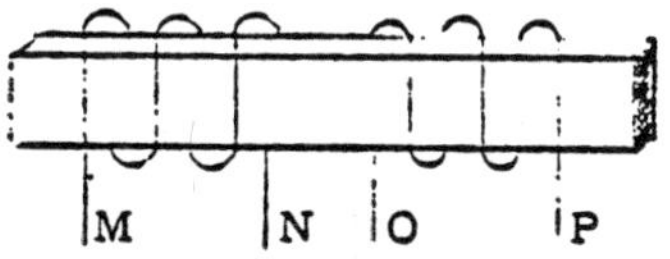

For maximum inductance in the circuit to the left, _N to P_ must be connected to _M to O_. Sec. 5-9.

14.   (5H, 1/5H) Compressing a coil would_____its inductance. Sec. 5-11.

16.   (increased or doubled) Work problem 10 page 78.

18.   (90 degrees) The wave forms shown indicate a circuit of pure_____ Sec. 5-13.

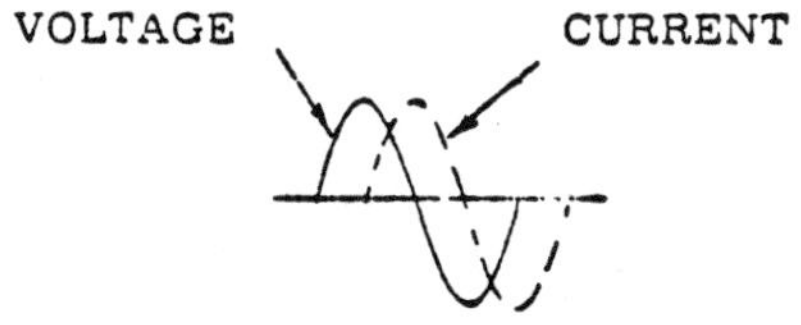

20.   (primary, secondary) Eddy current losses are reduced by using_____cores. Sec. 5-17.

22.   (400) Because of the losses in a transformer, the secondary power is_____than the primary power. Sec. 5-24.

24.   (250 turns) This completes the recheck study for unit 5.

87. A certain amplifier has a 40 db gain. If the output was 9 watts the input would be:

    a. 6 mw.
    b. .9 mw.
    c. 9 mw.
    d. 1 watt.
    e. none of these.

88. Two coils of .4 H and .8 H are connected in series and are 180 degrees out of phase. If the mutual inductance is .2 H the total inductance would be:

    a. .4 H.
    b. .8 H.
    c. 1.2 H.
    d. .32 H.
    e. none of these.

89. A 10 db gain is equal to a power gain of:

    a. 10.
    b. 100.
    c. 3.16.
    d. 20
    e. none of these.

90. The video and aural carriers are separated by:

    a. 1.25 Mhz
    b. 3 Mhz
    c. 4.5 Mhz
    d. 10 Mhz
    e. none of these

91. In the signal shown the video is moving from:
    a. white to gray to black.
    b. gray to black to white.
    c. black to gray to white.
    d. gray to white to black.
    e. none of these.

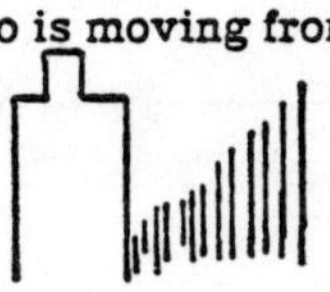

92. Overmodulation is shown on a trapezoidal pattern by:

    a. a trapezoid.
    b. a triangle.
    c. a triangle with a line coming out of the vertex.
    d. a vertical line.
    e. a horizontal line.

93. The approximate modulation percentage illustrated is:

    a. 0.
    b. 15.
    c. 50.
    d. 75.
    e. 100.

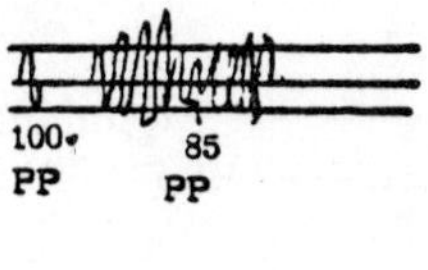

94. The output ripple frequency of a three phase half wave power supply having a 60 hertz input is:

    a. 60 hz.
    b. 120 hz.
    c. 240 hz.
    d. 180 hz.
    e. 360 hz.

1. An air core inductor made of No. 18 copper wire has an inductance of .3 H. When an iron core is added the inductance would be
    a. above .3 H
    b. below .3 H   d. .6H
    c. .3 H   e. 1.5 H

2. A certain coil has 1,600 turns with an inductance of .4 henry. When the turns are increased to 2,000 turns, the new inductance would be
    a. .4 H
    b. .625 H   d. 1 H
    c. .85 H   e. none of these

3. The total inductance of five 1 Henry inductors connected in parallel without coupling would be
    a. 5 henrys
    b. 1/5 henrys   d. 25 henrys
    c. 1 henry   e. none of these

4. Two coils having an inductance of .5 Henry and .9 Henry are connected in series with a mutual inductance of .3 Henry and the fields in phase. The total inductance is
    a. .8 H
    b. 2 H   d. 4.5 H
    c. 1.7 H e. 2.7 H

5. For maximum inductance connect

    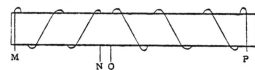

    a. M to P
    b. N to O
    c. O to P
    d. M to O
    e. M to N

6. If two coils are connected in series and the coefficient of coupling is .5, the mutual inductance would equal

    a. $1/2 \ \sqrt{L_1 \ L_2}$
    b. $2 \ \sqrt{L_1 \ L_2}$
    c. $L_1 + L_2$
    d. $2 (L_1 + L_2)$
    e. none of these

7. When the frequency of a signal fed to an inductance increases, the impedance
    a. decreases
    b. increases   d. varies
    c. stays the same e. none of these

8. Wrapping the turns of a coil tighter
    a. raises inductance
    b. lowers the inductance   d. increases the DC resistance
    c. decreases capacitance   e. lowers the inductive reactance

9. Core losses can be increased by using
    a. solid low permeability iron core
    b. laminated iron core   d. an open secondary
    c. copper windings   e. none of these

10. The inductance of a coil can be determined by
    a. the number of turns
    b. the ratio of the diameter to the length of the coil
    c. the diameter of the wire used
    d. the diameter of the coil
    e. the number of turns and the ratio of the diameter to the length of the coil (Assume single layer air core coil, close wound and a known gage of wire.)

11. The cores of inductors are laminated to
    a. increase permeability
    b. decrease permeability
    c. decrease eddy current losses
    d. increase eddy currents
    e. counteract Miller effect

80. When there is no modulation in an AM transmitter the antenna curent is 6A. At 100% modulation the antenna current is

    a. 6A.
    b. 12 A.
    c. 6 X 1.225 A.
    d. 6 X 1.500 A.
    e. none of these.

81. The circuit shown is a

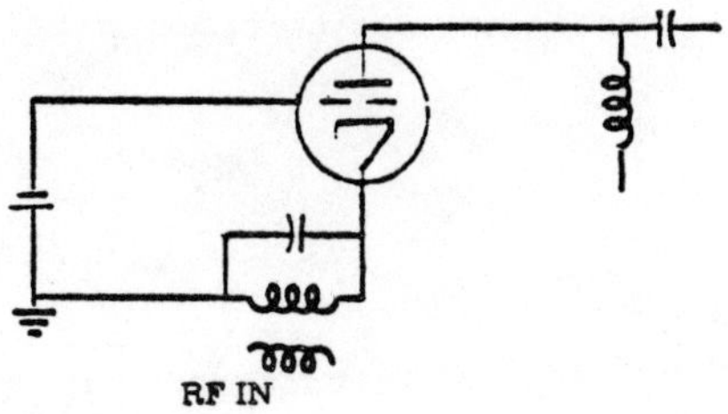

    a. cathode follower.
    b. grounded grid amplifier.
    c. voltage doubler.
    d. frequency doubler.
    e. degenerative feedback amplifier.

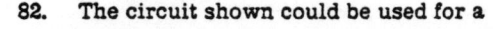

RF IN

82. The circuit shown could be used for a

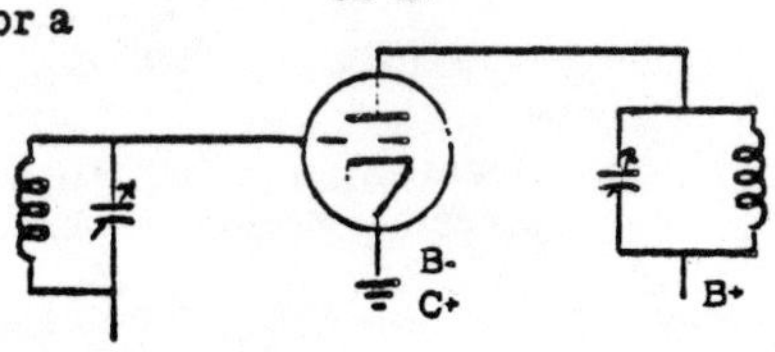

    a. tripler.
    b. AF amplifier.
    c. RF amplifier.
    d. RF oscillator.
    e. none of these.

83. An AM broadcast station licensed for an output of 500 watts would be in violation if it

    a. used 200 watts in the sidebands.
    b. used 300 watts in the sidebands.
    c. used 515 watts of carrier power.
    d. used 480 watts of carrier power
    e. 100% modulation.

84. The diagram below is the circuit used to

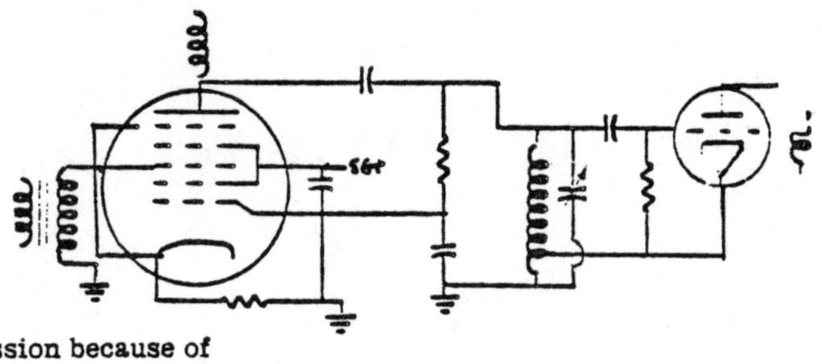

    a. inject capacitance.
    b. inject inductance.
    c. measure carrier shift.
    d. double voltage.
    e. double frequency.

85. Lighthouse tubes are used in UHF transmission because of

    a. the close spacing of the elements.
    b. their high interelectrode capacitance.
    c. the high power capabilities
    d. the wide spacing of the elements.
    e. none of these.

86. A top hat is sometimes used on an antenna to

    a. effectively lengthen the antenna.
    b. effectively shorten the antenna.
    c. stabilize it in the wind.
    d. discharge static.
    e. none of these.

12. The phase shift shown below is caused by

   a. pure capacitance
   b. pure inductance
   c. pure resistance
   d. a combination of the above
   e. matched impedance

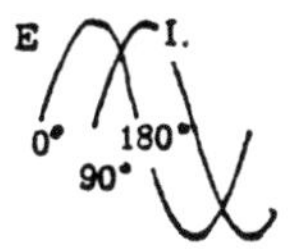

13. The total inductance of the circuit below assuming no coupling is

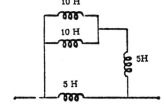

   a. 7.5 H
   b. 10 H
   c. 3.33 H
   d. 30 H
   e. none of these

14. A certain coil has 400 turns with an inductance of .4 Henry. When the turns are increased to 500 turns the new inductance would be
   a. .4 H
   b. .625 H   d. 1 H
   c. .85 H   e. none of these

15. Inductance in a single layer air wound coil is partially proportional to
   a. length squared
   b. the number of turns   d. the square root of the number of turns
   c. the number of turns squared   e. none of these

16. The primary of a transformer has 100 turns and the primary current is 1 ampere. If the secondary current is .25 amperes, the number of secondary turns (assuming 100% power transfer) would be
   a. 25 turns
   b. 50 turns   d. 200 turns
   c. 100 turns   e. 400 turns

17. If a .5 h and a .9 H coil are connected in series with a mutual inductance of .3 H with fields 180° out of phase, the total inductance is
   a. .8 H
   b. 2 H   d. 4.5 H
   c. 1.7 H   e. 2.7 H

18. Eddy current are currents that are
   a. circulating in the secondary winding
   b. circulating in the primary winding   d. induced in iron cores
   c. capacitor currents   e. a and b above

19. The inductance of a coil is
   a. greater with more turns
   b. greater with an air core   d. inversely proportional to the number of turns
   c. greater with an iron core   e. a and c

20. In the circuit below, as the frequency is increased, the output voltage will

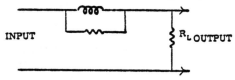

   a. increase
   b. decrease
   c. remain the same
   d. increase then decrease
   e. decrease then increase

21. Core losses are not determined by the
   a. Eddy currents
   b. Hysteresis
   c. size of wire on winding
   d. Air gap
   e. frequency

22. A certain coil has 1600 turns with an inductance of .4 Henry. When the turns are increased to 2000 turns, the new inductance would be
   a. greater than 400 mH.
   b. less than 400 mH
   c. 200 mH
   d. 100 mH
   e. none of these

72. In the diagram of question 68, the aural carrier frequency is indicated at point

    a. a.
    b. b.
    c. c.
    d. d.
    e. e.

73. The wave envelope patern shows a modulation percentage of about·

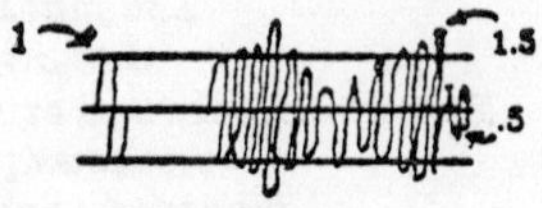

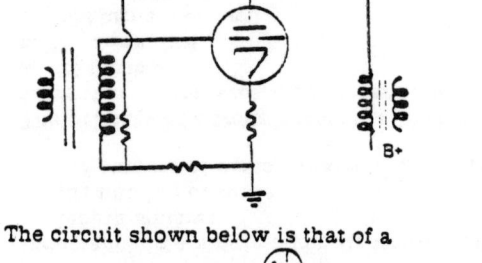

    a. 5%
    b. 20%
    c. 50%
    d. 60%
    e. 90%

74. An antenna that is 400 feet long is operating on 600 Khz The ratio of its physical length to its electrical length is

    a. .243 to 1.
    b. .308 to 1.
    c. .569 to 1.
    d. .176 to 1.
    e. none of these.

75. A limiter stage is used in an FM receiver to

    a. limit the frequency.
    b. limit the amplitude variations.
    c. produce gain.
    d. provide degenerated signals.
    e. none of these.

76. In FM broadcasting amplification of frequencies above 2,000 cycles is referred to as·

    a. degneration.
    b. attenuation.
    c. de-emphasis.
    d. neutralization.
    e. pre-emphasis.

77. The circuit shown below is that of a

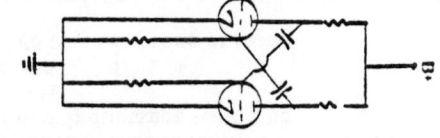

    a. degenerative feedback circuit.
    b. neutralized RF amplifier.
    c. leecher line.
    d. multivibrator.
    e. phase shift oscillator.

78. The circuit shown below is that of a

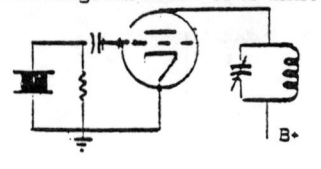

    a. degenerative feedback circuit.
    b. neutralized RF amplifier.
    c. leecher line.
    d. multivibrator.
    e. phase shift oscillator.

79. In the diagram below is is unnecessary to use

    a. a ground on the cathode.
    b. the capacitor in the grid circuit.
    c. a ground return on the crystal.
    d. the tube.
    e. the resistor in the grid circuit.

Unit 6 CAPACITANCE

1. The practical device that has the property of capacitance is the capacitor. A capacitor is a much used component in electronics. It consists of two electrostatic plates (usually metal) separated by a direct current insulator called a <u>dielectric.</u> The unit of capacitance is the <u>farad, microfarad</u> - $\frac{1}{1,000,000}$ farad, or picofarad - $\frac{1}{1,000,000,000,000}$ farad. The later two units are practical units. The symbol for capacitance is C. The schematic drawings for capacitors are shown.

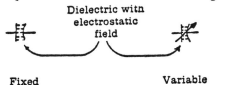

Dielectric with
electrostatic
field

Fixed   Variable

Increased capacitance
obtained by paralleling
plates

A simple capacitor is composed of two_____separated by a_____.

4. **(twice)** If mica with a K (dielectric constant) of 6 is used instead of rubber with a K of 2, the capacitance is tripled (assuming equal dielectric dimensions). If a mica dielectric with K of 6 is used instead of glass with a K of 3, the capacitance would be_____.

7. **(polarity)** The energy (ability to do work) stored in a capacitor is always returned to the circuit and cannot be dissipated in the capacitor. Energy can only be dissipated in a resistor: The formula for energy is:

$$En = \frac{CE^2}{2}$$

Where En = energy in watt - sec.
C = Capacitance in farads
E = Volts

This formula shows that the energy stored in a capacitor is directly proportional to_____ and to_____.

10. **(frequency, capacitance)** If in the example below the frequency was tripled the capacitive reactance would be one third as much.

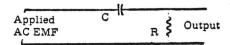

Applied
AC EMF   C   R   Output

Therefore, the current flow through R and the voltage drop across R (I X R) would be three times its former value.

If in the example above the applied emf frequency was lowered, the current through R and the voltage across R would be_____LOWER_____.

13. **(lead, 90)** A good memory crutch is:

E   L   I   the   I   C   E   man
E - Voltage
L - Inductance
I - Current

I - Current
C - Capacitance
E - Voltage

ELI shows current I lagging voltage E
L identifies it as an inductive circuit.

ICE shows current I leads voltage E
C identified it as a capacitive circuit.

The lead or lag in a pure capacitive or pure inductive circuit is 90 degrees regardless of the amount of capacitance or inductance in the circuit. This concludes unit 6.

65. The inductance in the resonant circuit below is

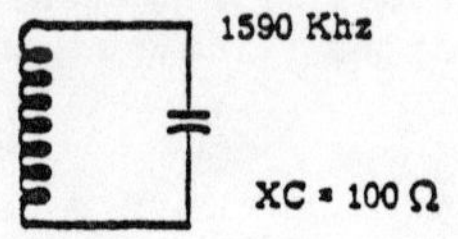

    a. 100 mh.
    b. 200 mh.
    c. 300 mh.
    d. 400 mh.
    e. none of these.

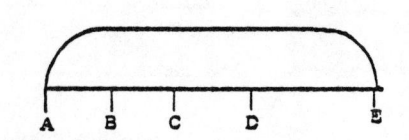

1590 Khz

$XC = 100 \Omega$

66. The output stage of an FM transmitter has a plate voltage of 1,000 V and a plate current of 300 ma. The final is 60% efficient and the loss in the transmission line is 50 W. If the field gain is 2 the effective radiated power is

    a. 260 W.
    b. 520 W.
    c. 130 W.
    d. 300 W.
    e. none of these.

67. An amplifier has a gain of 30 db and an output of 6 W. If o db = 6 mw the input equals

    a. 10 db.
    b. 20 db.
    c. 0 db.
    d. 20 db.
    e. none of these.

68. The video carrier would appear at

    a. A
    b. B
    c. C
    d. D
    e. E

A   B   C   D   E

69. The frequency tolerance of an international B.C. station is

    a. .001%.
    b. .002%.
    c. .003%.
    d. .004%.
    e. .005%.

70. The primary service area of a TV station is

    a. within a radius of 50 miles.
    b. within a radius of 100 miles.
    c. the area of a circle having a radius of approximately the line of sight.
    d. line of sight plus 50 miles.
    e. none of these.

71. In the diagram below the required audio power would be

    a. 300 watts.
    b. 400 watts.
    c. 500 watts.
    d. 800 watts.
    e. none of these.

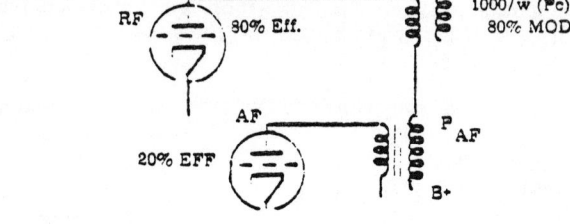

RF 80% Eff.   1000/w (Pc) 80% MOD

AF   P AF

20% EFF   B+

2. **(electrostatic plates, dielectric)** Capacitance may be defined as the ability of a capacitor to store a charge of electrons. The capacitance is directly proportional to the area of the plates and the dielectric constant. It is inversely proportional to the dielectric thickness (or spacing between plates). Whereas doubling the area of the plates doubles the capacitance, doubling the space cuts the capacitance to one half. If half of the plates were eliminated in an air dielectric capacitor (effectively reducing plate area to one half) the capacitance would be_____ as great as before.

5. **(doubled)** Because the dielectric has to withstand different voltages in different circuits, each capacitor has a voltage rating. Voltages in excess of the rating may puncture the dielectric permitting current flow. It is a known fact that capacitors are more subject to breakdown than any other electronic circuit component. The most unstable component in a circuit (highest break down rate) is the _____ .

8. **(capacitance, voltage squared)** The quantity of electricity stored in a capacitor is equal to C X E. If a capacitor is charged with a certain quantity of electricity (in coulombs) and then connected in parallel to two other equal but uncharged capacitors, the voltage across the combination drops to one third the voltage across the single capacitor. This is true because the capacitance increases three times when three equal capacitors are placed in parallel. Note:

    Q = E X C

    Fixed quantity   1/3 as great   3 times as great

    Since no charge was added or subtracted Q is a fixed quantity. If 120V. DC was placed across a 4 Mfd. capacitor. it would receive a charge of .00048 coulombs. If the capacitor was then disconnected from the voltage source and connected in parallel with two other 4 Mfd. capacitors, the voltage across the combination would be_____.

11. **(lower)** If a resistor was placed in parallel with C. the total restriction to current flow in the series R would be similarly affected. That is, increased frequency would result in increased current flow through the series R and would result in an increase in voltage drop. The exact nature of this restriction with a capacitor in parallel with a resistance will be dealt with in a later unit. If the frequency is steadily decreased in the example below the output voltage will _DECREASE_.

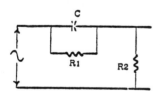

59. An FM transmitter is modulated 80% by a 1000 hertz tone. A 10,000 hertz tone of the same amplitude would modulate the transmitter

    a. 60%.
    b. 70%.
    c. 80%.
    d. 90%.
    e. 100%.

60. A 1000 watt daytime station having an antenna current of 5A is required to reduce its power to 400 watts at night. The antenna resistance is

    a. 20 ohms.
    b. 30 ohms.
    c. 40 ohms.
    d. 50 ohms.
    e. none of these

61. The circuit shown below is used for
    a. measuring high AC voltage.
    b. measuring high RF voltage.
    c. testing high current.
    d. measuring carrier shift.
    e. none of these.

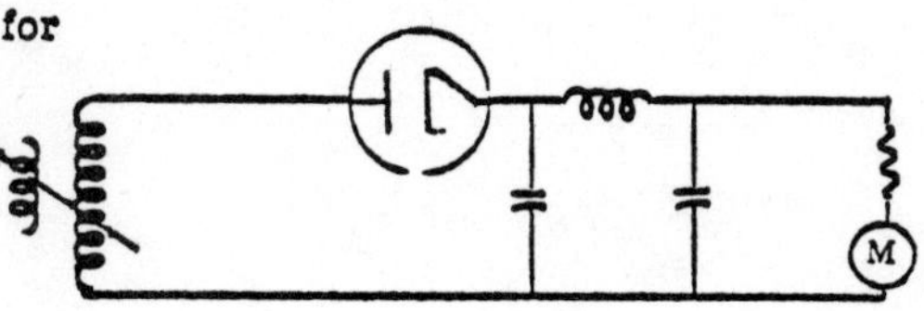

62. In the diagram below

    a. the resistor should be removed.
    b. the capacitor in the grid circuit should be removed.
    c. the position of the resistor and the grid capacitor should be interchanged.
    d. the plate should be grounded.
    e. the grid should be connected to B+

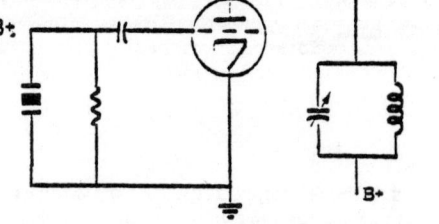

63. This is a diagram of a/an

    a. electron coupled oscillator.
    b. grounded grid amplifier.
    c. multivibrator.
    d. reactance tube modulator.
    e. push push amplifier.

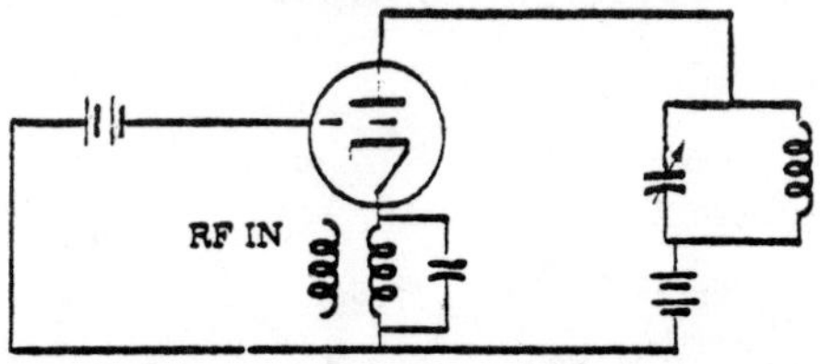

RF IN

64. A 1 kw output from a certain broadcast station antenna produces a field strength of 160 mv per meter at 1,000 meters. If the power is increased to 9 kw, the field strength at a distance of 4,000 meters would be

    a. 40 mv.
    b. 120 mv.
    c. 260 mv.
    d. 400 mv.
    e. none of these.

3. **(one half)** Use of a substance like mica for separating the plates of a capacitor will increase the ability of a capacitor to store a charge compared to air plate separation. Since it has been demonstrated that mica having the same physical dimensions as air used to separate capacitor plates stores a charge of approximately 6 times as much, the dielectric constant of mica is approximately 6. If rubber having a dielectric constant of 2 is used instead of air, the stored charge would be_____ __ __ as great.

6. **(capacitor)** An electrolytic capacitor utilizes a thin oxide coating for a dielectric. See the arrangement below:

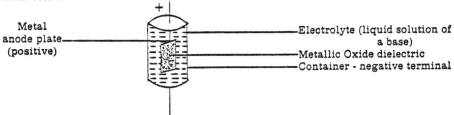

Metal anode plate (positive) —— Electrolyte (liquid solution of a base) — Metallic Oxide dielectric — Container - negative terminal

This provides for a minimum plate separation and maximum capacitance. This capacitor is made for direct current circuits and it is necessary to observe polarity when placing it in a circuit. One lead of this type capacitor is connected to the positive side of the circuit potential. The other lead is connected to the negative side of the circuit potential. It is necessary to observe_____ when using an electrolytic capacitor in a direct current circuit.

9. **(40 volts)** A capacitor will pass alternating current but will restrict its flow by an amount determined by its <u>capacitive reactance</u>. By formula:

$$X_c = \frac{1}{2\text{ pi}FC}$$

Where X_c = capacitive reactance
F = frequency in hertz
C = capacitance in farads

This shows the restriction (capacitive reactance) to be inversely proportional to_____and
_____.

12. **(decrease)** In the last unit we found that a pure inductance in a sine wave AC circuit caused the current to lag the voltage 90 degrees. In the pure capacitance circuit with an applied value of the wave voltage the current leads the voltage 90 degrees as shown.

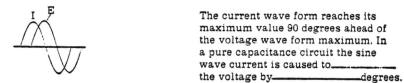

The current wave form reaches its maximum value 90 degrees ahead of the voltage wave form maximum. In a pure capacitance circuit the sine wave current is caused to_____ the voltage by_____degrees.

51. The phasing of antenna currents in standard broadcast antennas is important to

    a. prevent transmission line loss.
    b. produce maximum power output.
    c. give a certain directivity pattern.
    d. top loading.
    e. all the above.

52. A standard broadcast station must have

    a. a frequency meter.
    b. a modulation monitor.
    c. auxiliary transmitter.
    d. a and b.
    e. a, b and c.

53. If two antenna towers operating on 2000 khz are separated by 216 degrees, they are physically separated by approximately

    a. 216 feet.
    b. 1080 feet.
    c. 150 meters.
    d. 297 feet.
    e. 65 feet.

54. The frequency tolerance of an FM broadcast station is

    a. 002%.
    b. 20 cycles.
    c. 75 Khz.
    d. 2000 hertz.
    e. none of these.

55. If a 5 Mhz signal is FM modulated using a deviation of 5 Khz, the highest frequency would be

    a. 5 Khz.
    b. 10 Mhz.
    c. 5.010 Mhz.
    d. 12 Khz.
    e. It can't be determined from this information.

56. The antenna current along a properly matched transmission line

    a. is equal to the induced voltage times the line impedance.
    b. varies sinusoidally.
    c. is not affected by the length.
    d. is 72 ohms.
    e. none of these.

57. A VU meter showing 20 VU units represents a power gain of

    a. -10db.
    b. -20db.
    c. 20 db.
    d. 10 db.
    e. 60 db.

58. If the modulation percentage in an AM transmiter is increased from 80% to 100%, the increase in antenna current would be

    a. 6.5%.
    b. 15%.
    c. 20%.
    d. 22.5%.
    e. 7.5%.

Unit 6 CAPACITANCE

Recheck Programmed Instruction Using Shraders Electronic Communication

1. A simple_____ is formed by two metallic plates separated by a non conducting substance. Sec. 6-1.

3. (farad, microfarad, or picofarad) Capacitance may be defined as the property of a circuit to oppose any change in_____. Sec. 6-1.

5. (the dielectric constant, plate area, dielectric thickness) The use of a dielectric with a dielectric constant of 4 instead of 2 would_____the capacitance. Sec. 6-2.

7. (one half) The amount of energy stored in an electrostatic field is directly proportional to_____ and_____. Sec. 6-5.

9. (300 V) It is generally necessary to observe polarity when using_____capacitors. Sec. 6-7.

11. (stator, rotor) Most capacitor types are named for their_____Sec. 6-9.

13. (frequency, capacity) If the reactance of a capacitor is 30 ohms at 1000 hertz, it will be 15 ohms at 2000 hertz. Note the example below.

As applied emf frequency increases

Capacitive reactance decreased

and current flow increases through R producing increased output voltage.

On the other hand. decreasing the frequency would impede the current flow to a greater extent and _____the output voltage across R. Sec. 6-13.

15. (sum) Figuring total capacitance for a series circuit is like figuring total resistance for a_____circuit. Sec. 6-15.

17. (200v) In a purely capacitive circuit the current_____the voltage by_____degrees. Sec. 6-15.

44. Three phase is preferable to single phase in a power supply because

   a. its more available.
   b. it takes less filter.
   c. it takes more tubes.
   d. it can deliver more current.
   e. each phase in three phase has a higher voltage.

45. In a series RLC circuit, the capacitive reactance exceeds the inductive reactance at a certain frequency. It must therefore be concluded that

   a. the current leads the voltage.
   b. the voltage leads the current.
   c. the current and voltage are in phase.
   d. the circuit is resonant.
   e. there is a 90 degree phase displacement.

46. The plate voltage to the final tube of a broadcast station is 3000 volts. The plate current is 1 ampere. If the antenna resistance is 75 ohms and the antenna current is 6 amperes the output power is

   a. 2700 watts.
   b. 450 watts.
   c. 500 watts.
   d. 3000 watts.
   e. none of these.

47. The operating power of an FM station is determined

   a. by the direct method.
   b. by the indirect method.
   c. by either the direct or indirect method.
   d. from the driver stage.
   e. by a field strength meter.

48. The only current change with audio input in a properly tuned FM transmitter is in the

   a. final.
   b. buffer.
   c. multipliers.
   d. antenna.
   e. reactance tube modulator.

49. The secondary to primary voltage in a transformer is equal to

   a. the turns ratio.
   b. the turns ratio squared.
   c. multipliers.
   d. antenna.
   e. none of these.

50. The RMS voltage of a transformer secondary from center tap to one end is 500 volts. If this transformer is used in a full wave power supply using the center tap, the input filter capacitor must have a peak working voltage of

   a. 500 volts.
   b. 707 volts.
   c. 1000 volts.
   d. 250 volts.
   e. 600 volts.

2. (capacitor) The unit of capacitanc· .he_____ Sec. 6-1.

4. (voltage) Capacitance is directly proportional to_____and_____and inversely proportional to_____ Sec. 6-2.

6. (double) Doubling the distance between plates will cut the capacitance to_____. _____. Sec. 6-2.

8. (capacitance, voltage squared) Work problem 13 on page 94. Sec. 6-6. _____

10. (electrolytic) Variable capacitors have a set of_____or stationary plates and a set of _____or rotable plates. Sec. 6-8.

12. (dielectrics) Capactive reactance is inversely proportional to_____and_____ Sec. 6-13.

14. (reduce) A parallel resistor across the capacitance C would make no substantial change in this reduction. The total capacitance for capacitances connected in parallel is equal to their_____ Sec. 6-14.

16. (parallel) The voltage drop across the 4 Mfd capacitor in the illustration below would be_____ Sec. 6-16.

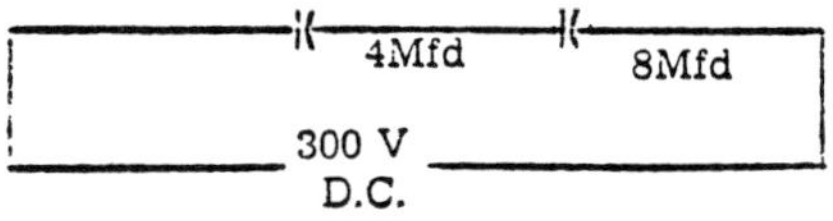

```
 _____||____||_____
|         4Mfd   8Mfd     |
|                         |
|_____ 300 V _____|
            D.C.
```

18. (leads, 90°) Capacitors are easily damaged by improper high voltages and by surge voltages. They have a high break down rate.

This concludes the recheck material for unit 6.

38. The accuracy of a remote reading antenna ammeter should be at least

   a. 1%.   c. 3%.
   b. 2%.   d. 4%.
                                               e. 5%.

39. Retrace signals are used to

   a. return the beam horizontally from left to right.
   b. return the beam vertically from top to bottom.
   c. return the beam horizontally from right to left.
   d. equalize voltages.
   e. none of these.

40. The total impedance of a .03 microhenry coil connected in series with a .03 microhenry coil without coupling at 2000 Khz is approximately

   a. 10 ohms.   c. 1000 ohms.
   b. 88 ohms.   d. 62 ohms.
                                               e. none of these.

41. In the circuit below the line current would be approximately

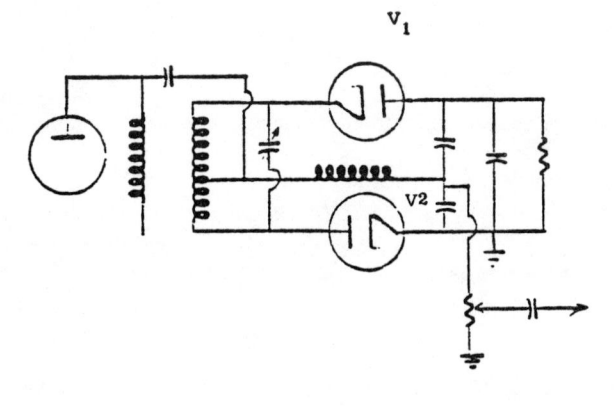

   a. 53.4 ma.
   b. 2.3 amps.
   c. .3 amps.
   d. 7.8 amps
   e. none of these.

42. If two identical coils were placed in series with the fields in phase and with a coefficient of coupling of .5, the total inductance would be equal

   a. $4L_1$ c. L_1
   b. $4L_2$ d. $3L_1$
                                               e. none of these.

43. In the circuit below

   a. V_1 is reversed.
 • b. V_2 is reversed.
   c. a discriminator is shown.
   d. the output is RF.
   e. a correct ratio detector is shown.

381

UNIT 6 CAPACITANCE

1. The phase shift shown below is caused by

   a. pure capacitance.
   b. pure inductance.
   c. pure resistance.
   d. a combination of the above
   e. none of these

2. If the amplitude of the applied signal is held constant and the frequency is steadily increased the output will

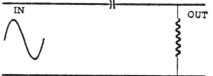

   a. increase.
   b. decrease.
   c. remain steady.
   d. increase for a while then decrease.
   e. none of these.

3. The most unstable component in a circuit (highest breakdown rate) is
   a. a crystal.
   b. a transformer.   d. a capacitor.
   c. a choke.   e. a wired connection

4. Two identical capacitors are connected in series and placed across 120 volts. They are disconnected without discharging and the two series capacitors are placed in parallel with a third identical capacitor. The voltage across this circuit would be
   a. 120 volts.
   b. 60 volts.   d. 20 volts.
   c. 40 volts.   e. none of the above.

5. If the amplitude of the applied signal in the circuit below is held constant and the frequency is steadily decreased the output will

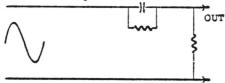

   a. increase.
   b. decrease
   c. remain steady.
   d. increase for a while then decrease.
   e. none of these

6. It is necessary to observe polarity when using
   a. resistors.
   b. oil capacitors.   d. chokes.
   c. electrolytic capacitors. e. transformers.

7. The energy stored in pure capacitance is directly proportional to
   a. the current
   b. the voltage.   d. the voltage squared.
   c. the current squared.   e. none of these.

8. If you doubled the distance between the two plates of an air capacitor you would
   a. double the capacitance.
   b. cut the capacitance in half.   d. decrease the voltage breakdown.
   c. not affect its capacitance.   e. none of these.

9. A material of twice the dielectric coefficient would
   a. double the capacitance.
   b. cut capacitance in half.   d. decrease the voltage breakdown.
   c. not affect capacitance.   e. none of these.

10. In order to determine the capacitance of a capacitor it is necessary to know
    a. the area of the plates.
    b. the type of dielectric.   d. the exact temperature.
    c. the dielectric thickness. e. a, b, and c.

11. In the circuit below, as the frequency is increased, the output will
    a. increase.
    b. decrease.
    c. remain the same.
    d. increase then decrease.
    e. decrease then increase.

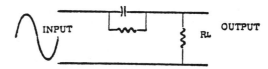

31. The usual means of protecting an antenna ammeter against lightening is

   a. to place a short across the meter when not in use.
   b. to use a high resistance meter movement.
   c. to use a movement with a high current capability.
   d. to use a horn gap.
   e. to use a series multiplier resistance.

32. The antenna current produced by an FM transmitter without modulation is 6 amperes. With 90% modulation the antenna current would be·

   a. 6 x 1.225 amperes.
   b. 6 amperes.
   c. 6 x 1.405.
   d. 7.3 amperes.
   e. 5.4 amperes·

33. The circuit enclosed with the dotted lines is used for

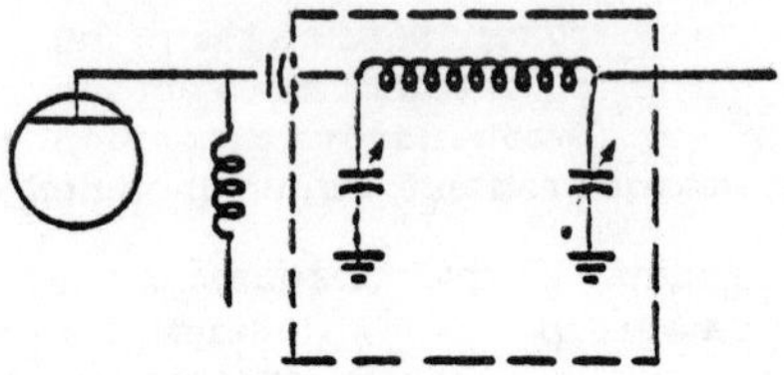

   a. generating harmonics.
   b. matching A high Z to A low Z
   c. parasitic oscillations.
   d. frequency doubling.
   e. feeding a push-pull circuit.

34. The circuit above is also effective in

   a. frequency tripling.
   b. paraphase amplifiers.
   c. cancelling feedback.
   d. reducing harmonics.
   e. none of these·

35. The type of transmission shown below is

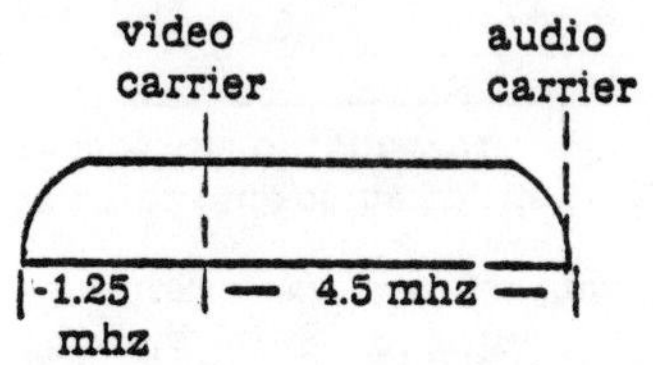

   a. single sideband.
   b. double sideband.
   c. vestigeal sideband·
   d. A3·
   e. none of these.

36. The action of an audio peak limiter produces·

   a. a negative bias by diode rectification.
   b. frequency modulation·
   c. line equalization·
   d. a positive grid bias voltage.
   e. time dealy of 75 microseconds.

37. AVC voltage in a receiver should be measured by a

   a. thermo couple.
   b. RF wattmenter·
   c. VOM.
   d. square law meter,
   e. VTVM·

Unit 7

ALTERNATING CURRENT CIRCUITS

1. The total restriction to the flow of an alternating current is called impedance. The unit of impedance is the ohm. The symbol is Z. Impedance is made up of three components - resistance, inductive reactance and capacitance reactance. It is important to remember that impedance in series, parallel or complex circuits is not equal to the simple algebraic sum of the resistance, inductive reactance and capacitive reactance. The unit of impedance is the _____.

8. **(500 ohms)** It will be remembered that pure inductance causes the AC current to lag the AC voltage by 90° and pure capacitance causes the AC current to lead the AC voltage by 90°. If resistance, inductance and capacitance are connected in a series circuit; the circuit current will lead or lag the circuit voltage depending on the amount of inductive reactance (X_L) or capacitive reactance (X_C) present. If more inductive reactance is present than capacitive reactance, the circuit current will lag the circuit voltage (less than 90°). It follows that if more capacitive reactance is present than inductive reactance, the circuit current will _____ the circuit voltage.

15. **(true)** The AC voltage times the AC current gives us a product that is referred to in the following three ways:
    1. Apparent power.
    2. Reactive power.
    3. VAR (voltage X amperes - reactive or VARS for the plural term)

    In a manner of speaking its always an inflated value for power since there are times during the cycle when current is going one direction while the voltage is built up in the opposite direction. True power is usually a large fraction of the apparent power but never equal to it. This fraction called power factor is numerically equal to:

    $COS\Theta$ (angle of lead or lag)

    or R/Z

    or $\dfrac{I^2R \text{ (true power)}}{IE \text{ (apparent power)}}$

    Power factor in an AC circuit is always _____ than 1.

SERIES AND PARALLEL AC CIRCUITS

22. **(161 ohms)** When inductive reactance and capacitive reactance are equal in a circuit, a condition known as resonance is achieved. In the series circuit resonance results in a low impedance to AC. If there is little resistance present the impedance is quite low. This is seen from the formula:

    $$Z = \sqrt{R^2 + (X_L - X_C)^2} = \sqrt{R^2 + 0} = \sqrt{R^2} = R$$

    The impedance of a series L C (inductance and capacitance) circuit is _____ at resonance.

42

24. An open transmission line having a conductor spacing of 10 inches and using conductors of a diameter of 5/16 inches has an impedance of about 500 ohms. If the spacing was changed to 5 inches and conductors having a diameter of 5/32 inches were used, the new impedance would be

    a. 72 ohms.
    b. 250 ohms.
    c. 690 ohms.
    d. 970 ohms.
    e. the same.

25. In the triode crystal oscillator shown

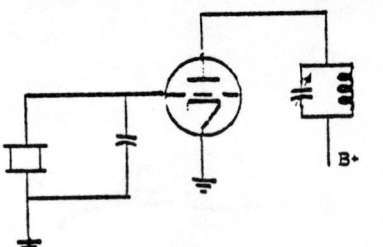

    a. the crystal should be in the cathode circuit.
    b. the plate tuned circuit should be grounded.
    c. the capacitor across the crystal should be replaced by a resistor
    d. the grid should be directly grounded.
    e. there should be no reason this circuit wouldn't work.

26. For the purpose of scanning, a wave form should be used that is

    a. a square wave.
    b. a triangular wave.
    c. a sine wave.
    d. a wave that rises linearly and falls quickly.
    e. none of these.

27. In a full wave power supply using a center tapped transformer with an end to end voltage of 1,000 volts and two tubes having 15 volt drops across them, the maximum inverse peak voltage occuring on either tube would be about

    a. 985 volts.
    b. 1,400 volts
    c. 707 volts.
    d. 2,000 volts
    e. none of these

28. The antenna resistance of a directional antenna system is measured by use of

    a. an impedance bridge at the base of each antenna
    b. an impedance bridge at the point of common supply
    c. an ohmeter at the base of each antenna
    d. an ohmeter at eastern most tower
    e. none of these

29. The transmitter at a 5 kw AM broadcast station must be able to

    a. broadcast on the ERI frequency
    b. transmit directional
    c. transmit high fidelity
    d. transmit FM
    e. be modulated 85%.

30. The field strength of a certain station is 200 millivolts per meter at one mile. If the power was tripled, the field strength would be 200 millivolts per meter at

    a. 2 miles.
    b. 1.73 miles
    c. 8 miles
    d. 1.414 miles.
    e. none of these.

2.   (ohm) Minimal impedance is offered to alternating current flow by a simple circuit consisting of a wire having high conductivity. For example, silver wire would offer negligible impedance to a 10 megahertz A.C. Silver wire conductors offer _____ impedance to A.C.

9.   (lead) The amount of lead or lag can be figured from a trigometric function. By formula:

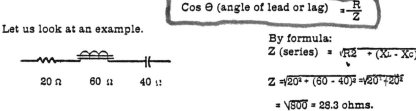

$$\text{Cos } \Theta \text{ (angle of lead or lag)} = \frac{R}{Z}$$

Let us look at an example.

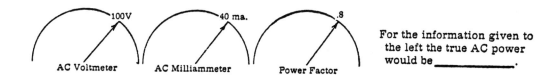

20 Ω   60 Ω   40 Ω

By formula:

$$Z \text{ (series)} = \sqrt{R^2 + (X_L - X_C)^2}$$

$$Z = \sqrt{20^2 + (60 - 40)^2} = \sqrt{20^2 + 20^2}$$

$$= \sqrt{800} = 28.3 \text{ ohms.}$$

$$\text{Cos } \Theta = \frac{R}{Z} = \frac{20 \text{ ohms}}{28.3 \text{ ohms}} = .707$$

If the Cos Θ = .707, the Θ (phase angle) is equal to 45°. (By calculator or table). Since the inductive reactance is greater than the capacitive reactance (60 compared to 40) the current in this circuit _____ the voltage.

16.   (less) If an AC voltmeter across a series circuit read 100 volts, an AC milliammeter read 50 ma. and the power factor was .9; then the true power would equal .050 (50ma) X 100 volts X .9 or 4.5 watts.

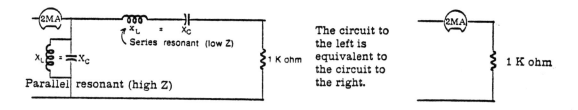

100V   40 ma.   .8

AC Voltmeter   AC Milliammeter   Power Factor

For the information given to the left the true AC power would be _____.

23.   (low) on the other hand parallel circuit resonance results in high impedance in an LC parallel circuit. It is so high that it is almost like an open circuit. The approximate equivalent AC circuit for series and parallel resonance is given below

The circuit to the left is equivalent to the circuit to the right.

If 2 milliamperes was flowing in the circuit, the voltage drop across the resistor would be _____ volts.

16. A Doherty amplifier is a

    a. Frequency doubler.
    b. push-pull amplifier.
    c. a parallel amplifier used for reducing harmonics.
    d. type of linear amplifier having an efficiency comparable to a Class C amplifier.
    e. none of these.

17. The field strength over average terrain varies

    a. directly with square of power.
    b. directly with distance squared.
    c. inversely with distance.
    d. inversely with the square of the distance.
    e. inversely with the square root of the distance.

18. The picture tube is changed from a small 4″ by 3″ tube to a larger 16″ x 12″ tube. The aspect ratio would then be:

    a. 4 to 3.
    b. 12 to 4.
    c. 6 to 4.
    d. 16 to 4.
    e. 12 to 3.

19. Two coils are connected in series so that their fields are out of phase. If $L_1 = .8H$, $L_2 = .5H$, and $M = .3H$, the total inductance would be:

    a. .4H
    b. 1.9H
    c. .6H.
    d. .7H.
    e. none of these.

20. In a television signal the blanking level is:

    a. 60%.
    b. 70%.
    c. 75%.
    d. 80%.
    e. 100%.

21. In a television signal the reference black level is:

    a. 60%.
    b. 70%.
    c. 15%.
    d. 75%.
    e. 100%.

22. In a television signal the reference white level is:

    a. 60%.
    b. 70%.
    c. 15%.
    d. 75%.
    e. 100%.

23. The wave envelope pattern shows a modulation percentage of about:

    a. 5%.
    b. 20%.
    c. 50%.
    d. 60%.
    e. 90%.

150   50

SERIES A.C. CIRCUITS

3.   (minimal or low) Let us first consider the impedance of a series circuit consisting of resistance, inductive reactance and capacitive reactance. The impedance in a series circuit is given by the formula:

$$Z \text{ (series)} = \sqrt{R^2 + (X_L - X_C)^2}$$

Where Z = impedance in ohms
   R = resistance in ohms
   X_C = capacitive reactance in ohms.
   X_L = inductive reactance in ohms

Note the example:

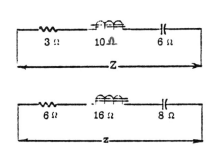

$$Z = \sqrt{3^2 + (10-6)^2} \qquad \sqrt{9+16}$$

$$= \sqrt{25} = 5 \text{ ohms.}$$

The impedance for the circuit at the left would be

10.   (lags).

The angle of lag in the circuit shown would be $= 45°$

$\cos \theta = \dfrac{R}{Z} = \dfrac{20}{20} =$

$\cos \theta = 1 = 45°$

17.   (3.2 watts) Knowing that power factor is equal to true power divided by the apparent power, we can solve for the power factor from the information given below:

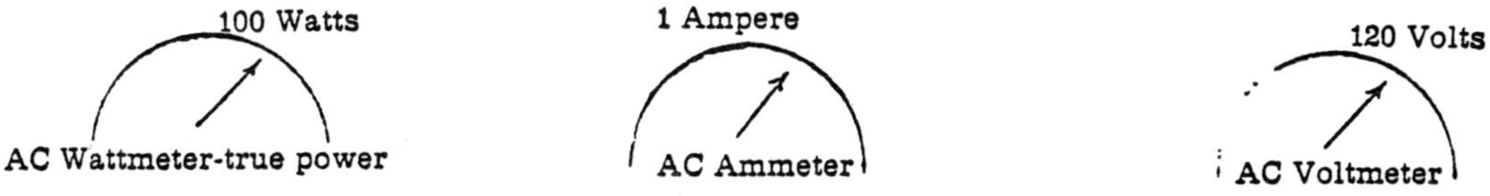

100 Watts   1 Ampere   120 Volts

AC Wattmeter-true power   AC Ammeter   AC Voltmeter

We solve by sutstituting in the formula:

P.F. (power factor) = $\dfrac{\text{True power (wattmeter reading)}}{\text{Apparent power (volts X amperes)}}$

$= \dfrac{100}{120} = .825 \text{ or } 82.5\%$

This means the true power is 82.5% of the IE (apparent) power. If a wattmeter reads 100 watts, an AC ammeter 2 amperes, and a AC voltmeter 70 volts; the power factor would be approximately

24.   (2 volts) This concludes unit 7.

9. If a 1500 khz standard AM broadcast transmitter is modulated by 100 to 15,000 hz of audio the highest resulting frequency would be

   a. 1500 Khz
   b. 1505 Khz
   c. 1503 Khz
   d. 1515 Khz
   e. 1530 Khz

10. The ratio of plate current change to grid voltage change is called

    a. amplification factor
    b. transconductance
    c. plate impedance
    d. stage gain
    e. impedance

11. Neutralization is accomplished in the circuit below by using a variable capacitor from

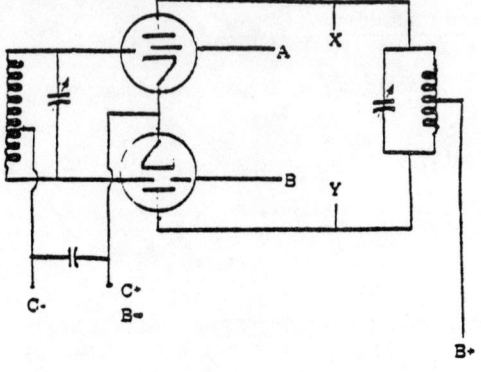

   a. a to b
   b. x to y
   c. a to y and b to x
   d. a to x
   e. b to y

12. Power losses in a transformer are

    a. hysteresis losses
    b. Eddy current losses
    c. I^2R
    d. inductance losses
    e. a, b, and c above

13. The circuit below is used for a

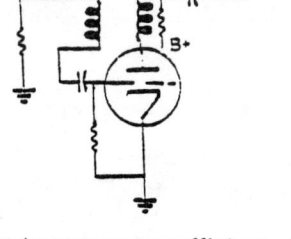

   a. RF attenuator
   b. vertical blocking oscillator
   c. neutralizer
   d. frequency doubler
   e. none of these

14. The temperaure coefficient of a low T. C. crystal is approximately

   a. plus or minus 1
   b. plus or minus 2
   c. plus or minus 3
   d. plus or minus 4
   e. plus or minus 5

15. In a video transmission there are

   a. 60 frames per second
   b. 60 fields per minute
   c. 120 lines per second
   d. 525 lines per second
   e. 30 frames per second

4. **(10 ohms)** Suppose we solved a series problem for impedance when resistance, inductance and capacitance were known. See the example below:

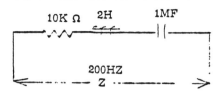

We first solve for X_L and X_C.

$X_L = 2 \text{ pi } F L = 6.28 \times 200 \times 2$
$= 2512$ ohms.

$X_C = \dfrac{1}{2 \text{ pi } F C} = \dfrac{1}{6.28 \times 200 \times 1 \times 10^6}$

$= \dfrac{159.000}{200} = 795$ ohms.

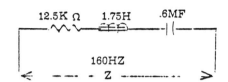

$Z = \sqrt{10,000^2 + (2512 - 795)^2} = 10,150$ ohms.

The impedance of the circuit to the left is approximately................ ....

11. **(45°).** A series circuit consists of 12 ohms of resistance, 64 ohms of capacitive reactance, and 64 ohms of inductive reactance. The phase angle would be   *ZERO* $Z = \sqrt{R^2}$ $\cos\theta = \dfrac{R}{Z}$

$Z = 12$ $\cos\theta = \dfrac{12}{12} = 0°$

PARALLEL AC CIRCUITS

18. **(.7)** Impedance in a parallel circuit may be figured up two ways:

   1. By an admittance method.
   2. By an assumed voltage method.

A brief discussion will first be given for the admittance method. By formulas:

$Z = \dfrac{1}{Y}$

$Y = \sqrt{G^2 + (B_L - B_c)^2}$ Where Z = parallel circuit impedance in ohms.

$G = \dfrac{1}{R}$
  Y = admittance
  G = conductance in mhos
  B_L = inductive susceptance
  B_c = capacitive susceptance

$B_L = \dfrac{1}{X_L}$

$B_c = \dfrac{1}{X_c}$

This is similar to the series impedance formula but deals with reciprocals (values divided into 1). The formula could be written using Z, R, X_L, and X_c as follows:

$$\frac{1}{Z} = \sqrt{\left(\frac{1}{R}\right)^2 + \left(\frac{1}{X_L} - \frac{1}{X_c}\right)^2}$$

The reciprocal of resistance is __CONDUCTANCE__ in mhos.

1. A six pole 60 cycle 3 phase induction motor would develop a speed of

   a. 5200 RPM
   b. 3600 RPM.
   c. 1800 RPM.
   d. 1200 RPM.
   e. none of these.

2. The field gain of a TV antenna is the ratio of the free space field intensity produced at 1 mile in the horizontal plane expressed in mv per meter for a 1 kw antenna input power to

   a. 137.6 mv/m
   b. 1.73 mv/m
   c. 2.21 mv/m
   d. 1.225 mv/m
   e. 3 mv/m

3. The bandwidth of an intercarrier IF stage in a television receiver should be

   a. 2000 Khz
   b. 4500 Khz
   c. 2 Khz
   d. 100 Khz
   e. none of these.

4. An RF frequency multiplier stage is not characterized by

   a. high bias
   b. high excitation
   c. distortion
   d. output circuit tuned to frequency of input circuit
   e. class C operation

5. Pre-emphasis is used in an FM transmitter to

   a. reduce parasitic oscillations
   b. cancel even harmonics
   c. attenuate high frquencies
   d. produce better signal to noise ratios on higher audio frequencies
   e. modulate the oscillator for frequency correction

6. The surge impedance of an open transmission line is not determined by

   a. size of conductors
   b. spacing between conductors.
   c. length of conductors
   d. ratio of spacing to diameter of conductors
   e. any of the above.

7. A 300 ft. broadcast antenna is operated on 2000 khz. If end effect is considered, the ratio of its physical length to wave length is approximately

   a. .243 to 1.
   b. .5 to 1.
   c. 1 to 1.
   d. 2 to 1.
   e. .642 to 1.

8. Two or more AM broadcast antennas are often fed by one transmitter for

   a. additional gain
   b. a directional effect
   c. generation single sideband
   d. higher signal to noise ratio
   e. none of these.

5. (12,500) Note that the two reactances X_L (app. 1750 ohms) and X_C (app. 1670 ohms) do not have a significant difference value. Since the net reactance (X_L - X_C) was a small value compared to the resistance, it can be disregarded. Therefore Z would be equal to $\sqrt{R^2}$ or to just R.

    In both the formula for X_L and X_C the expression 2 pi F is used. In a series circuit containing both inductive and capacitive reactance, 2 pi F will have the same value. For example, if 2 pi F is 1000 in a series circuit containing both inductance and capacitance; 1000 can be used for 2 pi F in both X_L and X_C formulas. If 2 pi F is equal to 1000, then the frequency is equal to 1000 divided by 2 pi (6.28) or _____hertz.

12. (zero) It is important to remember that although there may be a circuit lead or lag of less than 90°, there is a current lead of 90°, in the capacitor itself, a current lag of 90°, in the inductance itself, and no phase displacement in the resistor itself. The phase displacement in a resistor used in a series RCL circuit is _____.

19. (conductance) The conductance of the circuit shown is 1 divided by the total resistance or 1 divided by 50 ohms. This is equal to 1/50 or .02 mhos. We could also express it as 20,000 micromhos (moving the decimal 6 places to the right). Note that 2/100 is equal to 20,000/1,000,000.

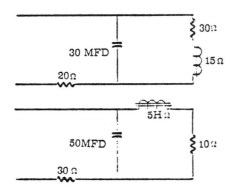

The total R in the circuit is equal to 20 + 30 or 50 ohms.
Conductance G = 1/50 or .02 mhos.
Conductance only involves resistors.

The condutance of the circuit to the left is- ----------- ---.-- .---.------micromhos.

46

18. If a TV broadcast transmitter is modulated 23% by a 1 KHz aural tone, the deviaton is
    a. 17.25 KHz.
    b. 5.75 KHz.
    c. 23 KHz.
    d. 30 KHz.
    e. 1 KHz.

19. The color burst on the back porch of the horizontal sync pulse is used
    a. to operate the blue gun in the C.R.T.
    b. to operate the red gun in the C.R.T.
    c. to provide signal for the TV receiver color killer.
    d. to sync the TV receiver vertical oscillator.
    e. to sync the TV receiver color oscillator.

20. The purpose of the blanking pulse is
    a. to cause the deflection coil currents to go from minimum to maximum.
    b. to interlace the odd and even lines.
    c. to cause the beam to move right to left.
    d. to blank the beam as it moves from right to left.
    e. none of these.

21. The mosaic plate in the TV camera is comparable to
    a. the speaker of an amplifier.
    b. the film in a camera.
    c. the receiver high voltage anode.
    d. the balanced FM modulator.
    e. all of the above.

22. If the operating power of the video transmitter at a TV station is 37 KW, the aural operating power should be approximately
    a. 37KW.
    b. 74KW.
    c. 18.5KW.
    d. 7.4KW.
    e. none of these.

23. The chrominance subcarrier frequency used in color TV broadcasts is
    a. 19 KHz.
    b. 3.58 KHz.
    c. 4.2 MHz.
    d. 4.5 MHz.
    e. 10.7 MHz.

6. **(159 hertz)** Ohm's law for alternating current circuits is very similar to the law for D.C. circuits. Note the formulas:

Substituting X_L for R in an inductive circuit.	Substituting X_C for R in a capacitive circuit.	Substituting Z for R in RL, RC, and RCL circuits
$I = \dfrac{E}{X_L}$	$I = \dfrac{E}{X_C}$	$I = \dfrac{E}{Z}$
$E = I\,X_L$	$E = I\,X_C$	$E = IZ$
$X_L = \dfrac{E}{I}$	$X_C = \dfrac{E}{I}$	$Z = \dfrac{E}{I}$

In the example below let us solve for circuit impedance, circuit current, and for the voltage across each circuit element.

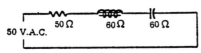

$$Z = \sqrt{50^2 + (60 - 60)^2}$$

$$= \sqrt{50^2} = 50 \text{ ohm}$$

I (circuit current) $= \dfrac{E}{Z} = \dfrac{50V}{50 \text{ ohms}} = 1$ ampere

E (across 50 ohm resistor) = IR = 1 X 50 or 50 volts.
E (across 60 ohm X_c) = I X L = 1 X 60 = 60 volts.
E (across 60 ohm X_L) = I X c = 1 X 60 = 60 volts

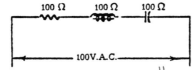

The voltage across the capacitance in the circuit to the left would be _____

13. **(zero)** The power dissipated in a "D.C. circuit" is equal to the voltage times the current. By formula:

APPARENT A-C POWER $\boxed{P = I \times E}$

Where P = power in watts
I = current in amperes
E = voltage in volts

In an alternating circuit the current is seldom in phase with the voltage so another formula must be used:

TRUE A-C POWER $\boxed{P = I \times E \times pf \text{ (power factor)}}$

Stated in words the true AC power is equal to the apparent AC power (IE) times some fraction equivalent to the power factor. The power factor is always less than 1. We can conclude from this formula that the true AC power is _____ than the product of the amperes times the volts (apparent power).

20. **(25,000 micromhos)** Now let us solve a parallel impedance problem using the admittance method.

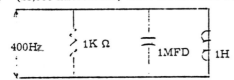

$$Z = \dfrac{1}{Y}$$

$$Y = \sqrt{G^2 + (B_L - B_c)^2}$$

Solving for G. $\quad G = \dfrac{1}{R} = 1/1000$ or .001 mhos - conductance

Solving for B_L $\quad B_L = 1/X_L \quad X_L = 2piFL = 6.28 \times 400 \times 1 = 2512$ ohms.

$\quad B_L = 1/2512$ or approximately .0004 - inductive susceptance.

Solving for B_c $\quad B_c = 1/X_c \quad X_c = \dfrac{1}{2\,pi\,F\,C} = \dfrac{1}{6.28 \times 400 \times 1 \times 10^{-5}}$ or approximately 400 ohms

Solving for Y. $\quad Y = \sqrt{.001^2 + (.0004 - .0025)^2} = \sqrt{.001^2 + .0021^2}$

$\quad = \sqrt{.000001 + .0000044} = \sqrt{.0000054}$

$\quad = .0025$ - admitttance.

Solving for Z $\quad Z = 1/Y = 1/.0025$ or approximately 400 ohms - impedance.

If in the example above the frequency was 600 hertz the impedance would be approximately _____ ohms.

11. The type of transmisson shown below is
    a. single sideband.
    b. double sideband.
    c. vestigeal sideband.
    d. A3
    e. none of these.

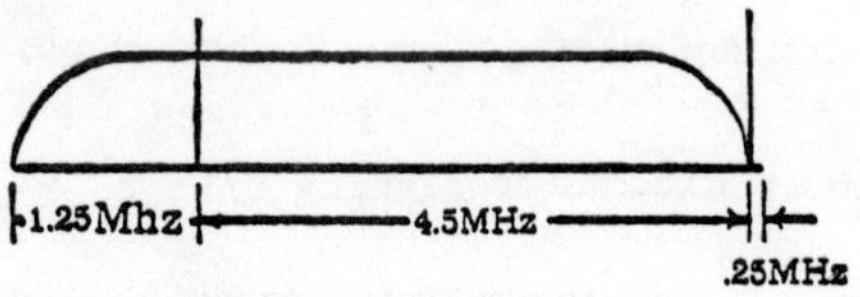

|-1.25Mhz |-------- 4.5MHz --------| |-
.25MHz

12. Retrace signals are used to
    a. return the beam horizontally from left to right.
    b. return the beam vertically from top to bottom.
    c. return the beam horizontally from right to left.
    d. equalize voltages.
    e. none of these.

13. In the diagram below the video carrier frequency is
    a. 87:75 MHz.
    b. 82 MHz.
    c. 83.25 MHz.
    d. 84.5 MHz.
    e. none of these.

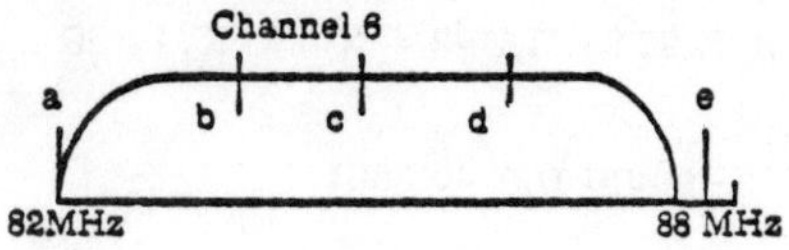

Channel 6
a   b   c   d   e
82MHz   88 MHz

14. In the diagram above the aural carrier frequency is indicated at point
    a. a.
    b. b.
    c. c.
    d. d.
    e. e.

15. The video and aural carriers are separated by
    a. 1.25 Mhz.
    b. 3 Mhz.
    c. 4.5 Mhz.
    d. 10 Mhz.
    e. none of these.

16. In the signal shown the video is moving from
    a. white to gray to black.
    b. gray to black to white.
    c. black to gray to white.
    d. gray to white to black.
    e. none of these.

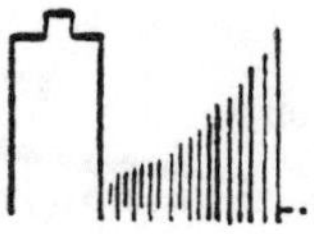

17. The primary service area of a TV station is
    a. within a radius of 50 miles.
    b. within a radius of 100 miles.
    c. the area of a circle having a radius of approximately the line of sight.
    d. line of sight plus 50 miles.
    e. none of these.

7. **(100 volts)** In solving for the impedance of a solenoid (coil) having inductance and resistance, it is only necessary to know the AC voltage and current. As was pointed out in the previous frame $Z = E/I$.

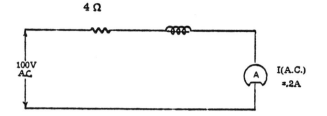

The impedance of the circuit
to the left would be_____

14. **(less)** Since power can only be dissipated in the resistance of an RCL AC circuit and since there is no phase displacement in the resistance itself, true AC power is also equal to I^2R or by formula:

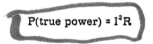

$$P(\text{true power}) = I^2R$$

Where P = true power in watts.
I = circuit current in amperes.
R = total resistance in series circuit.

TRUE POWER

Power factor is the ratio of _____ power to apparent power (IE).

21. **(270 ohms)** The assumed voltage method requires that you assume a voltage across the circuit. This same voltage must be used in every calculation involving the circuit voltage. Of course if a voltage is given in a problem, it should be used so that the currents involved will be actual values rather than relative values. See the example below where we use this method to solve for parallel circuit impedance.

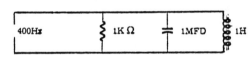

The same frequency and circuit components are used as we used when we solved for impedance by the admittance method.

$$Z = \frac{E}{I_{Line}}$$

$$I_{Line} = \sqrt{I_R{}^2 + (I_{XL} - I_{XC})^2}$$

$$I_R = E/R \quad I_{XL} = E/X_L \quad I_{XC} = E/X_C$$

Where Z = parallel impedance in ohms.
E = assumed or given voltage.
I_{Line} = current though parallel circuit.
I_R = current through resistance.
I_{XC} = current through capacitance.
I_{XL} = current through inductance.

Solving for X_L $X_L = 2\pi FL = 6.28 \times 400 \times 1 = 2512$ ohms - inductive reactance.

Solving for X_C $X_C = \dfrac{1}{2\pi F C} = \dfrac{1}{6.28 \times 400 \times 1 \times 10^{-6}} = 400$ ohms - capacitive reactance

Solving for I_{Line}. At this time we must assume a voltage if none is given. Suppose we assume a voltage of 100 volts. $I_R = E/R$ or 100v/1000 ohms = .1A $I_{XL} = E/X_L$ or 100v/2512 ohms = .04A
$I_{XC} = E/X_C$ or 100v/400 ohms = .25A

$$I_{Line} = \sqrt{I_R{}^2 + (I_{XL} - I_{XC})^2} = \sqrt{.1^2 + (.25 - .04)^2} = .25A \text{ (app.)}$$

Solving for parallel Z. $Z = E/I_{Line} = 100/.25$ or 400 ohms.

At a frequency of 1000 hertz, the impedance of the circuit above would be_____ .

1. In television broadcasting there are
   a. 30 frames a minute.
   b. 60 fields a second.
   c. 525 lines a second.
   d. 60 fields a minute.
   e. none of these.

2. The speaker monitor at a standard broadcast station is comparable to
   a. the antenna ammeter of a broadcast station.
   b. the final plae current meter of a standard broadcast station.
   c. the reflectometer at a television station.
   d. the antenna at a television station.
   e. the television monitor on a video transmission.

3. In standard television broadcasting the scanning period for one line is
   a. 1/60 sec.   d. 1/15750 sec.
   b. 1/525 sec.   e. none of these.
   c. 1/30 sec.

4. The bandwidth of an intercarrier IF stage in a television receiver should be
   a. 2000 khz.   d. 100 khz.
   b. 4500 khz.   e. none of these.
   c. 2 khz.

5. In a video transmission there are
   a. 60 frames per second.   d. 525 lines per second.
   b. 60 fields per minute.   e. 30 frames per second.
   c. 120 lines per second.

6. The picture tube is changed from a small 4″ X 3″ tube to a large 16″ X 12″ tube. The aspect ratio would then be
   a. 4 to 3.   d. 16 to 4.
   b. 12 to 4.   e. 12 to 3.
   c. 6 to 4.

7. In a television signal, the blanking level is
   a. 60%.   d. 80%.
   b. 70%.   e. 100%.
   c. 75%.

8. In a television signal, the reference black level is
   a. 60%.   d. 75%.
   b. 70%.   e. 100%.
   c. 15%.

9. In a teleision signal, the reference white level is
   a. 60%.   d. 75%.
   b. 70%.   e. 100%.
   c. 12.5%.

10. For the purpose of scanning a wave form should be used that is
    a. a square wave.
    b. a triangular wave.
    c. a sine wave.
    d. a wave that rises linearly and falls quickly.
    e. none of these.

Unit 7 ALTERNATING CURRENT CIRCUITS

Recheck Programmed Instruction Using Shrader's Electronic Communication

1. Resistance alone in a circuit produces . _____ phase difference between current and voltage. Sec. 7-1.

3. (lags, 90°) The impedance of a 3 ohm resistor in series with a 4 ohm inductive reactance would be _____. Sec. 7-2.

5. (300 ohms) The current in a series circuit consisting of five ohms of resistance and five ohms of inductive reactance would _____ the voltage by_____ degrees. Sec. 7-3.

7. (vectorially) Apparent power is equal to the product of the AC_____and AC _____. Sec. 7-5.

9. (apparent power) There are _____ ways of determining power factor in a series circuit. Sec. 7-6.

11. (apparently) The power factor of the readings given is_____ Sec.7-6.

13. (3 watts) From the information below the dissipated (true) power would be_____. Sec. 7-6.

15. (leads, 90°) The impedance of a series circuit composed of 3 ohms of resistance, 6 ohms of capacitive reactance, and 2 ohms of inductance is_____. Sec. 7-8.

17. (53%,leads) The power factor in the problem of frame #15 is approximately _____ . Sec. 7-8.

19. (zero) If the student has a problem with mathematics he should read all paragraphs of 7-9 and 7-10 and work all practice problems page 115. The answers can be found on page 116.

21. (admittance) Conductance in mhos is equal to the reciprocal of the _____. Sec.7-12.

23. (.0125 mhos or 12,500 micromhos) Generally speaking there is a lower impedance to a high frequency when the current path is made up of a conductor of high conductivity such as silver. Work problem 5 page 118.

25. (inductance) The impedance of a parallel resonant circuit is _____ and like an open circuit. Sec. 7-15.

27. (12 volts) This concludes the recheck material on Unit 7.

RECHECK PROGRAMMED INSTRUCTION USING SHRADER'S ELECTRONIC COMMUNICATION

3. (frequency, amplitude) The speaker monitor of the aural transmitter is comparable to the
    _____monitor of the video transmitter.   Sec. 25-1.

6. (deflection) For the purpose of scanning, a wave form should be used that has a_____ linear
    rise with a rapid _____ .   Sec. 25-4.

9. (4 to 3) In interlaced scanning there are_____ fields per second. _____ frames per second,
    _____ lines per field and_____ lines per frame.   Sec. 25-4.

12. (right, left) The blanking level is_____ %, the reference black level is_____ % and the white level
    is_____%.   Sec. 25-9.

15. (vestigial) In the diagram below the video carrier is located at_____ and the aural carrier at_____ .

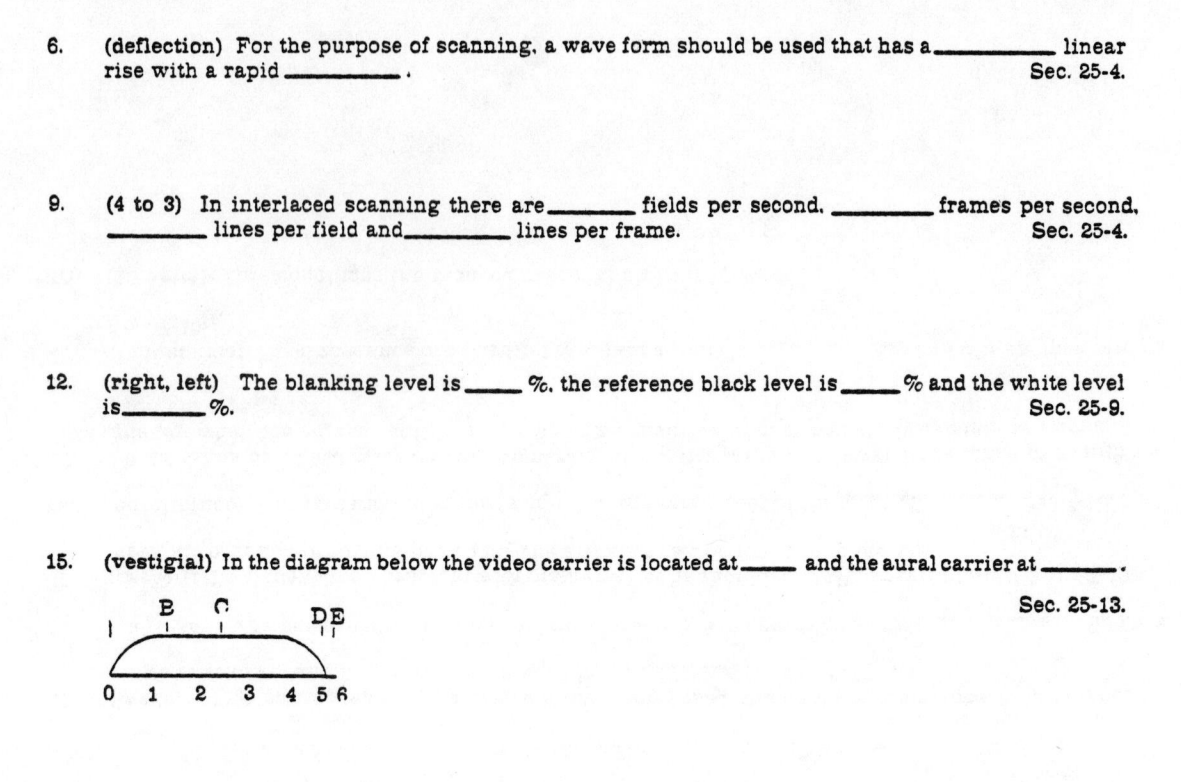
                                                                                   Sec. 25-13.

18. (4.5 Mhz , 70%) The bandwidth of an inter-carrier I.F. stage in a television receiver should be _____
    Mhz .   Sec. 25-17.

21. (3.58 Mhz, oscillator) This concludes the recheck of Unit 8.

Unit 7

2. (no or zero) In an RL circuit the current _____ the voltage by some less than_____. degrees. Sec. 7-2.

4. (5 ohms) The impedance of a solenoid coil having a resistance of 5 ohms, a current flow of .4 amperes, an applied voltage of 120 volts, and a frequency of 60 hertz; would be_____ ohms. Sec. 7-2.

6. (lag, 45°) In an AC circuit involving inductance, capacitance, and resistance in series; the voltage drops will add to equal the source voltage if they are added_____. Sec.7-4.

8. (current, voltage) Volt amperes is often used to mean_____Sec. 7-5.

10. (three) Power factor is in reality a comparison of the amount of power a circuit is actually using and what it is_____ using. Sec. 7-6.

12. (.90 or 90%) From the information below the true AC power is_____. Sec. 7-6.

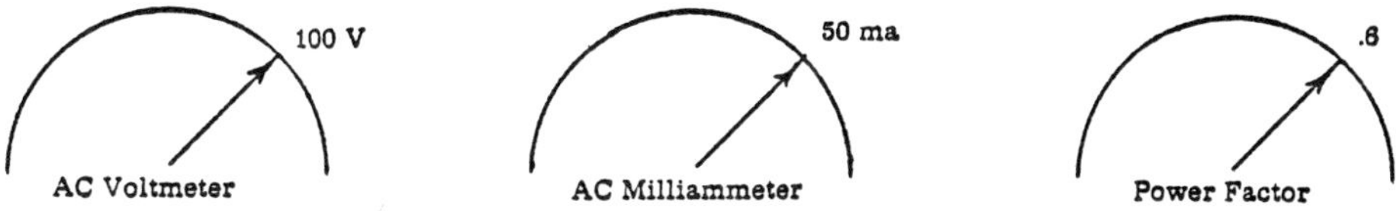

    100 V   50 ma   .6
    AC Voltmeter   AC Milliammeter   Power Factor

14. (120 X 60 X .6 or 4320 watts) In an RC series circuit the current _____the voltage by less than _____ degrees. Sec. 7-7.

16. (5 ohms) The phase angle in the problem #15 is approximately_____degrees and the current_____the voltage. Sec. 7-8.

18. (.6 or 60%) When Xc = XL in a series LC circuit the impedance is nearly _____. Sec. 7-8.

20. Impedance is equal to the reciprocal of_____. Sec. 7-12.

22. (resistance) The conductance in the circuit below would be _____. Sec. 7-12.

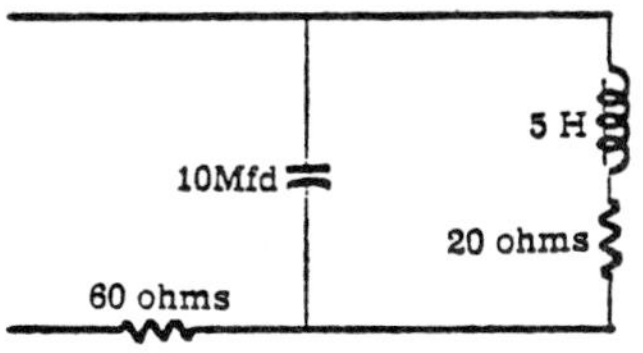

    5 H
    10Mfd
    20 ohms
    60 ohms

24. (.472, 21.2, 2A, 1.25A, 62.5 W) Capacitance and resistance in parallel are computed in the same way as _____and resistance in parallel. Sec. 7-14. (in impedance calculations)

26. (high) The voltage drop across the resistor in the circuit below would be _____ V.

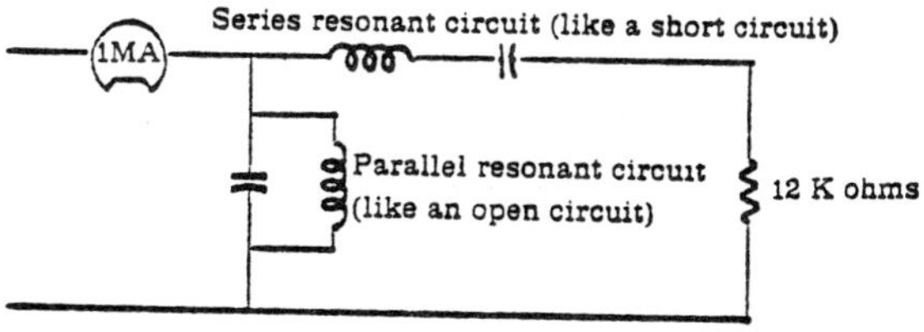

    1MA   Series resonant circuit (like a short circuit)
          Parallel resonant circuit (like an open circuit)   12 K ohms

50

RECHECK PROGRAMMED INSTRUCTION USING SHRADER'S ELECTRONIC COMMUNICATION

2.   (two, 25 Khz) The aural transmitter uses _____ modulation and the video transmitter uses _____ modulation.   Sec. 25-1.

5.   (15,750 Hz, 60 Hz) Two horizontal and two vertical coils form a _____ yoke.   Sec. 25-3.

8.   (flicker) If the picture tube is changed from a small 4″ X 3″ tube to a large 16″ X 12″ tube, the aspect ratio is _____ to _____ .   Sec. 25-4.

11.   (15,750) Retrace signals are used to return the beam horizontally from _____ to _____ .   Sec. 25-8.

14.   (black, gray, white) Since only a vestige of the lower sidebands is transmitted, the emission is termed _____ sideband.   Sec. 25-13.

17.   (6 Mhz) The aural carrier is _____ Mhz above the video carrier. Although the carrier power of the aural FM transmitter is usually 20% of the video transmitter power, it must be kept to a value of less than _____ %.   Sec. 25-13.

20.   (line of sight) The chrominance subcarrier has an approximate frequency of _____ Mhz . The color (subcarrier burst) is used for synchronizing the TV receiver color _____ .   Sec. 25-24.

Unit 7
ALTERNATING CURRENT CIRCUITS

1. A 10 Mhz current would be offered the least impedance by a
   a. copper strip 6 inches long and 2 inches wide.
   b. aluminum wire 6 inches long and 6 mils in diameter.
   c. 2 pf capacitor.
   d. one ohm wire wound resistor.
   e. silver wire 6 inches long and 6 mils in diameter.

2. Impedance is measured in:
   a. Farads
   b. Henrys d. Mhos
   c. Joules e. Ohms

3. The impedance of the circuit below at one khz is approximately
   a. 38.45
   b. 3845
   c. 161
   d. 6280
   e. none of these

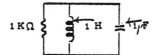

4. The impedance of the circuit above at two Khz is approximately
   a. 38.45 Ω
   b. 322 Ω d. 6280 Ω
   c. 80.5 Ω e. none of these

5. Conductance is the reciprocal of
   a. susceptance
   b. reactance d. a and b
   c. resistance e. b and c

6. The power in the circuit shown below would be
   a. A X V
   b. R_1 X R_2 X A^2
   c. A X V X P.F.
   d. (R_1 + R_2 + R_3) X A
   e. none of these

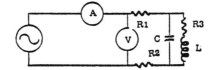

7. In the circuit shown 2 pi F is equal to 1,000. The approximate impedance is
   a. 8,000 Ω
   b. 300 Ω
   c. 5,000 Ω
   d. 12,500 Ω
   e. none of these

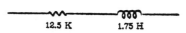

8. At resonance for the tank circuits shown below, the applied voltage would be
   a. 100 volts
   b. 12.5 volts.
   c. 63.2 mv.
   d. 12.5 mv.
   e. none of these

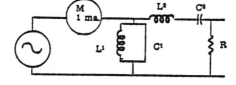

$L_1 = L_2$

$C_1 = C_2$

R = 12.5 K

9. From the information given below, the AC power would be
   a. 5 watts.
   b. 4,000 watts.
   c. 4 watts.
   d. 150.8 watts.
   e. none of these

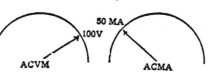

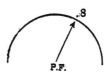

10. The power factor for the readings given is approximately
   a. 57%.
   b. 63%.
   c. 92%.
   d. 25%.
   e. 83%.

RECHECK PROGRAMMED INSTRUCTION USING SHRADER'S ELECTRONIC COMMUNICATION

1. A television transmitter is actually _____ transmitters coupled to a single antenna. 100% modulation of the aural signal results in a frequency swing of _____ Khz.   Sec. 25-1.

4. (video) The horizontal oscillator frequency is _____ Hz and the vertical oscillator frequency is _____ Hz.   Sec. 25-4.

7. (slow, retrace) To prevent _____ interlaced scanning is used.   Sec. 25-4.

10. (60, 30, 262½, 525) In standard television broadcasting, the scanning period for one horizontal line is equal to the reciprocal of _____ .   Sec. 25-8.

13. (75%, 70%, 12.5%) In the signal shown, the video is moving from _____ to _____

to _____ .

Sec. 25-9

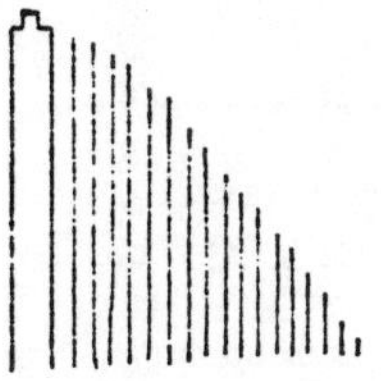

16. (B,D) The TV channel is _____ MHz wide.   Sec. 25-13.

19. (4.5 Mhz) Whereas the primary service area of a standard broadcast station is the area where there is no significant fading, the primary service area of a TV station is the area of a circle having a radius of approximately the line of sight.

The primary service area of a TV station is the area of a circle having a radius of approximately the _____ .

11. In the diagram below the voltage across the inductance would be
    a. zero.
    b. 1 volt.
    c. 10 volts.
    d. 100 volts.
    e. 1,000 volts.

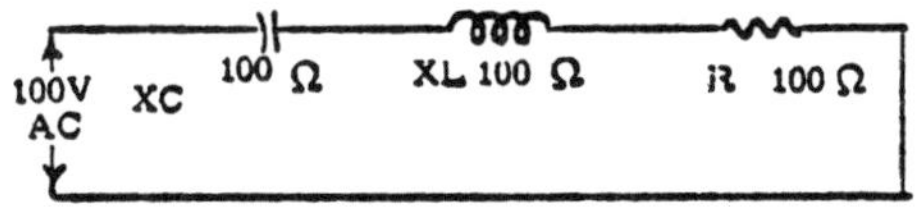

    100V AC XC 100 Ω XL 100 Ω R 100 Ω

12. The total condutance in the circuit below is
    a. 50 mhos.
    b. 20,000 micromhos.
    c. 65 mhos.
    d. 30 mhos.
    e. none of these.

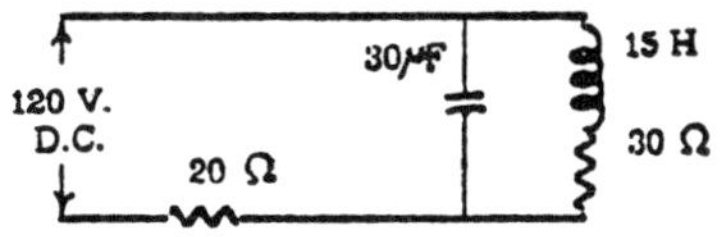

    120 V. D.C. 30 µF 15 H 20 Ω 30 Ω

13. 100 volts is applied to a solenoid having a resistance of 4 ohms. The resulting current flow is .2 amperes. The impedance of the solenoid is
    a. .08 ohms.
    b. 25 ohms. d. 750 ohms.
    c. 500 ohms. e. none of these.

14. A circuit having a true power of 138 watts, 115 volts of line voltage and drawing 1 1/2 amperes of current would have a power factor of
    a. 60%
    b. 70% d. 90%
    c. 80% e. 100%.

15. A series circuit having 10 ohms of resistance, 100 ohms of inductive reactance and 125 ohms of capacitive reactance will have
    a. 235 ohms of impedance.
    b. current leading the voltage.
    c. current lagging the voltage.
    d. a resistance that has a negligible effect on total Z.
    e. none of these.

16. In the circuit shown 2 pi F is equal to 1,000. The approximate impedance would be
    a. 8,000 ohms.
    b. 300 ohms.
    c. 5,000 ohms.
    d. 12,500 ohms.
    e. none of these.

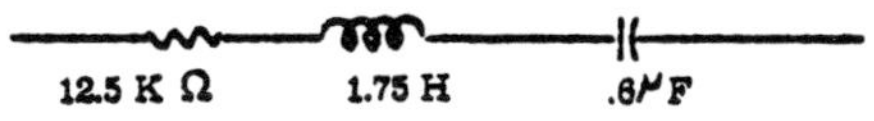

    12.5 K Ω 1.75 H .6 µF

17. A series RCL circuit consists of 12 ohms of resistance, 42 ohms of XC and 54 ohms of XL. The phase angle would be
    a. 45 degrees.
    b. 78.2 degrees. d. 33 degrees.
    c. 0 degrees. e. 27.5 degrees.

18. If in question number 17 the X_c is 54 ohms, the phase angle would be
    a. 45 degrees.
    b. 78.2 degrees. d. 33 degrees.
    c. 0 degrees. e. 27.5 degrees

19. The applied voltage in the diagram below is
    a. 1.25 volts.
    b. 12.5 volts.
    c. 125 volts.
    d. .125 volts.
    e. none of these.

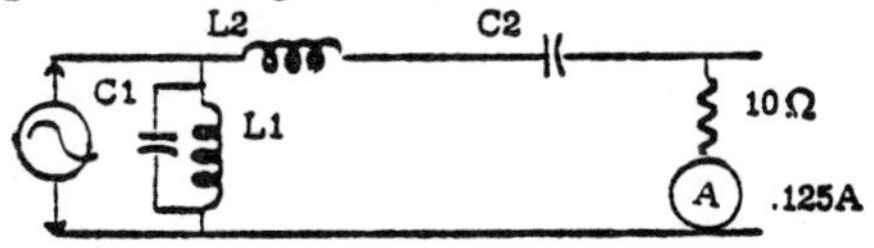

    L2 C2 C1 L1 10 Ω A .125A
    C1 = C2 L1 = L2 Both circuits are at resonance

20. The power in the circuit shown below could be (assume no resistance at L)
    a. A X V.
    b. R_1 X R_2 X A^2
    c. A X V X P.F.
    d. $(R_1 + R_2 + R_3)$ X A^2
    e. a or d.

    DC A R1 V R3 R2 L

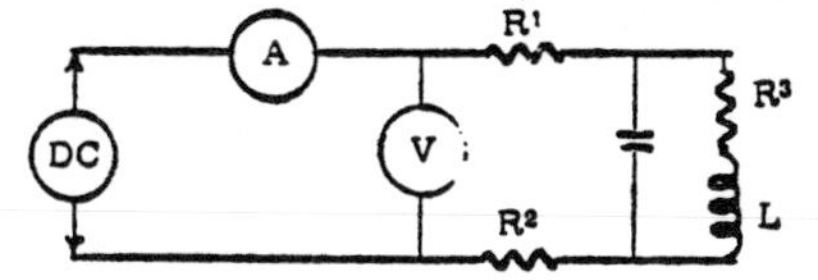

21. The indicated dissipated power is
    a. 1000 watts
    b. 125 X 65 watts.
    c. (125 X 65 X .65) watts.
    d. $\frac{125 \times 65}{65}$
    e. none of these.

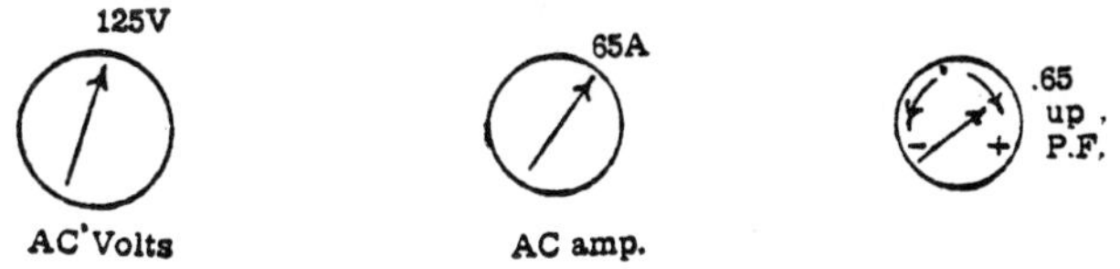

    125V AC Volts 65A AC amp. .65 up P.F.

52

4. (film, picture, 10 KW) The aural speaker monitor is comparable to the _____ monitor of the video transmitter.

8. (retrace) It is standard to use a width to heighth ratio for all U.S. TV of 4 to 3. This ratio is independent of the CRT size and is called aspect ratio. For all the reproduction of a complete picture there are two separate scans at the camera and the cathode ray tube. Note below:

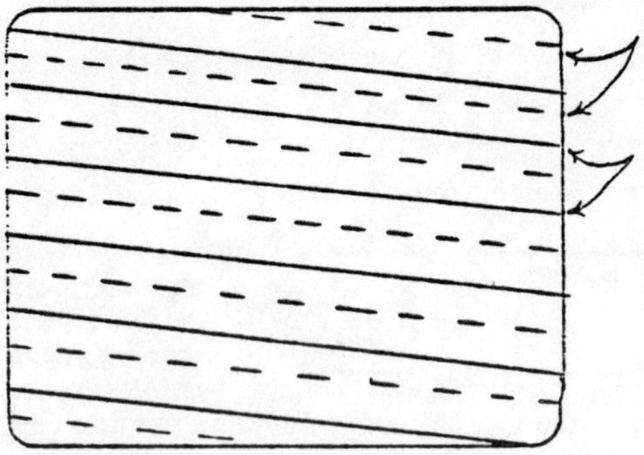

Odd line interlacing - 262½ lines.

Even line scanning - 262½ lines.

Two scans called fields complete one picture or a **frame.**

A frame has a total of 525 lines (262 ½ + 262½)

Only a few of the lines are shown.

There are 60 fields (partial pictures) a second, and 30 frames (complete pictures) a second. Interlaced scanning reduces flicker in video broadcasting.
Scanning is accomplished using_____ fields per second or_____ frames per second.

12. (75%, right, left) The reference white and reference black levels for video are_____ % and _____%.

16. (4500 Khz) In color TV transmissions a chrominance sub carrier (color burst) is transmitted on 3.58 Khz and appears on the sync pedestal on the back porch. It is used at the receiver to sync the color oscillator.

The chrominance sub carrier frequency is_____ Khz and is used to sync the TV receiver _____ oscillator.

22. In the circuit below
   a. the current through the resistor leads the voltage
   b. the voltage across the resistor leads the current.
   c. the impedance is 15 ohms.
   d. the current through the circuit leads the applied voltage.
   e. none of these.

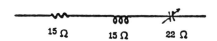

15 Ω   15 Ω   22 Ω

23. A circuit of pure capacitance and inductance with no resistance is connected to a power source. This circuit
   a. has a power factor of more than 1.
   b. has a power factor of 1.
   c. dissipates power in the form of heat.
   d. uses no power.
   e. b and c above.

24. The conductance of the circuit below is approximately
   a. .033 Ω
   b. 46 mhos.
   c. .0303 mhos.
   d. 13 Ω
   e. none of these.

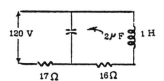

120 V   2 μF   1 H

17 Ω   16 Ω

25. The current lags the voltage by 45 ° in a circuit containing
   a. equal resistance and inductive reactance.
   b. equal resistance and capacitive reactance.
   c. all inductive reactance and no resistance.
   d. all capacitive reactance and no resistance.
   e. equal capacitive and inductive reactance.

26. The current leads the voltage by 45° in a circuit containing
   a. equal resistance and inductive reactance.
   b. equal resistance and capacitive reactance.
   c. all inductive reactance and no resistance.
   d. all capacitive reactance and no resistance.
   e. equal capacitance and inductance.

27. In the diagram below, the power delivered by the source is
   a. . 10 watts.
   b. .1 watts.
   c. 100 watts.
   d. 15 watts.
   e. none of these.

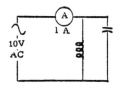

A   1 A   10V AC

3.   (vestigial) In order for a picture to be reproduced on the face of a receiver cathode ray tube, the electron beam at the receiver must be synchronized with the scanning beam at the transmitter. The beam at the receiver must start its scanning process in the upper left hand corner of the CRT at the exact moment that the beam at the camera starts in the upper left hand corner. Synchronized sawtooth waveforms move the beams from left to right and top to bottom.

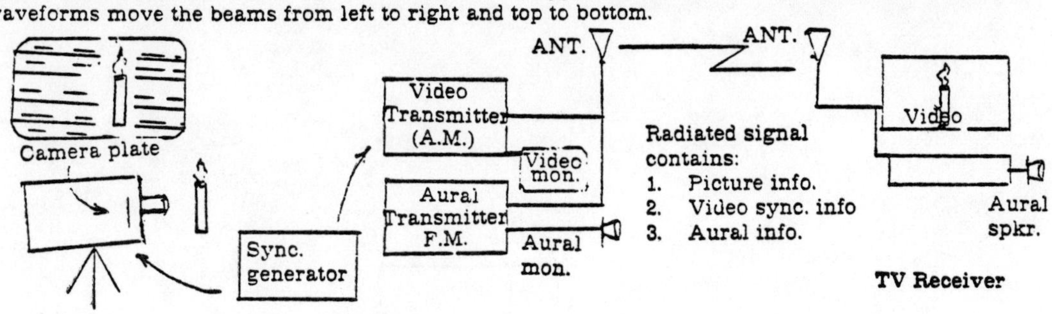

TV Transmitter

TV Receiver

Radiated signal contains:
1.   Picture info.
2.   Video sync. info
3.   Aural info.

As the camera image plate containing the optical image is scanned with an electron beam, electrical pulses modulate the transmitter. The image plate is somewhat like the film in a camera. The sound information is transmitted by the aural transmitter. The video and aural RF is mixed at the antenna and transmitted in a 6 Mhz. channel. The aural transmitter power output is 20% of the video transmitter power output. The output of both transmitters is monitored at the TV transmitter - a CRT circuit for monitoring video and an audio amplifier with speaker to monitor the aural transmission. The primary area of coverage for a TV signal is roughly the area of a circle having the radius of the line of sight.

The image plate in a TV camera is like the_____in a camera. The radiated signal from a TV transmitter contains_____, aural and sync information. If the video power output at a TV station was 50 KW, the aural power output should be_____KW.

7.   (scanning or deflection) The fast dropoff of a sawtooth wave is used for_____.

11.   (63.5 microseconds) 10% of this period is used to return (retrace) the beam to the left side of the picture. During the retrace, the beam is blanked by the application of a high negative bias to the CRT grid. This bias is provided by a blanking signal. The composite video signal for one horizontal line is shown with comparative level values below:

The Video shown for 1 line is changing from black to gray to white. After the beam reaches the bottom of the picture, the vertical retrace occurs and the beam is returned to the top of the left side of the CRT. During vertical retrace the beam is blanked by a vertical blanking pulse. The video blanking level is_____%.

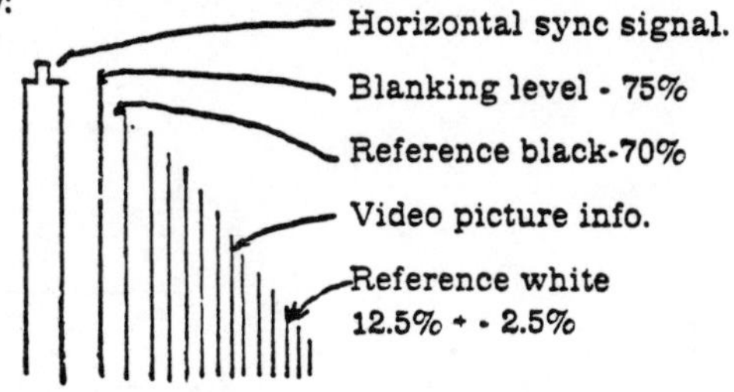

Horizontal sync signal.
Blanking level - 75%
Reference black-70%
Video picture info.
Reference white
12.5% + - 2.5%

During the blanking the beam returns from the_____side to the_____side of the CRT.

15.   (16,667 microsecs) Since the aural and video carriers are separated by 4.5 Mhz, the receiver I. F. bandpass must be at least this wide or_____Khz

Unit 8 RESONANCE AND FILTERS

1. The condition of resonance in a series or parallel circuit consisting of an inductance and a capacitance is obtained when the inductive reactance is equal to the capacitive reactance. ($X_L = X_C$) As was noted in Unit 7, the impedance of a series resonant LC circuit is generally low. The impedance of a parallel resonant circuit is generally quite high. The frequency for resonance in series and parallel LC circuits is given by the formula

FR in series or parallel

$$F_R = \frac{1}{2 \text{ pi} \sqrt{LC}}$$

Where F = the resonant frequency in hertz.
L = inductance in henrys.
C = capacitance in farads.

Since $\frac{1}{2 \text{ pi}} = \frac{1}{6.28} = .159$, the formula can be rewritten: $F = \frac{.159}{\sqrt{LC}}$

The addition of a series resistance in a series LC circuit will make a small (but in most cases negligible) change in the resonant frequency.

The addition of a parallel resistance in a parallel LC circuit will have no effect on the resonant frequency of the circuit.

The resonant frequency is inversely proportional to the square root of the product of _____ and _____.

6. **(500 ohms)** The approximate resonant frequency of a series circuit of 10 ohms resistance, 10 Mfd of capacitance, and 2 H of inductance would be_____.

11. **(.01 H)** The frequency of a parallel resonant LC circuit is not changed by the addition of parallel _____.

16. **(series)** Variations of the constant K low pass filter are shown below:

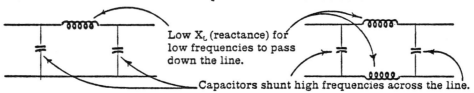

Low X_L (reactance) for low frequencies to pass down the line.

Capacitors shunt high frequencies across the line.

Unbalanced constant K
pi section low pass
filter

Balanced constant K
low pass filter

Inductors provide a low impedance path for the_____frequencies.

21. **(high pass)** The M stands for the ratio of the cut off frequency to the frequency of infinite attenuation, (no output). M derived filters unlike constant K filters contain series or parallel _TUNED_ circuits.

26. **(one tenth)** It is usual to make high frequency coils from large wire as the high frequency currents have a tendency to crowd to the outside surface of the wire. This effect is called _skin effect._ This concludes Unit 8.

2.   (4.5 MHz, 1.25 MHz, .25 MHz, 6.25 KHz) The lower video sidebands are called _____.

6.   (line of sight) The scanning action in the cathode ray tube (CRT) of the TV receiver is shown below:

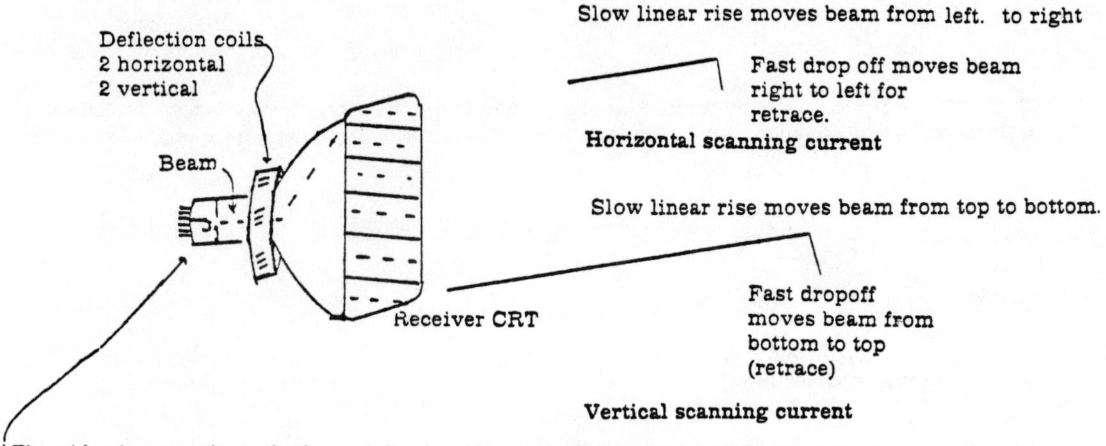

Deflection coils
2 horizontal
2 vertical

Beam

Receiver CRT

Slow linear rise moves beam from left. to right

Fast drop off moves beam right to left for retrace.

Horizontal scanning current

Slow linear rise moves beam from top to bottom.

Fast dropoff moves beam from bottom to top (retrace)

Vertical scanning current

The video input to the cathode ray tube provides variable bias to the grid cathode system causing the electron beam current to vary in intensity corresponding to light and dark picture areas as the beam is swept by the deflection circuits from right to left and top to bottom.

A sawtooth wave that has a slow linear rise and a quick drop off is used for horizontal and vertical_____.

10.   (4,3) Since there are 30 frames transmitted each second and each frame consists of 525 lines, there are 15,750 horizontal lines (525 X 30) transmitted in a second. The period of each horizontal line (cycle) is equal to the reciprocal of 15,750 or_____microseconds.

14.   (white, black) Since the field frequency is 60 Hertz, the vertical period is equal to the reciprocal of 60 or_____microseconds.

SERIES RESONANT CIRCUITS

2. (inductance, capacitance) Let us solve for the series resonant frequency of a circuit using the formula. If a series circuit consisted of an inductance of 100 MMfd and 200 Microhenrys, the resonant frequency is equal to:

$$F = \frac{.159}{\sqrt{100 \times 10^{-12} \times 200 \times 10^{-6}}} = \frac{.159}{\sqrt{2 \times 10^{-7}}} = \begin{matrix} 1,124,000 \text{ hertz} \\ \text{or } 1124 \text{ Khz.} \end{matrix}$$

If a 120 microhenry coil is tuned by a 120 MMfd (picofarad) capacitor, the resonant frequency is _____.

7. (35.6 hertz) A secondary tuned circuit may appear as though it is a parallel circuit, but actually it is a series tuned circuit because the voltage is first induced into the inductance. Note the illustration.

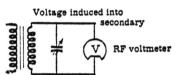
Voltage induced into secondary
V RF voltmeter

Since this is a series tuned circuit, the impedance is minimum at resonance and maximum current flows.

The meter would register high voltage at resonance and low voltage off resonance. When current is maximum the voltage across the inductance or capacitance is maximum.
As the tuning capacitor in the secondary was tuned through resonance the meter would go from minimum value to _____ value and then back to _____ value.

12. (resistance) If a resonant parallel circuit having resistance, capacitive reactance, and inductive reactance of 100 ohms has the resistance changed to 200 ohms; the resonant frequency is _____.

17. (low) The circuit shown is an example of a _____ filter.

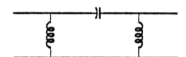

DECIBELS

22. (tuned) The decible is a logarithmic unit equivalent to one tenth Bel. The Bel is not a practical unit. One decibel is considered to be the smallest change (increase or decrease) in audio power that can be detected by the ear. The decibel is often used to compare two sound energy levels. The smallest change in sound intensity that can be detected by the ear is the _____.

1. It should be known that a television broadcast station has two transmitters. One is the video (picture) transmitter and the other is the aural (sound) transmitter. The carrier frequency of the Video A.M. signal is separated from the aural FM carrier by 4.5 MHz. The V.H.F. channel 2 is used to illustrate the frequency arrangement:

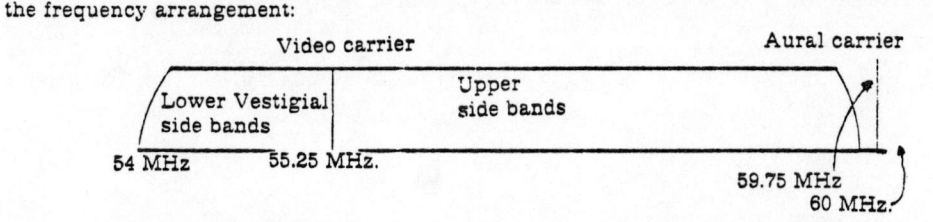

The lower sidebands are not complete and are called vestigial sidebands. Only the upper video sidebands are fully developed. The video carrier is 1.25 Mhz above the lower limit of the channel. The aural carrier is .25 Mhz below the upper limit of the channel.
The video carrier is amplitude modulated and the aural carrier is frequency modulated. 100% modulation of the aural carrier produces a deviation of ± 25 Khz. 50% modulation produces a deviation of 12.5 Khz.

The two carriers are separated _____ Mhz. The video carrier is _____ Mhz above the lower limit of the channel while the aural carrier is _____ Mhz below the upper limit of the channel. 25% modulation of the aural carrier produces a deviation of _____ Khz.

5. **(video)** The primary service area of a TV station is roughly the area of a circle having a radius of the _____ of _____.

9. **(60,30)** The aspect ratio (width to height) for all U.S. TV is _____ to _____.

13. **(12.5%, 70%)** The video shown is going from _____ to gray to _____.

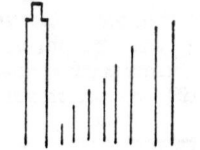

17. **(3.58, color)** This concludes Unit 8.

3. **(1325 Khz)** If a resistance is added in series to a series LC resonant circuit, the impedance increases as seen by the series formula:

$$Z = \sqrt{R^2 + (X_L - X_C)^2} = \sqrt{R^2 + 0^2} = R$$

In other words the impedance would theoretically be zero before the resistance was added and equal to the resistance after it was added. This is true in all series circuits. Since all LC circuits have some resistance, the series resonant impedance is low but not zero. If resistance is added in series to a series resonant LC circuit, the impedance _____.

PARALLEL RESONANT CIRCUITS

8. **(maximum, minimum)** If two identical parallel resonant circuits are connected in parallel, the resonant frequency of the combination is the same as either of the original circuits. This is true since the LC product is unaffected. Connected equal coils in parallel cuts the inductance to one half, but connected equal capacitances in parallel doubles the capacitance. The resonant frequency of a parallel circuit consisting of two identical resonant parallel tuned circuits is _____.

"CONSTANT K FILTERS"

13. **(unchanged)** In the two formulas $X_L = 2piFL$ and $X_C = \dfrac{1}{2piFC}$ it can be seen that inductive reactance is directly proportional to frequency and capacitive reactance is inversely proportional to frequency. This means that an inductance provides high reactance to high frequencies and a capacitor provides low reactance to high frequencies. It follows that an inductance provides low reactance to low frequencies and a capacitance high reactance to low frequencies. Note the examples of simple high and low pass filter circuits.

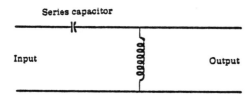

Series capacitor

Input   Output

High Pass Filter
(high frequencies easily passed
down the line by capacitance
having low reactance)

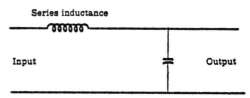

Series inductance

Input   Output

Low Pass Filter
(low frequencies easily passed
down the line by inductance
having low reactance)

The components across the lines above have low impedance (reactance) to the unwanted frequencies. A capacitance in series with one or both sides of a line provides a _____ pass circuit and an inductance in series with one or both sides of the line provides a _____ pass circuit.

18. **(unbalanced pi section high pass)** The circuit shown below is an example of a _____ filter.

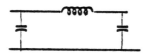

23. **(decibel)** By formula *for Power*

$$db \text{ (gain or loss)} = 10 \log \frac{P1}{P2}$$

Where db = decibels
    P1 = output when there is a gain:
       = input when there is a loss.
    P2 = input when there is a gain;
       = output when there is a loss.

For mathematical convenience P1 is always the larger of the two powers being considered. It can be shown that a 10 db gain is caused by a power ratio of 10 to 1 and that a 20 db gain is caused by a power ratio of 100 to 1. In the case of a 10 and 20 db loss the power ratios would be 1 to 10 and 1 to 100. A gain of 100 db represents the tremendous increase of power of 10^{10} or 10,000,000,000 times. An increase of power by ten times causes a _____ db gain, an increase of power by 100 times produces a _____ db gain and an increase of power by ten billion produces a _____ db gain.

1. The frequency tolerance of an international B.C. station is
   a. .001%.
   b. .002%.
   c. .003%.
   d. .004%.
   e. .005%.

2. The transmitter at a 5 Kw AM broadcast station must be able to
   a. broadcast on the ERI frequency.
   b. transmit directional.
   c. transmit high fidelity.
   d. transmit FM.
   e. be modulated 85%.

3. The action of an audio peak limiter produces
   a. a negative bias by diode rectification.
   b. frequency modulation.
   c. line equalization.
   d. a positive grid bias voltage.
   e. time delay of 75 microseconds.

4. The accuracy of a remote reading antenna ammeter should be at least
   a. 1%.
   b. 2%.
   c. 3%.
   d. 4%.
   e. 5%.

5. An audio limiter in an amplitude modulated transmitter depends on the principle of
   a. discrimination.
   b. deemphasis and preemphasis.
   c. mechanical rectification of three phase energy.
   d. developing a bias voltage by diode rectification of the audio signal.
   e. the piezo-electro effect.

6. The Austin ring transformer is used for
   a. balanced modulator.
   b. isolation of R.F. from the tower lights.
   c. a bridge rectifier in three phase circuits.
   d. reducing harmonics.
   e. preventing parasistic oscillations.

7. An H or T pad attenuator is used to
   a. amplify high audio frequencies.
   b. amplify low audio frequencies.
   c. achieve tone control.
   d. suppress harmonics.
   e. provide gain control without a mismatch of impedance.

8. A line equalizer is used at a broadcast station to
   a. attentuate audio harmonics.
   b. provide preemphasis for F.M. broadcasting.
   c. equalize the low and high audio frequencies.
   d. provide harmonics.
   e. none of these.

4. **(increases)**
Let us analyze a series RCL
resonant circuit solving for impedance,
circuit current, and individual
component voltage drops.

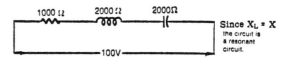

Since $X_L = X$ the circuit is a resonant circuit.

Solving for Z $Z \text{ (series)} = \sqrt{R^2 + (X_L - X_C)^2} = \sqrt{1000^2 + (2000 - 2000)^2} = 1000$
Solving for I $I = E/Z = 100/1000 = .1$ ampere.
Solving for E_R (voltage across the res.) $E_R = I \times R = .1 \times 1000 = 100V$
Solving for E_{XL} (voltage across the ind.) $E_{XL} = I \times X_L = .1 \times 2000 = 200V$
Solving for E_{XC} (voltage across the cap.) $E_{XC} = I \times X_C = .1 \times 2000 = 200V$

As is often the case the out of phase voltages across the inductance and capacitance are greater than the source voltage. If in the above example the resistance was 500 ohms, then the E_{XL}, E_{XC} would be_____volts.

9. **(the same as either of the original tuned circuits)** When a resistor is added across a parallel resonant LC circuit, it does not change the resonant frequency but it lowers the impedance of the circuit depending on its value.
The impedance of a parallel resonant LC circuit is_____by the addition of a parallel resistance.

.14. **(high, low)** Additional filter elements of inductance and capacitance can be connected in series and across the line for more pronounced effects. Some high pass filter variations are shown:

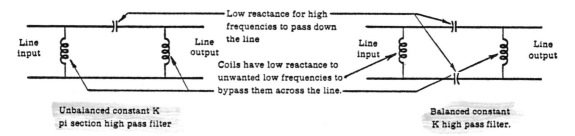

Unbalanced constant K pi section high pass filter

Balanced constant K high pass filter.

By the proper selection of inductance and capacitance the product of series and shunt impedances over a range of frequencies may be made to equal a fixed value. Such filters are called constant K filters. The configuration on the left above is called a pi section of filter because it resembles the greek letter π.
Filters having a product of series and shunt impedances that are equal to a constant over a range of frequencies are called _Constant K_ filters.

19. **(unbalanced pi section low pass)** Inductors are used in high pass filters connected in _____ with the line.

24. **(10db, 20db, 100db)** Current and voltage changes can also be interpreted in decibel gain or loss. By formulas:

$$\text{db (gain or loss)} = 20 \log \frac{E_1}{E_2} \quad \text{or} \quad 20 \log \frac{I_1}{I_2}$$

It can be shown that an increase of voltage by ten times produces a 20 db gain. Therefore a 20 db gain represents a power gain of_____ and a voltage gain of_____.

RECHECK PROGRAMMED INSTRUCTION USING SHRADER'S ELECTRONIC COMMUNICATION

2. **(85,100)** Attenuating an audio signal without a mismatch in impedance can be accomplished by a _____ or _____ pad attenuator.

4. **(low)** An audio peak limiter produces a negative bias by _____ rectification that is used to _____ the gain to prevent overmodulation.

6. **(2%, week)** An international broadcast station must maintain a carrier frequency tolerance of plus or minus _____ %.

5. (400V) The impedance of the circuit in this case would be_____.

10. (lowered) Let us solve for L in the parallel resonant circuit shown:

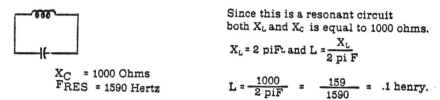

X_C = 1000 Ohms
F_{RES} = 1590 Hertz

Since this is a resonant circuit both X_L and X_C is equal to 1000 ohms.

$X_L = 2 \text{ pi} F L$ and $L = \dfrac{X_L}{2 \text{ pi } F}$

$L = \dfrac{1000}{2 \text{ pi} F} = \dfrac{159}{1590} = .1$ henry.

If X_C was equal to 100 ohms then the inductance would equal_____.

15. (constant K) The constant K filter does not employ series or parallel LC resonant circuits. Capacitors are used in high pass filters connected in ___SERIES___ with the line.

M DERIVED FILTERS

20. (parallel) A specialized filter using a series or parallel circuit either down the line or across the line is called an M derived filter. Note the four examples:

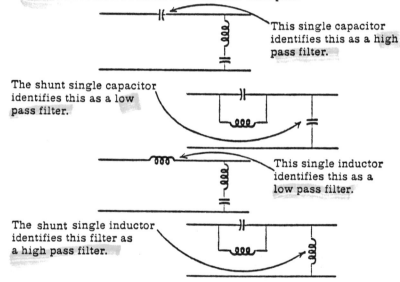

This single capacitor identifies this as a high pass filter.

The shunt single capacitor identifies this as a low pass filter.

This single inductor identifies this as a low pass filter.

The shunt single inductor identifies this filter as a high pass filter.

The M derived filters contain series and parallel tuned circuits and can be identified by the single reactive component. If a single inductor is in series down the line it is a low pass filter. If the single reactive component is an inductor across the line, the filter is a_____filter.

25. (100,10) The decibel is equivalent of_____bel.

UNIT 7 (Part 2)
BROADCAST STATIONS

RECHECK PROGRAMMED INSTRUCTION USING SHRADER'S ELECTRONIC COMMUNICATION

Review Recheck Unit 24 of the Part 1 Second Class Radiotelephone programmed instruction.

1. The F.C.C. requires that a broadcast station keep the highest peaks of modulation above______% and below______%. Sec. 24-2.

3. **(H, T)** Line equalizers are used to attenuate the______frequencies at the end of a long line. Sec. 24-6.

5. **(diode, reduce)** A remote reading antenna ammeter must have an accuracy of______% and must be calibrated once every______. Sec. 24-10.

7. **(.003%)** This concludes the recheck of Unit 7.

Unit 8 RESONANCE AND FILTERS

Recheck Programmed Instruction Using Shrader's Electronic Communication

1.   If the inductance is 150 ɥh and the capacitance is 150 ɥɥ fd (pfd) the resonant frequency is approximately_____. Sec. 8-1.

3.   (unchanged) This is true since the inductance is halved and the capacitance is doubled and the LC product is unchanged. An RF VTVM placed across the secondary of the circuit of figure 8-4 will read highest when the secondary is _____. Sec. 8-2.

5.   (6.5 ohms, 40A, 7000V, 7000V, 260V) The impedance, inductive voltage drop, and capacitor voltage drop in the circuit shown is_____ , _____. , and _____ . Sec. 8-2

7.   (low) If a resistance is added in series with a series resonant LC circuit the impedance_____.
Sec. 8-2.

9.   (high) If you add a parallel resistance to a parallel tuned LC circuit the impedance _____ .
Sec. 8-3.

11.   (unchanged) In the circuit shown the resonant frequency is 1590 Hertz.

The inductive reactance is equal to the capacitive reactance. (Since it is a resonant circuit). From the formula X_L equals 2 pi FL the inductance can be determined. It is_____. Sec. 8-3.

13.   (resistance, reactance, skin) particularly study the table page 135. A 10 db gain is equal to a power increase of_____times. Sec. 8-5.

15.   (1,100) A 20 db gain would be expressed as a power ratio of 100 to 1. The higher the Q of a resonant circuit, the _____ the bandwidth. Sec. 8-6.

17.   (constant K low pass) Because of its resemblance to the greek letter π it is referred to as a pi filter.

The circuit shown is an unbalanced pi section _____ filter. Sec. 8-8.

19.   (constant K) M is considered to be a ratio of the cut off frequency of_____. Sec. 8-8.

21.   (two) This concludes the recheck on Unit 8.

2.   **(85%)** If the audio levels are set for the occasional high peaks of audio that produce 100% modulation, the average audio amplitude is insufficient for maintaining 85% modulation. In order to obtain a higher average audio amplitude, it is necessary to use a peak limiter amplifier. If these peaks are higher than a predetermined level, part of the audio is rectified by diodes to produce a DC voltage for higher bias and a lower gain to an audio amplifier feeding the modulator. The general idea is shown:

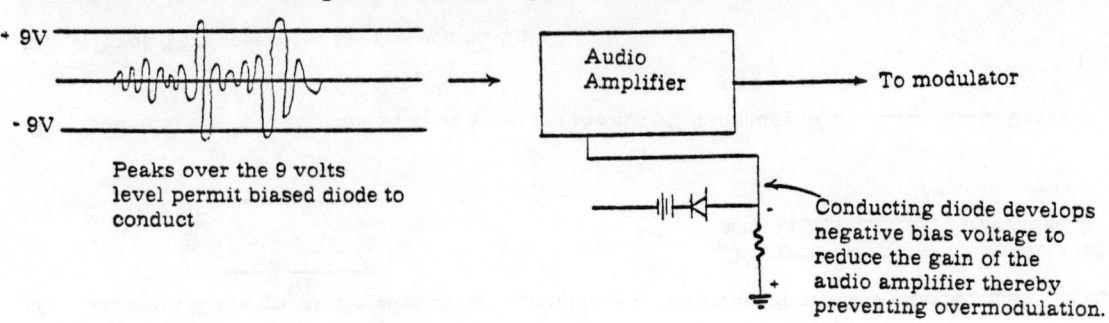

An audio peak limiter produces a negative bias by_____rectification.

4.   **(week, 2%)** International Broadcast stations operating on short waves (6-26 MHz) must maintain a frequency tolerance of plus or minus .003%. For example a station operating on 9.5 MHz must maintain their carrier frequency at 9.5 MHz plus or minus 285 Hz. (.00003 X 9,500,00).

An International Broadcast station operating on 11.7 MHz must maintain its carrier on 11.7 MHz plus or minus_____Hertz.

6.   **(low, high)** The power lines used to light the tower lights are in the strong field of the antenna when the station is on the air. To prevent RF pickup on the lines from lighting the tower lights, an isolation transformer called an Austin Ring transformer is used. The tower light isolation transformer is called an_____ _____transformer.

2. (1060 Khz) If two identical tuned parallel circuits are placed in parallel, the resulting resonant frequency would be _____. Sec. 8-1.

4. (resonant) Work problem 10 page 130. Sec. 8-2.

6. (2000 ohms, 150 V, 150V) In a series resonant LC circuit the impedance is_____ . Sec. 8-2.

8. (increases) The impedance of a practical paralleled resonant LC circuit is_____ . Sec. 8-3.

10. (decreases) On the other hand the resonant frequency of a parallel resonant LC circuit is unaffected by a parallel resistance. If you add a parallel resistance to a parallel tuned LC circuit the frequency is _____ . Sec. 8-3.

12. (.01 Henry) The Q (quality of a circuit) depends on _____ and the inductive or capacitive _____ . High frequency power inductors are often made with large wire to cut down on the losses due to electrons crowding to the surface of the wire. This effect is called_____. effect. Sec. 8-4.

14. (10) A 20 db loss is equal to a power ratio of _____ to _____ . Sec. 8-5.

16. (narrower) The circuit shown is a_____ filter. Sec. 8-8.

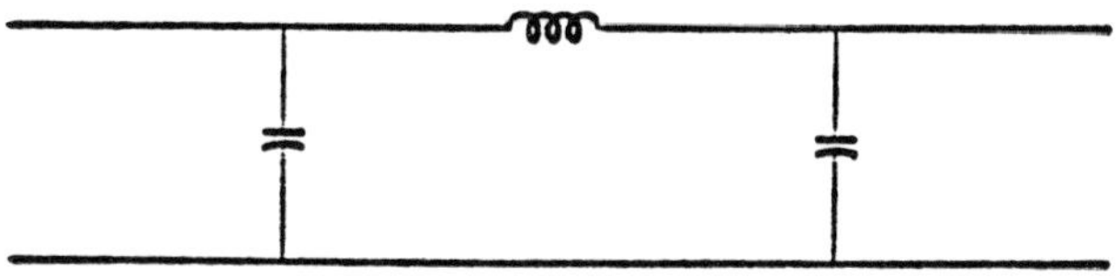

18. (high pass) A filter circuit designed with the product of the series and shunt impedances as a fixed value is called a _____filter. Sec. 8-8.

20. (infinite attenuation)

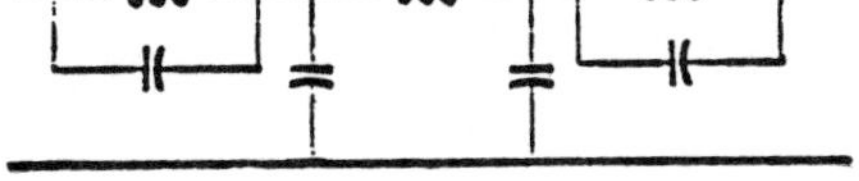

In the circuit shown there are _____ M derived low pass circuits. Sec. 8-8.

Review Unit 24 of the Part 1 Second Class Radiotelephone programmed instruction.

1. The rules and regulations of the Federal Communications Commission state that "The percentage of modulation shall be maintained as high as possible consistent with good quality of transmission and good broadcast practice. In no case is it to exceed 100% on negative peaks of frequent recurrence. Generally it should not be less than 85% on peaks of frequent recurrence. . . . ."

    A broadcast transmitter should maintain a modulation of at least_____% on peaks of frequent recurrence.

3. **(diode)** In the standard A.M. broadcast service, it is necessary to log the antenna current every three hours. Since the antenna ammeter is at the base of the antenna, it is not convenient for an operator to have to go some distance to the antenna to take a reading. In some cases the antenna may be a quarter of a mile from the transmitter.

    Therefore, the F.C.C. permits a station to use a remote reading antenna ammeter to be located right at the transmitter. This ammeter receives its excitation from a thermocouple located near the ammeter at the base of the antenna. The general idea is shown below:

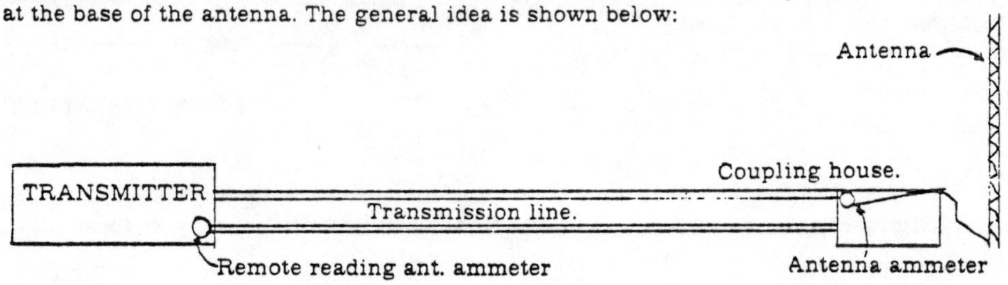

    The remote reading ammeter must be calibrated once a_____and must have an accuracy of _____%.

5. **(351 Hz)** Audio that travels great distances over TELCO lines (telephone lines) loses some of its high frequencies because the lines act like a giant capacitor. In order to equalize the highs and the lows arriving at the far end of a line, some of the low frequencies are by passed. This process is called line equalization. This is shown below:

    These two lines act like a capacitor.
    Remember the reactance of a capacitor is
    low at the high frequencies. $X_c = 1/2 piFC$

    A line equalizer is used to attenuate_____frequencies to compensate for the_____frequencies lost across the line.

7. **(Austin Ring)** This concludes Unit 7.

1. A 100 microhenry coil is tuned by a 100 pf capacitor. The resonant frequency would be approximately
    a. 15.9 Mhz.
    b. 159 Mhz.   d. 4.5 Mhz.
    c. 2.6 Mhz.   e. none of these.

2. The circuit shown below is that of a
    a. balanced low pass filter.
    b. unbalanced low pass filter.
    c. unbalanced pi section high pass filter.
    d. M derived low pass filter.
    e. M derived high pass filter.

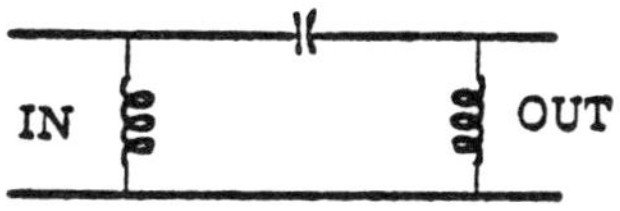

    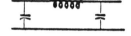

3. A 10 db gain represents a power gain of
    a. 1
    b. 10   d. 1,000
    c. 100   e. none of these.

4. The bandwidth of a tuned circuit depends on
    a. the capacitance of the circuit.
    b. the resistance of the circuit.   d. the Q of the circuit.
    c. the inductance of the circuit.   e. all of the above.

5. The circuit shown below is a
    a. high pass filter.
    b. low pass filter.
    c. high impedance circuit.
    d. low impedance circuit.
    e. de-emphasis circuit.

6. The impedance of the circuit below would be
    a. 2,000 Ω
    b. 3,000 Ω
    c. 8,000 Ω
    d. 1,140 Ω
    e. none of these

    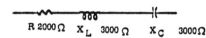

    R 2000 Ω X_L 3000 Ω X_C 3000 Ω

7. If there was 100 volts across the circuit above the voltage drop across the capacitor would be
    a. 100 volts.
    b. zero volts.   d. 5,000 volts.
    c. 150 volts.   e. none of these.

8. Under the same conditions (#6 and #7) the voltage drop across the inductor would be
    a. 100 volts.
    b. zero volts.   d. 5,000 volts.
    c. 150 volts.___ e. none of these.

9. A decibel is equivalent to
    a. ten bels.
    b. 1/10 bels.   d. 1 watt.
    c. 6 watts.   e. 10 watts.

10. An increase of power of 100 db represents
    a. 10 times the power.
    b. 100 times the power.   d. 10 times the voltage.
    c. 10^{10} times the power.   e. none of these.

11. The effect of current traveling along the outside of a conductor is called
    a. Pieso.
    b. Miller.   d. Skin.
    c. Dopler.   e. none of these.

12. If an RF VTVM was connected across the secondary of an IF transformer and the transformer was tuned through resonance the meter would
    a. go from maximum to minimum to maximum.
    b. go from minimum to maximum to minimum.
    c. go to zero at resonance.
    d. stay at maximum.
    e. none of these.

19. The E.R.P. from a certain transmitter is 3.93 watts. The antenna field gain is 1.2 and is fed with 130 ft. of RG 58 having a loss of 4.68 db/100 ft. The transmitter output power is approximately
    a. 2 watts.
    b. 5 watts.
    c. 10 watts.
    d. 11 watts.
    e. none of these.

20. A T network between the antenna and phasing control is used to
    a. divide the power.
    b. eliminate the need for separate antenna tuning.
    c. change power for night time operation.
    d. match impedances.
    e. all of the above.

21. The station to transmitter antenna link must be
    a. a folded dipole.
    b. a simple dipole.
    c. a vertical antenna.
    d. directional.
    e. a horizontal antenna.

22. Two coaxial feedlines are used to feed two in phase antennas operating on 98.3 MHz. The total coaxial cable length required would be approximately
    a. .6 meters.
    b. .3 meters.
    c. 4.21 meters.
    d. 3 meters.
    e. none of these.

23. On five different occasions the base current of one element of a five element directive array had five different values. The ratios of the different base currents to the reference antenna current are as shown. The out of tolerance ratio would be
    a. 3.8A and 1A.
    b. 4.7A and 1.27A.
    c. 3A and .79A.
    d. 3.35A and .71A.
    e. 3.8A to 1A

24. A certain A.M. broadcast transmitter has an output of 250 watts. If the modulation was increased from 80% to 100%, the antenna current would increase
    a. 6.6%.
    b. 9%.   d. 7.5%.
    c. 10%.   e. 15%.

25. A 3/4 wave transmission line is shorted at one end. The impedance at the other end is
    a. infinity.
    b. very low.
    c. very high.
    d. zero.
    e. 52 ohms.

26. A 1000 watt broadcast station has a daytime antenna current of 5 amperes. When the power is reduced to 400 watts for night time operation, the antenna impedance is
    a. 25Ω.
    b. 50Ω.
    c. 40Ω.
    d. 100Ω.
    e. none of these.

27. The power output of a directional broadcast antenna is calculated by multiplying the antenna current squared by the radiation resistance. These measurements are made at
    a. the common feed point.
    b. either tower.
    c. the tower having the highest radiation resistance.
    d. the tower having the highest antenna current.
    e. the tower having the lowest radiation resistance.

28. A certain 1/2 wave 800 ft. antenna radiates with an E.R.P. of 500 watts. The field strength of the signal 1 mile away is 336 mv per meter for the fundamental frequency and 47 microvolts per meter for the second harmonic. The second harmonic is attenuated
    a. 67 dbs.
    b. 70 dbs.   d. 80 dbs.
    c. 77 dbs.   e. 120 dbs.

13. If two identical tuned parallel circuits are placed in parallel, the resulting resonant frequency would be
   a. double.
   b. half.
   c. the same as for either alone.
   d. four times as high.
   e. none of these.

14. -20 db or twenty db down represents
   a. a voltage ratio of 1/20.
   b. a voltage ratio of 1/100.
   c. a power ratio of 1/10.
   d. a power ratio of 1/100.
   e. none of these.

15. In the circuit shown below there are
   a. two M derrived circuits.
   b. three M derrived circuits.
   c. no M derrived circuits.
   d. four high pass filter circuits.
   e. none of these.

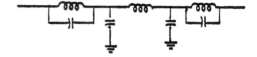

16. A resonant parallel circuit having capacitive and inductive reactance of 100 ohms each, has the resistance changed to 1000 ohms. The resonant frequency is now
   a. 1/10 the first frequency.
   b. 10 times the first frequency.
   c. 1000 Khz.
   d. 100 Khz.
   e. unchanged.

17. The frequency of resonance 1,590 hz. L is
   a. 1 henry.
   b. .01 henry.
   c. 10 henrys.
   d. 1 μF
   e. none of these.

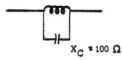

$X_C = 100\ \Omega$

18. In a series resonant LC circuit
   a. the impedance is infinity.
   b. the impedance is zero.
   c. the impedance is high
   d. the impedance is low
   e. the impedance is 72 ohms.

19. In a parallel resonant LC circuit the impedance is
   a. infinity.
   b. zero
   c. high.
   d. low.
   e. 72 ohms.

20. If resistance is added in series to a series resonant LC circuit the impedance
   a. increases.
   b. decreases.
   c. equals twice the resistance.
   d. equals the capacitive reactance.
   e. equals the inductive reactance.

21. A series network has a .6 ohm resistor, a capacitor of 20 Microfarad. and a coil of 1.57 henry. The resonant frequency is
   a. 1 Mhz.
   b. 5,230 Khz.
   c. 3420 Khz.
   d. 2.78 Mhz.
   e. none of these.

22. If you have a parallel LC circuit at resonance
   a. the impedance is zero with no resistance.
   b. the impedance increases when you add a resistor in parallel.
   c. the impedance decreases when you add a resistor in parallel.
   d. the impedance is infinity.
   e. the impedance is not affected by parallel resistance.

23. The resistance of a resonant RCL circuit is changed from 100Ω to 1000Ω. The resonant frequency is now
   a. 1/10 the first frequency.
   b. 10 times the first frequency.
   c. 1000 Khz.
   d. 100 Khz.
   e. unchanged.

24. A filter circuit designed with the product of the series and shunt impedance as a fixed value is called
   a. a constant K filter.
   b. a M derrived filter.
   c. a 60 cycle filter.
   d. a band pass filter.
   e. a band step filter.

10. The antenna resistance of a directional antenna system is measured by use of
   a. an impedance bridge at the base of each antenna.
   b. an impedance bridge at the point of common supply.
   c. an ohmmeter at the base of each antenna.
   d. an ohmmeter at eastern most tower.
   e. none of these.

11. The field strength of a certain station is 200 millivolts per meter at one mile. If the power was tripled, the field strength would be 200 millivolts per meter at
   a. 2 miles.
   b. 1.73 miles.
   c. 8 miles.
   d. 1.414 miles.
   e. none of these.

12. The usual means of protecting an antenna ammeter against lightening is
   a. to place a short across the meter when not in use.
   b. to use a high resistance meter movement.
   c. to use a movement with a high current capability.
   d. use a horn gap.
   e. to use a series multiplier resistance.

13. The circuit enclosed with the dotted lined for
   a. generating harmonics.
   b. matching a high Z to a low Z.
   c. parasitic oscillations.
   d. frequency doubling.
   e. feeding a push-pull circuit.

14. The circuit above is also effective in
   a. frequency tripling.
   b. paraphase amplifiers.
   c. cancelling feedback.
   d. reducing harmonics.
   e. none of these.

15. A 1 kw output from a certain broadcast station antenna produces a field strength of 160 mv per meter at 1,000 meters. If the power is increased to 9 kw the field strength at a distance of 4,000 meters would be
   a. 40 mv.
   b. 120 mv.
   c. 260 mv.
   d. 400 mv.
   e. none of these.

16. The ouput stage of an FM transmitter has a plate voltage of 1,000 V and a plate current of 300 ma. The final is 60% efficient and the loss in the transmission line is 50 W. If the field gain is 2, the effective radiated power is
   a. 260 W.
   b. 520 W.
   c. 130 W.
   d. 300 W.
   e. none of these.

17. An antenna that is 400 feet long is operating on 600 kcs. The ratio of its physical length to its electrical length is
   a. .243 to 1.
   b. .308 to 1.
   c. .560 to 1.
   d. .176 to 1.
   e. none of these.

18. A top hat is sometimes used on an antenna to
   a. effectively lengthen the antenna.
   b. effectively shorten the antenna.
   c. stabilize it in the wind.
   d. discharge static.
   e. none of these.

25. An M derived filter is used primarily for
    a. a constant attenuation over a range of frequencies.
    b. achieving a sharper cut off.
    c. pre-emphasis.
    d. deemphasis.
    e. 60 cycle filter.

26. The impedance of a series resonant circuit containing no resistance is
    a. infinite.
    b. zero
    c. equal to that of a parallel resonant circuit.
    d. one-half that of a parallel resonant circuit.
    e. low but not zero.

27. An example of an M derived low pass filter is

    a.

    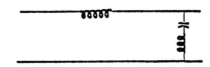

    b.

    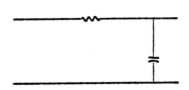

    c.

    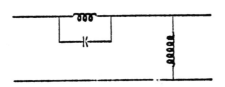

    d.

    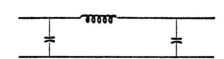

    e. none of these.

ANTENNAS

1. A properly terminated transmission line is shortened. In order to maintain the proper termination it is
   a. necessary to consider the line length.
   b. necessary to consider the resistance points.
   c. necessary to consider the capacitive reactance points.
   d. necessary to consider the inductive reactance points.
   e. not necessary to do anything.

2. The input power to the final stage of a transmitter is 500 watts. The stage efficiency is 65%. The efficiency of the transmission line is 80%. If the antenna has a field gain of 1.4, the effective radiated power (ERP) is approximately
   a. 4160 watts.
   b. 1040 watts.
   c. 260 watts.
   d. 3000 watts.
   e. none of these.

3. The field strength of a certain station is 500 milivolts per meter at one mile. If the power was tripled, the field strength would be 500 millivolts per meter at
   a. 3 miles.
   b. 1.73 miles.
   c. 9 miles.
   d. .707 miles.
   e. 1.414 miles.

4. The field gain of a TV antenna is the ratio of the free space field intensity produced at 1 mile in the horizontal plane expressed in mv per meter for a 1 kw antenna input power to
   a. 137.6 mv/w.
   b. 1.73 mv/w.
   c. 2.21 mw/w.
   d. 1.225 mv/w.
   e. 3 mv/w.

5. The surge impedance of an open transmission line is not determined by
   a. size of conductors.
   b. spacing between conductors.
   c. length of conductors.
   d. ratio of spacing to diameter of conductors.
   e. any of the above.

6. A 300 foot broadcast antenna is operated on 2000 Khz. If end effect is considered the ratio of its physical length to wave length is approximately
   a. .243 to 1.
   b. .5 to 1.
   c. 1 to 1.
   d. 2 to 1.
   e. .642 to 1.

7. Two or more AM broadcast antennas are often fed by one transmitter for
   a. additional gain.
   b. a directional effect.
   c. generating single sideband.
   d. higher signal to noise ratio.
   e. none of these.

8. The field strength over average terrain varies
   a. directly with square of powr.
   b. directly with distance squared.
   c. inversely with distance.
   d. inversely with the square of the distance
   e. inversely with the square root of the distance.

9. An open transmission line having a conductor spacing of 10 inches and using conductors of a diameter of 5/16 inches has an impedance of about 500 ohms. If the spacing was changed to 5 inches and conductors having a diameter of 5/32 inches were used, the new impedance would be
   a. 72 ohms.
   b. 250 ohms.
   c. 690 ohms.
   d. 970 ohms.
   e. the same.

1. The vacuum tube may eventually be replaced by more efficient solid state devices such as the transistor. Since there is much electronic equipment that still uses the vacuum tube it is still necessary to make a study of this device. The common types of vacuum tubes include the diode, triode, tetrode, and pentode. These types are based upon the useful elements or electrodes in the tube as follows:

> Diode - two useful electrodes - cathode and anode (also called the plate).
> Triode - three useful electrodes - cathode, anode and control grid.
> Tetrode - four useful electrodes - cathode, anode, control grid and screen grid.
> Pentode - five useful electrodes - cathode, anode, control grid, screen grid and suppressor grid (or beam forming plates).

Vacuum tubes are typed according to the number of useful _____ .

7. (7) As a tube gets older, the cathode coating loses its emissive power. This causes low plate current. This is the most common cause of tube failure. The most common cause of tube failure is the loss of _____ .

13. (20) (The symbol $\triangle$ pronounced delta is used to indicate change. By formula:

VOLTAGE
AMPLIFICATION $\quad$ $Mu = \dfrac{\triangle Ep}{\triangle Eg}$ $\qquad$ Where Mu = Voltage amplification of vacuum tube

$\triangle Ep$ = change in plate voltage
$\triangle Eg$ = change in grid voltage

It would be correct to say that Mu was equal to delta Ep/delta Eg but not Ep/Eg. If the vacuum tube plate voltage was caused to change 60 volts with a grid voltage change of 4 volts, the voltage amplification would be_____ .

THE VACUUM TUBE SCREEN GRID

19. (decreasing) The tetrode not only has the anode, cathode, and control grid of the triode but has the screen grid in addition. This grid is placed between the control grid and the anode. Note the arrangement:

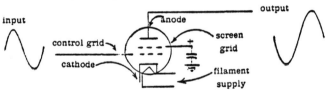

The screen is at ground potential for AC signals (because of the low reactance capacitor between it and ground) and at positive DC potential. The screen grid serves two functions:

1. It reduces the electrostatic capacitance effect between the anode and the control grid preventing the output at the plate from feeding back to the input at the grid.
2. It helps accelerate electrons to the plate. Some electrons are drawn to the positive screen grid.

One purpose of the screen grid is to decrease the_____ .

25. (30,000 ohms) If Rp is 10,000 ohms, RL should be at least _____ ohms for maximum efficiency.

64

RECHECK PROGRAMMED INSTRUCTION USING SHRADER'S ELECTRONIC COMMUNICATION

2.   (240 meters, .254) A 400 ft antenna operating on 600 KHz has a ratio of physical length to electrical wavelength of_____to 1.   sec. 20-7.

4.   (500 ohms) Two or more A.M. broadcast transmitters are often fed by one transmitter to produce a_____ effect in radiation pattern.   Sec. 20-18.

6.   (matching, harmonics) The antenna ammeter can be protected against lightning by placing a _____ across it when it is not in use.   Sec. 20-24.

8.   (directional) If a 4 meter antenna has 12 mv of signal induced into it, the field intensity is _____ millivolts per meter.   Sec.20-26.

10.   (inversely) If the field strength of a station is 300 mv at one mile, it will be approximately _____ mv at three miles.   Sec. 20-26.

12.   (1.73) A 1 KW output from a certain broadcast station antenna produces a field strength of 160 mv per meter (at 1000 meters). If the power is increased to 9 KW, the field strength at a distance of 4000 meters would be_____ mv/m.   Sec. 20-26.

14.   (four) The input power to the final stage of a transmitter is 1500 watts. The stage efficiency is 66 2/3%. The transmission line efficiency is 80%. If the antenna has a field gain of 1.5, the effective radiated power (E.R.P.) is_____watts.   Sec. 20-28.

16.   (two) This concludes the Recheck on Unit 6.

2. **(electrodes)** The cathode, as seen below, is common to all vacuum tubes. When the cathode is heated it gives off negative electrons which are attracted to positive electrode(s) within the vacuum tube and sometimes controlled in their flight by other negative electrodes in the vacuum tube. Two types of cathodes are illustrated:

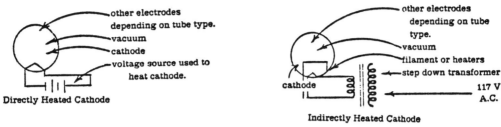

The cathode is used to emit or give off _____.

8. **(electron emission)** Some vacuum tubes have directly heated tungsten cathodes impregnated with thorium. As the thorium on the cathode burns off the emission is reduced. This type of thoriated tungsten cathode can be reactivated by doubling the filament voltage for a short period of time (1 or 2 seconds) and then reducing the voltage to a value slightly above normal value for a longer period of time (20 minutes or so)._____direct cathode filaments can be reactivated.

14. **(15)** Because voltage amplification only deals with changing (or AC) values, it is called a dynamic characteristic. (as opposed to static - or nonchanging values). Another **dynamic characteristic** is the **mutual conductance** or **trans-conductance** of a vacuum tube. This characteristic is defined as the ability of a tube to conduct an AC signal. By formula:

OR TRANSCONDUCTANCE

$$Gm = \frac{\Delta Ip}{\Delta Eg}$$

Where Gm = mutual conductance in mhos.
Δ Ip = change in plate current
Δ Eg = change in grid voltage

Remember conductance is the reciprocal of resistance. Since resistance is equal to E/I, conductance is equal to I/E. Transconductance only deals with changing delta values. Transconductance in mhos is the ratio of delta_____divided by delta_____

20. **(electro-static capacitance)** The DC polarity of the screen grid is_____*POSITIVE*_____.

26. **(50,000 ohms)** The plate voltage of a vacuum tube circuit may be considered as the voltage from plate to cathode. If we use a B power supply rather than a battery, the usual vacuum tube circuit is as shown:

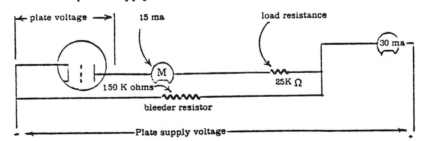

Let us use this diagram to solve for the plate voltage. Note that the circuit is a parallel circuit. Since there is a total current flow of 30 ma and a plate current of 15 ma, we can assume that the bleeder current is 15 ma (30-15).

Solving for the plate supply voltage.

    E = IR   E = .015 (15ma) X 150,000 ohms
           E = 2250 volts.
Solving for the voltage across the load.

    E = IR E = .015 (15 ma) X 25,000 ohms   E = 375V.

Solving for the plate voltage.

Plate voltage = Supply voltage - Load voltage
Ep = 2250 - 375 = 1875 volts.

If the total current was 20 ma instead of 30 ma, the plate voltage would be_____.

RECHECK PROGRAMMED INSTRUCTION USING SHRADER'S ELECTRONIC COMMUNICATION

Review Recheck Unit 20 of Part 1 Second Class Radiotelephone programmed instruction.

1. A 200 ft. antenna is to be operated at 1250 KHz. Its wavelength at this frequency is _____ meters. The ratio of the physical length in meters to the electrical wavelength in meters is _____ to 1.
    Sec. 20-7

3. (.244) An open transmission line having a conductor spacing of 2 inches and using conductors of .064 inch diameter has an impedance of approximately 500 ohms. If both the separation and the wire diameter were doubled, the approximate impedance would be _____ohms.   Sec. 20-13

5. (directional) A Pi network and a T network are useful for _____ the plate impedance to the antenna and they reduce the transfer of _____ to the antenna.   Sec. 20-24.

7. (short) The impedance of an antenna is measured at the base of the antenna using an impedance bridge. If a directional antenna is used with two antennas, the sytem antenna impedance is measured at the point of common R.F. supply. The antenna impedance of a _____ antenna system using two antennas is measured at the point of common R. F. supply.   Sec. 20-25.

9. (3mv/m) The ground wave over seawater (and average terrain) varies _____ with distance from the station antenna.   Sec. 20-26.

11. (100 mv) The field strength of a certain station is 150 mv per meter at one mile. If the power was tripled the field strength would be 150 mv per meter at _____ miles.   Sec. 20-26.

13. (120mv/m) A field gain of 2 is equivalent to a power gain of _____.   Sec. 20-28.

15. (1800 watts) If a simple diode produces a 137.6 mv/m signal, a 275.2 mv/m signal represents a field gain of _____.Sec. 20-28.

3. **(electrons)** Electrons that are emitted and attracted to other electrodes are replenished by connecting the negative side of a voltage source to the cathode and the positive side through a load to the positive electrode or electrodes of the vacuum tube. See the arrangement below:

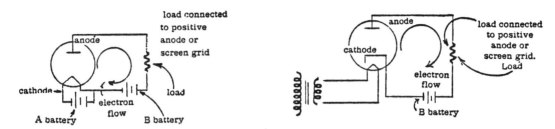

Note that the electron flow is from the negative side of the voltage source to the cathode. Since only the cathode emits electrons, current can never flow within the tube from other electrodes to the cathode. In a properly connected tetrode, screen grid current cannot flow to the _____.

9. **(thoriated tungsten)** When direct current is used on a directly heated cathode, it is common practice to periodically reverse the polarity of the A battery or voltage source to provide longer tube life. Direct current voltage polarity is reversed in directly heated cathodes to provide _____ .

15. **(Ip, Eg)** At higher frequencies the capacitance between the control grid and the cathode must be considered. This capacitance is called **input capacitance**. At high frequencies the low reactance of this capacitance in the usual tube may short out the input signal. To get around this the grid and cathode size and placement must be considered in the tube design. Note below:

When using triode tubes at higher frequencies, it is important to consider_____ capacitance.

THE VACUUM TUBE SUPPRESSOR GRID AND BEAM FORMING PLATES

21. **(positive)** Negative electrons hitting the positive anode of a vacuum tube dislodge a number of electrons. These electrons are referred to as **secondary emission**. Primary emission is from the cathode. The field interferes with the proper control of electrons in their flight to the anode. The pentode contains a third grid that generally is connected to the cathode and placed near the anode in such a manner as to force secondary emission electrons back into the plate. Since the suppressor grid may be connected to the cathode, its operated with a___ZERO___potential with respect to the cathode.

27. **(375 volts)** If the vacuum tube was pulled out of the circuit (#26) or if the filaments to the indirectly heated cathode was open, the tube would act like an open circuit. In the latter case the plate voltage would rise to the value of the supply voltage since there would be no plate current and no voltage drop across the load. If the filament to an indirectly heated cathode was open, the plate voltage would _____ .

6. **(directional, match)** At the higher FM and television frequencies directional arrays are used to achieve maximum horizontal line of sight coverage and minimum sky wave radiation. Any RF radiation towards the ionized layers surrounding the earth are lost since they simply penetrate the layers and are not reflected back to the earth. If these signals were not directed down towards the horizon, it would take higher power to produce the same field strengths as those produced by the directional arrays. The effectiveness of directional arrays is determined by their field or power gains. The power output of an AM or TV directional antenna is given as **EFFECTIVE RADIATED POWER** (E.R.P.) rather than its actual radiated power. If a directive antenna array having an actual radiated power of 1 KW produces the same field strength at a certain location one mile away as a non directional antenna having an actual radiation power of 2 KW at the same distance, the power gain is 2. See the example below:

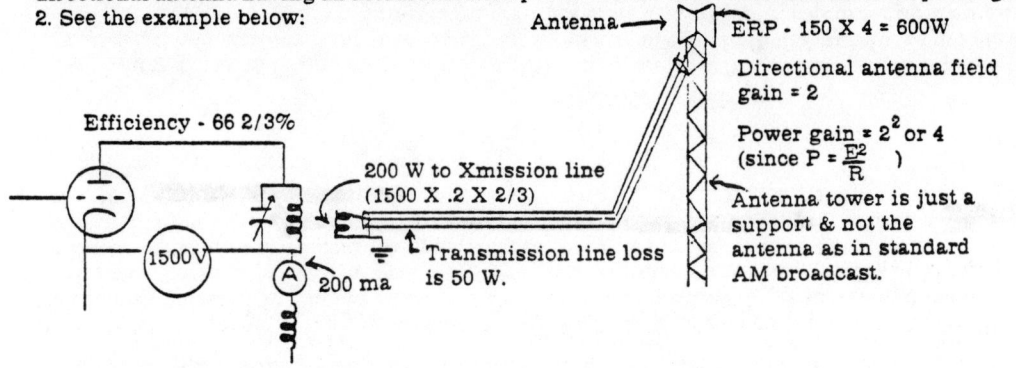

The output stage of an FM transmitter has a plate voltage of 1200 volts and a plate current of 300 ma. The final is 66 2/3% efficiency and the loss in the transmission line is 40 watts. If the field gain is 2, the effective radiation power (E.R.P.) is _____ watts. If the power gain is 2, the E.R.P. is _____ watts.

12. **(Pi Net)** This Pi Net is useful in matching a _____ Z to a low Z and is effective in reducing the flow of _____ to the transmission line and antenna.

18. **(2 meters)** The question is sometimes asked - By what percent does the antenna current increase when the modulation is increased from 80% to 100%?

By formula: I_{Ant} (mod) $= \sqrt{1 + M^2/2} \times I_{Ant.}$ (unmod.)

For 100% modualation the antenna current is equal to $\sqrt{1 + 1/2}$ or 1.225A

For 80% modulation the antenna current is equal to $\sqrt{1 + .8^2/2}$ or 1.15 A
The increase is .075A

Note - this assumes that the unmodulated antenna curent is 1 ampere.

The increase of .075 A expressed as a percent of the original current at 80% modulation is .075/1.15 X 100 or 6.5% (app)

The antenna curent increases _____ % when the modulation is increased from 75% to 100%.

4. (cathode) If current flows in electrodes other than the cathode it must flow out of the electrode. This is in contrast to the cathode current flow which is always into the cathode. Therefore, the sum of the electrode currents is equal to the cathode current as shown by block diagram:

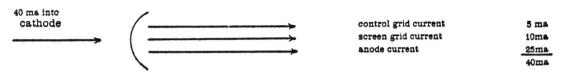

40 ma into cathode		control grid current	5 ma
		screen grid current	10ma
		anode current	25ma
			40ma

Current into cathode (40ma) = total current out of other electrodes (40ma). In a tetrode circuit the grid current flow is 2 ma, the screen grid current flow is 4 ma and the plate current is 30 ma. The cathode current would be_____ma.

10. (longer tube life) The current flow from the cathode of a tube can be increased by use of a hot gas like mercury vapor. This gas also serves to regulate the voltage output of any system using this gas filled tube as a rectifier (to change AC to DC). A steady output voltage can be achieved in a rectifier by using a _____ tube.

16. (input) Because is takes time for electrons to move from cathode to plate, high frequency vacuum tubes are designed with their electrodes close together. Otherwise, the signal input polarity might change before the electrons got past the control grid on their flight to the plate. By placing the electrodes close together the transit time can be reduced and higher frequencies can be applied at the input. Lighthouse and other UHF tubes are construced in this manner. The transit time for electrons to move from cathode to plate in UHF tubes in reduced by_____

22. (zero) Beam power tubes are comparable to pentodes. These tubes substitute beam forming plates for the suppressor grid. The physical arrangement in suppressor grid and beam power tubes is shown below:

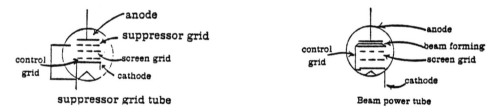

suppressor grid tube   Beam power tube

In addition to the function of reducing secondary emission the beam forming plates channel the electron stream into a narrow channel. This reduces the space charge. The beam forming plates in a beam power vacuum tube serve to channel the_____.

28. (rise) This concludes Unit 9. Now make the audio visual review and take the unit test.

5. **(three)** In standard broadcasting it is often necessary for a station to use two or more antennas for directional broadcasts. The general arrangement is shown below:

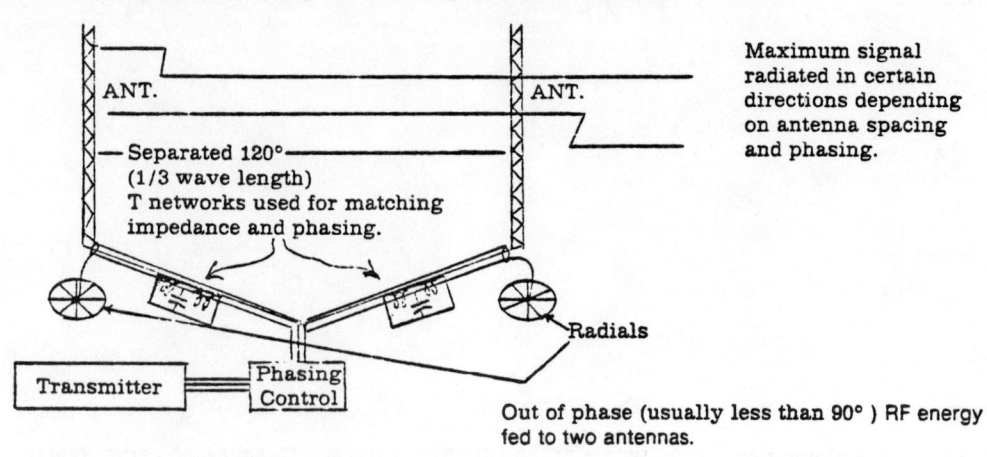

Maximum signal radiated in certain directions depending on antenna spacing and phasing.

Out of phase (usually less than 90°) RF energy fed to two antennas.

The phased signals from the two antennas reenforce each other in certain directions and cancel in other directions. Directional antennas are used to 1.) prevent interference with other stations operating in other cities on the same frquency and 2.) give the best coverage to certain areas.

Two or more AM broadcast antennas are often fed by one transmitter for a _____ effect. T networks are used between phasing control and the antenna to _____ impedances and for some phasing effects.

Pi Net Coupling

11. **(.256)** There is a distinct advantage in using a Pi Net Coupler to couple the final tube(s) to the transmission line. They are:
     1.) A Pi Net is a low pass filter. Harmonic energy can't easily pass to the transmission line and to the antenna through a Pi Coupler. This prevents harmonic energy from being radiated.
     2.) A Pi Net matches the high plate impedance of the final tube(s) to the low impedance transmission line for the maximum transfer of energy.

The Pi Net Coupler is shown below:

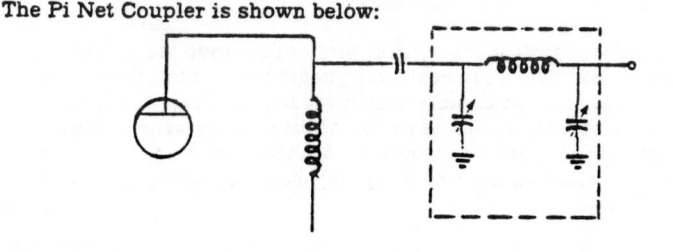

The circuit enclosed within the dotted lines is a_____ _____Coupler.

17. **(directional)** When two antennas are fed in phase for directional effect, the feedlines each are ½ wave length long. Such antennas operating on 100 MHz require feed lines that are approximately 1.5 meters long. (WL equals V/F or 3 X 10⁸/ 1 X 10⁸ or 3 meters --- ½ WL equals .5 X 3 or 1.5 meters). The two feed lines have a total length of 3 meters.

The approximate total length of the 2 feed lines used to feed two in phase antennas operating on 150 MHz would be_____meters.

5.   **(36 ma)** In a tetrode vacuum tube the grid current flow is 1 ma, the screen grid current flow is 10 ma, and the cathode current is 40 ma. The plate current would be_____ ,

THE VACUUM TUBE ANODE OR PLATE

11.   **(gas filled tube)** The anode which is also referred to as the plate in a vacuum tube has a positive DC potential. Such a tube with cathode and anode is called a diode and is useful in changing AC to DC.

When anode is positive, current is drawn causing a voltage drop across the load - when negative no current flows and there is no voltage drop across the load.

As electrons hit the positive plate, heat is generated. Although there may be other positive electrodes in a vacuum tube, most of the heat has to be dissipated by the plate. Vacuum tubes are rated as to how much power can be safely dissipated as heat. A tube having a power dissipation rating of 30 watts can dissipate_____watts in itself without damage.

17.   **(placing the electrodes closer together)** A special triode filled with an inert gas containing a control grid controls only the start of plate current flow. This tube shown is a thyratron. Current flow through the tube is by ion conduction.

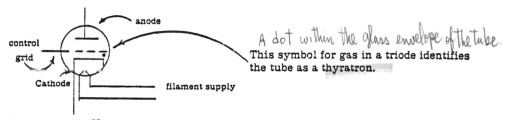

A dot within the glass envelope of the tube.
This symbol for gas in a triode identifies the tube as a thyratron.

In a THYRATRON:

When the grid voltage is negative, no plate current flows. When it is made positive, plate current flows. Changing the grid voltage back to a negative value will have no effect on the plate current after the tube is once conducting. To stop the plate current flow after it has been triggered into conduction by a positive voltage on the grid, the cathode or plate circuit must be opened or the anode voltage must be reduced to a low value. The thyratron triode tube can be identified by the _____ symbol in the schematic tube diagram.

MISCELLANEOUS VACUUM TUBE INFORMATION

23.   **(electron stream)** Now let us deal with the plate load. In some cases the load is a resistor and in others its often an inductor. The output is usually taken from across the load to ground. The value of the load in ohms makes a great difference in output power. Current flow from the plate supply voltage source flows through both the vacuum tube and the load. See the diagrams below:

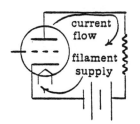

The AC output power taken here comes from plate supply voltage source.

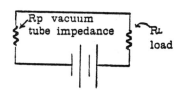

Three important generalizations can be made about the load in a vacuum tube triode:
1.   For maximum output taken at the load, the load impedance Rʟ must equal the plate tube impedance Rp. If Rp is 10,000 ohms, then Rʟ must equal 10,000 ohms for maximum output. *POWER.*
2.   For maximum undistorted output the Rʟ must be twice the vacuum tube plate impedance. If Rp is 10,000 ohms, Rʟ must be 20,000 ohms.
3.   For maximum efficiency (more output per input) Rʟ must be high compared to Rp. If Rp is 10,000 ohms Rʟ should be 50,000 ohms or greater. (5 times or greater). *for RL compared to Rp.*
If Rp is 20,000 ohms, Rʟ must be_____ohms for maximum power output.

4. **(1.73 miles)** The field gain of a TV antenna is the ratio of the free space field intensity produced at one mile in the horizontal plane expressed in millivolts per meter for a 1 KW antenna input power to 137.6 mv. 137.6 mv is a standard and is the approximate field strength produced at one mile when a simple dipole is being supplied 1 KW of power.

If a certain antenna produces a field strength of 275 mv at one mile when being fed a KW of power, it is said to have a field gain of 2 (275/137.6)

If a 1 KW input to a certain antenna produces a field strength of 412.8 mv/m, it's field gain is_____ .

10. **(410')** If a Marconi antenna is not equal to one fourth of the electrical wavelength, it can be altered electrically by a series inductor or capacitor to resonate on the proper frequency. The ratio of the actual physical length to the electrical wavelength must be known before any antenna alterations are made. This ratio is calculated with both the physical and electrical lengths in the same units. For example the ratio of a 300 foot antenna to the electrical wavelength of a signal on 800 Khz is

$$\frac{300'}{(3 \times 10^6 / 8 \times 10^5) \times 3.28} \quad = \quad \frac{300 \text{ ft}}{1230 \text{ ft}} \quad = \quad .244 \text{ to } 1$$

The ratio of a 210 ft antenna to the electrical wavelength of the antenna operating on 1200 Khz. is _____to 1.

16. **(short)** Many broadcast stations deliver their audio from the studio to the transmitter by using the telephone line. However some broadcast stations generate their modulated R.F. right at the studio and then transmit it on a directional antenna to the transmitter in the country. F.C.C. requires directional antennas to be used when such a studio to transmitter link (STL) is used.

The STL antennas must be_____.

6. **(29 ma)** In a directly heated cathode circuit using a low AC voltage it is necessry to connect the circuit ground connection to the center tap of the secondary of the filament transformer as shown:

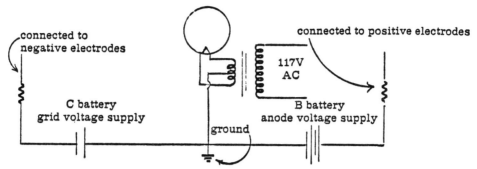

This provides a neutral point of connection so that the electrode voltages do not rise and fall and produce hum (60 cycle) in the output circuits.

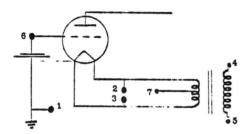

For proper operation of this circuit (to the left) point 1 should be connected to point ___SEVEN (7)___.

THE VACUUM TUBE CONTROL GRID

12. **(30 watts)** The triode vacuum tube has three useful electrodes. The additional electrode is the control grid. In most cases, this grid is made negative with respect to the cathode. Voltage amplification is achieved by varying the negativeness of the control grid. The negative charge repels electrons in their flight from cathode to plate. The amount of repulsion is determined by how negative the grid is. Note the example:

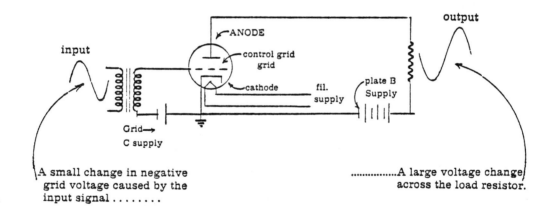

The input signal is connected to the control grid voltage supply in series so that the negativeness of the grid rises and falls. The change in positive plate voltage (plate to cathode) divided by the change in negative grid voltage (control grid to cathode) is called voltage amplification and is symbolized as mu (greek letter μ). If the plate voltage is caused to change 40 volts by a change in grid voltage of 2 the mu is_____ .

18. **(gas)** Control of the thyratron plate current can be regained by_____the anode voltage.

24. **(20,000)** If Rp is 15,000 ohms, R∟ should be _____ ohms for maximum undistorted output.

3. **(100 mv)** Field strength at a certain spot varies directly with the square root of the power. If the power is tripled, the field strength is the square root of three times as much (or 1.73X). If the field strength of a certain station is 400 mv per meter at one mile, it will be 400 mv per meter at two miles if the power is quadrupled. This is figured as follows:

$$400 \text{ mv} \quad X \quad \tfrac{1}{2} \quad X \quad \sqrt{4} \quad = 400 \text{ mv.}$$

Original field strength   **Distance factor.**   **Power factor**

The field strength of a certain station is 500 mv per meter at one mile. If the power is trippled, the field strength would be 500 mv per meter at_____miles.

9. **(18.18 W)** The physical length of most standard broadcast station antennas is approximately one fourth the electrical wavelength. For example the physical length of an antenna cut to operate on 1000 Khz can be found as follows:

$$\text{Electrical wavelength} = \frac{\text{Velocity (of a radio wave)}}{\text{Frequency in Hertz}} = \frac{3 \times 10^8}{1 \times 10^6}$$

$$= 3 \times 10^2 \text{ or } 300 \text{ meters}$$

Since one meter equals 3.28 ft, the electrical wavelength above would be 3.28 X 300 or 984 ft.

A quarter wave antenna should have a physical length of one fourth of 984 ft or 246 feet.

The physical length of a quarter wavelength antenna operating on 600 KHz should be approximately _____feet long.

15. **(impedance bridge)** A vertical antenna may pick up an electrostatic charge when struck by lightning or by the movement of air currents.
This shorting switch should be closed when the antenna meter is not in use. Any charge will discharge through the switch protecting the meter.

V. ANT.

To transmitter →

Horn gap arrestor. Any build up of antenna charge will ionize the air in the gap and a discharge spark follows.
Ground radials.

The usual means of protecting an antenna ammeter against lightning is to place a_____ across the ammeter when it's not in use.

21. **(77.5 Db)** This concludes Unit 6. Now do the Recheck.

RECHECK PROGRAMMED INSTRUCTION USING SHRADER'S ELECTRONIC COMMUNICATIONS

1. For high power amplification_____must be used. Sec. 9-1.

4. (emission) This is the most often cause of tube failure. To reactivate a vacuum tube, remove the plate voltage and raise the filament voltage two or three times the normal value for_____ seconds. Sec. 9-3.

7. (increased) The plate current in a vacuum tube is essentially_____proportional to plate voltage. Sec. 9-5.

10. (550 volts)

    For proper operation connect point 4
    to_____. Sec. 9-7.

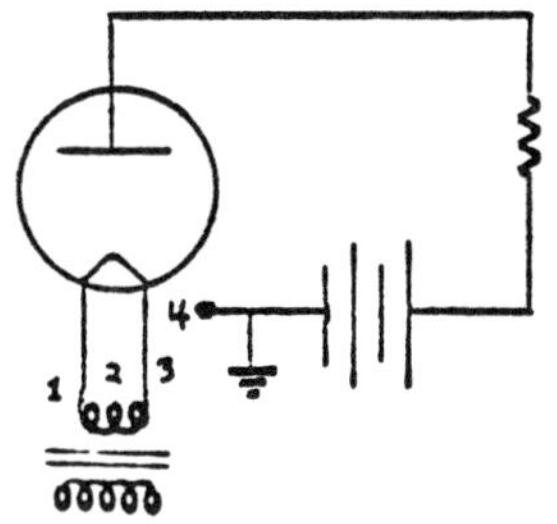

13. (reverse) Plate current will flow in a diode when the plate is_____. Sec. 9-9.

16. (reduced) The schematic symbol shown is for the _____. Sec. 9-13.

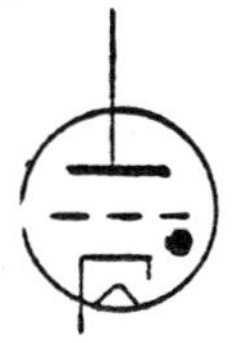

19. (amplification factor) it is symbolized by the greek letter _____. Sec. 9-15.

22. (bias) The maximum power output from a vacuum tube is obtained when the load impedance is equal to the_____. Sec. 9-20.

25. (high) The electrons moving from the plate out into the vacuum are known as_____ electrons. Sec. 9-25.

28. (cathode) The_____in a beam power tube are used to channel the electron stream. Sec. 9-27.

31. (inductance, transit, interelectrode) The spacing between electrodes in UHF tubes such as the light house tube is_____. Sec. 9-37.

34. (100 volts) If the plate dissipation rating of a tube is 20 watts, it means the tube can safely dissipate 20 watts of heat internally. If a tube is rated at 30 watts of plate dissipation, it can safely dissipate _____watts in itself without damage. Sec. 9-23.

2.   (100 mv/m) Field strength varies over average terrain inversely with distance. If the field strength is 200 mv at one mile from a transmitter antenna, it will be 100 mv at two miles. This is assuming that there is no change in the transmitted power. If the field strength of a station was 400 mv at one mile, it would be _____ mv at 4 miles.

8.   (4.4 to 1.2) Another type of E.R.P. (effective radiated power) problem involves decibels. Note the diagram below:

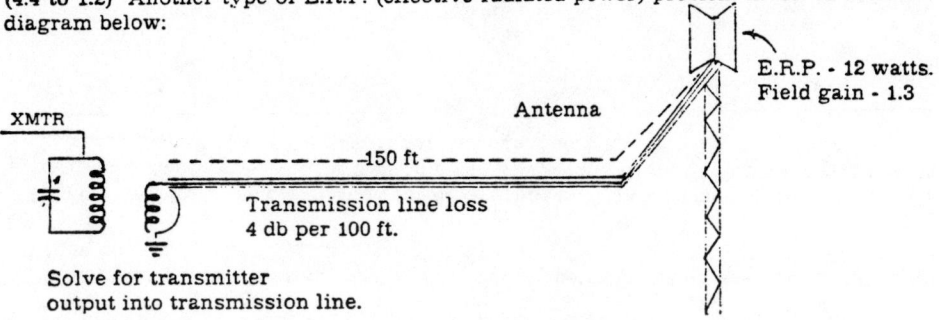

E.R.P. - 12 watts.
Field gain - 1.3

XMTR

Antenna

--------- 150 ft ----------

Transmission line loss
4 db per 100 ft.

Solve for transmitter
output into transmission line.

Working backwards, power fed to the antenna is $12/1.3^2$ (ERP/Power gain) or 7.1 watts. Note power gain is field gain squared.

The transmission line loss is 1.5 X 4 db or 6 db. (150/100 X 4)

Using the decibel formula for power, the transmitter output power can be solved for

$$Db = 10 \log\left(\text{Transmitter output power}\,/\,\text{Power delivered to the antenna}\right)$$

$6 = 10 \log \dfrac{\text{Transmitter output power}}{7.1W}$ $\log \dfrac{\text{Transmitter power}}{7.1} = 6/10 \text{ or } .6$

Xmtr Pwr/7.1 = antilog .6 or 3.98   Xmtr Pwr Out = 7.1 X 3.98 or 28.27 watts.

The ERP for a certain transmitter is 6 W. The field gain is 1.1. The antenna is fed with 120 ft. of coax having a loss of 4.7 db per 100 ft. The transmitter output into the transmission line is _____ watts.

14.   (500 ohms) The impedance is unchanged because the ratio of 2D to d is unchanged. Whereas line impedance can be calculated, the impedance of an antenna is measured at the base of an antenna using an impedance bridge.

If a directional antenna is used with two antennas, the system antenna impedance is measured with an impedance bridge at the point of common R.F. supply.

The antenna resistance (impedance) of a directional antenna system is measured by use of an _____ _____ at the point of common R. F. supply.

20.   (40 ohms) Harmonic attenuation can be determined using the formula

$Db = 20 \log E1/E_2$ where E1 is the fundamental field strength and E2 the harmonic field strength.

If the fundamental field strength is 300 mv per meter and the second harmonic field strength is 40 microvolts (.04 mv) at 1 mile from the antenna, the attenuation is _____ Dbs.

2. **(vacuum tubes)** Alternating current is used to heat the filaments whenever possible because of its more_____. Sec. 9-2.

5. **(a few)** Then bring the filament voltage down to_____times the normal voltage for 10 minutes or longer. Sec. 9-3.

8. **(directly)** The load in a vacuum tube usually is connected somewhere in the_____circuit. Sec. 9-6.

11. **(point 2)** In order to reduce voltage variations from AC filament supply voltages to direct cathodes and reduce hum in the output circuits, grid and plate supply returns are made to filament transformer _____. Sec. 9-7.

14. **(positive)** The hot cathode mercury vapor tube has an advantage over the high vacuum rectifier •because the gas in the tube provides a relatively_____voltage drop providing a steady output voltage. Sec. 9-11.

17. **(thyratron)** The AC resistance between cathode and plate is called_____. Sec. 9-14.

20. **(Mu or ·μ)** Theoretically, if the plate load resistance is infinite, the gain of the stage will equal _____. Sec. 9-16.

23. **(plate impedance)** Maximum undistorted power is obtained in a triode when the load impedance is at least_____plate load impedance. Sec. 9-22.

26. **(secondary emission)** The purpose of the screen in a vacuum tube is to reduce the_____ capacitance. Sec. 9-26.

29. **(deflection plates)** The suppressor grid normally is at zero potential with respect to the_____ . Sec. 9-28.

32. **(small)** It is significant to remember that all the current flows in at the cathode. The cathode current is equal to the sum of the currents flowing out of all other electrodes. In a tetrode vacuum tube circuit the grid current flow is 1.4 ma, the screen grid current is 3.6 ma and the cathode current is 40 ma. The plate current would be_____.

35. **(30 watts)** This concludes Unit 9 Recheck.

UNIT 6 (Part 2)

ANTENNAS

Review Unit 20 of the Part 1 Second Class Radiotelephone Programmed Instruction.

Field Strength

1. Field strength is measured in terms of millivolts or microvolts per meter of receiving antenna. Note the example given:

Receiving antenna 20 meters long

1000 millivolts

R. F. VOLTMETER

The field strength per meter of antenna would be

$\frac{1000 \text{ mv}}{20}$ or 50 mv per meter.

If a 10 meter antenna produced a 1000 mv signal the field strength would be_____mv/meter.

7. **(800 watts, 400 watts)** For a proper directional pattern both the phase and current of an antenna in a directional array affects the field pattern. For instance, in a five antenna directional array both the phase and the base current of each individual antenna have to be adjusted so that the proper field pattern results. The ratio of the individual base antenna current to that of the reference antenna in the array is specified as a licensed value. This ratio may not vary more than 5%.

If a particular antenna in a five element array, has ratios of base current to the reference antenna base current on five different occasions of 3.2 to 1, 2.9 to .91, 4.4 to 1.2, 3.2 to 1 and 3 to .94; the out of tolerance ratio would be _____ .

MISCELLANEOUS

13. **(high, harmonics)** The impedance of an open transmission line can be calculated by the formula

$Z = 276 \text{ Log } 2D/d$ Where Z is line impedance, D is distance between wires and d is the diameter of the wires.

If an open transmission line has a conductor spacing of 10 inches using conductors of a diameter of 5/16 inches, the line impedance is

$= 276 \text{ Log } \frac{20}{5/16}$ $= 276 \text{ Log } 20 \times 16/5 = 276 \text{ Log } 64$

$= 276 \times 1.81$ or 500 ohms.

If the spacing was changed to 5 inches and wire diameters to 5/32 inches, the line impedance would be _____ohms.

19. **(8.4%)** The power output of a directional antenna array is found by using Pout $= I^2$ R where I is the common feedpoint current and R the antenna impedance taken at the common point. The power output of an antenna system having a common feed point current of 5 A and an impedance of_____ohms is 1000 watts.

3.   (general availability) The loss of emissive cathode oxide coating could cause low_____.
     Sec. 9-3.

6.   (1½) The life expectancy of a vacuum tube is_____by using low filament voltage.
     Sec. 9-4.

9.   (plate) In the circuit below the plate voltage is _____volts. Sec. 9-7.

12. (center tap) To lengthen the life of the filaments in a DC transmitter circuit it is common practice to
     _____ the polarity of the filament supply voltage. Sec. 9-8.

15. (constant) After once fired a thyratron will not deionize until the plate potential is_____.
     Sec. 9-13.

18. (AC plate impedance) The ratio of $\triangle Ep/\triangle Eg$ is called the voltage_____. Sec. 9-15.

21. (mu) The negative DC voltage added in the grid circuit is known as the_____voltage.
     Sec. 9-17.

24. (twice) The maximum efficiency is achieved in a vacuum tube when the load impedance is_____
     with reference to the plate impedance. Sec. 9-22.

27. (electrostatic or interelectrode) It should be noted that the positive screen draws current from the
     cathode and a lesser amount by secondary emission from the plate. In no case will current flow from
     the screen to the cathode. Under no circumstances can the_____draw secondary emission
     current. Sec. 9-25 & 9-26.

30. (cathode) The requirements for all tubes operating at higher frequencies are to have minimum
     _____ in the leads, short_____time, and as little_____capacitance as
     possible. Sec. 9-37.

33. (35 ma) If the filament is open on a vacuum tube there can be no cathode emission or plate current.
     Therefore, the plate voltage will rise to the supply voltage level. (Since there is no voltage drop across
     the load resistor).

The plate voltage (plate to cathode)
in the circuit shown with SW 1 open
will be_____volts.

UNIT 5 (PART 2) TEST

FREQUENCY MODULATION

1. A limiter stage is used in an FM receiver to
   a. limit the frequency.
   b. limit the amplitude variations.
   c. produce gain.
   d. provide degenerate signals.
   e. none of these.

2. In FM broadcasting amplification of frequencies above 2,000 cycle is referred to as
   a. degeneration.
   b. attenuation.
   c. de-emphasis.
   d. neutralization.
   e. pre-emphasis.

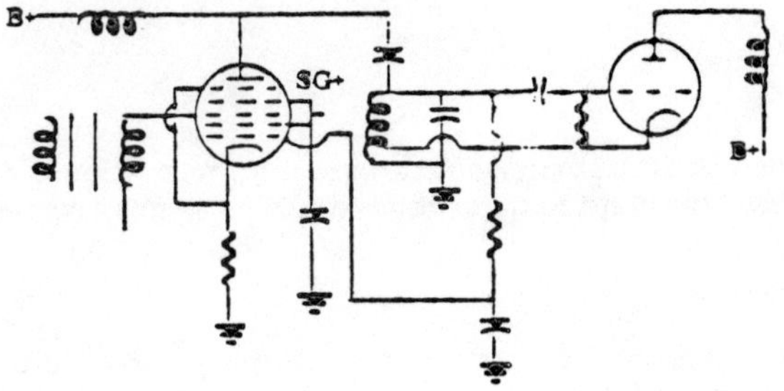

3. The diagram below is the circuit used to
   a. inject capacitance.
   b. inject inductance.
   c. measure carrier shift.
   d. double voltage.
   e. double frequency

4. Pre-emphasis is used in an FM transmitter to
   a. reduce parasitic oscillations.
   b. cancel even harmonics.
   c. attenuate high frequencies.
   d. produce better signal to noise ratios on higher audio frequencies.
   e. modulate the oscillator for frequency correction.

5. The antenna current produced by an FM transmitter without modulation is 6 amperes. With 90% modulation the antenna current would be
   a. 6 X 1.225 amperes.
   b. 6 amperes.
   c. 6 X 1.405 amperes.
   d. 7.3 amperes.
   e. 5.4 amperes.

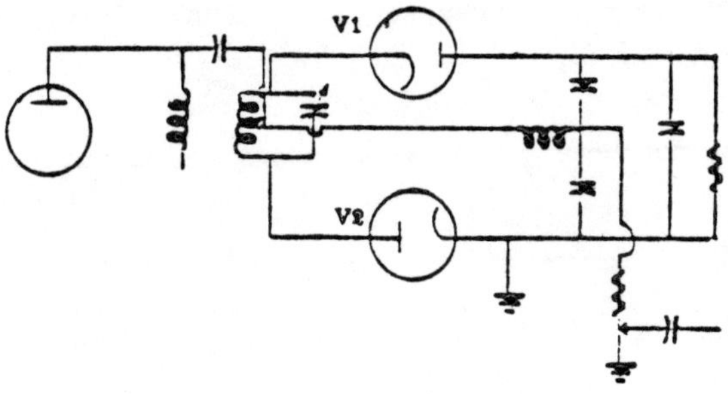

6. In the circuit
   a. V_1 is reversed
   b. V_2 is reversed.
   c. a discriminator is shown.
   d. the output is RF.
   e. a correct ratio detector is shown.

7. The operating power of an FM station is determined
   a. by the direct method.
   b. by the indirect method.
   c. by either the direct or indirect method.
   d. from the driver stage.
   e. by a field strength meter.

8. The only current change with audio input in a properly tuned FM transmitter is in the
   a. final.
   b. buffer.
   c. multipliers.
   d. antenna.
   e. reactance tube modulator.

9. The frequency of the pilot subcarrier used in FM stereo multiplex transmitting is
   a. 3.85 Khz
   b. 4.2 MHz.
   c. 19 KHz
   d. 4.5 MHz.
   e. 10.7 MHz.

1. One reason for using light house tubes at the high frequencies is
    a. the electrodes are far apart.
    b. the electrodes are close together. d. they are cheaper.
    c. they produce ultra violet light.   e. they provide for long transit time.

2. The grid and plate voltage return is often made to the center tap of a filament transformer to prevent
    a. parasitic oscillation.
    b. self oscillation.   d. degeneration.
    c. neutralization   e. hum modulation of the output signal.

3. In a lighthouse tube the transit time is cut to a minimum by
    a. special high voltage anodes.
    b. accelerator grids.
    c. placing the plate and cathode close together.
    d. separating the plate and cathode with insulator.
    e. none of these.

4. In a tetrode VT circuit the grid current flow is 1.5 ma. The screen grid current is 3.5 ma and the cathode current is 40 ma. The plate current flow would be
    a. 20 ma.
    b. 40 ma.   d. 45 ma.
    c. 35 ma.   e. none of these.

5. For maximum power output from a triode vacuum tube amplifier the ratio of R_L to R_P should be
    a. as low as possible.
    b. as high as possible. d. 1 to 1
    c. 2 to 1.   e. none of these.

6. For maximum undistorted power output from a triode vacuum tube amplifier the ratio of R_L to R_P should be
    a. as low as possible.
    b. as high as possible. d. 1 to 1.
    c. 2 to 1.   e. none of these.

7. For the maximum efficiency from a triode vacuum tube amplifier the ratio for R_L to R_P should be
    a. as low as possible.
    b. as high as possible. d. 1 to 1
    c. 2 to 1.   e. none of these.

8. In a tetrode VT circuit the grid current flow is 1.5 ma. The screen grid current is 3.5 ma and the plate current is 35 ma. The cathode current is
    a. 20 ma.
    b. 40 ma.   d. 50 ma.
    c. 35 ma.   e. 25 ma.

9. One of the identifying characteristics of UHF Tubes is
    a. they are bigger tubes.
    b. the grids are closer together. d. negative anodes.
    c. that higher voltage is used.   e. none of these.

10. The transconductance of a vacuum tube is equal to
    a. delta Ip/delta Eg.
    b. delta Ep/delta Eg. d. Gm/Rp.
    c. Ep/Ip.   e. none of these.

11. The diagram below is the diagram of a
    a. beam power tube.
    b. pentode.
    c. lighthouse tube.
    d. thyratron tube.
    e. none of these.

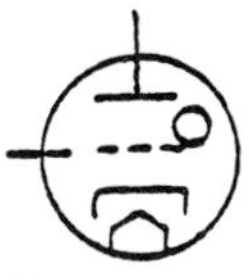

12. To lengthen the life of the filaments in a DC transmitter circuit, it is common practice to
    a. reduce the voltage to half value.
    b. double the DC voltage to the filaments.
    c. reverse the polarity of the filament supply voltage.
    d. water cool the tube.
    e. air cool the tube.

73

RECHECK PROGRAMMED INSTRUCTION USING SHRADER'S ELECTRONIC COMMUNICATION

2.   (6 amperes.) An audio grid voltage signal to the reactance tube modulator produces a plate _____ variation. Sec. 19-13

4.   (operating power) If the plate voltage of the final tube of an FM transmitter is 3000 volts at 200 ma and the efficiency factor is 66 2/3%, the operating power output would be_____watts. Sec. 19-18.

6.   (L + R, 19 Khz, L - R) This concludes Unit 4 Recheck.

13. In the diagram below the plate voltage is
     a. 1.875 volts.
     b. 375 volts.
     c. 2,250 volts.
     d. 150 volts.
     e. none of these.

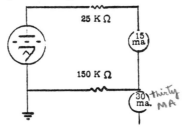

25 K Ω

15 ma

150 K Ω

30 ma. thirty MA

14. The deflection plates in a beam power tube are used to
     a. reduce interelectrode capacity.
     b. reduce primary emission.   d. neutralize the tube.
     c. channel the electron stream. e. none of these.

15. The hot cathode mercury vapor tube has an advantage over the high vacuum rectifier because
     a. the gas in the tube helps steady the output voltage.
     b. this tube provides for a steady flow of current.
     c. the filaments are at lower operating voltage.
     d. ionized gas prevents inverse feedback of current.
     e. they stand abuse.

16. Modulation of the output by 60 cycle hum can be reduced in an amplifier using direct cathodes by
     a. using a filament isolation transformer.
     b. making the plate and grid return to the filament transformer center tap.
     c. using a 60 cycle hum filter at the input.
     d. using a 60 cycle hum filter at the output.
     e. none of these.

17. To reactivate a vacuum tube
     a. use high plate voltage with no bias for eight hours.
     b. use high bias with no plate voltage for eight hours.
     c. use high plate voltage for short duration, then operate at normal voltage.
     d. with no plate voltage subject the filament to a momentary high voltage surge and then reduce to slightly lower than 20% above normal operating voltage.
     e. none of these.

18. If the filament to an indirectly heated cathode was opened
     a. the plate voltage would rise.
     b. the tube would conduct heavily.   d. there would be increased conduction.
     c. the grid would draw current.   e. the cathode would give off more electrons.

19. The loss of emissive cathode material could cause
     a. audio frequency noise.
     b. low plate current.   d. low plate voltage.
     c. grid current flow.   e. none of these.

20. The most common cause of tube failure is
     a. loss of emission.
     b. heater to cathode leakage.   d. wrong associated circuit components.
     c. shorted elements.   e. soft tubes.

21. The tube manual gives a tube as having a power dissipation of 50 watts. This means that
     a. the tube will dissipate 50 watts of power in itself without damage.
     b. The R_L should have a 50 watt rating.
     c. the tube will have 50 watts of useful output.
     d. the filament requires 50 watts.
     e. 50 watts will be dissipated in the grid circuit.

22. The purpose of the screen grid in a tetrode tube is to
     a. decrease the electrostatic capacitance.
     b. reduce secondary emission.   d. make the tube regenrative.
     c. channel electrons.   e. none of these.

23. In a properly connected screen grid vacuum tube circuit secondary emission screen current cannot flow to
     a. the plate.
     b. the cathode.
     c. the power supply.
     d. the control grid.
     e. the suppresser grid.

UNIT 5 (Part 2)
FREQUENCY MODULATION

RECHECK PROGRAMMED INSTRUCTION USING SHRADER'S ELECTRONIC COMMUNICATION

1. The antenna current produced by an FM transmitter without modulation is 6 amperes. With 90% modulation the antenna current would be __________ amperes. Sec. 19-3.

3. **(current)** The __________ __________ of FM transmitters may be determined by either the direct or indirect method. Sec. 19-18.

5. **(400 watts)** The whole multiplex modulating signal for an FM stereo broadcast consists of __________ audio, a __________ Khz pilot sub carrier, and the __________ stereophonic AC. Sec. 19-23.

24. In a tetrode VT amplifier the grid current flow is 7.5 ma. The screen grid current is 2.5 ma and the cathode current is 80 ma. The plate current flow is
    a. 20 ma.
    b. 90 ma.   d. 70 ma.
    c. 80 ma.   e. none of these.

25. The transconductance of a vacuum tube is equal to
    a. Ip/Eg.
    b. Ep/Eg.   d. Gm/Rp.
    c. Ep/Ip.   e. none of these.

26. To cutoff the plate current in a thyratron you could
    a. decrease the anode voltage.
    b. increase the grid bias.   d. open the grid circuit.
    c. use AC on the grid. _   e. none of these.

27. For proper operation connect
    a. 1 to 2.
    b. 1 to 5.
    c. 1 to 7.
    d. 2 to 5.
    e. 2 to 7.

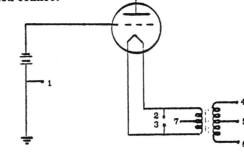

28. When using triode tubes at higher frequencies, it is important to consider
    a. transconductance.
    b. plate impedance.   d. skin effect.
    c. input capacitance.   e. none of these.

29. The suppressor grid of a tube is operated at a potential
    a. positive with respect to plate.
    b. negative with respect to grid.
    c. zero with respect to plate.
    d. zero with respect to cathode.
    e. none of these.

30. The polarity of the voltage used to supply DC voltage to a direct cathode is periodically reversed to
    a. increase the bias.
    b. decrease the bias.
    c. suppress parasitics.
    d. to balance out the emissive property.
    e. none of these.

31. The life of a vacuum tube will not be shortened by
    a. excessive screen current.
    b. insufficient filament voltage.
    c. excessive plate voltage.
    d. insufficient grid bias.
    e. excessive filament voltage.

32. The principal advantage of a tetrode over a triode is
    a. more power can be had.
    b. more voltage can be had.
    c. electrostatic capacitance is reduced and neutralization is not required.
    d. distortion is considerably reduced.
    e. efficiency is improved.

33. A small value of grid to plate capacitance is characteristic of
    a. tetrodes and pentodes.
    b. all vacuum tubes.   d. diodes.
    c. triodes.   e. none of these.

34. A voltage amplification (μ) of 50 means that
    a. a 50 volt signal at the grid appears as 1 volt at the plate.
    b. $\Delta I_p / \Delta I_g = 50$
    c. $\Delta Ip / \Delta Eg = 50$
    d. $\Delta Eg / \Delta Ep = 50$
    e. a 1 volt signal at the grid appears as 50 volts at the plate.

2. **(5 amperes)** The only current change with audio input in a properly tuned FM transmitter is in the _____ .

4. **(direct or indirect)** If the plate voltage to the final tube of an FM transmitter is 2000 volts and the plate current is 750 ma. & the efficiency factor is 66 2/3%, the operating output power would be _____ watts.

6. **(19 KHz)** This concludes Unit 4. Now do the Recheck.

1. Solid state devices, as the name implies, do not utilize a vacuum but are fabricated from solid crystalline materials. The most often used elements found in solid state devices are germanium or silicon with impurities of arsnic or gallium. These materials with their low impurity content are called semiconductors. Semiconductors are fabricated from_____or_____using controlled amounts of impurity.

8. (P, N) If the applied voltage was alternating current, current would flow through the load on one half cycle (forward bias) and current would not flow on the other half cycle (reverse bias). Therefore, the diode semiconductor is a rectifier with a DC output taken across the load. A rectifier changes AC to

_____,

15. (reverse) The ratio of the DC collector current to the DC base current (without signal) is called DC beta symbolized as hFE. Bv formula:

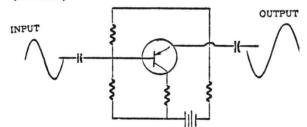

$$h_{FE} = \frac{I_C}{I_B}$$

Where h_{FE} = DC beta or current gain.
I_C = collector current
I_B = base current.

The currents in collector and base must be expressed in the same units.

The usual DC beta range is from 20-100. If the base current is .5 ma and the collector current is 20 ma, the DC beta hFE is -_____

22. (reversed)

INPUT

OUTPUT

In the transistor amplifier shown the_____ and_____ should be interchanged.

29. (electron, holes) Current flow in crystaline semiconductor material is always related to the outer valence electrons of an atom. Negative (N type) material has a surplus of valence electrons for co-valent bonding and positive (P type) material has a deficiency of valence electrons for complete co-valent bonding. The part of the atom concerned with current flow is the outer_____ electrons.

Review unit 19 of Part 1 Second Class Radiotelephone programmed instruction.

1. When using amplitude modulation, the antenna current increases 22½% for 100% modulation. When using frequency modulation, the antenna current does not change with modulation. The only current change in a properly tuned FM transmitter with audio input occurs in the reactance tube modulator. (Direct FM)

    The antenna current produced by an FM transmitter without modulation is 5 amperes. With 75% modulation the antenna current would be _____ amperes.

3. (reactance tube modulator) The operating power of an AM broadcast station is figured by the direct method:

    $$\text{Power output} = I^2 \text{ an. X Z (antenna impedance)}$$

    In FM, the operating power output can be determined by either the direct method (given above) or by the indirect method.

    In the indirect method the output power is determined by the formula:

    $$\text{Power output} = I_P \text{ (final plate) X } E_P \text{ (final plate) X F}$$
    Where F is an efficiency factor-usually around 65%.

    In FM broadcasting, the operating power is determined by either the _____ or _____ method.

5. (1000 watts) In modern FM stereo multiplex transmitting systems, three distinct signals are transmitted. They are a 19 Khz pilot sub carrier (for synchronizing), an L + R (left plus right) signal, and an L - R (left minus right) signal.

    The FM stereo sub carrier used in stereo multiplex transmissions is on _____ Khz

2. **(germanium or silicon)** Germanium or silicon atoms are linked together in crystalline form by a process of co-valent bonding. In this process one valence electron (outer orbit electron) is linked with one valence electron from a neighboring valence electron of another atom. Since there are four valence electrons in each germanium and silicon atom, each atom is linked in co-valent bonding with four other atoms.

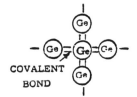

COVALENT
BOND

The four other atoms surrounding the central germanium atom are linked in like manner to other atoms in co-valent bonding

Crystalline germanium and silicon atoms are linked together by_____bonding.

9. **(DC)** The transistor is fabricated by sandwiching a thin slice of P type material between two sections of N type material or vice versa. Two types of triode transistors are shown:

 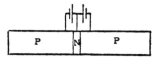

Note that each type has two junctions and two potential barriers. Triode transistors are either NPN or PNP in type. A triode transistor is comparable to two diodes connected back to back. A triode transistor has_____junctions.

16. **(40)** The ratio of collector current variation to the base current variation (when signal is applied) is called AC beta symbolized as h_{fe}. By formula:

$$h_{fe} = \frac{\Delta I_c}{\Delta I_b}$$

Where h_{fe} = AC beta or current gain.
ΔI_c = change in collector current.
ΔI_b = change in base current.

The change in collector and base currents must be expressed in the same units.

If the change of 24 ma of collector current is caused by a base current change of .4 ma, the h_{fe} is

_____.

23. **(emitter, collector)** The question might be asked - What causes the collector current to rise to such a high value when the forward bias to the base emitter circuit is increased? This is caused by the attraction of large collector voltage on the current carriers injected into the base. (electrons in an NPN and holes in a PNP). For proper operation the base emitter voltage might be as low as one tenth of the collector emitter voltage. The forward base emitter bias should be_____than the collector emitter voltage.

30. **(valence)** The emitter base junction capacitance can be reduced for high frequency transistor operation by the addition of a second base connection. Such a transistor is a tetrode transistor. These are used at___HIGH___frequencies because of their lower interelement capacitance.

8. In the diagram below the required audio power output would be
    a. 300 watts.
    b. 400 watts.
    c. 500 watts.
    d. 800 watts.
    e. none of these.

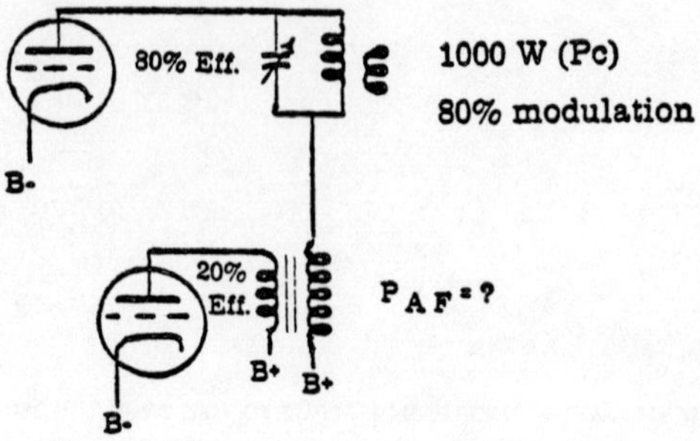

    80% Eff.   1000 W (Pc)

    80% modulation

    20% Eff. $P_{AF} = ?$

    B+ B+

    B-

9. The wave envelope pattern shows a modulation percentage of about

    a. 5%.
    b. 20%.
    c. 50%.
    d. 60%.
    e. 90%.

    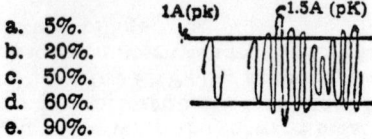

    1A(pk)   1.5A (pK)

10. Overmodulation is shown in a trapazoidal pattern by
    a. a trapazoid.
    b. a triangle.
    c. a triangle with a line coming out of the vertex.
    d. a vertical line.
    e. a horizontal line.

11. The approximate modulation percentage illustrated is
    a. 0.
    b. 15.
    c. 50.
    d. 75.
    e. 100.

    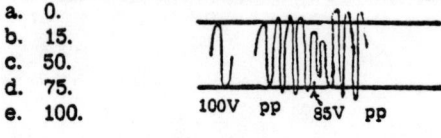

    100V pp   85V pp

12. The circuit below is used for
    a. measuring high AC voltage.
    b. measuring high RF voltage.
    c. testing high current.
    d. measuring carrier shift.
    e. none of these.

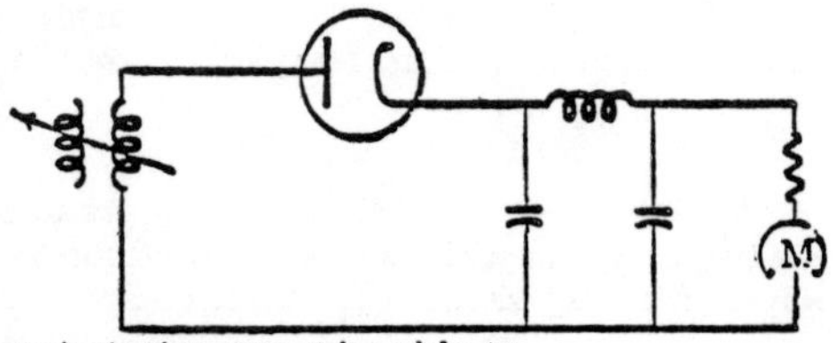

    M

13. The transmitter at an AM broadcast station must be able to
    a. broadcast on the ERI frequency.
    b. transmit directional.
    c. transmit high fidelity.
    d. transmit FM.
    e. be modulatd 85%.

3. **(co-valent bonding)** Pure or intrinsic germanium and silicon are insulators. By adding controlled amounts of an impurity, the crystalline materials are altered to become semiconductors. A semiconductor has a conductivity that lies between that of an insulator and a conductor. If the impurity is a substance like arsnic having five valence electrons, the germanium or silicon is left with more electrons that needed for complete co-valent bonding. These excess electrons are found in N type germanium or silicon and may be used to support conduction. If the impurity is a substance having three valence electrons like gallium, the germanium or silicon is left with too few electrons for complete co-valent bonding. These electron deficiences, referred to as holes, are found in P type germanium or silicon and may also be used to support conduction. Semiconductor conduction is either by_ELECTRONS_in N type material or by___HOLES___in P type material.

10. **(two)** The schematic symbols for transistors are shown as:

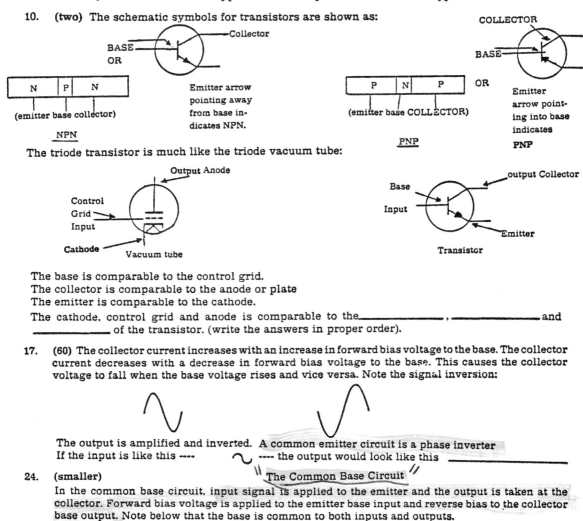

The triode transistor is much like the triode vacuum tube:

The base is comparable to the control grid.
The collector is comparable to the anode or plate
The emitter is comparable to the cathode.
The cathode, control grid and anode is comparable to the_____,_____and _____ of the transistor. (write the answers in proper order).

17. **(60)** The collector current increases with an increase in forward bias voltage to the base. The collector current decreases with a decrease in forward bias voltage to the base. This causes the collector voltage to fall when the base voltage rises and vice versa. Note the signal inversion:

The output is amplified and inverted. A common emitter circuit is a phase inverter
If the input is like this ---- ～ ---- the output would look like this _____

24. **(smaller)** The Common Base Circuit

In the common base circuit, input signal is applied to the emitter and the output is taken at the collector. Forward bias voltage is applied to the emitter base input and reverse bias to the collector base output. Note below that the base is common to both inputs and outputs.

NPN circuit showing both transistor symbols.

A positive voltage applied at the emitter with respect to the common base decreases the forward bias. This in turn decreases the collector current and reduces the voltage drop across the collector load. The net result is a positive going collector voltage with a positive going emitter. The input and output signals are in phase. A negative voltage at the emitter would increase the forward bias increasing the collector current and increasing the collector load voltage drop. The net result as seen above is a_NEGATIVE_going collector voltage which is produced by a negative going signal at the emitter.

31. **(high)** This concludes Unit 10.

1. When there is no modulation in an AM transmitter the antenna current is 6A. At 100% modulation the antenna current is
   a. 6A.
   b. 12A.
   c. 6 X 1.225A.
   d. 6 X 1.5A.,
   e. none of these.

2. A Doherty amplifier is a
   a. frequency doubler.
   b. push-pull amplifier.
   c. a parallel amplifier used for reducing harmonics.
   d. type of linear amplifier having an efficiency comparable to a Class C amplifier.
   e. none of these.

3. A standard broadcast transmitter has an output of 1000 watts. The efficiency of the modulated R. F. output tube is 80% and the efficiency of the modulator is 20%. If the transmitter is modulated 90% the modulator dissipates approximately
   a. 1000 watts.
   b. 2000 watts.
   c. 3000 watts.
   d. 405 watts.
   e. none of these.

4. For 100% modulation of an AM transmitter using voice frequencies the modulator output must be approximately
   a. 50% of the RF modulated amplifier input.
   b. 100% of the RF modulated amplifier input.
   c. 25% of the RF modulated amplifier input.
   d. 75% of the RF modulated amplifier input.
   e. none of these.

5. An AM broadcast station licensed for an output of 500 watts would be in violation if it
   a. used 100 watts in the sidebands.
   b. used 300 watts in the sidebands.
   c. uses 515 watts carrier power.
   d. used 480 watts of carrier power.
   e. 100% modulation.

6. If a 1500 khz standard AM broadcast transmitter is modulated by 100 to 15,000 hz of audio the highest resulting frequency would be
   a. 1500 khz.
   b. 1505 khz.
   c. 1503 khz.
   d. 1515 khz.
   e. 1530 khz.

7. The wave envelope pattern shows a modulation percentage of about

   a. 5%.
   b. 20%.
   c. 50%.
   d. 60%.
   e. 90%.

4. (electrons, holes) N or P type semiconductor material is electrically neutral. The excess or deficiency of electrons for co-valent bonding is created by the impurities. However, this excess or deficiency is only in terms of co-valent bonding. The overall positive proton charges are exactly equal to the negative electron charges found in the orbits surrounding the positive atomic nucleus. See the illustration:

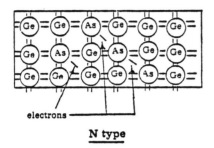

Ge - Germanium
As - Arsnic
Ga - Gallium

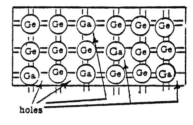

electrons

N type

holes

P type

N or P type semiconductor material is electrically_____.

11. (emitter, base, collector) Therefore, in most cases the input signal is applied at the_____ of the transistor and the output taken from the_____ of the transistor. (see diagram in #10)

18. (⌣) Let us see how this comes about in the common emitter circuit. Consider what happens on the positive half of the input signal in the NPN circuit.

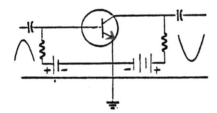

> A positive voltage into the base increases the forward bias increasing the collector current through the load resistor. This increases the voltage drop across the load and lowers the collector voltage.

If the input signal is negative going the output is_____ going.

25. (negative) Let us look at a PNP common base circuit.

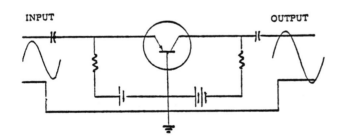

INPUT   OUTPUT

> As the emitter goes positive the forward emitter base bias increases. More collector current flows and there is a greater drop across the collector load resistor. Since the load resistor is connected to the negative terminal of the collector source voltage, a large voltage load drop makes the collector less negative or positive going. In the PNP common base circuit there is no phase inversion.

A positive going signal at the emitter of a PNP transistor causes both the emitter and collector currents to_INCREASE_.

RECHECK PROGRAMMED INSTRUCTION USING SHRADER'S ELECTRONIC COMMUNICATION

2.　(833 1/3 watts) The required sinusoidal audio output from the modulator for 100% modulation would be 1/2 X 833 1/3 watts or 416 2/3 watts.

For 80% modulation the required sinusoidal audio output would be_____watts.

4.　(1066 2/3 watts) The modulator tube would dissipate _____ watts in this case.

6.　(25%) Read all paragraphs of section 17-13. If an R. F. amplifier having an input of 1500 watts and an efficiency of 66 2/3% is modulated 100%, the power in the side band would be_____watts.

8.　(5250 watts)

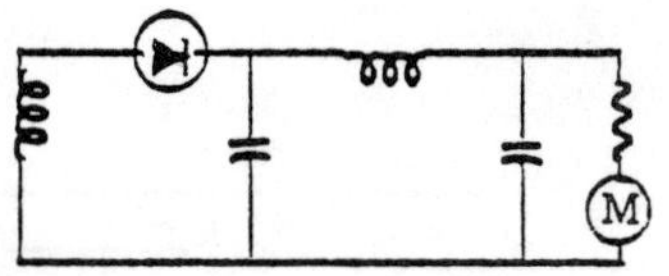

The circuit shown above is used for measuring_____ _____. Sec. 17-25

10.　(undistorted or symmetrical) This concludes Unit 4 recheck.

5. **(neutral)** When N type material is chemically joined with P type material some of the electrons of the N type material cross over from the junction to the P type material to fill the holes. This leaves the N type material region of the junction with too few electrons for electrical neutrality and the P type material in the region of the junction with too many electrons for electrical neutrality. In other words the N material in the region of the junction is positively charged (lacking electrons) and the P material in the region of the junction is negatively charged (having electrons). See the illustration:

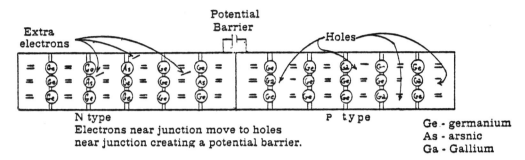

Extra electrons

Potential Barrier

Holes

N type

P type

Electrons near junction move to holes near junction creating a potential barrier.

Ge - germanium
As - arsnic
Ga - Gallium

The potential barrier at the junction is created by electrons in the N type material filling_____ in the P type material.

THE COMMON EMITTER CIRCUIT

12. **(base, collector)** In the much used common emitter circuit, the emitter is common to both the input and output signals. Both NPN and PNP circuits are shown:

NPN = -, +, +.
PNP = +, -, -.

IMPORTANT

Large reverse bias voltage.

NPN

Small forward bias voltage.

In both circuits:
1. The emitter current I_e = the base current I_b plus the collector current I_c. This is true in all transistor circuits.
2. The base to emitter bias is forward. (- to N or + to P)
3. The collector to emitter bias is reverse bias. (+ to N or - to P)
4. A little base current produces (by forward biasing) a large collector current flow.

The collector current is equal to the___EMITTER___current minus the___BASE___current.

19. **(positive)** A resistor may be placed in the emitter circuit for several reasons. It's often placed in the emitter circuit to prevent thermal run away. An over-heated transistor may have high emitter and collector current which in turn produces more heat. This cycle could destroy a transistor. To prevent this a series emitter stabilizing resistor (also called a swamping resistor) provides automatic bias stability. Increased emitter and collector current provide a lower forward bias to the base emitter circuit. This reduces the emitter and collector currents. If a transistor is heated the emitter and collector currents tend to___INCREASE___.

26. **(increase)**

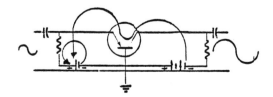

Since all the current flows in the input emitter circuit and only 97% or so of the total emitter flows in the collector, the current gain is 97/100 or .97. The common base current gain (output/input) is called alpha and is always less than 1.

As in the common emitter circuit the collector current is equal to the___EMITTER___current minus the___BASE___current.

UNIT 4 (Part 2)
AMPLITUDE MODULATION

RECHECK PROGRAMMED INSTRUCTION USING SHRADER'S ELECTRONIC COMMUNICATION

Review Recheck Unit 17 of Part 1 Second Class Radiotelephone programmed instruction.

1. Read all paragraphs Section 17-11.

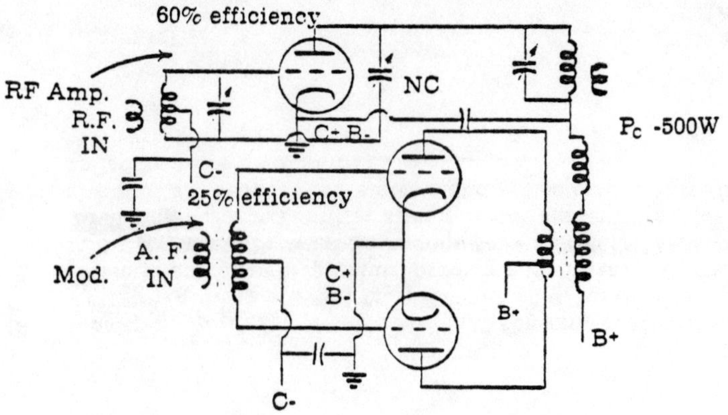

The R. F. amplifier input would be ________ watts.

3. **(266 2/3 watts)** The modulator input for 80% sinusoidal modulation would be ____________ watts. Sec. 17-11

5. **(800 watts)** Using voice frequencies for modulation, the modulator audio output should be approximately ____________ % of the DC power input to the modulated R.F. amplifier. Sec 17-11

7. **(500 watts)** An AM broadcast station is allowed to deviate from their assigned output power by plus 5% and minus 10%. A broadcast station using an output power of anything from 900 watts to 1050 watts is operating legally if their authorized output power is 1000 watts.

   A broadcast station authorized to use 5000 watts may use as much as ____________ watts.

9. **(carrier shift)** If there is no movement of the meter when a measurement is made using a carrier shift meter, there is ____________ modulation. Sec. 17-25

6. **(holes)** When N and P materials are joined in this manner, a diode semiconductor is formed. The potential barrier produced at the junction of the N and P type materials is an actual voltage. Its presence makes rectification possible. The diode rectifier will conduct when a voltage is applied to overcome the potential barrier and will not conduct if the potential barrier is increased. Note the diagrams:

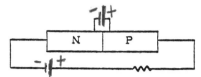

The applied votage is connected in such a manner as to reduce the potential barrier voltage. In this case current will flow. The diode is said to be "forward biased."

In "forward bias" the negative side of the applied voltage is connected to the _____N_____ type of material and the positive side of the applied voltage is connected to the _____P_____ type of material.

13. **(emitter, base)** By biasing a transistor in this manner a small base current produces a large collector current. In common emitter circuits the base to emitter bias is ___FORWARD___ bias.

20. **(increase)** A resistor may also be placed in the emitter circuit to provide an in phase output as well as the out of phase output at the collector. In this case both collector and emitter circuits would have load resistors. The circuit is used to provide two out of phase signals to feed a push-pull amplifier (to be discussed in a later unit). The phase inverter arrangement is as shown:

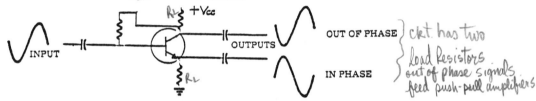

ckt. has two load Resistors. out of phase signals feed push-pull amplifiers.

The circuit shown above is a phase inverter used for supplying out of phase inputs for a _____ circuit.

27. **(emitter, base)** One other type of transistor circuit that is often used is the "common collector or emitter follower circuit." The input is to the base and the output is taken at the emitter.

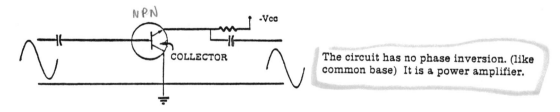

The circuit has no phase inversion. (like common base) It is a power amplifier.

Phase inversion of the output only takes place in the common ___EMITTER___ circuits.

4. **(1280 watts, 960 watts)**

For use in frames #4, #5, and #6.

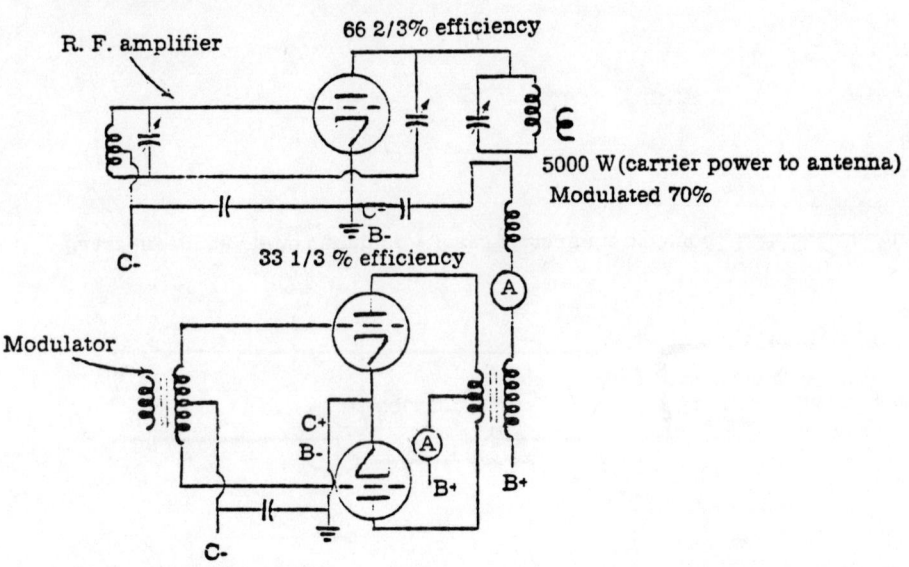

R. F. amplifier

66 2/3% efficiency

5000 W (carrier power to antenna)
Modulated 70%

33 1/3 % efficiency

Modulator

C+
B-

C-

C-

The R. F. amplifier input would be_____watts (5000 divided by 2/3)

8. **(150 watts)** The F.C.C. permits a power tolerance of plus 5% and minus 10% for a standard A.M. broadcast station. This means that a station licensed for 1000 watts output may use as high as 1050 watts (1000 W + 5% of 1000 watts) and as low as 900 watts (1000 watts minus 10% of 1000 watts)

A station with a licensed power of 500 watts may operate with a maximum power of _____ watts but with no less than_____watts..(output)

7. **(N, P)**

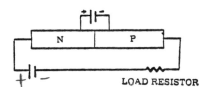

LOAD RESISTOR

The applied voltage is connected in such a manner as to increase the potential barrier.

In this case current will not flow. The diode is said to be reverse biased. In reverse bias the negative side of the applied voltage is connected to the _____P_____ type material and the positive side is connected to the _____N_____ type material.

14. **(forward)** The collector to emitter bias is _____REVERSE_____ bias. in a common-EMITTER ckt.

21. **(push-pull)** Forward bias for the base and reverse bias for the collector may be obtained from one battery. Two methods of using a single battery are shown:

1. <u>Voltage divider bias using emitter stabilizing resistor.</u>

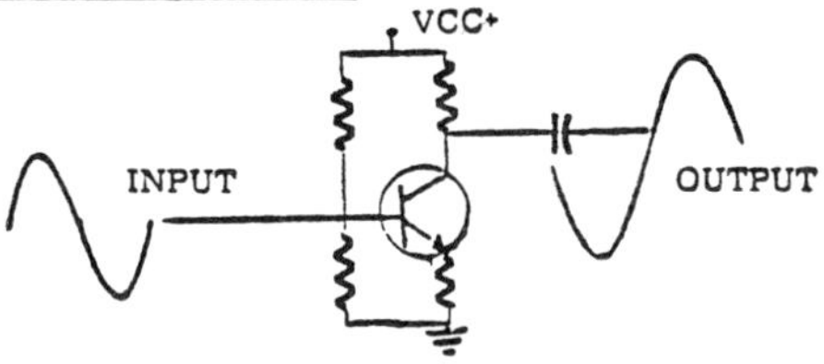

VCC+

INPUT   OUTPUT

The positive voltage at the base provides a forward bias that is lower than the collector reverse bias.

2. <u>Self bias.</u>

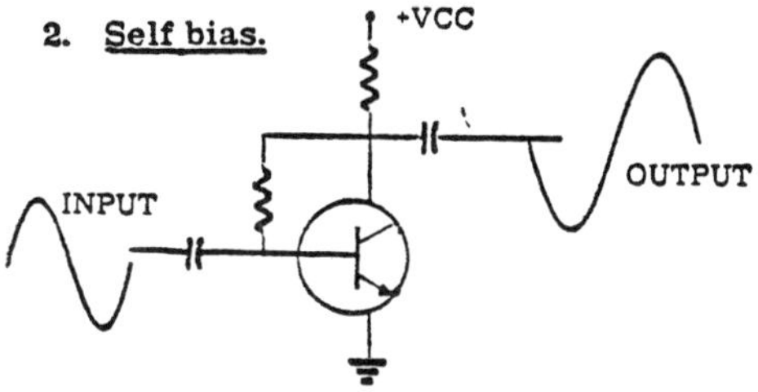

+VCC

INPUT   OUTPUT

The base resistor is returned to the positive collector for forward bias.

The PNP circuits are identical except the collector load resistor connects to the negative side of the battery.

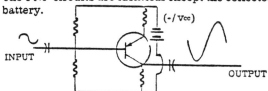

(-/Vcc)

INPUT   OUTPUT

In the circuit shown the battery polarity is _____REVERSED_____ (correct or reversed) for proper operation.

28. **(emitter)** In NPN transistors the majority of the current carriers are electrons traveling from minus to plus. In PNP transistors the majority of the current carriers are holes traveling from plus to minus. In all cases current flowing in the wires and resistors is electron flow from minus to plus. The majority NPN current carriers in the NPN transistor are _____ and the majority current carriers in the PNP transistor are _____ .

3. (1000 watts, 500 watts) If the modulator in the preceeding example was modulated 80%, the audio power output requirement would be found by the same formula

$$P_{AF} = P_{DC} \ X \ \frac{M^2}{2}$$

$_{or}$ = 1000 X .32 or 320 watts.

For 80% modulation and 25% modulator efficiency the modulator input would be _____ watts and _____ watts would be dissipated in the form of heat.

7. (5512.5 watts, 3675 watts) Since the sideband power comes from the audio, we can use the audio power formula in modified form to find the sideband power.

$$P_{SB} = P_C X \ \frac{M^2}{2}$$

Where P_{SB} IS THE POWER IN UPPER AND LOWER SIDEBANDS.
M IS MODULATION % WRITTEN DECIMALLY.
P_C IS THE CARRIER OUTPUT POWER

Since the maximum % modulation is 100%, the maximum sideband power permitted by F.C.C. is 1/2 ($1^2/2$) of the carrier power.

If the carrier power is 1000 watts, the maximum permissible sideband power is 500 watts.

If the carrier power is 300 watts the maximum permissible sideband power is _____ watts.

11. (rectifier.) This concludes Unit 4.

UNIT 10 BASIC SOLID STATE DEVICES

RECHECK PROGRAMMED INSTRUCTION USING SHRADER'S ELECTRONIC COMMUNICATIONS

1. Solid state devices control the flow of electrons along a solid piece of_____material.
    Sec. 10-1.

4. (germanium, silicon) Arsnic is used to produce_____type semiconductor material and
    gallium to produce_____type semiconductor material. Sec. 10-2.

7. (forward) The diode so biased has relatively little resistance. The barrier voltage at the junction has
    disappeared.

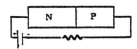

The bias shown is_____bias.
(+ to N and - to P) Sec. 10-3.

10. (NPN) The base emitter circuit should be_____biased and the collector emitter circuit
    should be_____biased. Sec. 10-6.

13. (180°)

This is a common_____circuit using
_____bias. Sec. 10-6.

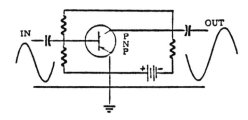

16. (emitter, collector)

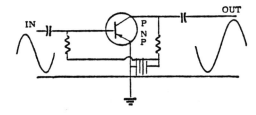

This is a common_____
circuit using_____bias.
Sec. 10-6.

19. (emitter, base, collector) Whereas the input to a common emitter circuit is to the base, the input to a
    common base circuit is to the_____. Sec. 10-9.

CORRECT

22. (increase) In all transistors the total current is found in the emitter. In other words the sum of the
    collector current and the base current is equal to the emitter current. In an amplifier without input
    the collector current is around 98% of the emitter current and the base current is around 2% of the
    emitter current. The collector current is equal to the_____current minus the base current.

25. (out) Better high frequency operation can be expected from_____transistors because they
    have less interelement_____. Sec. 10-5.

2. (1500 watts) Now let us tie a modulator on our modulated R. F. amplifier and adjust it for 100% modulation.

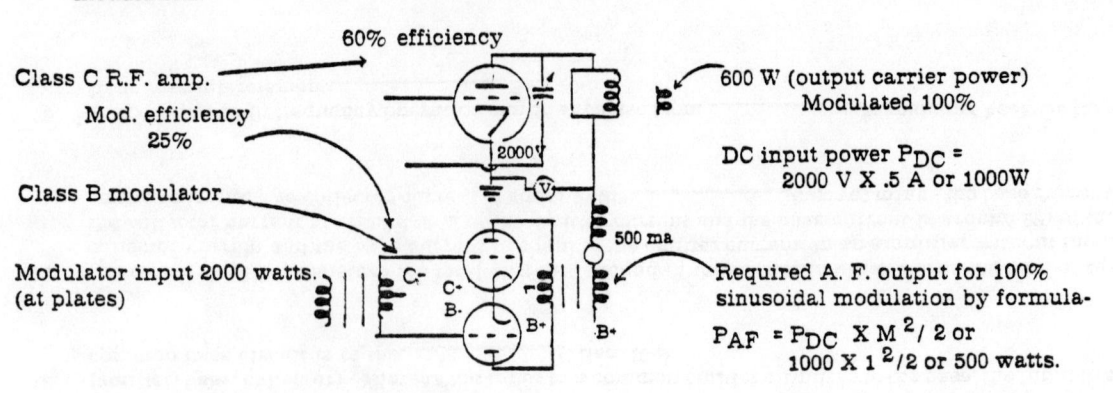

Class C R.F. amp.

Mod. efficiency 25%

Class B modulator

Modulator input 2000 watts. (at plates)

60% efficiency

2000 V

500 ma

600 W (output carrier power) Modulated 100%

DC input power P_{DC} = 2000 V X .5 A or 1000W

Required A. F. output for 100% sinusoidal modulation by formula—

$P_{AF} = P_{DC} \times M^2/2$ or 1000 X $1^2/2$ or 500 watts.

Since the modulator is 25% efficient, the input to the modulator (V X A) would be 500 divided by .25 (25%) or 2000 watts. 1500 watts is dissipated by the modulator in the form of heat. If the modulator had an efficiency of 50% the modulator input would have to be_____watts and_____ watts would be dissipated in heat.

6. (1837 watts) The modulator input power would be_____watts and_____watts would be dissipated in the modulator in the form of heat.

10. (400 watts) Symmetrical modulation results in equal positive and negative excursions in the modulated wave envelope. Note the example below:

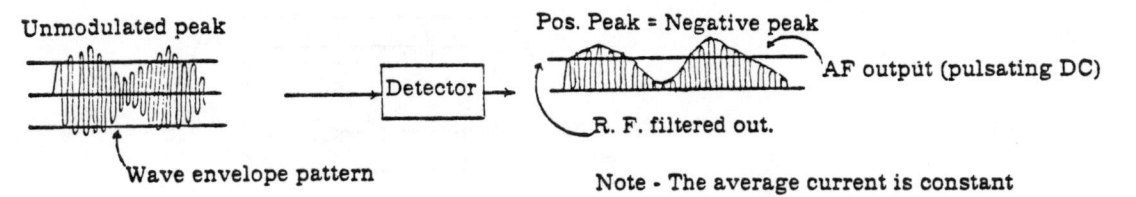

Unmodulated peak

Detector

Pos. Peak = Negative peak

AF output (pulsating DC)

R. F. filtered out.

Wave envelope pattern

Note - The average current is constant

If modulation was not symmetrical, the detected audio would have greater positive peaks than negative peaks or vice versa and the average current would not be constant.

Any R.F. rectifier with a filter can be used to determine if a modulated signal has carrier shift.

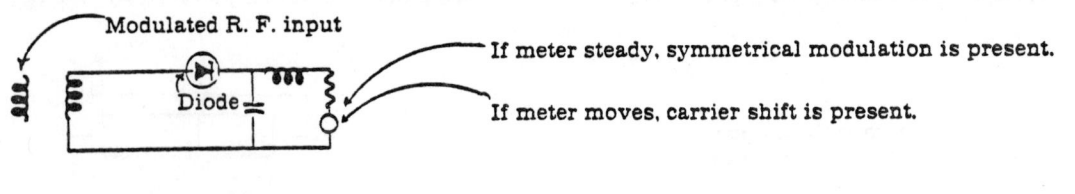

Modulated R. F. input

Diode

If meter steady, symmetrical modulation is present.

If meter moves, carrier shift is present.

Carrier Shift Detector

A carrier shift detector is an R.F. _____.

2. (semiconductor) The outer_____electrons of an atom are available for free interchange between atoms. Sec. 10-2.

5. (N, P) Insufficient electrons for complete covalent bonding produce a_____. Sec. 10-1.

8. (reverse) The reverse biased diode acts like a resistance of a_____value and the junction barrier voltage is much in evidence. Sec. 10-3.

11. (forward, reverse) The common emitter circuit shown is wrong because the_____to the emitter battery is in backwards. Sec. 10-6.

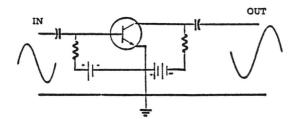

14. (emitter, voltage divider stabilized) Note the P type collector. It is connected through its load to the negative side of the battery. If this battery was reversed, it would easily ruin the transistor. A transistor can easily be damaged by_____bias on the collector. Sec. 10-6.

17. (emitter, self) The voltage used for the base emitter bias must be small compared to the collector emitter voltage. The values of resistances or batteries must be chosen with this in mind. For proper operation the base emitter forward bias voltage must be_____than the collector emitter reverse bias. Sec. 10-6.

20. (emitter)

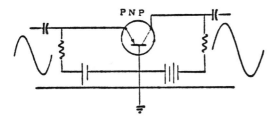

The PNP circuit shown is a common _____circuit and the output is _____(in, out of) phase with the input. Sec. 10-9

23. (emitter) Read all paragraphs 10-8.

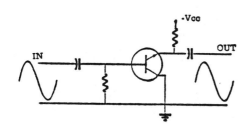

The NPN circuit shown is a common _____circuit with an output _____(in, out of) phase with the input. Sec. 10-10.

26. (tetrode, capacitance) Now take the Unit 10 test.

Review Unit 17 of the Part 1 Second Class Radiotelephone Programmed instruction.

1.   It is often necessary to consider the efficiency of both the modulated R. F. amplifier and the modulator.

Let us consider the modulated R. F. amplifier first. Note the example below:

60% Efficiency   Tube dissipates 400 W in form of heat.

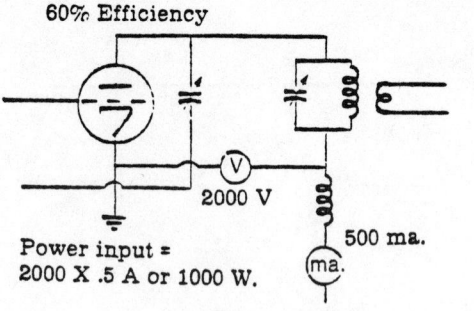

Power output to antenna
= .6 X 1000 W or 600 watts

2000 V

500 ma.

Power input =
2000 X .5 A or 1000 W.

1000 watts was put into the circuit, but only 600 watts was delivered to the antenna. 400 watts (1000 - 600) was dissipated by the tube as heat.

·If you knew only the power output and the efficiency, the input could be found by dividing the output by the efficiency. For example 600 W divided by .6 (60%) equals 1000 watts.

If the output was 1000 watts and the efficiency was 66 2/3%, the input power would be_____watts.

5.   (7500 watts) The required AF output for 70% sinusoidal modulation would be_____watts.

9.   (525 watts, 450 watts) The audio power output requirement of 50% of the R. F. amplifier DC power input for 100% modulation is based on the assumption that the audio is sinusoidal tone. If voice frequencies were used, the audio power output requirement is approximately 25% of the R. F. amplifier DC power input.

In order to modulate an R. F. amplifier having a DC power input of 1600 watts using speech audio frequencies, it would be necessary to have a modulator A. F. output of_____watts.

(Assuming 100% Modulation)

3.   (valence) Solid state devices are fabricated from_____or_____ . Sec.10-2.

6.   (hole)   The bias shown is_____bias.
               (- to n and + to P) Sec. 10-3.

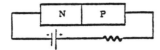

9.   (high)   The symbol shown is for a_____
                                                               transistor. Sec. 10-6.

12. (collector) Note that the common emitter output signal is out of phase (180°) with the input signal. It is
     the only amplifier configuration that inverts the output signal. It is comparable to the common
     cathode vacuum tube circuit in this respect. The output of a common emitter circuit is_____
     degrees out of phase with the input signal. Sec. 10-6.

15. (forward) Excessive heat causes increased current flow in the_____and_____
     circuits. Sec. 10-6.

18. (smaller) The cathode, grid, and plate of a vacuum tube are comparable to the_____,
     _____, and_____of a transistor. (put in proper order). Sec. 10-6.

21. (base, in) In the circuit in problem 20 the negative going part of the input signal would decrease the
     forward bias. This in turn decreases the collector current. Therefore, the collector load resistor
     voltage drop would decrease making the collector more negative or negative going. The positive
     portion of the input signal would increase the forward bias and cause a(n)_____emitter and
     collector current. Sec. 10-9.

24. (collector, in) By using a load resistor in both the emitter and collector circuits, we can construct a
     circuit with two outputs.

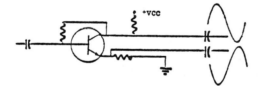

This circuit is a phase
inverter used to drive a
push pull amplifier.
Sec. 10-10. Also see Sec.
14-37.

The two outputs are_____(in, out of) phase with each other.

1. An R. F. frequency multiplier stage is not characterized by
    a. high bias
    b. high excitation
    c. distortion
    d. output circuit tuned to frequency of input circuit.
    e. class C operation.

2. The circuit shown could be used for a
    a. tripler.
    b. A. F. amplifier
    c. R. F. amplifier.
    d. R. F. oscillator.
    e. none of these.

3. The second harmonic of a certain signal appears on the dial of a frequency meter at 3105. This corresponds to 1620 KHz. If second harmonic energy of 1600 KHz appears at 3103, the fundamental frequency of the second harmonic energy appearing at 3104 would be (assuming a straight line relationship between frequency and dial reading)
    a. 1610 KHz.
    b. 3220 KHz.
    c. 805 KHz.
    d. 1000 KHz.
    e. none of these.

4. The output frequency of a transmitter is measured by measuring the second harmonic energy using a heterodyne frequency meter. The meter has a dial reading of 2101.0 for 1420 KHz and 2101.8 for 1440 KHz. Assuming straight line frequency dial calibrations, the fundamental frequency corresponding to a dial reading of 2101.3 would be
    a. 1427.5 KHz.
    b. 2855 KHz.
    c. 1430 KHz.
    d. 713.75 KHz.
    e. none of these.

5. A six pole 60 cycle 3 phase induction motor would develop a speed of
    a. 5200 RPM.
    b. 3600 RPM.
    c. 1800 RPM.
    d. 1200 RPM.
    e. none of these.

6. A second class radio telephone license cannot be used to operate and service
    a. a television broadcast station.
    b. a radiotelegraph station aboard a ship.
    c. an amateur radio station.
    d. a station requiring an aircraft license.
    e. any of the above.

7. AVC voltage in a receiver should be measured by a
    a. thermo couple.
    b. RF wattmeter.
    c. VOM.
    d. square law meter.
    e. VTVM.

1. A principle common to all transistors is that
    a. the collector base is forward biased.
    b. the emitter base is reverse biased.
    c. the collector is positive with respect to the base.
    d. the emitter is positive with respect to the base.
    e. the collector base bias is reverse bias.

2. One advantage of a tetrode transistor is that it operates well at
    a. low frequencies
    b. high frequencies.   d. high temperatures.
    c. low temperatures.   e. none of these.

3. In the circuit below
    a. the emitter bias is too high.
    b. the emitter bias is reversed.
    c. the collector bias is reversed.
    d. an NPN transistor is used.
    e. operation should be normal.

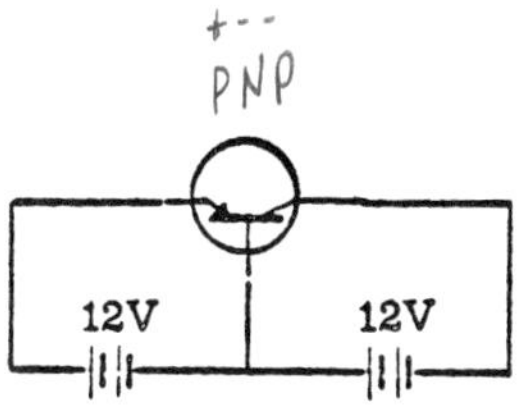

    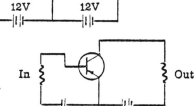

4. In the diagram below the
    a. collector bias is incorrect.
    b. emitter bias is wrong.
    c. point A should be grounded.
    d. the collector and base are 180° out of phase.
    e. the collector and base are in phase.

    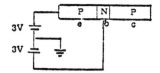

5. In the PNP common base transistor amplifier that is properly biased, the positive portion of the AC input signal causes
    a. the emitter base current to increase.
    b. the emitter base current to decrease.   d. no change in the emitter base current.
    c. the collector base current to decrease. e. none of these.

6. In a common base transistor circuit the
    a. output signal is in phase with the input.
    b. output signal is out of phase with the input.   d. input signal is applied to the collector.
    c. input signal is applied to the base.   e. current gain is figured in Beta.

7. In a common emitter transistor circuit the
    a. output signal is in phase.
    b. output signal is out of phase with the input.   d. input signal is applied to the collector.
    c. input signal is applied to the emitter.   e. current gain is figured in Alpha.

8. In the diagram
    a. the emitter is forward biased.
    b. the emitter is reverse biased.
    c. the emitter to base bias is zero.
    d. four diodes are shown.
    e. none of these.

9. The collector in a transistor is comparable to
    a. the anode in a VT.
    b. the control grid in a VT.   d. the screen grid in a VT.
    c. the cathode in a VT.   e. the suppressor grid in a VT.

10. The emitter in a transistor is comparable to
    a. the anode in a VT.
    b. the control grid in a VT.   d. the screen grid in a VT.
    c. the cathode in a VT.   e. none of these.

11. The transistor symbol shown is for a
    a. silicon transistor
    b. NPN transistor.   d. diode
    c. PNP transistor.   e. germanium transistor.

12. In the circuit shown
    a. the emitter if forward biased.
    b. the collector is reversed bias.
    c. a PNP transistor is used.
    d. is a typical phase inverter.
    e. all the above are true.

    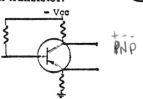

UNIT 3 (Part 2)

MISCELLANEOUS REVIEW

Review Units 16, 18, 21, and 23 of the Part 1 Second Class Radiotelephone programmed instruction. This is the original programmed writing of the author.

UNIT 3 (Part 2)

RECHECK MISCELLANEOUS REVIEW

Review Recheck Units 16, 18, 21, and 23 of the Part 1 Second Class Radiotelephone programmed instruction using Shrader's Electronic Communication book.

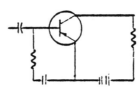

13. In the circuit shown below
    a. the collector is biased wrong.
    b. the emitter bias battery is reversed.
    c. there is no collector bias.
    d. there is no emitter bias.
    e. none of these.

14. Because of the reduction in base resistance and collector capacitance, the tetrode junction transistor has a better
    a. low frequency response.
    b. high frequency response. d. voltage gain.
    c. power capability   e. none of these.

15. In the common base transistor amplifier using a junction transistor, the collector current is equal to
    a. the emitter current.
    b. the base current.   d. the emitter current minus the base current.
    c. the emitter current plus the base current. e. none of these.

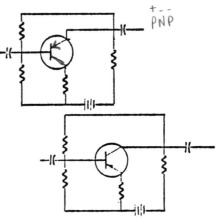

16. In the transistor amplifier shown
    a. the diagram is correct.
    b. there is no bias.
    c. the collector and emitter are reversed.
    d. the transistor is an NPN unit.
    e. none of these.

17. In the transistor amplifier shown
    a. there are no errors.
    b. the bias battery is in backwards.
    c. the collector and emitter are reversed.
    d. the transistor is an NPN unit.
    e. none of these.

18. A principle common to all transistor is that
    a. the collector base is forward biased.
    b. the emitter base is reverse biased.
    c. the collector is positive with respect to the base.
    d. the emitter is positive with respect to the base.
    e. the emitter base bias is forward bias.

19. A transistor can easily be damaged by
    a. forward bias on the emitter.
    b. forward bias on the collector. d. low bias on the emitter.
    c. insufficient excitation.   e. none of these.

20. The part of the atom concerned with current flow is the
    a. outer valence electrons.
    b. nucleus.   d. neutrons.
    c. inner electron shells.   e. none of these.

21. The bias shown is
    a. forward.
    b. reverse.
    c. positive.
    d. negative.
    .e. none of these

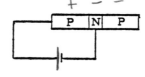

22. If a transistor is heated
    a. the temperature does not change.
    b. the base current decreases.
    c. the collector current increases.
    d. the collector current decreases and then rises.
    e. there is no appreciable effect.

23. The circuit
    a. is correct as drawn.
    b. will not work.
    c. is a common emitter circuit.
    d. is a common collector circuit.
    e. a and c above.

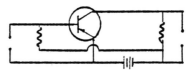

87

17. The plate voltage to the final tube of a broadcast station is 3000 volts. The plate current is 1 ampere. If the antenna resistance is 75 ohms and the antenna current is 6 amperes, the output power is
    a. 2700 watts.
    b. 450 watts.
    c. 500 watts.
    d. 3000 watts.
    e. none of these.

18. Grounded grid amplifiers are often used in high frequency circuits because
    a. they eliminate harmonic generation.
    b. they are good parasitic oscillators.
    c. they eliminate parasitics.
    d. grid neutralization can be used.
    e. they do not have to be neutralized.

19. A two tube class C R.F. amplifier with the grids connected in push pull and the plates in parallel would have an output frequency of
    a. the input frequency.
    b. twice the input frequency.
    c. an odd harmonic of the input frequency.
    d. all of the above.
    e. none of the above.

20. The circuit below is used to
    a. provide pre-emphasis
    b. provide de-emphasis.
    c. match impedance.
    d. generate harmonics.
    e. equalize harmonics.

21. The input to a push pull amplifier is 1000 volts at 3 amperes. If the efficiency factor is 80%, the power output would be
    a. 3000 watts.
    b. 3750 watts.
    c. 4000 watts.
    d. 2400 watts.
    e. none of these.

22. If the gain of A is infinite, the amplification factor is
    a. 17.
    b. 16.
    c. 15.
    d. 6..
    e. infinite.

23. Long sections of wave guides are not placed parallel to the earth in order to
    a. eliminate capacitance between wave guide and ground.
    b. eliminate inductance between wave guide and ground.
    c. eliminate dust and moisture accumulation.
    d. reduce harmonic energy.
    e. accellerate R.F. current flow.

24. The suppressor grid in a vacuum tube
    a. reduces interelectrode capacitance.
    b. is the second element from the cathode.
    c. is usually tied to the cathode.
    d. has a high positive potential with respect to the cathode.
    e. all of the above.

UNIT 11 POWER SUPPLIES

1. Electronic devices are powered, in most cases, by a direct current power source. Since it is easier to generate and distribute alternating current, it is often necessary to change AC to pure DC. In this case, a power supply consisting of a transformer, rectifier, and filter circuit may be called for. This is shown graphically below:

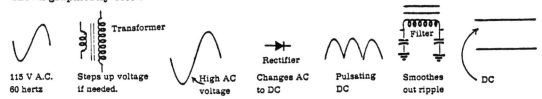

Transformer
115 V A.C.
60 hertz
Steps up voltage
if needed.
High AC
voltage
Rectifier
Changes AC
to DC
Pulsating
DC
Filter
Smoothes
out ripple
DC

Often in the case of a semiconductor the power source is a DC battery. Alternating current is changed to pulsating direct current by a ____________.

17. (rectification)

A+
Buffer
cap

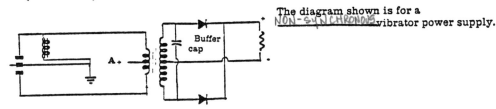

The diagram shown is for a NON-SYNCHRONOUS vibrator power supply.

33. (full, higher, half) A capacitance input filter circuit is shown connected to a full wave power supply.

Typical 8 Henry filter choke
600
V.
LOAD
Filter capacitors
Typical 16 MFD
Bleeder

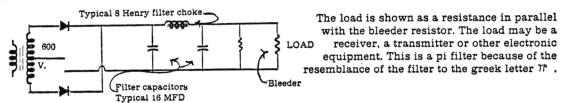

The load is shown as a resistance in parallel with the bleeder resistor. The load may be a receiver, a transmitter or other electronic equipment. This is a pi filter because of the resemblance of the filter to the greek letter π.

It is called capacitance input because a capacitor is closest to the cathodes of the circuit. Now let us see how this circuit filters.

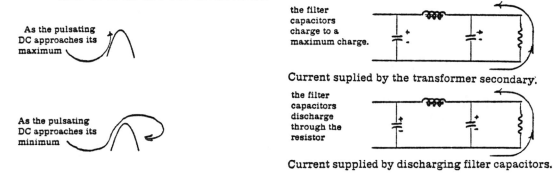

As the pulsating
DC approaches its
maximum

the filter
capacitors
charge to a
maximum charge.

Current suplied by the transformer secondary.

As the pulsating
DC approaches its
minimum

the filter
capacitors
discharge
through the
resistor

Current supplied by discharging filter capacitors.

When a filter capacitor is connected to the rectifier cathode, the filter circuit is said to be a Capacitance input filter.

49. (receiver) 300 volts plus will appear at point 1 as SW1 is ____________ and P. T.T. is ____________.

11. In the diagram below it is unnecessary to use

a. a ground on the cathode.
b. the capacitor in the grid circuit.
c. a ground return on the crystal.
d. the tube.
e. the resistor in the grid circuit.

12. The temperature coefficient of a low T.C crystal is approximately
a. plus or minus 1.
b. plus or minus 2.
c. plus or minus 3.
d. plus or minus 4.
e. plus or minus 5.

13. The circuit shown below is that of a

a. degenerative voltage feedback circuit.
b. neutralized RF amplifier.
c. inverse current feedback.
d. multivibrator.
e. phase shift oscillator.

14. This is a diagram of a/an

a. electron coupled oscillator.
b. grounded grid amplifier.
c. multivibrator.
d. reactance tube modulator.
e. push push amplifier.

15. The circuit shown is a
a. cathode follower.
b. grounded grid amplifier.
c. voltage doubler.
d. degenerative feedback amplifier.
e. frequency doubler.

16. Neutralization is accomplished in the circuit below by using a variable capacitor from

a. a to b.
b. x to y.
c. a to y and b to x.
d. a to x.
e. b to y.

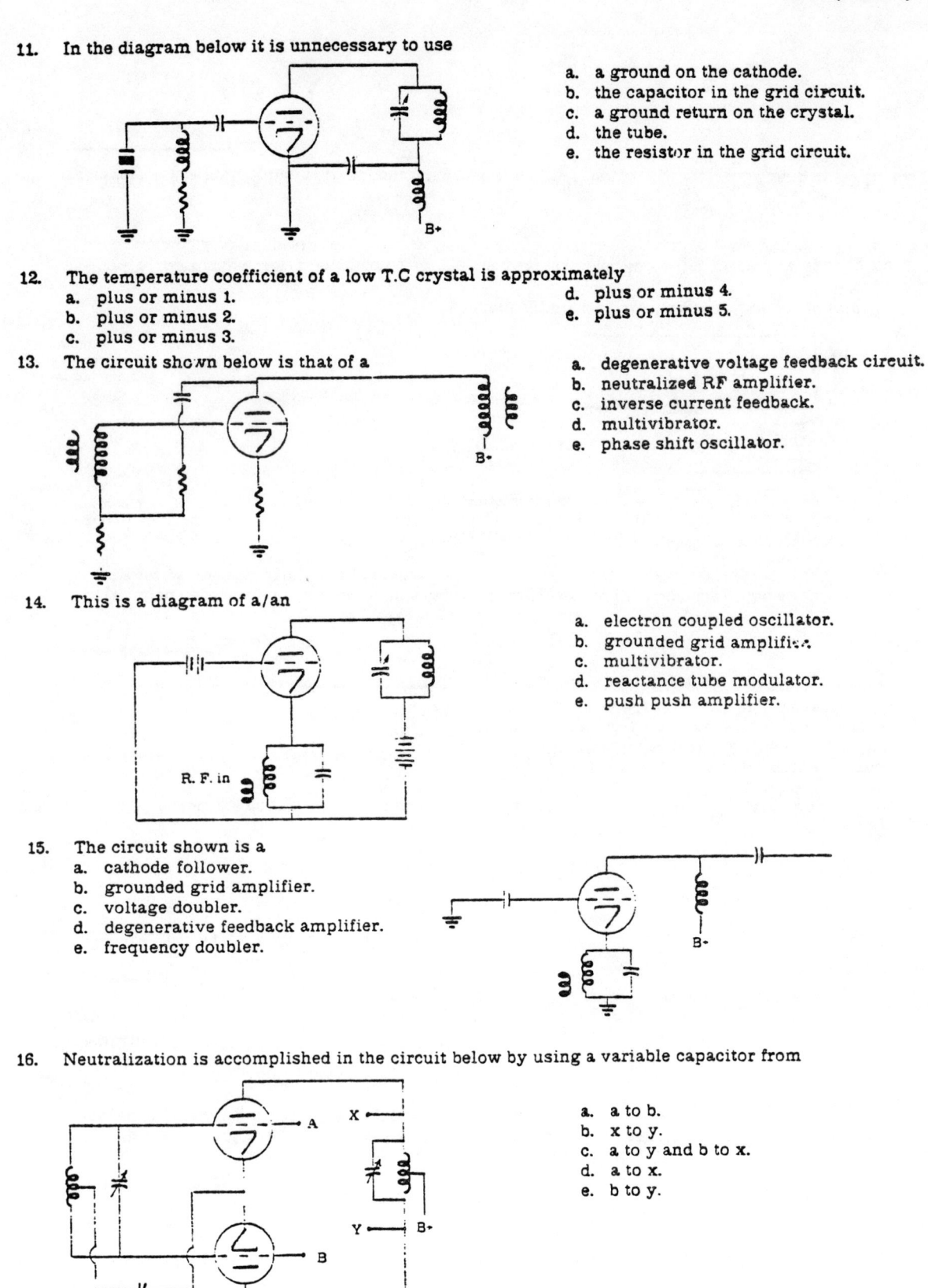

HALF WAVE RECTIFICATION

2. **(rectifier)** The simplest power supply uses a diode to change AC to DC. In some cases, the AC voltage may be stepped up first so the resulting DC voltage is sufficient. Let us look at a half wave circuit using a semiconductor diode rectifier.

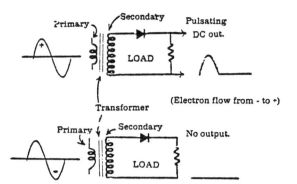

On the positive half cycle of the input, the anode is made positive with respect to the cathode and electrons flow through the load producing a voltage output. Note the PN diode is forward biased.

On the negative half cycle, the PN diode is reverse biased and no current can flow through the diode and load. Therefore, there is no output voltage drop.

Current will flow through a diode when the anode is _POSITIVE_.

18. **(non synchronous)**

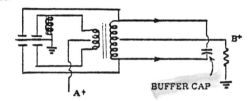

The diagram shown is for a _SYNCHRONOUS_ vibrator power supply.

34. **(capacitance)** The RC time constant must be greater than the period of the ripple cycle to completely fill in the gap during discharge. This means that the resistance of the bleeder must be large enough that the filter capacitors do not discharge too quickly.

Note that the current flow through the bleeder and load is continuous and always in the same direction. The voltage drop may be used to supply a source voltage for transistor and vacuum tube circuits.

The inductance of the choke has a tendency (explained by Lenz's law) to keep the current flowing at a steady rate providing a relatively steady voltage drop across the resistance. The input filter capacitance must withstand the total voltage drop across the series resistance and filter choke. This voltage is the peak supplied voltage. By formula: E peak equals $1.414 \times E_{RMS}$

Since only half of the total secondary voltage is used at any one time, the peak voltage on the input capacitor in this case (see diagram in #33) is 1.414×300 or 424.2 volts.

In a full wave rectifier circuit with capacitance input filter and a total secondary (end to end) voltage of 200 volts, the input filter capacitor should have a minimum voltage rating of _____ volts. The RC time constant of a filter should be ___greater___ than the ripple cycle period.

50. **(closed, closed)** If SW 1 is closed and P.T.T. is open, 300 V will appear at point _____ .

1. Lighthouse tubes are used in UHF transmission because of
   a. the close spacing of the elements.
   b. their high interlectrode capacitance.   d. the wide spacing of the elements.
   c. the high power capabilities.   e. none of these.

2. The ratio of plate current change to grid voltage change is called
   a. amplification factor.
   b. transconductance.   d. stage gain.
   d. plate impedance.   e. impedance.

3. Power losses in a transformer are
   a. hysteresis losses.
   b. Eddy current losses.   d. inductance losses.
   c. I²R losses.   e. a and b and c above

4. The output ripple frequency of a three phase half wave power supply having a 60 Hertz input is
   a. 60 Hertz.
   b. 120 hz.   d. 180 hz.
   c. 240 hz.   e. 360 hz.

5. In a full wave power supply using a center tapped transformer with an end to end voltage of 1,000 volts and two tubes having 15 volt drop across them, the maximum inverse peak voltage occurring on either tube would be about
   a. 985 volts.
   b. 1,400 volts.   d. 2,000 volts.
   c. 707 volts.   e. none of these.

6. Three phase is preferable to single phase in a power supply because
   a. it is more available.
   b. it takes less filter.   d. it can deliver more current.
   c. it takes more tubes.   e. each phase in three phase has a higher voltage.

7. The RMS voltage of a transformer secondary from center tap to one end is 500 volts. If this transformer is used in a full wave power supply using the center tap the input filter capacitor must have a peak working voltage of
   a. 500 volts.
   b. 707 volts.   d. 250 volts.
   c. 1000 volts.   e. 600 volts.

8. In the diagram
   a. the resistor should be removed.
   b. the capacitor in the grid circuit should be removed.
   c. the position of the resistor and the grid capacitor should be interchanged.
   d. the plate should be grounded.
   e. the grid should be connected to B+

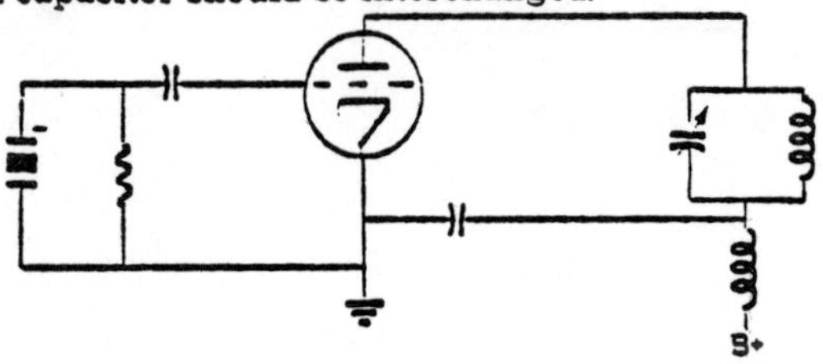

9. The circuit shown below is that of a

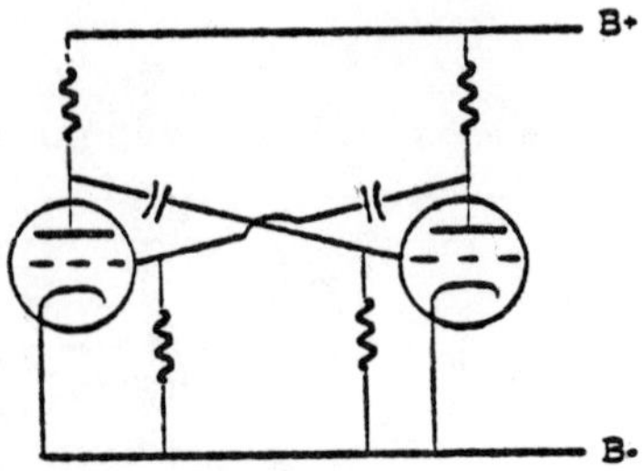

   a. degenerative feedback circuit.
   b. neutralized RF amplifier.
   c. Colpitts oscillator.
   d. multivibrator.
   e. phase shift oscillator.

10. In the triode crystal oscillator shown

    a. the crystal should be in the cathode circuit.
    b. the plate tuned circuit should be grounded.
    c. the capacitor across the crystal should be replaced by a resistor.
    d. the grid should be directly grounded.
    e. there should be no reason this circuit wouldn't work.

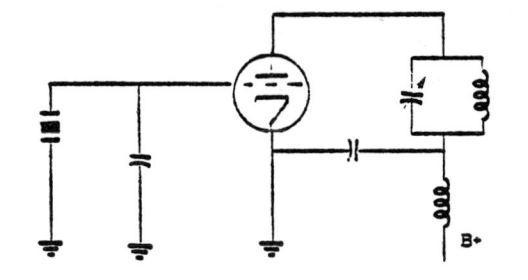

332

3. **(positive)** in a half wave rectifier the input and output ripple frequencies are the same. This is shown in the illustration below:

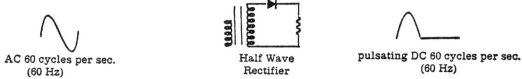

AC 60 cycles per sec.
(60 Hz)

Half Wave
Rectifier

pulsating DC 60 cycles per sec.
(60 Hz)

The vacuum tube diode rectifies on a different principle but with the same end result.

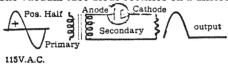

115V.A.C.

When the anode or plate is positive, the negative electrons are drawn from the cathode. This forms a low resistance path for the flow of electrons provided by the induced secondary voltage. Current flow through the load produces a pulsating DC output.

On the next half cycle the plate is negative and repels cathode electrons. Therefore, there is no current flowing through the load and no voltage drop across the load. If the input frequency to a half wave rectifier is 60 cycles per second, the output pulsating DC will have a frequency of_____ cycles per second.

19. **(synchronous)** Another source of AC from DC is provided by a multivibrator. The operation of the multivibrator will be discussed in another unit. The general arrangement is shown below:

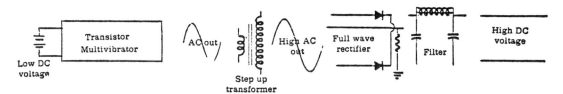

Low DC
voltage

Transistor
Multivibrator

AC out

Step up
transformer

High AC
out

Full wave
rectifier

Filter

High DC
voltage

The transistor oscillator uses the low voltage DC to generate AC. Such a device is called an inverter. Since there are no mechanical movements of parts, this system of deriving high DC voltage from low DC voltage has high efficiency. It is the only modern DC to DC power supply. Multivibrators are used in DC to DC power supplies because they have no_____ and are highly efficient.

35. **(141.4, greater)** Under light load condition with minimum voltage drop across the choke, the output voltage of a capacitance input filter being fed by a full wave rectifier is approximately equal to the peak value of the pulsating DC. This is equal to the peak value of 1/2 the total RMS voltage of the secondary.

An example of a heavy and light load situation might be as shown:

Heavy Load   Light Load

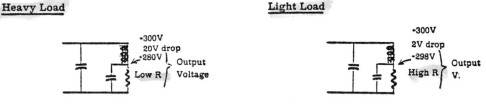

Note a 20 volt drop is shown when
load is heavy (low resistance for load)

Note a 2 volt drop across the choke when
load is light. (high resistance for load)

So the light load output voltage is figured in the same manner as the input filter capacitor voltage rating. But suppose you measured the DC output voltage and wanted to calculate the AC RMS voltage applied to the filter.

If E_{peak} equals 1.414 X E_{RMS} (1/2 total sec. V) then E_{RMS} equals $\frac{E_{peak}}{1.414}$ or .707 X E_{peak}

For example suppose the output voltage of a full wave transistor power supply using capacitance input filter was 12 volts. The RMS voltage input to the filter circuit would be .707 X 12 or 8.49 volts. A full wave rectifier circuit with a capacitance input filter has a DC output of 9 volts. The AC RMS voltage input to the filter would be approximately_____6 0_____volts.

51. **(2)** The P.T.T. switch is used to switch the_____from receiver to transmitter and to switch high voltage (600V plus) to the_____.

UNIT 2 (Part 2)

ACTIVE CIRCUITS REVIEW

Review Units 9, 11, 13, 14, 15, and 25 of Part 1 Second Class Radiotelephone programmed instruction. This is the original programmed writing of the author.

UNIT 2 (Part 2)

RECHECK ACTIVE CIRCUITS REVIEW

Review Recheck Units 9, 11, 13, 14, 15, and 25 of Part 1 Second Class Radiotelephone programmed instruction using Shrader's Electronic Communication Book.

4.   (60) Assuming sine wave input, the waveform output of a half wave rectifier looks like this
_____ .

FULL WAVE DOUBLER

20.   (moving parts) A much used full wave rectifying power supply operating off of commercial AC lines is the full wave doubler. A transformer may be used but usually is not required since the DC output is roughly twice the AC (RMS) voltage input. Note the circuit:

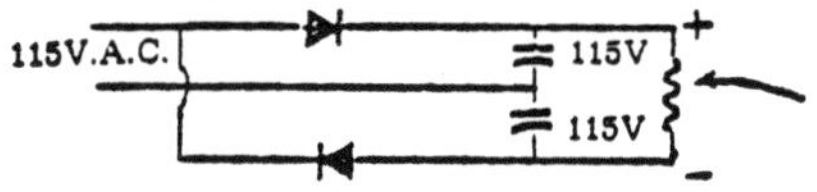

Approximately 230 volts DC when filtered

Let us examine its operation on each half cycle of input.

First: when the top diode anode is positive

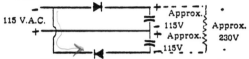

This diode is forward biased and will conduct. The large electrolytic capacitor has a much higher impedance than the diode, so most of the voltage drop is across the capacitor.

Second: When the bottom diode cathode is negative. (on next half cycle).

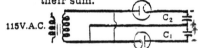

Now the bottom diode is forward biased and conducts. Most of the voltage drop is across the large electrolytic capacitor.

Since the two capacitors are in series and oppositely charged the total voltage delivered to the load is their sum.

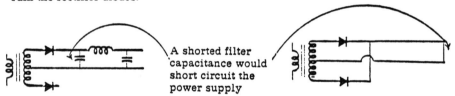

In the voltage doubler diagram shown the polarity of _____C2_____ is reversed.

36.   (6.3 volts) If a filter capacitor shorted out, this would put a heavy load on the power supply and would ruin the rectifier diodes.

A shorted filter capacitance would short circuit the power supply

This would place the entire RMS input voltage (1/2 end to end secondary voltage) across the diodes on alternate half cycles and shortly burn them out. If the diodes were tubes the plates would first get red hot. When a burned out power supply rectifier tube is replaced with a new tube, it is found that it gets red hot. This indicates that there is a shorted _____.

52.   (antenna, transmitter) This concludes Unit 11.

1. Two coils are connected in series so that their fields are out of phase. If L^1 = .8H, L^2 = .5H, and M = .3H, the total inductance would be
    a. .4H.
    b. 1.9H. d. .7H.
    c. .6H.   e. none of these.

2. If two identical coils were placed in series with the fields in phase and with a coefficient of coupling = .5 the total inductance would equal
    a. $4L_1$.
    b. $4 L_2$. d. $3 L_1$.
    c. L_1..   e. none of these.

3. The secondary to primary voltage in a transformer is equal to
    a. the turns ratio.
    b. the turns ratio squared. d. the square root of the turns ratio.
    c. the current ratio.   e. none of these.

4. Two coils are connected in series to that their fields are in phase. If L^1 = .8H, L^2 = .5H, and M = .3H, the total inductance would be
    a. .4H.
    b. 1.9H. d. .7H.
    c. .6H.   e. none of these.

5. Two coils of .4H and .8H are connected in series and are 180 degrees out of phase. If the mutual inductance is .2H the total inductance would be
    a. .4H.
    b. .8H.   d. .32H.
    c. 1.2H. e. none of these.

6. The inductance in the resonant circuit below is
    a. 100 mh.
    b. 200 mh.
    c. 300 mh.
    d. 400 mh.
    e. none of these.

    1.590 KHz

    X_C = 100 Ω

7. Y or admittance is the reciprocal of
    a. susceptance.   d. reactance.
    b. resistance.   e. impedance.
    c. conductance.

8. The total impedance of a .03 microhenry coil connected in series with a .03 microhenry coil without coupling at 200 khz is approximately
    a. 10 ohms.   d. 62 ohms.
    b. .88 ohms.   e. none of these.
    c. 1000 ohms.

9. In the circuit below, the line current would be approximately

    100V   20 Ω   10 Ω 25 Ω

    a. 53.4 ma.
    b. 2.3 amps.
    c. .3 amps.
    d. 7.8 amps.
    e. none of these.

10. In a series RLC circuit the capacitive reactance exceeds the inductive reactance at a certain frequency. It must therefore be concluded that
    a. the current leads the voltage.
    b. the voltage leads the current.   d. the circuit is resonant.
    c. the current and voltage are in phase. e. there is a 90 degree phase displacement.

11. An amplifier has a gain of 30 db and an output of 6 w. If O db = 6 mw the input equals
    a. 10 db.
    b. 20 db. d. .20 db.
    c. 0 db.   e. none of these.

12. A certain amplifier has a 40 db gain. If the output was 9 watts the input would be
    a. 6 mw.
    b. .9 mw. d. 1 watt.
    c. 9 mw.   e. none of these.

13. A 10 db gain is equal to power gain of
    a. 10..
    b. 100.   d. 20.
    c. 3.16. e. none of these.

Full Wave Rectification

5.   (∿) The usual full wave rectifier utilizes both halves of the input cycle to produce an output as shown:

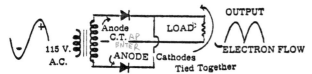

By using a center tap on the secondary of the transformer that is always negative to one anode or the other, current flows through the load on both half cycles of the input.

When the top anode is positive with respect to the center tap, current flow is from the center tap through the load and through the top diode (which is now forward biased). When the bottom anode is positive with respect to the center tap, current flow is from the center tap through the load in the same direction as before and then through the bottom diode (which is now forward biased). Note the output frequency is twice the input frequency:

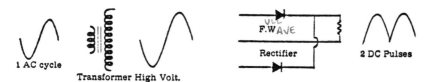

Only half of the transformer secondary voltage is used at any one time. Vacuum tube operation is very similar. If a 60 hertz input is applied to a full wave rectifier, the output ripple frequency will be 120 HZ (double) hertz.

21.   (C₂)

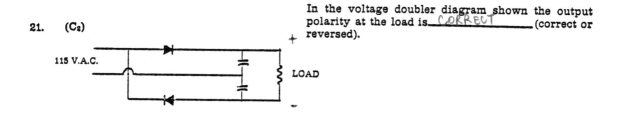

In the voltage doubler diagram shown the output polarity at the load is CORRECT (correct or reversed).

37.   (filter capacitor) To summarize, the features of a capacitance input filter are:
(1) High DC output voltage (up to $1.414 \times E_{RMS}$)
(2) Poor output voltage regulation. The voltage output varies considerable with different load currents.

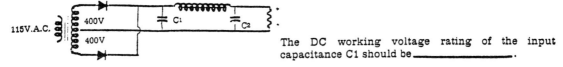

The DC working voltage rating of the input capacitance C1 should be _____ .

UNIT 1 (Part 2)

PASSIVE CIRCUITS REVIEW

Review Units 5, 7, and 8 of the Part 1 Second Class Radiotelephone programmed instruction. This is the original programmed writing of the author.

UNIT 1 (Part 2)

RECHECK - PASSIVE CIRCUITS REVIEW

Review Recheck Units 5, 7, and 8 of Part 1 Second Class Radiotelephone programmed instruction using Shrader's Electronic Communication book.

6.   **(120) Assuming sine wave input, the waveform output of a full wave rectifier looks like this** <u>   </u>

22.   **(correct)**

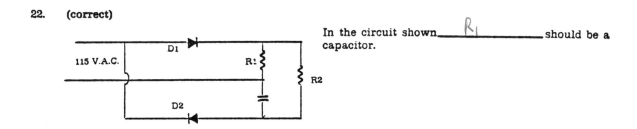

In the circuit shown ____R₁____ should be a capacitor.

38.   **(565 volts)** The output voltage from a choke input filter is .9 of the RMS voltage input to the filter under light loads. In other words the output is filtered to about the average value of the sine wave input. (Eavg equals .9 E(RMS)). One choke input circuit is shown below:

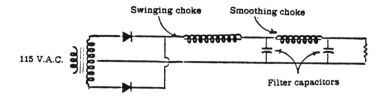

The features of the choke input filter are:
   (1) Low DC output voltage (up to .9 E(RMS)).
   (2) Good steady output voltage - good regulation.
   Output voltage doesn't change much at load under varying load conditions.
A smoothing choke has a low resistance and a comparatively fixed inductance. It steadys the current flow through the load circuit. The voltage drop across this choke is small but it varies under different loads.

The swinging choke is only used in power supplies delivering voltage to circuits where there are large load current variations. For example nearly all power supplies supplying voltage to class B modulators incorporate a swinging choke. This modulator will be discussed in a later unit. The unique property of the swinging choke is that it has an inductance that is inversely proportional to the load current (the inductance swings inversely with load current.) This provides a well regulated DC voltage output. A swinging choke should be used in a power supply for a class B_____.

PART II
THE FIRST-CLASS RADIOTELEPHONE LICENSE

7.   ($\sim$) Because of the center tap arrangement on the secondary, only_____of the secondary voltage is utilized at any one time.

23.   (R1) The full wave power supply using a center tapped secondary only utilized one half of the secondary voltage at any one time. In order to use the full secondary voltage at all times, a full wave...

Bridge Rectifier System
      using 4 diodes must be used. The circuit is as shown:

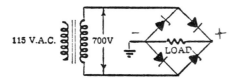

The output DC voltage is around 700 volts depending on the filter. Note there is no secondary center tap.

Now let us trace the circuit on both half cycles of input.

First when the top of the secondary is positive.

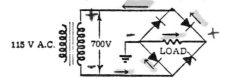

The arrows show the direction of current flow. Current flows into the cathode and out of the anodes of the two diodes that are forward biased on this half cycle.

Second when the bottom of the secondary is positive.

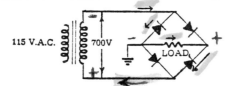

Now the current flows from the top end of the secondary through the two diodes that are forward biased. Most of the voltage drop is across the load.

The bridge rectifier power supply uses a transformer that has a secondary without a _CENTER TAP_

39.   (modulator) The output DC voltage regulation can easily be calculated. By formula:

$$\% \text{ Voltage Regulation} = \frac{E_{no\ load} - E_{load}}{E_{load}} \times 100$$

If there is no load on a power supply minimum current is drawn through the bleeder resistor. The voltage drop across the bleeder at the output is comparatively high because the high bleeder resistance is not shunted by a load.
But when the load resistance is added the high current is drawn through a much lower total parallel resistance resulting in a comparatively low DC voltage output. If the no load voltage is 400 volts and the load voltage is 300 volts, the % regulation is 33 1/3% as shown:

$$\% \text{ Voltage Regulation} = \frac{400 - 300}{300} \times 100 = 33\ 1/3\%$$

A certain power supply delivers 660 volts under no load condition. Under load condition it supplies 600 volts. The % regulation is_____.

294   Night time operation in broadcasting is done in the period of time from
     a. sunset to sunrise.
     b. 6 p.m. to 12 midnight.
     c. sunset to 12 midnight.
     d. 12 midnight to sunrise.
     e. 6 a.m. to 12 noon.

295   Frequency shift keying (F.S.K.) is designated as type
     a. A1 emission.
     b. A3 emission.
     c. A5 emission.
     d. F3 emission.
     e. F1 emission.

296   The magnetron is useful to generate
     a. VLF.
     b. MF.
     c. IF.
     d. SHF.
     e. VHF.

297.   In a traveling wave tube the RF input is applied at
     a. the attenuator.
     b. the cathode end of the helix.
     c. the cathode.
     d. repeller plate.
     e. control grid.

298.   Waveguides are commonly fed energy by
     a. a pick up loop.
     b. a leecher line.
     c. resistors
     d. low frequency generators.
     e. long lengths of open transmission line.

299.   Wave guides may not be used below UHF frequencies because
     a. the capacity is too great.
     b. the inductance is too great.
     c. the resistance is too great.
     d. the size would be prohibitive.
     e. they generate harmonics.

300.   Energy is propagated down a wave guide by
     a. diffussion.
     b. electrostatic fields.
     c. electromagnetic fields
     d. osmosis.
     e. b and c above.

8. (half) It is important to consider the maximum inverse voltage on a diode as an excessive negative voltage on the anode of a diode with respect to its cathode may ruin the semiconductor or tube. The maximum inverse voltage rating of a vacuum tube diode is generally higher than for a semiconductor solid state diode. Let us consider the negative voltage on the top anode when the lower diode is conducting.

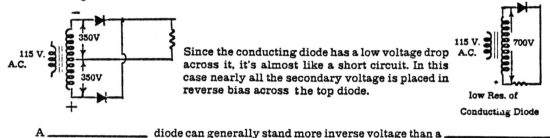

Since the conducting diode has a low voltage drop across it, it's almost like a short circuit. In this case nearly all the secondary voltage is placed in reverse bias across the top diode.

A _____ diode can generally stand more inverse voltage than a _____ .

24. (center tap) Since no center tap is used, the voltage delivered to the rectifiers is just___TWICE___ that delivered to the full wave power supply rectifiers using a transformer with a secondary center tap.

40. (10%) Although the bleeder provides a minimum load to a power supply, the power supply is said to be delivering a no load output with just a bleeder connected. The change in output voltage with the addition of a heavy load (low shunt impedance) is smaller if the bleeder resistance is made smaller. In other words, the % voltage regulation is better - - (low %) if bleeder resistance is used. Besides contributing to better voltage regulation a bleeder serves as a safety device since it will completely discharge the filter capacitors when the power supply is turned off. A service operator working on a power supply disconnected from the AC lines is only safe if a good bleeder resistance is in the circuit. Since there is little noticeable effect if the bleeder resistance is open, the filter capacitors should be discharged by using a screw driver with an insulated handle as an extra precaution. Although electrolytic capacitors are polarized and must not be connected in backwards, bleeders have no positive or negative end. Since there is little effect if the bleeder is open, a service operator should manually_____filter capacitors. Bleeder resistors_____(are or are not) polarized.

282. The paste in a dry cell contains the
    a. positive electrode.
    b. negative electrode.   d. resistance reducing agent.
    c. electrolyte.   e. iron oxide.

283. A discharged battery should be charged as soon as possible because
    a. the electrolytic solution would evaporate.
    b. the electrolyte would be neutralized.   d. the flaking of nickel cadium.
    c. of plate sulphation.   e. polarization sets in.

284. The best check on the charge of a lead acid battery is
    a. by a hydrometer.
    b. by a voltmeter with the battery under a heavy load.
    c. by a short circuit current test.
    d. by a voltmeter with the battery under light load.
    e. none of these.

285. If a battery is charged and the hydrometer reads low
    a. add a salt solution.
    b. add a base solution.   d. acid should be added.
    c. distilled water should be added.   e. alcohol should be added.

286. To change low DC voltage to high DC voltage, one could use a
    a. voltage divider.
    b. dynamometer.   d. capacitor.
    c. dynamotor.   e. dynatron oscillator.

287. A shunt DC generator is illustrated by circuit

288. The speed of a synchronous motor is determined by
    a. the number of fields.
    b. the frequency.   d. the load.
    c. the voltage.   e. the size of wire in the winding.

289. If the field in a shunt motor running without load came open
    a. the motor would stop.
    b. the motor would race.   d. there would be no noticeable effect.
    c. the field would burn out.   e. none of these.

290. The dynamotor output load changes are compensated for
    a. automatically.
    b. by a rheostat in the armature.   d. by a rheostat in the battery lead.
    c. by a rheostat in the field.   e. none of these.

291. The speed of a DC series motor is determined mainly by
    a. its load.
    b. its field strength.
    c. its voltage.
    d. its line frequency.
    e. number of poles.

292. It is necessary to keep radio frequency (R.F.) out of a generator to prevent
    a. harmonic generation.
    b. parasitic oscillations.
    c. eddy currents.
    d. burning out the armature.
    e. none of the above.

293 The experimental period in broadcasting is from
    a. sunset to sunrise.
    b. 6 p.m. to 12 midnight.
    c. sunset to 12 midnight.
    d. 12 midnight to sunrise.
    e. 6 a.m. to 12 noon.

9. **(vacuum tube, solid state)** We are now ready to figure the maximum inverse voltage across the top diode.

1st. We convert 700 volts RMS (effective) to peak value.
Since E peak equals 1.414 x E_{RMS}
E peak equals 1.414 x 700 or approximately 990 volts.

2nd. Since the voltage across the conducting diode is in the opposite direction to the total end to end secondary voltage on this half cycle, we must subtract the voltage from our peak voltage. Let us assume a voltage of 5 volts across the conducting diode.

E (maximum inverse voltage) equals E_{peak} - E diode or
equals 990 - 5 equals 985 volts.

To find the maximum inverse peak voltage on a diode in a full wave circuit multiply the total end to end secondary RMS voltage by_____ and subtract the voltage drop across the conducting diode. The secondary of a center tapped transformer has 500 volts each side of center tap. The voltage drop across either tube when conducting is 15 volts. The maximum inverse voltage rating of either tube should be at least _____ volts.

25. **(twice)** A bridge rectifier uses ___FOUR___ diodes as a minimum.

41. **(discharge, are not)** Better voltage regulation is often provided by use of a <u>gas filled cold cathode voltage regulator tube</u> or a <u>reverse biased Zener diode</u>. Although they operate on different principles, the end result is the same.

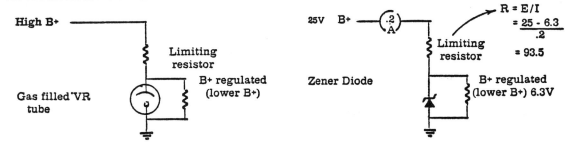

<u>In the VR tube</u>. If the load current changes, the amount of ionization in the VR tube changes. This changes the tube resistance. In effect the tube resistance increases when the load resistance decreases and vice versa. Therefore the parallel resistance of the tube and load remains about the same at all times. This provides a constant voltage drop.

<u>In the reverse biased Zenner diode</u>.

At a certain reverse biased voltage the Zener diode breaks down and conducts. If the voltage is increased the barrier area widens and the diode acts like a capacitor. This capacitance regulates the voltage to the zener voltage. This diode is manufactured by heavy doping at the junction. If the Zener diode and the load resistor drew .4 amperes, the limiting resistance should have a value of approximately _____ ohms.

270. If the frequency of a carrier must be held to within .002 percent, then the meter used to measure the frequency must be accurate to within
    a. .0005%
    b. .002%   d. .001%
    c. .00075%   e. .005%

271. In the diagram shown, the transmission line energy would cause the shorting bar lights to glow
    a. at 1/8 wavelength.
    b. at 1/4 wavelength.
    c. at 3/8 wavelength.
    d. at every even 1/4 wavelength.
    e. none of these.

1/8λ   1/4λ   3/8λ   1/2λ   1λ

272. In calibrating a secondary crystal oscillator standard with WWV it is not necessary to
    a. allow the crystal oscillator to warm up.
    b. tune WWV on a short wave receiver.
    c. turn on the internal BFO oscillator.
    d. beat a 100 kc crystal oscillator harmonic against WWV
    e. adjust a trimmer across the crystal for zero beat.

273. The reading on the vernier below is
    a. 30.2.
    b. 34.2.
    c. 40.5.
    d. 43.
    e. none of these.

274. A 5 Mhz signal is measured accurately as being off frequency 5000 hertz. The percent error in frequency is
    a. .01%
    b. .001%   d. .002%
    c. .02%   e. .1%

275. The carrier frequency of a station is the
    a. oscillator frequency.
    b. buffer frequency.   d. output frequency unmodulated.
    c. output frequency modulated.   e. none of these.

276. A heterodyne frequency meter having a straight line relationship between frequency and dial reading is used to measure the frequency of a station by measuring the second harmonic. If 1,600 Khz appears on the dial at 2,403 and 1,610 Khz appears on the dial at 2,408, the fundamental frequency of a signal on 2,405 would be
    a. 1,602 Khz
    b. 801 Khz   d. 805 Khz
    c. 1,605 Khz e. none of these.

277. The operating frequency of all radio stations is determined by comparison with the signals of station
    a. WWW of the FCC.
    b. WWV of the National Bureau of Standards.   d. WKW of Washington, D.C.
    c. KWK of the National Frequency Control Authority. e. NBS.

278. The electrolyte of a lead acid cell is
    a. hydrochloric acid.
    b. sulphuric acid.   d. lead oxide.
    c. sodium hydroxide. e. sal ammoniac.

279. When a battery is placed in storage it should be
    a. stored in a warm room
    b. drained and the electrolyte replaced with distilled water.   d. packed in ice.
    c. jarred to prevent sulfation.   e. none of these.

280. A 12 volt battery is rated at 100 ampere hours on an 8 hour basis. This battery will deliver
    a. 100 amperes for 1 hour.
    b. 10 amperes for 10 hours.   d. 25 amperes for 4 hours.
    c. 12.5 amperes for 8 hours. e. 100 amperes for 8 hours.

281. An A battery is
    a. a filament battery.
    b. an anode battery.
    c. control grid battery.
    d. screen grid battery.
    e. suppressor grid battery.

10. (1.414, 1399) If the primary voltage in #9 was 100 volts and the secondary voltage was 400 volts each side of center tap, the maximum inverse voltage would be approximately_____volts. The turns ratio primary to full secondary would be 1 to_____.

26. (four)

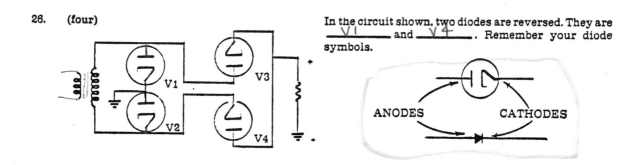

In the circuit shown, two diodes are reversed. They are _____V1_____ and _____V4_____. Remember your diode symbols.

ANODES   CATHODES

42. (46.75) Hot cathode rectifier tubes, filled with gas which ionizes with the application of plate voltage, also provides better voltage regulation at the output. A rectifier tube filled with mercury vapor has almost a constant 15 volt drop across the tube regardless of the load current.

Current flow within the tube is by ion conduction. The student is asked to remember that conduction within a vacuum tube is by electron flow. Using assumed values, compare the voltage outputs of vacuum tube and mercury vapor rectifier systems under the conditions of load and no load.

Vacuum Tube

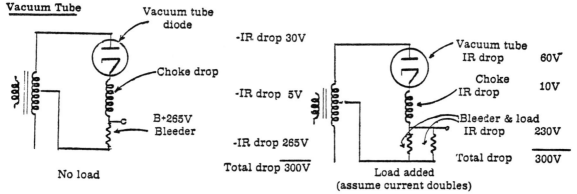

Note - the output dropped 35V under load

Mercury Vapor Tube

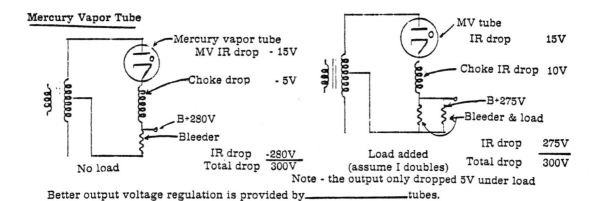

Note - the output only dropped 5V under load

Better output voltage regulation is provided by_____tubes.

258. If a 1/4 wave or 3/4 wave transmission line is shorted on one end, the impedance to the frequency at the other end is like
a. a short circuit.
b. an open circuit.   d. 500 ohms.
c. 600 ohms.   e. none of these.

259. Nitrogen is often used in concentric transmission lines to
a. separate the two lines.
b. radiate a signal.   d. keep moisture out of the lines.
c. produce black light.   e. produce conductivity.

260. A loop antenna used to receive a standard broadcast signal works best if
a. it is a horizontal loop.
b. it is vertical and the plane of the loop is perpendicular to the line of direction of the station.
c. it is a horizontal loop and the plane of the loop is perpendicular to the signal.
d. it is a vertical loop and the plane of the loop is parallel to the line of direction of the station.
e. none of these.

261. The wave form shown is typical of
a. the current on a Hertz half wave antenna.
b. the voltage on a Hertz half wave antenna.
c. the current on a 1/4 wave Marconi antenna.
d. the voltage on a 1/4 wave Marconi antenna.
e. none of these.

262. When the power output of a certain transmitter is 500 watts the antenna current is 7.07 amperes. When the power is raised to 750 watts the antenna current would be
a. 10.5 amperes.
b. 7.07 amperes.   d. 5 amperes.
c. 8.66 amperes.   e. none of these.

263. A loop antenna will receive
a. in all directions when in the horizontal plane.
b. in all directions when in the vertical plane.
c. in a very directive manner to vertical plane when in the horizontal plane.
d. in a very directive manner to horizontal plane when in the horizontal plane.
e. none of these.

264. A signal radiated by a horizontal antenna is best received by a
a. vertical antenna.
b. horizontal antenna.   d. loop stick antenna.
c. loop antenna.   e. Marconi antenna.

265. This circuit is used to
a. eliminate parasitics.
b. reduce harmonics.
c. match impedance.
d. pass harmonics.
e. none of these.

To Antenna

266. At a Marconi antenna the
a. DC resistance between the antenna and ground is near zero.
b. RF resistance between the antenna and ground is near zero.   d. the middle is grounded.
c. top end is grounded.   e. none of these.

267. A good substitute in a coaxial cable for nitrogen gas is
a. hydroflouric gas.
b. liquid oxygen.   d. dry air.
c. carbon dioxide.   e. nitrogen gas.

268. The final stage of a transmitter has a supply voltage of 600 volts. The final plate current is 300 ma. If the antenna resistance is 15 ohms and the antenna current is 3 amperes, the stage efficiency would be
a. 80%
b. 75%   d. 65%
c. 70%   e. 45%.

269. If the antenna ammeter reads 1.4 amperes at a 52 ohm point, the power radiated is
a. 72.8 watts.
b. 101.92 watts.
c. 37.1 watts.
d. 43.4 watts.
e. 26 watts.

11. (1116.8) The voltage ratio of the voltage from center to either end to the full secondary voltage is 1/2 to_____.

27. (V1, V4) It is common practice at Broadcast stations to obtain their high DC voltages for their transmitters by rectifying and filtering AC voltage from a 3 phase source. The circuit for rectifying 3 phase alternating current usually involves 3 transformers and three or six rectifying diodes. This circuit will be dealt with in Element four. Single phase and three phase voltage is shown graphically below:

Single phase   Three phase

There are the following advantages to using 3 phase: A-C

(1) Higher voltage output can be obtained than with single phase. By using the so called Delta Y transformer arrangement, the turns ratio step up of voltage is increased by a factor of $1.73 (\sqrt{3})$

(2) The pulsating DC rectified output has a higher ripple frequency and is easier to filter.
   (a) The 1/2 wave output frequency using 60 hertz input is 180 hertz. (3 times the input frequency)
   (b) The full wave output frequency using 60 hertz input is 360 cycles per second. (6 times the input frequency).

(3) Smaller wires can be used in wiring up the circuit. Less current is carried by each wire.

This ripple output frequency of a three phase power supply would be_____times the supply frequency for a half wave power supply and_____times the supply frequency for a full wave power supply.

43. (mercury vapor or gas) The characteristics of a gas filled rectifier tube are:

(1) Low internal tube resistance.
(2) Low constant voltage drop across the tube - approx. 15V.
(3) High current capabilities.
(4) Provides better output voltage regulation.

Before plate voltage is applied the mercury vapor tube must be_____to proper ionization temperature.

(5) The tube can't stand abuse. A brief overload will ruin tube.
6. The tube will only operate into choke input filters.
(7) Gas filled tubes must be warmed to ionization temperature before use. Filaments must be turned on 60 seconds or so before plate voltage is applied.

248. The circuit shown is a
   a. phase modulation circuit.
   b. electron coupled oscillator.
   c. voltage doubler.
   d. grounded grid amplifier.
   e. bridge power supply.

249. Modulation index defined is
   a. the ratio of the maximum deviation to the modulating audio frequency.
   b. the ratio of the maximum modulating audio frequency to the maximum RF swing.
   c. the product of the maximum RF swing and the modulating audio frequency.
   d. the deviation of the carrier frequency.
   e. none of these.

250. A licensed station in the public safety radio service can be tested
   a. once a month.
   b. when it is installed.   d. 12 midnight to sunrise.
   c. twice a year.   e. anytime the service or regulation of station requires it.

251. A limiter stage in an FM receiver should use
   a. a low mu triode.
   b. a low mu pentode.   d. a high mu pentode.
   c. a high mu triode.   e. a diode.

252. The authorized bandwith of an emission of a public safety station is defined as the width of the frequency band containing
   a. the carrier.
   b. the carrier and the upper sideband.
   c. the carrier and both sidebands.
   d. these frequencies upon which appears 99 percent of the radiated power.
   e. none of these.

253. "Type approval" when applied to equipment indicates that
   a. the manufacturer has submitted data concerning the equipment.
   b. the FCC has conducted tests on the equipment.
   c. the licensee has submitted data concerning the equipment.
   d. none of the above.
   e. the manufacturer approves the design.

254. The principal merit of frequency-modulated transmission is
   a. the reduction of the FM receiver's noise level.
   b. simpler circuits in both the transmitter and receiver.   d. simpler alignment procedures.
   c. the need for less bandwidth.   e. more audio is used.

255. The standing wave ratio on an antenna or transmission line is the ratio of
   a. the maximum voltage to the maximum current.
   b. the maximum current to the maximum voltage.
   c. the maximum voltage to the minimum voltage.
   d. the minimum current to the maximum current.
   e. none of these.

256. A transmitting antenna radiates
   a. an electrostatic field.
   b. an electromagnetic field.
   c. both an electrostatic and an electromagnetic field.
   d. a permanent field.
   e. none of these.

257. At 2 Mhz the antenna field strength is 120 mv per meter. At 4 Mhz it is 1200 microvolts per meter. The attenuation is
   a. 10 db.
   b. 20 db.
   c. 100 db.
   d. 40 db.
   e. none of these.

12. (1) It is interesting to note that there are situations where the AC input to a power transformer must be derived from a battery. At first thought it may appear foolish to go from pure DC to AC and then back to pure DC. However, some electronic equipment, such as a transmitter requires a higher DC voltage than that of a 6 or 12 volt battery. So the practical method is to change DC to AC so that a transformer may be used to step the voltage up. The general arrangement is shown:

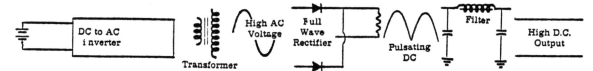

There are three ways of converting low battery DC voltage to high DC voltage. They are:

1. Change low DC to AC with a vibrator, step up the AC voltage with a transformer, and then rectify and filter the high AC voltage for high DC voltage.
2. Change the low DC to AC by applying it as collector voltage to a solid state transistor multivibrator. The AC can then be stepped up, rectified and filtered for high DC voltage. This circuit has no moving parts and is efficient. It is the modern method of changing low DC to high DC voltage.
3. Use the low DC voltage to turn the armature windings of a dynamotor. The moving armature has both a motor and a generator winding. The generated voltage is rectified mechanically by a commutator. This device will be discussed in a later unit.

There are_____common ways of changing low DC voltage to high DC voltage.

28. (3,6) The output ripple frequency of a half wave three phase power supply with a 60 cycle per second input would be__60 x 3__c/p/s.
    180

44. (brought or warmed) The normal voltage drop across a mercury vapor tube is approximately _____volts.

237. In FM broadcasting a frequency swing of plus or minus 60 kc represents a modulation percentage of
   a. 50.
   b. 60.   d. 80.
   c. 75.   e. none of these.

238. If you are aligning a mobile FM receiver with a limiter and discriminator you would first introduce your signal at
   a. the antenna.
   b. 1st IF amplifier.   d. the power amplifier.
   c. the last limiter IF amplifier.   e. the mixer.

239. Interference to an auto radio is produced by
   a. the ignition.
   b. the generator.   d. spark plugs.
   c. tire friction.   e. all the above.

240. For the best signal to noise ratio in FM broadcasting
   a. use greater frequency swing.
   b. use less frequency swing.   d. use split tuning.
   c. use omnidirectional antennas.   e. use none of these.

241. A Foster Seeley discriminator is used for
   a. an AM detector.
   b. producing a negative or positive control voltage.   d. low frequency amplification.
   c. high frequency amplification.   e. rectification.

242. The circuit shown is used for
   a. producing harmonics.
   b. scanning.
   c. injecting capacitance into an oscillator.
   d. reactance tube modulation.
   e. none of these.

243. The frequency tolerance of a public safety fixed base station operating above 50 Mhz is
   a. .0005%.
   b. .002%.   d. .01%.
   c. .003%   e. .02%.

244. The authorized bandwidth for narrow band FM is
   a. 5 Khz.
   b. 10 Khz.   d. 40 Khz.
   c. 20 Khz.   e. 60 Khz.

245. The bandwidth of a station is considered to be that of
   a. the band of frequencies containg 99% of the emitted energy.
   b. the carrier and lower sideband.   d. the carrier.
   c. the carrier and upper sideband.   e. none of these.

246. The AM portion of an FM signal is eliminated by the
   a. limiter.
   b. detector.   d. audio amlifier.
   c. discriminator.   e. sound trap.

247. The first step in tuning an FM mobile transmitter is
   a. apply voltage to final amplifier and tune.
   b. remove voltage from final amplifier and tune oscillator and multipliers.
   c. couple antenna to the final tank circuit.
   d. tune the multipliers to resonance.
   e. none of these.

13. (three)Low DC voltage can be changed to AC by interrupting and reversing the primary current in a transformer by a vibrator. This is done using either a nonsynchronous or synchronous vibrator power supply. Although this is an obsolete method, it is still the subject matter of various F.C.C. examination questions.

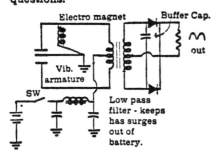

THE NON-SYNCHRONOUS CIRCUIT

As current flows from the negative ground lead of the battery through the electromagnet, the magnetic armature is pulled up. The upper contacts are thus closed shorting out the electromagnet winding. With no magnetic force to hold it, the spring steel armature reed swings back and the bottom contacts are closed, again shorting out the electromagnet winding. As the armature tries to straighten out, the contacts open and current again flows through the electromagnet winding. The cycle then begins all over again. In every case current flows through one half or other of the transformer primary. It is effectively AC as current flows up through one half the primary when the lower contact points are closed and down through the other half when the upper contact points are closed.

The vibrating armature is actually a single pole double throw switch. The low pass filter keeps the high voltage transients out of the positive lead of the battery. If these high voltage surges, caused by rapid switching, were not kept out of the battery lead; other devices such as lights might be burned out.

The secondary rectifying circuit is like other circuits except for the buffer capacitor (across the secondary.) This capacitor absorbs the high voltage transients caused by the rapid switching of the armature contacts. This prevents the vibrator contacts from sparking and burning out.

If the buffer capacitor has undue leakage, the vibrator contacts would slowly burn out. If the buffer capacitor was shorted out, there would be no high DC voltage developed. A buffer capacitor in a vibrator power supply reduces the _____ at the vibrator contact points.

29. (180) The circuit ripple frequency of a full wave three phase power supply with a 60 C.P.S. input would be___60 x 6___c.p.s.

360

45. (15 volts) Gas filled rectifiers require___choke___input filters.

100

227. The deviation ratio for NBFM would normally be
    a. 2.85.
    b. 5.   d. 7.
    c. 1.66.   e. 9.

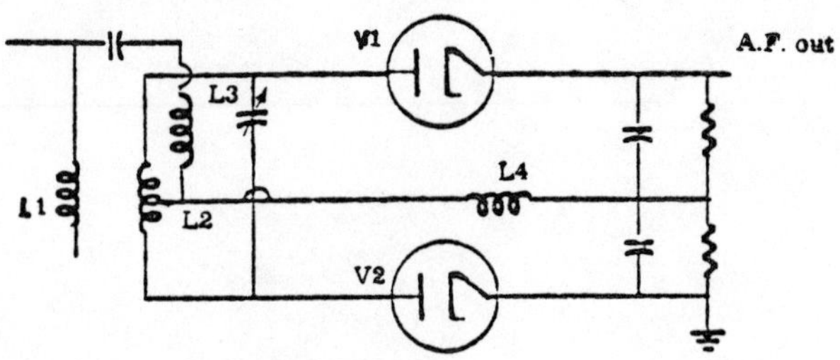

228. In the circuit shown below
    a. V1 is reversed.
    b. V2 is reversed.
    c. L3 is superfluous.
    d. V1 should be a triode.
    e. the grounding is wrong.

229. A reactance tube modulator changes the frequency of an oscillator by
    a. changing oscillator grid resistance.
    b. changing the oscillator plate voltage.
    c. injecting inductive or capacitive reactance in the oscillator tuned circuit.
    d. changing the oscillator cathode voltage.
    e. none of these.

230. Pre-emphasis is used in FM broadcasting to
    a. give extra amplification to audio frequencies above 2,000 cycles.
    b. attenuate audio frequencies above 2,000 cycles.   d. detect FM signals.
    c. modulate the oscillator.   e. provide phase inversion.

231. The maximum permitted power output for a Public Service base station is
    a. 3 watts.
    b. 60 watts.   d. 2,000 watts.
    c. 1,000 watts.   e. 5,000 watts.

232. A 25 khz frequency deviation of an RF signal caused by a 5 khz audio tone represents a deviation ratio of
    a. 1 2/3.
    b. 5.   d. 6.
    c. 10.   e. 75.

233. In both AM and FM transmitters, the % modulation is determined by the
    a. amplitude of the audio.
    b. frequency of the audio.   d. type of antenna used.
    c. frequency response.   e. RF frequency.

234. The circuit shown below is the circuit of a
    a. peak limiter.
    b. FM discriminator.
    c. ratio detector.
    d. voltage doubler.
    e. squelch system.

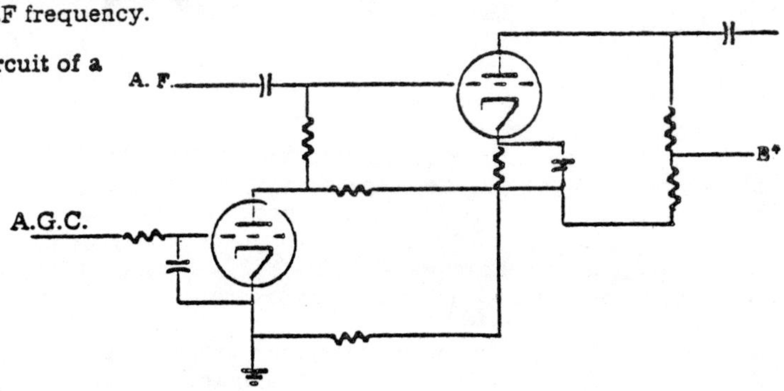

235. The circuit shown below is used for
    a. modulation.
    b. pre-emphasis.
    c. de-emphasis.
    d. voltage doubling.
    e. rectification.

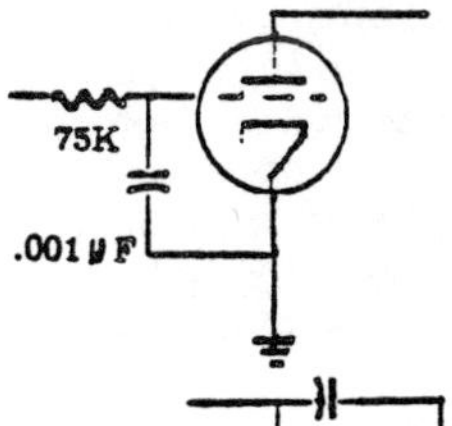

236. In the circuit shown below
    a. V1 is reversed.
    b. V2 is reversed.
    c. L3 should be replaced by a conductor.
    d. V1 should be a triode.
    e. none of these.

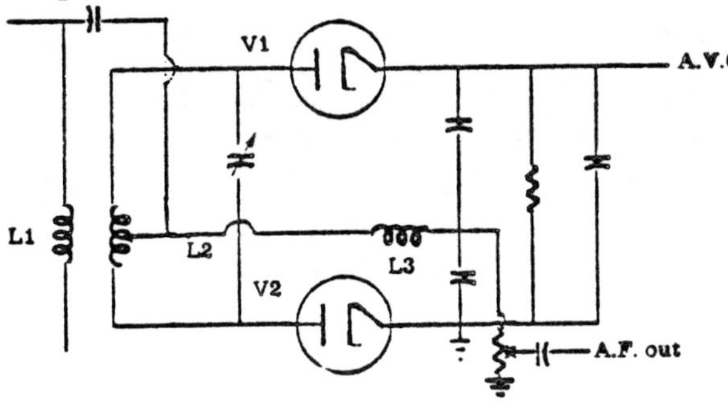

14. **(sparking)** If the buffer capacitor developed a partial short (undue leakage) the vibrator contact points gradually would ___BURN OUT___.

30. **(360)** Three advantages of a three phase rectifying power supply system are: The pulsating DC output is easier to ___FILTER___, higher output ___VOLTAGES___ can be obtained, and ___SMALLER___ wires can be used to carry the current.

Mobile Power Supply Circuits

46. **(choke)** It's quite usual today for mobile installations to use **balanced bridge** power supplies. This power supply is like the bridge power supply except a center tap is used on the secondary to obtain a voltage that is just one half the higher voltage taken between cathodes and anodes. Transmitter and receiver high voltages can both be derived from this single circuit. See below:

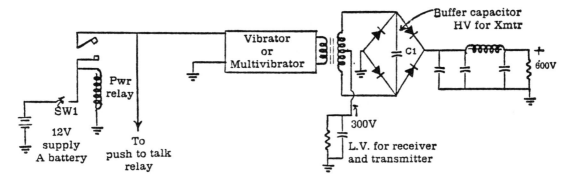

By using a center tap connection a lower voltage for receiver operation is obtained. When switch SW1 is turned on, the power relay is actuated to provide 12 volts for the power supply and for the push to talk switching relay. The push to talk switch is located on the microphone and is used to switch the antenna from receiver to transmitter and to switch high voltage from receiver to transmitter.
If the buffer capacitor ___C1___ was shorted out, this would short circuit the entire transformer secondary and there would be no output voltages.

216. The main disadvantage of the use of squelch circuit in a receiver is
    a. it can only be used with FM.
    b. weak signals interfere with strong signals.
    c. weak signals can't be received.
    d. there is objectionable background noise when no signal is received.
    e. the efficiency is poor.

217. The circuit shown below is that of a
    a. multivibrator.
    b. pentagrid converter.
    c. push push amplifier.
    d. push pull amplifier.
    e. dynatron oscillator.

218. In a superheterodyne receiver, the tuned signal is 1,500 Khz. The local oscillator is operating at 1,950 Khz. The image would be
    a. 1,500 Khz
    b. 1,950 Khz   d. 2,400 Khz
    c. 1,050 Khz   e. 2,850 Khz

219. A super regenerative receiver has
    a. low sensitivity.
    b. high sensitivity.   d. triple conversion.
    c. high selectivity.   e. images.

220. Radio telephone receivers with an oscillator operating near the IF frequency would be receiving
    a. MCW.
    b. CW.   d. FM.
    c. television.   e. standard broadcast.

221. An example of good tone control is

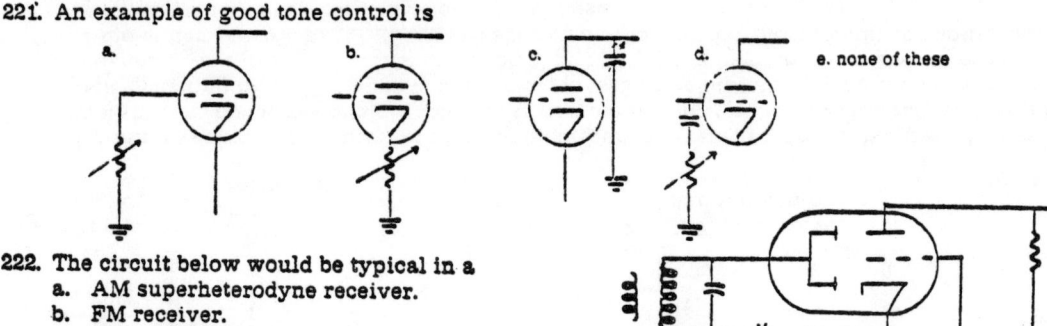

e. none of these

222. The circuit below would be typical in a
    a. AM superheterodyne receiver.
    b. FM receiver.
    c. TRF receiver.
    d. super regenerative receiver.
    e. AM transmitter.

223. A duo triode is
    a. in fact equivalent to two triodes in one envelope.
    b. used for halfwave rectification.
    c. used for a second detector.
    d. used as an RF amp.
    e. used as an AF amp.

224. When a stronger signal is tuned in a radio receiver, the AVC voltage
    a. goes high positive.
    b. goes low positive.   d. goes low negative.
    c. goes high negative.   e. goes to zero.

225. There is some noise level in a battery powered receiver because of
    a. unfiltered power supply A.C.
    b. the inherent noise level in each stage.   d. low Mu diodes.
    c. contact potential.   e. none of these.

226. If the grid return in a plate detector stage is made to the plus terminal instead of the negative termin of the bias battery, the
    a. bias is reduced.
    b. bias is increased.   d. the supply voltage to the plate increases.
    c. Ip decreases.   e. operation is normal.

15. **(burn out)** This choke in the battery lead serves to keep_____out of the battery leads.

31. **(filter, voltages, smaller)** The function of filter circuits is to smooth out the ripple, changing pulsating DC from the rectifier to pure DC as shown:

Half wave single phase.
    Large gaps must be
    filled in by filter

Pulsating DC

Filtered

High DC voltage

Full wave single phase
    Smaller gaps must be
    filled in by filter.

Pulsating DC

Filtered

High DC Voltage

Half wave three phase.
    Very small gaps must be filled in
    by filter.

Pulsating DC

Filtered

high DC voltage

The function of the filters to smooth out the____RIPPLE_____.

47. **(C1)**

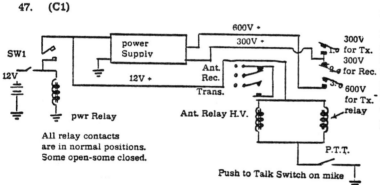

All relays operate from the 12V battery. Both 12 volts plus and minus must be present at a relay before it is activated. The negative side of the battery is permanently connected to the low voltage power relay. The positive side of the battery is connected by SW 1 to the low voltage power relay which in turn connects 12 volts positive to the antenna and H. V. relay.

With SW 1 open and PTT open - The power supply is turned off. The antenna is connected to the receiver. **With SW 1 on and PTT open (off)** - The power supply is on. The antenna and HV relays are not activated as the PTT is open. The antenna is still connected to the receiver. 300 volts + appears at point 2. **With SW1 closed and PTT closed** The power supply is on. The antenna and HV relays are activated. The antenna is disconnected from the receiver and connected to the transmitter. At point 1 there is 300V+ for the transmitter. At point 3 there is 600V+ for the transmitter. There is no voltage at point 2.

    The negative side of the battery is connected to the antenna and high voltage relays by the _____ switch.

204. In AM broadcasting 75% modulation would cause the antenna current to increase about
    a. 12.2%.
    b. 13.0%. d. 22.5%.
    c. 15.0%. e. 75.0%.

205. One hundred percent modulation is indicated by

206. A DC meter in a modulator plate circuit shows large variations. This is probably due to
    a. class A amplifier operation.
    b. class B amplifier operation. d. insufficient audio excitation.
    c. overmodulation. e. insufficient RF excitation.

207. If the first speech amplifier was overdriven, but the transmitter was not overmodulated, the output would be
    a. distorted.
    b. normal. d. lacking harmonics.
    c. undermodulated. e. rectified.

208. A crystal microphone is easily damaged by
    a. temperatures below 70 degrees F.
    b. shouting. d. excessive dryness.
    c. high temperatures. e. all the above.

209. A carbon mike is
    a. sensitive to high temperatures.
    b. a high impedance device. d. a high fidelity mike.
    c. subject to granule packing with exposure to moisture. e. little used today.

210. The bandwidth of an AM broadcast station is equal to
    a. half the modulating audio frequency.
    b. the modulating audio frequency.
    c. the carrier frequency.
    d. the carrier frequency plus the modulating audio frequency.
    e. twice the modulating audio frequency.

211. To prevent d nage to a crystal mike, it is necessary to
    a. keep it clean.
    b. keep it at room temperature. d. use high Z inputs.
    c. use low Z inputs. e. keep it out of the direct sunlight.

212. In a suppressed carrier SSB transmission
    a. one sideband and the carrier are used.
    b. two sidebands and the carrier are mixed and a frequency multiplier are used.
    c. frequency division is used in the final.
    d. two sidebands and no carrier are used.
    e. only one sideband is transmitted.

213. The ratio of the audio power to the input power of the final stage in 100% sinusiodal plate modulation is
    a. 25%.
    b. 30%. d. 100%.
    c. 50%. e. 200%.

214. Amplitude modulation for standard broadcast is maintained at
    a. 70%.
    b. 50%. d. 110%.
    c. 85%. e. none of these.

215. The circuit shown is used for
    a. plate modulation.
    b. grid modulation.
    c. cathode modulation.
    d. screen modulation.
    e. plate & screen modulation

16.   (hash voltage transients or surges)

Synchronous Vibrator Power Supply

This vibrator has an added set of contacts for mechanical rectification. The primary circuit operates in the same manner as before. The secondary voltage is mechanically switched by the second set of vibrator points so that the secondary center tap is always positive to which ever end of the secondary winding is grounded at the moment.

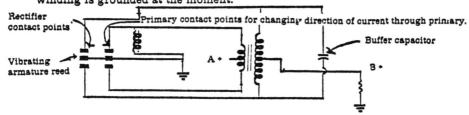

The synchronous vibrator power supply uses a second set of vibrator contact points for mechanical

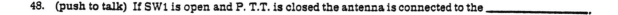

32.   (ripple) It is apparent that low frequency ripple (half wave single phase rectified DC) has large gaps to be filled in. Full wave single phase rectification results in twice the ripple frequency and smaller gaps have to be filled in by filter. Therefore, the higher ripple frequency is desirable as such an output is easier to filter. If the ripple frequency is not important half wave rectification should be used as such a circuit takes fewer parts. There are a few electronic circuits that do not require pure DC, such as a battery charger. In summary, it is easier to filter rectifier outputs having higher ripple frequencies.

Some recent power supply equipment converts 3 phase to 12 phase before rectification. The rectifier output of this supply requires very little filter. The output of a_____FULL_____wave rectifier is easier to filter because of its_____HIGHER_____ripple frequency.

If the ripple frequency was not important as a consideration it would be more economical to use a _____HALF_____ wave rectifier.

48.   (push to talk) If SW1 is open and P. T. T. is closed the antenna is connected to the _____.

191. The grid bias to the second stage is
    a. grid leak biasing.
    b. cathode resistor biasing.   d. supplied by a battery or power supply.
    c. contact potential biasing.   e. none of these.

192. If the excitation fails
    a. there is no grid leak bias to the second stage.
    b. there is no grid leak bias to the final stage.   d. the crystal will oscillate.
    c. the final tube has no protection and would burn out.   e. M6 would read high.

193. The type of coupling shown is

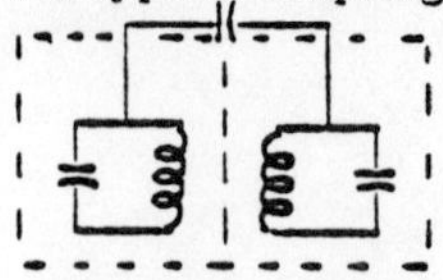

    a. inductive.
    b. capacitive.
    c. shielding.
    d. interelectrode.
    e. none of these.

194. A dummy antenna is constructed by use of
    a. a series choke and resistance.
    b. a parallel capacitance and resistor.   d. suitable resistors from 1 to 10 megohms.
    c. a small loop of wire.   e. a capacitor and resistor in series.

195. In a certain transmitter the final plate current was zero, the buffer plate current was zero, but the crystal oscillator plate current was higher than normal. This indicated
    a. self oscillation.
    b. parasitics.   d. excessive RF drive.
    c. a cracked crystal.   e. defective plate current meters.

196. Carbon resistors are preferred in transmitter power supplies as bleeder resistors because
    a. a wire wound resistor has inductance
    b. carbon is a poor conductor.   d. wire wound resistors tend to open or short out.
    c. carbon fuses.   e. none of these.

197. As doubler tank circuits are tuned through resonance, the plate current
    a. changes from maximum to minimum to maximum.
    b. changes from minimum to maximum to minimum.   d. is unaffected.
    c. goes to zero.   e. none of these.

198. The carrier frequency of a transmitter is the frequency of the
    a. oscillator.
    b. buffer.   d. output at zero % modulation.
    c. doubler.   e. none of these.

199. A buffer R.F. amplifier is used to
    a. shape a signal into a sine wave.
    b. provide a stable load for the oscillator.   d. generate parasitic oscillations.
    c. generate harmonics.   e. generate noise.

200. A buffer amplifier is used to
    a. improve the efficiency of an RF thermocouple.
    b. decrease the amplifier output.
    c. riase the Q of the oscillator.
    d. improve the frequency stability of the oscillator stage.
    e. multiply the frequency of the oscillator.

201. The percent modulation shown in the diagram be
    a. 100.
    b. 50.   d. 80.
    c. 75.   e. 54.

    Carrier
    5 units pp

    Modulated wave envelope
    7.7 units pp

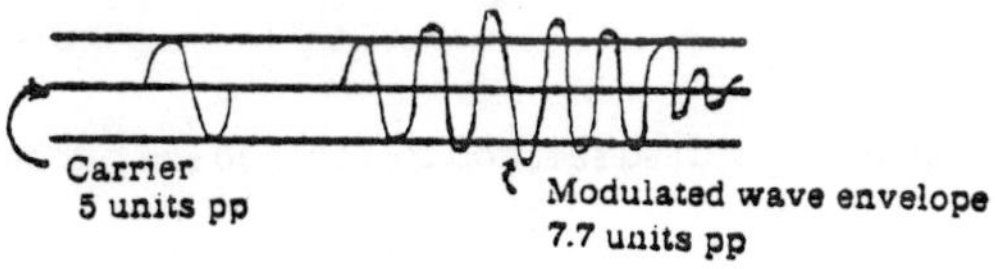

202. An RF linear amplifier can be operated in class B service with little or no distortion because of
    a. parasitic oscillations.
    b. flywheel effect.
    c. push-push operation.
    d. class C bias.
    e. none of these.

203. The block diagram below is that of a
    a. FM transmitter.
    b. SSB transmitter.
    c. AM transmitter.
    d. regenerative receiver.
    e. phase detector.

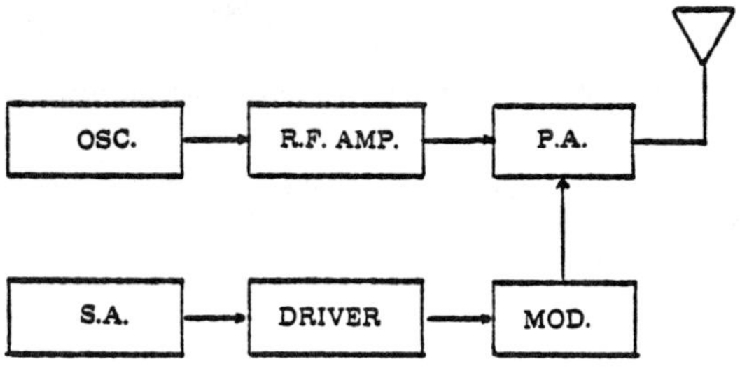

Recheck Programmed Instruction Using Shrader's Electronic Communication

1.   Power supplies usually convert AC to _____. Sec. 11-1.

CHAPTER 11 POWER SUPPLIES

7.   **(there are no mistakes)** The voltage ratio of the voltage from center tap to either end to the full secondary voltage is 1/2 to _____ . Sec. 11-4.

13.   **(141 volts)** Full wave rectification results in a higher ripple frequency and is easier to_____ .

19.   **(resistor)** A filter choke should have_____DC resistance. Sec. 11-12.

25.   **(warmed up)** This is done by turning the filament voltage on first. A mercury vapor rectifier system requires a _____ input filter. Sec. 11-5.

31.   **(120 Hz)** The ripple frequency output of a 3 phase 1/2 wave rectifier with a 60 hertz input is _____hertz and the ripple frequency output of a 3 phase full wave rectifier with 60 hertz input is _____hertz. Sec. 11-18.

37.   **(full load)** A low voltage power supply using a Zener diode for a regulator, has a 12 volts regulated output. If the maximum current through a dropping resistor from a supply voltage of 20 volts is 20 ma, the resistance should have a value of _____ . Sec. 11-25.

43.   **(efficient)** The output voltage of a three phase system using a Delta Y arrangement may be _____ per cent higher than the turns ratio of the transformers might indicate. Sec. 11-32.

49.   **(2)** 600 volts is applied to the transmitter when SW1 is closed and PTT is _____. See frame 47.

180. The oscillator of a transmitter uses a 2 Mhz crystal having a temperature coefficient of 10 cycles per degree centigrade per megacycle. The output frequency is normally 24 Mhz. When the crystal temperature changes 20 degrees C the output carrier frequency would be
    a. 24,000.4 Mhz.
    b. 23,999.6 Khz.   d. 23.9 Mhz.
    c. 24,000.4 Khz.   e. 24,004.8 Khz.

181. Telegraphy by frequency shift keying without the use of modulating audio frequency (FSK) is symbolized by
    a. F1.
    b. A3.   d. F3.
    c. A2.   e. A1.

182. Shields are used in RF circuits in order to
    a. reduce parasitic oscillation.
    b. reduce harmonic generation.   d. radiate energy.
    c. prevent unwanted coupling.   e. provide a heat sink.

183. In an RF amplifier the Ig is 5 ma, the Ip 30 ma, the supply voltage is 300 volts and the grid bias 40 volts. The value of the grid leak resistor would be
    a. 4,000 ohms.
    b. 6,000 ohms.   d. 10,000 ohms.
    c. 8,000 ohms.   e. none of these.

184. A buffer RF amplifier is used to
    a. shape a signal into a sine wave.
    b. isolate the final RF amplifier from the oscillator.   d. generate parasitic oscillations.
    c. generate harmonics.   e. generate noise.

185. In a grid leak biased RF amplifier the tube is easily harmed by
    a. too high plate current.
    b. too high screen current.
    c. too high grid current.
    d. too high cathode resistance.
    e. none of these.

186. If the 1,000 Khz crystal was inoperative
    a. M1 would read low.
    b. M2 would read high.   d. M5 would read low.
    c. M3 would read high.   e. none of these.

187. If C1 was shorted out
    a. M1 would read low.
    b. M2 would go to zero.   d. M5 would read low.
    c. M3 would read high.   e. M6 would read high.

188. If C3 was open
    a. M2 would read zero.
    b. M3 would read zero.   d. M6 would read zero.
    c. M5 would read high.   e. all of the above statements are true.

189. If the final plate was shorted to the final grid
    a. M1 would read zero.
    b. M2 would read zero.
    c. M4 would pin backwards.
    d. M6 would read high.
    e. none of these.

190. If the C- of the second tube shorted to ground
    a. M3 would read high.
    b. M3 would read zero.
    c. M4 would read high.
    d. M6 would read high.
    e. none of these.

2. (DC) Current will flow through a vacuum tube or semiconductor diode if the anode is _____ with respect to the cathode. Sec. 11-2.

8. (1) This circuit is capable of producing two separate rectified voltages, one is _____ the voltage of the other. Sec. 11-5.

14. (filter) The output of a capacitive input filter under light loads is equal to the peak voltage and under medium loads roughly_____ % of the peak value. Sec. 11-8.

20. (low) Swinging chokes are used in_____where there are large load variations such as required by a class B modulator. (to be discussed in a later unit). Sec. 11-13.

26. (choke input) Mercury vapor tubes can pass a relatively high _____. Sec. 11-5.

32. (180, 360)   The polarity of_____
                                                 is reversed. Sec. 11-22.

38. (400 ohms) In Figure 11-36 C² is the _____capacitor. It is used to reduce the sparking at the _____contacts. Sec. 11-30.

44. (73%) The three phase power supply can be wired with smaller wires since the load is distributed into more circuit conductors. Because of the higher ripple frequency 3 phase rectified current is easier to _____ . Sec. 11-32.

50. (closed) The push to talk switch is used to switch the_____ and the_____ . See frame 47.

169. In the circuit below it would be necessary to
    a. remove L5.
    b. remove C2.
    c. replace L1 with a conductor.
    d. remove L2.
    e. none of these.

170. When the RF final amplifier is turned through resonance the grid meter peaks. The peaking indicates
    a. overmodulation.
    b. insufficient RF excitation.   d. over excitation.
    c. the stage is not neutralized.   e. under modulation.

171. The strongest harmonic in the output of a push pull RF amplifier is the
    a. second.
    b. third.   d. fifth.
    c. fourth.   e. sixth.

172. The screen grid dropping resistor in an IF amplifier circuit is burned out. It is known that the screen grid voltage should be 250 volts, the screen grid current 5 ma, and that the plate voltage should be 300 volts. The value of the screen grid dropping resistor should be
    a. 5 K ohms.
    b. 10 K ohms.   d. 20 K ohms.
    c. 15 K ohms.   e. none of these.

173. Grid leak bias works because
    a. the grid attracts electrons.
    b. the grid repels electrons.   d. it has very low resistance.
    c. it has infinite resistance.   e. none of these.

174. Grid leak bias is developed
    a. in the plate circuit.
    b. in class A amplifiers.   d. in the cathode circuit.
    c. using battery or power supply bias.   e. by use of proper time constant in the grid circuit.

175. The wavelength of a 500 Mhz signal is
    a. 60 cm.
    b. .5 cm.   d. 1 meter.
    c. .06 cm.   e. none of these.

176. As compared to a Class A amplifier, a Class C amplifier
    a. has less distortion.
    b. requires less driving power.
    c. operates over the linear portion of its characteristics curve.
    d. operates over a greater part of its characteristic curve.
    e. has less efficiency.

177. If in an amplifier the grid current is .003 A, the grid voltage is 6 volts, the plate current is 40 ma, the plate voltage is 275 volts, and the plate dissipates 9 watts; the output power is
    a. 18.6 watts.
    b. 82.3 watts.   d. 2 watts.
    c. 10 watts.   e. 20 watts.

178. One harmonic of 480 khz is
    a. 500 Khz.
    b. 900 Khz.   d. 2400 Khz.
    c. 240 Khz.   e. 3250 Khz.

179. The circuit below is
    a. push pull amplifier.
    b. push push frequency doubler.
    c. an audio frequency amplifier.
    d. a voltage doubler.
    e. none of these.

3. **(positive)** Current flows through the load in a half wave rectifier when the_____of the diode rectifier is positive. The output waveform looks like this _____ . Sec. 11-3.

9. **(half or twice)** During the nonconductive half cycle in a half wave rectifier, the load current comes from the _____ Sec. 11-6.

15. **(85%)** A low voltage power supply with a capacitive input filter is used under light load conditions. It's DC output is 9 volts. The AC input (RMS) is approximately_____ volts. Sec. 11-8.

21. **(power supplies)** The inductance of a swinging choke is _____ proportional to the load current. Sec. 11-13.

27. **(current)** A center tapped full wave rectifier system using mercury vapor tubes has a secondary voltage of 400 volts each side of center tap. The approximate maximum inverse voltage that will be applied to either tube is _____. Sec. 11-16.

33. **(C_2)**

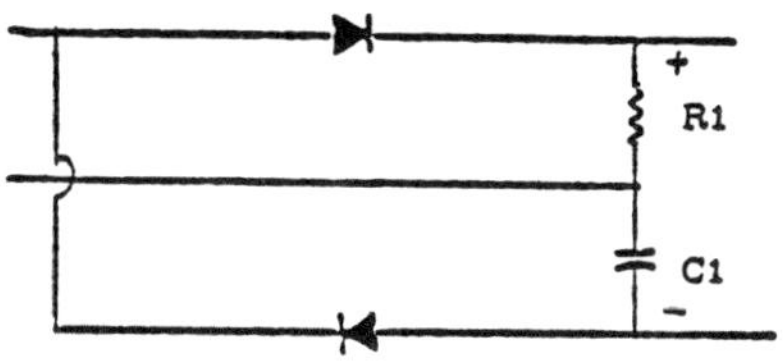

The component _____should be replaced by a_____ . Sec. 11-22.

39. **(buffer, vibrator)** In Fig. 11-36, C_1 and the RFC are used to reduce and intereference known as _____ . Sec. 11-30.

45. **(filter)** Usually filter capacitors are either across the load or across a series circuit consisting of the load and a filter choke. Therefore, a shorted filter capacitance puts a heavy load on the rectifier tube. In the case of a vacuum tube rectifier tube, a shorted filter would cause the plates to glow red hot. In the case of a mercury vapor rectifier tube, the gas would turn intensely blue green and the tube would quickly burn out. Red hot plates in a vacuum tube rectifier usually indicates a _____ filter capacitor.

51. **(antenna, high voltage)** This concludes the recheck.

162. If 3 cycles are complted in 1/50 of a second the frequency is
   a. 250 cycles/second.
   b. 150 hz.
   c. 167 hz.
   d. 50 hz.
   e. 100 hz.

163. In the diagram below it would be necessary to
   a. remove L5.
   b. remove C2.
   c. replace L3 with a conductor.
   d. replace C1 with a conductor.
   e. neutralize the amplifier.

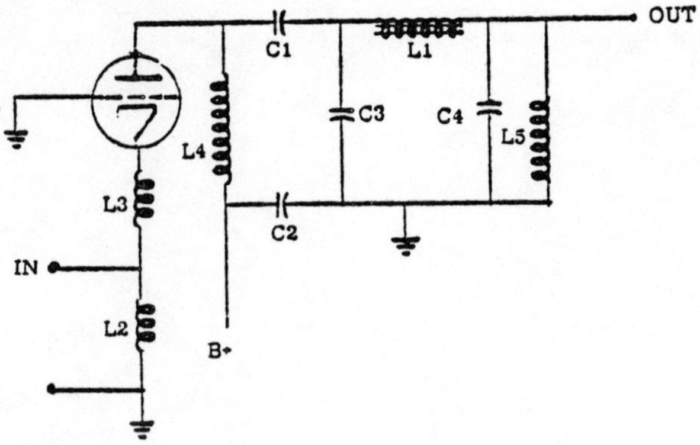

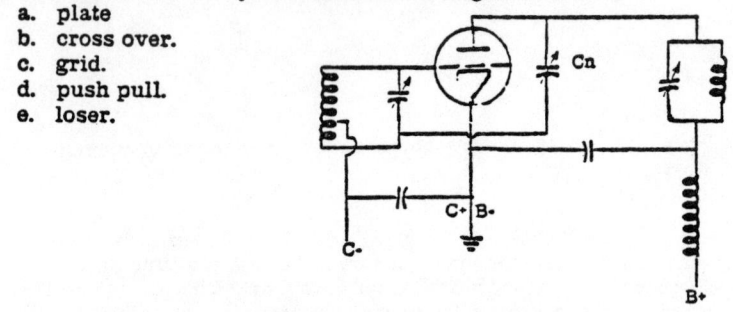

164. The neutralization system used in the diagram below is
   a. plate
   b. cross over.
   c. grid.
   d. push pull.
   e. loser.

165. In the diagram below the screen grid connection is
   a. correct.
   b. wrong, it should be conneced to cathode.
   c. wrong, it should be connected to plate.
   d. wrong, it should be connected to an SG plus voltage.
   e. wrong, it should be connected to the suppressor.

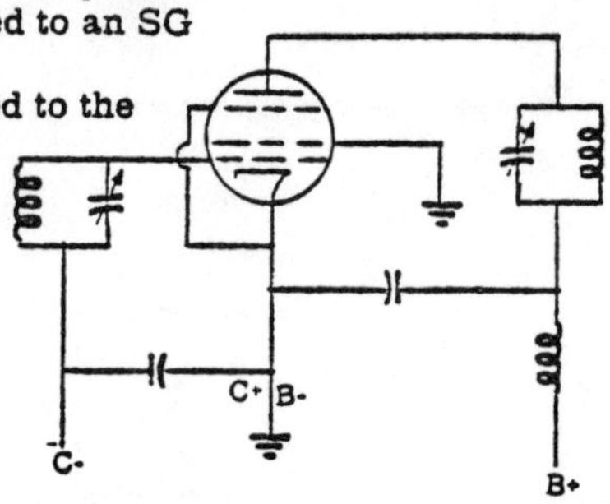

166. A single ended class C RF stage is used for
   a. voltage dividers.
   b. harmonic reduction.
   c. a multivibrator.
   d. a frequency doubler.
   e. push pull operation.

167. If the grid is not driven positive in a class C amplifier,
   a. there is no grid excitation.
   b. the grid excitation is low.
   c. the grid excitation is high.
   d. the bias will be too high.
   e. it will draw current.

168. The circuit below is used for
   a. push push amplification.
   b. push pull amplification.
   c. parallel operation.
   d. all the above.
   e. none of these.

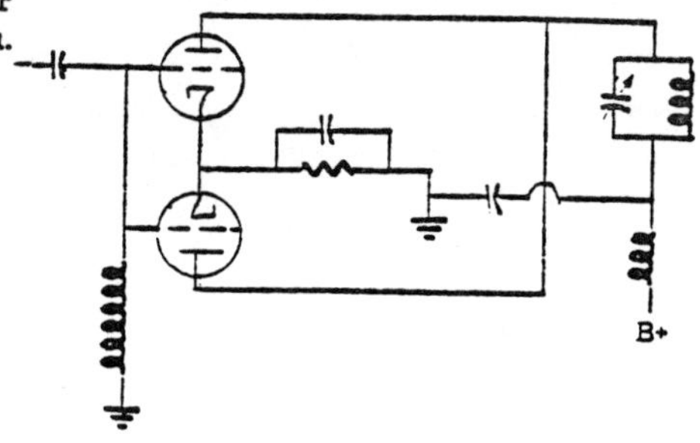

4. (anode, ⌐)

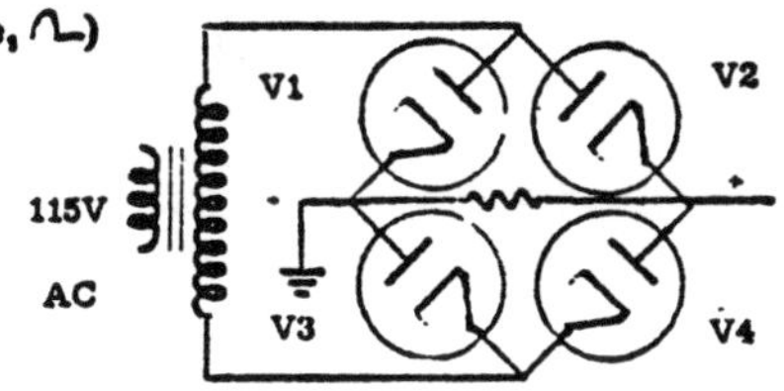

In the bridge circuit shown _____ and _____ are reversed. Sec. 11-4.

10. (charged filter capacitor) Inductance has the property to oppose any change in _____. Sec. 11-7.

16. (6.3 volts) Inductive (choke) input filter will have better regulation than capacitive input filter, but it will have _____ output voltage. Sec. 11-9.

22. (inversely) Duodiodes are constructed with two plates and two filaments in one _____. Sec. 11-14.

28. (1116v) Better voltage regulation is possible using _____ rectifier tubes. Sec. 11-17.

34. (R_1, capacitor) Read all paragraphs 11-23. Although filter capacitors have a positive and negative connection, bleeders are not polarized. Since there is little noticeable effect if a bleeder resistor comes open, an operator servicing a transmitter power supply that's turned off should make sure that there is no dangerous charge left in the _____. Bleeder Resistors are not _____. Sec. 11-23.

40. (hash) It would not be readily apparent if the buffer capacitance opened up, but eventually the vibrator contacts would burn up. A partially shorted buffer capacitor would cause the contact points of the vibrator to burn gradually and reduce the output voltage. If the buffer capacitor shorted out, this would short out the entire _____ winding. If it partially shorted out, the output voltage would be _____ and the vibrator contacts would burn gradually. If the buffer capacitor came open, operation would nearly be _____. Sec. 11-30.

46. (shorted) A vacuum tube or a mercury vapor tube has a higher inverse voltage rating than solid state diodes. When solid state diodes are used in high voltage application, it is customary to put several of them in a series string in order to withstand the applied voltage in the reverse direction. Solid state diodes usually have a lower _____ rating than tubes.

151. In the diagram below the total current flow is
    a. 10 ma.
    b. 20 ma.
    c. 30 ma.
    d. 40 ma.
    e. none of these.

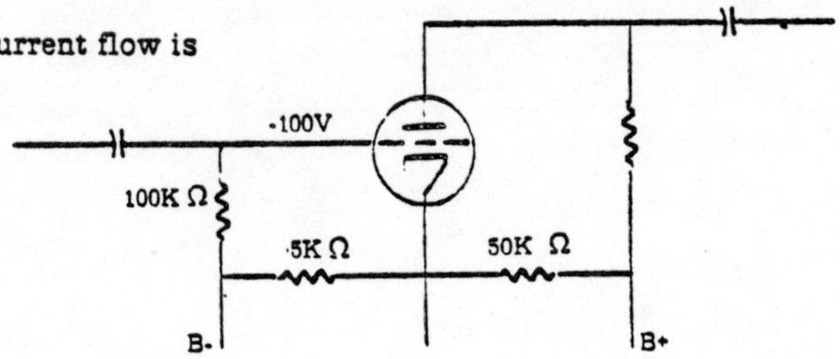

152. The circuit below is used for
    a. tone control.
    b. grid leak biasing.
    c. a paraphase amplifier.
    d. squelch control.
    e. volume control.

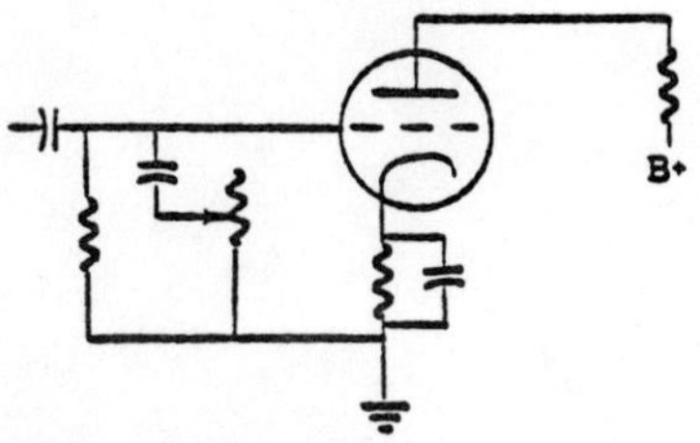

153. An open cathode by-pass capacitor would cause
    a. regeneration.
    b. decreased gain.   d. decreased degeneration.
    c. motor boating.   e. direct coupling.

154. There is no distortion with this amplifier with proper input when the grid voltage is between O and minus 20 volts. The maximum rms input for distortionless amplification would be
    a. 1 volt.
    b. 2.3 volts.
    c. 3.5 volts.
    d. 5 volts.
    e. 6.3 volts.

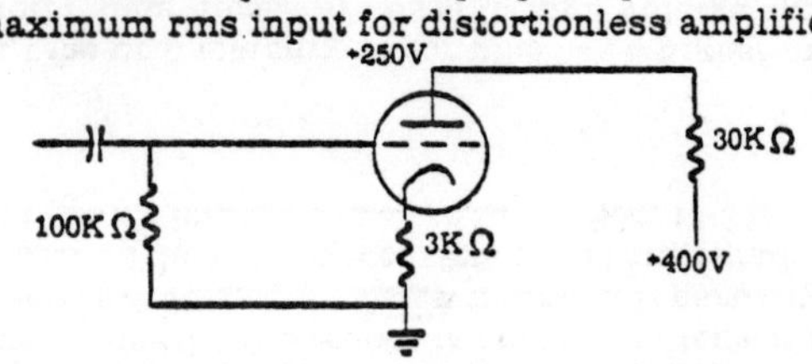

155. An amplifier having an output of 6 volts with an input of .006 volts has a gain of
    a. 60 db.
    b. 6 db.   d. 30 db.
    c. .6 db.   e. none of these.

156. The load should be matched to the output of an amplifier because this results in
    a. minimum current flow.
    b. maximum voltage output.   d. minimum harmonics.
    c. the maximum transfer of power.   e. audio degeneration.

157. One type of AF amplifier is characterized by
    a. no bias.
    b. no gain.   d. direct coupling.
    c. no amplification.   e. none of these.

158. When you plug in earphones to a receiver, all signals may be weak because of
    a. overloading.
    b. earphone magnets saturated.   d. weak input signals.
    c. impedance mismatch.   e. b and c above.

159. Link coupling is especially useful for coupling when components are
    a. located close to each other.
    b. widely separated.   d. within tolerance.
    c. running hot.   e. used in AF circuits.

160. In the circuit below
    a. the output would be on a frequency twice the input.
    b. the output frequency would be the same as the input.
    c. a push pull circuit is illustrated.
    d. a push push circuit is illustrated.
    e. there would be no output.

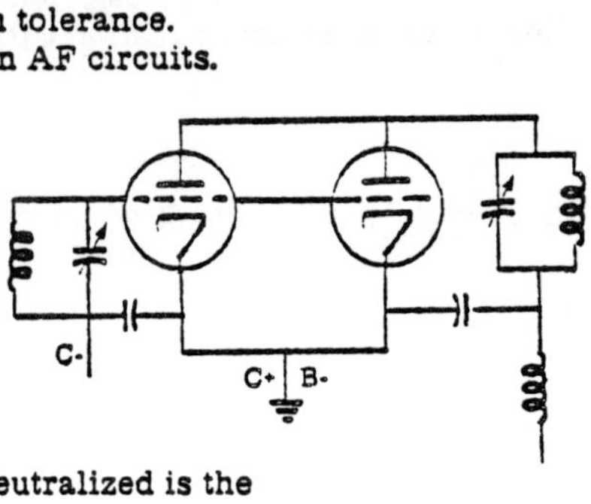

161. One triode RF amplifier that need not be neutralized is the
    a. push pull amplifier.
    b. common cathode circuit.   d. class C RF amplifier.
    c. grounded grid amplifier.   e. thermo trockle circuit.

314

5.   (VI, V4) Whereas the bridge circuit uses the full output voltage of the transformer secondary, the center tap circuit only uses_____of the secondary voltage at any one time. Sec. 11-4.

11.   (current) The input capacitor to a capacitive input filter charges to the_____value of the transformer AC applied to the filter. Sec. 11-8.

17.   (less) Whereas inductive input filters are always used with gas filled rectifiers, capacitive input filters are most often used with vacuum tube and semiconductor rectifiers. DC to DC power supplies starting with a low voltage battery and ending with a high DC voltage and using solid state rectifiers, usually use a _____ input filter.

23.   (envelope) Mercury vapor has nearly a constant voltage of _____volts across it with varying loads. Sec. 11-15.

29.   (mercury vapor) The ripple frequency output of a half wave rectifier using a 50 hertz input is _____ hertz. Sec. 11-18.

35.   (filter capacitors, polarized) A certain power supply has a no load output voltage of 400 volts and a full load output voltage of 300 volts. The percent regulation would be _____ . Sec. 11-24.

41.   (secondary, low, normal) The synchronous vibrator power supply has a second set of vibrator contacts that are used for mechanical_____. Sec. 11-30.

47.   (peak inverse voltage)   With SW1 open and PTT open the antenna is connected to the _____.

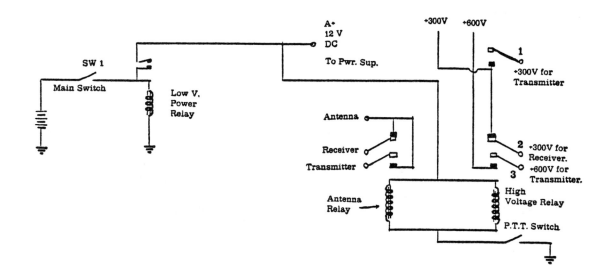

141. The circuit shown is a
    a. RF amplifier.
    b. voltage doubler.
    c. frequency multiplier.
    d. push push amplifier.
    e. Hartley oscillator.

142. The principal disadvantage of crystal-controlled oscillators is
    a. frequency instability more pronounced.
    b. high voltage requirements.   d. difficulty in changing operating frequencies.
    c. insufficient "drive" to the final,   e. high cost of crystals.

143. Amplifiers that are
    a. RF class B must be push pull.
    b. AF class B must use 2 tubes in PP.   d. RF linear amplifiers must be class A.
    c. final RF amplifiers must be class A.   e. RF class C take low bias.

144. The proper method for coupling high impedance earphones to a low impedance output would be by use of a
    a. series coil.
    b. series capacitor.   d. transformer.
    c. series resistor.   e. rectifier.

145. At any instant the phase of y with respect to x is
    a. 180 degrees out of phase.
    b. 90 degrees out of phase.
    c. 270 degrees out of phase.
    d. 45 degrees out of phase.
    e. in phase.

146. The plate current in the circuit below would be
    a. 5 ma.
    b. 5.5 ma.
    c. 100 ma.
    d. 20 ma.
    e. zero

147. The plate impedance of a certain tube amplifier is 10 K ohms. For maximum power output the load resistance should be
    a. 10 K ohms.
    b. 20 K ohms.   d. 40 K ohms.
    c. 30 K ohms.   e. infinity.

148. The circuit below would not work because
    a. the bias is low.
    b. the bias is high.
    c. there is no bias.
    d. it is not neutralized.
    e. of the resistance in the cathode circuit.

149. The voltage amplification of a typical cathode follower is
    a. 20.
    b. 10.
    c. 5.
    d. 2.
    e. less than unity.

150. In order to match a 4,000 ohms load into a 10 ohms speaker it would be necessary to use a transformer having a turns ratio of
    a. 1 to 1.
    b. 10 to 1.   d. 20 to 1.
    c. 15 to 1.   e. none of these.

313

6.   (one half)   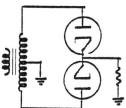   Tell what the mistake is in this circuit (if there is one)_____ .
Sec. 11-4.

12.   (peak) A full wave rectifier system using a capacitive input filter has a full secondary voltage of 200 volts (end to end). The input capacitance must have a working voltage rating of at least _____volts. Sec. 11-8.

18.   (capacitive) A filter capacitor must not discharge too fast or the output waveform will be jagged. The time for discharge must exceed the period of the ripple cycle. The RC time constant can be increased using a _____ instead of a choke in a filter. Sec. 11-11.

24.   (15 volts) Before anode voltage is applied, a mercury vapor tube must be_____ for 15 or 20 seconds. Sec. 11-15.

30.   (50 Hz)   The ripple frequency output of a full wave rectifier using a 60 hertz input is _____. Sec. 11-18.

36.   (33 1/3%) % regulation is equal to the ratio of difference output voltage under conditions of no load and full load to the _____load voltage times 100. Sec. 11-24.

42.   (rectification) The transistor oscillator is often used instead of a vibrator in a DC to DC supply in a multivibrator circuit because it has no moving parts and is more _____. Sec. 11-30.

48.   (receiver) With SW1 closed and PTT open there would be voltage at point _____. See frame 47.

128. In the diagram below the voltmeter should read
   a. 10 volts.   A1 = 12.5A
   b. 45 volts.   A2 = 2.5A
   c. 80 volts.   R2 = 9 Ω
   d. 100 volts.   R4 = 4 Ω
   e. none of these.

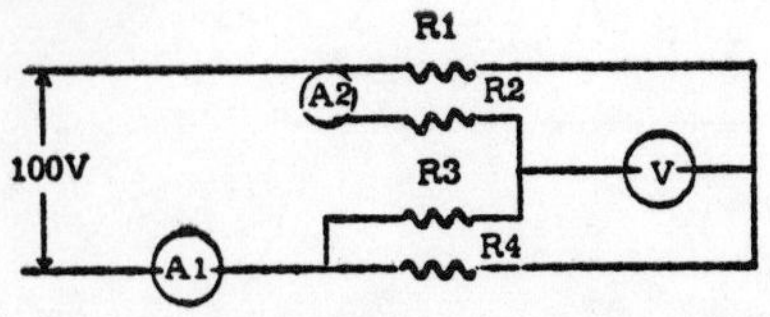

129. A VTVM is used to measure AC line voltage. The meter immediately rises to 150 volts and then slowly rises to 155 volts. This indicates
   a. internal RC time constant in the meter.
   b. the maximum line voltage is 150 volts.   d. oscillation.
   c. the meter is out of calibration.   e. none of these.

130. A 0 to 10 voltmeter has a total resistance of 150 ohms. To convert this meter to a 0 to 100 voltmeter, it would be necessary to add a series multiplier resistance of
   a. 1,345 ohms.
   b. 1,350 ohms.   d. 600 ohms.
   c. 1,500 ohms.   e. 752 ohms.

131. If you have a wattmeter you could find the current by use of the
   a. voltmeter.
   b. frequency meter.   d. grid dip meter.
   c. D'Arsonval meter.   e. pedometer.

132. An AC wattmeter used in a circuit with the voltage and current out of phase measures
   a. I X E.
   b. I X E X P.F.   d. reactive power.
   c. apparent power.   e. a and c.

133. The circuit shown is a
   a. phase shift oscillator.
   b. electron coupled oscillator
   c. voltage doubler.
   d. grounded Grid amplifier.
   e. bridge power supply.

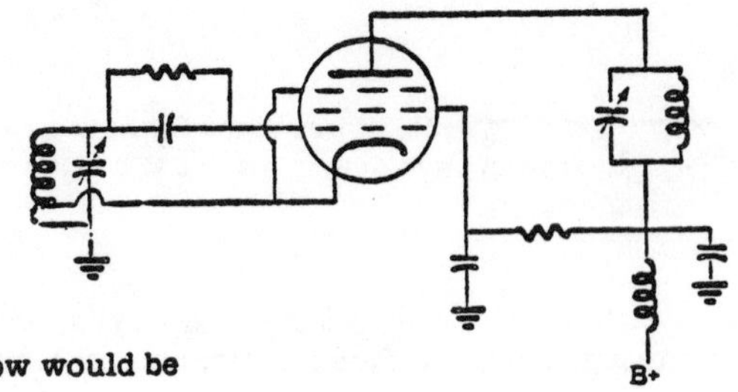

134. The output of the circuit shown below would be
   a. sawtooth taken at the plate.
   b. a square wave taken at the grid.
   c. a sawtooth taken at the grid of either tube.
   d. a sine wave taken at the plate.
   e. none of these.

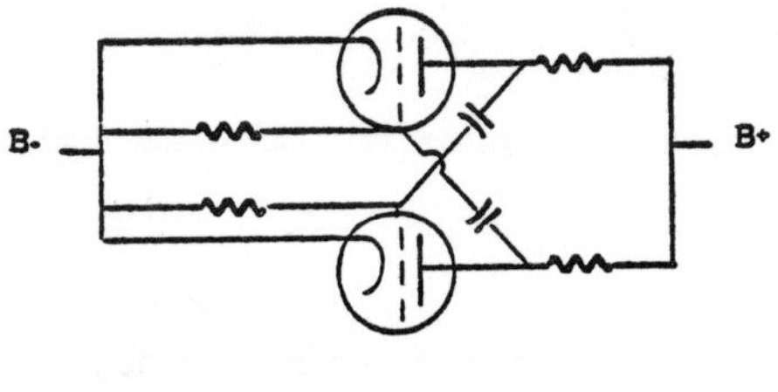

135. One characteristic of a Dynatron oscillator is
   a. negative resistance.
   b. negative feedback.   d. high output.
   c. positive feedback.   e. none of these.

136. Feedback in a T.P.T.G. Oscillator is obtained by
   a. detunning the plate circuit.
   b. detunning the grid circuit.   d. interelectrode capacitance.
   c. a capacitor between grid and plate.   e. inductance.

137. A Hartley oscillator needs
   a. positive feedback.
   b. an extremely high Q circuit.   d. negative feedback.
   c. B+ applied to a tap on a plate coil.   e. degeneration.

138. The frequency of a crystal can be appreciably changed by changing the temperature and by changing
   a. the transconductance.
   b. the plate voltage.   d. the grid resistance.
   c. the plate tank inductance.   e. the plate tank capacitance.

139. The advantage of an electron coupled oscillator is
   a. the load changes in the plate circuit have little effect on frequency.
   b. the output is coupled to the input.   d. it acts as a phase splitter.
   c. it is neutralized.   e. none of these.

140. To prevent the crystal in a oscillator from cracking it is necessary to
   a. use a Colpitts type.
   b. use a Hartley type.
   c. prevent excessive feedback.
   d. regulate the power supply.
   e. neutralize the oscillator.

1. A buffer capacitor in a vibrator power supply serves to
    a. load down the secondary.
    b. reduce sparking at the vibrator points. d. step down the secondary voltage.
    c. step up the secondary voltage.   e. double frequency.

2. A certain power supply delivers 660 volts under no load condition. Under load condition it supplies 600 volts. The % regulation is
    a. 60
    b. 20. d. 10.
    c. 100. e. 6.

3. The voltage ratio of the voltage from center tap to either end to the full secondary voltage of a full wave power transformer is
    a. 1 to 1.
    b. 1/2 to 1. d. 1 to 1/2.
    c. 1/4 to 1. e. 2 to 3.

4. In a mercury vapor power supply system
    a. the tube must be warmed before the plate voltage is applied.
    b. capacitance input filter must be used.
    c. the plate voltage must be applied before the filament voltage.
    d. 3 filament supplies are required.
    e. all the above are applicable.

5. When a burned out power supply rectifier tube is replaced with a new tube it is found that it gets red hot. This generally indicates
    a. a shorted filter capacitor.
    b. a bad new tube.   d. a mercury vapor tube is being used.
    c. a normal operation.   e. none of these.

6. In a non synchronous vibrator power supply the choke in the battery lead serves to
    a. prevent oscillation.
    b. provide better voltage regulation.   d. operate the vibrator.
    c. keeps hash voltage transients out of the battery leads. e. none of these.

7. If the bleeder resistor in a transmitter power supply opened up
    a. the transmitter would be inoperative.
    b. the final plate current would read low. d. the buffer would self oscillate.
    c. the antenna current would read low.   e. there would be little noticeable effect.

8. A swinging choke is used in
    a. audio amplifiers.
    b. RF amplifiers.   d. current amplifiers.
    c. voltage amplifiers. e. power supplies.

9. In a power supply, the filter capacitors must be of such value that
    a. the time constant is greater than the period of the ripple cycle.
    b. the time constant is smaller than the period of the ripple cycle. d. it will attenuate the signal.
    c. it will oscillate.   e. none of these.

10. The voltage in the primary of a transformer is 100 volts. The voltage in the secondary from CT to one end is 300 volts. The turns ratio primary to secondary is
    a. 1 to 3.
    b. 1 to 4. d. 100 to 200.
    c. 1 to 6. e. 100 to 500.

11. In order to make the diagram below correct it would be necessary to
    a. reverse the output polarity.
    b. reverse V1.
    c. reverse V2.
    d. replace the resistor with a capacitor.
    e. remove the capacitor.

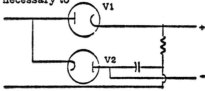

12. Mercury vapor rectifier tubes
    a. require a warm up period.
    b. require choke input filter.
    c. provide good voltage regulation.
    d. have about 15 volts drop across them while in use.
    e. all of the above.

115. Most broadcast stations use three phase supplies because
    a. less wiring is involved.
    b. the three phase transformers have a higher output voltage.   d. fewer parts are needed.
    c. fewer tubes are required.   e. all of the above.

116. If the buffer capacitor was open, the power supply load current would be
    a. higher.
    b. lower.   d. nearly normal.
    c. same.   e. none of these.

117. The regulation of a power supply is
    a. equal to the load voltage over the voltage without the load.
    b. the speed that the generator must be turned.   d. (ENL - EL)/EL.
    c. ENL - El.   e. none of these.

118. To change low DC voltage to high DC voltage use a
    a. rectifier.
    b. dynamotor.   d. transformer.
    c. dynamometer.   e. multiplier.

119. Polarity does not have to be observed when connecting
    a. an electrolytic cap.
    b. a bleeder resistor.   d. earphones.
    c. DC ammeter.   e. none of these.

120. In general the peak inverse voltage rating of a germanium diode is
    a. 15 volts.
    b. 100 volts.   d. higher than for a VT diode.
    c. 156 volts.   e. lower than for a VT diode.

121. A series diode regulator is used to regulate a 6.3 volt output. If the circuit is supplied 25v at .4 amps, the series limiting resistor should have a value of
    a. 200 ohms.
    b. 16.25 ohms.   d. 62.5 ohms.
    c. 21.1 ohms.   e. none of these.

122. The full wave power supply shown below is shown
    a. with reversed output polarity.
    b. with L and C interchanged.
    c. with capacitance input filter.
    d. without filter.
    e. correctly.

123. A resistor in series with a voltmeter lead will
    a. increase its full scale range.
    b. decrease its full scale range.   d. change it to a wattmeter.
    c. change it to an ammeter.   e. none of these.

124. A wattmeter measures
    a. current squared through its coils.
    b. voltage squared through its coils.   d. fequency.
    c. the voltage across the meter and the current through the meter.   e. energy.

125. In order to make the meter shown below read full scale for 135 volts, an additional series resistance must be added having a value of
    a. 3,700 ohms.
    b. approximately 1,420 ohms.
    c. approximately 470 ohms.
    d. approximately 1,690 ohms.
    e. none of these.

126. Higher current readings can be obtained with a DC ammeter by placing a
    a. choke in series with the ammeter.
    b. capacitor in shunt with the ammeter.   d. grounding one end of the ammeter.
    c. low resistance in shunt with the ammeter.   e. none of these.

127. To properly view a sine wave on a scope apply
    a. the sine wave to the vertical plates and a sawtooth wave to the horizontal plates.
    b. the sine wave to the vertical plates and a square wave to the horizontal plates.
    c. the sine wave to the horizontal plates and a sawtooth wave to the vertical plates.
    d. the sine wave to both the vertical and horizontal plates.
    e. none of these.

13. The ripple output fequency of a half wave three phase power supply would be
    a. the same as the supply frequency.
    b. twice the supply frequency.
    c. three times the supply frequency.
    d. four times the power frequency.
    e. six times the supply frequency.

14. In the diagram of the bridge power supply shown below the
    a. circuit is correct.
    b. the transformer center tap should be grounded.
    c. the electrodes of V1 are reversed.
    d. the electrodes of V2 are reversed.
    e. the diode plates of V1 and V2 should not be grounded.

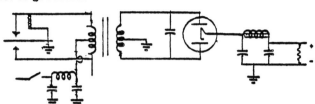

15. The diagram shown is that of
    a. a frequency doubler.
    b. push push amplifier.
    c. voltage doubler.
    d. non synchronous power supply.
    e. synchronous power supply

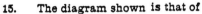

16. In the diagram below
    a. V1 is reversed.
    b. V2 is reversed.
    c. the output polarity is reversed.
    d. the mercury vapor tubes are used.
    e. there are no mistakes.

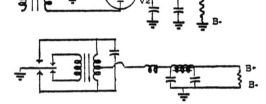

17. The diagram shown below is that of a
    a. frequency doubler.
    b. push push amplifier.
    c. voltage doubler.
    d. non synchronous power supply
    e. synchronous power supply

18. The output of a full wave three phase power supply with 60 cycle input would have a ripple frequency of
    a. 60 cycles/sec.
    b. 120 cycles/sec.
    c. 240 cycles/sec.
    d. 360 cycles/sec.
    e. 720/350 cycles/sec.

19. With Sw. 1 on and C1 shorted
    a. there would be excessive current flow through the filter choke.
    b. the current through the ammeter would rise.
    c. there would be no high voltage.
    d. there would be high voltage a point 2.
    e. the filter capacitors would short out.

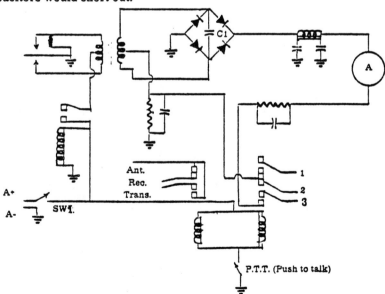

20. With Sw. 1 open and the push to talk switch closed
    a. the ammeter would indicate current flow.
    b. there would be voltage at point 2.
    c. there would be voltage at point 1.
    d. the antenna would be connected to the receiver.
    e. there would be none of these.

106. The diagram shown below is that of a
    a. frequency doubler.
    b. push pull amplifier.
    c. voltage doubler.
    d. non synchronous power supply.
    e. synchronous power supply.

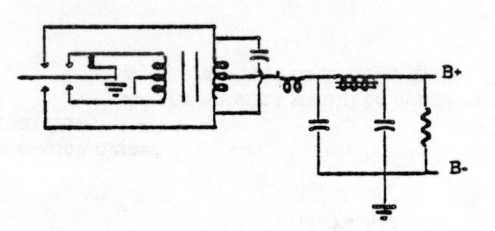

107. With Sw. 1 on and C1 shorted
    a. there would be excessive current flow through the filter choke.
    b. the current through the ammeter would rise.
    c. there would be no high voltage.
    d. there would be high voltage a point 2.
    e. the filter capacitors would short out.

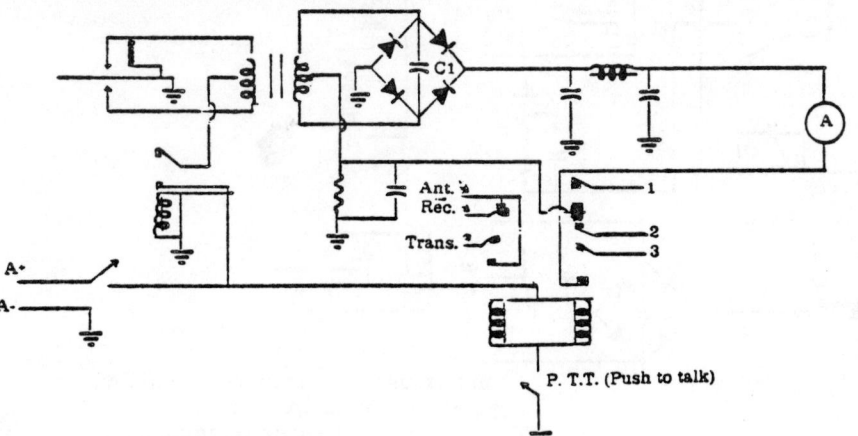

108. With Sw. 1 open and the push to talk switch closed
    a. the ammeter would indicate current flow.
    b. there would be voltage at point 2.
    c. there would be voltage at point 1.
    d. the antenna would be connected to the receiver.
    e. there would be none of these.

109. With Sw. 1 closed and the PTT open
    a. there would be voltage at point 2.
    b. there would be voltage at point 1.
    c. there would be voltage at point 3.
    d. the antenna would be connected to the transmitter.
    e. none of these.

110. To obtain 50 v DC from 100v DC use a(n)
    a. ammeter.
    b. converter.
    c. multiplier.
    d. voltage divider.
    e. inverter.

111. The PTT switch is used to
    a. actuate the vibrator.
    b. turn on the A supply.
    c. switch the antenna from receive to transmit.
    d. to switch the high voltage to the transmitter.
    e. switch the antenna from receive to transmit and to switch the high voltage to the transmitter.

112. It would be all right to use a half wave rectifier rather than a full wave if
    a. ripple was not important in output.
    b. regulation was not important.
    c. the filtering was insufficient.
    d. a bridge circuit was used.
    e. a voltage doubler was used.

113. The bridge power supply using a transformer differs from the usual full wave power supply using a transformer in that the bridge circuit
    a. uses a center tap connection to the secondary.
    b. delivers twice as much voltage to the rectifier tubes.
    c. can only be used for half wave rectification.
    d. delivers half as much voltage to the rectifier tubes.
    e. none of these.

114. In the bridge rectifier system shown
    a. the circuit is correct.
    b. the transformer center tap should be grounded.
    c. V1 and V2 are connected wrong.
    d. V3 and V4 are connected wrong.
    e. the output polarity is shown reversed.

21. With Sw. 1 closed and the PTT closed
    a. there would be voltage at point 3.
    b. there would be voltage at point 2.   d. there would be no high voltage.
    c. the antenna would be connected to the receiver.   e. none of these.

22. With Sw. 1 closed and the PTT open
    a. there would be voltage at point 2.
    b. there would be voltage at point 1.   d. the antenna would be connected to the transmitter.
    c. there would be voltage at point 3.   e. none of these.

23. To obtain 500v DC from 100v DC use a (n)
    a. ammeter.
    b. converter.   d. voltage divider.
    c. multiplier.   e. inverter.

24. The PTT switch is used to
    a. actuate the vibrator.
    b. turn on the A supply.
    c. switch the antenna from receive to transmit.
    d. to switch the high voltage to the transmitter.
    e. switch the antenna from receive to transmit and to switch the high voltage to the transmitter.

25. One advantage of a 3 phase power supply used with a high power transmitter is that
    a. it takes less parts.
    b. the DC output is easier to filter.   d. it requires no fuses.
    c. it will step up the power.   e. none of these.

26. The output of a half wave rectifier without filter would look like

27. In a DC to DC transistor multivibrator power supply
    a. capacitance input filter is usually used.
    b. a dynamotor is used.
    c. a vibrator is used.
    d. the rectifier filaments must be on before the high voltage is turned on.
    e. no transformer is used.

28. Multivibrators are used in DC to DC power supplies because
    a. they provide constant current.
    b. they provide constant voltage.   d. they require no transistors.
    c. they have no moving parts and are efficient.   e. none of these.

29. It would be all right to use a half wave rectifier rather than a full wave if
    a. ripple was not important in output.
    b. regulation was not important.   d. a bridge circuit was used.
    c. the filtering was insufficient.   e. a voltage doubler was used.

30. Delta Y transformers are used in 3 ∮ circuits because
    a. they have higher output voltage.
    b. it is the only possible connection.   d. they have an output of 220 volts single phase
    c. they have an output of 110 volts single phase.   e. none of these.

31. The bridge power supply using a transormer differs from the usual full wave power supply using a transformer in that the bridge circuit
    a. uses a center tap connection to the secondary.
    b. delivers twice as much voltage to the rectifier tubes.
    c. can only be used for half wave rectification.
    d. delivers half as much voltage to the rectifier tubes.
    e. none of these.

32. A full wave bridge rectifier with a capacitance input filter has a DC output of 9 v. The AC RMS input would be approximately
    a. 10 volts.
    b. 6.3 volts. d. 25 volts
    c. 18 volts e. 27 volts.

33. In a full wave rectifier circuit with a capacitance input filter and an AC input of 200 volts (total secondary RMS voltage) the filter capacitors should have a minimum voltage rating of
    a. 200 volts.
    b. 282 volts. d. 141 volts.
    c. 100 volts. e. 500 volts.

93. In the circuit shown below
   a. the collector is biased wrong.
   b. the emitter bias battery is reversed.
   c. there is no collector bias.
   d. there is no emitter bias.
   e. none of these.

94. In the transistor amplifier shown
   a. the diagram is correct.
   b. there is no bias.
   c. the collector and emitter are reversed.
   d. the transistor is an NPN unit.
   e. none of these.

95. A principle common to all transistors is that
   a. the collector base is forward biased.
   b. the emitter base is reverse biased.
   c. the collector is positive with respect to the base.
   d. the emitter is positive with respect to the base.
   e. the emitter base bias is forward bias.

96. A transistor can easily be damaged by
   a. forward bias on the emitter.
   b. forward bias on the collector.   d. low bias on the emitter.
   c. insufficient excitation.   e. none of these.

97. The part of the atom concerned with current flow is the
   a. outer valence electrons.
   b. nucleus.   d. neutrons.
   c. inner electron shells. e. none of these.

98. If a transistor is heated
   a. the temperature does not change.
   b. the base current decreases.   d. the collector current decreases and then rises.
   c. the collector current increases. e. there is no appreciable effect.

99. A certain power supply delivers 660 volts under no load condition. Under load condition it supplies 600 volts. The % regulation is
   a. 60.
   b. 20.   d. 10.
   c. 100.   e. 6.

100. The voltage ratio of the voltage from center tap to either end to the full secondary voltage of a full wave power transformer is
   a. 1 to 1.
   b. 1/2 to 1.   d. 1 to 1/2.
   c. 1/4 to 1.   e. 2 to 3.

101. When a burned out power supply rectifier tube is replaced with a new tube it is found that it gets red hot. This generally indicates
   a. a shorted filter capacitor.
   b. a bad new tube.   d. a mercury vapor tube is being used.
   c. a normal operation.   e. none of these.

102. In a non synchronous vibrator power supply the choke in the battery lead serves to
   a. prevent oscillation.
   b. provide better voltage regulation.   d. operate the vibrator.
   c. keeps hash voltage transients out of the battery leads.   e. none of these.

103. A swinging choke is used in
   a. audio amplifiers.
   b. RF amplifier.   d. current amplifiers.
   c. voltage amplifiers. e. power supplies.

104. In order to make the diagram below correct it would be necessary to
   a. reverse the output polarity.
   b. reverse V1.
   c. reverse V2.
   d. replace the resistor with a capacitor.
   e. remove the capacitor.

105. Mercury vapor rectifier tubes
   a. require a warm up period.
   b. require choke input filter.   d. have about 15 volts drop across them while in use.
   c. provide good voltage regulation. e. all of the above.

309

34. In the bridge rectifier system shown
   a. the circuit is correct.
   b. the transformer center tap should be grounded.
   c. V1 and V2 are connected wrong.
   d. V3 and V4 are connected wrong.
   e. the output polarity is shown reversed.

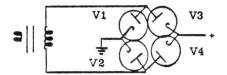

35. Most broadcast stations use three phase supplies because
   a. less wiring is involved.
   b. the three phase transformers have a higher output voltage.
   c. fewer tubes are required.
   d. fewer parts are needed.
   e. all of the above.

36. If C^1 was partially shorted
   a. the vibrator contacts would burn off quickly.
   b. the vibrator contacts would burn gradually.
   c. the output voltage would be high.
   d. the input voltage would be high.
   e. there would be no effect on the power supply.

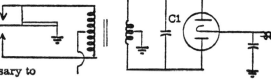

37. In the circuit below it would be necessary to
   a. reverse the output polarity.
   b. reverse V1.
   c. reverse V2.
   d. remove the capacitors and replace them with resistors.
   e. none of these.

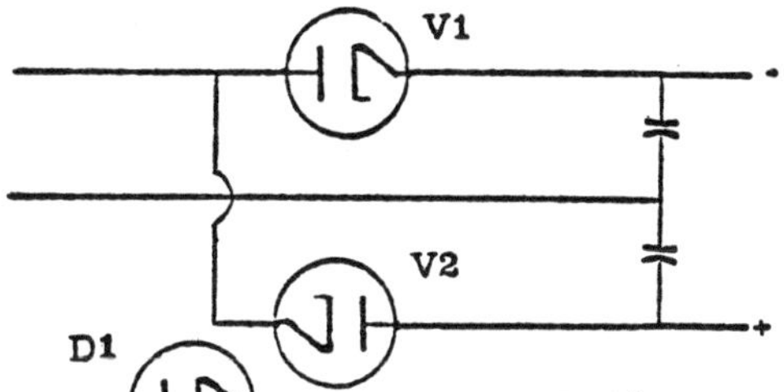

38. In the diagram below
   a. the polarity of the capacitor C^2 is reversed.
   b. D_1 diode is reversed.
   c. D_2 is reversed (diode).
   d. C1 should be removed.
   e. Point E should be grounded.

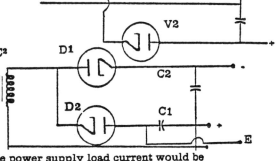

39. If the buffer capacitor was open the power supply load current would be
   a. higher.
   b. lower.
   c. same.
   d. nearly normal.
   e. none of these.

40. The regulation of a power supply is
   a. equal to the load voltage over the voltage without the load.
   b. the speed that the generator must be turned.
   c. ENL - EL.
   d. (ENL - EL)/EL.
   e. none of these.

41. A full wave power supply uses a transformer having a secondary voltage of 1000 volts from center tap to one end. The peak inverse voltage rating of mercury vapor rectifiers used in this circuit should be approximately
   a. 2830 volts.
   b. 2813 volts.
   c. 1400 volts.
   d. 1500 volts.
   e. none of these.

42. To change low DC voltage to high DC voltage use a
   a. rectifier.
   b. dynamotor.
   c. dynamometer.
   d. transformer.
   e. multiplier.

43. Polarity does not have to be observed when connecting
   a. an electrolytic cap.
   b. a bleeder resistor.
   c. DC ammeter.
   d. earphones.
   e. none of these.

44. A filter circuit designed with the product of the series and shunt impedance as a fixed value is called
   a. a constant K filter.
   b. an M derrived filter.
   c. a 60 cycle filter.
   d. a band pass filter.
   e. a band stop filter.

81. In a properly connected screen grid vacuum tube circuit secondary emission screen current cannot flow to
    a. the plate.
    b. the cathode.
    c. the power supply
    d. the control grid.
    e. the suppresser grid.

82. In a tetrode VT amplifier the grid current flow is 7.5 ma. The screen grid current is 2.5 ma and the cathode current is 80 ma. The plate current flow is
    a. 20 ma.
    b. 90 ma.
    c. 80 ma.
    d. 70 mA.
    e. none of these.

83. The transconductance of a vacuum tube is equal to
    a. Ip/Eg.
    b. Ep/Eg.
    c. Ep/Ip.
    d. Gm/Rp.
    e. none of these.

84. For proper operation connect
    a. 1 to 2.
    b. 1 to 5.
    c. 1 to 7.
    d. 2 to 5.
    e. 2 to 7.

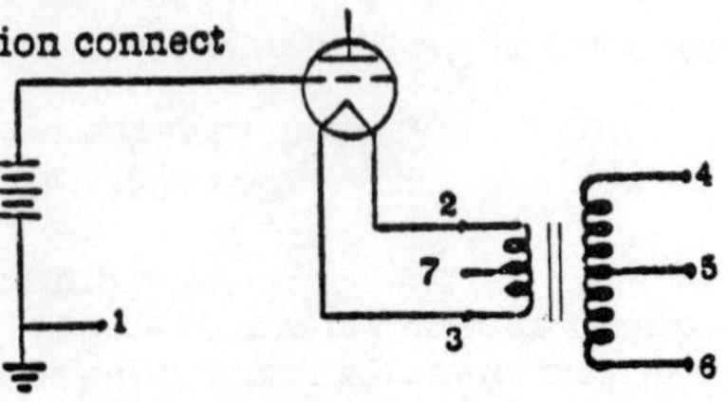

85. When using triode tubes at higher frequencies, it is important to consider
    a. transconductance.
    b. plate impedance.
    c. input capacitance.
    d. skin effect.
    e. none of these.

86. The polarity of the voltage used to supply DC voltage to a direct cathode is periodically reversed to
    a. increase the bias.
    b. decrease the bias.
    c. suppress parasitics.
    d. to balance out the emissive property.
    e. none of these.

87. A voltage amplification (μ) of 50, means that
    a. a 50 volt signal at the grid appears as 1 volt at the plate.
    b. $\Delta Ip/\Delta Ig = 50$.
    c. $\Delta Ip/\Delta Eg = 50$.
    d. $\Delta Eg/\Delta Ep = 50$.
    e. A 1 volt signal at the grid appears as 50 volts at the plate.

88. One advantage of a tetrode transistor is that it operates well at
    a. low frequencies.
    b. high frequencies.
    c. low temperatures.
    d. high temperatures.
    e. none of these.

89. In the diagram below the
    a. collector bias is incorrect.
    b. emitter bias is wrong.
    c. point A should be grounded.
    d. the collector and base are 180° out of phase.
    e. the collector and base are in phase.

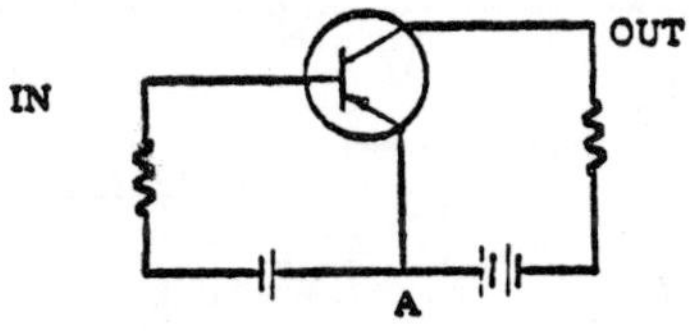

90. In a common base transistor circuit the
    a. output signal is in phase with the input.
    b. output signal is out of phase with the input.
    c. input signal is applied to the base.
    d. input signal is applied to the collector.
    e. current gain is figured in Beta.

91. The collector in a transistor is comparable to
    a. the anode in a VT.
    b. the control grid in a VT.
    c. the cathode in a VT.
    d. the screen grid in a VT.
    e. the suppressor grid in a VT.

92. The transistor symbol shown is for a
    a. silicon transistor.
    b. NPN transistor.
    c. PNP transistor.
    d. diode
    e. germanium transistor.

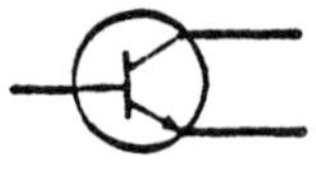

45. The secondary of a center tapped transformer has 350 volts each side of center tap. The peak inverse voltage rating of either tube used in full wave power supply with this transformer must have a peak inverse voltage rating of at least
   a. 350 volts.
   b. 495 volts.   d. 700 volts.
   c. 990 volts.   e. 824 volts.

46. In general the peak inverse voltage rating of a germanium diode is
   a. 15 volts.
   b. 100 volts.   d. higher than for a VT diode.
   c. 156 volts.   e. lower than for a VT diode.

47. A series diode regulator is used to regulate a 6.3 volt output. If the circuit is supplied 25v at .4 amps the series limiting resistor should have a value of
   a. 200 ohms.
   b. 16.25 ohms.   d. 62.5 ohms.
   c. 21.1 ohms.   e. none of these.

48. To obtain 100v DC from 500v DC use a(n)
   a. inverter.
   b. converter.   d. voltage divider.
   c. multiplier.   e. rectifier.

49. Voltage regulation in conventional power supplies is improved by
   a. proper fusing.
   b. a bleeder resistance.
   c. a filter condenser.
   d. high-resistance filter chokes.
   e. half wave rectifier.

50. The full wave power supply shown below is shown
   a. with reversed output polarity.
   b. with L and C interchanged.
   c. with capacitance input filter.
   d. without filter.
   e. correctly.

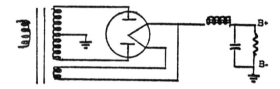

51. In the circuit shown below, an open capacitor C1 would
   a. cause the fuse to blow.
   b. reduce the output voltage to one half.
   c. have little noticeable effect.
   d. cause reverse polarity in output.
   e. none of these.

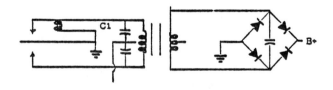

114

69. An example of an M derrived low pass filter is

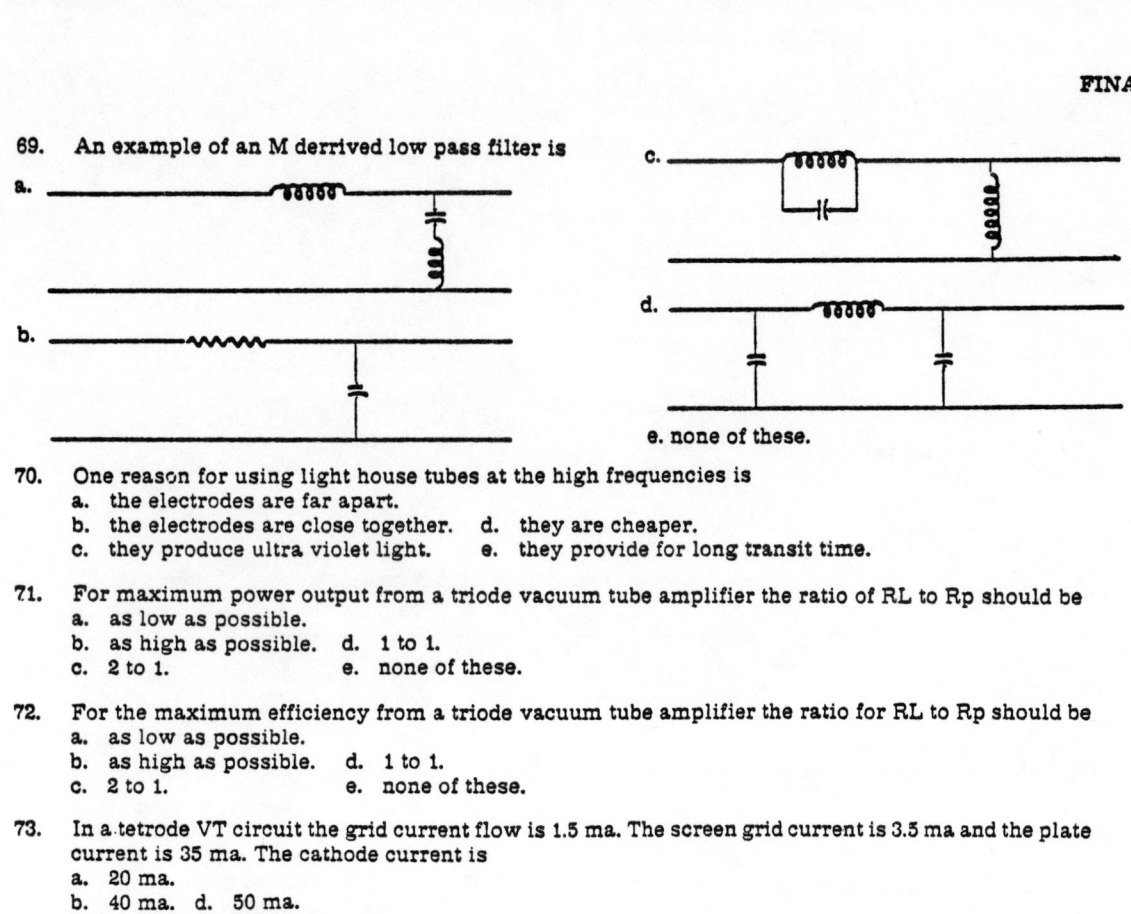

e. none of these.

70. One reason for using light house tubes at the high frequencies is
   a. the electrodes are far apart.
   b. the electrodes are close together.   d. they are cheaper.
   c. they produce ultra violet light.   e. they provide for long transit time.

71. For maximum power output from a triode vacuum tube amplifier the ratio of RL to Rp should be
   a. as low as possible.
   b. as high as possible.   d. 1 to 1.
   c. 2 to 1.   e. none of these.

72. For the maximum efficiency from a triode vacuum tube amplifier the ratio for RL to Rp should be
   a. as low as possible.
   b. as high as possible.   d. 1 to 1.
   c. 2 to 1.   e. none of these.

73. In a tetrode VT circuit the grid current flow is 1.5 ma. The screen grid current is 3.5 ma and the plate current is 35 ma. The cathode current is
   a. 20 ma.
   b. 40 ma.   d. 50 ma.
   c. 35 ma.   e. 25 ma.

74. The diagram below is the diagram of a
   a. beam power tube.
   b. pentode.
   c. lighthouse tube.
   d. thyratron tube.
   e. none of these.

75. To lengthen the life of the filaments in a DC transmitter circuit it is common practice to
   a. reduce the voltage to half value.
   b. double the DC voltage to the filaments.   d. water cool the tube.
   c. reverse the polarity of the filament supply voltage.   e. air cool the tube.

76. The deflection plates in a beam power tube are used to
   a. reduce interelectrode capacity.
   b. reduce primary emission.   d. neutralize the tube.
   c. channel the electron stream   e. none of these.

77. Modulation of the output by 60 cycle hum can be reduced in an amplifier using direct cathodes by
   a. using a filament isolation transformer.
   b. making the plate and grid return to the filament transformer center tap.
   c. using a 60 cycle hum filter at the input.
   d. using a 60 cycle hum filter at the output.
   e. none of these.

78. To reactivate a vacuum tube
   a. use high plate voltage with no bias for eight hours.
   b. use high bias with no plate voltage for eight hours.
   c. use high plate voltage for short duration, then operate at normal voltage.
   d. with no plate voltage subject the filament to a momentary high voltage surge and then reduce to slightly lower than 20% above normal operating voltage.
   e. all of the above.

79. The most common cause of tube failure is
   a. loss of emission.
   b. heater to cathode leakage.   d. wrong associated circuit components.
   c. shorted elements.   e. soft tubes.

80. The tube manual gives a tube as having a power dissipation of 50 watts. This means that
   a. the tube will dissipate 50 watts of power in itself without damage.
   b. the RL should have a 50 watt rating.
   c. the tube will have 50 watts of useful output.
   d. the filament requires 50 watts.
   e. 50 watts will be dissipated in the grid circuit.

1. The basic DC meter is a D'Arsonval current meter or galvanometer. Without any auxiliary equipment it consists of a moving coil mounted between the poles of a permanent magnet. The general arrangement is shown:

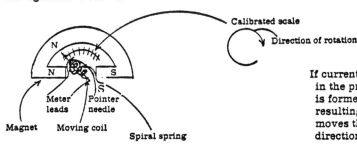

If current is caused to go through the coil in the proper direction, an electromagnet is formed with the polarities shown. The resulting repulsion and then attraction moves the needle pointer in the clockwise direction.

The DC meter is polarized. If the meter is connected in backwards the needle will spin backwards. The basic DC meter is a _____ current meter.

7. (40 K ohms)

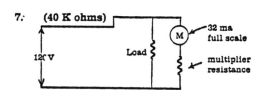

The multiplier resistance for this circuit

should be approximately_____.

13. (resistor)

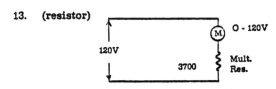

In order to make the voltmeter shown read full scale at 135 volts it would be necessary to have an additional series resistor.

It's value can be calculated as follows: It's full scale current before any changes are made is equal to the full scale voltage divided by the multiplier resistance (I=E/R) 120/3700 is .0324 A or 32.4 ma. The total multiplier resistance required to give full scale current with 135 volts applied is 135/.0324 or 4170. Since we already have 3700 ohms in the voltmeter circuit, we only need 4170 - 3700 or a little less than 500 ohms.

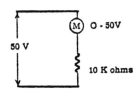

In order to make the voltmeter shown read full scale at 200 volts, it would be necessary to have an additional series resistance of _____ ohms.

19. (battery, resistors) The other ohmmeter using a D'Arsonval meter is a **Wheatstone Bridge**. Very accurate resistance measurements can be made with this device. Since the wheatstone bridge was discussed in Unit 2, it will not be discussed here. To accurately measure an unknown resistance one should use a_____.

25. (vertical) The sweep voltage generally is applied to the____HORIZONTAL____deflection plates.

57. In the diagram below, the power delivered by the source is
    a. 10 watts.
    b. .1 watts.
    c. 100 watts.
    d. 15 watts.
    e. none of these.

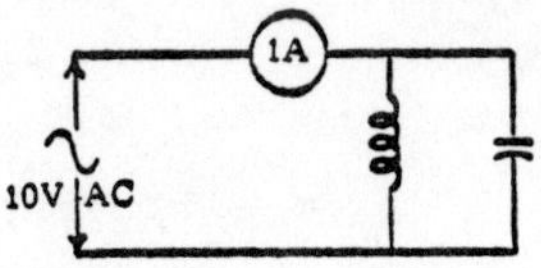

58. The circuit shown below is that of a
    a. balanced low pass filter.
    b. unbalanced low pass filter.
    c. unbalanced pi section high pass filter.
    d. M derrived low pass filter.
    e. M derrived high pass filter.

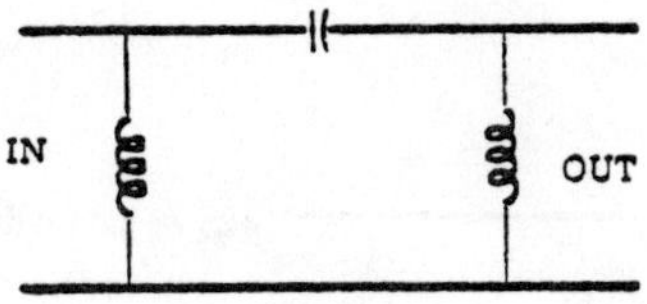

59. The bandwidth of a tuned circuit depends on
    a. the capacitance of the circuit.
    b. the resistance of the circuit.   d. the Q of the circuit.
    c. the inductance of the circuit.   e. all of the above.

60. The impedance of the circuit below would be
    a. 2,000 Ω.
    b. 3,000 Ω.
    c. 8,000 Ω.
    d. 1,140 Ω.
    e. none of these.

61. An increase of power of 100 db represents
    a. 10 times the power.
    b. 100 times the power.   d. 10 times the voltage.
    c. 10^{10} times the power.   e. none of these.

62. If an RF VTVM was connected across the secondary of an IF transformer and the transformer was tuned through resonance the meter would
    a. go from maximum to minimum to maximum.
    b. go from minimum to maximum to minimum.   d. stay at maximum.
    c. go to zero at resonance.   e. none of these.

63. -20 db or twenty db down represents
    a. a voltage ratio of 1/20.
    b. a voltage ratio of 1/100.   d. a power ratio of 1/100.
    c. a power ratio of 1/10.   e. none of these.

64. The frequency of resonance=1,590 hz. L is
    a. 1 henry.
    b. .01 henry.s
    c. 10 henry.s
    d. 1 MF.
    e. none of these.

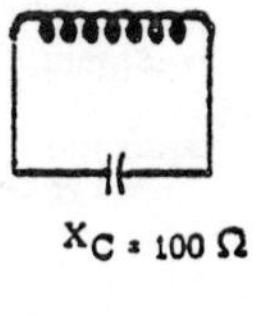

65. In a parallel resonant LC circuit the impedance is
    a. infinity.
    b. zero.   d. low.
    c. high.   e. 72 ohms.

66. If you have a parallel LC circuit at resonance
    a. the impedance is zero with no resistance.
    b. the impedance increases when you add a resistor in parallel.
    c. the impedance decreases when you add a resistor in parallel.
    d. the impedance is infinity.
    e. the impedance is not affected by parallel resistance.

67. A filter circuit designed with the product of the series and shunt impedance as a fixed value is called
    a. a constant K filter.
    b. a M derrived filter.   d. a band pass filter.
    c. a 60 cycle filter.   e. a band step filter.

68. The primary and secondary windings of a transformer are often broadly coupled (over coupled) in order to obtain
    a. greater selectivity.
    b. wider band pass.
    c. narrow band pass.
    d. high Q circuits.
    e. degeneration.

2. **(D'Arsonal)** Meters are calibrated in a metal or plastic case. A meter calibrated in a plastic case will not read correctly in a metal case as the metal will shunt some of the lines of force. The meter reading would be too low. A meter calibrated in a bakelite case and subsequently mounted in a steel case would give a _____ reading.

8. **(3750 ohms)** The sensitivity of the basic DC D'Arsonval meter is determined by the current required to produce full scale deflection. If it requires very little current, the meter is said to have high sensitivity. Voltmeter sensitivity is rated in ohms per volt. Since I = E/R, voltmeter sensitivity is the same as the basic DC meter sensitivity. By formula:

$$\text{Sensitivity} = \frac{R}{E}$$

Where sensitivity is in ohms per volt.

E is full scale voltage reading.
R is the resistance required to give full scale reading with the voltage E.

It should be noted that increasing the size of the multiplier resistance does not change the sensitivity of the meter but changes the voltage requirement for full scale. Typical voltmeter sensitivites are 1,000 ohms per volt for a 1 ma full scale meter and 20,000 ohms per volt for a 50 microampere meter. 20,000 ohms per volt represents the higher sensitivity of the two (it takes less current for full scale deflection). Typical vacuum tube voltmeters and solid state voltmeters have extremely high sensitivities on the order of 11 megohms per volt.

The ohms per volt sensitivity of a 0 to 50 voltmeter having an internal impedance of 50 K ohms would be _____ .

The Wattmeter

14. **(30K ohms)** A wattmeter is used in an AC circuit to measure true power. The arrangement of the circuit is shown:

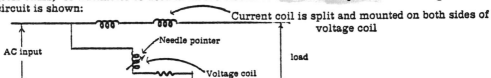

Current coil is split and mounted on both sides of voltage coil

The wattmeter is automatically corrected for power factor. In effect it measures voltage by the shunt coil, current by the series coil and power factor by the reactance of the two fields. By formula true power is equal to the AC voltage X AC current times power factor. If a wattmeter was used to measure DC power or AC true power delivered to a non reactive load, power factor does not have to be considered. In this case P = E X I. If the power was measured with a wattmeter and voltage was measured with a voltmeter, then the current could be calculated. If any two quantities were measured the third could be calculated. If you have a wattmeter reading in a non reactive circuit, you could calculate the current if you also had a _____ meter reading.

The Oscilloscope

20. **(Wheatstone bridge)** The oscilloscope is an instrument used for the examination of waveforms as to shape, amplitude, frequency and phase. The heart of the oscilloscope is the cathode ray tube (CRT) below:

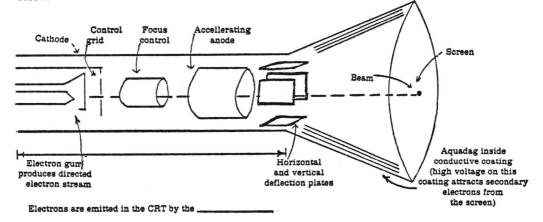

Electrons are emitted in the CRT by the _____

26. **(horizontal)** This concludes unit 12.

47. From the information given below, the AC power would be
    a. 5 watts.
    b. 4,000 watts.
    c. 4 watts.
    d. 150.8 watts.
    e. none of these.

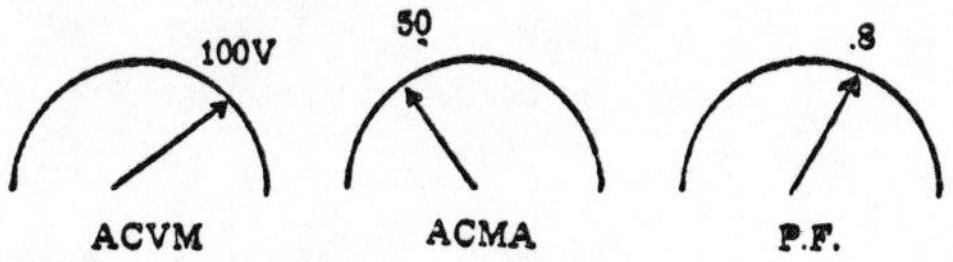

    100V   50   .8
    ACVM   ACMA   P.F.

48. The total conductance in the circuit below is
    a. 50 mhos.
    b. 20,000 micromhos.
    c. 65 mhos.
    d. 30 mhos.
    e. none of these.

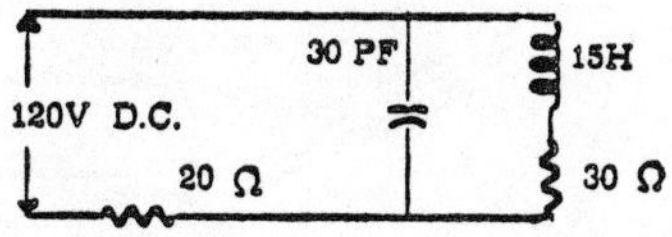

    30 PF   15H
    120V D.C.
    20 Ω   30 Ω

49. 100 volts is applied to a solenoid having a resistance of 4 ohms. The resulting current flow is .2 amperes. The impedance of the solenoid is
    a. .08 ohms.
    b. 25 ohms.   d. 750 ohms.
    c. 500 ohms.   e. none of these.

50. A series RCL circuit consists of 12 ohms of resistance, 54 ohms of X_e and 54 ohms of X_1. The phase angle would be
    a. 45 degrees.
    b. 78.2 degrees.   d. 33 degrees.
    c. O degrees.   e. 27.5 degrees.

51. The applied voltage in the diagram below is
    a. 1.25 volts.
    b. 12.5 volts.
    c. 125 volts.
    d. .125 volts.
    e. none of these.

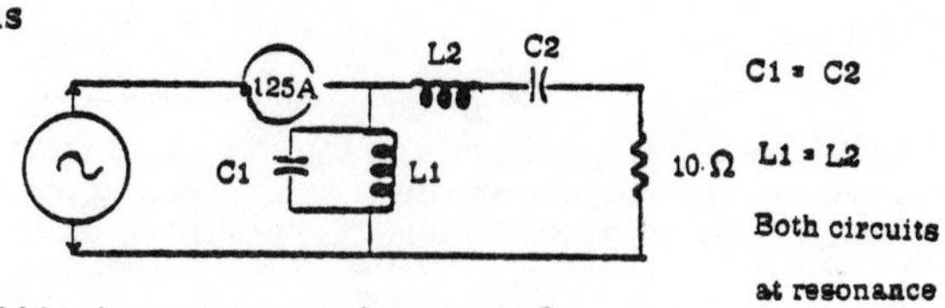

    125A   L2   C2 C_1 = C_2
    C1   L1   10 Ω L_1 = L_2
    Both circuits
    at resonance

52. The power in the circuit shown below would be (assume no resistance at L)
    a. A X V
    b. R_1 X R_2 X A^2.
    c. A X V X P.F.
    d. $(R_1 + R_2 + R_3)$ X A^2.
    e. a or d.

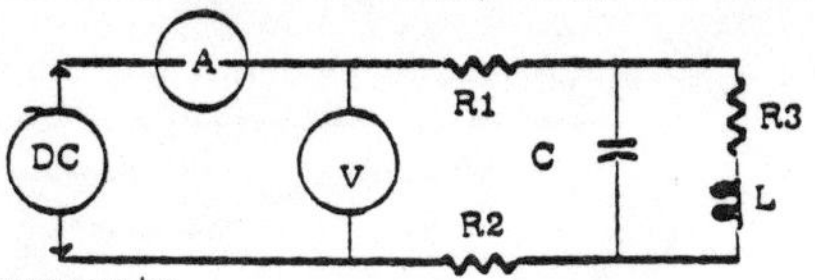

    A   R1   R3
    DC   V   C   L
    R2

53. The indicated dissipated power is
    a. 1000 watts.
    b. 125 X 65 watts.
    c. (125 X 65 X .65) watts.
    d. (125 X 65) / 65
    e. none of these.

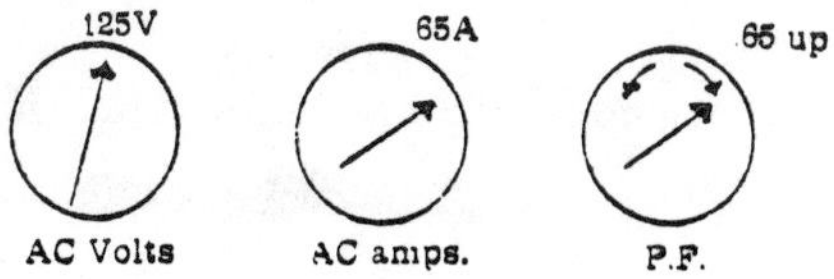

    125V   65A   65 up
    AC Volts   AC amps.   P.F.

54. In the circuit below
    a. the current through the resistor leads the voltage.
    b. the voltage across the resistor leads the current.
    c. the impedance is 15 ohms.
    d. the current through the circuit leads the applied voltage.
    e. none of these.

    15Ω   15Ω   22Ω

55. The conductance of the circuit below is approximately
    a. .033Ω.
    b. 46 mhos.
    c. .0303 mhos.
    d. 13Ω.
    e. none of these.

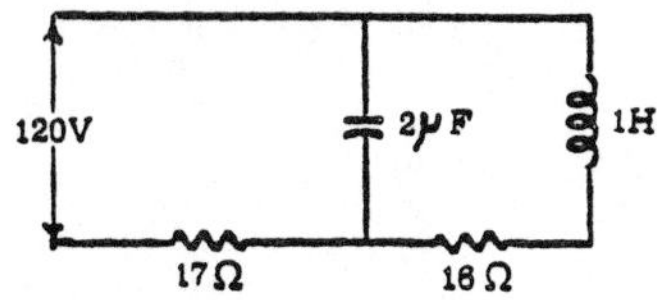

    120V   2 μF   1H
    17Ω   18 Ω

56. The current lags the voltage by 45° in a circuit containing
    a. equal resistance and inductive reactance.
    b. equal resistance and capacitive reactance.
    c. all inductive reactance and no resistance.
    d. all capacitive reactance and no resistance.
    e. equal capacitive and inductive reactance.

3.   (low) The current range of a D'Arsonval meter can be extended by use of a **shunt.** Consider a basic
      meter movement having a full scale deflection with 1 ma of current flowing. If the internal coil
      resistance is 12 ohms and it was shunted with a resistance of 3 ohms, then the total current would be 5
      ma when the pointer was at full scale. The arrangement shown provides an explanation:

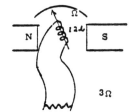

Pointer will move to full scale
      when 1 ma flows through coil.

At the same time 4 ma will go through the
shunt since the shunt resistance (3 ohms)
is 1/4 of the coil resistance (12 ohms).
Current flow is inversely proportional to
resistance. Therefore, four times as much
current will flow through the shunt.

The scale would be calibrated to read 5 ma full scale. (current of coil and shunt). Since it takes more
current now to obtain full scale reading, the sensitivity of the combination is lower.

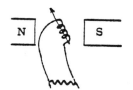

Full scale current = .5 ma

Coil resistance = 6 Ω

Shunt resistance = .6 Ω

The total full scale current in
the circuit shown is _____.

9.   (1000 ohms per volt) If a resistor is added in series with a voltmeter lead, the sensitivity of the meter
      is _____ and the full scale range is _____.

15.   (volt) The wattmeter reading in an AC circuit is in effect taking into account the __VOLTAGE__ of
      the shunt coil, the __CURRENT__ of the series coil and the power factor.

21.   (electron gun) The conductive coating on the inside of the CRT is called the _____
      coating.

35. Eddy currents are currents that are
    a. circulating in the secondary winding.
    b. circulating in the primary winding.
    c. capacitor currents.
    d. induced in iron cores.
    e. a and b above.

36. Core losses are not determined by the
    a. Eddy currents.
    b. Hysteresis.
    c. size of wire on winding.
    d. air gap.
    e. frequency.

37. A certain coil has 1600 turns with an inductance of .4 Henry. When the turns are increased to 2000 turns the new inductance would be
    a. greater than 400 mH.
    b. less than 400 mH.
    c. 200 mH.
    d. 100 mH.
    e. none of these.

38. The most unstable component in a circuit (highest breakdown rate) is
    a. a crystal.
    b. a transformer.
    c. a choke.
    d. a capacitor.
    e. a wire connection.

39. The phase shift shown below is caused by

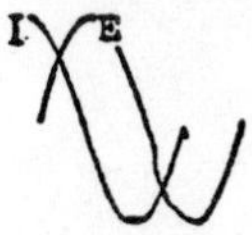

    I ⤬ E

    a. pure capacitance.
    b. pure inductance.
    c. pure resistance.
    d. a combination of the above.
    e. none of these.

40. Two identical capacitors are connected in series and placed across 120 volts. They are disconnected without discharging and the two series capacitors are placed in parallel with a third identical capacitor. The voltage across this circuit would be
    a. 120 volts.
    b. 60 volts.
    c. 40 volts.
    d. 20 volts.
    e. none of the above

41. It is necessary to observe polarity when using
    a. resistors.
    b. oil capacitors.
    c. electrolytic capacitors.
    d. chokes.
    e. transformers.

42. If you doubled the distance between the two plates of an air capacitor you would
    a. double the capacitance.
    b. cut the capacitance in half.
    c. not affect its capacitance.
    d. decreases the voltage breakdown.
    e. none of these.

43. In the circuit below, as the frequency is increased, the output will
    a. increase.
    b. decrease.
    c. remain the same.
    d. increase then decrease.
    e. decrease then increase.

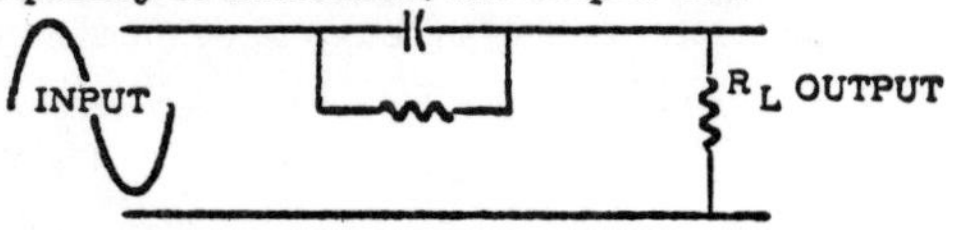

    INPUT R_L OUTPUT

44. A 10 Mhz current would be offered the least impedance by a
    a. copper strip 6 inches long and 2 inches wide.
    b. aluminum wire 6 inches long and 6 mils in diameter.
    c. 2 pf capacitor.
    d. one ohm wire wound resistor.
    e. silver wire 6 inches long and 6 mils in diameter.

45. The impedance of the circuit below at two KHz is approximately
    a. 38.45 Ω.
    b. 3845 Ω.
    c. 161 Ω.
    d. 6280 Ω.
    e. none of these.

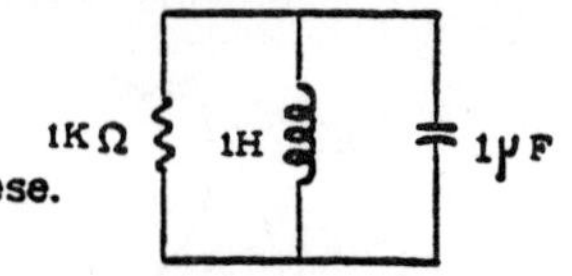

    1K Ω   1H   1μF

46. The power in the circuit shown below would be
    a. A X V.
    b. R_1 X R_2 X A^2
    c. A X V X P.F.
    d. $(R_1 + R_2 + R^3)$ X A
    e. none of these.

    A   R1   R3
    V   C
          R2   L

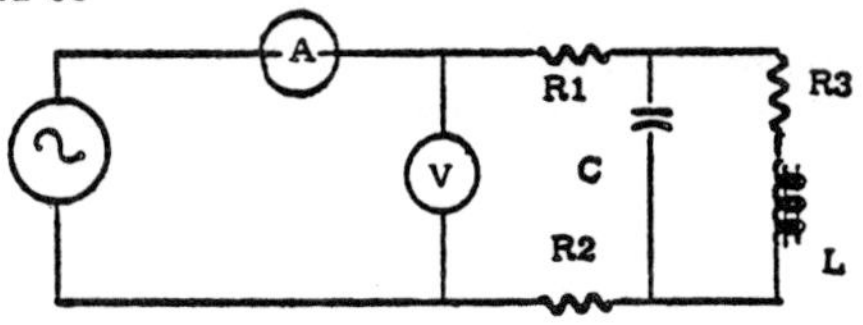

4. (5.5 ma) Higher current readings can be obtained with a DC ammeter by placing a ___SHUNT___ resistor in the meter circuit. The shunt reduces the __SENSITIVITY__ of the meter.

10. (unchanged, increased) Now let us see what we have to do to change a voltmeter for a higher full scale reading.

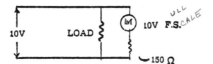

In the circuit to the left the full scale voltage is 10 volts. The full scale current is E/R or 10/150 = .066 2/3 amps = 66 2/3 ma

To extend the full scale to 100 volts we must add an additional series resistance to limit the current to 66 2/3 ma.

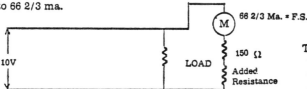

The total multiplier resistance must equal the total voltage (100V) divided by the full scale current (.066 2/3 amp.)
Rt = 100/.066 2/3 or 1500 ohms.

Since there is already 150 ohms in the circuit, the additional resistance would be 1500 - 150 or 1350 ohms.

An easier solution involves proportion. To limit the current to 66 2/3 ma it would take 10 times the resistance if 10 times the voltage is applied. 10 X 150 is 1500 ohms. Subtracting the original 150 ohms we find the added resistance needed is **1350 ohms.**

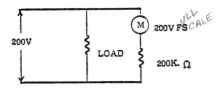

To extend this circuit scale reading to 300 volts, the additional series resistance

must have a value of _____.

16. (voltage, current) Voltmeters with a low sensitivity, such as 1000 ohms per volt are inaccurate when used to measure voltage in a high resistance circuit. Their low resistance when placed in parallel with a high circuit resistance drastically alters the circuit. See the example below:

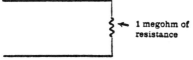 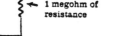 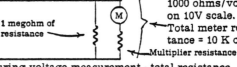

Before voltage measurement - total resistance is 1 megohm

During voltage measurement - total resistance of this parallel circuit is about 10K ohms.

This is called loading the circuit. The low impedance meter changed the circuit resistance from 1 megohm to approximately 10 K ohms. The circuit voltage drop with the meter connected would be about 1/100 th of its original value.

Vacuum tube or solid state voltmeters have a high sensitivity (11 megohm/volt) and do not load a circuit. When some vacuum tube voltmeters (VTVMs) are used to measure AC, the AC is first rectified and then applied as a DC bias to the vacuum tube circuit. It is sometimes necessary to wait a few seconds before taking a reading when using a VTVM. Special RC time constant networks or degenerative feedback circuits cause the meter pointer needle to settle down slowly.

For making voltage measurements in a high impedance circuit a __VACUUM TUBE__ volt meter should be used to prevent __LOADING__ of the circuit.

22. (aquadag) For proper display of a wave form the wave to be examined is amplified and fed to the vertical deflection plates. The horizontal plates are connected to a saw tooth sweep voltage. Suppose an oscilloscope was used to examine a 120 volt 60 cycle per second wave form. The diagram below shows such an arrangement:

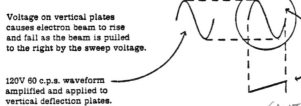

Voltage on vertical plates causes electron beam to rise and fall as the beam is pulled to the right by the sweep voltage.

As beam strikes flourescent screen this light pattern appears on face of CRT.

120V 60 c.p.s. waveform amplified and applied to vertical deflection plates.

Sawtooth voltage generated and amplified internally. It is applied to the horizontal deflection plates to pull beam to the right.

The horizontal sweep in an oscilloscope generally requires a __SAWTOOTH__ voltage.

22. The MF range is
    a. 20 to 30 Khz.
    b. 300 to 3.000 Khz.   d. 300 to 3.000 Mhz.
    c. 3 to 30 Mhz.   e. none of these.

23. 20 volts equals
    a. 28.28 peak volts.
    b. 56.56 peak volts.   d. 100 peak volts.
    c. 32 peak volts.   e. 70.7 peak volts.

24. A good high frequency insulator is
    a. rubber.
    b. bakelite.   d. glass.
    c. mica.   e. none of these.

25. An air core inductor made of No. 18 copper wire has an inductance of .3 H. When an iron core is added the inductance would be
    a. above .3 H.
    b. below .3 H.   d. .6 H.
    c. .3 H.   e. 1.5 H.

26. The total inductance of five 1 Henry inductors connected in parallel without coupling would be
    a. 5 henrys.
    b. 1/5 henry.   d. 25 henrys.
    c. 1 henry.   e. none of these.

27. For maximum inductance connect

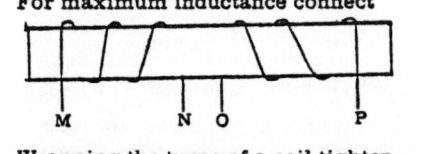

    a. M to P.
    b. N to O.
    c. O to P.
    d. M to O.
    e. M to N.

28. Wrapping the turns of a coil tighter
    a. raises inductance.
    b. lowers the inductance.   d. increases the DC resistance.
    c. decreases capacitance.   e. lowers the inductive reactance.

29. The inductance of a coil can be determined by
    a. the number of turns.
    b. the ratio of the diameter to the length of the coil.
    c. the diameter of the wire used.
    d. the diameter of the coil.
    e. the number of turns and the ratio of the diameter to the length of the coil (Assume single layer air core coil, close wound and a known gage of wire.)

30. The cores of inductors are laminated to
    a. increase permeability.
    b. decrease permeability.   d. increase eddy currents.
    c. decrease eddy current losses. e. counteract Miller effect.

31. The phase shift shown below is caused by 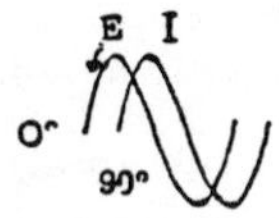
    a. pure capacitance.
    b. pure inductance.
    c. pure resistance.
    d. a combination of the above.
    e. matched impedance.

32. The total inductance of the circuit below assuming no coupling is 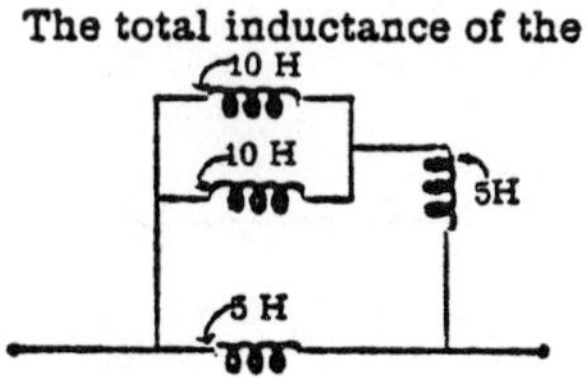
    a. 7.5 H.
    b. 10 H.
    c. 3.33 H.
    d. 30 H.
    e. none of these.

33. A certain coil has 400 turns with an inductance of .4 Henry. When the turns are increased to 500 turns the new inductance would be
    a. .4 H.
    b. .625 H.   d. 1 H.
    c. .85 H.   e. none of these.

34. If a .5H and a .9H coil are conneced in series with a mutual inductance of .3H with fields 180° out of phase, the total inductance is
    a. .8 H.
    b. 2 H.   d. 4.5 H.
    c. 1.7 H.   e. 2.7 H.

5. **(shunt, sensitivity)** When a D'Arsonval meter used as a current meter is placed in a circuit containing pulsating DC the deflection and reading will be directly proportional to the average current. The deflection and reading of a D'Arsonval meter in a pulsating DC circuit is directly proportional to the _AVERAGE_ current.

11. **(100 K)** Now we are ready to solve a more difficult problem. A 0 to 120 volt meter has an internal multiplying resistance of 3750 ohms. When an additional series resistance is added and 135 volts is applied, the meter reads 80 volts. Find the value of the added resistance.

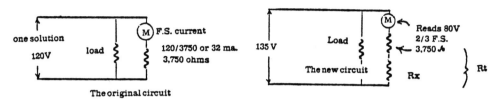

The original circuit

If the meter only reads 2/3 of full scale value (80/120), then the current in the new circuit must be 2/3 of full scale value. So the current in the new circuit is 2/3 of 32 ma or 21.33 ma. The total multiplying resistance must equal E/I or 135/.02133 or 6329 ohms. Rx = Rt - 3750 = 6329 - 3750 or **2579 ohms.**
A second solution. Perhaps an easier way of working the problem is by proportion. The additional resistance dropped the current to 2/3 value. In order to produce full scale current it would take 3/2 (2/3 inverted) as much voltage or 3/2 X 135 = 202.5 V. The total required multiplier resistance would be 202.5 divided by .032 A or 6329 ohms. Rx = Rt - 3750 = 6329 - 3750 or **2579 ohms.**
A 0 to 120V voltmeter has a multiplier resistance of 3700 ohms. When an additional series resistance is added to one side of the voltmeter and 350 volts is applied, the meter reads 79 volts (approx 80). The value of the additional resistance is approximately _____ ohms.

17. **(vacuum tube, loading)** A VTVM is used to measure AC line voltage. The meter rises to 100 volts and then slowly rises to 105 volts. This indicated either an internal _RC_ time constant network is being used or a degenerative feedback circuit is being used for meter _DAMPING_ .

23. **(sawtooth)** If a sine wave is applied to the vertical input of an oscilloscope using a sawtooth sweep voltage, the waveform displayed would be a _SINE_ wave.

12. If 100 v. D.C. is applied at point W with respect to ground, a voltmeter connected from point X to Z would read

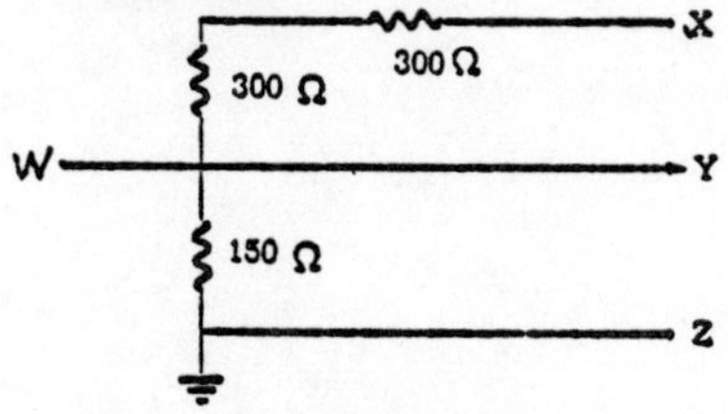

    a. 150 volts.
    b. 100 volts.
    c. 75 volts.
    d. 50 volts.
    e. 25 volts.

13. If you wanted to use a voltmeter to find the power dissipated by the application of a voltage from W to ground, you should

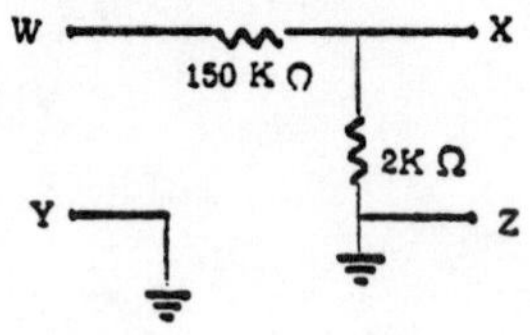

    a. measure the voltage across Y to Z. Square this voltage and divide by 2 K.
    b. measure the voltage across W to X. Divide by 150 K. Square this result and multiply by 152K.
    c. measure the voltage across W to X and multiply this by 152K.
    d. measure the voltage across X to Y and multiply this by 150K.
    e. none of these.

14. Energy is measured in units of
    a. kilowatt hours.
    b. kilowatts.   d. watts.
    c. ampere hours.   e. volts.

15. In order to dissipate the greatest amount of power, the load resistance should be

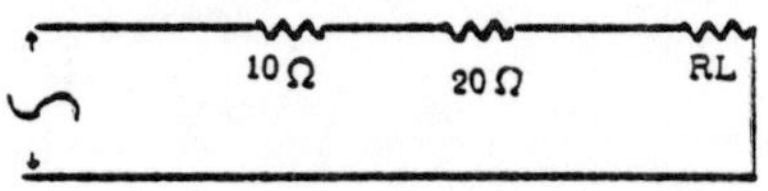

    a. 10 ohms.   d. high as possible.
    b. 20 ohms.   e. low as possible.
    c. 30 ohms.

16. A 12 volt battery has an internal resistance of .6 ohms. If a 2 watt 12 volt lamp is connected across the battery, the current is
    a. 220 ma.   d. 78 ma.
    b. 165 ma.   e. none of these.
    c. 32 ma.

17. In the diagram below

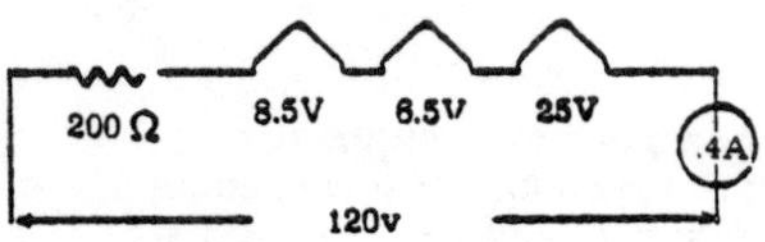

    a. there is no need for the dropping resistor.
    b. the resistance should have a value of 100 ohms.
    c. the resistance should have a value of 50 ohms.
    d. the circuit is ok.
    e. the circuit will not work.

18. A DC relay having a resistance of 700 ohms is made to operate with a current of .1 ampere. When operated from a 120 volt DC line the dropping resistor dissipates
    a. 8 watts.
    b. 4 watts.   d. 3 watts.
    c. 5 watts.   e. 25 watts.

19. A coil to a relay has an impedance of 500Ω, and operates on .1 amp. To operate correctly, a series resistor must be placed in the circuit. With 120V applied, the value of the dropping resistance should be
    a. 500Ω.
    b. 600Ω.   d. 800Ω.
    c. 700Ω.   e. none of these.

20. The RMS voltage of a sine wave is equal to
    a. Peak/ $\sqrt{2}$.
    b. Peak x$\sqrt{2}$.
    c. Peak to Peak/$\sqrt{2}$.
    d. Peak to Peak X $\sqrt{2}$.
    e. averaged value.

21. The EHF range of frequencies is
    a. 3 Mhz to 30 Mhz.
    b. 30 Mhz to 300 Mhz.
    c. 300 Mhz to 3,000 Mhz.
    d. 30,000 Mhz to 300,000 Mhz.
    e. none of these.

The DC Voltmeter using A Series Multiplier Resistor

6.   (average) The basic D'Arsonval meter can be converted to a voltmeter by the addition of a series multiplier resistor. Let us consider the circuit below:

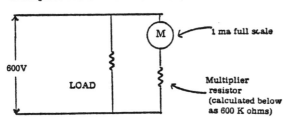

In order for this meter to read 600 V at full scale the current would have to be full scale current or 1 ma.

The multiplier resistance would have to limit the current to this value. It's resistance can be calculated by Ohm's law: R = E/I = 600 V / 1 ma. or 600 / .001 or 600 K ohms.

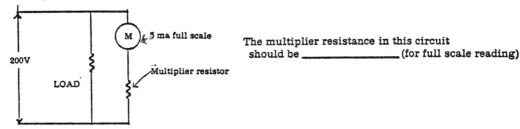

The multiplier resistance in this circuit should be _____ (for full scale reading)

12.   (12,400 ohms) A ___RESISTOR___ in series with a voltmeter lead will increase its full scale range.

18.   (RC, damping) An ohmmeter is used for measuring resistance and makes use of the D'Arsonval movement. One arrangement is shown below:

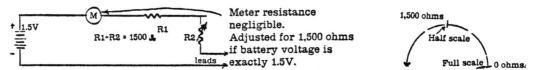

Meter resistance negligible.
Adjusted for 1,500 ohms if battery voltage is exactly 1.5V.

If the ohmmeter leads were shorted together, the current flow would be 1.5V/1,500 ohms or 1 ma. There would be full scale deflection indicating no resistance between meter leads. If 1,500 ohms was placed between the leads the meter current would be 1.5V (1,500 + 1,500) or .5 ma. The meter would read half scale and should be calibrated as indicated above. The variable series resistance is used to compensate for lower ohmmeter voltages as the battery goes down. An ohmmeter uses a D'Arsonval meter in series with a _____ and two _____ (one variable and the other fixed).

24.   (sine) The wave to be examined using an oscilloscope generally is applied to the ___VERTICAL___ input.

1. The copper wire which would carry current with a minimum loss would be
   a. No. 14.
   b. No. 12 d. No. 16.
   c. No. 20. e. No. 4.

2. A certain type of wire of certain dimensions has a resistance of 36 ohms per foot. Another wire of the same type and length but having a diameter of one third the first wire would have
   a. one third the resistance.
   b. one ninth the resistance. d. 9 times the resistance.
   c. 3 times the resistance.   e. the same resistance.

3. When there is a difference of potential between two points there exists
   a. an electrostatic field.
   b. current flow.   d. 100 volts of EMF.
   c. low resistance between points. e. none of these.

4. When an electron leaves an atom
   a. H_2 is formed.
   b. an ion forms.   d. a neutron is left.
   c. a proton is left. e. none of these.

5. A certain wire 36 feet long, has a resistance of 12 ohms per foot. If a second wire has the same length but a diameter of 1/3 the first wire, the resistance of the second wire is
   a. 3.888 ohms.
   b. 120 ohms.   d. 72 ohms.
   c. 1296 ohms. e. none of these.

6. The illustration below indicates

   a. 6 ohms of resistance.
   b. a resistor with a 10% tolerance.
   c. 2 ohms of resistance.
   d. 10 ohms of resistance.
   e. none of these.

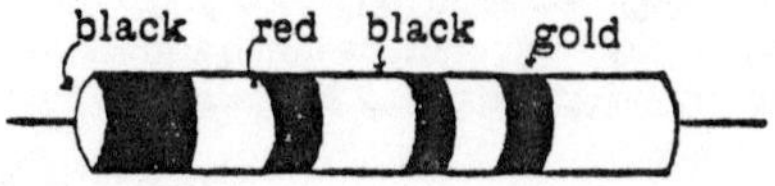

black red black gold

7. In the diagram below R_2 would have a value of

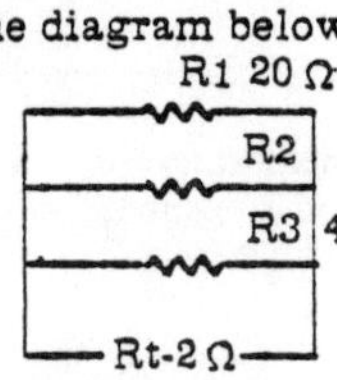

R1 20 Ω
R2
R3 4Ω
Rt-2 Ω

   a. 1 ohm.
   b. 2 ohms.
   c. 3 ohms.
   d. 4 ohms.
   e. 5 ohms.

8. The voltage across the 15 ohm resistor is approximately

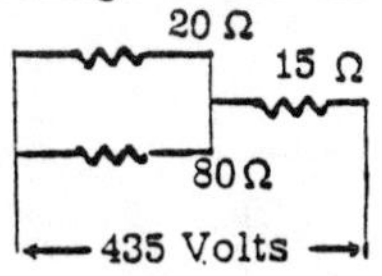

20 Ω
15 Ω
80 Ω
435 Volts

   a. 125 volts. d. 140 volts.
   b. 210 volts. e. 160 volts.
   c. 435 volts.

9. In the diagram shown, the voltage is

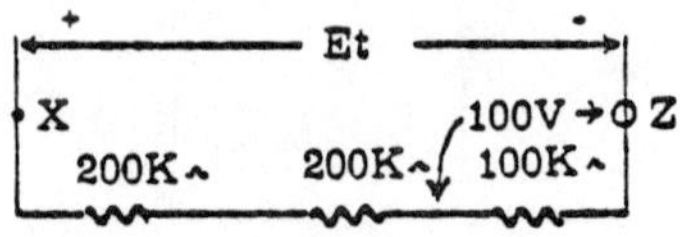

Et
X
200K   200K   100K
100V → Z

   a. 150 volts x to x.
   b. 300 volts x to z.
   c. 200 volts x to z.
   d. 500 volts x to z.
   e. 75 volts x to z.

10. The measured input to a transmitter was 242 watts. In 31 hours the energy consumed would be
    a. 242 watts.
    b. 7.5 kilowatts. d. 7.5 kilowatt hours.
    c. 31 kilowatts.   e. 18 watts.

11. In the diagram below the voltmeter should read

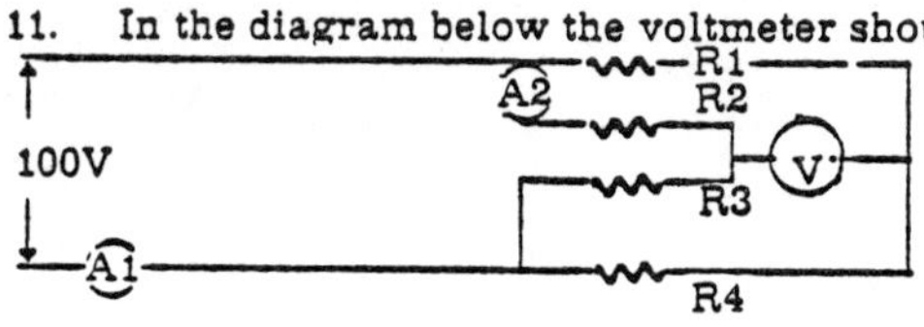

R1
A2 R2
100V
R3
V
A1
R4

   A1-12.5A
   A2-2.5A
   R2- 4Ω
   R4- 9Ω

   a. 10 volts.
   b. 45 volts.
   c. 80 volts.
   d. 100 volts.
   e. 0 volts

UNIT 12 MEASURING DEVICES

RECHECK PROGRAMMED INSTRUCTION USING SHRADER'S ELECTRONIC COMMUNICATION

1. Almost all meters in general use are_____type meters. Sec. 12-1.

3. (D'Arsonval) Meters calibrated for a bakelite panel would read_____for a steel panel. Sec. 12-2.

5. (2%) D'Arsonal meters generally have good scale_____. Sec. 12-3.

7. (shunt) An ammeter is always connected in_____in a circuit. Sec. 12-4.

9. (2.4 ma) If the range of a D'Arsonval meter is extended by use of a shunt, the device sensitivity is _____. Sec. 12-6.

11. (critically) A resistor in series with a voltmeter lead will _____ its full scale range. Sec. 12-9.

13. (300 K) A O to 150 voltmeter has a resistance of 50,000 ohms. When an additional resistance was placed in one of the meter leads and 300 volts was applied, the meter reads 100 volts. The additional series multiplier has an approximate value of_____. Sec. 12-9.

15. (300K) More accurate voltage readings will be obtained when high resistance circuits are being measured if the voltmeter has a _____sensitivity. Sec. 12-10.

17. (battery, resistors) For minimal loading of a high resistance circuit voltage should be measured using a meter like the_____volt meter. Sec. 12-13.

19. (VTVM) The power in a load in a DC circuit is measured by a wattmeter. The current in the circuit could be calculated if a_____ meter reading was also obtained. Sec. 12-23.

21. (voltage, current) Power factor is already allowed for when using a wattmeter so a wattmeter actually measures_____power. Sec. 12-3.

23. (17.5) Electrons are emitted in the CRT by the_____. Sec. 12-29.

25 (vertical) Horizontal sweep in an oscilloscope generally requires a_____wave. Sec. 12-29.

27. (sine) This concludes the recheck materials.

12. The symbol below represents a(n)
    a. OR gate.
    b. NAND gate.
    c. NOR gate.
    d. NOT gate.
    e. AND gate.

13. The truth table below describes a(n)
    a. OR gate.
    b. NAND gate.
    c. NOR gate.
    d. NOT gate.
    e. AND gate.

A	B	C
0	0	1
0	1	1
1	0	1
1	1	0

14. The unique output for the NAND circuit is
    a. logic 0.
    b. logic 1.   d. ambiguous.
    c. low.   e. b and d above.

15. And AND circuit followed by an inverter describes a(n)
    a. NOT circuit.
    b. NOR circuit.   d. OR circuit.
    c. NAND circuit.   e. AND circuit.

16. The symbol below represents a(n)
    a. NOT gate.
    b. NOR gate.   d. NAND gate.
    c. AND gate.   e. OR gate.

17. These symbol shown represents a(n)
    a. negative NOR gate.
    b. positive AND gate.   d. a or b above.
    c. positive NOR gate.   e. a or c above.

18. The truth table below describes a(n)
    a. common OR circuit.
    b. AND circuit.
    c. NOT circuit.
    d. NAND circuit.
    e. exclusive OR circuit.

A	B	C
0	0	0
0	1	1
1	0	1
1	1	0

19. NANDS and NORS are called
    a. unique gates.
    b. universal gates.   d. simple gates.
    c. exclusive gates.   e. none of these.

20. By connection or combination any of the other four gates can be formed from the
    a. NAND gate.
    b. OR gate.   d. AND gate.
    c. NOR gate.   e. a or c above.

21. Gates are like switches when component transistors are driven into
    a. cutoff.
    b. saturation.   d. a and b above.
    c. linear operation.   e. b and c above.

22. A good example of an inverter circuit is a
    a. common collector BJT circuit
    b. common base BJT circuit.   d. silicon diode.
    c. common emitter BJT circuit .   e. resistor.

23. Inverting the output of a NOR circuit forms a(n)
    a. OR gate.
    b. AND gate.   d. NAND gate.
    c. NOT gate.   e. NOR gate.

24. When more than two inputs are used the output will be logic 1 if
    a. all the inputs are logic 0 in an OR circuit.
    b. all the inputs are logic 1 in an AND circuit.   d. a and c above.
    c. any of the inputs are logic 1 in an OR circuit. e. b and c above.

2. (current) Practically all the DC meters used in commercial radio applications are of the same general type. These are known as a moving coil, galvanometer, or _____ meter. Sec. 12-2.

4. (wrong or low) Most general purpose meters are accurate to_____% or better. Sec. 12-2.

6. (linearity) The range of an ammeter can be extended by the use of a _____ . Sec. 12-4.

8. (series) If a 20 ohm 0 - 1 ma meter is connected across a 4 ohm resistance, it reads .4ma. The actual line current is _____. Sec. 12-5.

10. (decreased) If the pointer on a meter does rot settle down quickly, the meter is less than _____ damped. Sec. 12-7.

12. (extend or increase) To measure 300 volts with a 0 to 1 ma meter having negligible internal resistance, the multiplier resistor should have a value of_____ohms. Sec. 12-9.

14. (100K) In order to make the meter shown read full scale for 200 volts, an additional series resistor must be added having a value of_____ ohms. Sec. 12-9.

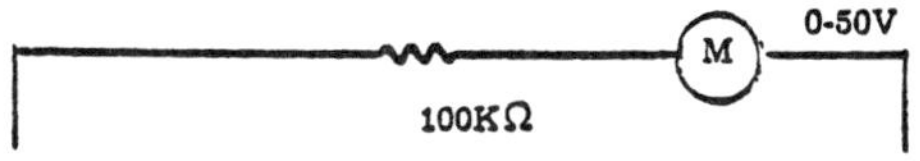

16. (high) An ohmmeter consists of a D'Arsonval meter, a_____and two_____. Sec. 12-11.

18. (vacuum tube) It is not necessary to observe polarity when measuring AC with an AC _____. Sec. 12-14.

20. (volt) The two coils of a wattmeter are the_____coil across the line and the_____ coil in series with the line. Sec. 12-23.

22. (true)

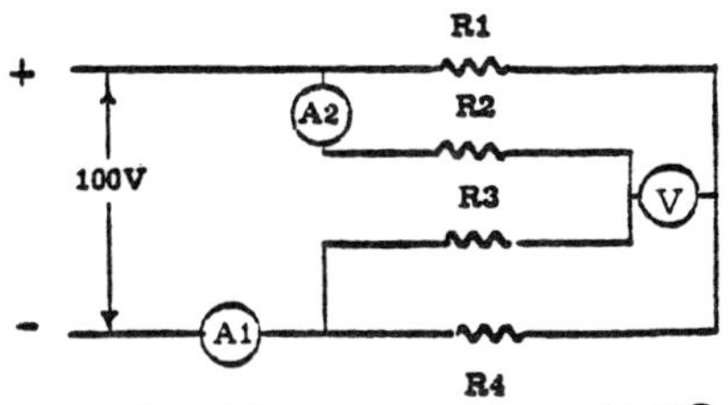

A1 = 12.5A   R2 = 9Ω
A2 = 2.5A   R1 = 4Ω

In the diagram shown the voltmeter should read _____ volts. Sec. 12-18.

24. (electron gun) When measuring a voltage with an oscilloscope, the voltage is applied to the _____plates. Sec. 12-29.

26. (sawtooth) If a sawtooth horizontal sweep is used the frequency of a sine wave input is displayed directly on the screen. if the leads of an oscilloscope are across a 60 c.p.s. 120V AC line, the displayed pattern would be a _____ wave. Sec. 12-29.

1. The two basic types of digital circuits are
    a. combinational and gates.
    b. decision making and gates.   d. flip flops and storage.
    c. combinational and sequential. e. sequential and storage.

2. The inverter gate has
    a. a logic 1 output with a logic 1 input.
    b. a logic 0 output with a logic 0 input.   d. a and b above.
    c. a logic 0 output with a logic 1 input.   e. b and c above.

3. The circuit shown below is a(n)
    a. AND gate.
    b. OR gate.
    c. NAND gate.
    d. NOT gate.
    e. NOR gate.

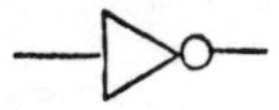

4. The AND gate output of the circuit below would be
    a. high.
    b. low.
    c. unique.
    d. 100 volts
    e. a or b above.

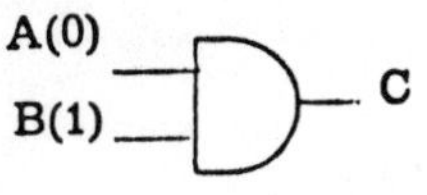

5. The A input in the circuit below would be
    a. logic 1.
    b. logic 0.
    c. grounded.
    d. low.
    e. any of the above.

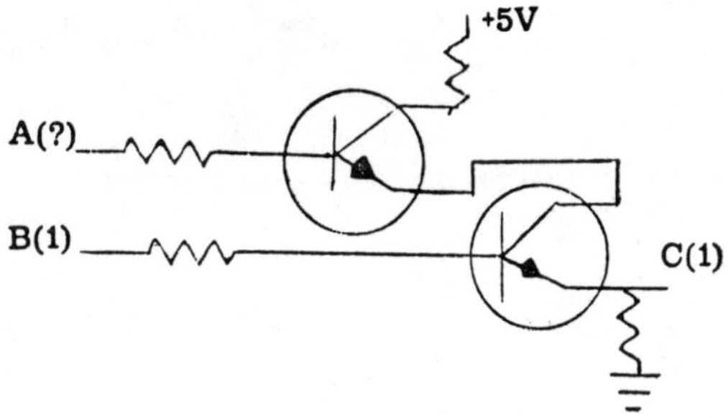

6. The unique output of an AND circuit is
    a. logic 0.
    b. logic 1   d. one half volt.
    c. zero volts.   e. ambiguous.

7. The unique output of a common OR circuit is
    a. logic 0.
    b. logic 1.   d. ambiguous
    c. low.   e. a and c above.

8. The truth table below describes a(n)
    a. NOT gate.
    b. AND gate.
    c. OR gate.
    d. NOR gate.
    e. NAND gate

A	B	C
0	0	0
0	1	0
1	0	0
1	1	1

9. A triangle followed by a circle (bubble) describes a(n)
    a. amplifier.
    b. inverter.   d. OR gate.
    c. AND gate.   e. NAND gate.

10. The output of the circuit below would be a logic 1 (high) if
    a. input A was a logic 1.
    b. input B was a logic 1.
    c. input A was a logic 0.
    d. input B was a logic 0.
    e. input A or input B was a logic 1.

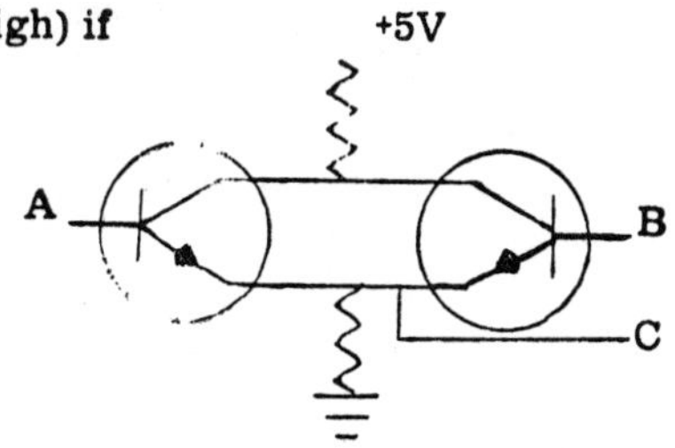

11. The circuit in question # 10 is a(n)
    a. OR gate.
    b. NOT gate.
    c. AND gate.
    d. NAND gate.
    e. NOR gate.

1. A resistor in series with a voltmeter lead will
   a. increase its full scale range.
   b. decrease its full scale range.
   c. change it to an ammeter.
   d. change it to a wattmeter.
   e. none of these.

2. The ohm per volt rating of an O to 50 volts voltmeter having an internal impedance of 50 K ohms would be
   a. 10.
   b. 100
   c. 1,000.
   d. 10,000.
   e. 100,000.

3. A 0 to 120 voltmeter has a resistance of 3,750 ohms. When an additional series resistance was placed in one of the meter leads and 135 volts was applied the meter read as shown below. The additional series multiplier has approximate value of
   a. 509 ohms.
   b. 630 ohms.
   c. 1,260 ohms.
   d. 2,580 ohms.
   e. none of these.

4. A wattmeter measures
   a. current squared through its coils.
   b. voltage squared through its coils.
   c. the voltage across the meter and the current through the meter.
   d. frequency.
   e. energy.

5. An additional series resistor was placed in the circuit below and when 350 volts was applied to the voltmeter circuit instead of 120 volts, the meter read 79 volts. The additional resistance must have had a value of
   a. 1,650 ohms.
   b. approximately 12,400 ohms.
   c. approximately 15,910 ohms.
   d. 782 ohms.
   e. none of these.

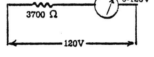

6. In order to make the meter shown below read full scale for 135 volts, an additional series resistance must be added having a value of
   a. 3,700 ohms.
   b. approximately 1,420 ohms.
   c. approximately 470 ohms.
   d. approximately 1,690 ohms.
   e. none of these.

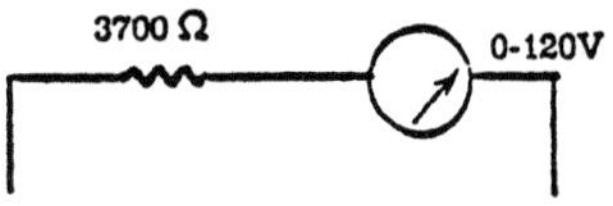

7. For the indicated frequency on the graph the output current would be

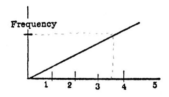

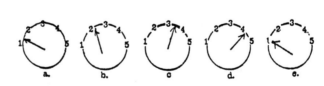

8. To accurately measure an unknown resistance one should use a
   a. Galvanometer.
   b. VTVM.
   c. Wheatstone Bridge.
   d. Dynamometer.
   e. Pedometer.

9. Higher current readings can be obtained with a DC ammeter by placing a
   a. choke in series with the ammeter.
   b. capacitor in shunt with the ammeter.
   c. low resistance in shunt with the ammeter.
   d. grounding one end of the ammeter.
   e. none of these.

10. To measure 200 volts with a 0 to 5 ma meter having negligible internal resistance, the multiplier resistor should have a value of
    a. 4 megohms.
    b. 1,000 ohms.
    c. 40,000 ohms.
    d. 10,000 ohms.
    e. none of these.

2. **(switch, linearity)** In a positive logic 2 input **AND** circuit, there will be a logic 1 output if input A is logic_____ and input B is logic _____. For all other inputs the output is a logic_____. Sec. 31-4

4. (A⎯⎤D⎯X , **truth table**) A 2 input **AND** circuit can be formed connecting two_____in B⎯⎤ _____in an emitter follower configuration. Sec. 31-4

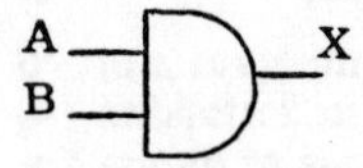

6. **(1, 1, 1)** The symbol for a 2 input **OR** circuit is _____ . There will be a logic 1 output in an **OR** circuit **OR** circuit if at least one of the inputs is logic_____. An **OR** circuit can be formed with 2 **BJT's** in _____ using an emitter following configuration. Sec. 31-5

8. **(inverter,** ⎯▷o⎯ **)** The triangle represents an _____ and the bubble the _____ . Sec. 31-6.

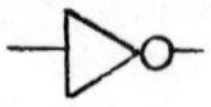

10. **(emitter)** An **AND** gate with an inversion bubble forms the _____ gate or a_____gate. Sec. 31-7

12. **(0, 1,** ⎯⎤Do⎯ **)** An inverter coupled to the output of an OR gate is called a_____gate or a_____ _____ gate. Sec. 31-8

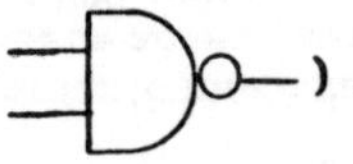

14. **(1, 0)** The symbol of a **NOR** gate is_____Sec. 31-8

16. **(1, 1,** ⎯⎤D⎯ **)** This concludes the recheck on unit 26.

11. A meter calibrated in a bakelite case and subsequently mounted in a steel framework would show
   a. lower reading for the same current.
   b. a higher reading for the same current.   d. a tendency to oscillate.
   c. no change in reading for the same current.   e. none of these.

12. A 0 to 120 voltmeter has a resistance of 3,750 ohms. When an additional series resistance was placed in one of the meter leads and 135 volts was applied, the meter read as shown below. The additional series multiplier has an approximate value of
   a. 10 K.
   b. 8,000 ohms.
   c. 3,000 ohms.
   d. 5,000 ohms.
   e. 1,200 ohms.

13. To properly view a sine wave on a scope apply
   a. the sine wave to the vertical plates and a sawtooth wave to the horizontal plates.
   b. the sine wave to the vertical plates and a square wave to the horizontal plates.
   c. the sine wave to the horizontal plates and a sawtooth wave to the vertical plates.
   d. the sine wave to both the vertical and horizontal plates.
   e. none of these.

14. In the diagram below the voltmeter should read
   a. 10 volts.
   b. 45 volts.
   c. 80 volts.
   d. 100 volts.
   e. none of these.

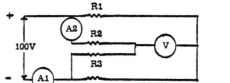

A 1 - 12.5A
A 2 - 2.5A
R 2 - 9Ω
R 4 - 4Ω

15. A VTVM is used to measure AC line voltage. The meter immediately rises to 150 volts and then slowly rises to 155 volts. This indicates
   a. internal RC time constant in the meter.
   b. the maximum line voltage is 150 volts.   d. oscillation.
   c. the meter is out of calibration.   e. none of these.

16. The leads of an oscilloscope are across a 60 cps 120V Ac line. On the screen you would see

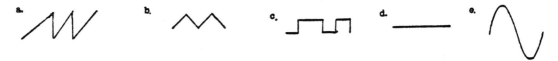

17. A 0 to 10 voltmeter has a total resistance of 150 ohms. To convert this meter to a 0 to 100 voltmeter, it would be necessary to add a series multiplier resistance of
   1. 1,345 ohms.
   b. 1,350 ohms.   d. 600 ohms.
   c. 1,500 ohms.   e. 752 ohms.

18. Electrons are emitted in the CRT by the
   a. aquadag coating.
   b. anode.
   c. phosphors.

19. If the range of a D'Arsonval meter is extended by use of a shunt
   a. its sensitivity is increased.
   b. its sensitivity is decreased.   d. it can be used as an electro-dynamometer.
   c. its suitable for a voltmeter.   e. it can be used to measure R.F.

20. If you have a wattmeter you could find the current by use of the
   a. voltmeter.
   b. frequency meter.   d. grid dip meter.
   c. D'Arsonval meter. e. pedometer.

21. Horizontal sweep in an oscilloscope generally requires
   a. square wave.
   b. a triangular wave.
   c. a sine wave.
   d. a sawtooth wave.
   e. a lissajou pattern.

RECHECK PROGRAMMED INSTRUCTION USING SHRADER'S ELECTRONIC COMMUNICATION

1. Unlike Bipolar Junction transistors, field effect transistors and vacuum tubes that are used to amplify a signal, these devices used in digital circuits act like a _____ and _____ is not a consideration. Sec. 31-1

3. (1, 1, 0) The symbol for the AND circuit is _____. The output for this circuit for all possible combinations of inputs can be shown by a _____ _____ . Sec. 31-4

5. (BJT's, series) In a positive logic 2 input **OR** circuit there will be a high output (logic 1) if input **A** is logic_____or input B is logic_____. In the circuit shown there will be a logic 1 also if both inputs are logic_____. Sec. 31-5

7. (⟩— ,1, parallel) A high signal can be changed to a low signal or vice versa by use of an _____ or **NOT** circuit. The symbol for this circuit is_____. Sec. 31-6

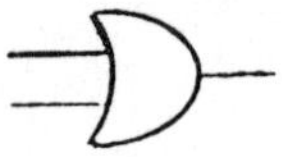

9. (amplifier, inversion) A good example of an inverter circuit is a common_____BJT circuit. Sec. 31-6

11. (NAND, NOT-AND) The unique output of a **NAND** circuit is a logic_____and only occurs when all inputs are logic_____. The **NAND** circuit symbol is _____ . Sec. 31-7

13. (NOR, NOT-OR) The unique output of a **NOR** circuit is a logic_____and only occurs when all inputs are logic_____ . Sec. 31-8

15. (⟩o—) The exclusive **OR** circuit will only have a logic 1 output if input A or input B is a logic_____but not if both are at logic_____ level. The symbol for an exclusive **OR** is_____. Sec. 31-9

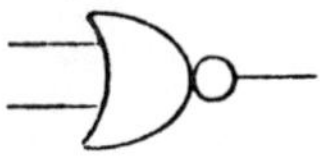

22. An AC VTVM has
   a. low internal impedance.
   b. no lead polarity.
   c. high sensitivity.
   d. lead polarity.
   e. none of these.

23. An AC wattmeter used in a circuit with the voltage and current out of phase measures
   a. I X E
   b. I X E X P.F.
   c. apparent power.
   d. reactive power.
   e. a and c.

24. Three fourths of one complete sine wave is equal to
   a. 90°.
   b. 60°.
   c. 270°.
   d. 360°.
   e. none of these.

25. A D'Arsonval meter put across the output of a full wave bridge rectifier using two 40 MFD filter capacitors and a 100K ohm bleeder resistor reads 9 volts peak. The RMS voltage is
   a. 7.07 volts.
   b. 9 volts.
   c. 8 volts.
   d. 6.36 volts.
   e. none of these.

26. In the circuit shown below each meter shows
   a. 1/2 the total current.
   b. twice the total current.
   c. the average total current.
   d. the actual current flowing.
   e. c or d above.

4. **(triangle, circle)** The **AND** gate has 2 inputs (sometimes more) and one output. Both inputs must be high before the output is high. This is the reason for the name. A **AND** B input must be high before C will be high. Note the **AND** symbol and the electro-mechanical equivalent circuit.

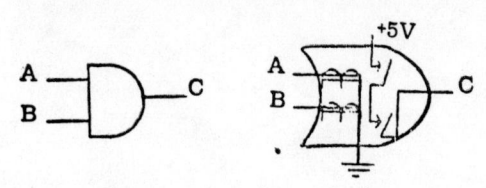

If inputs A and B are logic 1, the output C will be logic_____. If input A is logic 1 and input B is logic 0, the output C is logic_____.

8. **(1, high)** A **NOR** circuit is an **OR** circuit followed by an inverter. Again the inverter is symbolized by a small circle. The **NOR** symbol, the **NOR** electro-mechanical equivalent, and a **NOR** truth table is shown:

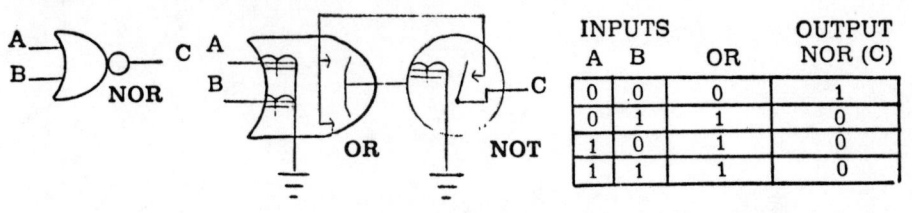

INPUTS A	B	OR	OUTPUT NOR (C)
0	0	0	1
0	1	1	0
1	0	1	0
1	1	1	0

The **NOR** output C would be logic 1 or high if both inputs A and B are a logic_____or_____.

12. **(1, high, high)** In the **NAND** circuit below, the A input must be_____if the B input is high.

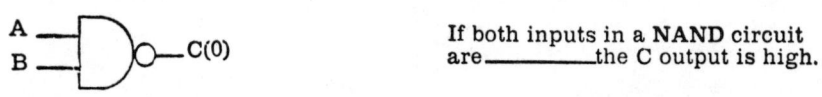

If both inputs in a **NAND** circuit are_____the C output is high.

16. **(NAND, NOR)** By inverting the inputs at a OR circuit a negative NOR circuit is formed. It's operation is identical to the **NAND** circuit. Note below that both circuits function alike.

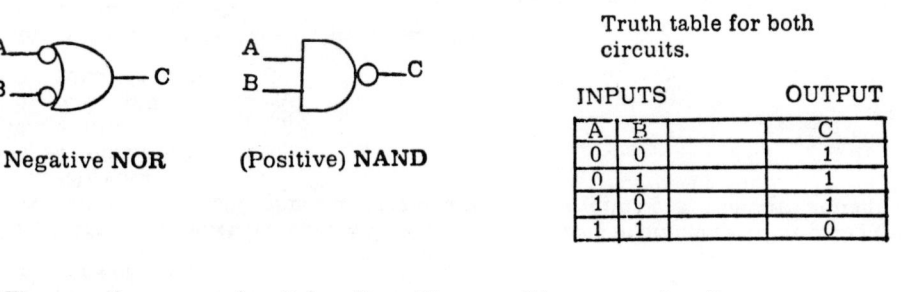

Negative **NOR**   (Positive) **NAND**

Truth table for both circuits.

INPUTS			OUTPUT
A	B		C
0	0		1
0	1		1
1	0		1
1	1		0

The negative_____circuit functions like a positive_____circuit.

1. An oscillator may be thought of as a device that converts direct current to alternating current. In one sense it's function is the opposite of that of a rectifier that changes AC to DC. Our study will deal with the following types of oscillators:

   (1) LC (inductance capacitance) oscillators   (3) RC (resistance capacitance) oscillators

   (2) Crystal oscillators.

           (a) Multivibrator oscillators

           (b) Relaxation oscillators

   An oscillator converts _____ to _____ .

7. (series fed Hartley)

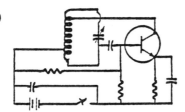

The circuit shown is a transistor series fed____HARTLEY____oscillator

(tapped coil

13. (size, shape) Crystals are cut from crystalline____QUARTZ____.

19. (plate) The oscillator power supply should be an____INDEPENDENT____and separate power supply.

25. (sawtooth, RC time constant) Another version of this neon bulb relaxtion oscillator substitutes a gas filled thyratron triode.

OUTPUT

SAWTOOTH WAVE

The value of negative voltage on the grid predetermines the amount of charge needed before the thyratron will ionize and discharge the capacitor. When the capacitor is discharged, the tube ionization ceases and the capacitor recharges. The output from the thyratron relaxation oscillator is a____SAWTOOTH____wave.

126

3. **(low, high)** The **NOT** gate has only one input and one output. The usual symbol for a **NOT** circuit is a triangle followed by a small circle as shown:

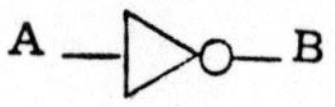

A is the input.
B is the output.

If A is logic 1, B is logic 0.
If A is logic 0, B is logic 1.

The symbol for a **NOT** circuit is a _____followed by a small _____.

THE UNIVERSAL GATES - The NAND and NOR

7. **(1, 1)** A **NAND** gate is composed of an **AND** followed by **NOT** (inverter). The inverter is symbolized by a small circle. The **NAND** symbol, the **NAND** electro-mechanical equivalents, and the **NAND** truth table are shown below:

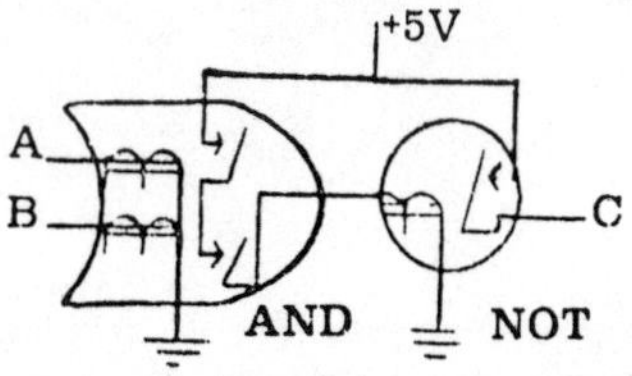

INPUTS			OUTPUT
A	B	AND	NAND (C)
0	0	0	1
0	1	0	1
1	0	0	1
1	1	1	0

The NAND C output is logic 0 (low), if the A and B inputs are logic_____or_____.

11. **(1, 1)** In the OR circuit below, the output C would be at logic_____ or_____.

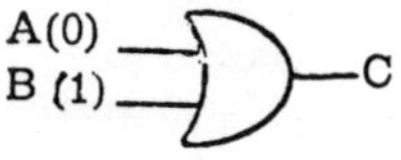

Either input A or B must be_____to get a high output

15. **(NANDS, NORS, universal)** By inverting the inputs at an AND circuit a negative NAND gate is formed. It operates like a NOR circuit. Note below that both circuits function alike.

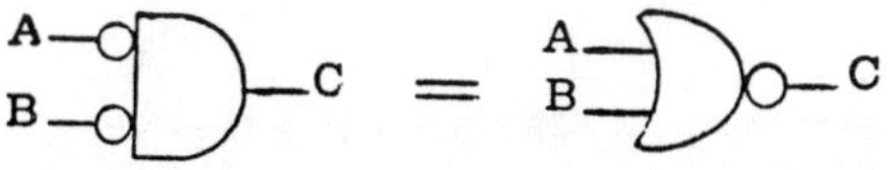

Negative **NAND**   (Positive) **NOR**

Truth table for both.

INPUTS			OUTPUT
A	B		C
0	0		1
0	1		0
1	0		0
1	1		0

The negative_____circuit is like a positive_____circuit.

2. **(DC, AC)** If a battery is connected to an LC tuned circuit and then disconnected, an interesting series of events take place.

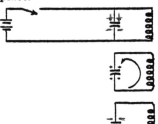

First when the battery is momentarily connected to the tuned circuit the capacitor is charged as shown.

Second the parallel inductor quickly discharged the capacitor. The direction of current flow is shown.

Third, the lines of force created when current went through the coil collapse and charges the capacitor in the opposite direction.

The capacitor is then discharged again through the coil - only this time in the opposite direction. This action of charge and discharge continues for a period of time determined by the circuit losses. The output waveform is a damped wave as shown:

If there was no resistance in the circuit, the charge and discharge would continue indefinitely without any decrease in amplitude.

This charge and discharge in a tuned circuit is called **oscillation**. The initial charge is supplied in a vacuum tube or solid state oscillator by just turning the power on. The initial surge of current through LC circuits as the voltage is applied starts the oscillatory process and is called shock excitation. Vacuum tube oscillators achieve greater stability by use of large capacitors and small inductance (High C to L) in their tuned circuits..

The initital LC circuit charge is achieved by ___SHOCK___ excitation. Greater frequency stability is achieved by using a high ___C to L___ ratio.

8. **(Hartley)** In a series fed Hartley oscillator the plate or collector current flows through the series ___FEEDBACK___ portion of the LC circuit.

14. **(quartz)** A common cut with a negative temperature coefficient is the ___X___ cut.

RC OSCILLATORS

20. **(independent)** The plate coupled multivibrator is an oscillator that uses the charge and discharge of capacitors through resistors. Whereas the output wave forms of LC oscillators are sine waves, RC oscillators produce either square wave or sawtooth outputs. The plate coupled multivibrator circuit is given below:

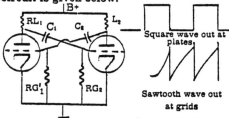

When plate voltage is applied, either V1 or V2 will conduct harder than the other tube due to small differences in tube emission or plate load resistances. C1 and C2 alternately charge to B+ values through their load resistors and discharge through the low impedance of the conducting tubes and the high resistance of the grid resistors.

The output would be a ___SQUARE___ wave at the plate and a ___SAWTOOTH___ wave at the grid.

26. **(sawtooth)** This concludes Unit 13.

THE UNIQUE GATES

2. **(combinational, sequential)** The combinational decision making gates are so called because DC pulses are either allowed or prevented to appear in the gate output depending on the condition of the inputs and the type of gate.

The simplest type of gate is the inverter or **NOT** gate. When the input is high or logic 1 in positive logic, the output is low or logic 0 and vice versa.

An electro-mechanical equivalent of the **NOT** gate is shown below:

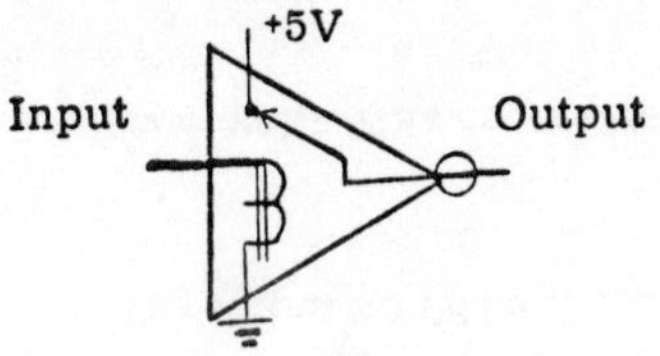

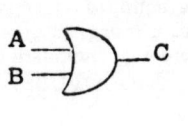

When the input is logic 1 (+5V), the output is logic 0 or_____. When the output is logic 0 (0V) the output is logic 1 (5V) or_____.

6. **(zero)** The **OR** gate has an output of logic 1 if either input A or B is logic 1.

The symbol, electro-mechanical equivalent, and truth table is shown:

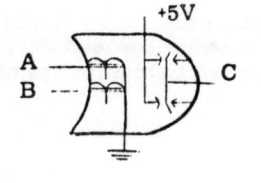 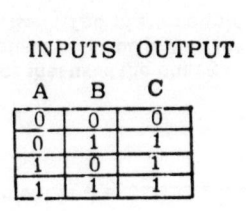

INPUTS		OUTPUT
A	B	C
0	0	0
0	1	1
1	0	1
1	1	1

OR gates may have more than 2 inputs.

If input A is logic 0 and input B is logic 1, the C output is logic_____ . The output C will be logic 1 if input A or input B is logic_____.

10. **(0, low, 0, low)** In the **AND** circuit below, the output C is a logic 1.

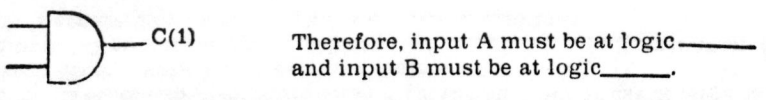

Therefore, input A must be at logic_____ and input B must be at logic_____.

14. **(1, low)** NANDS and NORS are called universal gates because by proper connection or grouping you can obtain any of the other four common gates.

Any of the five common gates can be obtained by using_____ or_____gates. These gates are called_____ gates.

18. **(cutoff, saturation)** This concludes unit 26.

3. (shock, C to L) In order to overcome the resistance in an LC circuit and provide for oscillations on a continuous basis the charge and discharge cycle is amplified and then fed back in phase to the original circuit. The arrangement below is typical:

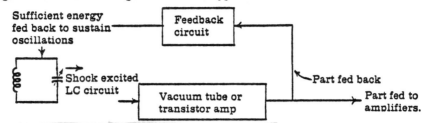

This in phase feedback insures continuous oscillation. This feedback is referred to as positive feedback. For sustained oscillations an oscillator needs_____ feedback.

9. (feedback) One common variation of the triode series fed Hartley oscillator is the pentode Electron Coupled Oscillator E.C.O.

The grid is ocassionally driven positive as the oscillatory signal is fed through C2. The grid then attracts electrons from the cathode. As the electrons leak off through R1 negative grid bias is developed. Shock excited LC tank circuit.

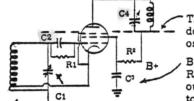

The output circuit above the dotted line amplifies the oscillator output.

By grounding the screen for RF by this capacity no plate output energy can feed back to the grid circuit.

The circuit under the dotted line is like a triode series fed Hartley oscillator. The screen grid acts as the anode or plate.

Bypassing the screen grid to ground eliminates the possibility of interelectrode capacity coupling of the output plate and input grid. The only coupling between output plate and input grid is through the electron stream and this is not significant. Therefore, any load changes, shorts or opens in the plate LC circuit cannot stop the oscillations in the electron coupled oscillator. This arrangement makes the E.C.O. a very stable oscillator Load changes in the plate circuit have very little effect on the oscillator frequency. This kind of oscillator is used typically as a pentagrid converter for the superheterodyne receiver (to be discussed later). There would be no ~~oscillation~~ if C2 was open. The E.C.O. would continue to oscillate if the capacitor _C4_ was open or shorted.

15. (X) The usual triode crystal oscillator is shown below:

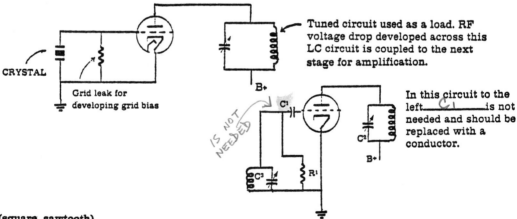

CRYSTAL

Grid leak for developing grid bias

Tuned circuit used as a load. RF voltage drop developed across this LC circuit is coupled to the next stage for amplification.

In this circuit to the left _C1_ is not needed and should be replaced with a conductor.

21. (square, sawtooth)

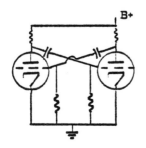

The circuit shown is that of a _PLATE COUPLED_ _MULTIVIBRATOR_ or _ASTABLE_ oscillator.

INTRODUCTION

1. Because of integrated circuit technology, the digital circuit is becoming common place in the design and implementation of electronics equipment. It is not necessary for in depth understanding of digital curcuits in terms of its electrical principles, but it is important to understand the logic involved. In a sense digital electronics is math oriented.

   There are two basic types of digital circuits:

   1) **COMBINATIONAL.** This type of circuit is also referred to as **DECISION MAKING** and **GATE logic.**

   2) **SEQUENTIAL.** This type of circuit is also referred to as **STORAGE** (memory) and **FLIP FLOP** logic.

   The two basic digital circuits are ———————————————— and ———————————————— .

5. (1.0) The operation of gate circuits can be shown by use of a device known as a truth table. Note the truth table for an **AND** gate:

   INPUTS OUTPUT

A	B	C
0	0	0
0	1	0
1	0	0
1	1	1

   Both A and B must be logic 1 for a C output of logic 1.

   If the input A is logic 1 and input B is logic 0, the output at C will be logic——————————— .

9. (**0, low**) Now let us review. In the **AND** circuit below, the output at C is at logic 0 or low.

   A ———⊐
   B ———⊐— C (0)   Therefore, either input A or input B is at logic——————or——————.

   It could also be true that both inputs A and B are at logic ——————or—————— .

13. (high, low) In the **NOR** circuit below, either input A or input B must be a logic——————.

    A ——
    B ——∑○— C'(0)   For an output that is high (logic 1) in a **NOR** circuit both A and B inputs must be——————————.

17. (**NOR, NAND**) The actual switching in an **IC** is done by alternately switching a transistor component into cutoff (open) and saturation (closed). A transistor may be used as a switch by alternately biasing it to ———————————and———————————— .

4. **(in phase or positive)** Feedback is provided in oscillators by coupling some output energy back to the LC circuit. This energy can be fed by inductive coupling or capacitive coupling.
A very popular circuit using inductive coupling for feedback is the series fed Hartley oscillator.

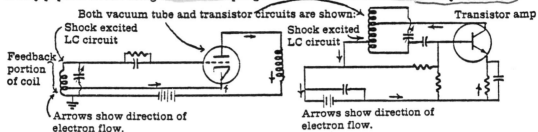

Both vacuum tube and transistor circuits are shown:
Shock excited LC circuit
Transistor amp
Shock excited LC circuit
Feedback portion of coil
Arrows show direction of electron flow.
Arrows show direction of electron flow.

In either case the LC tank circuit is shocked into oscillation. The output is amplified and the resulting plate or collector current change produces an in phase feedback to sustain oscillations. All series-fed Hartley oscillators have a tapped coil in the LC circuit providing inductive feedback through the L. C. circuit. The resistors from grid to ground through the LC circuit and from base to ground provide grid and base bias. The series fed Hartley oscillator uses an _INDUCTIVE (tapped coil)._ feedback to sustain oscillations.

10. **(oscillation, C4)** Plate load changes in an E.C.O. have very little effect on the _FREQUENCY_ of the oscillator.

16. **(C1)** The operating frequency of a crystal can be changed somewhat by shunting the crystal with a small trimmer capacitor.

This is called **rubberizing** a crystal.

A shunt capacitance is often used with a crystal in a crystal oscillator in order to _VARY its Freq._ .

22. **(plate coupled multivibrator)** The plate coupled multivibrator is called an **astable multivibrator** and is used as a sweep generator in television receivers. Other forms of the multivibrator are useful as frequency dividers and counters. The **bistable multivibrator** puts out one pulse for every two applied to its input and is a natural two to one frequency divider. Frequency dividers use a _BISTABLE_ multivibrator oscillator circuit.

1. The magnetron is useful to generate
   a. \LF.
   b. MF.
   c. IF.
   d. SHF.
   e. VHF.

2. A traveling wave tube is
   a. a hollow metal tube.
   b. a solid steel tube.
   c. a plastic tube.
   d. a rectangular wave guide.
   e. none of these.

3. In a traveling wave tube the RF input is applied at
   a. the attenuator.
   b. the cathode end of the helix.
   c. the cathode.
   d. repeller plate.
   e. control grid.

4. In a traveling wave tube a direct current source to an RF signal is accomplished by
   a. velocity modulating a beam of electrons to induce energy to an output coupling.
   b. negative resistance.
   c. secondary emission.
   d. frequency modulation.
   e. none of these.

5. Waveguides are commonly fed energy by
   a. a pick up loop.
   b. a leecher line.
   c. resistors.
   d. low frequency generators.
   e. long lengths of open transmission line.

6. The frequency at which a cavity in a magnetron resonates is determined by
   a. the filament voltage.
   b. the size of the cavity.
   c. the screen grid voltage.
   d. coupling method used.
   e. the external tuned circuit.

7. The best oscillator for use above 300 Mhz would be
   a. a Hartley.
   b. a multivibrator.
   c. a crystal.
   d. a Klystron.
   e. a Colpitts.

8. Copper coils are used in the T.W.T. tubes for
   a. input and output signals.
   b. the cathode electrode.
   c. the anode electrode.
   d. cross modulation.
   e. none of these.

9. Wave guides may not be used below UHF frequencies because
   a. the capacity is too great.
   b. the inductance is too great.
   c. the resistance is too great.
   d. the size would be prohibitive.
   e. they generate harmonics.

10. Copper magnetic coils are used around the T.W.T. tubes
    a. to direct the electron beam through the helix.
    b. for cathode electrodes.
    c. for anode electrodes.
    d. for cross modulation.
    e. none of these.

11. Energy is propagated down a wave guide by
    a. diffussion.
    b. electrostatic fields.   d. osmosis.
    c. electromagnetic fields.   e. b and c above.

5. **(inductive)** The vacuum tube or transistor series fed Hartley oscillator can be identified by the __TAPPED__ coil in the LC circuit.

11. **(frequency)** An older oscillator that uses capacitance feedback to sustain oscillation is the tuned *"T.P.T.G."* plate tuned grid oscillator. The feedback capacitance is the interelectrode capacitance between plate and grid.

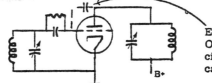

Oscillations start here in this LC circuit.

Equivalent plate to grid capacitance. Output energy is fed back to grid LC circuit through this interelectrode capacitance for sustained oscillation.

B+

Feedback in a Tuned plate tuned grid oscillator is obtained by __INTERELECTRODE__ capacitance. (T.P.T.G. oscillator).

17. **(vary it's frequency)** Excessive feedback in a crystal oscillator must be avoided or the crystal may be fractured and ruined. If a crystal oscillator doesn't have sufficient feedback through the interelectrode capacitance, it may be necessary to couple energy back from the output through a capacitor to the grid. To prevent the crystal in an oscillator from cracking, it is necessary to prevent _____ supply feedback.

23. **(bistable)** An obsolete oscillator that is still asked about in F.C.C. exams is the **Dynatron** oscillator. It is sufficient to say here that it works on the principle of secondary emission. The __"DYNATRON"__ oscillator works on the negative resistance principles.

130

2.   **(50)** Wave guides may not be used below UHF frequencies because the_____would be prohibitive. Sec. 26-2.

4.   **(electrostatic, magnetic)** Two common methods of coupling energy to a waveguide are by means of a single turn _____ and the other is the antenna _____ method. Sec. 26-4.

6.   **(klystron)** The frequency at which a magnetron operates is determined by the_____of the cavity. Sec. 26-8.

8.   **(vacuum)** External copper helixes are used in the T.W.T. for coupling the _____ and _____ signals. Sec. 26-9.

10.   **(cathode)** The electron beam through the main helix is directed by the_____induced into the helix. Sec. 26-9.

6.   (tapped)

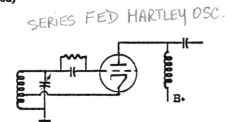

SERIES FED HARTLEY OSC.

The tapped coil in this circuit identifies it as a _SERIES_ _FED HARTLEY_ oscillator.

CRYSTAL OSCILLATORS

12.   (interelectrode) Commercial transmitter oscillators are used to generate a stable fixed frequency. By using a quartz crystal in place of a tuned LC circuit it is possible to obtain a high degree of frequency stability. The crystal has lumped inductance, capacitance, and resistance as shown:

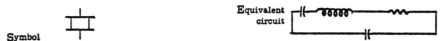

Symbol

Equivalent circuit

These crystals are precision cut from crystalline quartz. The size and shape of the cut determine their frequency. There are two common types of cuts:
   (1)   X cut. A 1 megahertz X cut crystal will change frequency from ten to twenty-five hertz for every degree centigrade change of temperature. It should be noted that if the temperature rises the frequency decreases and vice versa. This type of change is referred to as a negative temperature coefficient. Negative here signifies an inverse relationship between temperature and frequency.
   (2)   low temperature coefficient cut. These are cut along a different crystalline axis and are variously designated such as V, AT or GT. A 1 megahertz GT cut may only change frequency by 1 hertz for a 1 degree centigrade change in temperature. The frequency may either increase or decrease with an increase of temperature.
   X cut crystals are easier to manufacture.
   The resonant operating frequency of a crystal is determined primarily by it's _SIZE_ and _SHAPE_ .

18.   (excessive) Several things can be done for better frequency stability in a crystal oscillator circuit. They are:
   1.   Use an independent and separate power supply for the oscillator plate voltage supply. Any change in oscillator plate voltage can make a significant change in it's frequency.
   2.   Keep the crystal temperature constant. This requires a constant temperature oven.
   3.   Use crystals with low temperature coefficients.
   The frequency of a crystal can be appreciably changed by changing the temperature and by changing the _PLATE_ supply voltage.

RELAXATION OSCILLATORS
24.   (dynatron) The simplest relaxation oscillator utilizes a gas filled bulb.

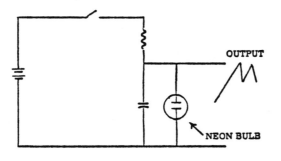

OUTPUT

NEON BULB

When voltage is applied, the capacitor charges through the resistor. The rate of charge is determined by the value of the resistance and capacitance. This determines the RC time constant.

At a certain voltage the neon ionizes and discharges the capacitance. When this happens, the ionization ceases removing the discharge path and the capacitor begins to charge again. An output taken across the capacitor is a sawtooth waveform. The frequency is determined by the RC time constant. The output of a relaxation oscillator is a _SAWTOOTH_ wave at a frequency determined by the _TIME CONSTANT_ of the resistance and capacitance.

UNIT 25 (CHAPTER 26) MICROWAVES

RECHECK PROGRAMMED INSTRUCTION USING SHRADER'S ELECTRONIC COMMUNICATION

1. Most microwave activity is from one to __________ ghz. Sec. 26-1.

3. **(size)** Energy is propagated down a wave guide by __________ and __________ fields. Sec. 26-2.

5. **(loop, probe)** A good oscillator for use above 300 Mhz would be the __________. Sec. 26-7.

7. **(size)** The traveling wave tube is a __________ tube with a glass envelope. Sec. 26-9.

9. **(input, output)** In a traveling wave tube the R.F. input is applied at the __________ end of the helix. Sec. 26-9.

11. **(signal)** This concludes the recheck on Unit 25 (Chapter 26)

RECHECK PROGRAMMED INSTRUCTION USING SHRADER'S ELECTRONIC COMMUNICATIONS

1. Alternating current may be produced by an _____ . Sec. 13-1.

3. (shock) For sustained oscillation in an LC oscillator the positive feedback energy must be _____ . Sec. 13-3.

5. (grid leak) The necessary feedback for sustained oscillations in a T.P.T.G. oscillator is through the _____ to _____ interelectrode capacitance. Sec. 13-6.

7. (series)

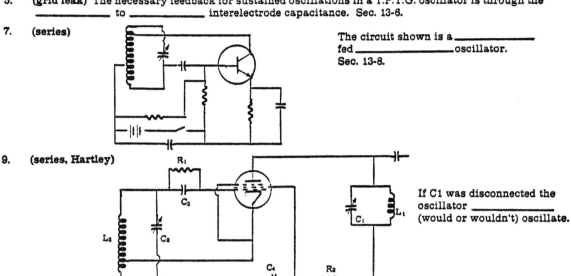

The circuit shown is a _____ fed _____ oscillator. Sec. 13-8.

9. (series, Hartley)

If C1 was disconnected the oscillator _____ (would or wouldn't) oscillate.

11. (electron coupled) If C3 in frame 9 was open the oscillator _____ (would or would not) oscillate. Sec. 13-11.

13. (would not) If L1 in frame 9 was open the oscillator _____ (would or would not) oscillate? Sec. 13-11.

15. (frequency) Crystals used in RF oscillators are cut from _____ Sec. 13-12.

17. (C1) The _____ of a crystal is determined primarily by it's size and shape. Sec. 13-12.

19. (vary its frequency) Excessive _____ may cause the crystal to crack. Sec. 13-12.

21. (frequency) It is customary for this reason to use a separate power supply for the oscillator. A common crystal cut with a negative temperature coefficent is the _____ cut. Sec. 13-13.

23. (10, 25, 1, 1) The Dynatron oscillator operates on the principle of _____ . Sec. 13-19.

25. (sawtooth)

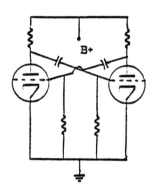

The circuit shown is a _____ oscillator. Sec. 13-21.

27. (sawtooth, square wave) This concludes Unit 13.

Waveguides

2. **(UHF)** Energy at these frequencies can be carried from one point to another by **waveguide** transmission lines. Energy travels down circular or rectangular waveguide pipes by electrostatic and electromagnetic fields. These waves are confined to an enclosed space. There is an infinite no. of ways these fields can arrange themselves. The general construction of a rectangular wave guide is shown:

Greater than ½ W. L. for lowest frequency.
½ W.L. for lowest frequency.

Waveguides are not used as transmission lines below the UHF band as their size would be prohibitive. Long level sections of waveguides are avoided to prevent the accumulation of dust and moisture.
Energy is propagated down a waveguide by _____ and _____ fields.
Long level sections of wave guides are avoided to prevent the accumulation of dust and _____ .

4. **(size)** Energy is coupled to and from a wave guide in three ways
    1) By coupling holes.

2 waveguide sections

Coupling holes.

Coaxial Cable

2) By a loop or a hook.

Waveguide section   Pickup loop

3) By an antenna probe.   Coaxial cable

Waveguide section 1/4 wave antenna probe

Energy is coupled to waveguide sections by _____ holes, pickup _____ or antenna _____ .

6. **(cavities)** It is common practice to use a _____ oscillator for the local oscillator of a receiver operating above 300 Mhz.

8. **(magnetron)** An important broadband microwave amplifier tube is the **traveling wave tube T.W.T.**

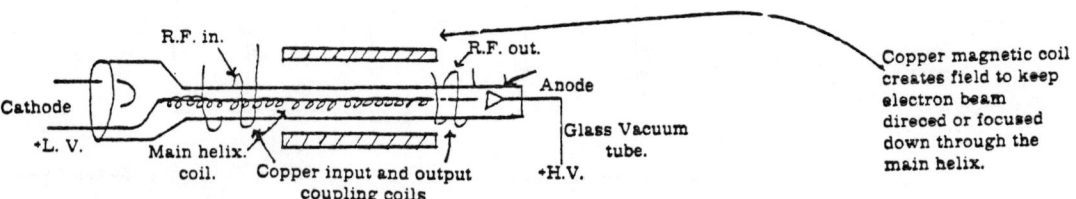

R.F. in.
R.F. out.
Anode
Cathode
+L. V.
Main helix. coil.
Copper input and output coupling coils
+H.V.
Glass Vacuum tube.
Copper magnetic coil creates field to keep electron beam direced or focused down through the main helix.

Induced R.F. into the main helix travels down the helix.
Electrons from the cathode travel through the center of the helix to the anode. They are prevented from going to the positive helix by the presence of the magnetic coil.

Although induced energy in the helix travels at the same rate as the electron beam, there is a greater path distance for the helix energy. Therefore, the electron beam moves faster horizontally from left to right than the induced energy in the helix. The interaction of the helix wave and the electron field causes the electrons to slow down and bunch. This change in velocity causes energy to be imparted to the R.F. output coil. The whole process is called velocity modulation.

Copper coils are used in the TWT for coupling _____ and _____ signals. The R.F. _____ signal is applied at the cathode end of the main helix.

10. **(glass vacuum)** Copper magnetic coils are used around the T.W.T. tubes for _____ _____ the elctron beam through the _____ .

2. **(oscillator)** Oscillators using capacitors and coils depend on _____ excitation. Sec. 13-2.

4. **(in phase)** _____ biasing is used in LC oscillators. Sec. 13-5.

6. **(grid, plate)** If the DC current flow in an LC oscillator flows through part of the coil of the LC circuit it is a _____ fed circuit. Sec. 13-7.

8. **(series, Hartley)**

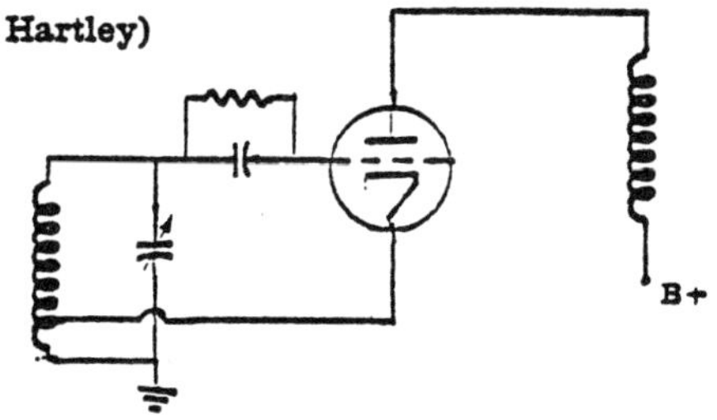

The circuit shown is a _____ fed _____ oscillator. Sec. 13-8.

10. **(would)** The oscillator in frame 9 is a _____ oscillator. Sec. 13-11.

12. **(would not)** If R1 in frame 9 was open the oscillator _____ (would or wouldn't) oscillate. Sec. 13-11.

14. **(would)** Load changes in the plate circuit of the electron coupled oscillator have little effect on it's _____ . Sec. 13-11.

16. **(quartz)**

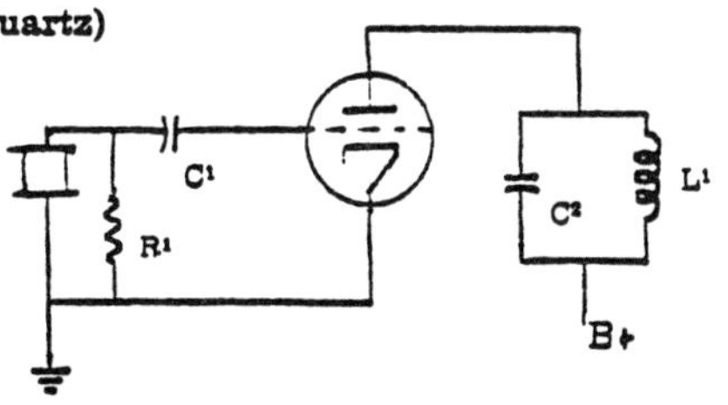

In the circuit to the left _____ is not needed and should be replaced by a conductor. Sec. 13-12.

18. **(frequency)** A shunt capacitance is often used with a crystal oscillator to _____ . Sec. 13-12.

20. **(feedback)** Changes in the oscillator plate voltage may vary appreciably the oscillator _____ . Sec. 13-12.

22. **(X)** X cut crystals have a range of about _____ to _____ hertz / C/MHz. A GT cut crystal has a range of about minus _____ to + _____ . Sec. 13-13.

24. **(secondary emission or negative resistance)** The output of a thyratron relaxation oscillator is a _____ wave. Sec. 13-20.

26. **(multivibrator)** In the circuit in frame 25 the voltage waveform at the grids is a _____ and at the plates a _____ . Sec. 13-21.

UNIT 25 MICROWAVES

Introduction

1. Microwave frequencies start in the UHF range (300-3000 Mhz) and extend into the SHF (3-30 Ghz) and EHF (30 Ghz up) ranges. At these frequencies a tuned circuit may consist of nothing but a cavity having lumped inductance and capacitance.

Microwaves start in the _____ range.

3. (electrostatic, electromagnetic, moisture) Waveguides are not used below the U.H.F. range as their _____ would be prohibitive.

5. (coupling, loops, probes) There are two common microwave oscillators:

1) The klystron oscillator is used in the superheterodyne microwave receiver as the local oscillator. The frequency of oscillation is primarily determined by the size of the internal cavity of the klystron. This tube contains a cathode, two grids, an anode, and a negative repeller plate.

2) The magnetron diode is used to generate a powerful microwave signal at the transmitter. Cathode electrons under the influence of two fields sweep past cavities in a cycloidal path shocking the tuned cavities into oscillation. The output frequency is determined by the size of the cavities.

The output frequency of both the klystron and the magnetron oscillator is determined by the physical size of the _____ .

7. (klystron) It is a common practice to use a _____ oscillator tube for the transmitter at UHF and SHF frequencies.

9. (input, output, input) The T.W.T. is a _____ _____ tube.

11. (focusing or directing, helix) This concludes Unit 25.

1. In the diagram below the oscillation would be completely stopped if
   a. C1 is shorted.
   b. C2 is shorted.
   c. primary of T1 is open.
   d. C4 is open.
   e. R2 is shorted.

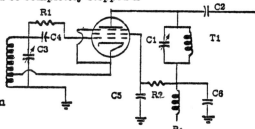

2. Crystals used in RF oscillators are cut from
   a. Galena.
   b. lead sulfide.   d. quartz.
   c. Rochelle Salts.   e. plastic.

3. A common crystal cut with a negative temperature coefficient is the
   a. X cut.
   b. Y cut.   d. Z cut.
   c. V cut.   e. none of these.

4. The circuit shown is a
   a. phase shift oscillator.
   b. electron coupled oscillator.
   c. voltage doubler.
   d. grounded Grid amplifier.
   e. bridge power supply.

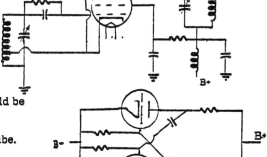

5. The output of the circuit shown below would be
   a. sawtooth taken at the plate.
   b. a square wave taken at the grid.
   c. a sawtooth taken at the grid of either tube.
   d. a sine wave taken at the plate.
   e. none of these.

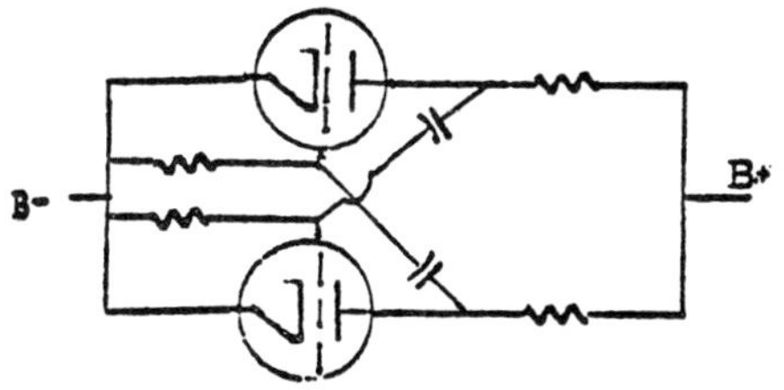

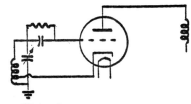

6. The output of the circuit shown above would be
   a. a square wave taken at the plate of either tube.
   b. a sine wave taken at the grid of either tube.   d. UHF.
   c. three times the input.   e. none of these.

7. A shunt capacitance is often used with a crystal in a crystal oscillator
   a. to vary its frequency.
   b. to lower the output.   d. to excite the crystal.
   c. to protect the crystal. e. as a temperature oven.

8. The oscillator shown below is a
   a. series fed Hartley.
   b. shunt fed Hartley.
   c. Colpitts shunt fed.
   d. crystal oscillator.
   e. Dynatron.

9. One characteristic of a Dynatron oscillator is
   a. negative resistance.
   b. negative feedback.   d. high output.
   c. positive feedback.   e. none of these.

10. A vacuum tube oscillates because of
    a. shock excitation in the grid LC circuit.
    b. resonance in the plate circuit.   d. electron coupling.
    c. neutralizing capacitance.   e. negative feedback.

11. Feedback in a T.P.T.G. oscillator is obtained by
    a. detunning the plate circuit.
    b. detunning the grid circuit.   d. interelectrode capacitance.
    c. a capacitor between grid and plate.   e. inductance.

12. The operating frequency of a crystal is determined primarily by
    a. the size and shape of the crystal.
    b. the type of oscillator circuit.   d. the grid RC time constant.
    c. the amount of feedback.   e. none of these.

1. Daytime broadcasting is from
    a. sunrise to 6 p.m.
    b. 6 a.m. local time to sunset.
    c. sunrise to sunset.
    d. 6 p.m. local time to midnight.
    e. none of these.

2. The experimental period in broadcasting is from
    a. sunset to sunrise.
    b. 6 p.m. to 12 midnight.
    c. sunset to 12 midnight.
    d. 12 midnight to sunrise.
    e. 6 a.m. to 12 noon.

3. Night time operation in broadcasting is done in the period of time from
    a. sunset to sunrise.
    b. 6 p.m. to 12 midnight.
    c. sunset to 12 midnight.
    d. 12 midnight to sunrise.
    e. 6 a.m. to 12 noon.

4. A line equalizer is used to
    a. attenuate high audio frequencies.
    b. attenuate low audio frequencies.
    c. cancel even harmonics.
    d. cancel odd harmonics.
    e. none of these.

5. Frequency shift keying (F.S.K.) is designated as type
    a. A1 emission.
    b. A3 emission.
    c. A5 emission.
    d. F3 emission.
    e. F1 emission.

6. Carbon resistors at Ultra High Frequencies (U.H.F.)
    a. appear to have decreased resistance.
    b. appear to have inductance and capacitance.
    c. will open at these high frequencies.
    d. will short at these high frequencies.
    e. none of these since carbon resistors are not used at U.H.F.

13. A Hartley oscillator needs
   a. positive feedback.
   b. an extremely high Q circuit.   d. negative feedback.
   c. B+ applied to a tap on a plate coil.   e. degeneration.

14. The diagram below is that of a(n)
   a. R.F.Doubler.
   b. R.F.amplifier
   c. A. F.amplifier.
   d. multivibrator.
   e. Hartley oscillator.

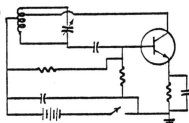

15. The frequency of a crystal can be appreciably changed by changing the temperature and by changing
   a. the transconductance.
   b. the plate voltage.   d. the grid resistance.
   c. the plate tank inductance.   e. the plate tank capacitance.

16. In the diagram below
   a. C1 is unnecessary.
   b. C2 is unnecessary.
   c. C3 is unnecessary.
   d. R1 is unnecessary.
   e. L1 is unnecessary.

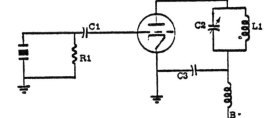

17. The circuit shown is that of a(n)
   a. R.F.amplifier.
   b. R.F. buffer
   c. reactance tube modulator.
   d. bridge rectifier.
   e. multivibrator.

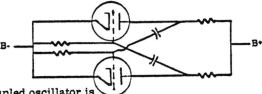

18. The advantage of an electron coupled oscillator is
   a. the load changes in the plate circuit have little effect on frequency.
   b. the output is coupled to the input.
   c. it is neutralized.
   d. it acts as a phase splitter.
   e. none of these.

19. The frequency of a crystal oscillator can be changed by
   a. varying the grid voltage.
   b. varying cathode voltage.   d. varying the grid leak resistance.
   c. capacitor is shunt with the crystal   e. none of these.

20. To stabilize the frequency of a crystal oscillator
   a. connect it to the same power supply used for the buffer.
   b. use a swinging choke.   d. keep the crystal at a constant temperature.
   c. store the crystal in a cool place when not in use.   e. none of these.

21. To prevent the crystal in a oscillator from cracking it is necessary to
   a. use a Colpitts type.
   b. use a Hartley type.   d. regulate the power supply.
   c. prevent excessive feedback.   e. neutralize the oscillator.

22. In order to considerably vary the frequency of a crystal oscillator
   a. vary the grid leak resistance.
   b. use a thicker crystal to raise the frequency.
   c. shunt the crystal with an inductance to raise the frequency.
   d. vary the plate tank inductance.
   e. vary the oscillator plate voltage.

2.   (sunrise, sunset) Night time operation in broadcasting is done in the period of time from local _____ to _____. Sec. 24-1.

4.   (midnight, sunrise) A line equalizer is used to attenuate _____ frequencies. Sec.24-6.

6.   (experimental) Tests made after construction has been completed and the station is licensed are called _____ or _____ tests. Sec. 24-9.

8.   (85%) The nature of any repairs made at a broadcast station should be recorded in the _____ log. Sec. 24-14.

10.   (final, modulator) After a public safety radio service has been authorized by a _____ _____ and before the installation has been completed, a _____ _____ must be applied for using the standard F.C.C. form 400. Sec. 19-19.

12.   (land) A land station in the land mobile service carrying on a service with land mobile stations is called a _____ station. Sec. 32-1.

14.   (citizens, 2nd) An A.M. carrier carrying no modulation or information is typed _____ . Amplitude modulated telephony with double side bands and carrier is typed _____. A.M. telephony with single sideband and suppressed carrier is typed _____ . Facsimile A.M. is typed _____ . Appendix E, page 766.

16.   (F1, F3) The height and lighting of a broadcast station tower is a concern of the F.C.C. and the _____. Sec. 24-23.

18.   (verification) Remote antenna current meters should be checked once a _____ and should have an accuracy of ___ %. Sec. 24-10.

23. The output for the circuit shown below should be

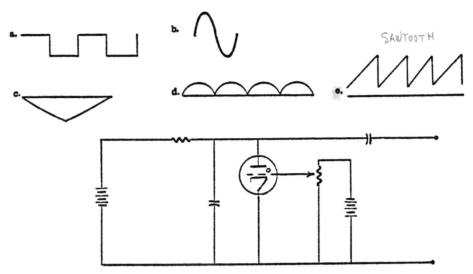

a.

b.

SAWTOOTH

c.

d.

e.

24. The circuit shown is a
   a R.F.amplifier.
   b. voltage doubler.
   c. frequency multiplier.
   d. push push amplifier.
   e. Hartley oscillator.

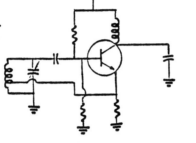

25. In order to improve the frequency stability of an oscillator
   a. temperature changes are introduced by means of blowers.
   b. a buffer stage should not be used.
   c. a high capacity to inductance ratio is employed. —HIGH C to L.
   d. a high inductance to capacity ratio is employed.
   e. plate voltage is varied.

26. The principal disadvantage of crystal-controlled oscillators is
   a. frequency instability more pronounced.
   b. high voltage requirements.
   c. insufficient "drive" to the final.
   d. difficulty in changing operating frequencies.
   e. high cost of crystals.

27. The temperature of a quartz crystal should
   a. vary according to the power plant.
   b. be kept constant.
   c. not be kept constant for considerable lengths of time.
   d. be kept as low as possible.
   e. vary according to voltage.

RECHECK PROGRAMMED INSTRUCTION USING SHRADER'S ELECTRONIC COMMUNICATION.

1.   Daytime broadcasting is from local_____ to_____. Sec. 24-1.

3.   (sunset,sunrise) The experimental period in broadcasting is from_____ to local_____. Sec. 24-1.

5.   (lower) Before a broadcast station can be constructed, it is first necessary to obtain a construction permit. Any tests made during the construction period must be made during the_____ period. Sec. 24-9.

7.   (service, program) Broadcast stations must maintain modulation peaks of at least_____%. Sec. 24-9.

9.   (maintenance)   Changes to be made in the_____ amplifier and_____ must have prior approval of the FCC. Sec. 24-17.

11.   (construction permit, station license) A station in the mobile service not intended to be used while in motion is called a _____ station. Sec. 32-1.

13.   (base) A citizen band station does not require an operators license. However, each C.B. station must have a station license. This station may be used for personal matters or business. The station input power is limited to 5 watts. Anyone servicing C.B. transmitters must have at least a 2nd class phone license. A radio station band that is used for personal matters and corporate business is the _____ band. A serviceman for C.B. transmitters should have at least a _____ class phone license.

15.   (Aϕ, A3, A3J, A4) Frequency keying telegraphy is typed_____ . F.M. telephony is typed _____ . Appendix E, page 766.

17.   (F.A.A. - Federal Aviation Agency) The authorized heighth of the broadcast station tower is given in the instrument of authorization (the license). The license of an operator normally may be posted at the place where he is on duty. A _____ card may be carried on the person of the operator when posting of the license is not required. Sec. 31-3.

19.   (week, 2%) This concludes the recheck on Unit 24.

1. The basic action of an audio amplifier is that of taking a weak electrical signal and using it to control the amplifier power supply current flowing through tube or transistor and their loads. The amplifier output is taken from the loads.
The main signal sources include:
   (1) Detected receiver signals.
   (2) Microphones.
   (3) Record player outputs from phono cartridges or tape heads.
   (4) Preamplifiers.
The main tube or transistor loads include:
   (1) Resistors. The output taken from this type of a load is fed generally to another radio amplifier for additional amplification.
   (2) Transformer primarys. Outputs across this load are either fed to an earphone, a speaker, or to another audio amplifier for additional amplification.
The signal input to an audio amplifier is used to control the ___CURRENT___ flow through the vacuum tube or transistor and their loads.

17. (shunt, inductive, close) In a single ended (one tube) series fed plate circuit using inductive coupling the DC plate current always flows through the transformer winding in the same direction as shown:

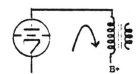

This has a tendency to magnetize the core or saturate the core in such a manner as to permanently magnetize it. This produces distortion.

There are two ways of preventing core saturation.

Use a series fed plate circuit of push pull amplifier design.

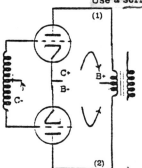

On one half cycle of the input plate current flows down through the primary, while on the other half cycle of the input plate current flows up through the primary. In effect both magnetizing and demagnetizing currents flow.

Use a shunt fed AF amplifier with inductive coupling.

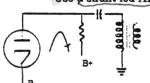

There are no magnetizing DC current flowing through the primary in this arrangement.

Shunt means parallel

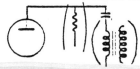

Core saturation in an inductive coupling system can be prevented by using pushpull series fed circuits or single ended ___SHUNT___ fed plate circuits. *which produces distortion*

33. (32, 16) If the state gain is 40, the Mu will be ___greater___ than 40.

137

3.   (sunset, sunrise) The experimental period is from local ＿＿＿＿＿＿ to local ＿＿＿＿＿＿ .

Broadcast Station logs

6.   (service; program) There are three logs required at the broadcast station:
   1) The program log must list times of identification (I.D.), nature of program, sponsor if program sponsored, and time and name of network operation.
   2) The operation log is a technical log listing final plate current readings, final plate voltage readings, antenna current readings, and frequency readings. These readings are logged every three hours. In addition this log must show the sign on and sign off time and any carrier interruption times.
   3) The maintenance log shows any test results, approved F.C.C. changes made (to final, modulator or antenna), experimental period tests, and antenna lighting inspection results. Many weekly maintenance items are entered in this log.

   The broadcast station must keep ＿＿＿＿＿＿＿＿＿＿＿ logs.

F.C.C. Definitions

9.   (construction permit, station license) There are three other types of stations that we should be able to define:
   1) Citizen band station. This is a station that may be used for personal matters or corporate business
   2) Base station. This is a land station in the land mobile service carrying on a service with land mobile stations.
   3) Land station. This is a station in the mobile service not intended to be used while in motion.

   A radio band that is used for personal matters and corporate business is the ＿＿＿＿＿ band.

12.   (base) Some of the more important transmitter emissions are listed below:

Amplitude modulation -
   AØ Carrier carrying no modulation.
   A1 Radiotelegraphy. On off keying.
   A3 Radiotelephony. Carrier with double sideband.
   A3A Radiotelephony. Reduced carrier with single sideband.
   A5 Video television

Frequency Modulation -
   F1 Frequency shift keying. used for radioteletype --- or for radiotelegraphy.
   F3 Frequency modulation radiotelephony.
   F4 Facsimile. used for transmission of stable images.
   F5 Aural television.

A carrier wave with no modulation is typed A＿. Amplitude modulation radiotelephony emissions with carrier and double sidebands is typed A＿.

Rules, Regulations, and Procedures

15.   (A1) All antenna proposals should be checked by the Federal Aviation Agency to see if there is any possibility of navigational hazard. The correct heighth of a licensed station antenna is listed on the instrument of authorization or on the station license. To determine if a proposed antenna would be an obstruction the ＿＿＿＿＿＿＿＿＿＿＿ should be consulted. The heighth of a broadcast station antenna is given on the ＿＿＿＿＿＿＿ license.

18.   (verification) The remote antenna current meter at a broadcast station must be checked against the antenna meter at the base of the antenna at least once a week. The accuracy of the remote meter must be within 2% of the antenna base current meter. The remote antenna current meter must read within ＿＿% of the antenna base current meter.

Vacuum Tubes

2.　(current) The basic action of an audio amplifier is illustrated for both vacuum tube and transistor circuits below:

4 volt peak to peak voltage swings negative grid from -6V to -4V and back to -6V and then to -8V.

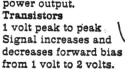

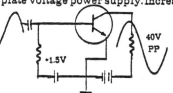

Negative grid repels cathode electrons.

High positive anode draws electrons.

Input signals add and subtract voltage to the fixed grid bias of -6V.

Changing plate current produces a variable voltage drop of 40 volts peak to peak across the load.

The amount of plate current varies with the negativeness of the grid. More current with low negative voltage (-4V) and less current with more negative voltage (-8V).

In this example a 4 volt (peak to peak) signal produced a 40 volt (peak to peak) output. The resulting output power is delivered by the plate voltage power supply. Increasing the supply voltage will result in a greater power output.

Transistors

1 volt peak to peak Signal increases and decreases forward bias from 1 volt to 2 volts.

40V PP

+1.5V

Most of emitter current flows in collector circuits.

Changing the forward bias changes the collector current. More current flows with high forward bias (2V) and less with lower forward bias (1V)

In this case a volt (PP) signal produced a 40V (PP) output. The resulting output is delivered by the collector power supply.

In the examples above the plate current flow in a vacuum tube is controlled by varying the negative voltage on the _CONTROL GRID_ and the collector current flow is controlled by varying the forward bias on the _BASE_ .

18.　(shunt)　The maximum transfer of energy using inductive (transformer) coupling can be accomplished by the proper choice of turns ratio. The formula for maximum transfer and proper impedance match is given by the ratio:

$$\frac{T_p}{T_s} = \sqrt{\frac{Z_p}{Z_s}}$$

Where　T_p = primary turns　Z_p = primary impedance

　　　　T_s = secondary turns　Z_s = secondary impedance

As an example consider what turns ratio primary to secondary is required to properly match the 20K ohm plate load impedance of a vacuum tube to a 5 ohm speaker.

$$\frac{T_p}{T_s} = \sqrt{\frac{20000}{5}} = \sqrt{4000} = 63 \text{ to } 1$$

This means for every turn in the secondary there would be 63 turns in the primary. In order to match a 4,000 ohm load into a 10 ohm speaker it would be necessary to use a transformer having a turns ratio of ___20___ to 1.

A.F. Amplifier Input and Output Phase

34.　(greater)　Two types of audio amplifiers should be discussed here - the common cathode and the common plate or cathode follower.

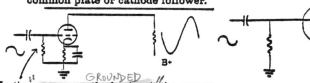

In the **common cathode circuit** the output is taken across the plate load resistor and is 180° out of phase from the grid input signal. _VOLTAGE GAIN greater than unity._

In the **common plate or cathode follower** the output is taken across the cathode resistor and is in phase with the input signal. The voltage gain is less than 1 (unity)

Sometimes the term grounded cathode or grounded plate are used instead of common cathode and common plate.

Whereas the common cathode amplifier has a voltage gain of greater than unity and an output that is out of phase with the input, the common plate or cathode follower amplifier has a voltage gain of _LESS_ _THAN UNITY_ and has an output that is _IN_ phase with the input.

2. (sunrise, sunset) The nighttime broadcast period is from local _____ to local _____.

5. (construction; equpment; experimental) After the construction has been completed and before the station license has been granted _____ or _____ tests may be made on the air.

Miscellaneous Station Information

8. (maintenance) In the public Safety Radio Services (fire, police, etc.) there is one F.C.C. form - Form 400 - that serves the following purposes:
    1) New station authorizations for base, fixed, or mobile stations.
    2) License application of any class of station upon the completion of construction.
    3) Modification of construction permit or station license.

    F.C.C. Form 400 should be used for modification of a _____ _____ or _____ _____.

11. (land) A land station in the land mobile service carrying on a service with land mobile stations is called a _____ station.

14. (facsimile) On off keying is referred to as A_____ radiotelegraphy.

17. (second class radiotelephone) If a licensed serviceman works at more than one station, he may satisfy the F.C.C. operator license requirement by posting his license at the station of principle employment and by carrying a verification card. A traveling transmitter serviceman can satisfy the F.C.C. operator license requirement if he posts his license at the place of principle employment and carries a _____ card.

20. (UHF) This concludes Unit 24.

VACUUM TUBE AUDIO AMPLIFIER GRID BIASING

3.　(control grid, base) In order for a control grid to control the flight of electrons from cathode to anode, it must have a negative voltage on it with respect to the cathode. When the signal is added the negative value fluctuates in such a manner that the resulting plate current flow also fluctuates.

　　　　The arrangement may be thought of as a valve.

There are five methods of biasing used in vacuum tube audio amplifiers:
　　(1) Automatic or cathode resistor biasing.
　　(2) Battery or power supply biasing.
　　(3) Voltage divider biasing.
　　(4) Contact potential biasing.
　　(5) Automatic volume control biasing.

In order for the control grid to control cathode electrons, it must be ___NEGATIVE___ with respect to the cathode.

19.　(20 to 1) A speaker output transformer designed to match 4,000 ohms to 4 ohms should have a turns ratio of _____ to 1.

35.　(less than unity, in) The push-pull common cathode audio amplifier requires two inputs that are equal amplitude and 180° out of phase with each other. This can be accomplished in the following ways:

(1) Use a transformer with a center tapped secondary.

To push pull grids

(2) Use a phase inverter.

(a) Combination common cathode　　　　　　　(b) Twin triode phase inverter
　　and common plate amplifier

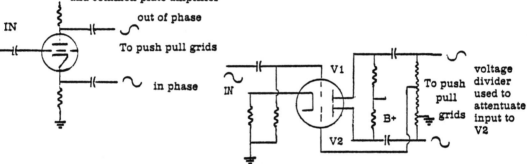

A push-pull audio amplifier requires input signals, that are ___EQUAL___ in amplitude and ___180°___ degrees out of phase.

UNIT 24 RADIO STATIONS

Introduction

1. The following facts concerning the standard broadcast service should be known:
   1) The band extends from 535 Khz to 1605 Khz.
   2) Except for low power daytime stations, the channels are 10 Khz wide. Therefore, the maximum modulating audio frequency allowed is 5 Khz.
   3) The frequency tolerance is 20 hertz or .002% for the mid frequency of 1000 Khz.
   4) There are 3 broadcast periods:
      a. Daytime - Local sunrise to local sunset
      b. Nightime - Local sunset to local sunrise
      c. Exprimental - Local midnight to local sunrise
   5) The primary service area is the area where there is no fading.

   The daytime broadcasting period is from local _____ to local _____.

Broadcast Station Tests

4. (midnight; sunrise) Before a broadcast station is constructed, a **construction permit** (C.P.) is required. During the construction and after the transmitter is installed, **equipment tests** may be made during the experimental period. (Midnight to sunrise) Upon completion of the station construction and until the station has been licensed, the station may be tested on the air on the construction permit frequency. This test is called a **service or program test**.
   Before a broadcast station can be built, a _____ permit must be secured from the F.C.C. Tests conducted during the period covered by the permit are called _____ tests and must be made during the _____ period.

7. (three) F.C.C. approved changes to the final, modulator, or antenna must appear in this _____ log.

10. (citizen's) A station in the mobile service not intended to be used while in motion is called a _____ station.

13. (Aϕ, A3) Stable images are telecast by a station using _____ .

16. (Federal Aviation Agency, station) Citizen band transmitters are all F.C.C. type approved and may not be serviced by any one. It requires a second class Radiotelephony license to service the citizens band transmitter. The citizen band transmitter may be adjusted and tuned by the holder of the _____ license.

Other Information

19. (2%) Carbon resistors that have an equal distribution of carbon throughout a ceramic binder do not work well in UHF transmitters as these high frequencies only travel on the surface. Because of this skin effect carbon resistors cannot be used at _____ .

4. **(negative)** The most common biasing system used in vacuum tube audio amplifiers is the automatic or cathode resistance method.

As current flows up through the cathode resistor, there is a voltage drop that may be used for grid bias.

Note: With a tetrode audio amplifier to find the cathode current only add the values of the screen and the plate currents - do not count the voltage nor grid current since they do not flow in an audio amplifier.

Note that even though there is a. 500K ohm resistor from grid to ground, there is no voltage drop across the resistor since grid current does not flow in an audio amplifier.

Therefore, the -6V at the bottom of the cathode resistor also appears at the control grid of the tube. The grid bias in this case results when 15 ma of plate (or cathode) current flows through the 400 ohm cathode resistor. The voltage drop is equal to .015 X 400 (I X R) or 6 volts. If a screen grid tube was used, the cathode current would be equal to the sum of the plate and screen currents. The value of grid bias developed in a tube having a plate current of 30 ma, a cathode current of 40 ma, and a cathode resistance of 500 ohms is _____20_____ volts. → 500Ω × 40 MA.

20. **(31.6 to 1)** If the voice coil of a permanent magnet speaker was used as a load in a vacuum tube plate circuit without using a matching transformer, there would be a serious mismatch of impedance and distortion would result. In addition the insulation between the voice coil and the frame work of the speaker would probably be inadequate for the high plate voltage. The breakdown of insulation might burn out the voice coil. If the voice coil of a PM speaker was inserted from the plate of a vacuum tube to the plus side of the power supply, there would be severe __DISTORTION__ in the output and the voice coil might burn out.

36. **(equal, 180°)** The circuit of the twin triode phase inverter is used to supply an input signal to a __PUSH-PULL__ amplifier.

1. The speed of a DC motor is determined by
    a. the number of bar segments in the commutator.
    c. the size of the commutator.
    c. the applied voltage.
    d. the motor load.
    e. c and d above.

2. To change low DC voltage to high DC voltage, one could use a
    a. voltage divider.
    b. dynamometer.
    c. dynamotor.
    d. capacitor.
    e. dynatron oscillator.

3. A shunt DC generator is illutrated by circuit

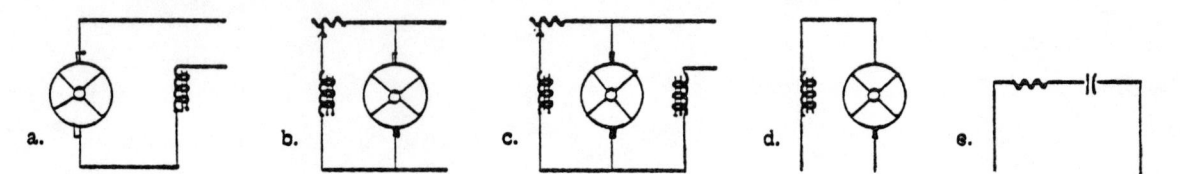

a.   b.   c.   d.   e.

4. If a high powered transmitter is powered by a generator, it is customary to protect the generator armature by
    a. using a capacitor in series with the supply lines.
    b. using a choke across the generator output.
    c. using an RF choke in series with the supply lines.
    d. grounding both sides of the generator output.
    e. none of these.

5. The speed of a synchronous motor is determined by
    a. the number of fields.
    b. the frequency.
    c. the voltage.
    d. the load.
    e. the size of wire in the winding.

6. If the field in a shunt motor running without load came open
    a. the motor would stop.
    b. the motor would race.
    c. the field would burn out.
    d. there would be no noticeable.
    e. none of these.

7. The dynamotor output load changes are compensated for
    a. automatically.
    b. by a rheostat in the armature.   d. by a rheostat in the battery lead.
    c. by a rheostat in the field.   e. none of these.

8. The purpose of the commutator brush assembly on a generator is to
    a. provide AC output.
    b. mechanically rectify the generator output.   d. reduce harmonics.
    c. eliminate interference.   e. none of these.

9. A dynamotor is used to
    a. step up DC voltage.
    b. step down DC voltage.   d. step up DC power.
    c. step up AC voltage.   e. measure power factor.

10. The speed of a DC series motor is determined mainly by
    a. its load.
    b. its field strength.   d. its line frequency.
    c. its voltage.   e. number of poles.

11. It is necessary to keep radio frequency (R.F.) out of a generator to prevent
    a. harmonic generation.
    b. parasitic oscillations.
    c. eddy currents.
    d. burning out the armature.
    e. none of the above.

5. (20) The value of grid bias developed in a tube having a plate current of 40 ma, a cathode current of 50 ma, and a cathode resistor of 500 ohms is _____25_____ volts.

        500 × .050 ↗

21. (distortion) The secondary impedance of a transformer is 10K ohms and the primary is working out of an impedance of 20 ohms, there would be a maximum transfer of energy if the transformer had a turns ratio of _____ to 1.

MOTOR BOATING IN A.F. AMPLIFIERS

37. (push-pull) A low audio frequency oscillation due to feedback and regeneration is called **motorboating**. The general idea is shown in block diagram:

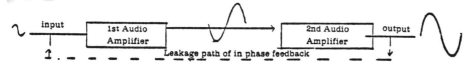

This feedback builds up again (regenerates) and if the amplitude of the feedback is sufficient, the whole amplifier may oscillate at a low audio frequency. The resultant sound is a form of severe distortion called **motorboating**.

Two feedback leakage paths are readily identifiable:

   (1) In phase feedback producing regeneration may occur if the output of one stage is coupled to the input of another stage by stray inductances and capacitance. This may result if components or wires associated with one stage are mounted too close to the components or wires of another stage.

   (2) In phase feedback may occur through a power supply common to two stages. The secret in preventing this type of feedback leakage is to keep audio frequencies out of the power supply by **decoupling**. A common way of decoupling is by an RC network.

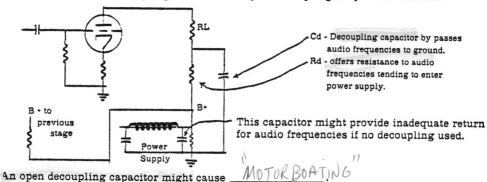

Cd - Decoupling capacitor by passes audio frequencies to ground.

Rd - offers resistance to audio frequencies tending to enter power supply.

This capacitor might provide inadequate return for audio frequencies if no decoupling used.

An open decoupling capacitor might cause _____"MOTORBOATING"_____

2. (motor) A _____ converts mechanical energy into electrical energy. Sec. 23-1.

4. (rectify) In a series D.C. generator the _____ is in series with the _____ . Sec.23-8.

6. (shunt). If a high powered transmitter is powered by a generator, it is customary to protect the generator armature by using an _____ in series with the ungrounded line and a _____ across the line. This forms a _____ pass filter. Sec. 23-13.

8. (generator) This D.C. series motor has a high _____ torque. Sec. 23-15.

10. (race) The speed of a DC motor is determined by the applied _____ and the motor load. Sec. 23-16.

12. (frequency) The dynamotor is a form of the DC _____ . Sec. 23-24.

14. (low, high) Although the speed of a dynamotor is not generally regulated, it could be done by putting a rheostat in the _____ load. Sec. 23-24.

6. **(25 volts)** In the circuit shown. plate current flows from the ground through the cathode resistor, through the tube, and then back to the plus side of the plate supply source voltage.

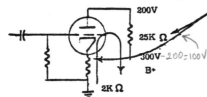

As it flows a voltage drop is developed across the cathode resistance and the plate load resistance. In this case the plate current flow through the load resistance of 25K ohms causes a 100 volt drop. It can be concluded that the current flow is 100V/25K or 4 ma. The same current flows through the cathode resistance causing a biasing voltage drop of .004 A (4ma) X 2K ohms or 8 volts.

Since the signal input voltage varies the bias voltage, care must be taken to avoid excessive signal drive or distortion will result. If in the example below the bias must be kept between 0 and negative 22 volts for distortionless amplification, the input signal must not exceed 14 volts peak to peak or 7 volts peak.

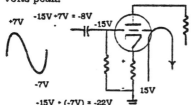

The bias would vary between -8V and -22V with the application of signal and distortionless operation would result.

If the signal peak voltage is 7 volts, the RMS voltage would be .707 X 7 (707 X Epk) or about 4 volts. The cathode resistor bias voltage in the circuit shown would be ____9____ volts. There is no distortion with the amplifier to the left when the grid bias is kept between 0 and -20V. The maximum RMS voltage signal input for distortionless amplification would be approximately _____ volts.

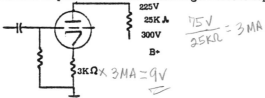

22. **(22.3 to 1)** Direct coupling has become a popular coupling method in recent years with the advent of solid state devices. However, in both vacuum tube and transistor circuits this method of coupling has one outstanding advantage.
A direct coupled amplifier is a high fidelity amplifier and can amplify signals without distortion or attenuation down to below 1 hertz.
Note in the circuit below there are no capacitive or inductive components.

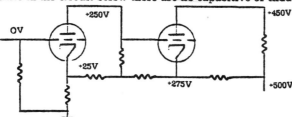

Direct coupling means the output plate of one stage is directly connected to the input grid of the next stage.

If you direct coupled a number of vacuum tube stages an extremely high voltage power supply is required. The low power supply voltage requirement for direct coupled transistor stages makes direct coupling desirable for solid state circuitry. Direct coupling is used in audio frequency amplifiers for amplifying signals down to below ____ONE____ hertz.

38. **(motorboating)** If the output connections of a stage came too close to the input of another stage ___MOTOR BOATING___ might result.

UNIT 23 MOTORS AND GENERATORS

RECHECK PROGRAMMED INSTRUCTION USING SHRADER'S ELECTRONIC COMMUNICATION

1. A ____________ converts electrical energy into mechanical energy. Sec. 23-1.

3. **(generator)** The purpose of the commutator brush assembly on a generator is to mechanically ____________ the generator output. Sec. 23-6.

5. **(armature, field)** The DC generator shown is a ____________ generator. Sec. 23-9.

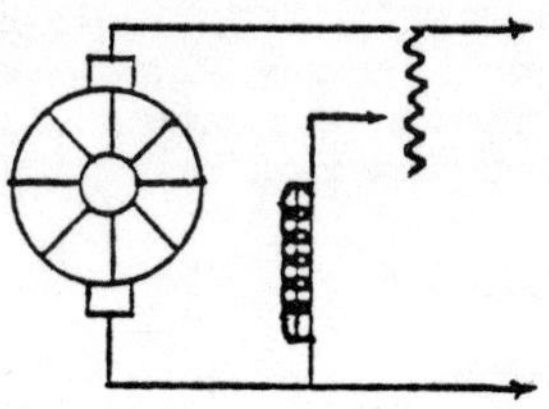

7. **(RF choke, capacitor, low)** A DC motor is the same machine as a DC ____________. Sec. 23-14.

9. **(starting)** If the field in a shunt motor running without load came open, the motor would ____________. Sec. 23-16.

11. **(voltage)** The speed of a synchronous motor is determined by the number of poles and the ____________. Sec. 23-20.

13. **(motor generator)** The dynamotor can be used for changing a ____________ DC voltage to a ____________ DC voltage. Sec. 23-24.

15. **(battery)** This concludes Unit 23.

7. **(9V, 6.36V)** In order to get maximum gain from an audio amplifier with cathode resistor biasing, it is necessary to bypass the resistor with a large capacitor. This is illustrated below:

Unbypassed

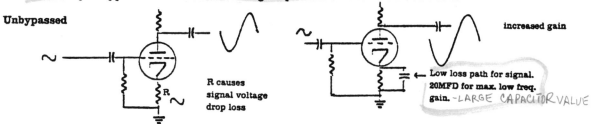

R causes
signal voltage
drop loss

Low loss path for signal.
20MFD for max. low freq.
gain. -LARGE CAPACITOR VALUE

increased gain

The small interelectrode capacitance in a vacuum tube permits some regenerative feedback. If the output is reduced because of the signal loss across an unbypassed cathode resistor, there isn't as much signal to produce feedback. Such a circuit is degenerative in effect.

If there is more output signal present in the plate circuit due to cathode resistor bypassing, there will be more feedback. Such a circuit is said to be regenerative. Although high regenerative circuits have more voltage gain, they have greater distortion. (lack high fidelity)

Although more gain is achieved by use of a cathode resistor bypass capacitor, the end result is poor ___FIDELITY___ .

VACUUM TUBE PLATE LOADS

23. **(1 hertz)** The output voltage to be delivered to a succeeding stage or to a speaker is taken from the plate load. The plate load value is determined by the desired output condition.

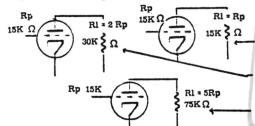

For maximum output power the load RL must be equal to the tube impedance between cathode and plate.
For maximum undistorted output power the load RL must be twice the tube impedance between cathode and plate. 15KΩ × 2 = 30KΩ
For maximum efficiency the load RL must be much larger than Rp. -grid Resistor 15KΩ

RP
√15KΩ×5
Resistor one
R₁ = 75KΩ
on schematic

The plate impedance of a certain tube amplifier is 20K ohms. For maximum power output the load impedance should be ___20KΩ___ ohms.

39. **(motorboating)** Another form of motor boating results from the use of long RC time constants in RC coupling. If this time constant is too long, there may be a build up of electrons on the control grid.

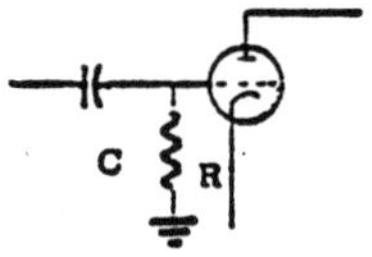

If C is too large or R is too large or open, motorboating may occur.

An open grid resistor may cause ___MOTORBOATING___.

4.   (commutator) The field used for producing magnetic lines of force may be generated by an electro-magnet winding around pole pieces. If the field is generated by placing the winding in series with the armature winding...The DC generator is a series generator. If the field winding is in parallel with the armature, the DC generator is a shunt generator. By diagram:

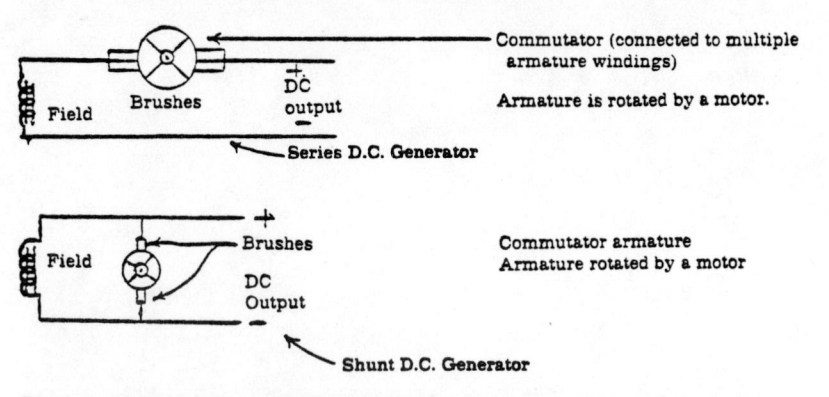

These generators are called self excited generators. If an external voltage source is used to excite the field, the DC generator does not supply the EMF for the field. If the field of a D.C. generator is in parallel with the armature winding, it is called a _____ generator.

The Dynamotor

8.   (1200 R.P.M.) The dynamotor is a type of motor generator. The armature has both a motor and generator winding. The field is common to both windings.

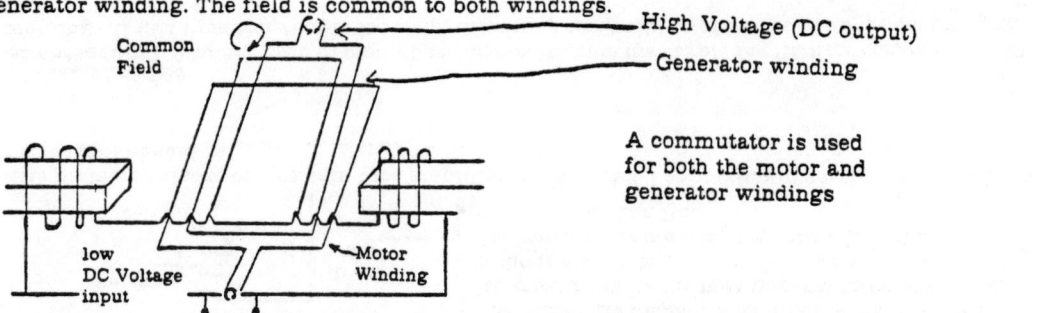

The dynamotor takes a low D.C. voltage input and delivers a high D.C. output voltage. It does the same thing for D.C. as a transformer does for A.C.

The output voltage is difficult to regulate. To some extent it can be done by a rheostat in the low voltage battery lead.

A dynamotor is used to step up _____ voltage.

12.   (R.F.; capacitors) This concludes Unit 23.

8.   (fidelity) In the ideal high fidelity low distortion amplifier, it is desirable to eliminate all feedback and regeneration.

In summary:

  (1) Automatic cathode resistor biasing without a bypass capacitor produces degeneration (less feedback)

  (2) Automatic cathode resistor biasing with a bypass capacitor produces regeneration (more feedback and more gain). *but less fidelity.*

If Ck in the amplifier shown becomes "open," the circuit would become ___DEGENERATIVE___ (degenerative or (regenerative)

If Ck becomes "shorted" the grid bias would ___FALL___ and the plate current would ___RISE___.

24.   (20K ohms) For maximum undistorted output the load impedance should be ___40KΩ (twice R grid___ ohms. (see #23) *Follows question 23.*

R load (the previous) value

MISCELLANEOUS

40.   (motorboating) If the power output of an audio amplifier is to be raised, it is necessary to raise the plate voltage. The output power of an audio amplifier can be increased by increasing the ___PLATE___ voltage.

3. **(alternating)** If the alternator output is mechanically rectified, the device is called a DC generator. The rectifier in a DC generator takes the form of a **commutator**.

The side of the loop that is cutting lines of force as it moves down is always connected to the positive brush.

The side of the loop that is cutting lines of force as it moves up is always connected to the negative brush.

Brushes
+Commutator (split ring)

DC output +

The output of an alternator can be mechanically rectified by the _____.

7. **(race)** Two common AC motors are the induction and synchronous motors. Their speeds can be figured by the formula:

$$\text{Speed in R.P.M. m} = \frac{\text{Frequency (cps)}}{\text{Pairs of Poles (per phase)}} \times 60$$

The speed of a 3 phase AC motor having six poles per phase and in input frequency of 60 hz would be _____.

D.C. Generator Supply Line Filtering

11. **(rheostat, battery)** In order to prevent R.F. currents from coming back from a high power transmitter to a generator power supply, a low pass filter is used. Series R.F.C. has high reactance to R.F.

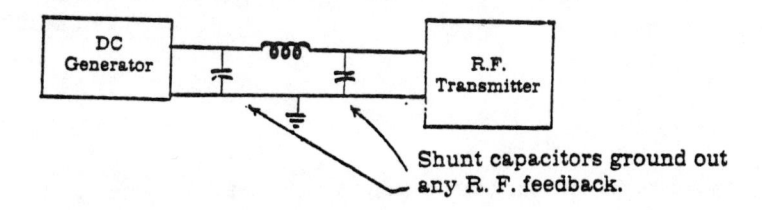

Shunt capacitors ground out any R. F. feedback.

If this filtering was not done, R.F. could burn out the D.C. generator armature winding.

If a high powered transmitter is powered by a D.C. generator, it is customary to protect the generator armature by using a _____ choke in series with the supply line and _____ in parallel across the line.

9.   (degenerative, fall, rise) In an ideal high fidelity amplifier it is desirable to have _____ *NO FEEDBACK* (positive, negative or no) feedback.

25.   (40 K ohms) For maximum efficiency the load impedance should be at least _____ $100 K\Omega \rightarrow$ (*value greater than plate Z*) (see #23) *follows Question 23.* *of 75KΩ*

41.   (plate) The gain in DBs of an amplifier can be determined by the formula:

$$DB = 20 \log \frac{E_1}{E_2}$$

$$DB = 20 \log \frac{I_\phi}{I_3}$$

Assuming equal input and output impedance.

If for example the input voltage was .005 volts and the output voltage was 5 volts, the gain in DBs would be 20 log 1000 or 20 X 3 = 60 DBs.

If an amplifier has an output of 6 volts with an input of .006 volts the gain would be _____ *60 DBS* DBs.

Generators

2.   **(transducers)** The simplest generator is the AC alternator. As the loop is rotated in a magnetic field, an AC voltage is generated. One end of the loop is terminated in a rotating slip ring. The other end of the loop is terminated in another slip ring. The output voltage is collected from the slip rings by brushes.

The rotating winding in a practical alternator consists of many turns and is called a rotating armature.

The output of an alternator is _____ current.

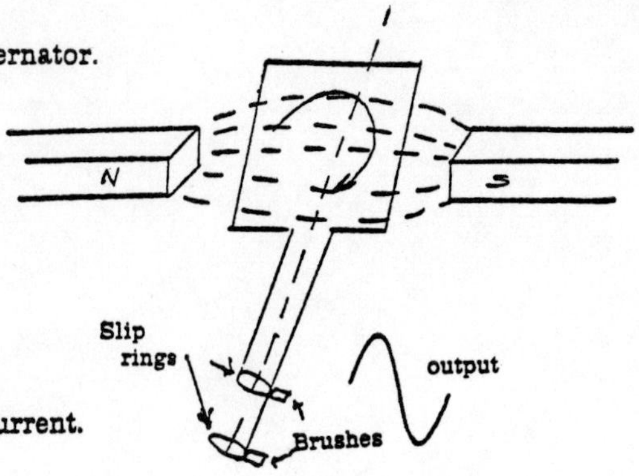

6.   (**load**) If the field winding came open in an operating shunt motor, the motor would _____.

10.   **(dynamotor)** The dynamotor output load changes are compensated for by a _____ in the _____ lead.

10. **(no)** Grid bias is measured at the grid with respect to the cathode. If the grid return resistor is open, then the cathode resistor bias voltage cannot be applied to the grid. In this case the grid is said to be floating.

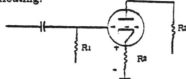

This circuit would not work because ___R1___

is not returned to the negative side of the bias resistor.

26. **(100K ohm)** Often a high impedance pair of earphones is used as a load. The variable plate current through the earphones varies the magnetic attraction for the earphone diaphragms.

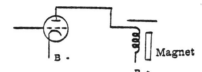

Earphones are polarized. If current flows the wrong direction through the windings the magnets are demagnitized.

If earphones used as a plate load are connected with the wrong polarity, the permanent magnets may ___DE-MAGNETIZED___.

42. **(60 DBs)** AC hum in the output of an audio amplifier can be reduced or eliminated by:
(1) Using well filtered power supplies.
(2) Using tubes with indirect cathodes.
(3) Using center tapped filament connections to the ground grid and plate returns when using direct cathodes. This provides a neutral point for grid and plate returns.

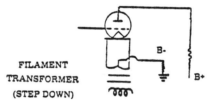

FILAMENT
TRANSFORMER
(STEP DOWN)

To eliminate hum in an audio amplifier using direct cathodes, the grid and plate returns should be returned to the ___CENTER TAP___ on the filament transformer.

Introduction

1. A device that changes one kind of energy into another kind is called a **transducer**. Both motors and generators are transducers. Generators change mechanical energy into electrical energy. Motors change electrical energy into mechanical energy. Motors and generators are _____ .

Motors

5. (shunt) The DC series and shunt motors are much like the DC series and shunt generators. However, the motor has an electrical input with a mechanical torque output. The rotation is a result of the interaction of the armature and stationary fields. The series motor works on either AC or DC and will start under heavy mechanical loads.

   The shunt DC motor will only work with a DC input.

   Both circuits are shown:

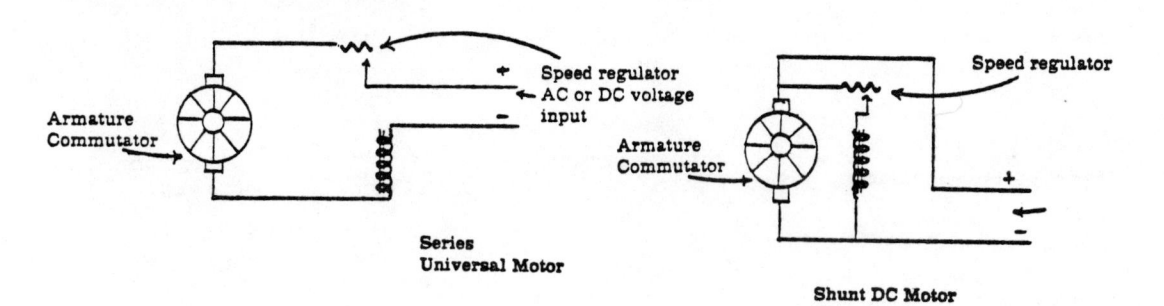

Series
Universal Motor

Shunt DC Motor

If field coil comes open motor will race.

   The speed of a DC motor is determined by the mechanical load and the DC voltage input, but mainly by the load. The speed is determined mainly by the_____and the applied voltage.

9. (D.C.) To change low DC voltage to high DC voltage, one could use a _____ .

11. **(R1)** Let us examine a cathode resistor biased circuit in terms of the direction of current flow.

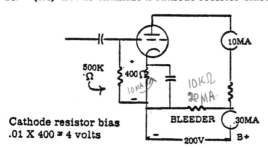

30 ma of current flows in two parallel paths from the negative terminal of the power supply to the positive terminal. 10 ma flows up through the cathode resistor. 20 ma flows through the bleeder resistor.

The value of the bleeder resistance would be = E/I or 200/.02A pr 10KΛ

Cathode resistor bias
.01 X 400 = 4 volts

If in the circuit above the plate current was 15 ma and the total power supply current was 20 ma, the grid bias voltage would be _____ volts and the value of the bleeder resistance would be _____ ohms.

CLASSES OF AMPLIFIERS "A", "AB", "B".

27. **(demagnetized)** There are three main classes of audio amplifiers: Class A, class AB, and class B. The class A amplifier is biased for high fidelity operation. The graph of the grid voltage plate current characteristics is shown for a triode class A amplifier:

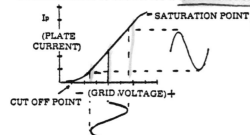

The class A amplifier negative bias voltage is set at the mid point on the linear part (straight line part) of the curve. Heavy line shows linear portion of curve.

As the signal changes the negativeness of the bias from the fixed quiescent bias voltage value, the plate current rises and falls.

Since the output plate current wave form looks like the input signal voltage, the amplifier is said to be high in fidelity (faithfullness in reproduction). Plate current flows during the entire input cycle.

The class A amplifier is biased to the _MID_ point of the _liNEAR_ portion of the EgIp curve.

43. **(center tap)** Two tubes can be combined in a **parallel circuit** for twice the output power. Note the diagram below:

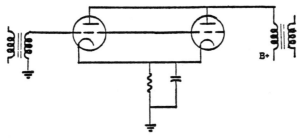

It is seen in the diagram that like electrodes in the two tubes are connected in parallel - hence the name parallel circuit.

Two tubes connected in parallel provide _TWICE_ the power as one tube alone.

1. The electrolyte of a lead acid cell is
   a. hydrochloric acid.
   b. sulphuric acid.   d. lead oxide.
   c. sodium hydroxide.   e. sal ammoniac.

2. When a battery is placed in storage it should be
   a. stored in a warm room
   b. drained and the electrolyte replaced with distilled water.
   c. jarred to prevent sulfation.
   d. packed in ice.
   e. none of these.

3. A 12 volt battery is rated at 100 ampere hours on an 8 hour basis. This battery will deliver
   a. 100 amperes for 1 hour.
   b. 10 amperes for 10 hours.
   c. 12.5 amperes for 8 hours.
   d. 25 amperes for 4 hours.
   e. 100 amperes for 8 hours.

4. The plates of an Edison cell are immersed in
   a. HCL.
   b. H_2SO_4.   d. water.
   c. KOH.   e. NH_4Cl.

5. An A battery is
   a. a filament battery.
   b. an anode battery.
   c. control grid battery.
   d. screen grid battery.
   e. suppressor grid battery.

6. The paste in a dry cell contains the
   a. positive electrode.
   b. negative electrode.
   c. electrolyte.
   d. resistance reducing agent.
   e. iron oxide.

7. The depolarizing agent in a dry cell is
   a. carbon.
   b. salamoniac.   d. manganese dioxide.
   c. sodium hydroxide.   e. iron oxide.

8. A discharged battery should be charged as soon as possible because
   a. the electrolytic solution would evaporate.
   b. the electrolyte would be neutralized.
   c. of plate sulphation.
   d. the flaking of nickel cadium.
   e. polarization sets in.

9. A battery charger tube uses
   a. a high vacuum with a carbon filament.
   b. an injected inert gas.
   c. a high vacuum with a carbon.
   d. a tetrode.
   e. none of these.

10. A ship board battery should be grounded by use of
    a. number 14 wire.
    b. a long copper wire.
    c. several different lengths of wire.
    d. a short lead to a common point.
    e. none of these.

11. The best check on the charge of a lead acid battery is
    a. by a hydrometer.
    b. by a voltmeter with the battery under a heavy load.
    c. by a short circuit current test.
    d. by a voltmeter with the battery under light load.
    e. none of these.

12. If a battery is charged and the hydrometer reads low
    a. add a salt solution.
    b. add a base solution.   d. acid should be added.
    c. distilled water should be added.   e. alcohol should be added.

274

12. **(6V, 40 K)** A simple method of biasing a vacuum tube is by use of a battery or bias power supply. This arrangement is shown:

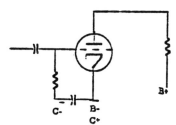

Battery or low
voltage power
(C supply)

In this circuit negative grid bias is supplied
by use of a＿＿＿＿＿＿＿or low voltage power supply.

28. **(mid, linear)** The class A amplifier is a＿＿＿HIGH＿＿＿ fidelity amplifier.

44. **(twice)** By the proper choice of a capacitor in series with a variable resistor certain frequencies can be shunted across the input or output of an audio amplifier to provide tone control.

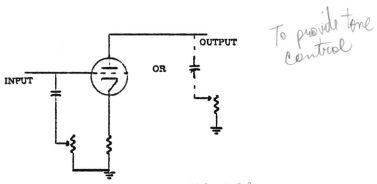

To provide tone
control

A tone control consists of a series＿＿CAPACITOR＿＿and variable resistor.
This control can be used in either the＿＿INPUT＿＿or＿＿OUTPUT＿＿of the audio amplifier circuit.

2. (A, B, C) The depolarizing agent in a dry cell is _____ _____ . Sec. 22-2.

4. (electrolyte) The output voltage of a good dry cell is approximately _____ volts. Sec. 22-2.

6. (sulfuric acid) A discharged battery should be charged as soon as possible because of plate _____ . Sec. 22-3.

8. (1.280) The best check on the charge of a lead acid battery is by using a _____. Sec. 22-5.

10. (acid) A 12 volt battery is rated at 100 ampere hours on an 8 hour basis. This battery will deliver _____ amperes for 8 hours. Sec. 22-7.

12. (argon) When a battery is placed in storage, it should be charged, the _____ drained and replaced with distilled water. Sec. 22-9.

14. (potasium hydroxide - KOH) A shipboard _____ should not be grounded. Sec. 28-1.

13. **(battery)** Audio amplifiers are sometimes biased by use of a voltage divider as shown:

No voltage drop across
grid resistor as no
current flows here.

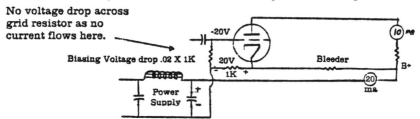

Biasing Voltage drop .02 X 1K

The total current 20 ma flows through biasing resistor developing 20 volts bias - 1,000 ohms X .02A.

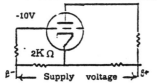

The total current flow from B- to B+ in the circuit shown would be _____ ma.

29. **(high)** The class B amplifier is biased at the cut off point on an EgIp curve.

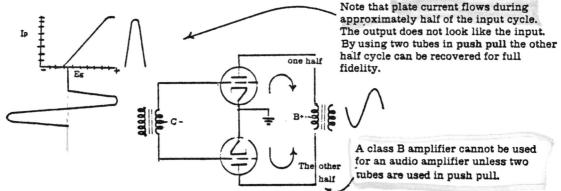

Note that plate current flows during approximately half of the input cycle. The output does not look like the input. By using two tubes in **push pull** the other half cycle can be recovered for full fidelity.

A class B amplifier cannot be used for an audio amplifier unless two tubes are used in push pull.

In push pull circuits all even harmonic (2nd, 4th, etc.) current from the two tubes arrive at the output 180° out of phase and cancel.

Class B audio frequency amplifiers can be used if two tubes are used in _PUSH-PULL_ for high fidelity operation. In this circuit all _EVEN_ harmonics are cancelled.

45. **(capacitor, input, output)** To get high fidelity reproduction from an audio amplifier it is necessary to neutralize the interelectrode capacity effect between the anode and the grid. Any feedback through this capacitance can be cancelled by an opposite degenerative inverse feedback. In the diagram shown inverse voltage feedback is provided through an RC network.

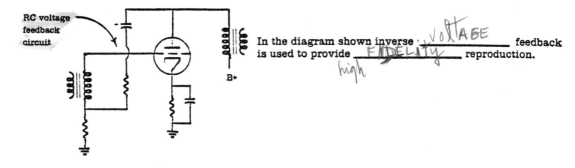

In the diagram shown inverse _VOLTAGE_ feedback is used to provide _FIDELITY_ reproduction. _high_

UNIT 22 BATTERIES

RECHECK PROGRAMMED INSTRUCTION USING SHRADER'S ELECTRONIC COMMUNICATION

1. Batteries used to heat vacuum tube filaments are called_____batteries. Plate voltage supply batteries are called_____batteries. A battery used to bias the grid of a vacuum tube is called a_____battery. Sec. 22-1.

3. (manganese dioxide) The paste in a dry cell contains the_____. Sec. 22-2.

5. (1.5 volts) The electrolyte of a lead acid cell is_____. Sec. 22-3.

7. (sulphation) The fully charged lead acid battery has an electrolyte with an approximate specific gravity of_____. Sec. 22-4.

9. (hydrometer) If a battery is charged and the hydrometer reads low, it will be necessary to add_____. Sec. 22-5.

11. (12.5A) One common battery charger rectifier tube uses_____gas. Sec. 22-8.

13. (electrolyte) The plates of an Edison cell are immersed in_____ _____. Sec. 22-10.

15. (battery or DC source) This concludes Unit 22.

14. **(5 ma)** Contact and automatic volume control bias will be discussed in Unit 18 with AM Receivers.

30. **(push pull, even)** The bias point for class AB is half way between the quiescent point of bias for the class A and the bias point for class B.

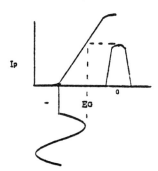

The class of operation shown is class _____B_____ .

46. **(voltage, high fidelity)** This concludes Unit 14.

3.   (electrolyte) A battery cell is composed of two _____ metals and an electrolyte.

6.   (manganese dioxide) The output voltage of a good dry cell is approximately _____ volts.

9.   (sulphuric) When a battery is placed in storage, the electrolyte should be replaced with _____ _____.

The Edison Cell

12. (hydrometer; acid) The Edison battery is a rugged battery used in trucks and laboratories. The cell has a positive electrode of nickle and nickle hydrate, a negative electrode of iron, and an electrolyte of potassium hydroxide (KOH).

The full charged cell voltage is approximately 1.3 volts. The battery consists of 5 cells in series.

The electrolyte of an Edison cell is _____ .

15. (1.5 V) When a battery is charged, current is forced back through the battery in opposite direction from the discharge. A typical battery charger is shown:

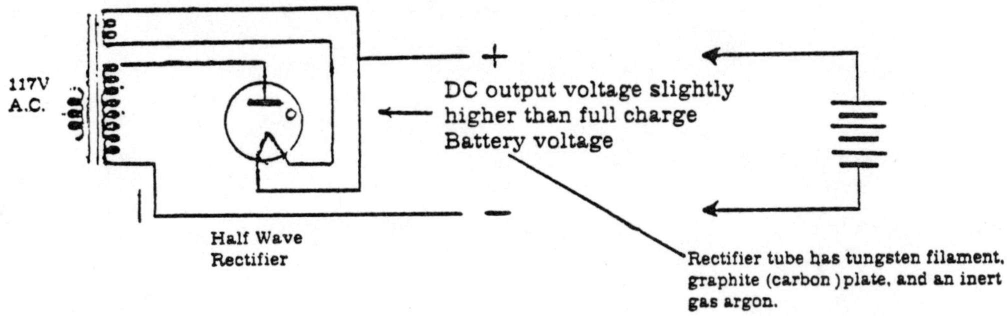

117V
A.C.

+

DC output voltage slightly
higher than full charge
Battery voltage

−

Half Wave
Rectifier

Rectifier tube has tungsten filament,
graphite (carbon) plate, and an inert
gas argon.

The battery charge tube usually contains the inert gas _____ .

18. (grounded) This concludes Unit 22.

VACUUM TUBE INTERSTAGE COUPLING

15. The most common method of coupling the output of one audio amplifier stage to the next is by capacitive coupling. This method is also referred to as resistance coupling and RC coupling.

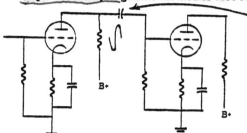

Voltage drop across load resistance in plate circuit is connected to the grid of the next stage through a low loss capacitor. The value of the capacitance must be of such a size as to provide a low impedance at the lowest frequency used. An .01 Mfd is usual for audio frequencies.

Coupling AF energy to a succeeding stage by a capacitor is referred to as capacitive coupling or _RESISTANCE_ coupling or _R-C_ coupling.

VOLTAGE AMPLIFICATION

31. (B) The stage voltage amplification of an amplifier is equal to the output voltage divided by the input signal voltage. The maximum possible voltage amplification is only theoretical and is symbolized by the greek letter Mu or μ.

The practical stage voltage amplification is given by formula:

$$V.A. = \frac{Mu\ R_L}{R_p \cdot R_L}$$

Where V.A. is amplification.
   Mu is the maximum voltage amplification obtainable.
   R_L is the plate load resistance
   R_p is the internal cathode to plate tube impedance.

If the Mu of a tube is given as 48, the R_L load impedance is 20 K ohms, and R_p plate impedance is 10 K ohms; the voltage amplification would equal:

$$\frac{48 \times 20.000}{10,000 + 20.000} \qquad \text{or } 48 \ 2/3 = 32$$

This would mean that the peak to peak output voltage would be 32 times as great as the peak to peak voltage of the signal input.

If the Mu of a tube is given as 100, the R_L as 15 K ohms, and the R_p as .045 megohms: the voltage amplification of the stage would be_____ .

2.   (**Filament or heater; plate; grid bias**) A battery is made up of a combination of cells. A cell is constructed by immersing two dissimilar metals in a water solution of an acid, base or salt. The water solution is an electrolyte. Chemical action within the cell produces an EMF. A water solution of an acid, base or salt is called an _____ .

5.   (**carbon; zinc**) The depolarizing agent used to prevent hydrogen from collecting at the anode is _____ .

The Lead Acid Cell

8.   (**sal ammoniac**) The construction of a lead acid cell is shown below.

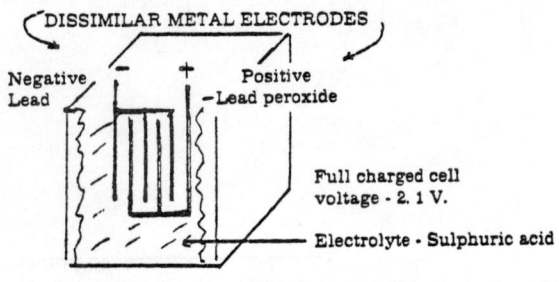

When three cells are connected in series, the battery voltage is 6.3 volts. When six cells are connected in series, the battery voltage is 12.6 volts.

The best way to check a lead acid battery is by use of a specific gravity test using a hydrometer. The specific gravity of the electrolyte of a fully charged battery cell should be approximately 1.280. This means the electrolyte would weigh 1.28 times as much as pure water.

If a voltage under load test shows the battery fully charged and yet the specific gravity is below 1.280, acid should be added to the electrolyte until the proper reading is obtained. This could only happen if some of the electrolyte had been spilled.

When a lead acid battery is placed in storage, the electrolyte should be drained and replaced by distilled water.

A lead acid battery should be charged often. If discharge continues too long, the plates become excessively sulphated. Such a battery is difficult to charge.

The electrolyte of a lead acid cell is a water solution of _____ acid.

11.   (**plate**) The best check on the charge of a lead acid cell is made by using a _____ . If this test shows the specific gravity is low and yet a voltage test shows the cell fully charged, _____ should be added to the electrolyte.

14.   (**negative**) The full charged cell voltage of a dry cell is _____ V.

17.   (**12.5 A**) The negative terminal of a ship board battery is not grounded to the metal hull of the ship. This eliminates any cathodic current flow from hull to the sea water and prevents corrosion from electrical currents.

The negative terminal of a ship board battery is not _____ to the metal hull.

16. (resistance, RC) Transformer or inductive coupling is used for impedance matching between an AF amplifier and a speaker It is also used for phase inversion for feeding a push pull amplifier.
Examples of inductive coupling are shown:

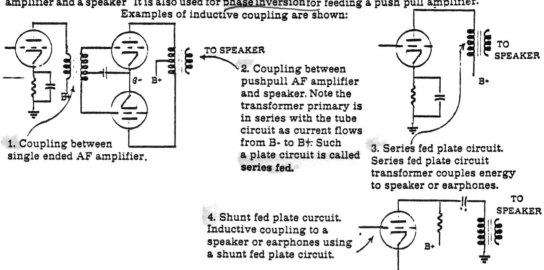

1. Coupling between single ended AF amplifier.

2. Coupling between pushpull AF amplifier and speaker. Note the transformer primary is in series with the tube circuit as current flows from B- to B+. Such a plate circuit is called series fed.

TO SPEAKER

3. Series fed plate circuit. Series fed plate circuit transformer couples energy to speaker or earphones.

4. Shunt fed plate curcuit. Inductive coupling to a speaker or earphones using a shunt fed plate circuit.

TO SPEAKER

Note that in the shunt fed plate circuit DC plate current does not flow through the transformer primary.

If the primary and secondary windings of a transformer are close together, the coupling is said to be broadly coupled and a wider audio frequency range is passed.

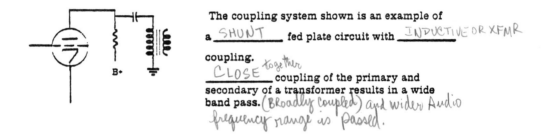

The coupling system shown is an example of a ___SHUNT___ fed plate circuit with ___INDUCTIVE OR XFMR___ coupling.
___CLOSE___ together coupling of the primary and secondary of a transformer results in a wide band pass. (Broadly coupled) and wider Audio frequency range is passed.

32. (25) If the stage gain V.A., RL and Rp is given we can solve for Mu. For example suppose the stage gain was 30, the RL 20K ohms, and the Rp 10 ohms.

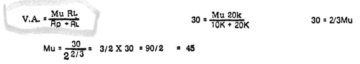

$V.A. = \frac{Mu\ R_L}{R_p + R_L}$

$30 = \frac{Mu\ 20k}{10K + 20K}$

$30 = 2/3 Mu$

$Mu = \frac{30}{2\ 2/3} = 3/2 \times 30 = 90/2 = 45$

Note that the Mu is greater than the V.A. stage gain.

If the V.A. is 16, the RL 20K ohms, and Rp 20K; the Mu would be _____ .

The voltage amplification of a tube is somewhat similar to the voltage gain of the high gain operational amplifier (OP AMP). The actual gain is always less than the theoretical gain. The amplification factor is equal to the feedback impedance divided by the input impedance. If the feedback impedance of an Op. Amp. was 12,000 ohms and the input impedance was 750 ohms, the stage gain would be_____ .

UNIT 22 BATTERIES

Introduction

1. Batteries that are used for vacuum tube circuits are classes as
    1. A batteries. These are used to supply the voltage for filaments or heaters.
    2. B batteries. These are used to supply the voltage for the plate circuits of vacuum tubes.
    C. C batteries. These are used to supply the grid voltage for biasing vacuum tubes.

    An A battery is a _____ supply battery.

    A B battery is a _____ supply battery.

    A C battery is a _____ supply battery.

The Dry Cell

4. (dissimilar) The construction of a dry cell is shown below.

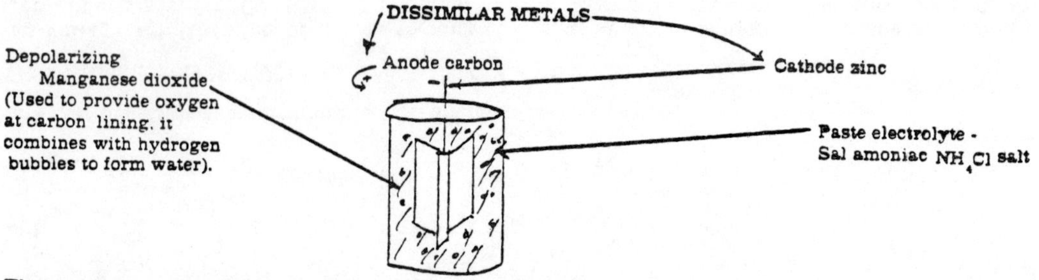

DISSIMILAR METALS

Depolarizing
  Manganese dioxide.
(Used to provide oxygen
at carbon lining. it
combines with hydrogen
bubbles to form water).

Anode carbon

Cathode zinc

Paste electrolyte -
Sal amoniac NH_4Cl salt

The manganese dioxide is called a depolarizing agent. It prevents hydrogen from collecting at the anode carbon by supplying oxygen for water formation. Hydrogen could prevent further chemical action but water aids chemical action.

The cell voltage of a dry cell is approximately 1.5 volts. The dry cell anode is_____and the cathode is_____ .

7. (1.5 volts) The paste electrolyte in a dry cell is_____salt.

10. (distilled water) A discharged lead acid battery should be charged as soon as possible because of _____ sulphation.

Miscellaneous

13. (KOH) The three cells are compared below:

Type of Cell	Electrolyte	Neg. Electrode	Pos. Electrode	Voltage
Dry Cell	Salt (NH_4Cl)	Zinc	Carbon	1.5 V
Lead Acid Cell	Acid (H_2SO_4)	Lead	Lead peroxide	2.1 V
Edison Cell	Base (KOH)	Iron	Nickle and Nickle Hydrate	1.3 V

The short words in each case indicate the _____electrode.

16. (argon) The capacity of a battery indicates how long it will discharge at a given current. A 100 ampere hour battery would discharge at a 10 amp rate for 10 hours.

A 100 ampere hour battery would discharge at a _____ampere rate for 8 hours.

UNIT 14
AUDIO FREQUENCY AMPLIFIER

RECHECK MATERIAL USING SHRADER'S ELECTRONIC COMMUNICATION

1.   When it is necessary to drive a speaker an audio _____ amplifier must be used. Sec. 14-2.

5.   (Mu) A certain amplifier has a tube with a Mu of 80, a load resistance of 15 K Ω, a plate impedance of .045 megohms. The plate current is 16 ma. The gain of the stage would be _____. Sec. 14-4.

9.   (30K Ω)

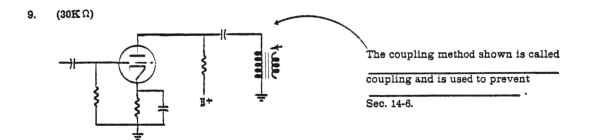

The coupling method shown is called _____ coupling and is used to prevent _____ . Sec. 14-6.

13.   (five) If in Figure 14-8 the biasing resistance is 1K ohm and the developed bias is 20 volts, the total circuit current flow is _____ ma. Sec. 14-13.

17.   (first) To eliminate hum in an audio amplifier using direct cathodes a _____ filament transformer should be used for grid and plate voltage returns. Sec. 14-17.

21.   (motorboating, decoupling) Class A power amplifiers may use a single tube but Class B power amplifiers must use two tubes in _____ _____ . Sec. 14-22.

25.   (demagnetized) Earphones in Fig. 14-26b are coupled to the tube by means of a _____ Sec. 14-30.

29.   (parallel)

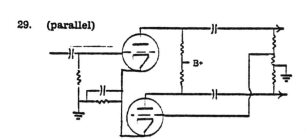

The circuit to the left is used to supply input signal to a _PUSH_ _PULL_ amplifier. Sec. 14-39.

33.   _(in phase)_ At any instant the phase of Z with respect to Y is _180° OUT OF PHASE_ .

153

13. The maximum allowable frequency for a 5 mhz signal having a .002% tolerance is
   a. 5,000,100.1 hertz.
   b. 5,000,200.1 hertz.   d. 5,000,100.0 hertz.
   c. 5,005,000.1 hertz.   e. none of these.

14. The frequency of a transmitter should be checked if
   a. an AF tube is changed.
   b. an RF buffer tube is changed.   d. an oscillator tube is changed.
   c. a final RF tube is changed.   e. the antenna is changed.

15. The carrier frequency of a station is the
   a. oscillator frequency.
   b. buffer frequency.   d. output frequency unmodulated.
   c. output frequency modulated.   e. none of these.

16. A 5 Mhz oscillator has a frequency tolerance of .002%. If this oscillator frequency is measured with a meter that has a tolerance of .002%, the maximum reading that would be safely within tolerance would be
   a. 5,001,000.1 Hz.
   b. 5,000,100.1 Hz.   d. 5,000,000.0 Hz.
   c. 5,101,000.0 Hz.   e. 5,005,000.0 Hz.

17. A transmitter having an output frequency of 16 Mhz and an oscillator frequency of one eighth the output is being used. If the maximum allowable deviation of frequency is .02%, the crystal may vary
   a. 16 MHz.
   b. 8 MHz.   d. 20 KHz.
   c. 2 Hz.   e. none of these.

18. An absorption wave meter could be used to
   a. make a pecision frequency measurement.
   b. neutralize an RF amplifier.   d. tune an IF amplifier.
   c. rubberize a crystal.   e. none of these.

19. If a transmitter has an assigned frequency of 25 MHz, but is actually on 25.0025 MHz unmodulated and 24.495 MHz modulated, it is operating
   a. legally if the tolerance is .001%.
   b. illegally if the tolerance is .001%.   d. a and b above.
   c. illegally if the tolerance is .002%.   e. b and c above.

20. A heterodyne frequency meter having a straight line relationship between frequency and dial reading is used to measure the frequency of a station by measuring the second harmonic. If 1,600 Khz appears on the dial at 2,403 and 1,610 Khz appears on the dial at 2,408, the fundamental frequency of a signal on 2,405 would be
   a. 1,602 Khz.
   b. 801 Khz.   d. 805 Khz.
   c. 1,605 Khz.   e. none of these.

21. If you make a change in a transmitter that might possibly change the frequency, you should
   a. notify the F.C.C. in Washington, D.C.
   b. notify the District F.C.C. Engineer.
   c. measure the frequency.
   d. notify WWV.
   e. all the above.

22. When using a secondary frequency standard, it is important to
   a. let the equipment warm up before using.
   b. disregard WWV calibration.
   c. check findings with F.C.C.
   d. check every half hour for at least 8 hours.
   e. all of the above.

23. The operating frequency of all radio stations is determined by comparison with the signals of station
   a. WWW of the FCC.
   b. WWV of the National Bureau of Standards.
   c. KWK of the National Frequency Control Authority.
   d. WKW of Washington, D.C.
   e. NBS.

24. The reading on the vernier below is
   a. 31.90.
   b. 32.04.
   c. 31.84.
   d. 31.94.
   e. none of these.

2. (power)

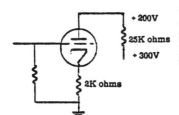

+ 200V

25K ohms

+ 300V

2K ohms

There is no distortion with this amplifier with proper input when the grid voltage is between 0 and minus 20 volts. The maximum RMS input for distortionless amplification would be _____ volts. Sec. 14-2.

6. (20) There are _____ methods of audio coupling. Sec. 14-5.

10. (inductive or transformer, core saturation)

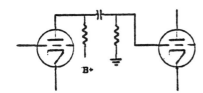

B+

The coupling method shown is called, _____ . Sec.14-7.

14. (20 ma) If in Figure 14-9, RK is 200 Ω and the plate current is 25 ma, the grid bias would be _____ volts. Sec. 14-14.

18. (center tapped) The generally used method of varying the signal to the grid of an amplifier is to use a voltage divider in the grid circuit. This takes the form of a _____ . Sec. 14-17.

22. (push pull)

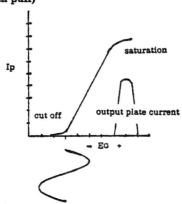

Ip

saturation

cut off

output plate current

- EG +

The EG Ip curve shown illustrates class_____ operation. Sec. 14-29.

26. (transformer) The secondary impedance of a transformer is 20KΩ and the primary is working out of an impedance of 20 ohms. There would be a maximum transfer of energy if the transformer had a turns ratio of _____ to 1. Sec. 14-33.

30. (push pull) Grounding the _____ of the filament transformer is usually effective in decreasing hum. Sec. 14-39.

34. (180° out of phase) It should be remembered that by passing the cathode resistor with a capacitor will provide a low loss path across the resistor and increase the output at the plate (Point Z in #32). This would make the circuit regenerative and no signal output would be available at the cathode (Point Y in #32). By passing the cathode biasing resistor makes a circuit _____ .

1. The best approved method of measuring frequency is by use of
   a. a grid dip meter.
   b. a watt meter.
   c. a calibrated frequency meter.
   d. pedometer.
   e. a thermocouple meter.

2. If the frequency of a carrier must be held to within .002 percent, then the meter used to measure the frequency must be accurate to within
   a. .0005%.
   b. .002%.
   c. .00075%.
   d. .001%.
   e. .005%.

3. The reading on the vernier below is
   a. 40.8.
   b. 30.8.
   c. 30.2.
   d. 34.5.
   e. none of these.

4. In the diagram shown, the transmission line energy would cause the shorting bar lights to glow
   a. at 1/8 wavelength.
   b. at 1/4 wavelength.
   c. at 3/8 wavelength.
   d. at every even 1/4 wavelength.
   e. none of these.

5. A frequency standard that is not a secondary standard is
   a. a temperature controlled crystal oscillator.
   b. a calibrated frequency meter.
   c. a calibrated receiver.
   d. the National Bureau of Standard WWV.
   e. none of these.

6. In calibrating a secondary crystal oscillator standard with WWV it is not necessary to
   a. allow the crystal oscillator to warm up.
   b. tune WWV on a short wave receiver.
   c. turn on the internal BFO oscillator in the receiver.
   d. beat a 100 kc crystal oscillator harmonic against WWV.
   e. adjust a trimmer across the crystal for zero beat.

7. At 1.000 Khz a broadcast station is allowed a frequency tolerance of
   a. .002% of the carrier frequency.
   b. .002% of the upper sideband frequency.
   c. .002% of the lower sideband frequency.
   d. plus or minus 20 Khz.
   e. none of these.

8. In the diagram below the arrow is pointing to
   a. 31 MHz.
   b. 31.95 MHz.
   c. 39.5 MHz.
   d. 32.5 MHz.
   e. 33 MHz.

9. The reading on the vernier below is
   a. 30.2.
   b. 34.2.
   c. 40.5.
   d. 43.
   e. none of these.

10. A frequency meter with an internal calibrating oscillator which was calibrated properly is used to check a receiver frequency of 21.14 Mhz. It would not be necessary to
    a. tune the dial to approximately 21 Mhz.
    b. turn the receiver on.
    c. let the frequency meter warm up.
    d. let the receiver warm up.
    e. calibrate the crystal with WWV.

11. A transmitter licensed to operate on 1210 khz could be operating illegally although the frequency was measured with accurate equipment because the transmitter was being modulated because sidebands fall outside of
    a. .002%.
    b. .01%.
    c. .05%.
    d. 1%.
    e. 2%.

12. A 5 mhz signal is measured accurately as being off frequency 5000 hertz. The percent error in frequency is
    a. .01%.
    b. .001%.
    c. .02%.
    d. .002%.
    e. none of these.

3. (5.66V) With a bias value of 12 volts, (see #2), an_____VRMS can be accommodated before grid current is drawn, assuming no distortion when the grid voltage is from 0 to 24 volts.

7. (4) Transformer coupling is also called _____ coupling. Sec. 14-6.

11. (resistance of capacitive or RC) The circuit of Fig. 14-7 can be used to amplify frequencies down to _____ without distortion. Sec. 14-9.

15. (5 volts) For a 500 Ω cathode resistance opeation on frequencies down to 50 hz, the cathode by pass capacitor should have a value of_____ Mfd. Sec. 14-14.

19. (Potentiometer) The grid shunt capacitance circuit shown is used for _____control. Sec. 14-18.

23. (B) Since plate current flows for 1/2 of the input cycle the output is distorted if a single tube is used. The full output wave form can be obtained by using a _____ Class B audio amplifier. Sec. 14-29.

27. (31.6) In order to match a 4,000 ohm load into a 10 ohm speaker, it would be necessary to use a transformer having a turns ratio of_____ to 1. Sec. 14-33.

31. (center tap) The plate supply voltage is the voltage reading when a voltmeter is placed across the _____. The plate voltage is the voltage when a voltmeter is placed between _____and_____. Sec. 14-41.

35. (regenerative) When cathode resistor biasing is used in an audio frequency amplifier the negative voltage developed is connected to the grid through a grid resistor (usually 500 KΩ). If this resistor is open the grid is said to be floating.

The amplifier shown is not biased because the grid resistor is _____.

155

2. **(external)** If the frequency of a carrier must be held to within .002%, then the meter used to measure the frequency must be accurate to within_____%. Sec. 21-2.

4. **(.002%)** A transmitter licensed to operate on 1000 Khz could be operating illegally if the sidebands fall outside of a 10 Khz bandwidth. The top of the upper sideband should be within .002% of _____ Khz. Sec. 21-1.

6. **(.1%)** The maximum allowable frequency for a 2 Mhz signal having a tolerance of .002% is_____ hz. Sec. 21-2.

8. **(5,000,000 hz)** A transmitter having an output frequency of 16 Mhz and an oscillator frequency of one eighth the output is being used. If the maximum allowable deviation of frequency is .02%, the crystal may vary_____hertz. Sec. 21-2.

10. **(31.95)**

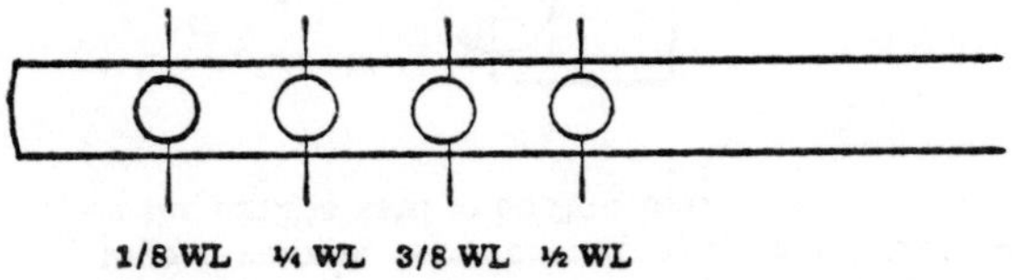

1/8 WL   ¼ WL   3/8 WL   ½ WL

In the diagram shown, the transmission line energy would cause the shorting bar lights to glow at every even _____ wave length (or every half wave length).   Sec. 21-4.

12. **(poor)** The primary standard of frequency measurement is _____. Sec. 21-6.

14. **(B.F.O.)** This is true since both WWV and the oscillator beat together as inputs to the receiver. (B.F.Os are only used to detect unmodulated signals). A frequency standard that is not a secondary standard is_____. Sec. 21-7.

16. **(Frequency meter)**

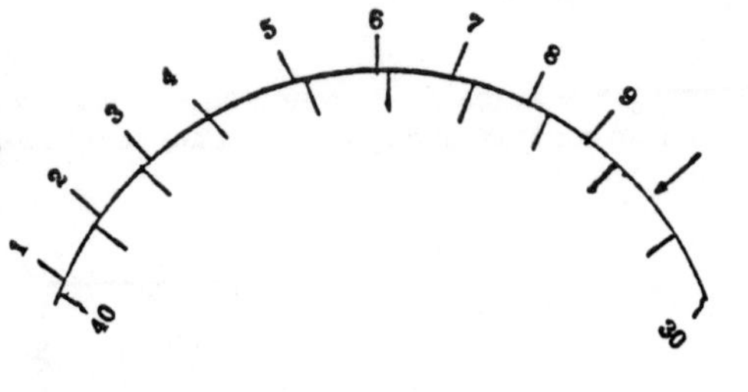

The dial reading on the vernier would be _____ Sec. 21-9

18. **(zero)** The frequency of a transmitter should be checked if any change is made in the oscillator stage. If the oscillator tube is changed the transmitter_____should be checked.

20. **(47.6)** This concludes Unit 21 recheck.

4.   (8.48V) The stage gain is always less than_____.   Sec. 14-4.

8.   (inductive) The plate impedance of a certain amplifier is 15K   . For maximum undistorted power output the load impedance should be_____ohms. Sec. 14-6.

12. (below 1 hz or DC) There are _____ methods of biasing audio frequency   amplifiers. Sec. 14-10.

16. (20 Mfd) Contact potential is only used in the_____stage of audio amplifiers. Sec. 14-5.

20. (tone) The low frequency audio oscillations are called _____and can be often eliminated by _____ the plate load circuit. Sec. 14-28.

24. (push pull) Care must be taken to connect earphones connected directly in the output circuit of an amplifier (Fig. 14-26a) correctly so that current flows the right direction through the earphones. Otherwise the permanent magnets become _____ . Sec. 14-30.

28. (20)

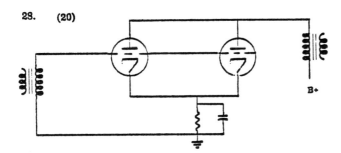

The circuit shown is a _____ circuit. Sec. 14-34.

32. (power supply, cathode, plate) Before we leave the chapter of A.F. amplifiers a word should be said about the phase of the output of the three types of amplifiers. The output of a common cathode or common emitter amplifier is 180° out of phase with the input.
The output of all other types of amplifiers including common grid, common base, common plate, and common collector are in phase with the input signal.
If an input is put in at the grid of an amplifier and an output is taken at the cathode there is no voltage amplification and no phase reversal. If an output is taken at the plate, there will be 180° phase reversal and voltage amplification.

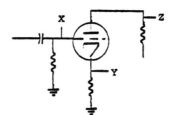

At any instant the phase of Y with respect to X is_____.

36. (open) This concludes the recheck instruction for Unit 14.

UNIT 21 MEASURING FREQUENCY

RECHECK PROGRAMMED INSTRUCTION USING SHRADER'S ELECTRONIC COMMUNICATION.

1. To make sure the transmitter is on frequency some _____ measuring device must be used periodically. Sec. 21-1.

3. (.001%) At 1000 Khz a standard broadcast station is allowed a frequency tolerance of 20 hz or _____ % of the carrier frequency. Sec. 21-2.

5. (1005 Khz) A 5 Mhz signal is measured as being off frequency 5000 hertz. The % error is _____. Sec. 21-2.

7. (2,000,040 hz) A 5 Mhz oscillator has a frequency tolerance of .002%. If this oscillator frequency is measured with a meter that has a tolerance of .002%, the maximum reading that would be safely within tolerance would be _____ hz. Sec. 21-2.

9. (400 hertz) In the diagram shown the arrow is pointing to _____ . Sec. 21-3.

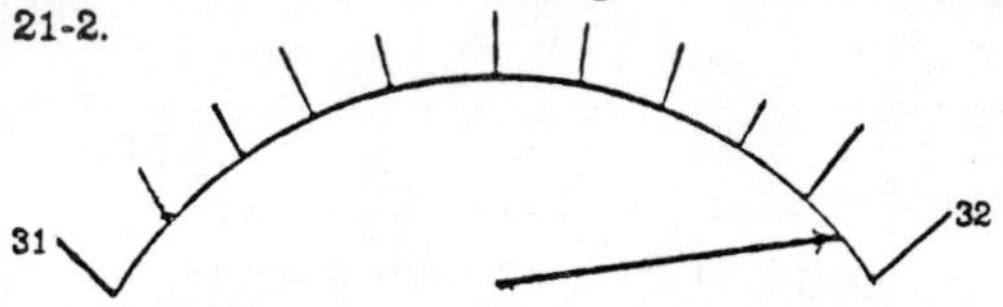

11. (quarter) A grid dip meter has _____ accuracy in frequency measurements. Sec. 21-5.

13. (WWV or the National Bureau of Standards) In calibrating a secondary crystal oscillator with WWV, it is not necessary to use a receiver with an internal _____ . Sec. 21-7.

15. (WWV or National Bureau of Standards) The best frequency measurement can be made by using a calibrated _____ . Sec. 21-9.

17. (31.4) The internal calibrating crystal should be calibrated by adjusting one of its harmonics to _____ beat with WWV. Sec. 21-9.

19. (frequency) The dial reading on the vernier and the calibrated scale shown would be _____ .

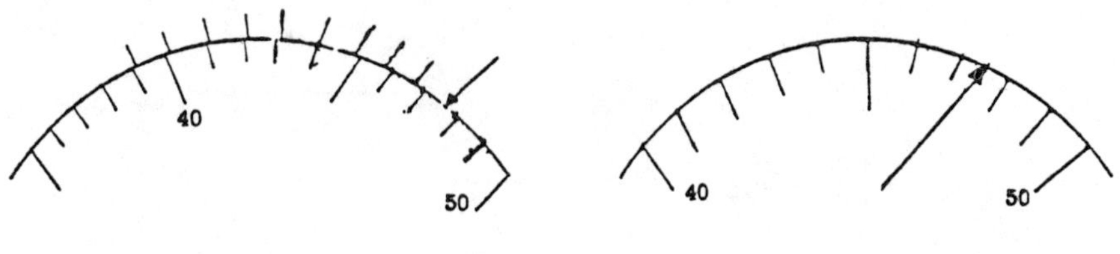

UNIT 14   AUDIO FREQUENCY AMPLIFIERS

1. Motor boating in an audio amplifier may be caused by
   a. unbalanced resistors in the filament circuits.
   b. a grounded filament circuit.
   c. an open decoupling capacitor.
   d. a shorted decoupling capacitor.
   e. none of these.

2. Amplifiers that are
   a. RF class B must be push pull.
   b. AF class B must use 2 tubes in PP.
   c. final RF amplifiers must be class A.
   d. RF linear amplifiers must be class A.
   e. RF class C take low bias.

3. The proper method for coupling high impedance earphones to a low impedance output would be by use of a
   a. series coil.
   b. series capacitor.
   c. series resistor.
   d. transformer.
   e. rectifier.

4. A vacuum tube amplifier having a stage gain of 50 has a
   a. Mu of less than 50.
   b. Mu greater than 50.
   c. current gain of 50.
   d. voltage gain of 50.
   e. voltage and current gain of 50.

5. At any instant the phase of y with respect to x is
   a. 180 degrees out of phase.
   b. 90 degrees out of phase.
   c. 270 degrees out of phase.
   d. 45 degrees out of phase.
   e. in phase.

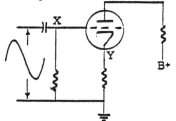

6. If Ck was shorted in the amplifier below
   a. the amplifier would oscillate.
   b. the grid bias would be raised.
   c. there would be degeneration.
   d. the plate current would increase.
   e. the plate current would decrease.

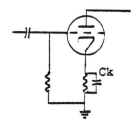

7. If Ck became open in the amplifier of question #6
   a. the amplifier would begin to howl and start to oscillate.
   b. there would be no grid bias.
   c. there would be degeneration.
   d. there would be regeneration.
   e. none of these.

8. The plate output power of a stage can be increased by
   a. using higher plate voltage.
   b. using higher grid bias.
   c. using higher plate load values.
   d. a and c above.
   e. none of these.

9. The circuit shown below is
   a. a multivibrator.
   b. a driver for a class C RF amp.
   c. the input circuit for a PP power amp.
   d. the input circuit for a crystal mike.
   e. none of these.

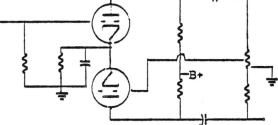

10. The plate current in the circuit below would be
    a. 5 ma.
    b. 5.5 ma.
    c. 100 ma.
    d. 20 ma.
    e. zero.

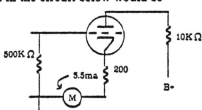

4.   (.01%)   When solving for a maximum allowable frequency when there is a known tolerance, we must convert the % tolerance to the decimal equivalent before multiplying. For example, the maximum allowable frequency for a 3 Mhz signal having a tolerance of .002% is 3 Mhz + (.00002 X 3 Mhz) = 3.00006 or 3,000,060 hz. The maximum allowable frequency for a 2 Mhz signal having a tolerance of .002% is _____ hz.

Primary and Secondary Frequency Standards

8.   (400 hertz)   The primary standard of frequency in this country is given by continuous radio broadcast by WWV and WWVH. These stations are operated by the National Bureau of Standards, from near Ft. Collins, Colorado and Hawaii. They are simultaneous broadcasts on 5, 10, and 15 Mhz. WWV (near Ft. Collins) also broadcasts on 2.5 and 25 Mhz. Both a standard of time and frequency is given.

The primary standard of frequency is that of the _____ _____ _____ _____ using WWV or WWVH.

12.   (even)   The transmitter frequency should be measured every time there are any changes in the _____ circuit.

11. The secondary impedance of a transformer is 20 K ohms and the primary is working out of an impedance of 20 ohms. There would be a maximum transfer of energy if the transformer had a turns ratio of
   a. 10 to 1.
   b. 1.000 to 1.   d. 31.6 to 1.
   c. 3.73 to 1.   e. none of these.

12. A certain amplifier has a tube with an mu of 100, an R1 of 15K ohms and an Rp of .045 megohms. The plate current is 20 ma. The gain of the stage would be
   a. 100
   b. 66 2/3   d. 25.
   c. 50.   e. 27.

13. The plate impedance of a certain tube amplifier is 10 K ohms. For maximum power output the load resistance should be
   a. 10 K ohms.
   b. 20 K ohms.   d. 40 K ohms.
   c. 30 K ohms.   e. infinity.

14. In the circuit shown, the highest input RMS voltage that could be used without distortion is
   a. 3 volts.
   b. 6.3 volts.
   c. 8 volts.
   d. 10 volts.
   e. 12 volts.

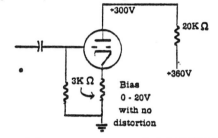

15. The circuit below would not work because
   a. the bias is low.
   b. the bias is high.
   c. there is no bias.
   d. it is not neutralized.
   e. of the resistance in the cathode circuit.

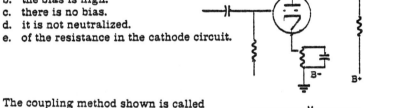

16. The coupling method shown is called
   a. RC coupling.
   b. impedance coupling.
   c. transformer coupling.
   d. double impedance coupling.
   e. inductive coupling.

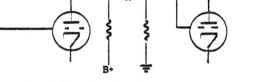

17. The voltage amplification of a stage is 16. The plate load resistance is 10 K ohms and the plate impedance is 10KΩ. The mu of the tube is
   a. 16.
   b. 20.   d. 24.
   c. 22.   e. none of these.

18. The voltage amplification of a typical cathode follower is
   a. 20.
   b. 10.   d. 2.
   c. 5..   e. less than unity.

19. In order to match a 4,000 ohms load into a 10 ohms speaker it would be necessary to use a transformer having a turns ratio of
   a. 1 to 1.
   b. 10 to 1.   d. 20 to 1.
   c. 15 to 1.   e. none of these.

20. Motor boating in an audio amplifier might be caused by
   a. grid and plate connections of stages being too close to each other.
   b. degeneration.
   c. an open cathode by-pass capacitor.
   d. inverse feedback.
   e. none of these.

3.   (.002%) Percent error is figured the same way as % frequency tolerance. Suppose a station is assigned a frequency of 6 Mhz and it is operating on 6.006 Mhz (or 6000 hertz off)

The % error = $\dfrac{\text{Numerical error}}{\text{Correct frequency}}$ X 100

Both the numerical error and the correct frequency must be in the same units (hertz or Khz or Mhz)

% error = $\dfrac{6000 \text{ hz}}{6,000,000 \text{ hz}}$ X 100 = $\dfrac{600,000}{6,000,000}$ = .1%

A 5 Mhz signal is measured as being off frequency by 500 hertz. The error is_____%.

7.   (5 Mhz) When a transmitter using multipliers is used, the same frequency tolerance applies to the oscillator as to the output carrier frequency.

A transmitter having an output frequency of 12 Mhz and an oscillator frequency of one twelfth the output, has a maximum allowable deviation of .02%. The oscillator may vary .0002 X 1 Mhz or 200 hertz.

A transmitter having an output frequency of 16 Mhz and an oscillator frequency of one eighth the output has a frequency tolerance of .02%. The crystal oscillator may vary_____ hertz.

11.   (frequency meter) The shorting bar lamps glow in a Lecher line at every_____ quarter wave length.

15.   (28.8) If this reading is 28.8 Mhz and is second harmonic energy, then the fundamental frequency would be 14.4 Mhz. This concludes unit 21.

21. The right polarity on earphones should be observed when using them as a series plate load in a vacuum tube in order to
    a. prevent demagnetization of the earphones.
    b. prevent radiation of harmonics.
    c. prevent parasitics.
    d. prevent self oscillation.
    e. none of these.

22. If the voice coil of a PM speaker was inserted from the plate of a VT to the plus side of the power supply
    a. high fidelity would result.
    b. all even harmonics would be cancelled.
    c. all odd harmonics would be cancelled.
    d. the speaker voice coil would burn out.
    e. none of these.

23. In the diagram below the total current flow is
    a. 10 ma.
    b. 20 ma.
    c. 30 ma.
    d. 40 ma.
    e. none of these.

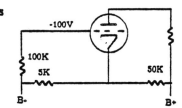

24. R1 would have a value of
    a. 5 K ohms.
    b. 10 K ohms.
    c. 30 K ohms.
    d. 300 K ohms.
    e. 50 K ohms.

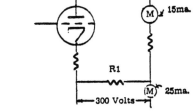

25. The circuit below is used for
    a. tone control.
    b. grid leak biasing.
    c. a paraphase amplifier.
    d. squelch control.
    e. volume control.

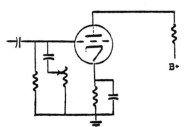

26. An open cathode by-pass capacitor would cause
    a. regeneration.
    b. decreased gain.
    c. motor boating.
    d. decreased degeneration.
    e. direct coupling.

27. In a resistance coupled AF amplifier the coupling capacitor should have a value so as to
    a. provide high impedance at low frequencies.
    b. provide low impedance at lowest frequency used.
    c. have high impedance at all frequencies.
    d. provide motor boating.
    e. have no reactance.

28. There is no distortion with this amplifier with proper input when the grid voltage is between O and minus 20 volts. The maximum rms input for distortionless amplification would be
    a. 1 volt.
    b. 2.3 volts.
    c. 3.5 volts.
    d. 5 volts.
    e. 6.3 volts.

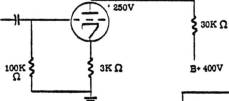

29. This circuit would be used for
    a. feeding a PP circuit.
    b. phase modulation.
    c. amplitude modulation.
    d. amplifying signals above 10 khz.
    e. amplifying signals below 1 hz.

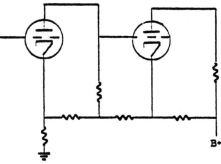

2. **(20, .002%)** The AM station is allowed upper and lower sidebands of 5 Khz. This means a station assigned to 1000 Khz can modulate their carrier with audio frequencies up to 5 Khz to produce sidebands extending to 1005 Khz (USB) and 995 Khz (LSB). The highest and lowest sidebands must be within 20 hertz (or .002%) of these frequencies. The total channel bandwidth of an AM broadcast station is 10 Khz.

The highest and lowest sidebands should not extend higher or lower than _____% of 1005 Khz and 995 Khz for a station operating on 1000 Khz.

6. **(.001%)** If a frequency meter had the same accuracy as the frequency tolerance, you could be sure that a signal was within tolerance only if it was set by meter on the exact assigned frequency. This would be true since there is the possibility that the frequency meter would be off in the same plus or minus direction as the signal.

A 5 Mhz oscillator has a frequency tolerance of .002%. If this oscillator frequency is measured with a meter that has a tolerance of .002%, the maximum reading that would be safely within tolerance would be _____ Mhz.

Frequency Measuring Devices

10. **(Beat Frequency Oscillator)** The frequency of a transmitter should be measured when: It's first installed, there is a change in any of the oscillator stage components, and at least once a year.

The common frequency measuring devices include:

(1) An absorption wave meter. This device can be used for a rough frequency measurement or for an R.F. indicator for neutralizing.

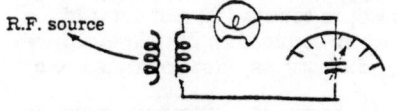

R.F. source

Calibrated tuning capacitor dial

When this tuned circuit is tuned to resonance with the R.F. source, the R. F. indicator (a lamp bulb here) indicates maximum R.F. When the bulb lights a reading is taken from the calibrated dial.

(2) Grid Dip oscillator. When an oscillator with a milliameter in the grid is tuned to the same frequency as the coupled dead LC tank circuit, energy is absorbed from the oscillator grid circuit. The grid current dips and the frequency is read from a calibrated dial.
Most grid dip oscillators incorporate an absorption wave meter. Measurements made with an absorption wave meter or a grid dip oscillator are not very accurate.

(3) A calibrated receiver. If a receiver is calibrated by using a secondary frequency standard, fair accuracy in frequency measurement can be made.

(4) A heterodyne frequency meter. A calibrated frequency meter is actually a receiver containing a calibrated oscillator. The output of the calibrated oscillator is beat with the incoming signal to be measured. When zero beat is achieved, a reading is taken from a vernier dial. This is one of the most accurate frequency measuring devices available.

(5) Lecher transmission lines. This measuring device is used at the high frequency of 100 Mhz and up. It is a method of measuring a frequency with a meter stick.

R.F. source   high current loops form every even quarter wave length (every 1/2 W.L.)

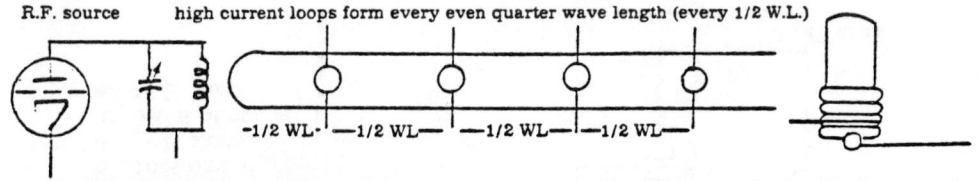

—1/2 WL— —1/2 WL— —1/2 WL— —1/2 WL—

If a pilot bulb shorting bar is placed across these points, it will light. The measured distance between the 1/2 WL points where the bulb lights is one half wave length. The full wave length is twice this distance. The frequency can be figured by dividing the velocity of a radio wave by the wave length.

One of the most accurate frequency measuring devices is the calibrated _____ .

14. **(5.66 Mhz)** In measuring frequency with a frequency meter an indirect reading on a vernier scale must be made. This reading is looked up in a book and interpreted as a specific frequency.

The vernier dial is illustrated below:

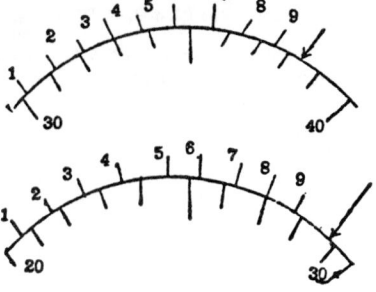

The index points to 38 and a decimal part more. The decimal part is indicated where a vernier scale mark is directly above a dial scale mark.

The reading on this vernier is 38.4.

The vernier dial reading shown is _____ •

30. A speaker output transformer designed to match 4000 ohms to 4 ohms should have a turns ratio of
   a. 4000 to 4.
   b. 16.000 to 16.   d. 2 to 1.
   c. 31.6 to 1.   e. none of these.

31. If the amplifier is designed to operate at 50 Hz, the value of C² should be approximately
   a. 2 MFD.
   b. .25 MFD
   c. 20 MFD.
   d. 5 MFD.
   e. none of these.

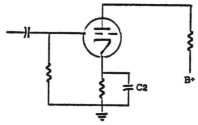

32. An amplifier having an output of 6 volts with an input of .006 volts has a gain of
   a. 60 db.
   b. 6 db.   d. 30 db.
   c. .6 db.   e. none of these.

33. To eliminate hum in an amplifier use a
   a. center tap filament connection to ground.
   b. decoupling.   d. plate neutralization.
   c. grid neutralization.   e. a phase splitter.

34. The value of grid bias developed on a tube having a plate current of 40 ma, a cathode current of 50 ma, and a cathode resistor of 500 ohms is
   a. 25 volts.
   b. 50 volts.   d. 80 volts.
   c. 19 volts.   e. none of these.

35. The class operation show is
   a. A.
   b. B.
   c. C.
   d. D.
   e. none of these.

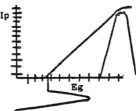

36. The usual amplifier circuit provides
   a. positive feedback.
   b. negative feedback.   d. oscillation.
   c no feedback.   e. none of these.

37. The load should be matched to the output of an amplifier because this results in
   a. minimum current flow.
   b. maximum voltage output.   d. minimum harmonics.
   c. the maximum transfer of power.   e. audio degeneration.

38. In the audio amplifier shown, plate current would decrease if
   a. R₃ is shorted out.
   b. C₂ is shorted out.
   c. R₂ increases.
   d. R₁ is open.
   e. C₁ is open.

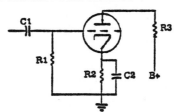

39. Impedance matching is primarily necessary for
   a. miniaturization of equipment.
   b. economy of design.
   c. reduction of harmonic transfer.
   d. maximum transfer of power.
   e. minimum voltage transfer.

UNIT 21 MEASURING FREQUENCY

Frequency Tolerance

1. For minimum interference problems, it has been necessary for the F.C.C. to set frequency tolerances for the various services. These are expressed in either hertz or in terms of percentage of assigned frequency. For instance, the standard AM broadcast station is allowed a frequency tolerance of plus or minus 20 hertz. At the mid frequency of 1000 Khz this is a frequency tolerance of .002% as shown:

$$\% \text{ Frequency tolerance} = \frac{\text{Numerical tolerance}}{\text{Assigned frequency}} \times 100$$

$$= \frac{20 \text{ hz}}{1,000,000 \text{ hz}} \times 100 = .002\%$$

The standard AM broadcast station must stay within _____ hertz of their assigned frequency. This is _____ % at the mid band frequency of 1,000 Khz.

5. (2,000,040 hz) In order to insure greater accuracy in measurement, frequency measuring devices must have an accuracy of no more than one half the frequency tolerance. If the frequency tolerance of the service is .004%., the measuring device should be .002% accurate. If the frequency of a carrier must be held to within .002%, the frequency meter must be accurate to within _____%.

9. **(National Bureau of Standards)** A frequency measuring device that is N.B.S. related is called a secondary frequency standard.
    A secondary frequency standard consists of:

    1) A multivibrator oscillator that generates many harmonics.
    2) A crystal oscillator to synchronize the fundamental frequency of the multivibrator. This crystal oscillator is rubberized by placing a trimmer capacitor across it's crystal. If this capacitor is tuned so that one of the harmonics of the synchronized multivibrator is zero beat with a WWV signal, the secondary standard is WWV related.

    The basic arrangement for calibrating a secondary frequency standard is shown below:

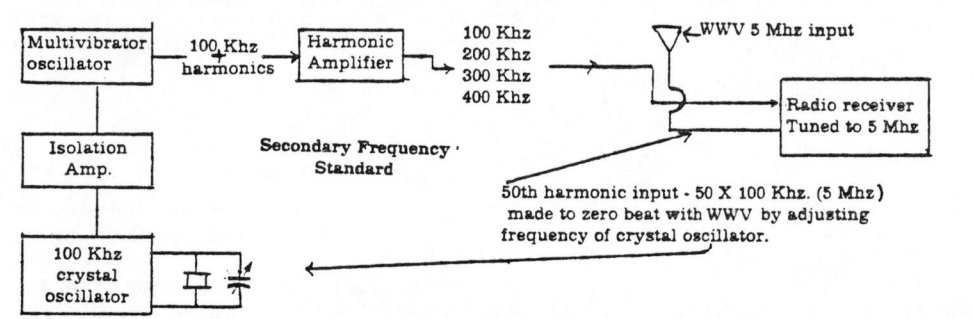

Since there are two signal inputs to the calibrated receiver, they beat together. When the 100 Khz crystal oscillator frequency synchronizes the multivibrator so that it's 50th harmonic is exactly on 5 Mhz, there is a zero beat with WWV and the secondary standard is calibrated so that all harmonics are WWV related. It is important that no internal receiver beat frequency oscillator (BFO) be used in this calibration. When calibrated the secondary frequency standard can be used to accurately calibrate receivers or other frequency measuring devices.

In calibrating a secondary frequency standard, it is not necessary to use a receiver with an internal _____ _____ _____ .

Dial Readings

13. (oscillator) Many frequency measuring devices have direct or indirect dial calibrations. Usually the frequency of a radio receiver can be read directly from a dial. An example is shown:

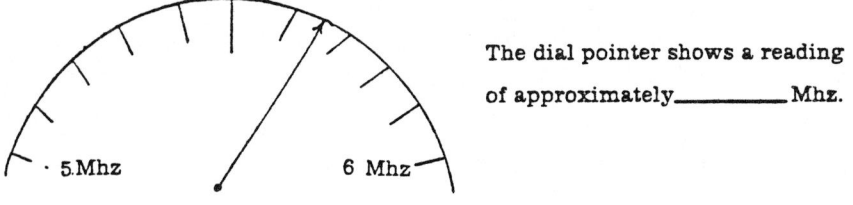

The dial pointer shows a reading

of approximately _____ Mhz.

40. Removing the cathode by-pass capacitor in an audio stage will
   a. increase distortion.
   b. decrease distortion.
   c. increase gain.
   d. none of the above.
   e. cause regeneration.

41. When a push pull circuit is used for an audio frequency amplifier
   a. there is no grid bias.
   b. even harmonics are cancelled.
   c. odd harmonics are cancelled.
   d. all harmonics are cancelled.
   e. oscillation is prevented.

42. One type of AF amplifier is characterized by
   a. no bias.
   b. no gain.
   c. no amplification.
   d. direct coupling.
   e. none of these.

43. In the circuit shown below
   a. there is no bias.
   b. there is no gain.
   c. there is no amplification.
   d. a DC amplifier is shown.
   e. the C - voltage is wrongly applied.

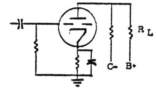

44. When you plug in earphones to a receiver all signals may be weak because of
   a. overloading.
   b. earphone magnets saturated.
   c. impedance mismatch.
   d. weak input signals.
   e. b and c above.

45. The primary and secondary windings of a transformer are often broadly coupled (over coupled) in order to obtain
   a. greater selectivity.
   b. wider band pass.
   c. narrow band pass.
   d. high Q circuits.
   e. degeneration.

29. This circuit is used to

a. eliminate parasitics.
b. reduce harmonics.
c. match impedance.
d. pass harmonics.
e. none of these.

From P.A.

To antenna

30. The impedance of a transmission line should
   a. match the output impedance of the transmitter.
   b. be 72 ohms.
   c. 300 ohms.
   d. 500 ohms.
   e. none of these.

31. At a Marconi antenna the
   a. DC resistance betweenthe antenna and ground is near zero.
   b. RF resistance between the antenna and ground is near zero.
   c. top end is grounded.
   d. the middle is grounded.
   e. none of these.

32. A vertically polarized wave is
   a. best received by a vertical antenna.
   b. best received by a horizontal antenna.
   c. best received by a loop.
   d. best received by an L shaped antenna.
   e. none of these.

33. A quarter wave transmission line is shorted at one end. The impedance at the other end is
   a. low.
   b. high.
   c. 720 ohms.
   d. 50 ohms.
   e. zero ohms.

34. The resonate frequency of an antenna can be lowered by
   a. placing inductance in series with the antenna.
   b. placing a capacitance in series with the antenna.
   c. shorten the length of the antenna.
   d. placing a resistance in series with the antenna.
   e. grounding the center of the antenna.

35. A good substitute in a coaxial cable for nitrogen gas is
   a. hydroflouric gas.
   b. liquid oxygen.
   c. carbon dioxide.
   d. dry air.
   e. nitrogen gas.

36. Standing waves are caused by
   a. high voltage.
   b. high percentage modulation.
   c. impedance mismatch.
   d. high current.
   e. nitrogen gas.

37. The antenna current would increase if
   a. the antenna coupling was increased.
   b. the final plate voltage was increased.
   c. the final plate current was decreased.
   d. the antenna anmeter was shunted.
   e. the antenna was shortened.

38. Cable shielding used as a transmission line should be grounded
   a. at both ends usually.
   b. at one end.
   c. through a resistor.
   d. through a choke.
   e. through a capacitor.

39. The final stage of a transmitter has a supply voltage of 600 volts. The final plate current is 300 ma. If the antenna resistance is 15 ohms and the antenna current is 3 amperes the stage efficiency would be
   a. 80%.
   b. 75%.
   c. 70%.
   d. 65%.
   e. 45%.

40. Stacking the elements on a directional antenna
   a. improve reception.
   b. makes reception poor.
   c. decreases received antenna current.
   d. is not advised.
   e. does not affect reception.

41. Radio interference from other services can be reduced by using
   a. shielded antennas.
   b. wave traps.
   c. heterodyne oscillators.
   d. underground antennas.
   e. all of the above.

42. If the antenna ammeter reads 1.4 amperes at a 52 ohm point, the power radiated is
   a. 72.8 watts.
   b. 101.92 watts.
   c. 37.1 watts.
   d. 43.4 watts.
   e. 26 watts.

UNIT 15 RADIO FREQUENCY AMPLIFIERS

1. Special care must be taken in the design and maintenance of radio frequency circuits. A few of the things to remember are:
    (1) Component leads and wires between components should be kept short. This reduces stray inductances and capacitances that might affect a circuit adversely.
    (2) All ground returns within an R.F. circuit (stage) should be made to one point. Otherwise induced voltages in conductors between grounds would affect proper operation.
    (3) To prevent unwanted coupling and self oscillation R.F. coils should be shielded.
        Component leads and wires between components should be kept_____.

15. (maximum, maximum, minimum, maximum) The plate current in an R.F. amplifier decreases as the tank circuit is tuned to resonance because the impedance of a parallel tuned circuit is ___HIGH.___ at resonance.

29. (link, harmonics) Pi network coupling is commonly used to couple the high impedance energy from an RF amplifier to the low impedance of an antenna.

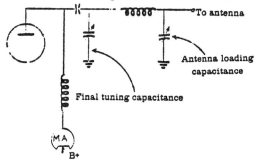

The pi net is a low pass filter that serves the following functions:
(1) It reduces harmonic transfer since it is a low pass filter.
(2) It matches the high plate impedance of the tube to the low impedance of the antenna.

The Pi net is a_____pass filter.

43. (.6 meters, 60 centimeters) Proper drive to an R.F. amplifier is a necessity. If the tuned circuits preceding an R.F. amplifier are tuned out of resonance, this may cause heavy plate current to flow in the amplifier. In protected circuits this would cause a plate circuit breaker to blow preventing damage to the tube. Although tuning may be done by adjusting a variable capacitor, it is sometimes done by adjusting the position of a powdered iron core or slug. This method of tuning is called variable permeability tuning. In the circuit below individual variable inductance tuning is provided by using two slugs.

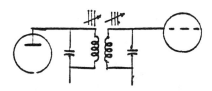

Off resonance tuning may cause heavy_____current to flow in the succeeding R.F. amplifier stage. If two slugs are used in tuning an R.F. transformer, the tuning is said to be _____ variable inductance tuning.

162

15. A shorted stub used to reduce second harmonic energy should be
    a. 1/4 the WL of the fundamental frequency.
    b. 1/8 the WL of the fundamental frequency. d. 1 WL long.
    c. 1/2 the WL of the fundamental frequency. e. none of these.

16. The wave form shown is typical of
    a. the current on a Hertz half wave antenna.
    b. the voltage on a Hertz half wave antenna.
    c. the current on a 1/4 wave Marconi antenna.
    d. the voltage on a 1/4 wave Marconi antenna.
    e. none of these.

17. One common cause of fading in a car radio receiver is
    a. absorption of the pavement.
    b. the RF shading of a hill.   d. poor connections.
    c. reflection by the pavement. e. none of these.

18. The wave form shown is
    a. the voltage on a half wave Hertz.
    b. the current on a half wave Hertz.
    c. a differentiated square wave.
    d. an integrated saw tooth wave.
    e. the output ripple of a full wave power supply.

19. A change in the physical length of an antenna will
    a. raise the resonant frequency.
    b. lower the resonant frequency.   d. overload the receiver.
    c. increase the antenna losses.   e. change the electrical characteristics.

20. When the power output of a certain transmitter is 500 watts the antenna current is 7.07 amperes. When the power is raised to 750 watts the antenna current would be
    a. 10.5 amperes.
    b. 7.07 amperes.   d. 5 amperes.
    c. 8.66 amperes.   e. none of these.

21. If an inductor is placed in series with an antenna the
    a. resonant frequency would increase.
    b. the resonant frequency would decrease.   d. the SWR would increase.
    c. the SWR would decrease.   e. parasitics would increase.

22. A loop antenna will receive
    a. in all directions when in the horizontal plane.
    b. in all directions when in the vertical plane.
    c. in a very directive manner to vertical plane when in the horizontal plane.
    d. in a very directive manner to horizontal plane when in the horizontal plane.
    e. none of these.

23. Guy wires should be used for a vertical antenna tower
    a. using copper wire.
    b. at a 45 degree angle.   d. with grounding and no insulators.
    c. with insulated segments.   e. as a ground plane.

24. The degree of antenna coupling to the final stage of a transmitter determines
    a. the final grid bias.
    b. the plate current to the final.   d. antenna directivity.
    c. the oscillator frequency.   e. none of these.

25. A 1/4 wave length antenna for a certain frequency is cut to resonate as a 1/4 wave length antenna on a higher frequency. At the higher frequency
    a. the skip distance is increased.
    b. the skip distance is decreased.   d. the ionosphere produces more bending.
    c. the radiation pattern is changed. e. the skip distance is the same.

26. A signal radiated by a horizontal antenna is best received by a
    a. vertical antenna.
    b. horizontal antenna.   d. loop stick antenna.
    c. loop antenna.   e. Marconi antenna.

27. If the antenna current decreases with amplitude modulation this may be
    a. caused by poor power supply regulation.
    b. negative carrier shift.   d. asymmetrical modulation.
    c. caused by low R.F. excitation of the final amplifier.   e. all the above.

28. When coupling a 52 ohm line to a 52 ohm point on an antenna the feed line should be
    a. 1/4 W.L.
    b. 1/2 W.L.   d. 1 W.L.
    c. 100 meters.   e. any length desired.

2.   (short) All ground returns within an R.F. stage should be made to _____.

16. (high) So far we have been dealing with multigrid R.F. amplifiers that are internally neutralized to prevent feedback from the output plate circuit to the input grid circuit. When a triode is used as a common cathode R. F. amplifier and the output is tuned to the same frequency as the input, the feedback from the plate to the grid must be neutralized or self oscillation may occur.

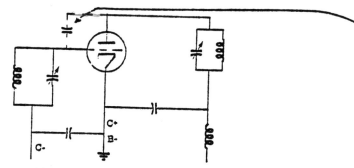

Interelectrode capacitance from plate to grid. Feedback through this capacitance will cause the amplifier to become an oscillator generating a new unwanted frequency.

Three types of neutralization of triodes will be discussed:
(1)   plate
(2)   grid
(3)   push pull

A triode R.F. amplifier using the common cathode circuit must be neutralized to prevent ___SELF. OSCILLATION.

FREQUENCY MULIPLIERS
30. (low) The simple frequency multiplier uses one tube. A frequency doubler is shown. The output is tuned to twice the frequency of the input.

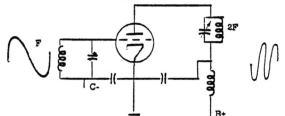

It requires no neutralization. It is biased class C and requires high excitation.

Each plate current pulse charges tuning capacitor. Flywheel action produces two output cycles for each input cycle.

A single ended class C R.F. triode amplifier without neutralization is useful as a frequency _____.

44. (plate, individual) This concludes Unit 15.

1. The standing wave ratio on an antenna or transmission line is the ratio of
    a. the maximum voltage to the maximum current.
    b. the maximum current to the maximum voltage.   d. the minimum current to the maximum current.
    c. the maximum voltage to the minimum voltage.   e. none of these.

2. A transmitting antenna radiates
    a. an electrostatic field.
    b. an electromagnetic field.   d. a permanent field.
    c. both an electrostatic and an electromagnetic field.   e. none of these.

3. A type of antenna that receives best from all directions in the horizontal plane is a
    a. horizontal dipole.
    b. horizontal beam.   d. vertical loop.
    c. vertical ground plane antenna.   e. loop stick.

4. When coupling a 72 ohm line to a 72 ohm point on an antenna the feed line should be
    a. 1/4 W.L.
    b. 1/2 W.L.   d. 1 W.L.
    c. 100 meters.   e. any length desired.

5. The antenna illustrated in the diagram below is a
    a. loop.
    b. quarter wave.
    c. eighth wave.
    d. half wave.
    e. full wave.

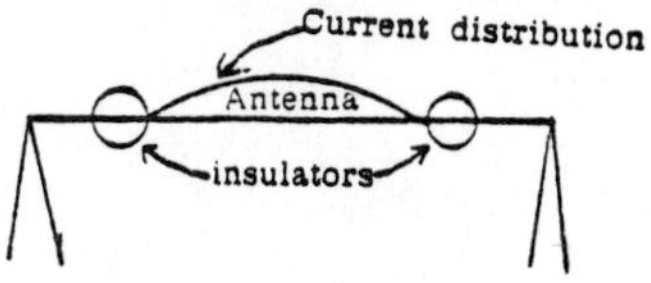

6. At 2 Mhz the antenna field strength is 120 mv per meter. At 4 Mhz it is 1200 microvolts per meter. The attenuation is
    a. 10 db.
    b. 20 db.   d. 40 db.
    c. 100 db.   e. none of these.

7. A shorted or open stub is sometimes inserted in the middle of a half wave antenna to act as
    a. a resistor.
    b. a capacitor.   d. an impedance matching device.
    c. an inductor.   e. a rectifier.

8. If a 1/4 wave or 3/4 wave transmission line is shorted on one end, the impedance to the frequency at the other end is like
    a. a short circuit.
    b. an open circuit.   d. 500 ohms.
    c. 600 ohms.   e. none of these.

9. A signal radiated by a vertical antenna is best received by
    a. vertical antenna.
    b. horizontal antenna.   d. loop stick antenna.
    c. loop antenna.   e. Hertz antenna.

10. Nitrogen is often used in concentric transmission lines to
    a. separate the two lines.
    b. radiate a signal.   d. keep moisture out of the lines.
    c. produce black light.   e. produce conductivity.

11. A parasitic antenna is used to
    a. change polarization.
    b. change the radiated frequency.   d. prevent parasitic oscillation.
    c. attenuate a signal.   e. give additional gain and directivity.

12. A loop antenna used to receive a standard broadcast signal works best if
    a. it is a horizontal loop.
    b. it is a vertical and the plane of the loop is perpendicular to the line of direction of the station.
    c. it is a horizontal loop and the plane of the loop is perpendicular to the signal.
    d. it is a vertical loop and the plane of the loop is parallel to the line of direction of the station.
    e. none of these.

13. Top loading an antenna has the effect of
    a. increasing the electrical wave length.
    b. decreasing the electrical wave length.   d. stabilizing the antenna in the wind.
    c. decreasing the power.   e. none of these.

14. A capacitor placed in series with a Marconi antenna will
    a. increase its resonant frequency.
    b. decrease its resonant frequency.   d. double the radiated power.
    c. change the radiated frequency.   e. effectively lengthen the antenna.

Class A R.F. Amplifiers

3.   (one point) Radio frequency amplifiers used in receivers are usually class A amplifiers using cathode resistor bias. The EgIp curve and a typical circuit are shown:

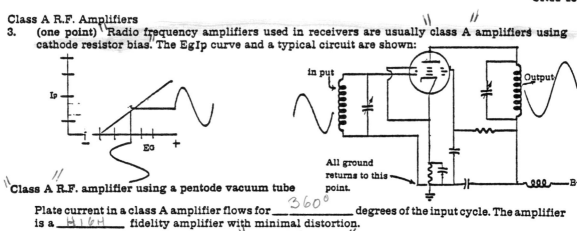

Class A R.F. amplifier using a pentode vacuum tube

All ground returns to this point.

Plate current in a class A amplifier flows for ___360°___ degrees of the input cycle. The amplifier is a ___HIGH___ fidelity amplifier with minimal distortion.

17.   (self oscillation) The general idea of plate neutralization is as shown:

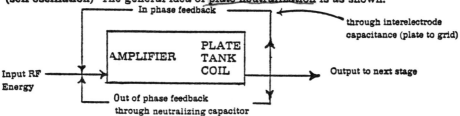

The planned out of phase feedback cancels the in phase feedback. The actual circuit is shown below:

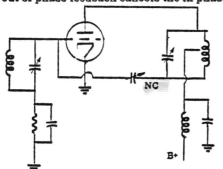

In phase feedback through plate to grid capacitance.

Out of phase feedback through the neutralizing capacitor.

B+ is connected to the coil center tap - otherwise plate bypass capacitor would ground out any RF at bottom of plate tank coil.

The value of the neutralizing capacitor must equal the interelectrode capacitance for complete neutralization.
In plate neutralization the neutralizing RF is fed from the ___bottom___ of the plate tank circuit coil and B+ must be applied at the coil ___CENTER TAP___.

31.   (doubler) The push push frequency doubler is a double tube R.F. circuit operating Class C.

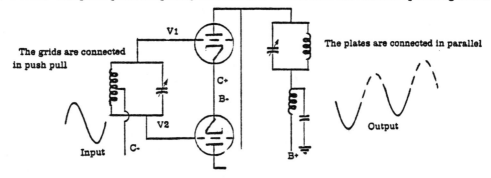

The grids are connected in push pull

The plates are connected in parallel

When V1 receives positive half cycle of input, a plate current pulse flows through tank circuit. Flywheel effect supplies other half of output cycle. When V2 receives positive pulse input (on other half of cycle of input) a plate current pulse flows through tank circuit. Flywheel effect supplies the other half of this cycle. The end result is two output cycles for one input cycle.

The frequency doubler can be identified by the fact that the grids are connected in _____ and the plates in _____.

3. **(increases)** Another major cause of fading for mobile communications is the R. F. shading of mountains and hills. One common cause of fading in a car radio receiver is _____ of a hill. Sec. 20-3.

6. **(voltage, half, current)** A capacitor placed in series with an antenna will _____ the antenna and _____ its resonant frequency. Sec. 20-11.

9. **(antenna, plate)** The standing wave ratio on an antenna is the ratio of maximum _____ or _____ to the minimum _____ or _____. Sec. 20-12.

12. **(any length, one)** An antenna that transmits or receives equally well in all directions is the _____ antenna. Sec. 20-13.

15. **(repeats, open)** If a 1/4 wave or any odd quarter transmission line has a high terminal impedance for a particular frequency, it will have a _____ impedance at the other end. Sec. 20-16.

18. **(one fourth)** Stacking the elements of a driven array produces greater _____ . Sec. 20-18.

21. **(vertical, parallel)** A horizontal loop is _____ _____ in the horizontal plane. Sec. 20-22.

24. **(insulated)** The degree of antenna coupling to the final stage of a transmitter determines the final _____ current and the resulting antenna current. Sec. 20-24.

27. **(40 db)** This circuit is used to reduce _____. Sec. 20-27.

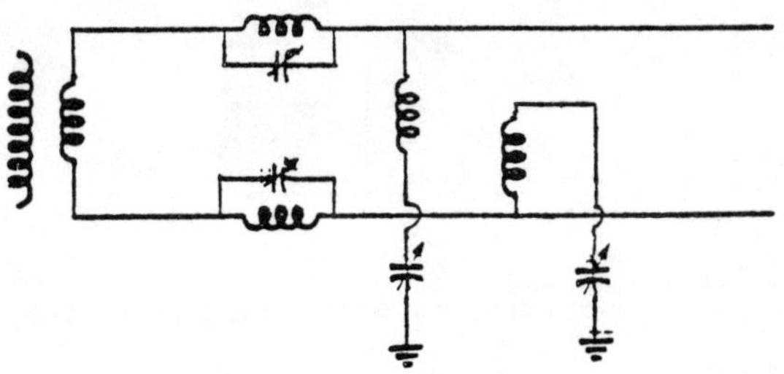

30. **(75%)** This concludes the recheck on Unit 20.

4. (360°, high) Let's take a close look at the screen grid circuit in the class A amplifier.

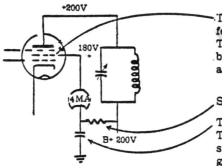

The screen provides internal neutralization of feedback voltage.
The screen reduces the interelectrode capacitance between the plate and grid preventing feedback and oscillation.

Screen grid voltage dropping resistance.

This capacitor is a screen bypass capacitor. The screen is at the ground potential for R.F. so that any feedback from the plate circuit is grounded and does not reach the grid input circuit.

The DC positive voltage on the screen helps accelerate the electrons on their way to the anode. Some electrons are attracted to the screen.
The screen grid reduces the _INTERELECTRODE CAPACITANCE_ between anode and grid eliminating the need for external NEUTRALIZATION .

18. (bottom, center tap) The general idea of grid neutralization is shown below:

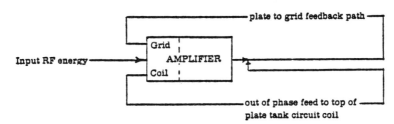

The actual circuit is as shown:

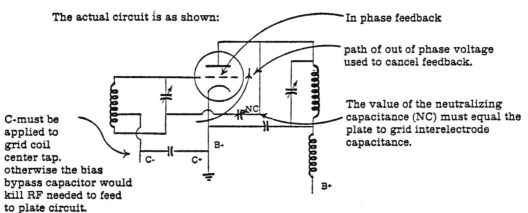

In phase feedback

path of out of phase voltage used to cancel feedback.

The value of the neutralizing capacitance (NC) must equal the plate to grid interelectrode capacitance.

C-must be applied to grid coil center tap. otherwise the bias bypass capacitor would kill RF needed to feed to plate circuit.

In grid neutralization the neutralizing RF voltage is fed from the __bottom__ of the grid tank coil and C-bias voltage must be applied at the grid coil __CENTER TAP__ .

32. (push pull, parallel)

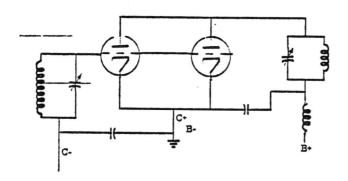

These two tubes are connected in in __PARALLEL__.

Since these triodes are not neutralized, the circuit must be a frequency __MULTIPLIER__.

2. **(electrostatic, electromagnetic, horizontally)** At higher frequencies skip distance (between end of ground wave and beginning of reflected skywave)_____. Sec. 20-2.

5. **(horizontal, electrostatic)** The b. antenna illustrated shows the _____ distribution for _____ wave antenna. The a. antenna illustrated shows _____ distribution for a half wave antenna. Sec. 20-9.

8. **(lengthen, decrease, length)** The impedance of a transmission line should be matched to the _____ on one end and to the _____ impedance of the tube on the other end. Sec. 20-12.

11. **(mismatch)** Coaxial cables that are terminated in their characteristic impedance may be any length. Although there will be some attenuation with long lengths, there will be no mismatch. To avoid the pickup of R.F. between ground connections to the shield of coax cable, there should only be one ground on a coax transmission line. When coupling a 72 ohm line to a 72 ohm point on an antenna, the feed line should be _____ _____. Coax cable should be grounded at _____ point. Sec. 20-12.

14. **(36.5 Ω, zero)** A half wave transmission line _____ its terminal impedance. A quarter wave transmission line will invert impedance. Therefore, a 1/4 wave transmission line shorted on one end would have high impedance like an _____ circuit on the other end (for a particular frequency). Sec. 20-16.

17. **(impedance matching)** Another use of the shorted stub is to short circuit 2nd harmonic energy. Note the example:

1/2 wave length stub for 2nd harmonic energy. Short circuit (low impedance) is repeated at feedpoint for 2nd harmonic energy. The fundamental energy is unaffected since a 1/2 wave stub for the 2nd harmonic would be a 1/4 wave for the fundamental. A shorted stub used to reduce 2nd harmonic energy would be _____ wave length of the fundamental. Sec. 20-16.

20. **(gain)** A loop antenna used to receive a standard broadcast signal works best if it is a _____ loop and the plane of the loop is _____ to the line of direction of the station. Sec. 20-22.

23. **(increasing, decreasing)** Guy wires should be used with _____ segments. Sec. 20-23

26. **(nitrogen, moisture)** At 2 Mhz the antenna field strength is 120 mv per meter. At 4 Mhz it is 1200 microvolts per meter. The attenuation is _____ dbs. Sec. 20-27.

29. **(8.66 amperes)** The final stage of a transmitter has a supply voltage of 600 volts. The final plate current is 300 ma. If the antenna resistance is 15 ohms and the antenna current is 3 amperes, the stage efficiency would be _____%. Sec. 20-30.

5. **(interelectrode capacitance, neutralization)** From assumed values given in the diagram in #4 we can calculate the necessary value for the dropping resistor. Since the plate voltage is 200 volts and the screen voltage should be 180 volts, we need to drop the voltage 20 volts. The required screen current is given as 4 ma. Therefore, the resistance equals 20V/4ma or 5000 ohms.

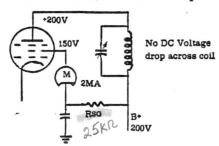

The screen dropping resistance in the circuit shown should have a value of_____ohms.

19. **(bottom, center tap)** Push pull triode RF neutralization consists of a combination of plate and grid neutralization:

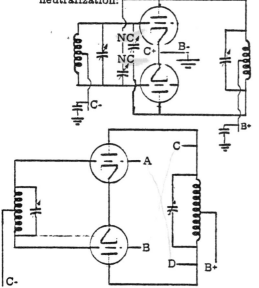

It requires two neutralizing capacitors. Each capacitor is connected from the grid of one tube to the plate of the other tube. Both the B+ and C- connections are to center taps.

Neutralizing capacitors should be connected from point___A___ to point___D___.
And from point to___B___ to point___C___.

33. **(parallel, multiplier)** A push pull circuit can be used as a tripler but not as a doubler as all even harmonics are cancelled by push pull connection.

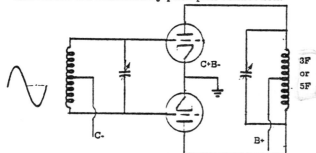

Output is tuned to odd harmonics frequencies. No 2nd or 4th harmonic energy is present in output.

3rd Harmonic

Lower order harmonic energy is stronger than the higher harmonic energy (3rd is stronger than 5th and 5th is stronger than 7th, etc.)

The predominant harmonic present in the output of a push pull RF amplifier (other than the 1st) is the _____Third_____harmonic.

RECHECK PROGRAMMED INSTRUCTION USING SHRADERS ELECTRONIC COMMUNICATION

1. A transmitting antenna radiates _____ and _____ fields. In Fig. 20-1 the radiated wave is _____ polarized because the electrostatic lines are parallel to the earths surface. Sec. 20-1 and Sec. 20-6.

4. (R.F. shading) A signal radiated by a horizontal antenna is best received by a _____ antenna. The polarization of the radiated wave is considered to be in the direction of the _____ field of the antenna. Sec. 20-6.

7. (shorten, increase) An inductor placed in series with an antenna will _____ the antenna and _____ its resonant frequency. The resonant frequency of an antenna can be changed also by changing antenna _____. Sec. 20-11.

10. (voltage, current; voltage, current) Standing waves are caused by impedance _____. Sec. 20-12.

13. (vertical) The theoretical surge impedance between ground and the lower end of a Marconi 1/4 wave antenna is _____ but the DC resistance is near _____ . Sec. 20-14.

16. (low) A shorted or open stub is often inserted in the middle of a half wave antenna to act as a _____ _____ device. Sec. 20-16.

19. (gain) Parasitic antennas give additional _____ and directivity. Sec. 20-20.

22. (omni directional) Top loading has the effect of _____ the electrical wavelength or _____ its resonant frequency. Sec. 20-23.

25. (plate) Dry air or_____ is often used in concentric transmission line to keep_____ out of the lines. Sec. 20-24.

28. (harmonics) When the antenna power of a certain transmitter is 500 watts the antenna current is 7.07 amperes. When the power is raised to 750 watts, the antenna current would be _____ amperes. Sec. 20-30.

CLASS C R.F. AMPLIFIERS.

6.   **(25K ohms)** Radio frequency amplifiers used in transmitters are class C amplifiers biased by grid leak biasing. The Eg1p curve for class C operation is shown: "CLASS C"

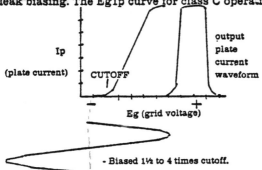

Plate current flows for less than ½ of the input cycle. The output waveform is very distorted. The efficiency is high.

- Biased 1½ to 4 times cutoff.

Even though a sine wave input is used, the class C R.F. amplifier current waveform is badly _distorted_. Plate current flows for less than ___HALF___ of the input cycle. The efficiency is ___HIGH___ .

20.   **(A,D,B,C)**

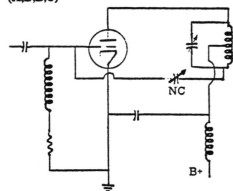

In the circuit ___PLATE___ neutralization is shown.

MISCELLANEOUS INFORMATION

34.   **(third)** Transmitter RF amplifiers are designed so radio frequency energy is kept out of the power supply:

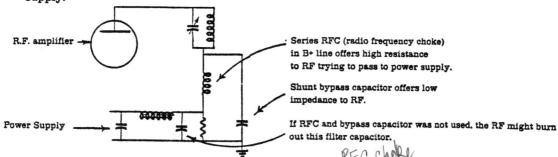

R.F. amplifier →

Power Supply →

: Series RFC (radio frequency choke) in B+ line offers high resistance to RF trying to pass to power supply.

Shunt bypass capacitor offers low impedance to RF.

If RFC and bypass capacitor was not used, the RF might burn out this filter capacitor.

RF from an amplifier is kept out of the power supply by using an ___RFC choke___ in series with the B+ line and a ___capacitor___ in shunt with the power supply.

The Quarter Wave Antenna

7.　(**lengthens; lower**) The quarter wave vertical antenna is called a **Marconi** antenna. Actually the complete Marconi system is a half wave antenna with one quarter wave length extending above ground and one quarter wave in the ground radials. The general arrangement is shown:

The tower is the antenna and is 1/4 wave length long.

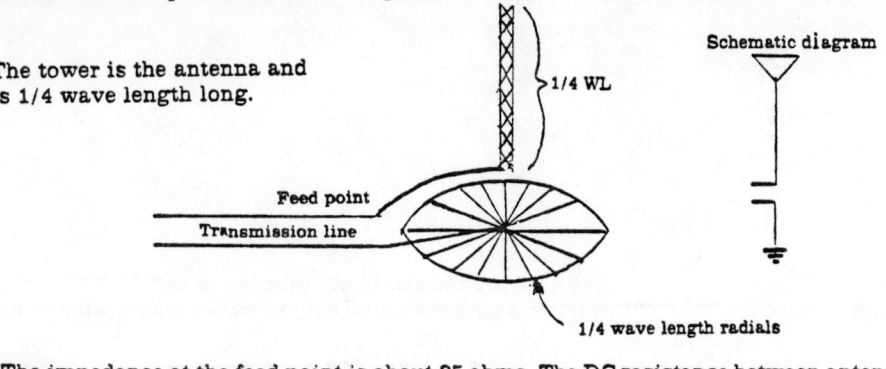

Schematic diagram

1/4 WL

Feed point

Transmission line

1/4 wave length radials

The impedance at the feed point is about 35 ohms. The DC resistance between antenna and ground is about zero.

This antenna is equi-directional (or non directional) either as a transmitting or receiving antenna. This means that it receives or transmits equally well to or from all directions.

If the antenna is elevated above a building and a few radials are placed under the antenna but in the air, the antenna is known as a ground plane vertical. This antenna is also a nondirectional antenna.

The vertical Marconi is a _____ wave antenna having a feed point impedance of about _____ ohms and the DC resistance from the antenna to ground is near_____.

14.　(**gain; directivity**) R.F. energy is carried from the transmitter to the antenna or from the antenna to a receiver by a transmission line. There are several kinds of lines. Three of them are as follows:

1) An open twin line. The characteristic impedance of this transmission line is determined by the size of wire used and the spacing between wires. It's impedance is independent of its length. The wires are held apart at regular intervals by insulators called feeder spreaders.

Parallel lines

Insulators

2) Coaxial cables. The characteristic impedance of this line is determined by the conductor sizes the spacing between conductors, and the type of dielectric material. It's impedance is independent of its length. 50 and 72 ohm cables are common.

Center conductor

Solid dielectric

Braided copper shield.

The braided copper outer shield should be grounded at one point only to prevent R.F. pickup between grounded points.

3) Hollow concentric lines. The inner wire is held away from the inner surface of the outer conductor. In order to prevent moisture condensation on the inside of a concentric line, nitrogen or dry air is used to fill the hollow tube. Again the characteristic impedance is dependent on the conductor sizes and spacing. It is independent of length.

Hollow tube

Insulating bead

The characteristic impedance of transmission lines is determined by conductor _____ and _____. The impedance is independent of the line _____.

21.　(**impedance; harmonic**) An improperly terminated transmission line does not deliver all of its power to the antenna. The amount of reflected power is determined by the amount of mismatch.

Reflected power causes standing waves of current and voltage to form on the transmission line. The degree of match is indicated by the **standing wave ratio. (S.W.R.)**

This ratio may take two forms:

1) It is the ratio of the transmission line impedance to the feed point impedance. By formula:

$$\text{S.W.R.} = \frac{Z \text{ line}}{Z\text{ant. (at feed point)}}$$

2) It is the ratio of the maximum voltage or current on a transmission line to the minimum voltage or current. By formula:

$$\text{SWR} = \frac{E\text{max}}{E\text{min}} \text{ or } \frac{I\text{max}}{I\text{min}}$$

In either case there is perfect match or termination if the ratio is 1 to 1.

Standing wave ratio is the ratio of maximum_____or_____to the minimum _____, or_____on a transmission line.

28.　(**higher**) Mountains or hills may cause_____ _____.

7.   (distorted, half, high) An R.F. using grid leak biasing only depends on high excitation.

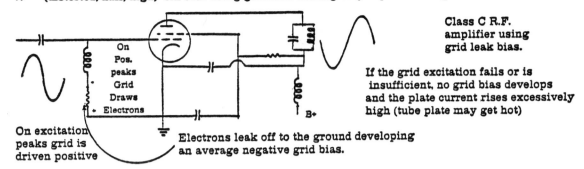

On excitation
peaks grid is
driven positive

Class C R.F.
amplifier using
grid leak bias.

If the grid excitation fails or is
insufficient, no grid bias develops
and the plate current rises excessively
high (tube plate may get hot)

Electrons leak off to the ground developing
an average negative grid bias.

The grid current flow is from the grid through an RFC and grid leak to ground.

On the positive excitation peaks the grid __ATTRACTS__ electrons. The electrons leak off to the __GROUND__
and develop an average negative voltage on the grid.

21. (plate) Neutralization is accomplished in the following manner:
    (1) Disconnect the B+ from the power supply.
    (2) Apply excitation to the stage being neutralized.
    (3) Tune the plate tank circuit for maximum RF output. A neon bulb touched to the plate end of the
         tank circuit coil is a good indicator. If there is any RF indication the stage is not neutralized..
    (4) Tune the neutralizing capacitor(s) until there is no RF output.
    (5) Repeat step 3 and 4 until no RF output can be obtained. The amplifier is now neutralized.
    If an RF triode amplifier is neutralized the grid current meter will not peak when the plate circuit is
    tuned through resonance.
    The first step in neutralizing is to disconnect the __B+__ from the power supply.

35. (RFC choke, capacitor) The input power to an RF amplifier is determined by multiplying the plate
     voltage by the plate current.

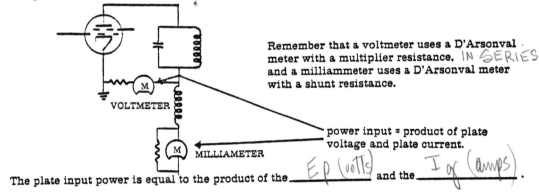

Remember that a voltmeter uses a D'Arsonval
meter with a multiplier resistance, __IN SERIES__
and a milliammeter uses a D'Arsonval meter
with a shunt resistance.

power input = product of plate
voltage and plate current.

The plate input power is equal to the product of the __EP (volts)__ and the __I of (amps)__ .

6. **(shortens; higher)** Top loading an antenna effectively _____ the antenna causing it to resonate at a _____ frequency.

13. **(gain)** Parasitic antennas are often incorporated in a beam to give an array additional gain and directivity. Parasitic elements of a beam are placed near a driven element and are excited by induced voltages. The induced voltages are re-radiated either back towards the driven element or in the opposite direction. If the parasitic element is about .2 wave length from the driven element and is slightly longer than the half wave length dimension, it becomes a reflector. If the parasitic element is about .1 wave length from the driven element and is slightly shorter than 1/2 wave length, it becomes a director.

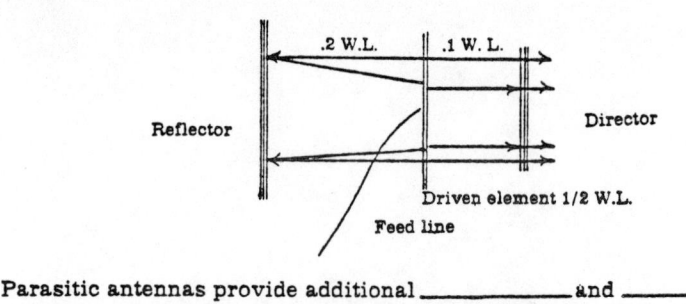

Parasitic antennas provide additional _____ and _____ .

20. **(high resistance - like an open; half)** A 1/4 wave length or 1/2 wave length open or shorted transmission line can be used as an impedance matching device. Such a line is called a stub.
Two examples of matching by a stub are given:

1) Matching a 300 ohm line to the 72 ohm feed point at the center of a 1/4 wave length antenna.

2) Shorting out 2nd harmonic energy at the feed point with a stub.

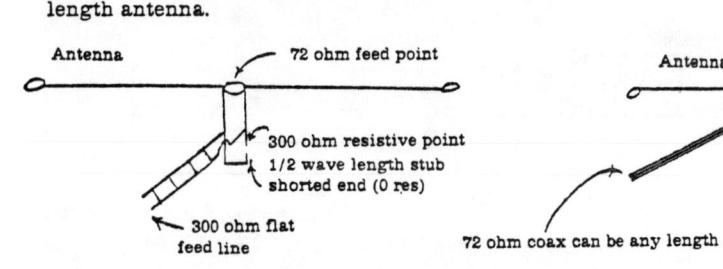

It should be noted that the fundamental frequency is not shorted out at the feed point as a 1/2 WL stub for the 2nd harmonic is a 1/4 WL stub for the fundamental. For the fundamental frequency the shorted 1/4 WL stub resistance is inverted to a high resistance at the feed point end.

A stub used with an antenna may be used as an _____ matching device or to reduce 2nd _____ energy.

27. **(75%)** Now one last word about radiation. When high frequency energy leaves an antenna, it takes two paths:

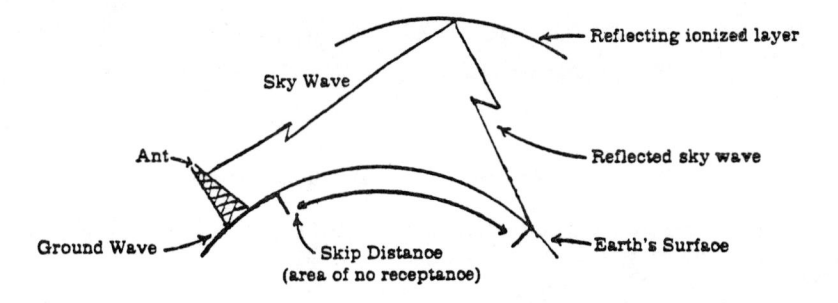

There is an area between the end of the ground wave (50 miles or so from the station) and the beginning of the reflected sky wave called skip distance. As the frequency increases the skip distance increases since the reflected wave of the higher frequency hits further out on the earth's surface. Reception may even be poor in the reflected wave area due to the changing altitude of the ionized layer or due to the R.F. shading of a hill or mountain.

Skip distance increases with _____ frequencies.

8. (attracts, ground) If the excitation to the grid fails, the plate current ___RISES___ and may ruin the tube.

22. (B+) A good RF indicator for neutralizing is a _NEON BULB_ . if the grid meter shows a pronounced peak when the plate circuit is tuned to resonance, this indicates the amplifier _IS NOT_ (is or is not) neutralized

36. (plate voltage, plate current) In figuring frequency from the period of a wave we simply invert the period. For example if the period of a cycle is 1/100 of a second, the frequency is 100/1 hertz or 100 hertz.

    If two cycles are completed in 1/100 second the frequency is _____ hertz.

169

5.   (change; higher; lower) A capacitor placed in series with an antenna effectively _____ the antenna and it resonates at a _____ frequency.

Beam Antennas

12.   (equi-directional) If two vertical half wave antennas are fed in phase energy when they are separated by a half wave length, a greater gain and directivity is experienced. This is illustrated below:

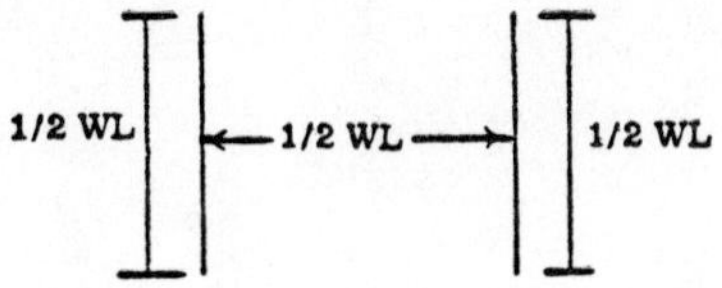

1/2 WL |←— 1/2 WL —→| 1/2 WL

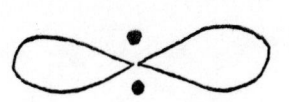

Tops of antnnas

Radiaton pattern in horizontal plane.

Two vertical antennas driven
simultaneously by in phase
energy. This process is
called stacking.

Stacking the elements of a driven array produces greater_____in given directions.

19.   (flat, any length)   If a transmission line is terminated in some impedance other than it's characteristic impedance, it is a tuned line with alternate resistance and reactance points along its length. Two extremes of mismatch are shown:

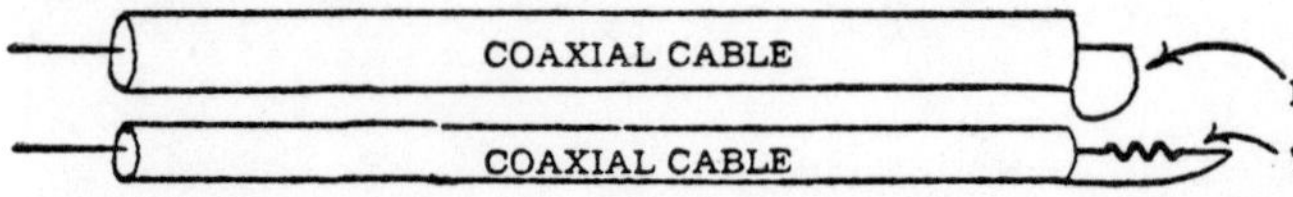

COAXIAL CABLE — Low resistance, termination in a short.

COAXIAL CABLE — Terminated in an open (or high resistance)

The characteristics of a mismatched line are these: 1) The termination resistance is repeated back down the line every half wave length.2) The termination resistance is inverted back down the line every odd quarter wave length.(low resistance becomes high resistance and vice versa) 3) Much of the power traveling down the line will be reflected back to the source. These characteristics are summarized by using parallel lines:

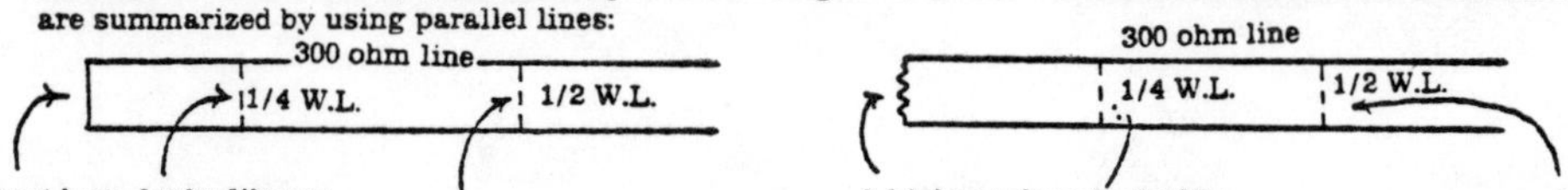

___300 ohm line___
1/4 W.L.   1/2 W.L.

300 ohm line
1/4 W.L.   1/2 W.L.

A short here looks like an   or a short here
            open here

A high res. here looks like   or high res.
            low res. here   here.

At certain intermediate points the lines are either resistive or reactance. They can only be powered at resistive points. If a 1/4 W.L. transmission line is shorted on one end, it has a_____ resistance on the other end. The resistance of a 1/2 W.L. is repeated every_____W.L. if the line is improperly terminated.

26.   (8.66 amperes) The efficiency of the final stage of a transmitter is equal to the antenna output power divided by the final plate input power. By formula:

$$\% \text{ Efficiency} = \frac{I^2 (ant) \times R (ant)}{Ip \times Ep} \times 100$$

If the final stage of a transmitter has a supply voltage of 600 volts, the final plate current is 300 ma, the antenna resistance is 15 ohms and the antenna current is 3 amperes; the stage efficiency is _____ %.

9. (rises) The amount of grid bias developed by the grid leak biased amplifier is a function of the time constant of the RC coupled circuit.

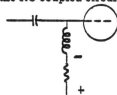

Increasing grid leak resistance value increases RC time constant and produces higher bias voltage.

Grid leak-biasing is developed by use of proper RC _TIME CONSTANT_ .

23. (neon bulb, is not) It is only necessary to neutralize common cathode RF triode amplifiers of the equivalent common emitter RF triode amplifier. It is not necessary to neutralize:
    (1) Multiple grid tube amplifiers containing a screen grid. The screen provides internal neutralization.
    (2) Triodes used as multipliers. There can be no feedback for regeneration if the output is on a different frequency than the input. Triode doublers, triplers and quadruplers do not need to be neutralized.
    (3) Grounded grid amplifiers need not be neutralized.

Any plate circuit feedback is grounded out at the grid and cannot reach the cathode input.

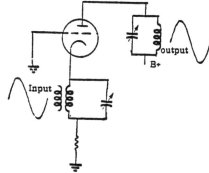

Only common _CATHODE_ triode RF amplifiers need be neutralized.

37. (200) If the oscillator of a transmitter having three doublers and one tripler drifts 2Khz, the drift in the output would equal: $\frac{2}{osc.}$ X $\frac{2\ X\ 2\ X\ 2}{three\ doublers}$ X $\frac{3}{tripler}$ or 48 Khz.

If the oscillator of a transmitter having two doublers and three triplers drifts 1 Khz, the drift in the output would be____108____ Khz.

4. **(voltage)** There are several ways the resonant frequency of an antenna can be changed:
    1) Change its length. A shorter antenna resonates at a higher frequency. A longer antenna resonates at a lower frequency.
    2) Place an inductance in series with the antenna as shown:

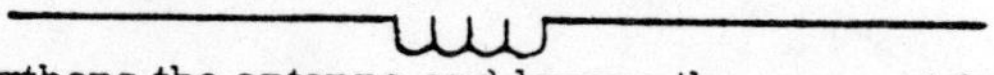

    This effectively lengthens the antenna and lowers the resonant frequency.
    3) place a capacitor in series with an antenna as shown:

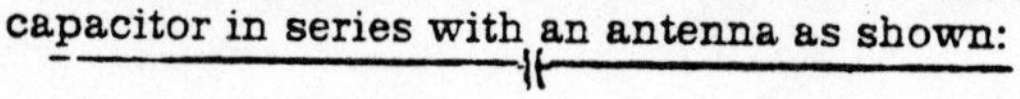

    This effectively shortens the antenna and raises the resonant frequency.
    4) Top load a vertical antenna.

    A wheel structure on top of a low frequency antenna increases the antenna inductance and the antenna capacitance from the top of the antenna to the ground. The net result is to effectively lengthen an antenna and to lower its resonant frequency.

    Changing the length of an antenna will_____ its resonant frequency. A shorter antenna will resonate at a _____frequency. A longer antenna will resonate at a _____ frequency.

11. **(vertical; parallel)** If the loop antenna was laid over on its side, it would become a horizontal loop antenna. Since it would be impossible to place a horizontal loop in a position so that its plane would not be parallel to the line of direction of a station, it is an equi-directional antenna. (Equi-directional, omni-directional and non-directional all mean the same thing.)
    The horizontal loop is an _____ _____ antenna in the horizontal plane.

18. **(antenna)** If a transmission line is terminated (matched) in its characteristic impedance, it is a _____ line. The length of a 72 ohm coax cable terminated with 72 ohms could be _____.

25. **(10 ohms)** If the output power was 750 watts in this 10 ohm antenna, the current could be calculated using our power formula:

    $P = I^2 \times R$ $750 = I^2 \, 10$ $I^2 = 750/10 = 75$ and I would $= $ _____amps.

10. (time constant) When there is no excitation, the grid does not draw any electrons and no current flows through the grid leak. Therefore the grid is at the same potential as the cathode and zero bias results. Without a negative voltage on the grid to repel cathode electrons on their way to the plate, the plate current can rise to an excessively high value and possibly ruin the tube. The plate would get red hot. It is therefore customary to add some protective cathode resistor bias. If the excitation fails, the plate current rises somewhat causing a voltage drop across a cathode resistance. This voltage is used as protective bias.

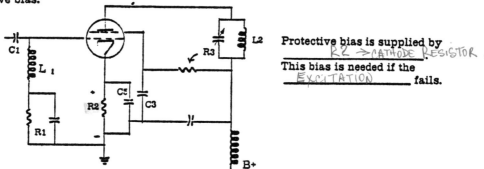

Protective bias is supplied by ___R2 →CATHODE RESISTOR___.
This bias is needed if the ___EXCITATION___ fails.

24. (cathode)

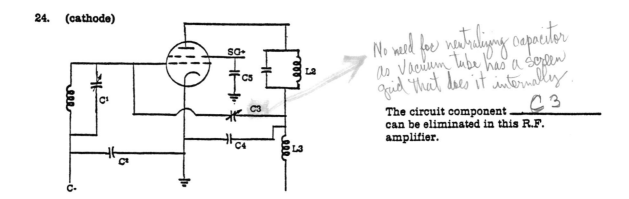

No need for neutralizing capacitor as vacuum tube has a screen grid that does it internally.

The circuit component ___C3___ can be eliminated in this R.F. amplifier.

38. (108) The radio frequency choke used in a shunt fed RF circuit constitutes the load. If some of the turns are shorted out the output RF voltage would be decreased.

A shorted RFC in a shunt fed RF circuit would change the ___LOAD___ impedance.

3.   (current; half)

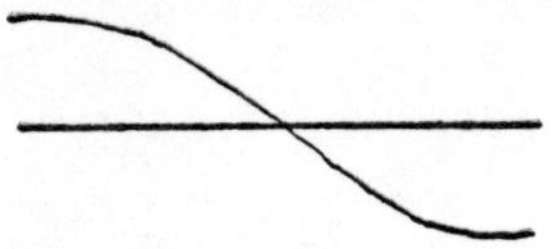

The illustration shown represents

_____ distribution

along a half wave antenna.

The Loop Antenna

10. (insulated) The loop antenna consists of a tuned loop having inductance and capacitance. It is used usually for receiving and is placed in the vertical plane. R.F. energy induced into the loop from a direction perpendicular to the plane of the loop is self cancelling. The illustration shows why:

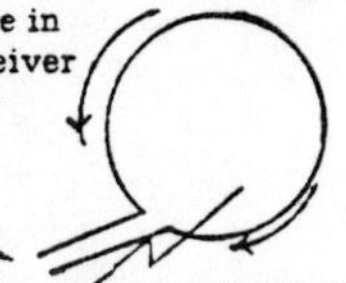

Although the resultant currents are in phase, when they arrive at the receiver from oposite sides of the loop they are out of phase and cancel.

To receiver

At a particular instant in time equal induced voltages will produce currents of equal amplitude as shown by the arrows.

R.F. signal coming at right angles to plane of loop.

If a signal comes from a direction that is in a line parallel to the plane of the loop, voltage is induced into one side of the loop first and then into the other side a little later. Therefore, the induced voltages are not simultaneously induced and seldom have the same amplitude.

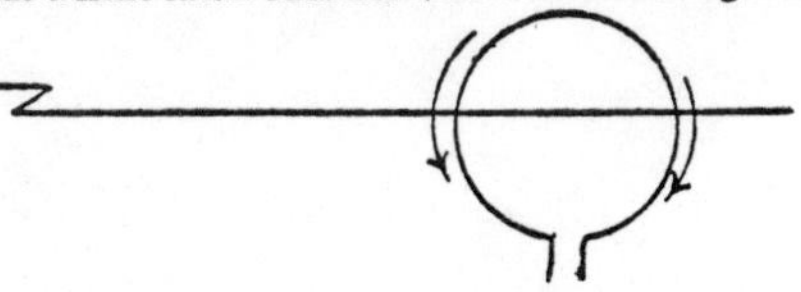

R.F. Source

A vertical loop is bi-directional and receives best from a direction that is in a line that is parallel with the plane of the loop.

To receiver

A directional loop antenna used to receive a standard broadcast signal works best if it is a _____ loop and the plane of the loop is _____ to the line of direction at the station.

17. (nitrogen; moisture) For the maximum transfer of energy from a transmitter final to the antenna the transmission line impedance should be matched on both ends. Note the examples:

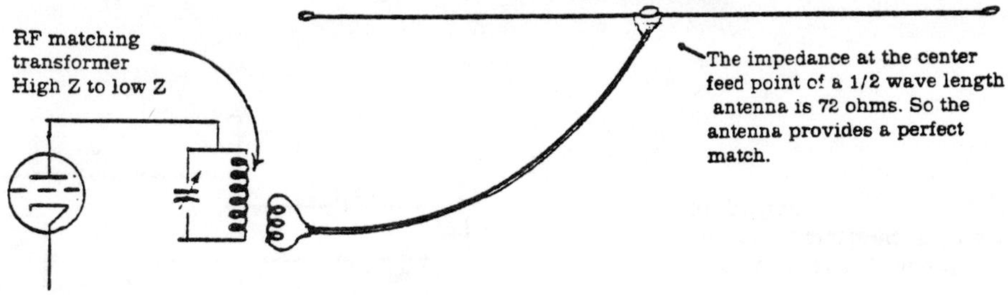

1/2 Wave length

RF matching transformer High Z to low Z

The impedance at the center feed point of a 1/2 wave length antenna is 72 ohms. So the antenna provides a perfect match.

If the line is matched (terminated in its characteristic impedance) it is said to be a flat line and the 72 ohm coax can be cut to any convenient length.

The impedance of a transmission line should be matched to the _____ impedance on one end and to the transmitter on the other end.

24. (traps) Antenna output power is figured by formula:

$$P = I^2R$$

The degree of antenna coupling to the final stage of a transmitter determines the final plate current and the resulting antenna current.

If the antenna resistance is 15 ohms and the antenna current is 3 amperes, the output power is 3^2 X 15 or 135 watts.

If the output power is 500 watts and the antenna current is 7.07 amperes we can substitute in the formula and find the antenna resistance. It would be equal to $500/7.07^2$ or _____ ohms.

250

11. (R2, excitation) An R. F. amplifier has ample protection against the loss of bias if it is biased Class C by a battery or power supply.

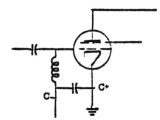

If this amplifier loses excitation the battery or power supply holds the grid high negative and no plate current can flow.

When high excitation drives grid positive on peaks, both grid and plate current flows.
If the bias supply shorts out the tube would be zero biased and the plate current would rise excessively.
A cathode resistor would be used in this circuit to protect the tube against the loss of bias.

If an R.F. Class C amplifier was biased by a battery or a power supply and the excitation failed, there would be ___NO___ plate current. If the bias supply was shorted out, there would be ___HIGH___ plate current.

25. (C₃) A triode RF amplifier will not need to be neutralized if it is a __MULTIPLIER__ or is a grounded __GRID__ amplifier.

39. (load) Spurious frequencies may be generated in an R.F. amplifier by the inductance and capacitance due to long component leads. These frequencies are generally V.H.F. frequencies and are called parasitic oscillations. As the name implies useful power is robbed from an R.F. amplifier by these unwanted parasitic oscillations. These oscillations often result in eratic tuning and may cause a tube plate to run hot. Parasitic oscillations can be minimized by using short leads, parasitic chokes, and by proper placement of leads.
If a pushpull R.F. amplifier tunes erratically and one tube gets hot, __PARASITIC__ oscillations are probably being generated.

2. **(half; electromagnetic; electrostatic)** The resonant transmitting antenna has standing waves of voltage and current which vary sinusoidally along the length of the antenna.

Current distribution

Voltage distribution

⊢— 1/2 wave length —⊣

The current is at a maximum at the center of the antenna and at a minimum on the ends. The voltage is at a minimum at the center and at a maximum at the ends.

⊢— 1/2 W.L. —⊣

The illustration represents _____
distribution along a _____ wave antenna.

9. **(equi-directional)** It is often necessary to support a vertical antenna by use of guy wires. These wires must be insulated segments that are not resonant harmonic lengths. This will prevent absorption and re-radiation.

Glazed porcelain or pyrex insulators.

radials

Guy wires should have _____ segments to prevent re-radiation.

16. **(one)** Dry air or _____ is often used in concentric transmission lines to keep _____ out of the lines.

Miscellaneous

23. **(One; one)** Harmonics are often reduced in the transmission line so that they never reach the antenna to be radiated. One system uses series and parallel traps in the line to reduce the transfer of 2nd and 3rd harmonic energy.

Transmission line.

To antenna

These parallel traps are tuned to resonance for 2nd harmonic energy. They offer high Z to the flow of 2nd harmonic energy but do not impede the fundamental energy. Remember a parallel resonant circuit has high impedance to the frequency for which it is resonant and low impedance for all other frequencies.

These series tuned traps are tuned to resonance for 3rd harmonic energy. They offer low Z to this energy flowing to the ground.

2nd and 3rd harmonic energy can be reduced by using _____ in the transmission line.

30. **(vertical)** This concludes Unit 20.

12. **(no, high)** The output plate current in a class C amplifier flows for less than 1/2 of the input cycle. The current waveform is a pulsating DC current with an AC characteristic as shown:

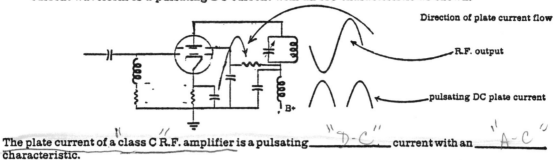

The plate current of a class C R.F. amplifier is a pulsating ___"D-C"___ current with an ___"A-C"___ characteristic.

GROUNDED GRID AMPLIFIERS

26. **(multiplier, grid)** Two typical grounded grid amplifiers are shown:

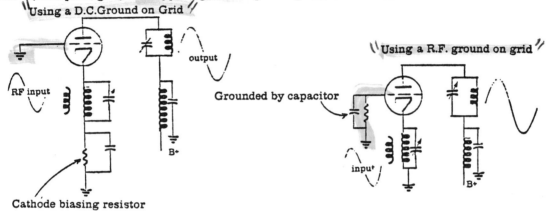

Any RF feeding back to cathode input is grounded. Grid here acts like the screen in a multigrid tube. The input is into the cathode-the output is taken at the plate.

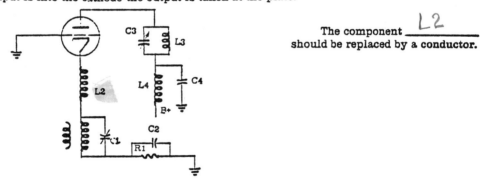

The component ___L2___ should be replaced by a **conductor.**

40. **(parasitic)** Parasitic chokes are constructed by using a few turns of wire (no. 12 is common) around a small 2 watt resistor (47 ohms is common). These chokes may be inserted in series in the grid, screen grid, or plate leads to prevent parasitic oscillation. Parasitic chokes are constructed by wrapping a few turns of wire around a ___47___ ohm ___2___ watt resistor.

The Half Wave Antenna

1. An antenna is a tuned circuit having lumped inductance and capacitance. If the antenna is approximately one half wave length long (or any odd half wave length), the antenna is resonant for the frequency for which it is one half wave length long. The transmitting and receiving antenna constitute an R.F. transformer.

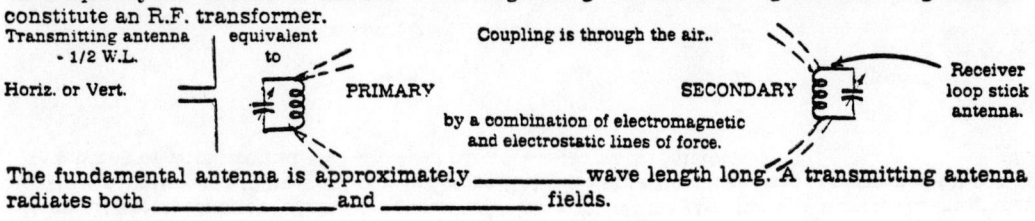

The fundamental antenna is approximately _____ wave length long. A transmitting antenna radiates both _____ and _____ fields.

8. **(quarter; 35; zero)** The vertical Marconi and ground plane antenna is _____ directional.

15. **(size; spacing; length)** In order to avoid ground loops (pickup of RF between grounds) coax cable should be grounded at _____ point.

22. **(voltage; current; voltage; current)** A flat line should have a S.W.R. of _____ to _____ .

29. **(R.F. shading)** A radiated wave is composed of two compenents:
    1. An electromagnetic field. This is the kind of field that surrounds a coil when current is flowing through its winding.
    2. An electrostatic field. This is the kind of field that exists between the plates of a charged capacitor. These two fields travel together in a wave front and are at right angles to each other. The wave is described as being either vertically or horizontally polarized. It is vertically polarized if the electrostatic component is perpendicular to the earth and horizontally polarized if the electrostatic component is parallel to the earth. Note the example below:

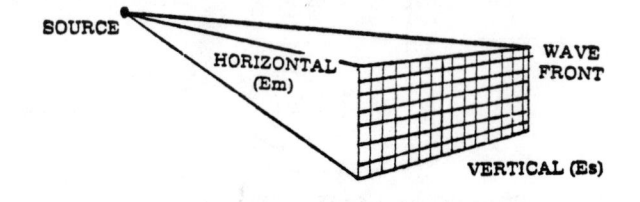

The wave above is _____ polarized.

13. **(DC , AC)** The output from the plate tank circuit is in the form of complete cycles (distorted). A pulse of plate current charges the tank circuit capacitor. During the portion of the input cycle when no plate current flows the charged capacitor discharges in the opposite direction from the original plate current pulse through the tank circuit inductance. This effect is called the **Flywheel Effect.**

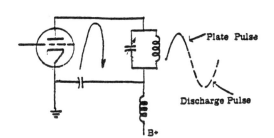

The nearly complete R.F. output cycle from a class C amplifier is provided for by the ___FLYWHEEL___ effect.

27. **(L2)** The grid of one grounded grid amplifier is connected directly to the ground. The other circuit grid is grounded for RF by a ___CAPACITOR___.

41. **(47, 2)** If the wave length of any radio frequency is known, its frequency can be calculated by use of the formula:

$$F = \frac{V}{W.L.}$$ Where F is the frequency in kilohertz.
    V is the velocity of a radio wave in kilometers (300,000 Km/sec.)
    WL is the wave length in meters

Thus the frequency of a 300 meter wave length if 300,000/300 or 1000 Khz.
The frequency of a 200 meter wave length is _____ Khz.

48. Modulation index defined is
   a. the ratio of the maximum deviation to the modulating audio frequency.
   b. the ratio of the maximum modulating audio frequency to the maximum RF swing.
   c. the product of the maximum RF swing and the modulating audio frequency.
   d. the deviation of the carrier frequency.
   e. none of these.

49. The input power of a public safety station should be measured
   a. twice a year.
   b. whenever a change is made in the transmitter.   d. when the station is first licensed.
   c. every three months.   e. b and d above.

50. A licensed station in the public safety radio service can be tested
   a. once a month.
   b. when it is installed.   d. 12 midnight to sunrise.
   c. twice a year.   e. anytime the service or regulation of station requires it.

51. A de-emphasis circuit is used
   a. pass high audio frequencies.
   b. to pass low audio frequencies.   d. in an AM transmitter.
   c. in an FM transmitter.   e. in a phase modulator.

52. A limiter stage in an FM receiver should use
   a. a low mu triode.
   b. a low mu pentode.   d. a high mu pentode.
   c. a high mu triode.   e. a diode.

53. The authorized bandwidth of an emission of a public safety station is defined as the width of the frequency band containing
   a. the carrier.
   b. the carrier and the upper sideband.
   c. the carrier and both sidebands.
   d. those frequencies upon which appears 99 percent of the radiated power.
   e. none of these.

54. In the diagram shown below
   a. V1 is reversed.
   b. V2 is reversed.
   c. V1 and V2 are reversed.
   d. the ground is in the wrong place.
   e. there are no mistakes.

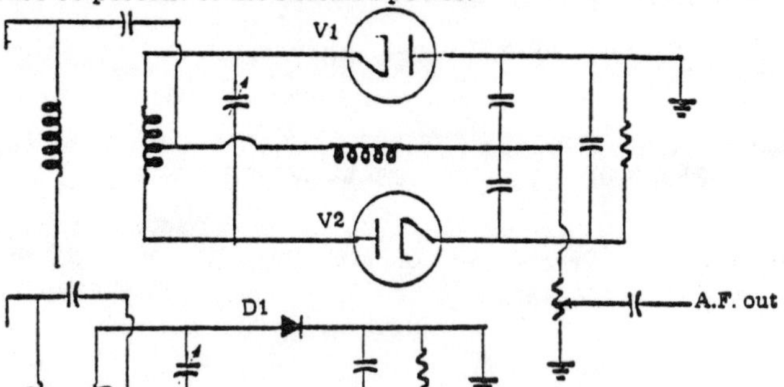

55. In the diagram shown below
   a. D1 is reversed.
   b. D2 is reversed.
   c. D1 and D2 are reversed.
   d. the ground is in the wrong place.
   e. this is a correct discriminator.

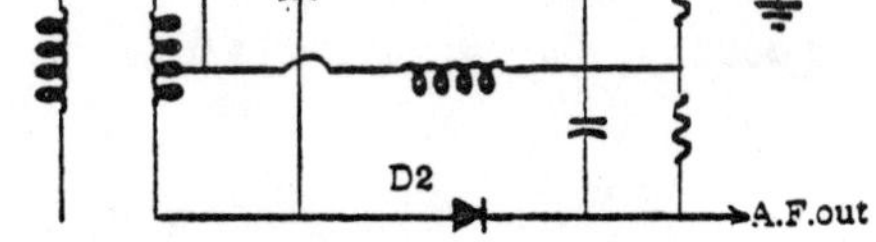

56. "Type approval" when applied to equipment indicates that
   a. the manufacturer has submitted data concerning the equipment.
   b. the FCC has conducted tests on the equipment.
   c. the licensee has submitted data concerning the equipment.
   d. none of the above.
   e. the manufacturer approves the design.

57. Stations in the Public Safety Radio Services may be operated without a station authorization for a period
   a. not to exceed 3 months.
   b. not to exceed 10 days.   d. not to exceed 72 hours.
   c. not to exceed 48 hours.   e. none of the above.

58. The maximum authorized bandwidth of Public Safety stations operating between 25 and 50 Mhz is
   a. 20 Khz.
   b. 10 Khz.   d. 150 Khz.
   c. 30 Khz.   e. 5 Khz.

59. The principal merit of frequency-modulated transmission is
   a. the reduction of the FM receiver's noise level.
   b. simpler circuits in both the transmitter and receiver.   d. simpler alignment procedures.
   c. the need for less bandwidth.   e. more audio is used.

60. One way to reduce interference to a car radio would be to use
   a. heavy battery cables.
   b. negative ground.   d. resistors in the spark plug leads.
   c. positive ground.   e. horizontal antennas.

247

14. (flywheel) It is important that we understand how to use D'Arsonval milliammeters and voltmeters in Class C.R.F. transmitter amplifiers.

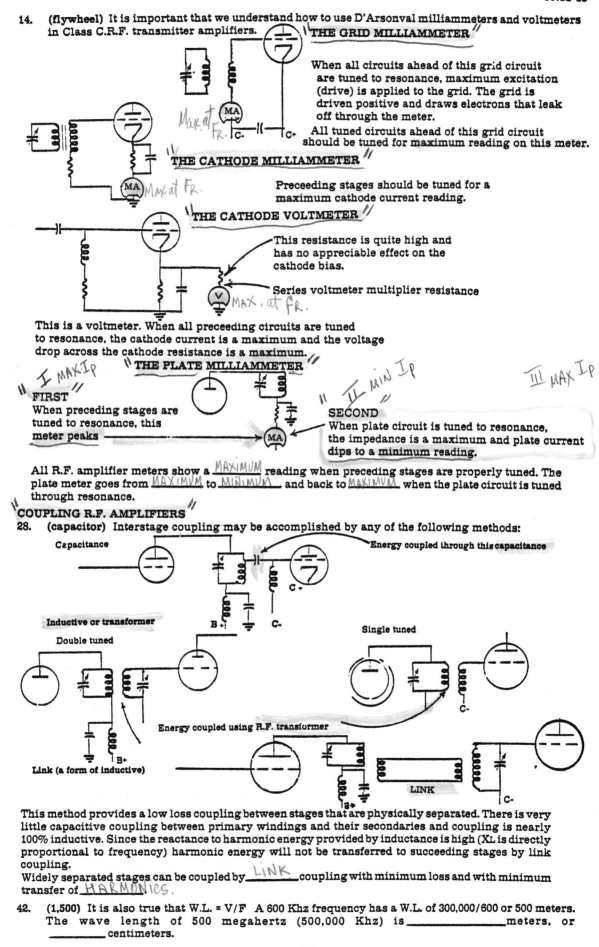

THE GRID MILLIAMMETER

When all circuits ahead of this grid circuit are tuned to resonance, maximum excitation (drive) is applied to the grid. The grid is driven positive and draws electrons that leak off through the meter.

All tuned circuits ahead of this grid circuit should be tuned for maximum reading on this meter.

THE CATHODE MILLIAMMETER

Preceeding stages should be tuned for a maximum cathode current reading.

THE CATHODE VOLTMETER

This resistance is quite high and has no appreciable effect on the cathode bias.

Series voltmeter multiplier resistance

This is a voltmeter. When all preceeding circuits are tuned to resonance, the cathode current is a maximum and the voltage drop across the cathode resistance is a maximum.

THE PLATE MILLIAMMETER

FIRST
When preceding stages are tuned to resonance, this meter peaks

SECOND
When plate circuit is tuned to resonance, the impedance is a maximum and plate current dips to a minimum reading.

All R.F. amplifier meters show a MAXIMUM reading when preceding stages are properly tuned. The plate meter goes from MAXIMUM to MINIMUM and back to MAXIMUM when the plate circuit is tuned through resonance.

COUPLING R.F. AMPLIFIERS

28. (capacitor) Interstage coupling may be accomplished by any of the following methods:

Capacitance

Energy coupled through this capacitance

Inductive or transformer

Double tuned

Single tuned

Energy coupled using R.F. transformer

Link (a form of inductive)

LINK

This method provides a low loss coupling between stages that are physically separated. There is very little capacitive coupling between primary windings and their secondaries and coupling is nearly 100% inductive. Since the reactance to harmonic energy provided by inductance is high (X_L is directly proportional to frequency) harmonic energy will not be transferred to succeeding stages by link coupling.

Widely separated stages can be coupled by LINK coupling with minimum loss and with minimum transfer of HARMONICS.

42. (1,500) It is also true that W.L. = V/F A 600 Khz frequency has a W.L. of 300,000/600 or 500 meters. The wave length of 500 megahertz (500,000 Khz) is _____ meters, or _____ centimeters.

36. The direct FM transmitter frequency can be stabilized by using
   a. an AVC circuit.
   b. an AGC circuit.   d. a power supply.
   c. an AFC circuit.   e. 60 cycles.

37. The authorized bandwidth for narrow band FM is
   a. 5 Khz.
   b. 10 Khz.   d. 40 Khz.
   c. 20 Khz.   e. 60 Khz.

38. Pre-emphasis improves signal to noise ratio of
   a. high modulating audio frequencies.
   b. low modulating audio frequencies.   d. frequencies below 100 hz.
   c. rubberized crystal.   e. none of these.

39. The bandwidth of a station is considered to be that of
   a. the band of frequencies containing 99% of the emitted energy.
   b. the carrier and lower sideband.   d. the carrier.
   c. the carrier and upper sideband.   e. none of these.

40. The sidebands created in FM are created by
   a. final plate power.
   b. input power.   d. carried frequency.
   c. modulating power.   e. none of these.

41. The frequency swing is checked on an FM station by
   a. checking oscillator frequency and varying tuning dial.
   b. checking oscillator frequency and modulating internally.   d. checking upper and lower frequency.
   c. checking upper frequency.   e. none of these.

42. The AM portion of an FM signal is eliminated by the
   a. limiter.
   b. detector.   d. audio amplifier.
   c. discriminator.   e. sound trap.

43. The first step in tuning an FM mobile transmitter is
   a. apply voltage to final amplifier and tune.
   b. remove voltage from final amplifier and tune oscillator and multipliers.
   c. couple antenna to the final tank circuit.
   d. tune the multipliers to resonance.
   e. none of these.

44. Narrow band public safety FM stations should limit their deviation to
   a. 5 Khz.
   b. 10 Khz.   d. 20 Khz.
   c. 15 Khz.   e. 30 Khz.

45. A disadvantage of wide band FM over narrow band FM is
   a. wideband FM requires excessive power.
   b. wideband FM is not high fidelity.
   c. wideband FM requires more equipment.
   d. wideband FM requires excessive use of the space assigned to FM.
   e. none of these.

46. The advantage of indirect FM over direct FM is
   a. higher fidelity.
   b. it takes less A.F. power.   d. no limiter is required.
   c. 100% modulation is assured.   e. none of these.

47. The circuit shown is a
   a. phase modulation circuit.
   b. electron coupled oscillator.
   c. voltage doubler.
   d. grounded grid amplifier.
   e. bridge power supply.

UNIT 15

RECHECK PROGRAMMED INSTRUCTION USING SHRADER'S ELECTRONIC COMMUNICATION

1.   Wires and leads between the component parts of an R.F. circuit must be kept_____ . Sec. 15-1

8.   (high, lower) The grid current _____ somewhat when the plate tuned circuit is tuned to resonance. Sec. 15-5.

15.   (parallel or pushpull) In the Frequency Doubler circuit shown, the two tubes are connected in _____ . Sec. 15-18

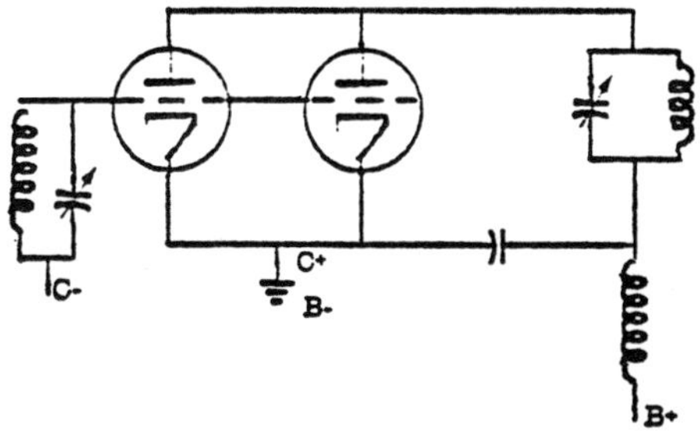

22.   (link) The coupling method shown is _____ _____ coupling. Sec. 15-11.

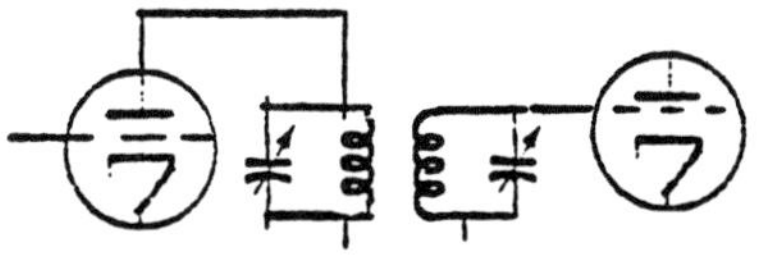

29.   (interelectrode) The neutralization method shown is_____ neutralization. Sec. 15-13.

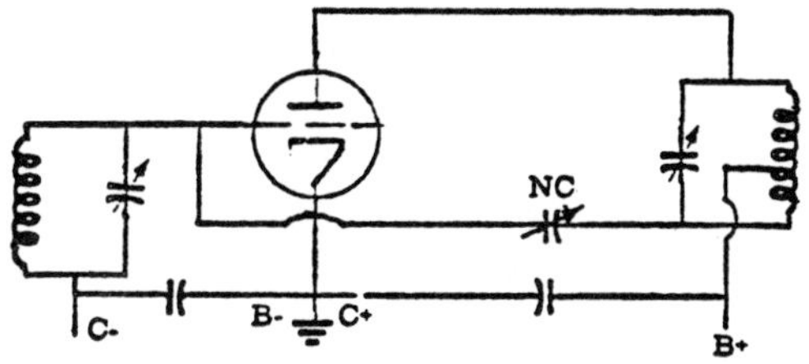

36.   (plate power supply voltage) Any form of a R.F. wavemeter may be used to check neutralization. A simple device, however, is a _____ bulb held to the plate end of the tank coil. Sec. 15-15.

43.   (push pull, parallel) The oscillator of a transmitter having two doublers and three triplers drifts 2 Khz. The drift in the output would be _____ Khz. Sec. 15-21.

50.   (choke, capacitor) This concludes the recheck programmed instruction on Unit 15.

176

24. A common way of reducing interference to a communications receiver is
    a. install traps in the antenna.
    b. bypass the armature of the auto generators in the neighborhood.
    c. by increasing the selectivity of the receiver.
    d. block off the neighborhood roads.
    e. none of these.

25. If the frequency of interference to an auto radio increased as the car speed increased, it would be well to
    a. put a tuned circuit in the antenna.
    b. put a capacitor in series to the antenna.   d. place a choke between the starter and generator field.
    c. put a choke from antenna to ground.   e. place a capacitor between generator armature and ground.

26. For the best signal to noise ratio in FM broadcasting
    a. use greater frequency swing.
    b. use less frequency swing.   d. use split tuning.
    c. use omnidirectional antennas.   e. none of these.

27. In the circuit shown below
    a. V1 is reversed.
    b. V2 is reversed.
    c. a discriminator is used.
    d. L3 should be replaced by a conductor.
    e. there are no mistakes.

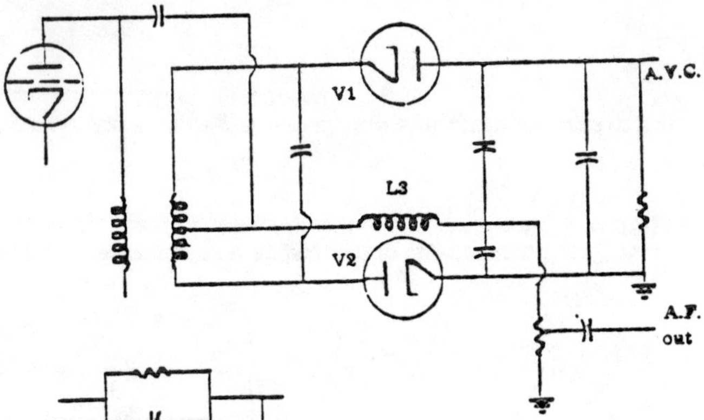

28. The circuit below shows
    a. pre-emphasis.
    b. de-emphasis.
    c. tone control.
    d. half wave rectification.
    e. none of these.

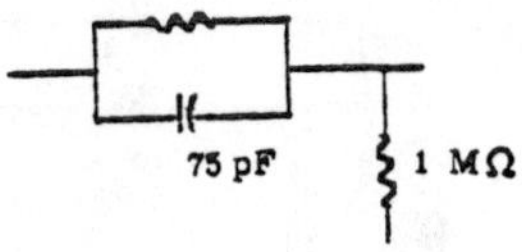

29. A Foster Seeley discriminator is used for
    a. an AM detector.
    b. producing a negative or positive control voltage.   d. low frequency amplification.
    c. high frequency amplification.   e. rectification.

30. A Foster Seeley discriminator in an FM receiver
    a. is fed by the output of a de-emphasis circuit.
    b. has a DC output voltage that is proportional to the input frequency.   d. is a good detector.
    c. decreases objectionable noises.   e. none of these.

31. The circuit shown is used for
    a. producing harmonics.
    b. scanning.
    c. injecting capacitance into an oscillator.
    d. reactance tube modulation.
    e. none of these.

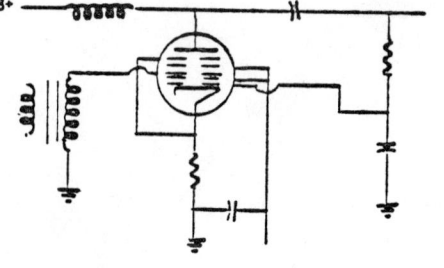

32. A public safety station operating with an output power of more than 3 watts on frequencies from 20 to 25 Mhz must maintain a frequency tolerance of
    a. .01%.
    b. .02%.   d. .04%.
    c. .03%.   e. .05%.

33. The frequency of a non-crystal controlled public safety station should be checked every
    a. 30 days.
    b. 60 days.   d. six months.
    c. 90 days.   e. year.

34. The frequency tolerance of a public safety fixed base station operating above 50 Mhz is
    a. .0005%.
    b. .002%.   d. .01%.
    c. .003%.   e. .02%.

35. If a 2Khz sine wave is used to modulate an FM transmitter, the sidebands will be separated
    a. 2Khz.
    b. 4Khz.   d. 6Khz.
    c. 5Khz.   e. none of these.

2. (short) If the screen requires a current of 5 ma and a potential of 150 V with a power supply voltage of 200 V, the screen dropping resistor should have a value of _____ ohms. Sec. 15-2.

9. (rises) The input power to the final stage of a transmitter is determined by multiplying the _____ times the _____ . Efficiency is the ratio of power _OUTPUT_ to power _INPUT_.   Sec. 15-6.

16. (parallel) The predominant harmonic (whole number multiple of input frequency) present in the output of a push pull RF amplifier is the _____ (second or third) harmonic. Sec. 15-9.

23. (inductive or transformer) The coupling method shown is_CAPACITIVE_coupling. Sec. 15-11.   OR IMPEDANCE

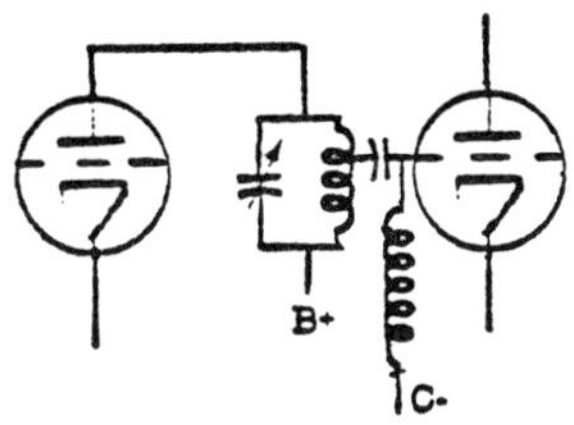

30. (plate) When using plate neutralization, the plate tank coil is _____ for applying B+. If B+ was applied to the bottom of the coil, this would put an RF ground at the bottom of the coil and there would be no_____ for neutralization. Sec. 15-13.

37. (neon) If the grid meter of a triode R.F. amplifier fluctuates when the plate circuit tank capacitor is tuned through resonance, the amplifier is not _____ . Sec. 15-16.

44. (216 Khz) If 3 cycles are completed in 1/50 of a second, the frequency is_____ hz. Sec. 15-22.

13. The modulation percentage of a Public Safety station using more than three watts should be checked
    a. every 30 days.
    b. every 60 days.   d. every six months.
    c. every 90 days.   e. none of these.

14. De-emphasis is used in a (an)
    a. AM detector.
    b. FM detector.   d. AM receiver.
    c. AM transmitter.   e. super regenerative receiver.

15. In both AM and FM transmitters, the % modulation is determined by the
    a. amplitude of the audio.
    b. frequency of the audio.   d. type of antenna used.
    c. frequency response.   e. RF frequency.

16. The circuit shown below is the circuit of a
    a. peak limiter.
    b. FM discriminator.
    c. ratio detector.
    d. voltage doubler.
    e. squelch system.

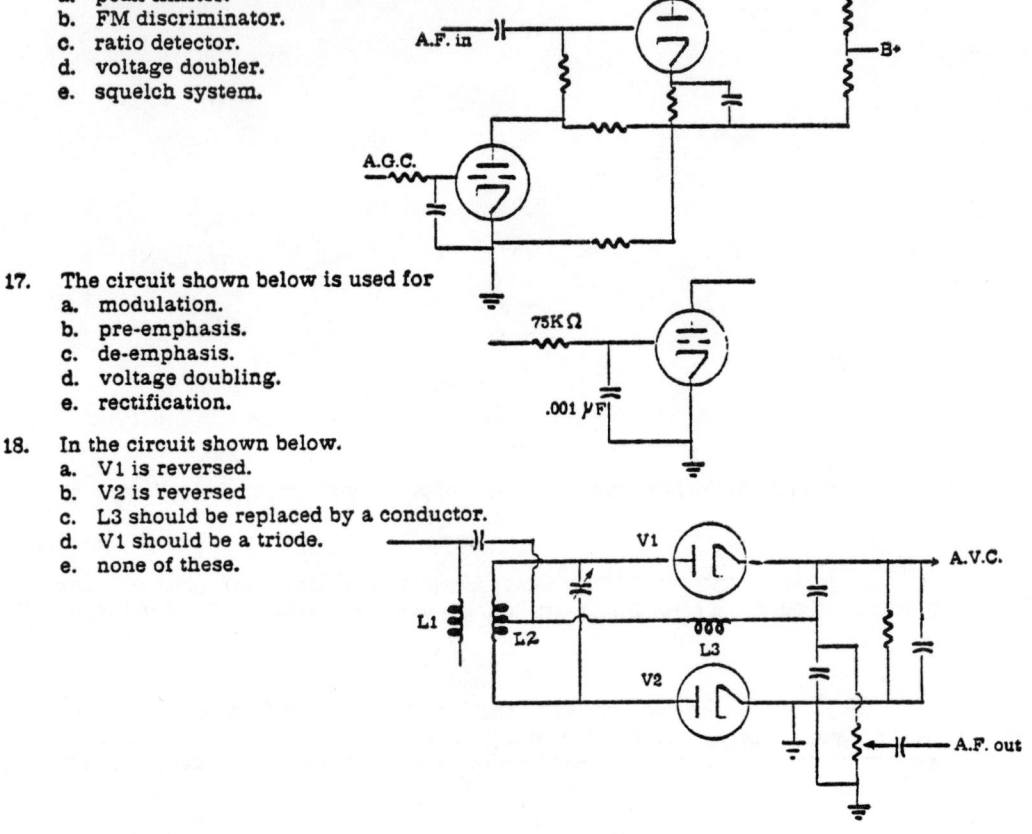

17. The circuit shown below is used for
    a. modulation.
    b. pre-emphasis.
    c. de-emphasis.
    d. voltage doubling.
    e. rectification.

18. In the circuit shown below.
    a. V1 is reversed.
    b. V2 is reversed
    c. L3 should be replaced by a conductor.
    d. V1 should be a triode.
    e. none of these.

19. In FM broadcasting a frequency swing of plus or minus 60 Khz represents a modulation percentage of
    a. 50.
    b. 60.   d. 80.
    c. 75.   e. none of these.

20. The advantage of Narrow Band FM over wide band FM is
    a. it has a better signal to noise ratio.
    b. it uses a shorter antenna.   d. it covers a wider spectrum.
    c. it has 8 times the audio punch.   e. none of these.

21. If you are aligning a mobile FM receiver with a limiter and discriminator you would first introduce your signal at
    a. the antenna.
    b. 1st IF amplifier.   d. the power amplifier.
    c. the last limiter IF amplifier.   e. the mixer.

22. Interference to a car radio that occurs only when the car is moving would likely be caused by
    a. ignition.
    b. electrostatic charge picked up on the tires.   d. the spark plugs.
    c. the generator.   e. the distributor.

23. Interference to an auto radio is produced by
    a. the ignition.
    b. the generator.   d. spark plugs.
    c. tire friction.   e. all the above.

3.　(10K) All ground leads of an R.F. amplifier must be brought to＿＿＿＿＿and kept physically short. Sec. 15-2.

10.　(plate power supply voltage, plate current, output, input) If there is insufficient grid excitation, the grid will not be driven ＿＿＿＿＿ and will not draw current. Sec. 15-7.

17.　(third) Whereas like electrodes are tied together in a parallel RF amplifier, the＿＿＿＿＿ are connected to opposite ends of a center tapped input tuned circuit and the＿＿＿＿＿ are connected to opposite ends of a center tapped output tuned circuit in push pull circuits. Sec. 15-9.

24.　(capacitive or impedance) The coupling method shown is ＿＿＿＿＿ coupling. Sec. 15-11.

31.　(center tapped, feedback) The neutralization method shown is＿＿＿＿＿neutralization. Sec. 15-14.

38.　(neutralized) In order to neutralize the circuit shown it would be necessary to connect a variable capacitor between＿＿＿ and ＿＿＿;
and＿＿＿＿＿and＿＿＿＿＿
Sec. 15-17.

45.　(150 hz) To prevent hum modulation in the output of an R.F. amplifier using direct cathodes, the grid and plate returns are connected to the filament transformer＿＿＿＿＿. Sec. 15-23.

1. The deviation ratio for NBFM would normally be
   a. 2.85.
   b. 5.   d. 7.
   c. 1.66.   e. 9.

2. Deviation ratio is defined as
   a. the ratio of the maximum RF swing to the maximum modulating audio frequency.
   b. the ratio of the maximum modulating audio frequency to the maximum RF swing.
   c. the product of the maximum RF swing and the modulating audo frequency.
   d. the deviation of the carrier frequency.
   e. none of these.

3. Before a Public Safety Radio Service station is established, it is necessary to
   a. check with the F.A.A. to determine the need.
   b. have $100,000 in escrow.   d. all of the above.
   c. submit F.C.C. form 400 for radio station authorization.   e. none of the above.

4. In the circuit shown below
   a. V1 is reversed.
   b. V2 is reversed.
   c. L3 is superfluous.
   d. V1 should be a triode.
   e. the grounding is wrong.

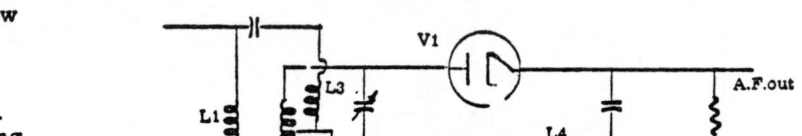

5. A reactance tube modulator changes the frequency of an oscillator by
   a. changing oscillator grid resistance.
   b. changing the oscillator plate voltage.
   c. injecting inductive or capacitive reactance in the oscillator tuned circuit.
   d. changing the oscillator cathode voltage.
   e. none of these.

6. Pre-emphasis is used in FM broadcasting to
   a. give extra amplification to audio frequencies above 2,000 cycles.
   b. attenuate audio frequencies above 2,000 cycles.   d. detect FM signals.
   c. modulate the oscillator.   e. provide phase inversion.

7. De-emphasis is used in the FM receiver to
   a. detect an FM signal.
   b. modulate FM.   d. amplify FM signals of certain frequencies.
   c. properly phase FM.   e. to compensate for pre-emphasis.

8. The frequency of a crystal controlled Public Safety station using more than three watts should be checked every
   a. 30 days.
   b. 60 days.   d. six months.
   c. 90 days.   e. year.

9. The maximum permitted power output for a Public Service base station is
   a. 3 watts.
   b. 60 watts.   d. 2,000 watts.
   c. 1,000 watts. e. 5,000 watts.

10. Public Safety Radio Service stations using amplitude modulation should maintain modulation peaks of at least
    a. 50%.
    b. 70%.   d. 90%.
    c. 85%.   e. 100%.

11. A 25Khz frequency deviation of an FM signal caused by a 5Khz audio tone represents a deviation ratio of
    a. 1 2/3.
    b. 5.   d. 6.
    c. 10.   e. 75.

12. In the example of #11, there would be 8 significant sidebands and a total bandwidth of
    a. 10 Khz.
    b. 240 Khz.
    c. 25 Khz.
    d. 50 Khz.
    e. 80 Khz.

4. **(one point)** Small signal RF amplifiers are operated class_____ and RF power amplifiers are operated class_____. Sec. 15-3.

11. **(positive)** The value of grid leak bias is determined by the excitation and the size of the _____ resistor. If a transmitter tube using grid leak biasing becomes inoperative and very hot, this indicates loss of _____. Sec. 15-7.

18. **(grids, plates)** If DC plate current flows through the coil of the tuned tank circuit, the circuit is said to be_____ fed. If the DC plate current flows through a radio frequency choke without going through the coil of the tuned circuit, the circuit is said to be_____ fed. Sec. 15-10.

25. **(link)** Common cathode triode RF amplifiers with input and output on the same frequency require _____ to prevent self_____. Sec. 15-12.

32. **(grid)** The C- bias must be applied to the grid tank coil at the _____ in order to avoid RF grounding of the bottom of the coil. Sec. 15-14.

39. **(A,D; B,C)** Since the plate circuit is not tuned to the same frequency as the input in a frequency doubler it is not necessary to_____the stage. Sec. 15-21.

46. **(center tap)** In this circuit there is no need for_____. Sec. 15-24.

Class A grounded grid amplifier

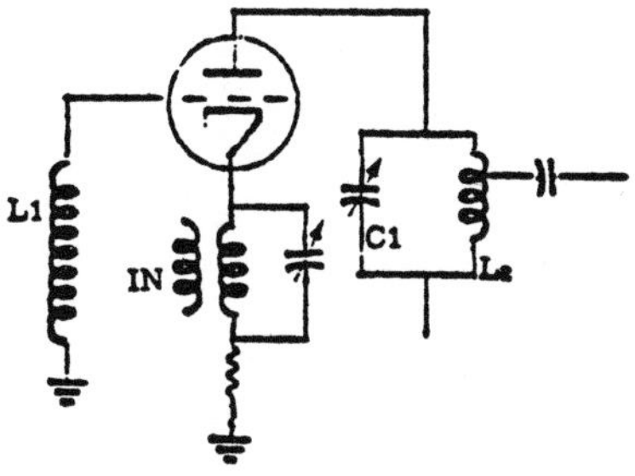

4. (amplitude)   In FM broadcasting a deviation of 60 Khz represents a % modulation of _____ % . Sec. 19-3.

8. (8, 240 Khz, modulating audio) If a 3 Khz sine wave is used to modulate an FM transmitter, the sidebands will be spaced _____ Khz apart. Sec. 19-3.

12. (V2, L1, ground). Read all paragraphs 19-7.

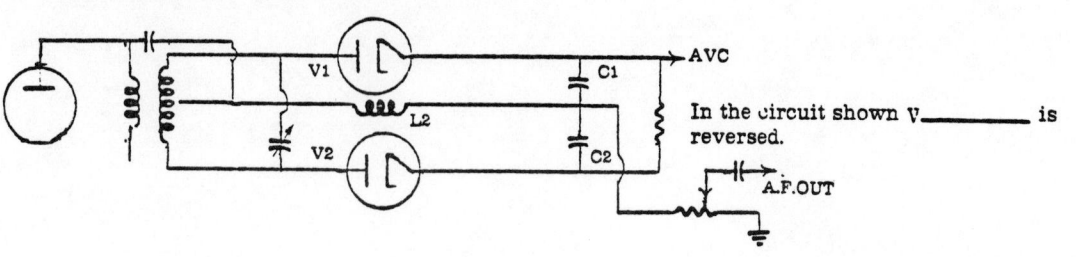

In the circuit shown V_____ is reversed.

16. (high - above 2000 hz)   A pre-emphasis circuit is a _____ pass filter consisting of a _____ capacitance shunted by a _____ . Sec. 19-10.

20. (noise, squelch) The circuit shown is that of a _____ circuit. When there is no carrier input to the receiver the AVC voltage is _____ and V_____ is cut off. Sec. 19-11.

24. (capacitive, inductive) See Figure 19-15. The 100 K ohm resistor and the 50 pF capacitor constitute a phase shifting network. This provides a lagging voltage to the oscillator and in effect provides _____ reactance. Inverting the phase shift, network would provide capacitive reactance to the oscillator LC circuit. Sec. 19-13.

28. (diodes) Although low noise results using narrow band FM with weak signals, wide band FM has a better overall signal to noise ratio. A better signal to noise ratio can be obtained in FM by use of _____ _____ FM. (Using a wide frequency swing). Sec. 19-17.

32. (20 Khz, 5 Khz)   The maximum power output for a public safety station (base) is_____ watts. Sec. 19-19.

36. (.0005%) Public Safety transmitters using more than 3 watts should be checked for input_____ to the final stage, _____ of the carrier, and _____ percentage. This should be done when it is first licensed, whenever a change is made, and at least once a _____ . The frequency of non crystal controlled transmitters must be checked every 30 days. Sec. 19-19.

40. (final, approval, acceptance) Interference that occurs only when the car is moving is caused by _____ _____ . Sec. 19-21.

44. (spark plug) This concludes the recheck of unit 19.

5.   (A, C) In normal class C RF amplifier (condition 4), the RF signal induces a voltage having a peak value _____ than the bias voltage. Sec. 15-4.

12. (grid leak, grid excitation) Because of this danger, many class C amplifiers use either an external bias supply or some _____ bias. Sec. 15-7.

19. (series, shunt) The radio frequency choke in the shunt fed circuit of Fig. 15-9b is used as a load to develop an A.C. voltage drop which is coupled to the tuned circuit. If the turns in the RFC were shorted out, this would change the plate load and the R.F.output would _____ .

26. (neutralization, oscillation) It is not necessary, in most cases, to neutralize_____ or _____tubes. Sec. 15-12.

33. (center tap) In the RF amplifier shown the neutralizing path should use a _____ instead of a _____ . Sec. 15-14.

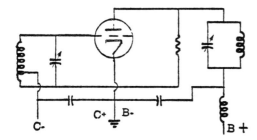

40. (neutralize) Two tubes can be used in a frequency doubler if they are connected in _____ but not in _____ . Sec. 15-21.

47. (L₁) In this circuit _____ should be replaced by a conductor. Sec. 15-24.

Class A G.G.Amplifer

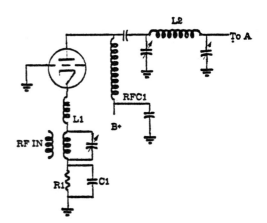

3. **(75 Khz)** % modulation in both AM and FM is determined by the _____ of the audio. Sec. 19-3.

7. **(5 or 75 Khz/15 Khz, 1 2/3 or 5 Khz/3 Khz)** With a deviation ratio of 5, there will be _____ significant sidebands. With a modulation audio of 15 Khz and 75 Khz deviation, the possible sideband width would be _____ Khz. The sidebands are created by the _____ power. Sec. 19-3.

11. **(frequency)** In the circuit shown _____ is reversed, _____ is superfluous, and the _____ is connected to the wrong point. Sec. 19-61.

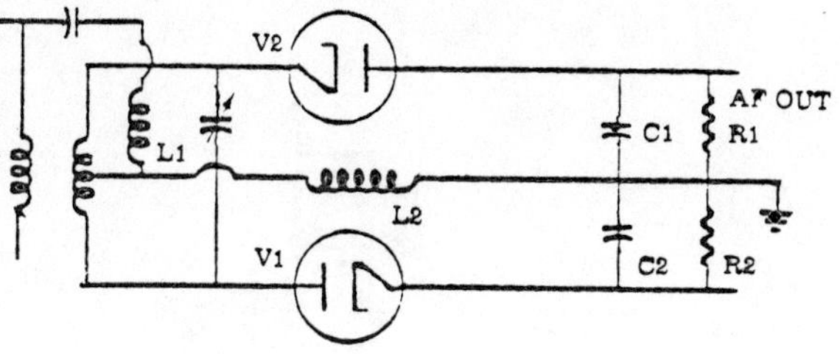

15. **(low)** Pre-emphasis improves the signal to noise ratio of _____ modulating audio frequencies. Sec. 19-10.

19. **(pre-emphasis, low, 75 microseconds)** FM receivers produce considerable _____ when no carrier is being received. To prevent this a _____ circuit is used. Sec. 19-11.

23. **(maximum)** The reactance tube modulator changes the frequency of an oscillator by injecting _____ or _____ reactance across the oscillator LC circuit. Sec. 19-13.

27. **(reactance tube, inductance or inductive reactance)** The variable bias provided by an audio signal provides a variable junction capacitance when using Varactor or Varicap _____ . Sec. 19-14.

31. **(amplitude, third, first)** The authorized bandwidth for narrow band FM modulation (25 to 450 Mhz) is _____ Khz with a _____ Khz deviation. Sec. 19-19.

35. **(99%)** The frequency tolerance of a public safety fixed base station operating above 50 Mhz is _____ %. Sec. 19-19.

39. **(30)** The first step in tuning an FM mobile transmitter is to open up the _____ plate circuit. Licensed transmitting equipment is said to have _____ if the F.C.C. tests its characteristics and _____ if the F.C.C. accepts the manufacturers data. Sec. 19-20.

43. **(ignition)** The major source of ignition noise is from the _____ . Sec. 19-21.

6. (greater) Plate current flows for less than _____ of the input cycle in a Class C amplifier. Class C efficiency is _____ with _____ distortion. Sec. 15-4.

13. (cathode resistor) Electron flow through the grid leak R^1 would be from the _____ to the _____ . If capacitor C^1 was shorted out, there would be no _____ and plate current would _____ excessively. Sec. 15-7.

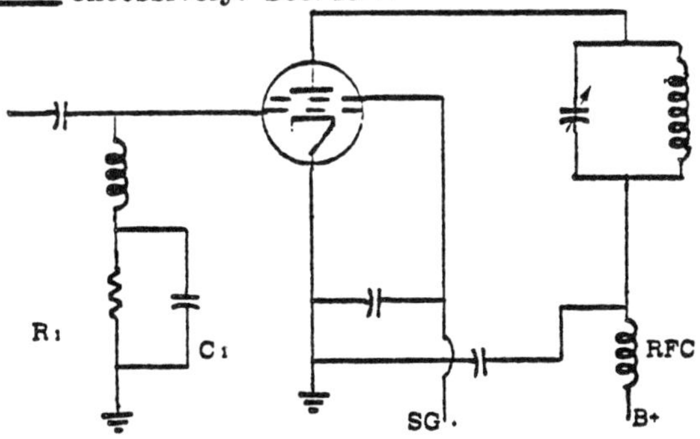

R_1 C_1 SG.   RFC   B+

20. (decrease) _____ coupling is useful to couple circuits that are widely separated. Sec. 15-11.

27. (tetrode, pentode) A _____ resistance will not only provide neutralization at the frequency to which the amplifier is tuned but will prevent _____ oscillations. Sec. 15-12.

34. (capacitor, resistor) In the diagram shown, there is no need to use _____ . Sec. 15-12.

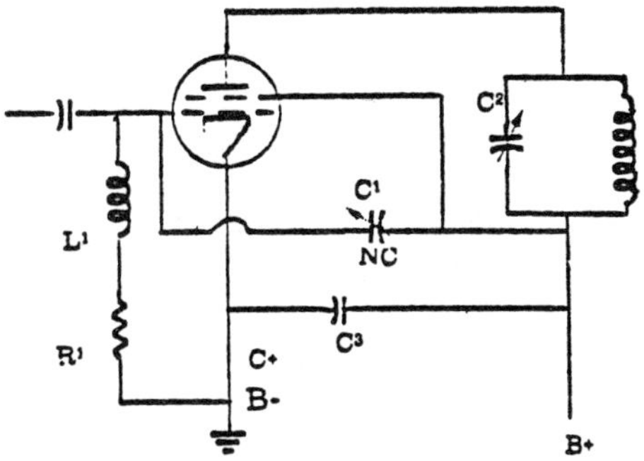

C^2 C^1 NC L^1 R^1 C+ B- C^3 B+

41. (parallel, push pull) High harmonic output requires high _____ voltage, high _____ voltage, high plate voltage and a high _____ tank circuit. Sec. 15-21.

48. (L^1) The grid in a grounded grid RF amplifier is either at ground DC potential or at _____ ground potential. Therefore, there is no need to _____ an RF grounded grid amplifier. Sec. 15-24.

2.   (amplitude)   100% modulation in FM broadcasting is defined as a deviation of plus or minus _____ Khz. Sec. 19-3.

6.   (deviation, modulation) The deviation ratio in FM broadcasting is _____ . In narrow band frequency modulation the maximum deviation is 5 Khz and the maximum audio frequency is 3 Khz. The deviation ratio would be _____ . Sec. 19-13. Frame 12

10.   (FM, control voltage) The output voltage of the discriminator is proportional to the change in input _____ . Sec. 19-6.

14.   (limiter) It is usual to use a _____ Mu pentode tube in a limiter stage. Sec. 19-9.

18.   (pre-emphasis, 75 microseconds) See the de-emphasis circuit in dotted lines of Fig. 19-6b. A de-emphasis circuit is used at the receiver to compensate for _____ at the transmitter. It is a _____ pass filter with a _____ microsecond time constant. Sec. 19-10.

22.   (limiter) If a voltmeter is connected across the IF secondary for tuning, preceeding circuits should be tuned for _____ voltage indication. Sec. 19-12.

26.   (automatic frequency control) The circuit shown is a _____ modulator used for injecting _____ into an oscillator circuit. Sec. 19-13.

30.   (phase, audio) The frequency swing of an FM signal is measured by measuring the _____ of the discriminator audio output. An operator performing routine duties needs only a _____ _____ class license with a B.C. endorsement. Except for educational FM stations a daily inspection of transmitting & monitoring equipment must be made by the holder of a _____ class license.

34.   (.01%) The band width of a public safety transmission is considered to be that of the band of frequency containing _____% of the emitted energy of the transmitter. Sec. 19-19.

38.   (70%) A Public Safety station can be tested any time service is required. Identification of a Public Safety station should be made at least every _____ minutes. Sec. 19-19.

42.   (capacitor) The major source of noise in a mobile receiver is from the _____ system. Sec. 19-21.

7. (half, high, high) The plate current in an R.F. amplifier decreases as the tank circuit is tuned to resonance because a parallel tuned circuit has a _____ impedance at resonance and a _____ impedance off resonance. Sec. 15-5.

14. (grid, ground, grid bias, rise) To produce twice the power output possible from one tube, two tubes may be connected in _____ or _____ . Sec. 15-8.

21. (link) The transfer of harmonics is minimized by the use of _____ coupling. Sec. 15-11.

28. (losser, parasitic) The neutralizing capacitor must have a value of capacitance equal to the _____ capacitance of the tube. Sec. 15-13.

35. (C_1 - it's not necessary to neutralize a tetrode) The first step in neutralizing a triode RF amplifier is to turn off the _____. Sec. 15-15.

42. (bias, driving, Q) The push push doubler uses two tubes with the grids connected in _____ and the plates in _____ . Sec. 15-21.

49. (R.F., neutralize) Radio frequency energy must be kept out of power supplies for two reasons. 1. High values of R.F. energy might burn out filter capacitors. 2. R.F. energy in a power supply could be fed back to previous stages and cause unwanted oscillations.
There are two decoupling components used to prevent RF from reaching the power supply.

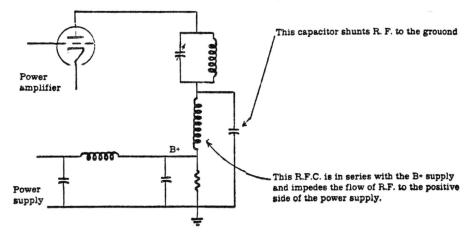

This capacitor shunts R. F. to the grouond

Power amplifier

B+

Power supply

This R.F.C. is in series with the B+ supply and impedes the flow of R.F. to the positive side of the power supply.

Radio frequency from an amplifier is kept out of the power supply by using a _____ in series with the high voltage plus lead or a _____ in shunt (parallel) with the power supply.

RECHECK PROGRAMMED INSTRUCTION USING SHRADER'S ELECTRONIC COMMUNICATION

1.   FM receivers are not sensitive to_____variations and static. Sec. 19-1.

5.   (80%) The ratio of the maximum deviation to the maximum audio frequency used is called _____ ratio. The ratio of the maximum deviation to a particular audio frequency is called _____ index.

9.   (3 Khz) The Foster Seeley descriminator is used as an _____detector and for producing a negative or positive _____ _____ from a change in frequency. Sec. 19-6.

13. (V_1) The AM portion of an FM signal is eliminated by the_____ . Sec. 19-9.

17. (high, series, resistance) The circuit shown is a_____ circuit. It has a time constant of_____ micro-seconds. Sec. 19-10.

.001 μF
75K
2K Ω

21. (squelch, low, V_1) If you are aligning a mobile FM receiver with a limiter and a discriminator, you would first introduce your signal to the grid of the last_____ I. F. stage. Sec. 19-12.

25. (inductive) A discriminator is used with direct FM for_____ . This stabilizes the FM transmitter frequency. Sec. 19-13.

29. (wide band) In indirect phase FM modulation, the modulator comes between the oscillator and the multipliers. Less audio power is requied for 100% modulation in indirect modulation.

The circuit shown is a _____ modulator. The advantage of indirect FM modulation is that it takes less _____ power. Sec. 19-17. Fig. 19-20a.

OSC.
B+
B+

33. (2000 watts) A Public Safety station using an output power of 3 watts or more in a frequency band from 20-25 Mhz must maintain a frequency tolerance of _____%. Sec. 19-19.

37. (power, frequency, modulation, year) A station using FM in the Public Safety service should maintain modulation peaks of at least_____%. Sec. 19-19.

41. (Wheel Static) If the frequency of intereference to an auto radio receiver increased as the car speed increased, it would be well to put a_____between generator armature and ground. Sec. 19-21.

239

1.   To check neutralization of a triode RF amplifier one should use
     a. a wattmeter.
     b. a tachometer.   d. a Strobescope.
     c. a potentiometer. e. a neon bulb.

2.   A class C amplifier is noted for
     a. a small driving requirement.
     b. low bias.   d. high fidelity.
     c. distorted output. e. low efficiency.

3.   Link coupling is especially useful for coupling when components are
     a. located close to each other.
     b. widely separated. d. within tolerance.
     c. running hot.   e. used in AF circuits.

4.   In the circuit below
     a. the output would be on a frequency twice the input.
     b. the output frequency would be the same as the input.
     c. a push pull circuit is illustrated.
     d. a push push circuit is illustrated.
     e. there would be no output.

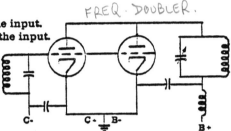

FREQ. DOUBLER.

5.   The input power to the final stage of a transmitter is determined by
     a. dividing the input voltage by the input current.
     b. multiplying the input voltage by the input plate current.
     c. dividing the plate voltage of the preceeding stage by the final plate current.
     d. a wattmeter.
     e. none of these.

6.   One triode RF amplifier that need not be neutralized is the
     a. push pull amplifier.
     b. common cathode circuit. d. class C RF amplifier.
     c. grounded grid amplifier. e. thermo trockle circuit.

7.   In the circuit shown, there is no need for
     a. L1.
     b. L2.
     c. L3.
     d. C1.
     e. C2.

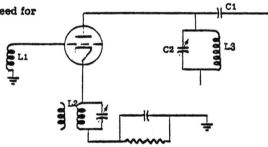

8.   In order to neutralize the circuit below it would be necessary to connect a variable capacitor between
     a. x and y.
     b. x and ground.
     c. b and ground.
     d. a and b.
     e. (x and b) and (a and y)

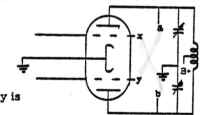

9.   If 3 cycles are completed in 1/50 of a second, the frequency is
     a. 250 cycles/second.
     b. 150 hz.   d. 50 Hz.
     c. 167 hz.   e. 100 hz.

10. In the circuit below it would be necessary to
     a. remove L5.
     b. remove C2.
     c. remove the ground and run B+ to L3.
     d. remove L2.
     e. none of these.

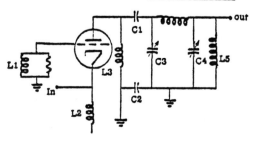

9. **(7.5)** In addition to the deviation of the carrier, we must consider sidebands. Just as in amplitude modulation an upper and lower sideband is generated when an audio frequency beats with an RF frequency, sidebands are created in frequency modulation. Not only the fundamental audio tones beat with the R.F. to create sidebands, but so do the audio harmonics. let us consider what happens if 2 Khz of audio having 2nd and 3rd harmonics beat with 100 mhz:

100 Mhz		USB 100.002 Mhz	Up 2 Khz
2 Khz	→	100 Mhz	
		LSB 99.998 Mhz	Down 2 Khz

100 Mhz		USB 100.004 Mhz	Up 4 Khz
4 Khz	→	100 Mhz	
(2nd harmonic)		LSB 99.996 Mhz	Down 4 Khz

100 Mhz		USC 100.006 Mhz	Up 6 Khz
6 Khz	→	100 Mhz	
(3rd harmonic)		LSB 99.994 Mhz	Down 6 Khz

In this example three upper sidebands and three lower side bands are generated. Note the graphic representation.

6 Khz USB (carrier + 6 Khz) created by 3rd harmonic
4 Khz USB (carrier + 4 Khz) created by 2nd harmonic
2 Khz USB (carrier + 2 Khz) created by fundamental
Carrier
2 Khz LSB (carrier - 2 Khz)
4 Khz LSB (carrier - 4 Khz)
6 Khz LSB (carrier - 6 Khz)

The total bandwidth in the example above would be_____Khz. If a 3 Khz audio frequency sine wave with its harmonics is used to modulate an FM transmitter, the sidebands will be spaced _____ Khz apart.

18. **(low, V_1)** A receiver with a squelch circuit cannot receive_____signals.

27. **(2000)** Because of the importance of public safety stations, they should be continuously maintained. The law allows for testing at any time that service is required. A public safety station should be tested when _____ is required.

36. **(capacitor, armature)** Some interference can be eliminated in mobile reception by using receivers with highly selective circuits. Mobile receiver interference can be reduced by using _____ circuits.

11. In the diagram below it would be necessary to
    a. remove L5.
    b. remove C2.
    c. replace L3 with a conductor.
    d. replace C1 with a conductor.
    e. neutralize the amplifier.

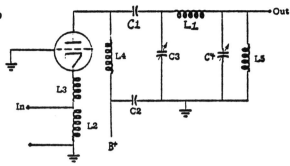

12. The predominant harmonic present in the output of a push pull RF amplifier is the
    a. second.
    b. third.   d. fifth.
    c. fourth.   e. sixth.

13. Radio frequency from an amplifier is kept out of the power supply by using
    a. a capacitor in series with the high voltage plus load.
    b. a capacitor across the power supply.   d. a filter shoke.
    c. an RF choke in shunt with the power supply.   e. none of these.

14. The oscillator of a transmitter having two doublers and three triplers drifts 2 Khz. The drift in the output frequency would be   A   27
    a. 36 Khz
    b. 73 Khz   d. 216 Khz
    c. 108 Khz   e. none of these.

15. RF can be kept out of a B supply battery by using
    a. a capacitor in series with the supply lines.
    b. an RF choke in series with the suppy lines.   d. positive ground.
    c. an RF choke across the battery.   e. neutralization.

16. The neutralization system used in the diagram below is
    a. plate.
    b. cross over.
    c. grid.
    d. push pull.
    e. losser.

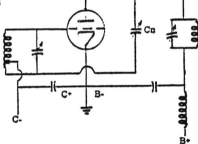

17. If the turns in an RFC used in the plate circuit of a shunt fed RF amplifier were shorted out
    a. this would change the plate load.
    b. this would keep RF out of the power supply.   d. harmonics would reappear.
    c. this would result in more RF output.   e. none of these.

18. In the diagram below the screen grid connection is
    a. correct.
    b. wrong, it should be connected to cathode.
    c. wrong, it should be connected to plate.
    d. wrong, it should be connected to an SG plus voltage.
    e. wrong, it should be connected to the suppressor.

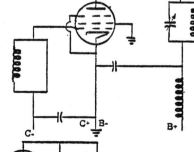

19. In the RF amplifier below the neutralization path
    a. should use a capacitor rather than a resistor.
    b. should use a choke rather than a resistor.
    c. should be a short circuit.
    d. is correct.
    e. none of these.

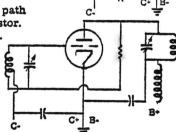

8. **(1 2/3)** The ratio of the maximum deviation in FM transmissions to a particular audio frequency is called modulation index. By formula:

$$\text{Modulation index} = \frac{\text{maximum deviation (100\% modulation)}}{\text{audio frequency used}}$$

If 10,000 hz audio was used for a test in FM broadcasting, the modulation index would be

17. **(V_1, amplitude)** Noise impulses and weak signals cause a receiver to provide high voltage gain (see page 223 in Unit 18). A squelch circuit will cut off a stage during periods when no signal is being received. This will eliminate noisy static during standby periods. It also prevents the reception of weak signals. An audio squelch circuit is shown:

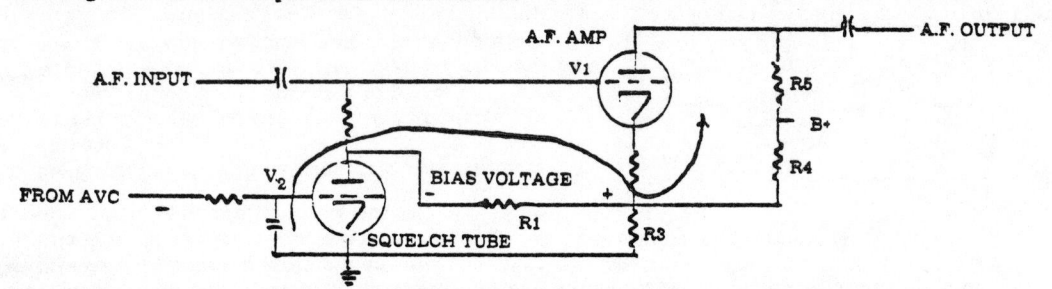

When no carrier (or weak signal) is present the low negative AVC voltage on the grid of V_2 permits high plate current to flow through R_1 on its way to B+. The high voltage drop across R_1 provides high negative bias on V_1 and cuts the tube off. There will be no A.F. output noise as weak signals are squelched.

When a normal signal is being received the AVC voltage is high negative and cuts V_2 off. V_1 is now biased as a class A amplifier by a voltage divider resistance network. V_1 now acts as a normal audio amplifier.

When there is no carrier input to the receiver, the AVC voltage to the squelch tube is negative and V_____ is cut off.

26. **(70%)** The law permits mobile transmitters in the public safety service to have power ratings of up to 60 watts. Public safety base transmitters may have power capabilities to 2000 watts. The maximum power output for a public safety base station is _____ watts.

35. **(resistance)** Generator hash can be reduced by the use of a _____ between the generator _____ and ground.

20. A single ended RF amplifier using a triode and no neutralization could be used for
   a. a straight through frequency amplifier.
   b. a frequency doubler.
   c. a dynamometer.
   d. power amplifier.
   e. none of these.

21. A single ended class C RF stage is used for
   a. voltage dividers.
   b. harmonic reduction.
   c. a multivibrator.
   d. a frequency doubler.
   e. push pull operation.

22. RF nutralization isn't necessary for
   a. push pull amplifiers.
   b. triode amplifier.
   c. a two grid tube amplifier.
   d. VHF.
   e. UHF.

23. If the grid is not driven positive in a class C amplifier
   a. there is no grid excitation.
   b. the grid excitation is low.
   c. the grid excitation is high.
   d. the bias will be too high.
   e. it will draw current.

24. An amplifier with a sinusoidal waveform input has maximum efficiency when operated in
   a. class A.
   b. class B.
   c. class C.
   d. class AB.
   e. none of these.

25. The first step in neutralizing an RF amplifier is
   a. tune up the input circuit.
   b. tune the plate circuit for maximum output.
   c. tune neutralizing capacitor for no output.
   d. disconnect the plate supply B+ lead.
   e. none of these.

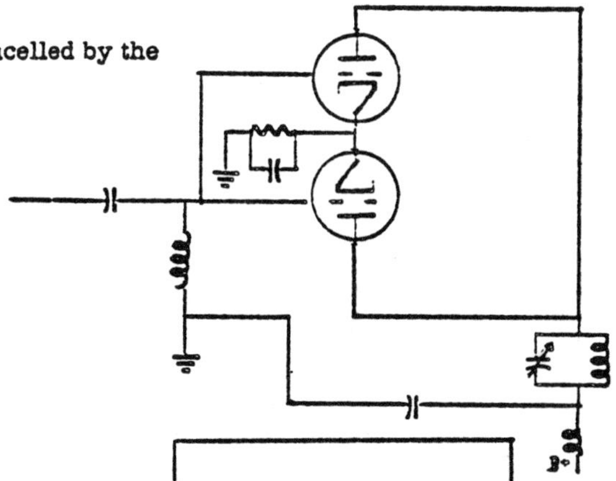

26. Second harmonic energy is effectively cancelled by the
   a. parallel RF amplifier.
   b. push pull RF amplifier.
   c. push push RF amplifier.
   d. frequency doubler.
   e. grounded grid amplifier.

27. The circuit shown is used for
   a. push pull amplification.
   b. push push amplification.
   c. parallel operation.
   d. all the above.
   e. none of these.

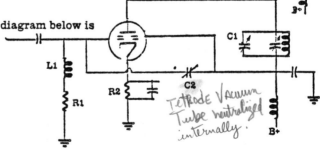

28. The component not needed in the diagram below is
   a. R1.
   b. L1.
   c. C1.
   d. C2.
   e. R2.

Tetrode Vacuum Tube neutralized internally.

29. When an amplifier tube tank circuit is tuned through resonance the grid current peaks. This indicates
   a. low plate voltage.
   b. antenna coupling is too loose.
   c. excessive RF drive.
   d. the tube inter electrode capacity is not neutralized.
   e. none of these.

30. In the circuit shown a short in C1 would cause
   a. M1 to pin backwards.
   b. M1 to burn out.
   c. M2 to read low.
   d. the tube plate to get red hot.
   e. excessive drive.

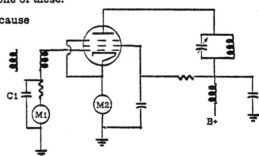

185

7.   (5) In narrow band FM transmissions the maximum deviation is 5 Khz and the maximum audio frequency used for speech is 3 Khz, the deviation ratio for narrow band FM transmissions is _____.

16.   (limiter, low) Another popular FM detector is the **Ratio Detector.**

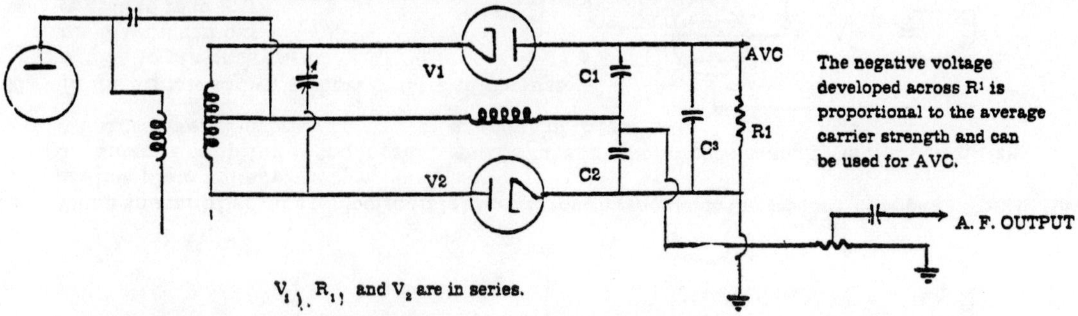

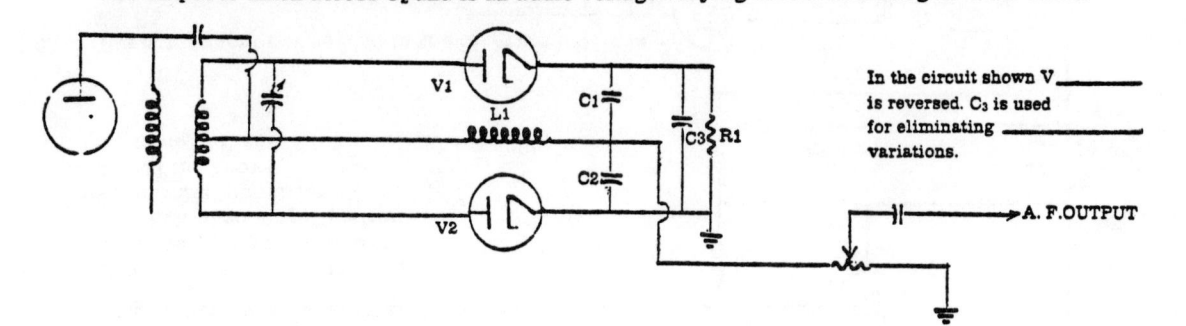

The negative voltage developed across R¹ is proportional to the average carrier strength and can be used for AVC.

V_{1}, R_{1}, and V_{2} are in series.

Amplitude variations are filtered out by C_3 so that the ratio detector requires no limiter.
At the center frequency the voltages across C_1 and C_2 are equal.
Above the center frequency E_{C2} will be higher than E_{C1}.
Below the center frequency E_{C1} will be higher than E_{C2}.
The output is taken across C_2 and is an audio voltage varying around some negative DC value.

In the circuit shown V_____ is reversed. C_3 is used for eliminating _____ variations.

A. F. OUTPUT

25.   (30) Amplitude modulated public safety stations should maintain modulation to a minimum of 70%.

AM public safety stations must maintain modulation percentages of at least _____%.

34.   (tires) Spark plug and ignition noise can be reduced by using _____ in spark plug and ignition coil lead.

236

31. In the circuit below it would be necessary to
    a. remove L5.
    b. remove C2.
    c. replace L1 with a conductor.
    d. remove L2.
    e. none of these.

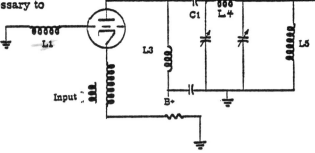

32. When the RF final amplifier is turned through resonance the grid meter peaks. The peaking indicates
    a. overmodulation.
    b. insufficient RF excitation.
    c. the stage is not neutralized.
    d. over excitation.
    e. under modulation.

33. If a transmitter tube using gridleak biasing became inoperative and very hot, this probably indicates
    a. excessive drive.
    b. loss of excitation and biasing.
    c. excessive bias.
    d. the tube is neutralized.
    e. none of these.

34. The plate current in an RF amplifier decreases as the tank circuit is tuned to resonance because
    a. the plate load impedance increases.
    b. the plate load impedance decreases.
    c. the stage is not neutralized.
    d. the state is neutralized.
    e. of split tuning.

35. In replacing components in RF circuits
    a. make several ground returns.
    b. don't touch soldered points.
    c. keep leads short.
    d. work with power on.
    e. none of these.

36. As the plate circuit of a tube using an indirect cathode is tuned through resonance
    a. the heater current dips.
    b. the heater current rises.
    c. the plate current dips.
    d. the plate current rises.
    e. none of these.

37. Electron flow in the grid circuit of a grid leak biased tube is
    a. from ground to grid.
    b. from grid through the grid leak to ground.
    c. from grid to plate.
    d. from grid to screen grid.
    e. not possible.

38. The slugs shown in the circuit below are used for
    a. coupling.
    b. tuning the circuits to resonance.
    c. decoupling.
    d. frequency doubling.
    e. none of these.

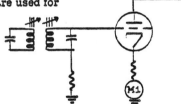

39. When the circuits preceeding the R.F. amplifier shown above are tuned to resonance
    a. M1 will peak.
    b. M1 will dip.
    c. M1 will remain unchanged.
    d. M1 will be pinned backwards.
    e. none of these.

40. The strongest harmonic in the output of a push pull RF amplifier is the
    a. second.
    b. third.
    c. fourth.
    d. fifth.
    e. sixth.

41. The screen grid dropping resistor in an IF amplifier circuit is burned out. It is known that the screen grid voltage should be 250 volts, the screen grid current 5 ma, and that the plate voltage should be 300 volts. The value of the screen grid dropping resistor should be
    a. 5 K ohms.
    b. 10 K ohms.
    c. 15 K ohms.
    d. 20 K ohms.
    e. none of these.

42. Plate current flows in a class C RF amplifier for
    a. entire input cycle.
    b. 1/2 input cycle.
    c. less than 1/2 input cycle.
    d. 3/4 input cycle.
    e. none of these.

6. **(wide band)** The ratio of the maximum deviation to the maximum audio frequency used is called deviation ratio. By formula

$$\text{Deviation Ratio} = \frac{\text{Maximum deviation (for 100\% modulation)}}{\text{Maximum audio frequency used}}$$

In wide band FM broadcasting the maximum deviation is 75 Khz and the maximum audio frequency for high fidelity reproduction is 15 Khz.

The deviation ratio for wideband FM broadcasting would be_____.

15. **(V_1, L_1, ground)** In order to insure that the output of the discriminator detector is the result of frequency deviation and not amplitude variations a limiter circuit must proceed the discriminator.

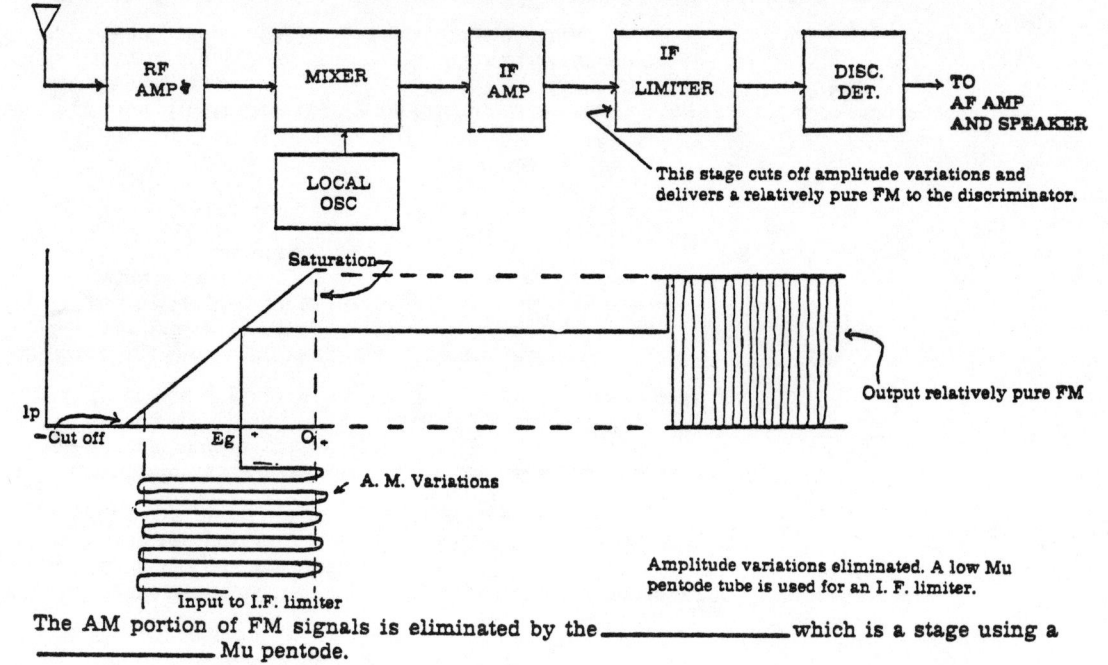

This stage cuts off amplitude variations and delivers a relatively pure FM to the discriminator.

Output relatively pure FM

Amplitude variations eliminated. A low Mu pentode tube is used for an I. F. limiter.

The AM portion of FM signals is eliminated by the_____which is a stage using a _____ Mu pentode.

24. **(year)** The frequency of a non crystal controlled public safety transmitter should be checked every _____ days.

33. **(ignition)** An interference present only while a mobile is in motion is caused by the pick up of static on the_____.

43. If the bias battery to an RF amplifier tube was reversed putting a positive voltage on the grid, the
    a. plate current would decrease.
    b. plate current would increase.   d. operation would be normal.
    c. there would be no output.   e. the stage would oscillate.

44. Grid leak bias works because
    a. the grid attracts electrons.
    b. the grid repels electrons.   d. it has very low resistance.
    c. it has infinite resistance.   e. none of these.

45. It is not necessary to neutralize an RF amplifier tube at high frequencies if
    a. a single ended triode is used.
    b. push pull triodes are used.
    c. triodes are shielded from all other stages.
    d. screen grid tubes are used.
    e. metal envelope tubes are used.

46. 600 meters has a wavelength is equivalent to
    a. 500 Khz.
    b. 600 Khz.   d. 1200 Khz.
    c. 300 Khz.   e. none of these.

47. The output current wave form of a class C amplifier has
    a. a DC component with AC characteristics.
    b. no distortion.   d. low amplitude.
    c. square wave characteristics.   e. none of these.

48. Class C works best with
    a. class A bias.
    b. linear amplifiers.   d. distorted output current waveform.
    c. sine wave output.   e. class B bias.

49. Grid leak bias is developed
    a. in the plate circuit.
    b. in class A amplifiers.   d. in the cathode circuit.
    c. using battery or power supply bias.   e. by use of proper time constant in the grid circuit.

50. If a push pull RF amplifier tunes erratically and one tube shows excessive color, the trouble might be
    a. high frequency parasitic oscillations.
    b. low B plus.   d. excessive modulation.
    c. an open coupling capacitor.   e. one side of the antenna is not grounded.

51. In the diagram below, there is no need for
    a. C1.
    b. C2.
    c. C3.
    d. C4.
    e. a and b above.

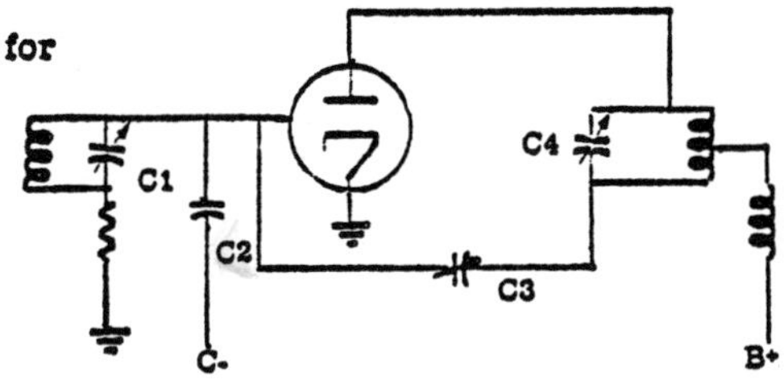

52. The wavelength of a 500 Mhz signal is
    a. 60 cm.
    b. .5 cm.   d. 1 meter.
    c. .06 cm. e. none of these.

53. The velocity of a radio wave in free space
    a. increases with frequency increase.
    b. decreases with frequency decrease.   d. increases with antenna height.
    c. increases with power.   e. is constant.

54. The plate voltage and the plate current to the final amplifier of a transmitter is 1230 volts and 325 ma. If the output power is 230 watts, the plate efficiency is approximately
    a. 56%.
    b. 63%   d. 75%.
    c. 68%. e. none of these.

55. As compared to a Class A amplifier, a Class C amplifier
    a. has less distortion.
    b. requires less driving power.
    c. operates over the linear portion of its characteristics curve.
    d. operates over a greater part of its characteristic curve.
    e. has less efficiency.

56. In a Class C vacuum tube amplifier, efficiency may run as high as
    a. 85%.
    b. 100%.   d. 200%.
    c. 50%.   e. 95%.

5. **(amplitude)** In narrow band frequency modulation for speech communications, the deviation is generally plus or minus 5 Khz for 100% modulation. The characteristics of N.B. FM are:

(1) It conserves spectrum. The bandwidth is 20 Khz.
(5 Khz up + 5 Khz down + 10 Khz guard channel).

(2) The signal to noise ratio is lower for N.B. FM. In other words wide band FM has a better signal to noise ratio.

A better signal to noise ratio can be obtained using_____FM.

14. **(FM, control)** The diode plates of the discriminator are connected to the opposite ends of the discriminator transformer secondary. The output is taken from the ungrounded cathode. These are two identifying features of the discriminator.

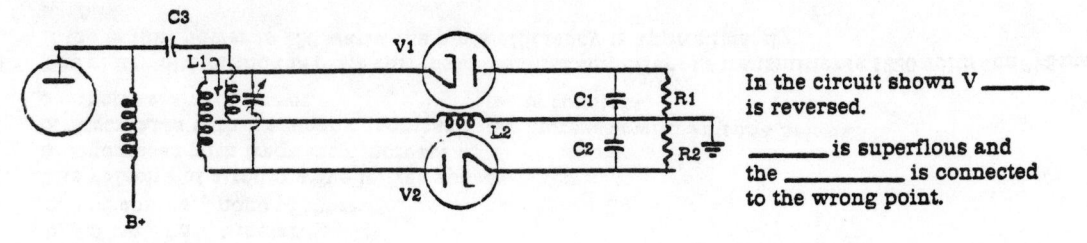

In the circuit shown V_____ is reversed.

_____is superflous and the _____ is connected to the wrong point.

23. **(.0005%, .01%)** With the initial installation and once every year crystal controlled public safety transmitters should be checked for:

1. Frequency (a non crystal controlled transmitter every 30 days).
2. Modulation %
3. Power.

These three same checks should be made when any change is made in a transmitter.

The power, frequency and modulation percentage of a public safety transmitter should be checked at least once every_____.

32. **(final or power amplifier)** Much of the interference to a mobile FM receiver is caused by:

(1) Spark plug and ignition noise. This is the most common source of interference. It can be cured by placing resistance in the spark plug and ignition coil leads.

(2) Generator hash. This can be eliminated by placing a capacitance between generator armature and ground. (.25 mfd usual).

(3) Static pickup on tires. This is only heard while the mobile unit is in motion. Hub cap discharge springs can be used to eliminate such interference.

The most common mobile receiver interference is from spark plug and _____ noise.

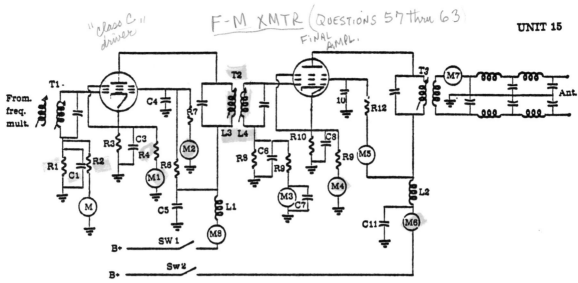

"class C" driver   F-M XMTR (QUESTIONS 57 thru 63)   UNIT 15
FINAL AMPL.

57. The coupling used between driver and final is
 a. single tuned coupling.
 b. impedance coupling.
 c. adjustable mutual inductance.
 d. individual adjustable inductance.
 e. capacitance coupling.

58. The driver for this FM transmitter is probably operated
 a. class A.
 b. class AB.
 c. class B.
 d. class C.
 e. class D.

59. If R2 in the driver stage has a much greater resistance than R1 and C1 is shorted,
 a. the readings of M3 and M4 would decrease.
 b. the readings of M3 and M5 would increase.
 c. the readings of M4 and M6 would increase.
 d. the readings of M1 and M3 would decrease.
 e. none of these.

60. While the transmitter was left unattended by a licensed operator, a self-appointed electronics expert decided to tune the transmitter. He turned the adjusting screws in L3 and L4. The circuit breakers opened, cutting the transmitter off of the air. The circuit breakers probably opened because
 a. of the shifting of the transmitter frequency.
 b. the increase in mutual inductance between L3 and L4 increased the drive to the final stage causing a great increase in final stage plate current.
 c. grid drive reduced to the final stage, reducing final stage bias and thus increasing final plate current.
 d. some turns in L3 or L4 were likely shorted by the adjusting screwdriver of perhaps shorted to ground.
 e. none of these.

61. It would be wrong or an unnecessary step for retuning the transmitter after T2 had been tampered with to
 a. open switch S2, close S1 and turn on power.
 b. tune L3 for minimum reading on M2.
 c. tune L4 for maximum reading on M3.
 d. close switch S2.
 e. tune primary of T3 for minimum reading on M5 and for correct reading on M6 and also retune secondary if required.

62. M2 is
 a. a voltmeter reading the plate voltage on the driver.
 b. an ammeter reading screen current
 c. a voltmeter reading screen voltage.
 d. an ammeter reading plate and screen current.
 e. a voltmeter reading grid voltage.

63. R4
 a. is a voltmeter multiplier resistor for M1.
 b. works in connection with R3 to properly proportion the current through M1.
 c. keeps M1 from being damaged by high voltage surges.
 d. blocks AC signal from M1.
 e. none of these.

4. **(80%)** Recall that in amplitude modulation the sinusoidal audio output had to be 50% of the DC input to the modulated R.F. power amplifier for 100% modulation. In AM and FM % modulation is determined by the_____ of the audio.

13. **(change or deviation)** The discriminator may be used as an _____ detector or to develop frequency_____ voltages.

22. **(5 Khz, 20 Khz, 10)** The frequency tolerance of an N.B. FM station on 460 Mhz would be_____% and on 22 Mhz it would be _____ %.

31. **(I. F. limiter)** The first step in tuning a mobile transmitter is to disconnect or open the plate circuit of the final power amplifier. Then the oscillator and multiplier circuits can be tuned without the danger of excessive current in the final while tuning the earlier stages.

    The first step in tuning a mobile FM transmitter is to open the plate circuit of the_____ .

64. The RF output power of a transmitter is supplied by the
    a. vacuum tubes.
    b. DC supply.
    c. bias supply.
    d. filament supply.
    e. screen grid supply.

65. The output power of the final RF amplifier may be raised by
    a. increasing the input drive.
    b. increasing the final plate voltage.
    c. decreasing the load.
    d. a and b above.
    e. a, b, and c above.

66. If in an amplifier the grid current is 3 ma, the grid voltage is 6 volts, the plate current is 40 ma, the plate voltage is 275 volts, and the plate dissipates 9 watts; the output power is
    a. 18.6 watts.
    b. 82.3 watts.
    c. 10 watts.
    d. 2 watts.
    e. 20 watts.

3. (75Khz) If the frequency was caused to deviate 37.5 Khz, the percent modulation would be 50% (37.5 Khz =.5 or 50%) 60 Khz of deviation would represent a modulation of _____%.

12. (200 khz) The Foster Seeley Discriminator FM detector is the most important mobile FM receiver. It changes frequency variations into audio frequency outputs.
The Amplitude of the audio output is directly proportional to the deviation.
The Frequency of the audio output is determined by the rate of change (back and forth across the carrier frequency) of the frequency modulation.

The diagram of the discriminator is shown below.
I.F. energy fed through 2 paths.
(1) by inducatance (2) by a comparator capacitor

Rectified currents flow in opposite directions through R_1 and R_2. At center I.F. frequency voltage drops across R_1 and R_2 are equal and opposite. The net voltage from the top of R_1 to ground is zero.

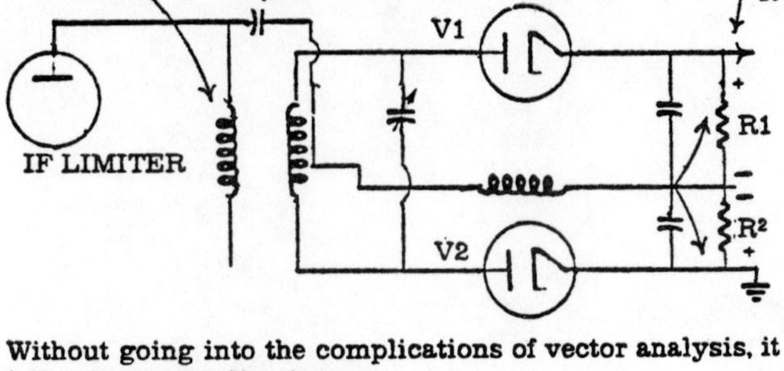

Without going into the complications of vector analysis, it is sufficient for this study to make the following generalizations:
1. At the center I.F. frequency (usually 10.7 mhz) V_1 and V_2 conduct equally. The total voltage drop across R_1 and R_2 is zero.
2. At frequencies higher than the center I.F. frequency V_1 conducts harder than V_2. The greater voltage drop across R_1 leaves a positive voltage at the output.
3. At frequencies lower than the center I.F. frequency V_2 conducts harder than V_1. The greater voltage drop across R_2 leaves a negative voltage at the output.
This action is illustrated in the following diagrams using assumed voltage values:

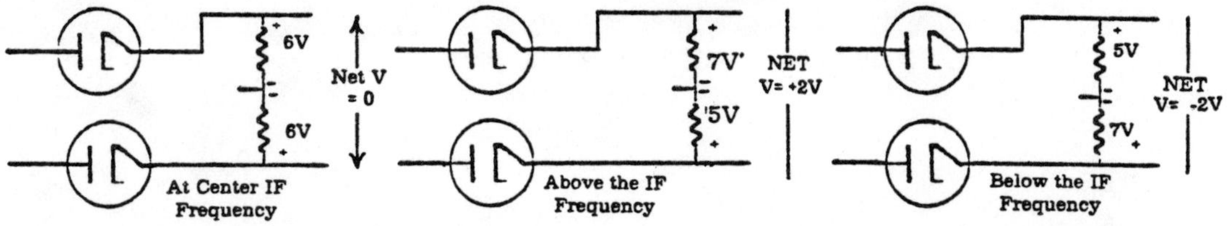

The Foster Seeley discriminator is an FM detector and can be used also for developing frequency control voltages. The latter principle is used in the automatic frequency control circuits for transmitter and receivers. The output voltage of a discriminator is proportional to frequency _____.

PUBLIC SAFETY RADIO SERVICE
21. (phase, audio) Most of the public safety stations, such as fire and police, use narrow band FM transmitters and receivers. These stations are allowed:

1. A frequency deviation of plus or minus 5 Khz
2. A 20 Khz channel bandwidth.
3. A frequency tolerance of .01% in 20-25 Mhz band. N.B. FM deviation should be_____ Khz for 100% modulation. The N.B. FM channel is_____Khz wide.
4. A frequency tolerance of .0005% above 50 Mhz.
5. Operation up to 10 days without station authorization in an emergency. A P.S. station can be operated_____days without authorization.

MISCELLANEOUS

30. (low pass, receiver, compensate) The first step in tuning an FM mobile receiver is to tune the output of the last I. F. limiter stage. A signal generator on the I. F. frequency should be connected to the grid of this stage and the discriminator tuned circuits tuned for zero output voltage.

The first stage to be tuned in a mobile FM receiver is the last_____.

"Harmonic Reduction."

1. The dummy antenna is a low radiation device used for testing a transmitter without putting it on the air. The dummy antenna provides the same resistive load as an actual antenna would itself. It consists of a non inductive resistance immersed in transformer oil connected in series with a coupling capacitor.

Capacitance used to cancel reactance of R.F. pick up inductance

ALSO. In Series with

Non inductive resistor.

R.F. pick up inductance

Dummy Antenna

The dummy antenna is a _____ LOW _____ radiation device consisting of a _____ RESISTOR _____ connected in series with a _____ CAPACITOR _____ .

6. (third) Link coupling is a form of inductive coupling and is especially useful in coupling stages that are widely separated.

LINK

It is a low impedance and low loss coupling system. It minimizes the transfer of harmonics.

Link coupling is anoher form of _____ INDUCTIVE _____ coupling.

11. (voltage, multipliers, isolate) Note that the buffer bias is by battery or power supply. If the excitation fails, the buffer is held by the fixed bias to cut off and no plate current flows. M2 and M3 would go to zero.
    If C5 was open, there would be no excitation and M2 and M3 would go to _____ .

16. (R5) With normal excitation the grid and plate current are tuned in preceeding stages by tuning for a peak. Also the cathode current in M5 would peak. When the first doubler plate circuit is tuned to resonance at the harmonic frequency, the plate current dips. Tuning the tuned circuits in the stages ahead of the first doubler to resonance will cause the first doubler grid, cathode, and plate current to _____ .

21. (rise) Note that there is no need for neutralization of this tube as the output frequency is double that of the input frequency.
    It is necessary to neutralize a grounded cathode triode R.F. amplifier if the output frequency is _____ the input frequency.

26. (zero, high, R7) M 9 in the power amplifier is a voltmeter. The series multiplier resistance R 8 is high (usually in the megohms). Although R 8 and M 9 provide a parallel path of resistance to R 7, the total resistance is essentially that of R 7. If R 8 opens up, the plate current at M 10 would be _____ .
    If R 8 shorts out, the plate current at M 10 would _____ .

31. (F1, background) Resistors used in transmitter circuits are either carbon or wire wound. Wire wound resistors are often used in the higher power applications. However, it's safer to use carbon resistors in transmitter power supply bleeder circuits as wire wound resistors tend to open or short. A carbon resistor may change value but seldom opens up or shorts.
    The _____ resistor has a tendency to develop opens or shorts.

2. **(frequency, amplitude)** If in FM broadcasting (88 to 108 Mhz) enough amplitude of audio was used to cause the frequency to deviate up and down 75 Khz, 100% modulation is achieved (by definition). This is shown graphically for a 100 Mhz carrier.

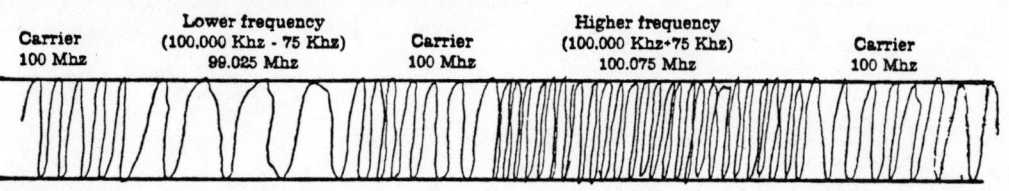

| Carrier
100 Mhz | Lower frequency
(100,000 Khz - 75 Khz)
99.025 Mhz | Carrier
100 Mhz | Higher frequency
(100,000 Khz+75 Khz)
100.075 Mhz | Carrier
100 Mhz |

In FM broadcasting a deviation of_____Khz is considered to be 100% modulation.

F M RECEIVERS

11. **(240 Khz)** Only a few of the upper audio frequencies are transmitted and bandwidths of 200 Khz are provided for in FM receivers. The FM receiver is a superheterodyne. It differs from the AM receiver in that it has an FM detector and in some cases limiters, automatic frequency control and squelch circuits. In general, an FM receiver has the minimum circuits shown:

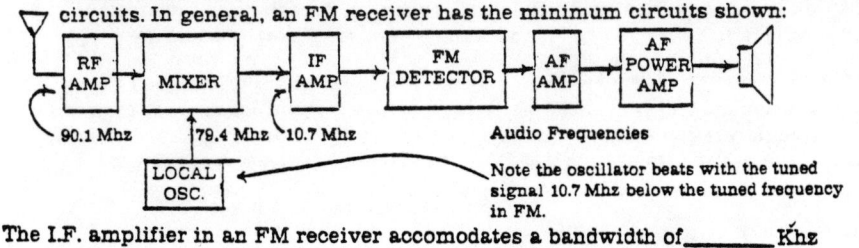

The I.F. amplifier in an FM receiver accomodates a bandwidth of_____Khz

20. **(inductive, capacitive, reactance tube)** In indirect phase FM modulation, the modulator comes in between the oscillator and the multipliers. Less audio power is required for 100% modulation.

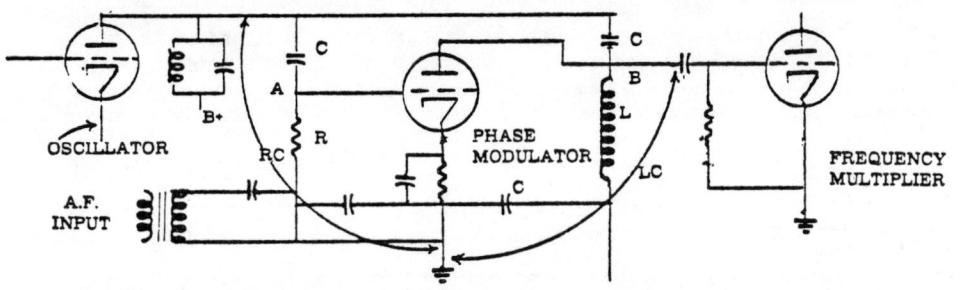

The output of the oscillator is fed into two circuits. The left hand circuit is an RC circuit. The one on the right is a LC circuit. The voltage at B will have two out of phase components (with that at A): one due to the LC network and the other due to the tube amplified voltage from A. This will produce one resultant out of phase voltage with the oscillator output. When audio is applied at A the phase is shifted in accordance with the amplitude of the audio signal. This phase shift results in frequency modulation.

The_____modulator is indirect frequency modulation. Indirect modulation does not require as much_____power for 100% modulation.

29. **(transmitter, high pass, 75 microsecond)** To compensate for the extra boost the high frequency audio received at the transmitter, A **De-emphasis circuit** must be used at the receiver. The resulting audio at the speaker represents a balanced signal to noise ratio for all audio frequencies. A de-emphasis circuit is a low pass filter and is shown below:

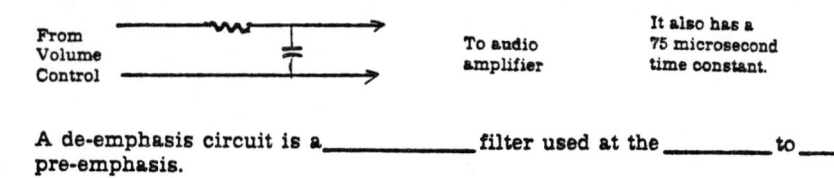

From Volume Control → To audio amplifier

It also has a 75 microsecond time constant.

A de-emphasis circuit is a_____filter used at the_____to_____for pre-emphasis.

231

2. (low, resistor, capacitor) The output of a transmitter is often coupled to an antenna through a filter. Two common filters are shown:

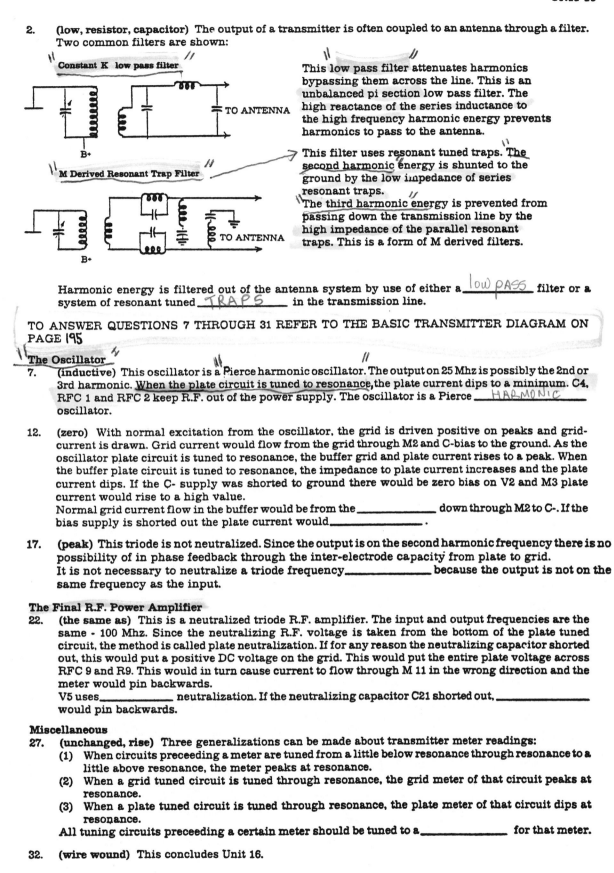

Constant K low pass filter

TO ANTENNA

B+

This low pass filter attenuates harmonics bypassing them across the line. This is an unbalanced pi section low pass filter. The high reactance of the series inductance to the high frequency harmonic energy prevents harmonics to pass to the antenna.

M Derived Resonant Trap Filter

TO ANTENNA

B+

This filter uses resonant tuned traps. The second harmonic energy is shunted to the ground by the low impedance of series resonant traps.
The third harmonic energy is prevented from passing down the transmission line by the high impedance of the parallel resonant traps. This is a form of M derived filters.

Harmonic energy is filtered out of the antenna system by use of either a __low pass__ filter or a system of resonant tuned __TRAPS__ in the transmission line.

TO ANSWER QUESTIONS 7 THROUGH 31 REFER TO THE BASIC TRANSMITTER DIAGRAM ON PAGE 195

The Oscillator

7. (inductive) This oscillator is a Pierce harmonic oscillator. The output on 25 Mhz is possibly the 2nd or 3rd harmonic. When the plate circuit is tuned to resonance, the plate current dips to a minimum. C4, RFC 1 and RFC 2 keep R.F. out of the power supply. The oscillator is a Pierce __HARMONIC__ oscillator.

12. (zero) With normal excitation from the oscillator, the grid is driven positive on peaks and grid-current is drawn. Grid current would flow from the grid through M2 and C-bias to the ground. As the oscillator plate circuit is tuned to resonance, the buffer grid and plate current rises to a peak. When the buffer plate circuit is tuned to resonance, the impedance to plate current increases and the plate current dips. If the C- supply was shorted to ground there would be zero bias on V2 and M3 plate current would rise to a high value.
Normal grid current flow in the buffer would be from the _____ down through M2 to C-. If the bias supply is shorted out the plate current would _____ .

17. (peak) This triode is not neutralized. Since the output is on the second harmonic frequency there is no possibility of in phase feedback through the inter-electrode capacity from plate to grid.
It is not necessary to neutralize a triode frequency_____ because the output is not on the same frequency as the input.

The Final R.F. Power Amplifier

22. (the same as) This is a neutralized triode R.F. amplifier. The input and output frequencies are the same - 100 Mhz. Since the neutralizing R.F. voltage is taken from the bottom of the plate tuned circuit, the method is called plate neutralization. If for any reason the neutralizing capacitor shorted out, this would put a positive DC voltage on the grid. This would put the entire plate voltage across RFC 9 and R9. This would in turn cause current to flow through M 11 in the wrong direction and the meter would pin backwards.
V5 uses_____ neutralization. If the neutralizing capacitor C21 shorted out, _____ would pin backwards.

Miscellaneous

27. (unchanged, rise) Three generalizations can be made about transmitter meter readings:
   (1) When circuits preceeding a meter are tuned from a little below resonance through resonance to a little above resonance, the meter peaks at resonance.
   (2) When a grid tuned circuit is tuned through resonance, the grid meter of that circuit peaks at resonance.
   (3) When a plate tuned circuit is tuned through resonance, the plate meter of that circuit dips at resonance.
   All tuning circuits preceeding a certain meter should be tuned to a_____ for that meter.

32. (wire wound) This concludes Unit 16.

UNIT 19 FREQUENCY MODULATION

BASIC FM PRINCIPLES

1. Amplitude modulation is the process of beating an audio signal with an R. F. signal in a non linear device to produce an amplitude modulated wave with upper and lower sidebands.

Frequency modulation is the process of varying the frequency of a signal in accordance with speech or music. The general idea of FM is shown:

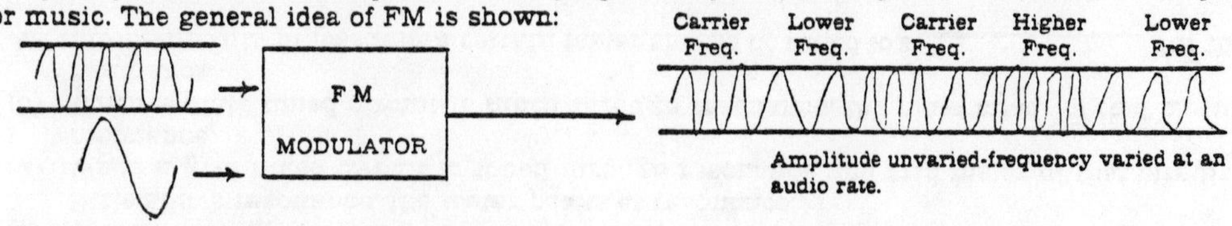

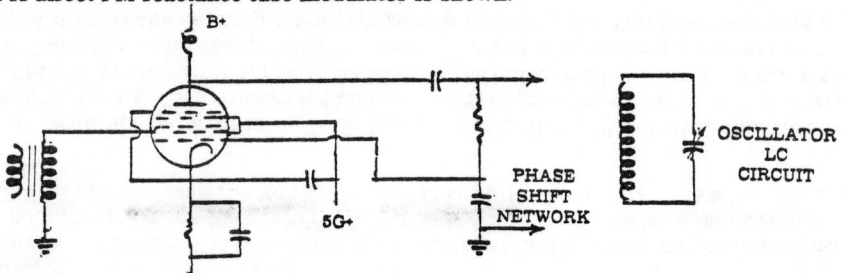

Amplitude unvaried-frequency varied at an audio rate.

The **rate of change** from a lower frequency to a higher frequency and vice versa is equal to the **frequency of the audio.**

The amount of change of frequency up or down from the carrier frequency is called **deviation** and is determined by the **amplitude** of the audio.

The rate of change is determined by the _____ of the audio signal.

The amount of change in frequency is determined by the _____ of the audio.

10. (12 Khz, 3 Khz) In FM broadcasting where audio frequencies up to 15 khz are used and deviations up to 75 Khz are used, the deviation ratio is 5. With this deviation ratio there are eight significant sidebands. The sidebands are spaced 15 Khz apart and extended 120 Khz above the carrier and 120 Khz below the carrier. (8 X 15 Khz = 120 Khz). Although there may be more than eight harmonics present, they are not of sufficient strength to create sidebands of any significant amplitudes. The number of significant sidebands can be determined by Bessel Functions. In general, the number of significant sidebands increases with increased deviation ratios.

The total bandwidth in FM broadcasting is _____ Khz

FM TRANSMITTERS

19. (weak) Direct FM is accomplished by injecting inductive or capacitive reactance in the tank circuit of an oscillator. It has the effect of changing the inductance or capacity of the tuned circuit at an audio rate. A direct FM reactance tube modulator is shown.

An audio input varies the gain of the modulator tube and produces a variable reactance which is fed to the oscillator circuit. This arrangement injects inductive reactance. If the phase shift network was inverted, capacitive reactance would be injected into the oscillator LC circuit.

In direct FM the oscillator frequency is changed by injecting _____ or _____ reactance into the oscillator grid circuit. The _____ modulator is a direct FM modulator.

PRE-EMPHASIS AND DE-EMPHASIS

28. (service) Because there are more noises generated in the vacuum tube and transistor circuits above 2000 hz than below 2000 hz, the signal to noise ratio at the higher audio frequencies would be poor unless compensated for.
   Therefore, audio frequencies above 2000 hertz are given additional boost at the transmitter. This is accomplished by a high pass filter having a time constant of 75 micro-seconds. The circuit is called a **pre-Emphasis circuit** and is shown below:

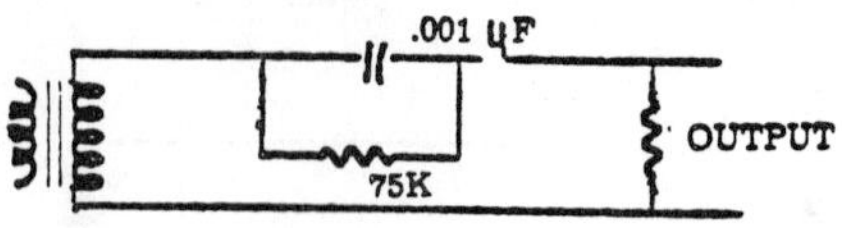

The pre-emphasis circuit is used at the _____ . It is a _____ filter with a _____ microsecond time constant.

37. (selective) This concludes Unit 19.

230

3. **(low pass, traps)** R. F. coupling between stages is accomplished by a capacitive or inductive effect or by both. By use of shielding either the electromagnetic inductive or electrostatic capacitive coupling can be eliminated.

Some forms of coupling are shown:

1) _Inductive and capacitive coupling._

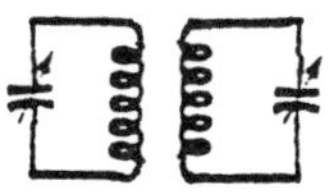

This is mostly inductive coupling. Some capacitive coupling is provided by the capacity between windings.

2) "_Inductive coupling._"

Faraday shield

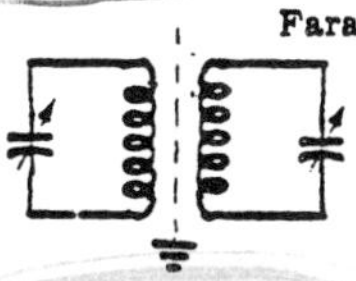

The Faraday copper shield eliminates any capacity effect between windings. The coupling is inductive. Harmonic energy transfer is blocked as inductance has a high reactance to the high frequency harmonics.

3) _Capacitive coupling._

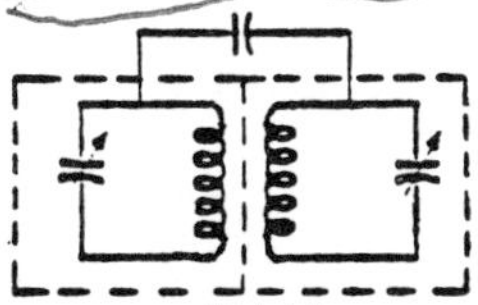

Shield

The coils are shielded from each other in this circuit and the only coupling is through the external capacity. Harmonic energy is transferred with capacitive coupling. The capacitive reactance would be low for the high frequency harmonic energy.

ABOVE FIGS. Harmonic energy transfer is minimized by circuit _2 (inductive ckt high X_L to H-F's)_ _high read._ and passed easily by circuit _3 (CAPACITIVE), LOW X_c TO H-F's_

8. **(harmonic)** If the circuit crystal quits oscillating for any reason, grid leak bias is not developed and the plate current rises. There would be no RF output. If the filament circuit to the oscillator tube came open, there would be no cathode emission and the tube would act like an open circuit. M1 would fall to zero.

If the crystal was defective, the plate current at M1 would _RISE_

If the filament circuit of V1 was open, the plate current at M1 would _FALL TO ZERO_ .

13. **(grid, rise)** It is not necessary to neutralize the buffer amplifier with external neutralization because the screen grid is grounded by C6 for R.F. and prevents feedback from the plate circuit to the grid. R2 is a small resistor placed in the grid circuit to suppress parasitic oscillations.

It is not necessary to neutralize the buffer amplifier because the tube is a _____ with a _____ grid. If R2 was shorted out, there would be the possibility of the generation of _____ oscillations.

The Second Doubler

18. **(doubler)** This doubler does not have protective bias. If the excitation is removed, the grid will not draw current and no grid leak biasing will develop. The rise in plate current with zero bias on the tube would ruin the tube.

If C 14 was open, there would be no _____ and the plate current would _____ and ruin the tube.

23. **(plate, M 11)** A shunt fed R.F. amplifier is shown below:

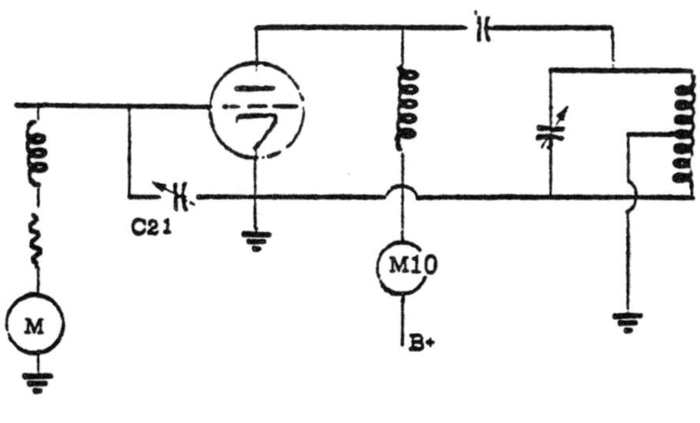

C21

M10

B+

M

Here the neutralizing capacitor is connected to the plate tank coil which is grounded at the center tap. If this capacitor shorts out, the amplifier grid would be grounded resulting in zero bias and high plate current.

If C 21 was shorted out M 10 would read

28. **(peak)** Tuning the plate circuit through resonance causes the meter of that circuit to go from _____ reading to a _____ reading and back to a _____ reading. In other words you tune for a _____ in plate current.

192

9. The disadvantage of plate power detection compared to grid leak detection is
   a. poor high frequency response.
   b. it requires a separate power supply for biasing.
   c. the plate power supply would require more voltage.
   d. it requires the use of a pentode.
   e. it requires the use of a duo diode triode tube.

10. Radio telephone receivers with an oscillator operating near the IF frequency would be receiving
    a. MCW.
    b. CW.   d. FM.
    c. television.   e. standard broadcast.

11. An example of a good tone control is

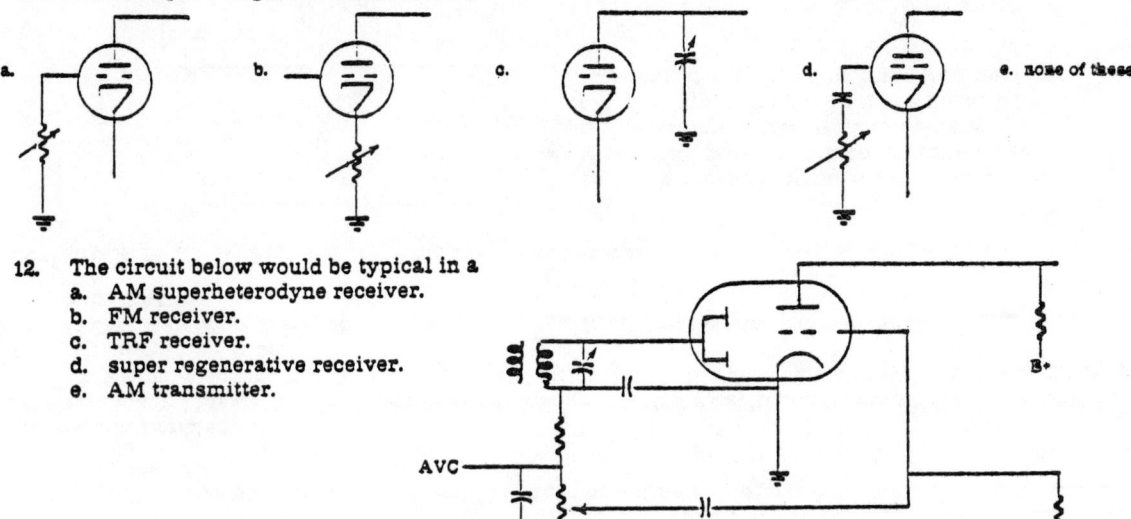

a.   b.   c.   d.   e. none of these

12. The circuit below would be typical in a
    a. AM superheterodyne receiver.
    b. FM receiver.
    c. TRF receiver.
    d. super regenerative receiver.
    e. AM transmitter.

    AVC

13. For greater sensitivity and selectivity the receiver antenna coupling should be
    a. tightly coupled.
    b. loosely coupled.   d. impedance coupled.
    c. inductively coupled. e. none of these.

14. A duo triode is
    a. in fact equivalent to two triodes in one envelope.
    b. used for halfwave rectification.   d. used as an RF amp.
    c. used for a second detector.   e. used as an AF amp.

15. The selectivity of a receiver may be increased by
    a. loose coupling.
    b. tighter coupling.   d. high plate voltage.
    c. more grid bias.   e. none of these.

16. When a stronger signal is tuned in a radio receiver, the AVC voltage
    a. goes high positive.
    b. goes low positive.   d. goes low negative.
    c. goes high negative. e. goes to zero.

17. There is some noise level in a battery powered receiver because of
    a. unfiltered power supply A.C.
    b. the inherent noise level in each stage.
    c. contact potential.
    d. low Mu diodes.
    e. none of these.

18. If the grid return in a plate detector stage is made to the plus terminal instead of the negative terminal of the bias battery, the
    a. bias is reduced.
    b. bias is increased.   d. the supply voltage to the plate increases.
    c. Ip decreases.   e. operation is normal.

19. The purpose of a "squelch" circuit is to
    a. reduce the signal strength of the incoming signal.
    b. render the receiver inoperative when no carrier wave is present.
    c. increase the strength of all incoming signals.
    d. turn off the transmitter when safe voltage is not maintained.
    e. amplify the audio.

4. (2, 3) Harmonics are always integral multiples of the fundamental frequency. The third harmonic of 600 Khz is 3 X 600 or 1800 Khz. The fifth harmonic of 480 Khz is _____ Khz.

9. (rise, fall to zero) If C4 shorted out, this would put a short circuit on the power supply. M1 would rise to an excessive value unless a fuse blew. If C4 was shorted out there would be no R.F. output and M2 in the next stage would go to zero. If C4 became open there will be little or no effect on operation as its sole purpose is to keep R.F. out of the power supply. This low level R.F. would do no probable damage to the oscillator power supply.
    If C4 shorted out the plate current as indicated by M1 would be very _____ .
    If C4 opened up the oscillator output would be _____ .

The First Doubler
14. (tetrode, screen, parasitic) The plate output circuit is tuned to twice the frequency of the input. If the grid circuit marked Z2 is tuned to the same frequency as the plate circuit of the buffer amplifier marked Z1, the output in the doubler plate circuit is the second harmonic frequency. Note the doubling occurs in the plate circuit. If Z2 was tuned to twice the frequency of Z1, there would be very little input to the grid and very little harmonic energy in the plate circuit. There would be very little harmonic output if Z2 was tuned to _____ the frequency that Z1 was tuned to.

19. (grid bias, rise) Since this is the second doubler, the original oscillator output frequency (25 Mhz) has been increased to 50 Mhz. So the input frequency to the second doubler is 50 Mhz.
    The output frequency of this stage would be _____ Mhz.

24. (high) The carrier frequency of a transmitter is the unmodulated output frequency of the final R.F. power amplifier. If the neutralizing capacitor became open, the stage would develop self oscillation and radiate spurious radiations. These radiations would be in addition to the carrier output frequency of 100 Mhz.
    The carrier frequency is the output frequency of V_____. If C 21 is open, there will be _____ _____ .

29. (maximum, minimum, maximum, dip) Precautions should be taken to prevent unwanted coupling of a stage back to an earlier stage as this could cause self oscillation. Shielding is often used to prevent _____ coupling.

1.   The main disadvantage of the use of squelch circuit in a receiver is
     a. it can only be used with FM.
     b. weak signals interfere with strong signals.
     c. weak signals can't be received.
     d. there is objectionable background noise when no signal is received.
     e. the efficiency is poor.

2.   A super regenerative receiver has
     a. low sensitivity.
     b. high selectivity.
     c. images.
     d. low selectivity.
     e. triple conversion.

3.   The image frequency for the superheterodyne receiver shown is
     a. 1.910 Khz.
     b. 455 Khz.
     c. 1,455 Khz.
     d. 645 Khz.
     e. none of these.

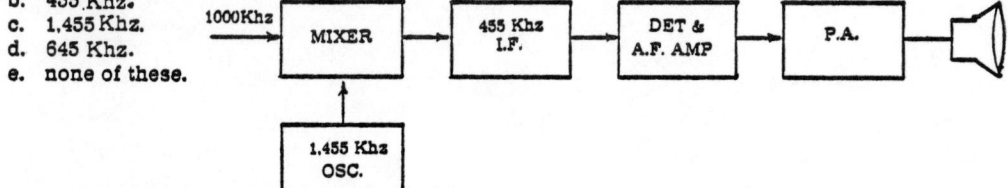

4.   The circuit shown below is that of a
     a. multivibrator.
     b. pentagrid converter.
     c. push push amplifier.
     d. push pull amplifier.
     e. dynatron oscillator

5.   In a superheterodyne receiver, the tuned signal is 1,500 Khz. The local oscillator is operating at 1950 Khz. The image would be
     a. 1.500 Khz.
     b. 1.950 Khz.
     c. 1.050 Khz.
     d. 2.400 Khz.
     e. 2.850 Khz.

6.   A regenerative receiver is tuned for maximum amplification for a radio telephone signal. It should be adjusted
     a. just before oscillation.
     b. just into oscillation.
     c. for minimum regeneration.
     d. for best neutralization.
     e. minimum peak output.

7.   A superheterodyne receiver tuned to 5.6 Mhz has an I. F. of 455 Khz. The local oscillator would be operating on
     a. 5,145 Khz.
     b. 45,016 Khz.
     c. 5.6 Mhz.
     d. 5,455 Khz.
     e. 6,055 Khz.

8.   A super regenerative receiver has
     a. low sensitivity.
     b. high sensitivity.
     c. high selectivity.
     d. triple conversion.
     e. images.

5. (2400 Khz) All harmonics can be minimized by use of the following:
    1) Link or inductive coupling.
    2) High Q circuits - large capacitors and small inductors.
    3) Low bias. Class A, AB, or B
    4) Low excitation
    5) Faraday shields

    In addition even harmonics are minimized by use of push pull circuits (2nd, 4th, 6th, etc.). The strongest low order harmonic present in the output of a push pull R.F. amplifier would be the _THIRD_ harmonic.

The Buffer

10. (high, about normal) This is a standard capacity coupled voltage amplifier. It is usual for the buffer to proceed the frequency multipliers. The buffer serves to isolate the oscillator from load changes in the multipliers and final power amplifier. This insures a stable oscillator frequency.
    The buffer is usually a standard capacitive coupled _____ amplifier following the oscillator and preceeding the frequency _____ . This stage serves to _____ the oscillator from load changes in succeeding stages.

15. (twice) The stage uses grid leak bias with protective cathode resistor bias. If excitation failed, there would be no grid leak bias (since the grid would not be driven positive to draw electrons). The plate current would rise and some automatic bias would be developed by the resistance in the cathode circuit. The bias would shift from class C with excitation to class A or AB without excitation. The plate current rise with no excitation would not be sufficient to ruin the tube.
    The resistance that provides protective bias in the event of the failure of excitation is marked _____ in the diagram.

20. (100 Mhz) If C 15 was shorted, this would put the grid on the ground and there would be zero bias. M7 would fall to zero. With C 15 shorted, the plate current at M8 would _____ .

25. (V5, spurious radiatons) If the plate radio frequency choke RFC 7 of the previous stage is open, there will be no excitation to the power amplifier. M11 will read _____ and M10 will read_____ R_____ will provide protective bias.

30. (unwanted) This transmitter could be keyed to produce a carrier that goes on and off at a coded rate. Such a transmitter is a CW (continuous wave) transmitter. Another type of CW transmitter is the frequency shift keyed (F 1 or FSK) transmitter. In this system the carrier is left on and the frequency is shifted. This covers objectionable background noise at the receiver.
    Telegraphy by frequency shift keying is symbolized by F_____ or FSK and covers objectionable _____ noise at the receiver.

2. **(detector)** It takes no local power to_____ a modulated wave. Sec. 18-3.

4. **(crystal)** A plate power detector requires a_____ power supply voltage. Sec. 18-4.

6. **(B)** The detector circuit operates with little distortion if it is a _____ detector. One example of this detector is the _____ detector. Sec. 18-5.

8. **(grid, plate)** A regenerative receiver is tuned for maximum amplification for an A3 radiotelephone signal. Regeneration should be adjusted for just under the value for_____. Sec. 18-7.

10. **(audodyne, A1)** The super regenerative detector has_____ sensitivity and_____ selectivity. Sec. 18-8.

12. **(6.055 Mhz)** A superheterodyne receiver tuned to 1000 Khz has an I. F. of _____ Khz if the local oscillator is tuned to 1455 Khz. Sec. 18-10.

14. **(A1 or CW code)** This oscillator is called a_____ oscillator. Sec. 18-10.

16. **(mixer)** The local oscillator used in the pentagrid converter circuit of Fig. 18-18 is a_____ type. Sec. 18-12.

18. **(loose, over)** Since the selectivity of tuned circuits requires loose coupling and high sensitivity requires tight coupling, a compromise is usual. The best method of adjusting coupling for R.F. tuned circuits is by using inductive coupling.

   For greater sensitivity or selectivity_____ coupling is used. Sec. 18-13.

20. **(high)**

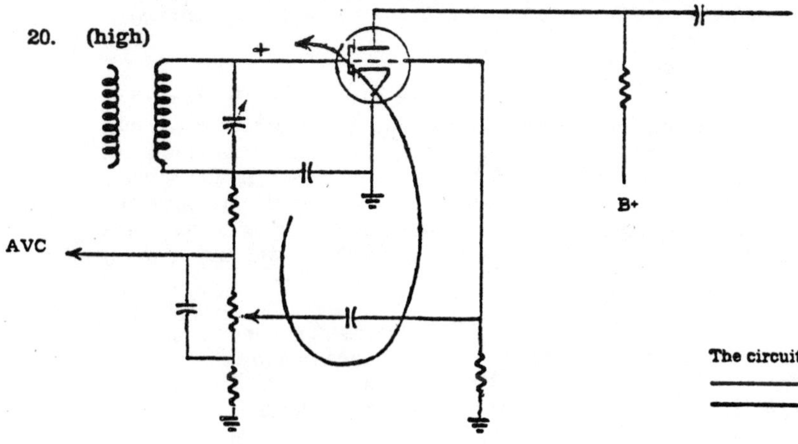

B+

AVC

The circuit shown is the typical A.M. _____ detector and first _____ amplifier. Sec. 18-14.

22. **(weak)** In a superheterodyne receiver the tuned signal is 1000 Khz. The local oscillator is operating on 1455 Khz. The image frequency would be _____ Khz. Sec. 18-23.

THE R.F. SECTION OF A BASIC TRANSMITTER

DiAGRAM USED FOR QUESTIONS (7 thru 31).

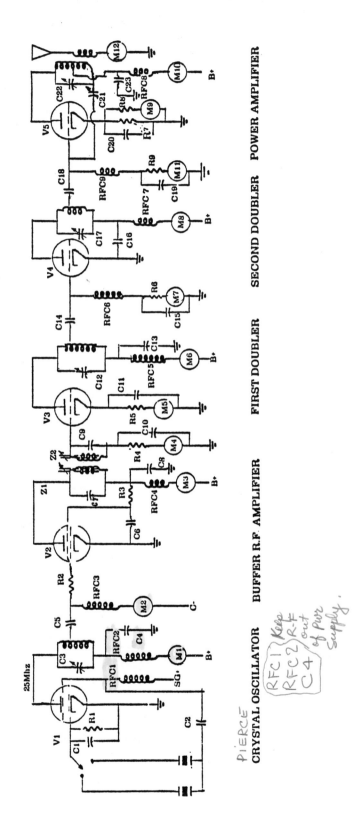

| PIERCE CRYSTAL OSCILLATOR | BUFFER R.F. AMPLIFIER | FIRST DOUBLER | SECOND DOUBLER | POWER AMPLIFIER |

RFC1
RFC2 Keep R-F out of Pwr supply.
C 4

195

1.   To change inaudible R.F. to audible frequency AC, a _____ is needed. Sec. 18-1

3.   (detect or demodulate) Figure 18-4 shows a simple complete receiver. The _____ detector receiver requires no local power supply. Sec. 18-3.

5.   (high) The reason for this is that both plate voltage and the high class B cathode biasing voltage must be supplied by the power supply.

A plate power detector is biased as a class _____ circuit. Sec. 18-4.

7.   (linear, diode) The grid leak detector detects in the _____ circuit and amplifies in the _____ circuit.

9.   (oscillation) A regenerative detector that breaks into oscillation is called an _____ and can be used for receiving a A ____ code signal. Sec. 18-7.

11.   (high, poor) A superheterodyne receiver tuned to 5.6 Mhz has an I.F. of 455 Khz. The local oscillator should be tuned to _____ Khz. Sec. 18-10.

13.· (455 Khz) A radio telephone receiver with an oscillator operating near the I. F. frequency would be receiving _____ signals. Sec. 18-10.

15.   (beat frequency or BFO) The output of the R. F. amplifier is fed to the _____ . Sec. 18-11.

17.   (series fed Hartley) The selectivity of the I.F. can be increased by _____ coupling. The sensitivity of the I. F. can be increased by _____ coupling. Sec. 18-13.

19.   (inductive) When a strong signal is tuned in a radio receiver, the A.V.C. Voltage is _____ negative. Sec. 18-14.

21.   (second or diode, audio) The main disadvantage of a squelch circuit in a receiver is that _____ signals can't be received. Sec. 18-16.

23.   (1910 Khz) This concludes unit 18.

UNIT 16 BASIC TRANSMITTERS

RECHECK PROGRAMMED INSTRUCTION USING SHRADER'S ELECTRONIC COMMUNICATION

Begin by reviewing Unit 15 Recheck programmed instruction.

1. A dummy antenna is composed of _____ and _____ in series. Sec. 16-7.

3. (LOW) There is less objectional background noise in the reception of _____ emissions than when a coded carrier is turned on and off as in A1 emission. Sec. 16-13.

5. (oscillator, capacitance) A grid leak biased stage has no bias when there is no _____ . The stage may also employ _____ resistor bias as a safety bias. Sec. 16-15.

7. (push push) The oscillator of a transmitter uses a 2 Mhz crystal having a temperature coefficient of 10 hertz per degree centigrade per megahertz. The output carrier frequency is normally 24 Mhz. When the crystal temperature falls 20 degrees centigrade, the output carrier frequency would be _____ Khz. (Assume a negative temperature coefficient). Sec. 16-17.

9. (2400 Khz) See Fig. 16-23, page 370 and see diagram figure 20 - 47 page 524.

The two transmission line circuits shown are for the purpose of reducing _____ radiation.

11. (harmonic)

The type of coupling shown is _____ or _____ coupling. Sec. 16-19 and reread Sec. 15-11.

The top circuit is a constant K _____ pi filter and the bottom one is a type of the M derived filter using wave _____ . Sec. 16-18.

13. Read all paragraphs Sec. 16-24.

15. (crystal) If the crystal failed to operate, there would be no grid leak bias and M1 would _____ .

17. (R.F.) If C4 shorted out to ground M1 would read _____ .

19. (battery, power supply) If C5 was open, the excitation would be lost and M2 and M3 would read _____ .

21. (tetrode, screen grid) Assuming normal operation, the M3 reading shows a _____ when the plate circuit of V2 is tuned to resonance.

23. (low) Protective bias is provided in V3 by R_____ .

25. (doublers) If C14 was open, excitation to V4 would be lost and M8 would read _____ .

27. (grid leak) As C17 is tuned to resonance M11 would _____ .

29. (grid leak, cathode) If C18 comes open, M12 will read_____ .

31. (plate, M11) Operation would be nearly normal if R_____ in the power amplifier was open.

33. (zero) M9 is a_____ .

7. (good, poor) Major Armstrong hit upon the idea that the best selectivity and sensitivity could be achieved in a radio receiver if high quality circuits could be used for R.F. ahead of the detector. It happens that a circuit having a certain high quality (high Q) for one frequency will not have a high quality for other frequencies. By changing all tuned frequencies to one frequency, Major Armstrong was able to achieve maximum selectivity and sensitivity. This one frequency is called the Intermediate Frequency (I.F.). Follow a 1000 Khz modulated signal through Armstrong's Super Heterodyne Receiver.

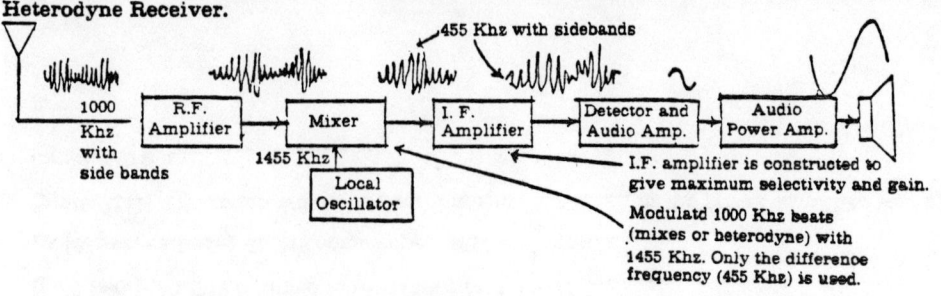

If 1400 Khz is tuned the oscillator tuning is automatically changed to 1855 Khz (by gang tuning R.F. amp and oscillator capacitors.)

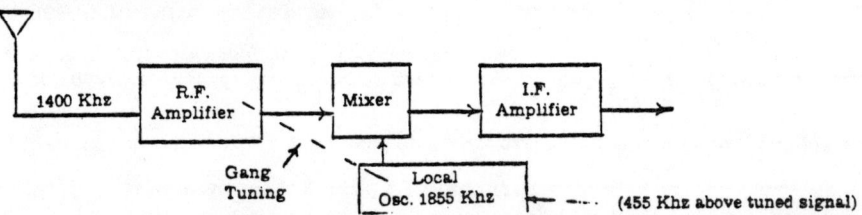

As a result all frequencies are changed to the intermediate frequencies where they receive treatment with high quality circuits.

If the I.F. is 455 Khz, the oscillator must be tuned 455 Khz higher than the tuned signal.

Nearly all amplitude modulation, frequency modulation, and television receivers are super heterodyne receivers. Even in battery operated receivers, there is some noise level due to the inherent noise in each stage.

A super heterodyne receiver tuned to 5.6 Mhz has an I.F. of 455 khz. The local oscillator should be operating on _____ Khz. All receivers have some noise due to the inherent noise of each _____ .

14. (high, low) A.V.C. voltage is developed in the _____ detector circuit and should be measured by using a _____ .

2. (resistance, capacitance) A dummy antenna is a _____ radiation device. Sec. 16-7.

4. (F1 or FSK) The buffer R.F. amplifier is used to provide a stable load to the _____ preventing any interaction with the power amplifiers. The buffer shown in Fig. 16-19 is a _____ coupled voltage R.F. amplifier. Sec. 16-15.

6. (excitation, cathode)

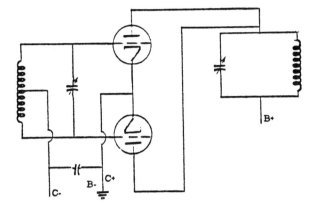

The circuit shown is a _____ .

frequency doubler. Sec. 16-17.

8. (24, 004.8 Khz) The fifth harmonic of 480 Khz is _____ Khz. Sec. 16-17.

10. (harmonic, low pass, traps) Link coupling, High Q circuits, low bias, low excitation and Faraday shields are all used to reduce _____ radiation. Sec. 16-18.

12. (capacitance, impedance) To answer the following questions refer to the diagram on page 202.

14. In the V1 circuit the output frequency is determined by a _____ .

16. (rise) RFC2 and C4 are used to keep _____ out of the power supply.

18. (high) V2 is biased class C by _____ or _____ _____ biasing.

20. (zero) It is not necessary to neutralize V2 because the tube is a _____ containing a _____ .

22. (dip) If Z2 was tuned to twice the frequency of Z1, the output of V3 would be _____ .

24. (R5) It is not necessary to neutralize V3 and V4 because they are frequency _____ .

26. (high) V4 uses _____ bias.

28. (peak) V5 is biased by _____ biasing and _____ resistor protective bias.

30. (zero) V5 uses _____ neutralization. If C21 shorts out M _____ will pin backwards.

32. (R8) If C5 was open M11 would read _____ .

34. (voltmeter) This concludes Unit 16. Now retake Unit 16 test.

6. **(oscillation)** Major Armstrong discovered that maximum amplification occurs in a regenerative receiver at the point of oscillation. Unless such a receiver was tuned to zero beat with the oscillator, there would be a bothersome squeal when receiving a modulated signal with carrier. If the carrier of the received signal was on 1000 Khz and the oscillator was operating on 1001 Khz, a 1 Khz audio squeal would result. The need for critical tuning would be a serious disadvantage. To get maximum amplification without the possibility of the squeal, Armstrong designed a **Super Regenerative Receiver**. In this scheme the three circuit receiver was made to go in and out of oscillation at a supersonic rate. The circuit is shown:

Energy added here causes circuit to go in and out of oscillation at supersonic (above 15 Khz) rate.

Supersonic frequency (usually 25 Khz) from a quench oscillator.

Although the amplification is great, the selectivity is very poor.

A super regenerative receiver has _____ sensitivity and _____ selectivity.

13. **(two)** The second detector is a diode detector. The upper and lower sidebands are beat with the carrier frequency to produce the audio frequency. Using the traditional explanation for detection, the modulated wave is rectified by the diodes (connected in parallel) and the R.F. is filtered out leaving only audio frequencies. A combination detector and A. F. amplifier is shown:

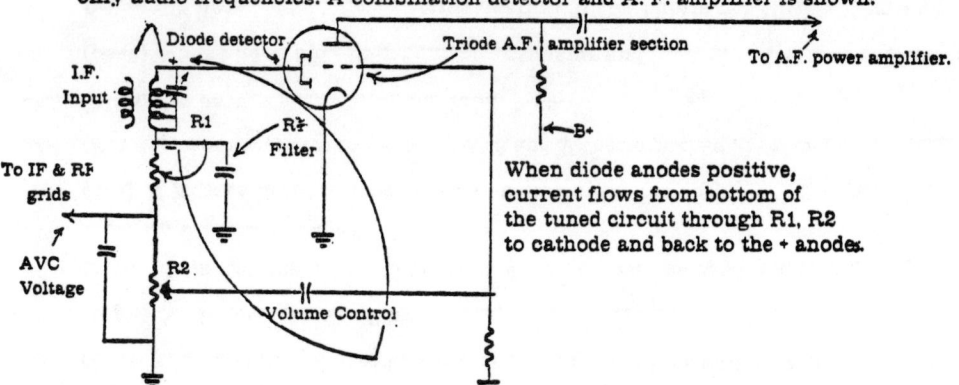

When diode anodes positive, current flows from bottom of the tuned circuit through R1, R2 to cathode and back to the + anodes.

Audio voltage drop across R2 coupled to grid of triode audio amplifier. The voltage drop across the volume control R2 is used to provide automatic volume control bias to the I.F. and R.F. stages. If a strong signal is fed to the detector, a high negative voltage is developed across R2. This is fed to the I.F. and R.F. grids producing low signal voltage gains in these stages.

If the signal fed to the detector is a weak signal, a low AVC negative voltage is developed across R2. This low negative voltage is used to bias I.F. and R.F. stages with a low negative voltage and high voltage amplification results.

Since this resistor has a high value of resistance, AVC voltage should be measured by a meter that will not load the circuit. A V.T.V.M. should be used.

When a stronger signal is tuned in a radio receiver, the AVC voltage goes _____ negative and the I.F. and R.F. stage gains are _____.

20. **(loose, close)** This concludes unit 18.

THE R.F. SECTION OF A BASIC TRANSMITTER

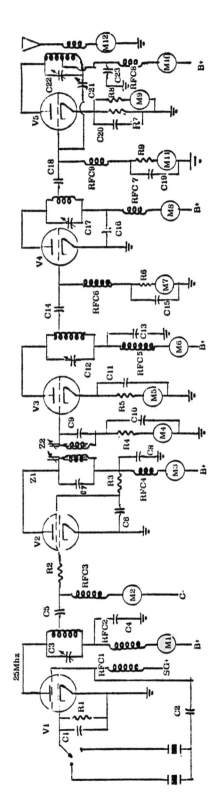

CRYSTAL OSCILLATOR   BUFFER R.F AMPLIFIER   FIRST DOUBLER   SECOND DOUBLER   POWER AMPLIFIER

5. **(frequency)** The **three circuit regenerative receiver** incorporates the Armstrong oscillator with grid leak detection.

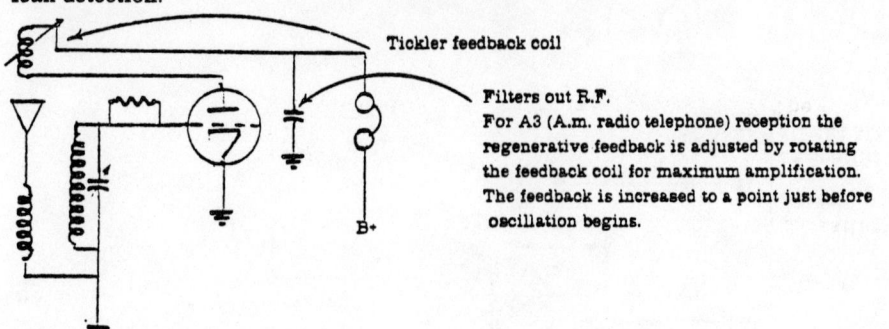

Tickler feedback coil

Filters out R.F.
For A3 (A.m. radio telephone) reception the regenerative feedback is adjusted by rotating the feedback coil for maximum amplification. The feedback is increased to a point just before oscillation begins.

For A1 (continuous wave or code) reception, the feedback coil is rotated until the circuit oscillates. Incoming unmodulated signals beat with the oscillator frequency to produce an audio output. Such a code receiver is called an **autodyne**.

A regenerative receiver is tuned for maximum amplification for an amplitude modulation radio telephone signal by adjusting feedback to a point just before_____ begins.

12. **(series fed)** The pentagrid converter changes high R.F. signal frequencies to lower intermediate frequencies. Because of this change, it is often referred to as the first detector. The second detector changes the intermediate frequencies to audio frequencies. This is shown by block diagram.

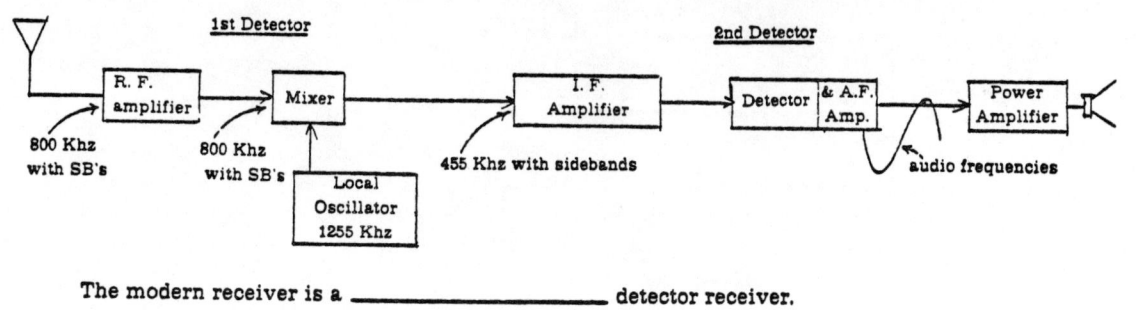

The modern receiver is a _____ detector receiver.

19. **(inductive)** The best selectivity is achieved by using_____coupling. The best sensitivity is achieved by using_____coupling.

1. A dummy antenna is
   a. made out of plastic.
   b. a parasitic element.   d. an oscillator.
   c. a low radiation device.   e. none of these.

2. One harmonic of 480 khz is
   a. 500 Khz.
   b. 900 Khz.   d. 2400 Khz.
   c. 240 Khz.   e. 3250 Khz.

3. One advantage of FSK over A1 CW is that
   a. a wider band is used.
   b. the constant carrier reduces objectionable background noises.
   c. transmitter tubes run cooler.
   d. transmitter tubes run at higher efficiency.
   e. none of these.

4. In the diagram shown Z2 is tuned to twice Z1 with high Q circuits. The output would be
   a. normal at 1 Mhz.
   b. normal at 2 Mhz.
   c. normal at 3 Mhz.
   d. very low.
   e. none of these.

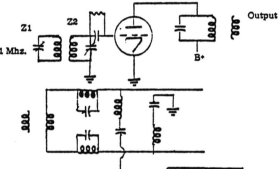

5. The circuit shown below is used for
   a. reducing harmonics.
   b. reducing parasitics.
   c. coupling to a frequency doubler.
   d. producing harmonics.
   e. none of these.

6. The circuit below is
   a. push pull amplifier.
   b. push push frequency doubler.
   c. an audio frequency amplifier.
   d. a voltage doubler.
   e. none of these.

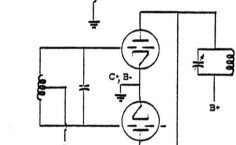

7. The grid bias developed in the circuit below would be
   a. 75 volts.
   b. 100 volts.
   c. 150 volts.
   d. 750 volts.
   e. zero.

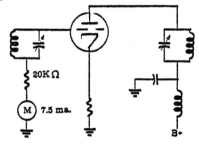

8. A buffer RF amplifier is used to
   a. shape a signal into a sine wave.
   b. prevent load changes from reflecting to oscillator.   d. generate parasitics oscillations.
   c. generate harmonics.   e. generate noise.

9. The oscillator of a transmitter uses a 2 Mhz crystal having a temperature coefficient of 10 cycles per degree centigrade per megacycle. The output carrier frequency is normally 24 Mhz. When the crystal temperature changes 20 degrees C, the output carrier frequency would be
   a. 24,000.4 Mhz.
   b. 23,999.6 Khz.
   c. 24,000.4 Khz.
   d. 23.9 Mhz.
   e. 24,004.8 Khz.

199

Receivers

4. (high) We have already examined the simple detector receiver. This receiver lacks two things:
(1) selectivity and (2) sensitivity
Selectivity is the ability of a receiver to select one frequency and reject other nearby frequencies.
Sensitivity is the ability of a receiver to give ample amplification to weak signals. The tuned R. F.
receiver provides some fair amount of selectivity. The block diagram below shows the general
arrangement.

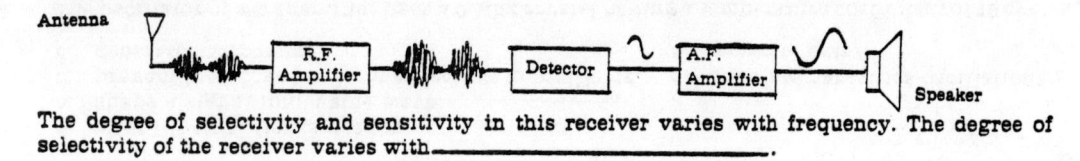

The degree of selectivity and sensitivity in this receiver varies with frequency. The degree of
selectivity of the receiver varies with _____.

11. (2400 Khz) In most cases the mixer and local oscillator are incorporated in one tube envelope in the
pentagrid converter. A typical circuit is shown:

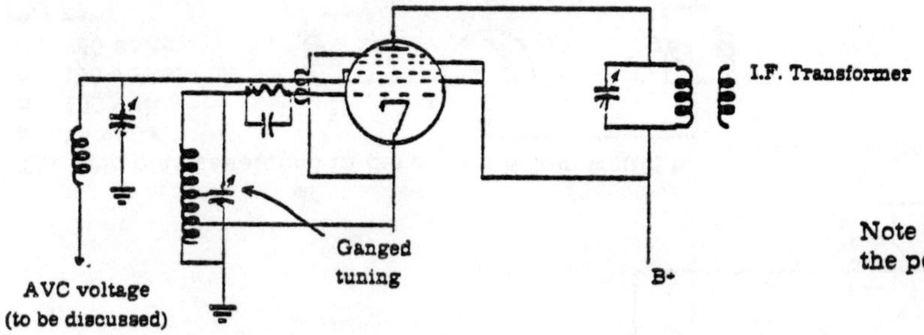

Note there are five grids in
the pentagrid converter.

The oscillator section of this pentagrid oscillator is a _____ Hartley or electron
coupled oscillator.

18. (code or Cw or A1 or A3J) The amount of inductive coupling from the antenna to the receiver or
from one R. F. (or I.F.) stage to another determines the selectivity of a stage. Inductive coupling
makes it possible to come up with a good compromise.

Close coupling
provides greater
sensitivity

Loose coupling
provides greater
selectivity

For best sensitivity of selectivity, the antenna coupling should be _____.

10. Telegraphy by frequency shift keying without the use of modulating audio frequency (FSK) is symbolized by
   a. F1.
   b. A3.
   c. A2.
   d. F3.
   e. A1.

(THIS DIAGRAM IS FOR PROBLEMS 11 THROUGH 15)

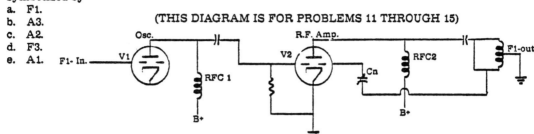

11. If Cn was shorted there would be
   a. proper neutralization.
   b. no plate current in V1. d. high plate current in V2.
   c. no plate current in V2. e. a direct short on the power supply.

12. If Cn was open there would be
   a. proper neutralization.
   b. spurious emissions due to self oscillations. d. no oscillation.
   c. no plate current in V1. e. parasitic oscillations.

13. If RFC1 was open there would be
   a. high plate current in V1.
   b. high plate current in V2. d. self oscillation.
   c. high grid bias in V2. e. no plate voltage to V2.

14. If RFC1 was shorted there would be
   a. V2 would not be neutralized.
   b. high plate current in V2. d. a short on the power supply.
   c. the possibility of low RF drive to the RF amp. e. b and c above.

15. If RFC2 was open there would be
   a. no plate current in V1.
   b. no plate current in V2. d. parasitic oscillations in V2.
   c. self oscillation in V2. e. no plate voltage to V1.

16. Shields are used in RF circuits in order to
   a. reduce parasitic oscillation.
   b. reduce harmonic generation. d. radiate energy.
   c. prevent unwanted coupling. e. provide a heat sink.

17. In an RF amplifier the Ig is 5 ma, the Ip 30 ma, the supply voltage is 300 volts and the grid bias 40 volts. The value of the grid leak resistor would be
   a. 4,000 ohms.
   b. 6,000 ohms. d. 10,000 ohms.
   c. 8,000 ohms. e. none of these.

18. A Buffer RF amplifier is used to
   a. shape a signal into a sine wave.
   b. isolate the final RF amplifier from the oscillator. d. generate parasitic oscillations.
   c. general harmonics. e. generate noise.

19. In a grid leak biased RF amplifier the tube is easily harmed by
   a. too high plate current.
   b. too high screen current.
   c. too high grid current.
   d. too high cathode resistance.
   e. none of these.

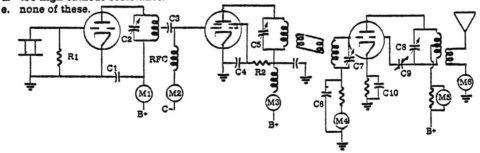

3. **(grid, plate)** The plate power detector operates like a class B amplifier. Cathode resistor bias is used. The detector is biased near cutoff. Since the bias is of a high value and since it has to be supplied by the plate voltage supply, a high supply voltage must be used. For example:

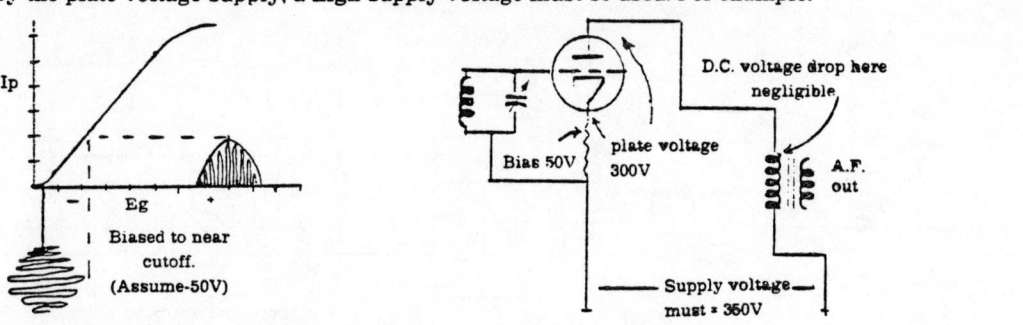

The disadvantage of plate power detection compared to grid leak detection is a _____ plate supply voltage is required.

·10. **(changes; intermediate)** A superheterodyne receiver is subject to image interference from strong local signals on certain frequencies. Look at the example below:

A strong local signal on 1510 Khz picked up on grid of mixer:

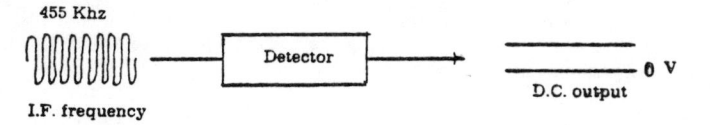

600 Khz from antenna or R.F. amplifier.

600 Khz beats with 1055 Khz oscillator producing I.F. of 455 Khz (1055-600)

1510 Khz (image frequency) beats with 1055 Khz oscillator frequency producing an I.F. of 455 Khz. (1510-1055)

Two I. F. signals result

An image frequency is as high above the local oscillator frequency as the oscillator is above the tuned frequency. Shielding and R.F. amplifiers can be used to reduce image interference. In a superheterodyne receiver the tuned signal is 1510 Khz. The local oscillator is operating at 1950 Khz. The image would be _____ Khz.

17. **(weak)** Receivers used for the reception of A1 (code) or A3J (single sideband) use a beat frequency to produce an audible output.

When a single R.F. frequency is detected in the conventional receiver, the output is direct current with no audible characteristics.

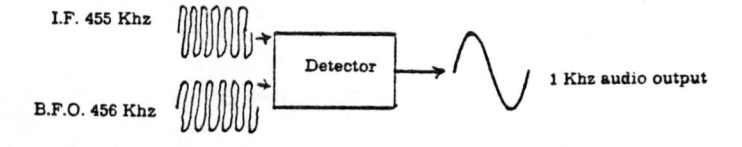

By injecting another oscillator generated frequency the I.F. carrier can be heard.

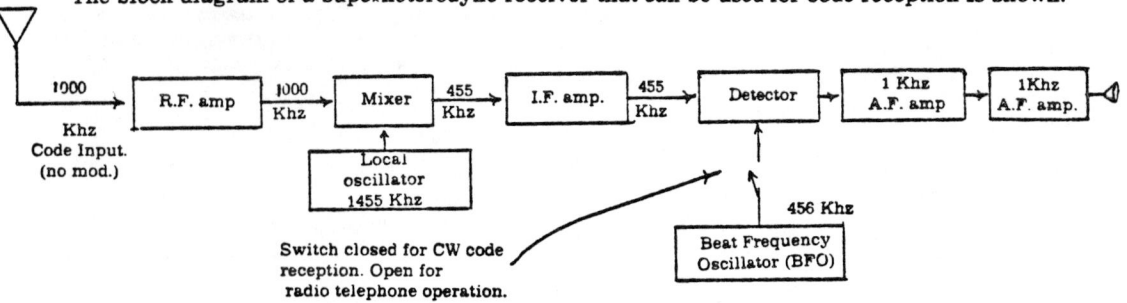

The block diagram of a superheterodyne receiver that can be used for code reception is shown:

Radio receivers with an oscillator operating near the I. F. frequency would be receiving _____ signals.

20. If the 1,000 kc crystal was inoperative
   a. M1 would read low.
   b. M2 would read high.
   c. M3 would read high.
   d. M5 would read low.
   e. none of these.

21. If C1 was shorted out
   a. M1 would read low.
   b. M2 would go to zero.
   c. M3 would read high.
   d. M5 would read low.
   e. M6 would read high.

22. If C3 was open
   a. M2 would read zero.
   b. M3 would read zero.
   c. M5 would read high.
   d. M6 would read zero.
   e. all of the above statements are true.

23. If the final plate was shorted to the final grid
   a. M1 would read zero.
   b. M2 would read zero.
   c. M4 would read pin backwards.
   d. M6 would read high.
   e. none of these.

24. If the C- of the second tube shorted to ground
   a. M3 would read high.
   b. M3 would read zero.
   c. M4 would read high.
   d. M6 would read high.
   e. none of these.

25. The grid bias to the second stage is
   a. grid leak biasing.
   b. cathode resistor biasing.
   c. contact potential biasing.
   d. supplied by a battery or power supply.
   e. none of these.

26. If the excitation fails
   a. there is no grid leak bias to the second stage.
   b. there is no grid leak bias to the final stage.
   c. the final tube has no protection and would burn out.
   d. the crystal will oscillate.
   e. M6 will read high.

27. The type of coupling shown is

   a. inductive.
   b. capacitive.
   c. shielding.
   d. interelectrode.
   e. none of these.

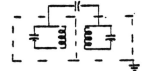

28. In the diagram below
   a. a Pierce oscillator is shown.
   b. the oscillator is tuned to an overtone of the crystal frequency.
   c. a dynatron oscillator is shown.
   d. the RF output frequency is a fraction to the crystal input frequency.
   e. a and b

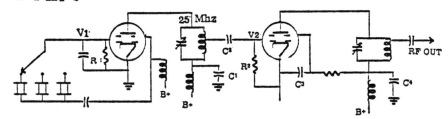

29. In the circuit above there would be the least change in the RF output if
   a. R1 was open.
   b. R2 was shorted.
   c. C1 was open.
   d. C2 was open.
   e. C3 was shorted.

30. If the filaments to V1 were open
   a. the current would increase in V1.
   b. the plate current would increase in V2.
   c. the plate current would decrease in V2.
   d. a and b are correct.
   e. b and c are correct.

31. A dummy antenna is constructed by use of
   a. a series choke and resistance.
   b. a parallel capacitance and resistor.
   c. a small loop of wire.
   d. suitable resistors from 1 to 10 megohm.
   e. a capacitor and resistor in series.

2. **(diode)** The diode detector is a linear detector. The resulting audio is without distortion. The grid leak detector is a square law detector. The output signal is proportional to the square of the input signal. A grid leak detector is shown below.

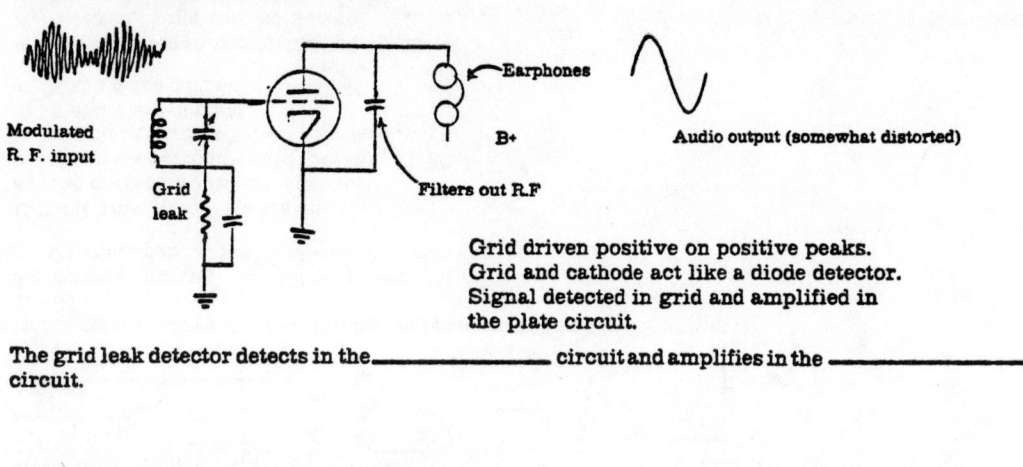

Modulated
R. F. input

Grid leak

Earphones

B+

Filters out R.F

Audio output (somewhat distorted)

Grid driven positive on positive peaks.
Grid and cathode act like a diode detector.
Signal detected in grid and amplified in
the plate circuit.

The grid leak detector detects in the_____ circuit and amplifies in the _____ circuit.

9. **(1055 Khz)** The superheterodyne receiver_____all frequencies to one frequency called the _____ frequency.

16. **(low, high)** Noise impulses act like weak signals and cause a receiver to provide high voltage gain. This is no problem with broadcast reception as the presence of a moderate to strong signal overrides the weak static. The I.F. and R.F. stage amplifications are low. If, however, a receiver was used to monitor police or public safety transmissions; there would be periods of time when there would be no signal present into the monitoring receiver. The AVC bias developed by static or noise would be low negative causing I.F. and R.F. stages to give maximum voltage gain. There would be extreme noise reception every time the transmitter carrier was cut off. This would be unpleasant to listen to. In order to quiet a receiver between transmission the low negative AVC voltage can be used to operate a **Squelch** circuit. The squelch circuit is used to cut off an I.F. or AF amplifier when weak or no signals are received. It would be impossible to receive a weak signal in a receiver using a squelch circuit. This latter circuit will be discussed further in Unit 19.
The disadvantage of a squelch circuit is_____ signals cannot be received.

32. In a certain transmitter the final plate current was zero, the buffer plate current was zero, but the crystal oscillator plate current was higher than normal. This indicated
    a. self oscillation.
    b. parasitics.
    c. a cracked crystal.
    d. excessive RF drive.
    e. defective plate current meters.

33. Carbon resistors are preferred in transmitter power supplies as bleeder resistors because
    a. a wire wound resistor has inductance.
    b. carbon is a poor conductor.
    c. carbon fuses.
    d. wire wound resistors to open or short out.
    e. none of these.

(This diagram for problems 34 through 37)

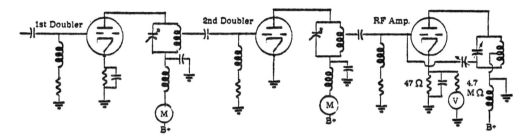

34. As the doubler tank circuits are tuned through resonance, the plate current
    a. changes from maximum to minimum to maximum.
    b. changes from minimum to maximum to minimum.
    c. goes to zero.
    d. is unaffected.
    e. none of these.

35. If the 4.7 megohm resistor in the voltmeter circuit is open
    a. the R.F. amp. bias would increase.
    b. the R.F. amp. bias would decrease.
    c. the amplifier operation would be normal.
    d. the amplifier plate current would increase.
    e. the amplifier plate current would decrease.

36. Equipment damage might result if
    a. B+ was removed from the R.F. amp.
    b. B+ was removed from the 2nd doubler.
    c. B+ was applied to the R.F. amp. after B+ was applied to the two doublers.
    d. the drive was removed from the 2nd doubler.
    e. none of these.

37. If the doubler tuned circuit was turned off resonance
    a. the R.F. amp. plate current would remain unchanged.
    b. the 2nd doubler plate current would increase.
    c. the 2nd doubler plate current would decrease.
    d. there would be no bias to the 1st doubler.
    e. there would be no bias to the 2nd doubler.

38. The carrier frequency of a transmitter is the frequency of the
    a. oscillator.
    b. buffer.
    c. doubler.
    d. output at zero % modulation.
    e. none of these.

39. The fifth harmonic of 480 Khz is
    a. 500 Khz.
    b. 900 Khz.
    c. 240 Khz.
    d. 2400 Khz.
    e. 3250 Khz.

40. A buffer R.F. amplifier is used to
    a. shape a signal into a sine wave.
    b. provide a stable load for the oscillator.
    c. generate harmonics.
    d. generate parasitic oscillations.
    e. generate noise.

41. A buffer amplifier is used to
    a. improve the efficiency of an RF thermocouple.
    b. decrease the amplifier output.
    c. raise the Q of the oscillator.
    d. improve the frequency stability of the oscillator stage.
    e. multiply the frequency of the oscillator.

Amplitude Modulation Detection

1. The one essential task of a receiver is to demodulate or detect a modulated R.F. wave. The simplest receiver is a diode detector. This receiver takes no local power source. A conventional explanation treats a modulated wave envelope with diode rectification:

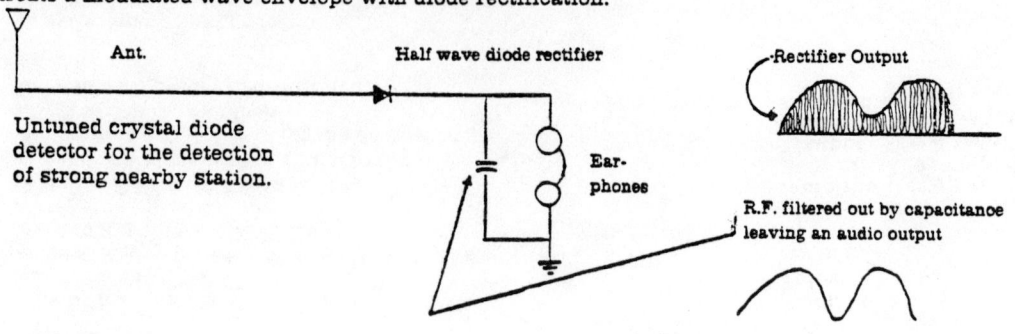

Ant.

Half wave diode rectifier

Rectifier Output

Untuned crystal diode detector for the detection of strong nearby station.

Ear-phones

R.F. filtered out by capacitance leaving an audio output

Demodulation can also be explained on the basis of upper and lower sidebands with carrier:

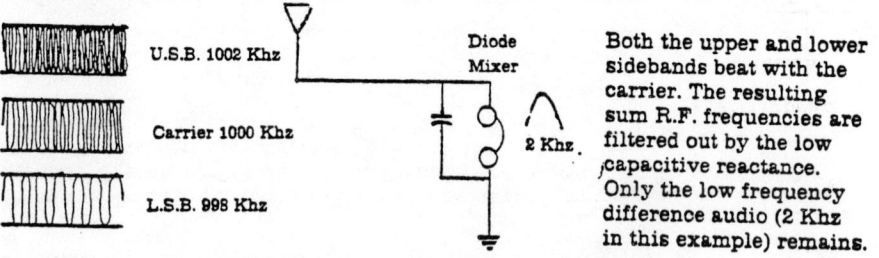

U.S.B. 1002 Khz

Carrier 1000 Khz

L.S.B. 998 Khz

Diode Mixer

2 Khz

Both the upper and lower sidebands beat with the carrier. The resulting sum R.F. frequencies are filtered out by the low capacitive reactance. Only the low frequency difference audio (2 Khz in this example) remains.

The_____ detector receiver requires no local power supply.

8. **(6055 Khz, Stage)** In a superheterodyne receiver the tuned signal is on 600 Khz and the I. F. is on 455 Khz. The local oscillator frequency is on_____Khz.

15. **(second, VTVM)** Variable Mu or remote cutoff I.F. and R.F. amplifier tubes make automatic volume control possible. The EgIp curve shows no sharp cutoff.

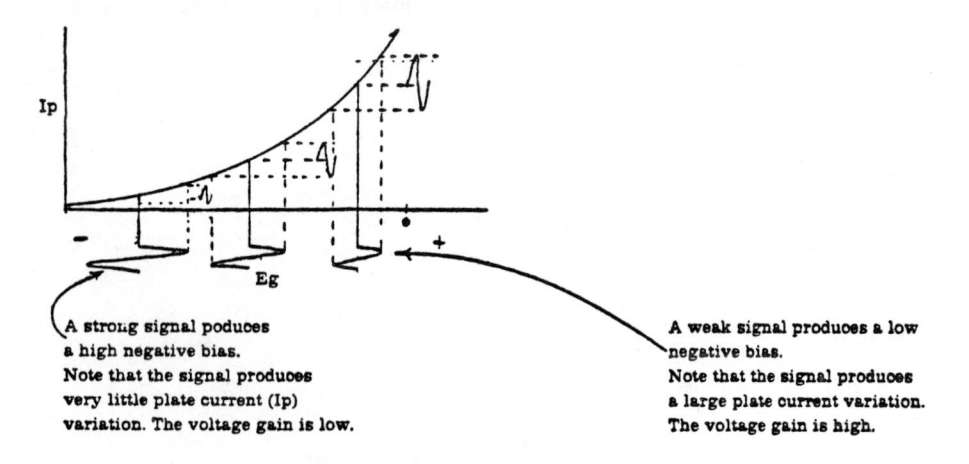

Ip

Eg

A strong signal poduces a high negative bias. Note that the signal produces very little plate current (Ip) variation. The voltage gain is low.

A weak signal produces a low negative bias. Note that the signal produces a large plate current variation. The voltage gain is high.

Weak input signals produce a _____ negative bias for I.F. and R.F. stages. This results in a _____voltage gain for these stages.

UNIT 17 AMPLITUDE MODULATION

1.

Introduction

Amplitude modulation is the process of mixing (or heterodyning) an audio signal with an R.F signal in a non linear device. This results in several new frequencies in addition to the original audio and R.F. When two such frequencies are mixed in modulation, we obtain 1) the sum; 2) the difference; 3) the original audio; 4) the original radio frequency; and 5) some R.F. harmonics. The general idea is shown:

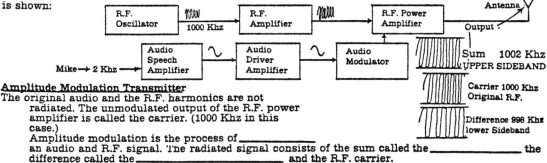

Amplitude Modulation Transmitter

The original audio and the R.F. harmonics are not radiated. The unmodulated output of the R.F. power amplifier is called the carrier. (1000 Khz in this case.)

Amplitude modulation is the process of_____ an audio and R.F. signal. The radiated signal consists of the sum called the_____ the difference called the_____ and the R.F. carrier.

9. Modulation Systems

(50%, 100%) The common types of modulation can be identified by where the audio is introduced into the modulated radio frequency amplifier. The general arrangement is shown below:

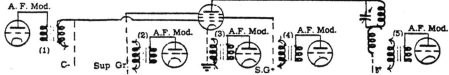

If the secondary of the modulator transformer is used to introduce audio at point:
1) modulation is called control grid modulation.
2) modulation is called suppressor grid modulation.
3) modulation is called cathode modulation.
4) modulation is called screen grid modulation.
5) modulation is called plate modulation.

Normally only one electrode receives the audio but combined screen and plate modulation is occasionally used. This is done by introducing the audio into the plate circuit and then connecting the screen to the bottom of the plate tank circuit through a dropping resistor. In plate modulation the audio is introduced into the_____circuit.

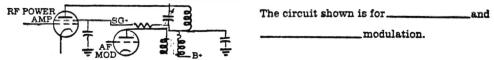

The circuit shown is for_____and _____ modulation.

17. (low level; linear) In our study of audio frequencies, we learned that three types of amplifiers can be used for distortionless amplification. They were

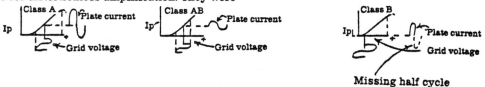

Missing half cycle supplied by using 2 tubes in push pull.

This is also true in radio frequency amplifiers. However, it is not necessary in R.F. circuits to use push pull circuits in Class B operation as the missing half cycle can be supplied by the flywheel action of a tuned tank circuits. (Discussed in Unit 15). Either single ended or push pull amplifiers may be used for linear amplifiers using any class of operation. If push pull circuits are used, even harmonics (2nd, 4th, 6th, etc.) are cancelled. Only the low order odd harmonics appear with any strength in the output. Class C output current is badly distorted and can not be used for a linear amplifier. A single ended class B amplifier can be used as a linear amplifier because of the_____effect. If a push pull linear amplifier is used, the_____ harmonics appear in the output.

26. A characteristic of the carbon button microphone is
    a. high sensitivity.
    b. wide frequency response.
    c. can be applied directly to the grid of an amplifier.
    d. non-sensitivity to vibration and handling.
    e. heat sensitive.

27. The output of an A.M. modulated R.F. amplifier contains
    a. the carrier frequency.
    b. a frequency equal to the sum of the carrier and modulating audio frequencies.
    c. a frequency equal to the difference between the carrier and modulating audio frequencies.
    d. all of the above.
    e. none of the above.

28. In amplitude modulation the modulation percentage is kept high to
    a. reduce distortion.
    b. reduce parasitics.
    c. reduce harmonics.
    d. provide improved inteligibility.
    e. reduce fidelity.

29. Amplitude modulation for standard broadcast is maintained at
    a. 70%.
    b. 50%.
    c. 85%.
    d. 110%.
    e. none of these.

30. The circuit shown is used for
    a. plate modulation.
    b. grid modulation.
    c. cathode modulation.
    d. screen modulation.
    e. plate & screen modulation.

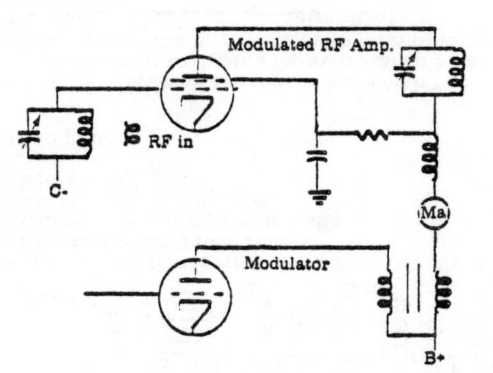

31. An AM transmitter has a carrier frequency of 20 Mhz. It is modulated with a single tone of 3 Khz that has a strong second harmonic. The highest frequency in the output would be
    a. 20.003 Mhz.
    b. 20.006 Mhz.
    c. 20.009 Mhz.
    d. 20.012 Mhz.
    e. none of these.

Microphones

2. (mixing or heterodyning, upper sideband, lower sideband) Acoustical or mechanical vibrations (speech, music, or other sounds) are converted to electrical audio signals by the microphone. The most common microphone is the **carbon single button mike.**

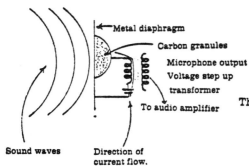

Air molecules are compressed and expanded by sound waves. This puts a variable pressure on the carbon granules. When the granules are compacted, more current flows. When less pressure is put on the diaphragm, less current flows.

The characteristics of this microphone are:
1) Low impedance
2) High output - near minus 30 db.
3) Granules may pack together with excessive moisture or mechanical shock.
4) Good for voice frequencies but has a characteristic hiss.

The carbon microphone has a _____ impedance, a _____ output, and is subject to _____ with excessive _____ or mechanical shock.

10. (plate, plate, screen grid) The most common type of modulation is plate modulaton.

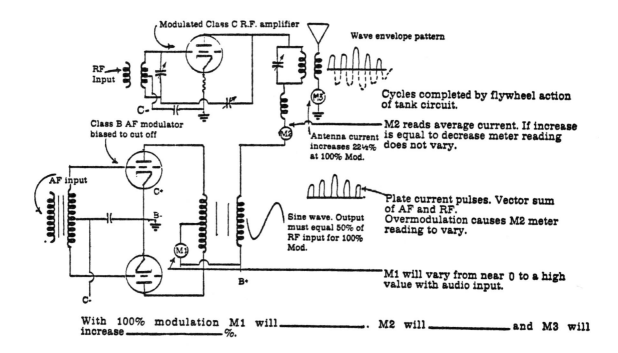

With 100% modulation M1 will _____. M2 will _____ and M3 will increase _____ %.

18. (flywheel, odd) Although a class C circuit cannot be used as a linear amplifier, there is a complex circuit in current use that has the high efficiency of a class C amplifier. It is called the **Doherty linear amplifier.**

The _____ amplifier is a linear amplifier having the efficiency of a Class C amplifier.

13. If the first speech amplifier was overdriven, but the transmitter was not overmodulated, the output would be
  a. distorted.
  b. normal.   d. lacking harmonics.
  c. undermodulated.   e. rectified.

14. A crystal microphone is easily damaged by
  a. temperatures below 70 degrees F.
  b. shouting.   d. excessive dryness.
  c. high temperatures. e. all the above.

15. If antenna current drops when modulation is applied in an AM transmitter, this indicates
  a. insufficient audio.
  b. insufficient RF excitation. d. frequency modulation.
  c. neutralization.   e. none of these.

16. If the bandwidth of a signal using A3 in 20 khz, the band width with A3A emission would be
  a. 5 khz.
  b. 10 khz.   d. 20 khz.
  c. 15 khz.   e. 40 khz.

17. A carbon mike is
  a. sensitive to high temperatures.
  b. a high impedance device.   d. a high fidelity mike.
  c. subject to granule packing with exposure to moisture.   e. little used today.

18. The bandwidth of an AM broadcast station is equal to
  a. half the modulating audio frequency.
  b. the modulating audio frequency.   d. the carrier frequency plus the modulating audio frequency.
  c. the carrier frequency.   e. twice the modulating audio frequency.

19. The input frequency to a push pull RF linear amplifier is 650 khz. The harmonics present in the output would be
  a. 1950, 3250, and 4550 khz.
  b. 1300, 2600, and 3900 khz.   d. the odd and even harmonics.
  c. the even harmonics.   e. none of these.

20. To prevent damage to a crystal mike, it is necessary to
  a. keep it clean.
  b. keep it at room temperature.   d. use high Z inputs.
  c. use low Z inputs.   e. keep it out of the direct sunlight.

21. The best way to measure percent modulation is by use of an
  a. oscilloscope.
  b. G.D.O.   d. ohmeter.
  c. voltmeter.   e. impedance bridge.

22. In the wave envelope pattern shown, the percentage of modulation is approximately
  a. 10.
  b. 50.
  c. 60.
  d. 75.
  e. none of these.

23. In a suppressed carrier SSB transmission
  a. one sideband and the carrier are used.
  b. two sidebands and the carrier are mixed and a frequency multiplier are used.
  c. frequency division is used in the final.
  d. two sidebands and no carrier are used.
  e. none of the above are applicable.

24. The bandwidth of emission in an AM transmission with a 2 Mhz carrier when modulated by audio whose highest frequency is 4,000 cycles is
  a. 2.004 Mhz
  b. 4.808 Mhz   d. 4 Khz
  c. 8 Khz   e. 2.008 Mhz

25. The ratio of the audio power to the input power of the final stage in 100% sinusiodal plate modulation is
  a. 25%.
  b. 30%.   d. 100%.
  c. 50%.   e. 200%.

3. (low, high, packing, moisture) The **crystal** microphone depends on the piezo electro effect for its operation. When certain crystalline substances such as rochelle salts are put under mechanical stress or are vibrated, a voltage is generated.

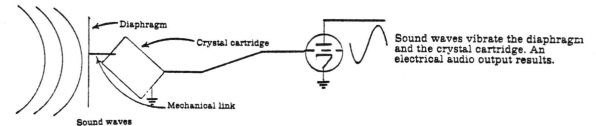

Sound waves vibrate the diaphragm and the crystal cartridge. An electrical audio output results.

The characteristics of the crystal microphone are:
1) High impedance
2) low output - near minus 60 db
3) Older models subject to damage by direct sunlight or excessive heat.
4) Subject to damage by excessive moisture
5) High fidelity

A new crystal ceramic microphone is now available that is not subject to damage by excessive heat.

The crystal microphone works on the_____ effect, has a_____impedance, a _____ output, and may be subject to damage by excessive_____or moisture.

11. (vary, not vary, 22½%) Overmodulation will cause M _____to vary.

Bandwidth

19. (Doherty) Since modulation results in frequencies representing the sum and difference of the carrier and modulating audio, the bandwidth of a standard broadcast transmission is equal to two times the audio frequency. For example:

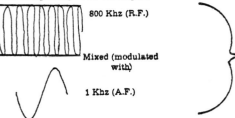

Results in

801 Khz (U.S.B.), 800 Khz (carrier) and 799 Khz (L.S.B.)

The bandwidth is from 801 Khz to 799 Khz = 2 Khz or twice the A.F. frequency.

The bandwidth of an A.M. Broadcast station is equal to_____the modulating audio frequency.

1. The percent modulation shown in the diagram below is
    a. 100.
    b. 50.
    c. 75.
    d. 80.
    e. 54.

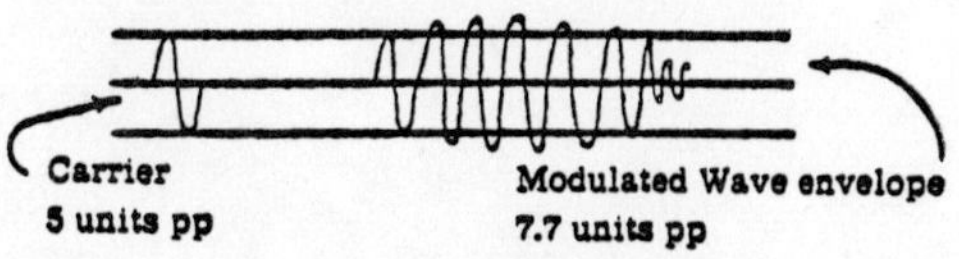

    Carrier
    5 units pp

    Modulated Wave envelope
    7.7 units pp

2. An RF linear amplifier can be operated in class B service with little or no distortion because of
    a. parasitic oscillations.
    b. flywheel effect.   d. class C bias.
    c. push-push operation.   e. none of these.

3. The block diagram below is that of a
    a. FM transmitter.
    b. SSB transmitter.
    c. AM transmitter.
    d. degenerative receiver.
    e. phase detector.

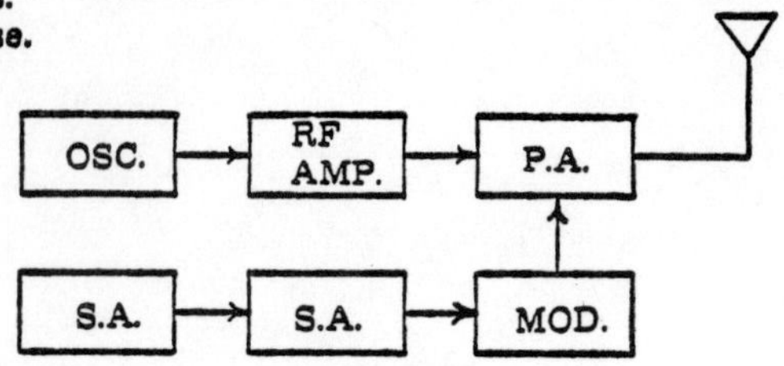

    OSC. → RF AMP. → P.A.

    S.A. → S.A. → MOD.

4. In the wave envelope pattern shown, the percentage of modulation is
    a. 10.
    b. 50.
    c. 60.
    d. 75.
    e. none of these.

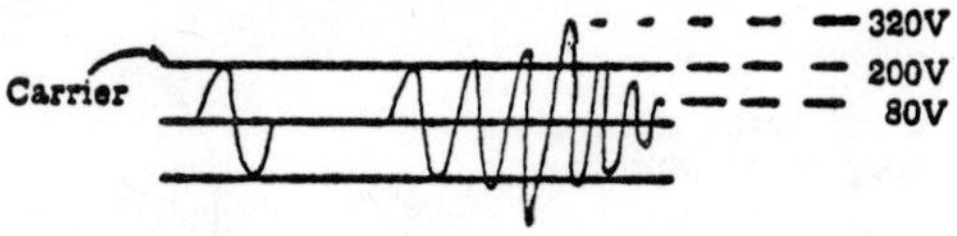

    Carrier
    320V
    200V
    80V

5. The Doherty amplifier is a
    a. voltage doubler.
    b. frequency multiplier.
    c. class A audio amplifier with low efficiency.
    d. RF linear amplifier having an efficiency comparable to a class C amplifier.
    e. type of multivibrator.

6. In AM broadcasting 75% modulation would cause the antenna current to increase about
    a. 12.2%.
    b. 13.0%.   d. 22.5%.
    c. 15.0%.   e. 75.0%.

7. one hundred percent modulation is indicated by

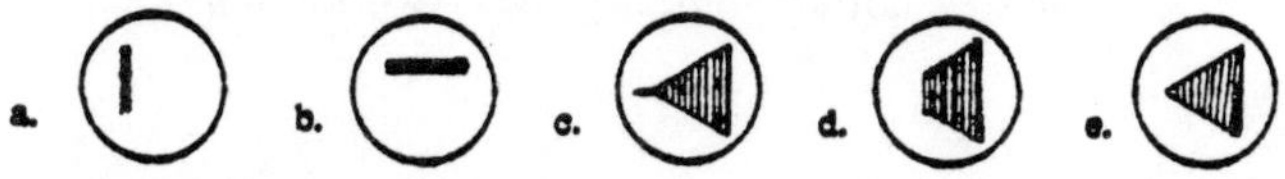

    a.   b.   c.   d.   e.

8. For 100% sinusoidal modulation the ratio of the audio power output to the modulated RF power input should be
    a. 0.5 to 1.0.
    b. 1.0 to 1.0.   d. 3.0 to 1.0.
    c. 2.0 to 1.0.   e. 4.0 to 1.0.

9. For 65% modulation the antenna current should increase
    a. 50.0%.
    b. 12.0%.   d. 22.5%.
    c. 10.0%.   e. none of these.

10. One characteristics of a crystal microphone is its
    a. low frequency response.
    b. poor fidelity at high frequencies.   d. high impedance.
    c. low impedance.   e. none of these.

11. A DC meter in a modulator plate circuit shows large variations. This is probably due to
    a. class A amplifier operation.
    b. class B amplifier operation.   d. insufficient audio excitation.
    c. overmodulation.   e. insufficient RF excitation.

12. Plate current variations in a properly designed RF amplifier might be caused by
    a. grid modulation.
    b. plate modulation.
    c. overmodulation.
    d. the flywheel effect.
    e. RF excitation.

4. (piezo electro, high, low, heat) Another microphone with a low output is the **dynamic** or **magnetic** microphone.

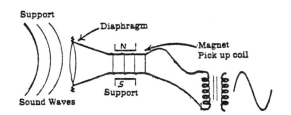

Support

Diaphragm

N

Magnet
Pick up coil

S
Support

Sound Waves

As sound waves strike the diaphragm, the coil moves in and out of the field of a permanent magnet generating an audio electrical wave.

This microphone is like a loud speaker in construction.
Its characteristics are:
1) low impedance
2) low output - near minus 65 db
3) high fidelity

The dynamic microphone is like a _____ in construction, has a _____ impedance and a _____ output.

12. (M2) The output waveforms are completed by the _____ action of the tank circuit.

20. (twice) Standard A.M. Broadcasts radiate A3 or double sideband frequencies with carrier. Some amateur and commercial transmission are made using A3A or single sideband transmissions with carrier. The bandwidth of an A3A emission is just half of that of an A3 emission.

If the bandwidth of a signal using A3 is 10 Khz, the bandwidth of an A3A emission is _____ Khz.

5.   (pack) All modulated R.F. stages are biased class _____ . Sec. 17-8.

10.   (plate) For 100% sinusoidal modulation, the ratio of the audio power, output to the modulated RF power input should be _____ to _____ . Sec. 17-11.

15.   (sidebands) The band width of an AM station is equal to _____ the modulating audio frequency. Sec. 17-14.

20.   (high) The best way to measure percent modulation is by use of an _____ . Sec. 17-21.

25.   (AB, B) Another type of linear amplifier, that is not mentioned here by name, is the Doherty. It has an efficiency of around 65% which is comparable to Class C efficiency. The _____ linear amplifier is comparable to the Class C amplifier in efficiency. Sec. 17-24.

30.   (negative) Insufficient R. F. _____ is the most frequent cause of _____ carrier shift. Sec. 17-26.

35.   (heat, high) If the first speech amplifier was overdriven (gain control set too high), audio _____ would result. Sec. 17-32.

Measuring Percent Modulation

5. (speaker, low, low) The best way to check percent modulation is by an oscilloscope. When the upper sideband, lower sideband, and carrier frequencies are fed by link coupling to the vertical input of an oscilloscope having an internal horizontal sawtooth sweep generator, a wave envelope pattern results. This pattern is the vector summation of the three frequencies.

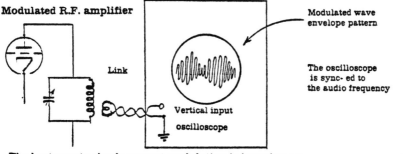

The best way to check percent modulation is by using an _____. The modulated R.F. is coupled to the _____ input.

Antenna Current

13. (flywheel) The antenna current as measured by the thermocouple R.F. ammeter increases by an amount determined by the percentage of modulation. By formula:

$$I_{Ant} \text{ (with modulation)} = \sqrt{1 + M^2/2} \text{ X Iant. (without modulation)}$$

For example with 75% modulation:

$$I_{ANT} \text{ (75\% mod)} = \sqrt{1 + 75^2/2} \quad \text{X } I_{ANT} \text{ (unmodulated)}$$

$$= \sqrt{1 + .5625/2} \quad \text{X } I_{ANT} \text{ (unmodulated)}$$

$$= \sqrt{1.28125} \quad \text{X } I_{ANT} \text{ (unmodulated)}$$

$$= 1.13 \quad \text{X } I_{ANT} \text{ (unmodulated)}$$

This means an increase in antenna current of 13% (1 X anything is itself - the increase is the .13 or 13%)

In the standard broadcast service the F.C.C. requires that the modulation be maintained to at least 85% in order to provide a greater intelligibility. 50% modulation would cause an increase in antenna current of _____%. For standard Broadcast Service, modulation must be maintained to _____% for greater intelligibility.

Miscellaneous

21. (5 Khz) If a class A audio amplifier is overdriven but not sufficiently to cause overmodulation, the output will be badly distorted.

Over driving an R.F. amplifier results in _____.

4. (high, heat, cold) Moisture may cause the carbon granules to_____. Sec. 17-4.

9. (spurious) The standard method of producing amplitude modulation is the transformer type _____ modulation. Sec. 17-11.

14. (output) At 100% modulation 1/3 of the total R.F. output is in the _____. Sec. 17-13.

19. (2Khz)

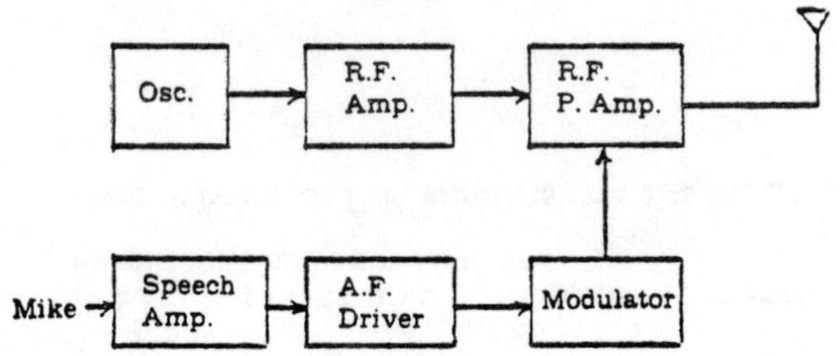

```
                                              ___
                                               \ /
                                                V
  +------+     +------+     +------+            |
  |      |     | R.F. |     | R.F. |------------+
  | Osc. |---->| Amp. |---->| P. Amp.|
  |      |     |      |     |      |
  +------+     +------+     +------+
                              ^
                              |
  +------+     +------+     +------+
  |Speech|     | A.F. |     |      |
Mike->| Amp. |--->|Driver|---->|Modulator|
  |      |     |      |     |      |
  +------+     +------+     +------+
```

The diagram to the left shows _____ level standard broadcast AM modulation. Sec. 17-20.

24. (push pull, fly wheel) Class_____ or_____ amplifiers give high efficiency than class A amplifiers. Sec. 17-22.

29. (low, linear) If antenna current drops when modulation is applied in an AM transmitter, this indicates_____carrier shift and may be due to insufficient R. F. excitation. Sec. 17-25.

34. (low, low, speaker) The older crystal microphones are subject to damage by_____ and moisture. Crystal Microphones have a_____ impedance. Sec. 17-30.

6. **(oscilloscope, vertical)** Percent modulation refers to the percent increase or decrease in antenna voltage or current. If modulation is symetrical and the increase or decrease in antenna voltage or current vary from the unmodulated peak values by a certain percentage, then it is only necessary to consider the increase. By formula:

$$\% \text{ modulation} = \frac{\text{E or I peak increase}}{\text{E or I peak unmodulated}} \times 100$$

For example:

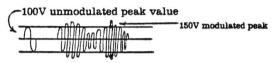

The increase is 50V.
The unmodulated peak is 100V.

$$\% \text{ Mod} = \frac{50}{100} \times 100$$

$$= 50\%$$

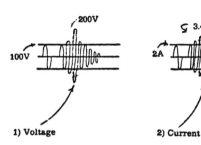

1) Voltage   2) Current

The percent modulation for the

examples shown is 1)_____

and 2)_____

14. **(6%, 85%)** 65% modulation would cause an antenna current increase of_____%.

22. **(distortion)** This concludes unit 17.

208

3. (sound variable) The carbon microphone has a relatively_____output and is not subject to detereation due to_____ or_____ . Sec. 17-4.

8. (50%, 100%, 30%) Overmodulation causes splatter or_____emissions. Sec. 17-10.

13. (plate) The operating power of a standard broadcast station is the_____power unmodulated. Sec. 17-13.

18. (four) Standard double sideband emissions with carrier are classed as A3. Single side band emissions with carrier result in one half the band width and are typed as A3A emissions. If 2 Khz of audio was used with 1,000 Khz of radio frequency in single sideband production, the band width would be_____ Khz. Sec. 17-15.

23. (50%, 100%, overmodulation) An R.F. Linear Amplifier can be operated in class B with little or no distortion by using a_____amplifier or by utilizing the_____ effect of a single ended stage. Sec. 17-22.

28. (modulated)

The modulation system shown is _____ level and block D must be a_____ R.F. amplifier. Sec. 17-20.

33. (14.8%) The dynamic microphone has a_____ impedance and a comparatively _____ output. It is similar in construction to a permanent magnet _____. Sec. 17-29.

38. (B) This concludes the recheck on Unit 17. Now retake Unit 17 test.

7. (100%, 70%) If the peak antenna voltage increases from 120 volts unmodulated to 168 volts modulated, the % modulation is _____%.

15. (10%) If the antenna current drops with modulation, it is usually because there is a negative carrier shift caused by insufficient R.F. excitation to the final R.F. power amplifier.

Note the decrease in antenna voltage or current is greater than the increase. This nonsymmetry is called **negative carrier shift**. it is a variation in amplitude (not in frequency) from a symmetrical wave form having equal increases and decreases.

In positive carrier shift, the increase in peak antenna current or voltage is greater than the decrease. Carrier shift represents **dynamic instability**. This instability is caused by poor power supply regulation, improper excitation, improper bias, or improper electrode voltages.

Downward deflection of antenna current is caused by negative carrier shift due to the lack of sufficient _____ to the modulated stage. Carrier shift is a variation in _____ and not in frequency.

2. (A3) The carbon button microphone in reality is a _____ resistor. Sec.17-4

7. (flywheel)

The percentage modulations shown are _____ , _____ , & _____ Sec. 17-10.

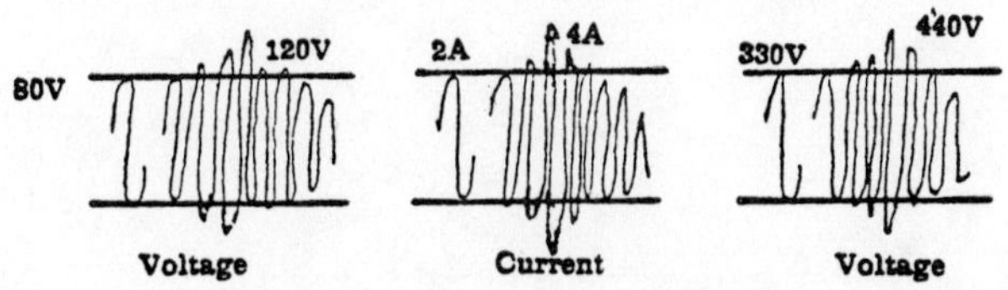

80V | 120V 2A | 4A 330V | 440V

Voltage   Current   Voltage

12. (plate, screen) If the screen dropping resistor R_1 was connected directly to B+, only _____ modulation would result. Sec. 17-12.

17. (mixing or beating or heterodyning) If in standard broadcasting 2 Khz of audio is beat with 1,000 Khz of radio frequency the band width would be _____ Khz. Sec. 17-15.

22. (zero)

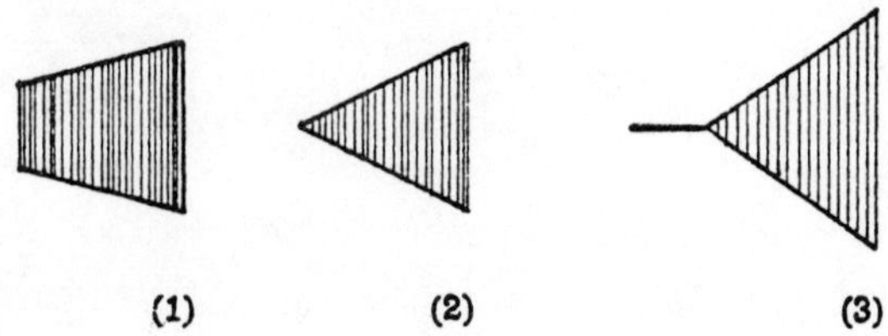

The modulations shown are _____ , _____ and _____ . Sec. 17-21.

(1)   (2)   (3)

27. (1800 Khz, 3000 Khz, 4200 Khz) Remember a push pull stage cancels even harmonics. An R.F. linear amplifier must be used to amplify a _____ radio frequency signals. Sec. 17-22.

32. (positive, frequency, amplitude) The student may find it easier to solve for modulated antenna current using the formula

$$I_{ant\text{-}modulated} = \sqrt{1 + \frac{M^2}{2}} \times I_{ant\text{-}unmodulated}$$

If its assumed that the unmodulated antenna current is 1 ampere then the formula can be written:

$$I_{ant\text{-}modulated} = \sqrt{1 + \frac{M^2}{2}}$$

If the modulation percentage is 65%, then the antenna current modulated is $\sqrt{1 + \frac{.65^2}{2}}$ times the unmodulated antenna current or 1.10 times the unmodulated current. This represents an increase of 10%. The antenna current would increase _____ % for 80% modulation. Sec. 17-28.

37. (overmodulation or carrier shift) A DC meter in a modulator plate circuit shows large variations. This is probably due to the normal operation of a Class _____ modulator as modulating audio is applied. Sec. 17-32.

8.   (40%) Another modulation pattern that can be obtained on an oscilloscope is the trapezoidal pattern.

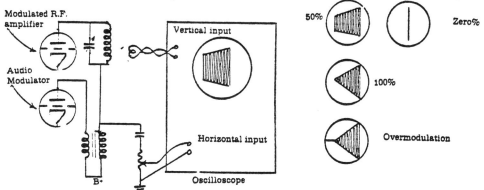

The percent modulation can be figured by measurement of the short and long side dimensions of the trapezoid:

D² ▨ D¹

$$\% \text{ modulation} = \frac{D1 - D2}{D1 + D2} \times 100$$

Suppose D1 = 140 V and D2 = 60V

$$\% \text{ modulation} = \frac{140 - 60}{140 + 60} \times 100$$

$$= \frac{80}{200} \times 100 = 40\%$$

For 100% modulation D2 would be zero and the figure becomes a triangle.

 (1)

The percent modulations shown are approximately

1)_____ and 2)_____.

Linear Amplifiers

16.   (R.F. excitation, amplitude) Now let us look at another classification of amplitude modulation systems. Modulation is either <u>high level</u> or <u>low level</u>

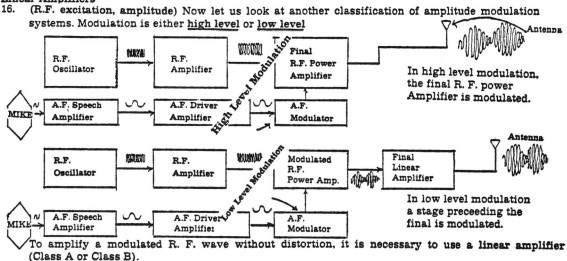

To amplify a modulated R. F. wave without distortion, it is necessary to use a linear amplifier (Class A or Class B).

If an R.F. amplifier stage preceeding the final is modulated, _____amplitude modulation occurs. The modulated R.F. can only be amplified by a _____ amplifier.

RECHECK PROGRAMMED INSTRUCTION USING SHRADERS ELECTRONIC COMMUNICATION

1. Amplitude modulated radio telephony emissions are classed as A____. Sec. 17-1.

6. (C) In single ended circuits (one tube) _____ action is responsible for the reproduction of the second half of the R.F. A-C cycle. Sec. 17-8.

11. (1, 2)

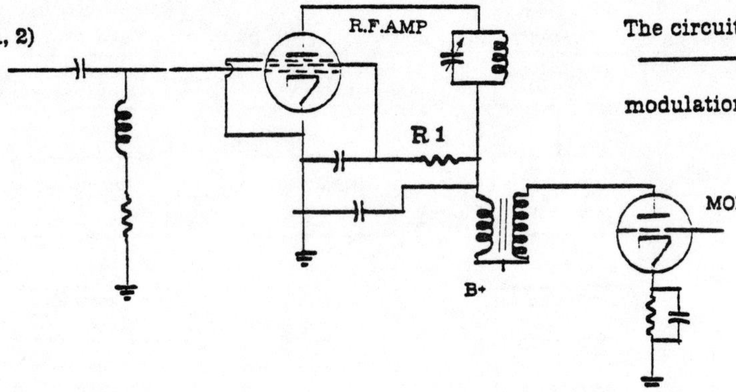

The circuit shown illustrates _____ and _____ modulation of a pentode. Sec. 17-12.

R.F.AMP

R 1

MODULATOR

B+

16. (twice) The production of sidebands in modulation deals with the theory of_____ . Sec. 17-14.

21. (oscilloscope)

The percent modulation shown is _____ . Sec. 17-21.

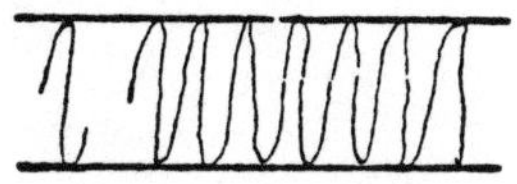

26. (Doherty) See Fig. 17-29. If the input frequency to this push pull R. F. linear amplifier is 600 Khz, the three lowest harmonics present in the output would be _____ , _____ , and _____ . Sec. 17-22.

31. (excitation, negative)

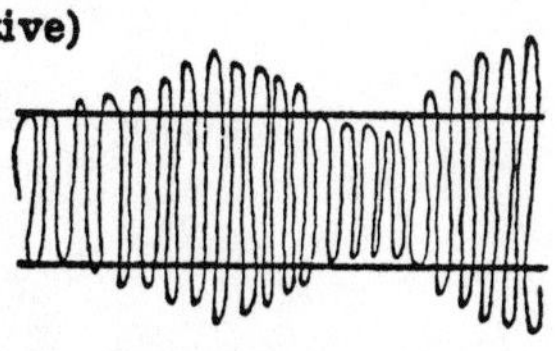

The wave envelope pattern shown indicates_____ carrier shift.

Carrier shift is not a variation in_____ but in_____ . Sec. 17-25.

36. (distortion) Plate current variations in a properly designed R. F. amplifier might be caused by _____ . Sec. 17-32.

KEY TO MULTIPLE CHOICE EXAMS
PART I

UNIT 1 - 1E, 2D, 3C, 4E, 5A, 6B, 7A, 8C, 9E

UNIT 2 - 1B, 2C, 3E, 4B, 5D, 6B, 7E, 8D, 9E, 10D, 11E, 12B, 13B, 14A, 15E, 16B, 17C, 18D,

UNIT 3 - 1C, 2A, 3C, 4C, 5C

UNIT 4 - 1A, 2B, 3D, 4D, 5B, 6B, 7E, 8A, 9E, 10C, 11C, 12C

UNIT 5 - 1A, 2B, 3B, 4B, 5D, 6A, 7B, 8A, 9A, 10E, 11C, 12B, 13C, 14B, 15C, 16E, 17A, 18D, 19E, 20B, 21C,
22A

UNIT 6 - 1A, 2A, 3D, 4C, 5B, 6C, 7D, 8B, 9A, 10E, 11A

UNIT 7 - 1A, 2E, 3C, 4C, 5C, 6C, 7D, 8B, 9C, 10E, 11D, 12B, 13C, 14C, 15B, 16D, 17A, 18C, 19A, 20E, 21C,
22D, 23D, 24C, 25A, 26B, 27A

UNIT 8 - 1E, 2C, 3B, 4E, 5B, 6A, 7C, 8C, 9B, 10C, 11D, 12B, 13C, 14D, 15A, 16E, 17B, 18D, 19C, 20A, 21E,
22C, 23E, 24A, 25B, 26B, 27A

UNIT 9 - 1B, 2E, 3C, 4C, 5D, 6C, 7B, 8B, 9B, 10A, 11D, 12C, 13A, 14C, 15A, 16B, 17D, 18A, 19B, 20A, 21A
22A, 23B, 24D, 25E, 26A, 27C, 28C, 29D, 30D, 31B, 32C, 33A, 34E

UNIT 10 - 1E, 2B, 3A, 4D, 5A, 6A, 7B, 8C, 9A, 10C, 11B, 12E, 13A, 14B, 15D, 16C, 17A, 18E, 19B, 20A, 21A,
22C, 23E

UNIT 11 - 1B, 2D, 3B, 4A, 5A, 6C, 7E, 8E, 9A, 10C, 11D, 12E, 13C, 14A, 15D, 16E, 17E, 18D, 19C, 20D, 21A,
22A, 23E, 24E, 25B, 26D, 27A, 28C, 29A, 30A, 31B, 32B, 33D, 34C, 35B, 36B, 37A, 38A, 39D, 40D,
41B, 42B, 43B, 44A, 45C, 46E, 47E, 48D, 49B, 50E, 51C

UNIT 12 - 1A, 2C, 3D, 4C, 5B, 6C, 7C, 8C, 9C, 10C, 11A, 12C, 13A, 14E, 15A, 16E, 17B, 18D, 19B, 20A, 21D
22B, 23B, 24C, 25D, 26E

UNIT 13 - 1D, 2D, 3A, 4B, 5C, 6A, 7A, 8A, 9A, 10A, 11D, 12A, 13A, 14E, 15B, 16A, 17E, 18A, 19C, 20D, 21C,
22E, 23E, 24E, 25C, 26D, 27B

UNIT 14 - 1C, 2B, 3D, 4B, 5E, 6D, 7C, 8A, 9C, 10B, 11D, 12D, 13A, 14B, 15C, 16A, 17E, 18E, 19D, 20A, 21A,
22D, 23B, 24C, 25A, 26B, 27B, 28C, 29E, 30C, 31C, 32A, 33A, 34A, 35B, 36C, 37C, 38C, 39D, 40B,
41B, 42D, 43E, 44E, 45B

UNIT 15 - 1E, 2C, 3B, 4A, 5B, 6C, 7A, 8E, 9B, 10C, 11C, 12B, 13B, 14D, 15B, 16C, 17A, 18D, 19A, 20B, 21D,
22C, 23B, 24C, 25D, 26B, 27C, 28D, 29D, 30D, 31C, 32C, 33B, 34A, 35C, 36C, 37B, 38B, 39A, 40B,
41B, 42C, 43B, 44A, 45D, 46A, 47A, 48D, 49E, 50A, 51B, 52A, 53E, 54A, 55D, 56A, 57D, 58D, 59C,
60C, 61E, 62C, 63A, 64B, 65E, 66D

UNIT 16 - 1C, 2D, 3B, 4D, 5A, 6B, 7C, 8B, 9E, 10A, 11D, 12B, 13B, 14E, 15B, 16C, 17C, 18B, 19A, 20E, 21B,
22E, 23C, 24A, 25D, 26B, 27B, 28E, 29C, 30B, 31E, 32C, 33D, 34A, 35C, 36D, 37B, 38D, 39D, 40B,
41D

UNIT 17 - 1E, 2B, 3C, 4C, 5D, 6B, 7E, 8A, 9C, 10D, 11B, 12C, 13A, 14C, 15B, 16B, 17C, 18E, 19A, 20E, 21A,
22E, 23E, 24C, 25C, 26A, 27D, 28D, 29C, 30E, 31B

UNIT 18 - 1C, 2D, 3A, 4B, 5D, 6A, 7E, 8B, 9C, 10B, 11D, 12A, 13C, 14A, 15A, 16C, 17B, 18A, 19B

UNIT 19 - 1C, 2A, 3C, 4C, 5C, 6A, 7E, 8E, 9D, 10B, 11B, 12E, 13E, 14B, 15A, 16E, 17C, 18A, 19D, 20E,
21C, 22B, 23E, 24C, 25E, 26A, 27E, 28A, 29B, 30B, 31D, 32A, 33A, 34A, 35A, 36C, 37C, 38A, 39A
40C, 41D, 42A, 43B, 44A, 45D, 46B, 47A, 48A, 49E, 50E, 51B, 52B, 53D, 54D, 55E, 56B, 57B, 58A,
59A, 60D

UNIT 20 - 1C, 2C, 3C, 4E, 5D, 6D, 7D, 8B, 9A, 10D, 11E, 12D, 13A, 14A, 15A, 16B, 17B, 18B, 19E, 20C,
21B, 22A, 23C, 24B, 25A, 26B, 27E, 28E, 29B, 30A, 31A, 32A, 33B, 34A, 35D, 36C, 37B, 38B, 39B,
40A, 41B, 42B

UNIT 21 - 1C, 2D, 3C, 4D, 5D, 6C, 7A, 8B, 9B, 10E, 11A, 12E, 13D, 14D, 15D, 16D, 17E, 18B, 19E, 20E, 21C,
22A, 23B, 24D

UNIT 22 - 1B, 2B, 3C, 4C, 5A, 6C, 7D, 8C, 9B, 10D, 11A, 12D

UNIT 23 - 1E, 2C, 3B, 4C, 5B, 6B, 7D, 8B, 9A, 10A, 11D

UNIT 24 - 1C, 2D, 3A, 4B, 5E, 6E

UNIT 25 - 1D, 2E, 3B, 4A, 5A, 6B, 7D, 8A, 9D, 10A, 11E

UNIT 26 - 1C, 2C, 3D, 4B, 5A, 6B, 7A, 8B, 9B, 10E, 11A, 12B, 13B, 14A, 15C, 16B, 17A, 18E, 19B, 20E,
21D, 22C, 23A, 24E

KEY TO MULTIPLE CHOICE EXAMS

PART I

FINAL EXAMINATION

1E, 2D, 3A, 4B, 5A, 6C, 7E, 8B, 9D, 10D, 11E, 12B, 13B, 14A, 15E, 16B, 17D, 18C, 19C, 20A, 21D, 22B, 23A, 24C, 25A, 26B, 27D, 28A, 29E, 30C, 31B, 32C, 33B, 34A, 35D, 36C, 37A, 38D, 39A, 40C, 41C, 42B, 43A, 44A, 45E, 46C, 47C, 48B, 49C, 50C, 51A, 52E, 53C, 54D, 55C, 56A, 57A, 58C, 59E, 60A, 61C, 62B, 63D, 64B, 65C, 66C, 67A, 68B, 69A, 70B, 71D, 72B, 73B, 74D, 75C, 76C, 77B, 78D, 79A, 80A, 81B, 82D, 83E, 84C, 85C, 86D, 87E, 88B, 89D, 90A, 91A, 92B, 93A, 94C, 95E, 96B, 97A, 98C, 99D, 100B, 101A, 102C, 103E, 104D, 105E, 106E, 107C, 108D, 109A, 110D, 111E, 112A, 113B, 114C, 115B, 116D, 117D, 118B, 119B, 120E, 121E, 122E, 123A, 124C, 125C, 126C, 127A, 128E, 129A, 130B, 131A, 132B, 133B, 134C, 135A, 136D, 137A, 138B, 139A, 140C, 141E, 142D, 143B, 144D, 145E, 146B, 147A, 148C, 149E, 150D, 151B, 152A, 153B, 154C, 155A, 156C, 157D, 158E, 159B, 160A, 161C, 162B, 163C, 164C, 165D, 166D, 167B, 168C, 169C, 170C, 171B, 172B, 173A, 174E, 175A, 176D, 177D, 178D, 179B, 180E, 181A, 182C, 183C, 184B, 185A, 186E, 187B, 188E, 189C, 190A, 191D, 192B, 193B, 194E, 195C, 196D, 197A, 198D, 199B, 200D, 201E, 202B, 203C, 204B, 205E, 206B, 207A, 208C, 209C, 210E, 211E, 212E, 213C, 214C, 215E, 216C, 217B, 218D, 219B, 220B, 221D, 222A, 223A, 224C, 225B, 226A, 227C, 228C, 229C, 230A, 231D, 232B, 233A, 234E, 235C, 236A, 237D, 238C, 239E, 240A, 241B, 242D, 243A, 244C, 245A, 246A, 247B, 248A, 249A, 250E, 251B, 252D, 253B, 254A, 255C, 256C, 257D, 258B, 259D, 260D, 261B, 262C, 263A, 264B, 265B, 266A, 267D, 268B, 269B, 270D, 271D, 272C, 273B, 274E, 275D, 276E, 277B, 278B, 279B, 280C, 281A, 282C, 283C, 284A, 285D, 286C, 287B, 288B, 289B, 290D, 291A, 292D, 293D, 294A, 295E, 296D, 297B, 298A, 299D, 300E.

PART II

UNIT 1 - 1D, 2D, 3A, 4B, 5B, 6E, 7E, 8E, 9D, 10A, 11C, 12B, 13A

UNIT 2 - 1A, 2B, 3E, 4D, 5B, 6B, 7B, 8B, 9D, 10C, 11B, 12A, 13A, 14B, 15B, 16C, 17A, 18E, 19B, 20C, 21D, 22B, 23C, 24C

UNIT 3 - 1D, 2A, 3C, 4D, 5D, 6E, 7E

UNIT 4 - 1C, 2D, 3B, 4C, 5B, 6D, 7C, 8B, 9C, 10C, 11B, 12D, 13E

UNIT 5 - 1B, 2E, 3B, 4D, 5B, 6E, 7C, 8E, 9C

UNIT 6 - 1E, 2E, 3B, 4A, 5C, 6E, 7B, 8C, 9E, 10B, 11B, 12A, 13B, 14D, 15B, 16B, 17A, 18A, 19D, 20D, 21D, 22D, 23D, 24A, 25C, 26C, 27A, 28C

UNIT 7 - 1C, 2E, 3A, 4B, 5D, 6B, 7E, 8C

UNIT 8 - 1B, 2E, 3D, 4B, 5E, 6A, 7C, 8B, 9C, 10D, 11C, 12C, 13C, 14E, 15C, 16A, 17C, 18B, 19E, 20D, 21B, 22D, 23B

PART II FINAL EXAMINATION

1D, 2A, 3B, 4D, 5D, 6C, 7E, 8B, 9D, 10B, 11C, 12E, 13B, 14A, 15E, 16D, 17C, 18A, 19D, 20C, 21B, 22C, 23C, 24E, 25C, 26D, 27B, 28B, 29E, 30B, 31A, 32B, 33B, 34D, 35C, 36A, 37E, 38B, 39C, 40E, 41D, 42D, 43E, 44B, 45A, 46A, 47C, 48E, 49A, 50B, 51C, 52D, 53D, 54E, 55E, 56C, 57C, 58A, 59C, 60C, 61D, 62B, 63B, 64B, 65E, 66B, 67C, 68B, 69C, 70C, 71B, 72E, 73C, 74A, 75B, 76E, 77A, 78D, 79B, 80C, 81B, 82A, 83B, 84B, 85A, 86A, 87B, 88B, 89A, 90C, 91A, 92C, 93B, 94D, 95E, 96B, 97C, 98C, 99D, 100C, 101B, 102B, 103C, 104C, 105B, 106E, 107A, 108C, 109B, 110E, 111C, 112A, 113C, 114E, 115B, 116D, 117B, 118D, 119D, 120A, 121B, 122C, 123A, 124C, 125D, 126E, 127D, 128C, 129A, 130C, 131E, 132B, 133C, 134B, 135D.